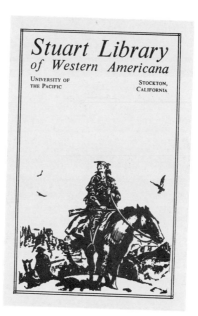

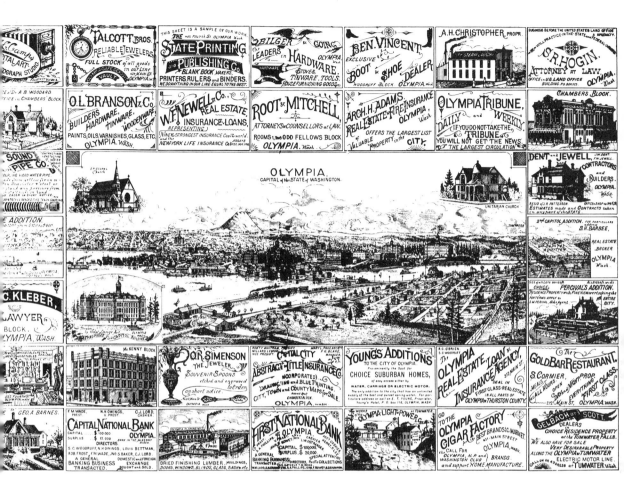

ROGUES, BUFFOONS
& STATESMEN

AGAIN THEY SWARM

Recorder cartoonist James North heralded the convening of another legislative session in 1905.

ROGUES, BUFFOONS & STATESMEN

By

GORDON NEWELL

HANGMAN PRESS

As Presented By

Superior Publishing Company

Of Seattle, Washington

Library of Congress Cataloging in Publication Data

Newell, Gordon R.
    Rogues, buffoons, and statesmen.

    Includes bibliographical references and index.
    1. Olympia, Wash.—History. 2. Washington (State)
—Politics and government. I. Title.
F899.05N48   979.7'79   75-2686
ISBN 0-87564-106-7

FIRST EDITION

Printed In
The United States of America

DEDICATION

This book is dedicated to the Washington State Library, the repository of 120 years of Washington state and territorial history, and to its helpful staff. Very special appreciation goes to Hazel Mills, Nancy Pryor and Mary Flinton of the library's Washington Room, without whose patience, guidance and assistance the task of researching and writing would have been impossible.

ACKNOWLEDGEMENTS

Valuable historic photographs were made available by Truman Schmidt of the Olympia Brewing Company, Ken Hopkins, director, and Del McBride, curator of the State Capital Historical Museum, Ray Olsen, sergeant at arms, Washington State House of Representatives, Donald Baker, former President of the State Federation of Teachers, and Pat Haskett, maritime artist and researcher. The author's thanks are extended to them.

"Politicians unintentionally are frequently funnier than comedians".
. . . *Will Rogers*

INTRODUCTION

This is really two stories in one ... the story of the capital city, which is the stage upon which the frequently comic drama of state politics is played, and the story of the actors in that continuing drama ... the rogues, buffoons, statesmen and less colorful individuals who have played out their great and little parts in the limelight and the backstage shadows.

Olympia, the capital city of Washington, presents in microcosm the hopes and fears, the foibles and the fads, of all the people who, over 120 years, have cast their votes to determine the cast of characters in that never-ending circus, state politics. The changing scenery and sound affects of the town portray the changing environment in which, year by year, the performance has been staged.

The performers include governors, senators, lobbyists, clerks, bureaucrats, drunks and psychopaths; crusaders, shakedown artists, reformers and outright thieves; Republicans, Democrats, Populists, Bull Moosers and Communists . . . but they all have one thing in common . . . a role in the sometimes funny, sometimes frightening and frequently downright unbelievable show we call state politics. Much of what is recorded here of their doings appears in no civics book or political science text, but it is nonetheless essential knowledge to anyone who wants to probe behind the pomp and circumstance and ritualistic confusion of state government.

The Legislature is the main attraction ... the major public spectacle. In the marbled halls of House and Senate the political institution which is often referred to as the very keystone of our democratic government is on view periodically to the wondering gaze of those who pay the bills for it all. And, as Frank Trippett wrote in his superbly analytical book on state legislatures, "The States: United They Fell",

"From Little Rock to Olympia, from Austin to Montpelier, the legislature is a sight to behold."

The casual viewer of this strange phenomenon will probably find its routine of methodical chaos more boring than exciting most of the time, but one never knows when drama will erupt, as a brief review of past performances makes clear. It is too late to view such past marvels as the representative from Walla Walla who flourished a loaded revolver under the nose of his opponent in a floor debate, or the senator from Sumner who arrived at the legislative chambers upon the back of a mule and preceded by a brass band, or the solon from Seattle who kicked an assistant sergeant at arms in the head and paralyzed him for life, or the freshman legislator from Thetis who complained to the Speaker that he had been bribed and was rewarded for his honesty by impeachment proceedings, or the platoon of bootleggers who helped the legislature of 1919 get drunk enough to vote for prohibition, or the new lawmaker who rose to announce that he could die happy, now that he had spoken before the august body to which he had been elected .. . and then dropped dead, or the lieutenant governor who summoned a barbershop quartette to sing soothing melodies to quell an incipient riot on the floor of the Senate, or the outraged liberal from King county who galloped the length of the House chambers to punch the head of the *Spokesman-Review's* political writer.

But the state legislature is an institution which seems to encourage periodic outbreaks of bizarre behavior while striving mightily for "decorum". If one watches closely, one never knows what may develop. After all, even Abraham Lincoln as a member of the Illinois Legislature, was moved to make a spectacular leap from a second story window of the capitol in an effort to prevent a quorum being mustered by the Democrats to do in the Whigs.

Those who believe that history must be solemn, humorless and boring to have merit won't like this book and shouldn't buy it. State politics may be costly, bumbling, frustrating and frequently mendacious, but it has one saving grace ... it's essentially comical. If this book makes it possible for the reader to chuckle a bit as he daily impoverishes himself paying the countless nuisance taxes inflicted upon him by his elected representatives, it will have served its purpose.

One other thing . . . this is the story of what happened at the capitol. It does not pretend to explain *why* capitol politicians and bureaucrats behave in the seemingly incomprehensible ways they do.

That's another book . . . and I'm working on it now.

Gordon Newell
Olympia, Washington

CONTENTS

CHAPTER ONE
In the Beginning
1845-1853

The new governor and his embryonic capital city had several things in common on the dark and drizzly evening of Saturday, November 26, 1853. Both were small, muddy, rain-soaked and far from fragrant.

The governor, Isaac I. Stevens of Massachusetts, graduate of West Point (at the head of his class of 1839) and late major, United States Army, wasn't much over five feet tall. As a child he had toiled from dawn to dusk on his father's hardscrabble New England farm and in the mills of Andover. The brutal labor had overtaxed his strength and afflicted him with ruptures which would cause him pain throughout his relatively short life. He killed the pain with large and frequent doses of straight whiskey. He had just crossed a continent, much of it a howling wilderness, on foot and surveying a route for a transcontinental railway as he went. From the Columbia River he had traversed the bone-breaking trail the settlers called a wagon road to the head of Puget Sound, and he needed a drink, a bath and a hot meal.

For a while, according to a cherished legend of the old settlers, it appeared that he might get none of these at Olympia, the metropolis of the Puget Sound country and future capital of the commonwealth of Washington which President Franklin Pierce had assigned him to organize. Most of the town's white population of 150 and a number of the Indians who inhabited flee-infested huts along the downtown mudflats were on hand to welcome the new territorial governor and the civic leaders had done all they could within their very limited resources to make his welcome a memorable one.

George E. Blankenship, native son and a local historian who seldom let cold facts interfere with a good story, told it this way:

"Great preparations were made for the governor's reception. He arrived ahead of his party and in an unostentatious way asked for admission to the dining room (of the town's only hotel). He was informed that there was no time to lose on strangers, as they were 'getting ready for a great doin's'. Saying he was hungry, Stevens asked for a snack in the kitchen, which was furnished him. He then went outside where he met a stranger, who complained that the governor was late in arriving. 'Why I am the man you are looking for', said Stevens. This announcement, made by the small travel-stained man was enough. The arrival was announced by vigorous beating on a circular saw hung from a post, and the first gubernatorial reception was fairly on".

According to other accounts, Stevens arrived with his railroad survey party a few days ahead of schedule and his reception was an impromptu affair at the Washington Hotel, a rambling wooden structure at the corner of 2nd and Main operated by Edmund Sylvester, the town's founding father, who pledged himself to "furnish man and beast with the best fare the market affords".

It is reasonable to assume that the little governor was indeed ahead of schedule. Despite his frail and undersized body, seemingly over-balanced by a huge, shaggily bearded head, Isaac Stevens operated at only one speed ... full steam ahead. This driving impetuosity was to secure him a place in history as Washington's most dynamic governor. It was also to bring him and his new territory close to the brink of disaster in the years immediately ahead.

Stevens' new territory had had its beginnings eight years earlier, in 1845, when Dr. John McLaughlin, the Hudson's Bay Company factor at Fort Vancouver on the Columbia River had tried to convince a big Kentucky wagon train master named Michael T. Simmons that he and his companions should file their land claims south of that watery barrier. The Canadian-American boundary line was

Edmund Sylvester, founding father of Olympia.

Governor Isaac I. Stevens

still in dispute, the company had long since staked its claim to thousands of acres of land on the Nisqually River on southern Puget Sound, and it hoped to make the Columbia the southern boundary of the British Empire in North America.

McLaughlin was a kindly man and he had treated the American pioneers well, but Mike Simmons didn't like to be hemmed in, even by a man he liked. He had just about decided to settle on the Willamette, but McLaughlin's arguments got his dander up and he decided to push on to Puget Sound.

In April, 1845, the Simmons wagon train stopped at Washougal while a baby, Christopher Columbus, was born to Mike Simmons' wife . . . the first American child to be born north of the Columbia. Then the train pushed on north, hacking a trail through the virgin forest as it went. Thus, building the legendary Cowlitz Trail foot by sweat-drenched foot, it worked its way to the southern tip of Puget Sound at the falls of the Des Chutes River. The 58-mile trip, which can today be made in well under an hour by freeway, took 15 days to complete.

Colonel Simmons was a Kentucky man of little education, much good nature and fierce loyalty to his friends. One of Mike Simmons' friends, a fur trader and frontiersman who had guided the party across the plains to the far Northwest, was George Bush. Bush was a Negro, or rather his father had been . . . a seaman from the British Indies. His mother had been white. That made him, in the terminology of the day, a mulatto, a man of color, and that section of the Constitution guaranteeing equal rights to everyone didn't apply to him. The gathering storm clouds of Civil War were bringing added racial bigotry and hatred to Missouri, where Bush and Simmons were neighbors, and it was partly to escape this that Simmons convinced his friend that they should make the great migration to the last frontier.

James McAllister, another of the party's family men, was looking for a lot of land where he could raise big crops and a big family in peace and security. Fate had decreed that his path would one day cross that of Isaac Stevens, who was then in the process of earning promotion from lieutenant to major for bravery at Contreras and Chapultepec on the staff of

9

General Winfield Scott. The result would be violent death for McAllister.

David Kindred and Gabriel Jones were also family men. Jesse Ferguson and Sam Crockett were bachelors. Peter Bercier had guided them from the last outpost of civilization on the Columbia, and they were met along the weary way by a sturdy Nisqually Indian named Leschi, whose homely, kind face smiled a welcome to his people's land. His welcome had practical aspects, too, for he brought them pack-horse loads of badly needed supplies.

Mike Simmons stayed at the Des Chutes falls, which were called Tum Water, staked a claim and named his town New Market, letting the Hudson's Bay men at Vancouver and Nisqually know that they had a new market to contend with . . . the first American settlement on Puget Sound.

Using water power from the falls, he built a sawmill and a grist mill, but while they were being built and the other settlers were getting in their crops, they survived by splitting and selling cedar shingles to Dr. Tolmie, Hudson's Bay factor at Fort Nisqually. The "King George men", as the Indians called the British, and the "Boston men" from the American states were rivals for an empire, but they were not enemies.

George Bush, a man of substance and some wealth by frontier standards, settled on a nearby fertile prairie, one of the few areas not covered with an impenetrable wilderness of virgin timber and jungle-like undergrowth. He planted the seeds and saplings he had brought with him across the plains and Bush Prairie became fruitful . . . a well-tilled and lovingly tended midwestern farm in the heart of a wilderness.

The McAllisters settled in the Nisqually Valley, in the midst of Leschi's people. Their first home was in two huge hollow cedar stumps until Leschi and his men helped them build a log farmhouse. There, the following spring, Mrs. McAllister gave birth to the first American child born in the Puget Sound country . . . a boy named James Benton.

The neighboring town of Olympia wasn't born until the next year, 1846, and then under a temporary and almost forgotten name. Edmund Sylvester and Levi Lathrop Smith arrived in October with a wagon train that included A. M. Poe, Daniel Kinsey, A. B. Rabbeson and Charles Eaton. Sylvester and Smith were partners, although about as unlike as two men can be, and they staked a joint claim on the site of what was to become Washington's capital city. Three months earlier a treaty between the United States and Great Britain had been ratified, extending the northwest boundary of American Territory to the Strait of Juan de Fuca.

Edmund Sylvester was a Maine fisherman who wanted to forget the cold seas and rocky soil of New England, Smith was an epileptic; cultured, solitary, with a call to the ministry which had been frustrated by ill health. Each filed on 320 acres. (The married men claimed 640 acres, although none of the new American lands had been surveyed and no homestead laws existed). Sylvester, weary of the sea, took an inland area later known as Chambers Prairie. Smith chose for his claim the land between the two southernmost waterways of Budd Inlet. The westerly inlet extended two miles north to Tum Water falls and new Market. The easterly inlet also wound north through tall timber to merge with the swampland of Moxlie creek. The two square acres of muddy peninsula between the two arms of Puget Sound formed a small oasis in the wilderness of virgin timber. It was here that Olympia would have its beginnings. The tidal range at the tip of Puget Sound is well over 20 feet. At low tide the peninsula extended nearly a mile south in the form of mudflats

Leschi, martyr in the Indians' fight for survival.

10

teeming with clams and oysters. At extreme high tide much of it was covered by salt water.

Under normal tidal conditions the small peninsula somewhat resembled the silhouette of a bear, and the area was called "Chetwoot" by the Indians . . . a Nisqually word meaning bear . . . and here the Suquamish and Duwamish tribes under Chief Seattle were accustomed to camp during the stormy winter months. Here, too, Smith built the first permanent structure in his embryonic town . . . a rude log cabin some 16 feet square.

The tragic figure of Levi Lathrop Smith was soon to depart from the rude stage of pioneer Olympia, or Smithfield, as he called his claim. He did not live to see any of the beginnings beyond the first crude cabin.

With the creation in 1848 of Oregon Territory, Smithfield was in Lewis County, Oregon territory, and in the first county elections that year, Smith was chosen as a representative to the Oregon provisional legislature. As he was traveling to New Market by canoe to begin his journey over the Cowlitz trail he was seized by an epileptic attack, fell into the water and was drowned. It is part of the dark tragedy of this lonely man that he did not live to glimpse even a hint of the beautiful city which was to grow from his rough shack between the empty bay and the primeval forests.

Sylvester and Smith had a partnership which provided for sole ownership by the survivor of both claims should one of them die. After Smith's death, Sylvester moved from his Chambers prairie claim and became the permanent occupant of his dead partner's cabin on tidewater.

It was not an impressive beginning, but 1847 and 1848 were years of modest progress. A trail was cleared between Smithfield and New Market in the late summer of 1847, making it possible to travel between the two settlements at any stage of the tide. The population of the Smithfield-New Market area had also increased by 1848. Early in 1847 a party consisting of the Davis family, Samuel Cool, A. J. Moore, Benjamin Gordon, Thomas W. Glasgow, Samuel Hancock and Leander C. Wallace arrived at New Market, followed shortly by the Packwood brothers, Elisha and William, who had scouted the area the previous year and now returned with their families, followed by J. B. Logan, A. D. Carnefix and Frank Shaw. Thomas Chambers, with his sons

David, Andrew, Thomas and McLain, along with George Shazer and a Mr. Baril arrived during the winter.

In 1848, too, the area became an educational center with the arrival of Father Pascal Ricard and a little band of Oblat missionaries, who built a church and mission school south of Smithfield on a section of wooded shoreland which is known to this day as Priest Point.

Soon afterward Samuel Hancock took a claim across the bay to the west and built a wharf and warehouse on relatively deep water, beyond the vast mudflats which emerged at each low tide to surround Smithfield with hundreds of square acres of spouting clams.

The wharf and warehouse were soon needed, for in 1849 many of the earliest settlers deserted the outpost on Puget Sound to join the California gold rush. A few prospered, among them Isaac Ebey, Benjamin Shaw, Sylvester and a couple of other pioneers. These enterprising men invested part of their profits in the little brig *Orbit,* which they loaded with general cargo and sailed to Puget Sound, landing at Hancock's wharf. There they loaded a cargo of piling for the return voyage to San Francisco, both cargoes paying a tidy profit.

Mike Simmons, who found the complexities of business life not to his liking, had in the meantime sold his New Market claim and its

Clanrick Crosby.

mills to a newcomer named Clanrick Crosby, a New England shipmaster with a high regard for a dollar.

Captain Clanrick had first heard about the Puget Sound country from his younger brother, Captain Nathaniel, who had been sent out by the United States government in command of the brig *O. C. Raymond* with supplies for the earliest American settlers. Captain Nat liked the new frontier and he believed in direct action. He sent word to Clanrick, back in Wicasset, Maine, to buy a ship and bring the family out. Clanrick forthwith purchased the 270-ton brig *Grecian,* loaded her with the Crosby goods and chattels, manned her with a crew of Crosbys and their kinfolk, and took her around Cape Horn to Portland. That voyage brought famous pioneers to New Market, from whence they overflowed to Smithfield. All but four of that ship's company (including the ship's black cook) were members of the Crosby clan.*

Clanrick Crosby gave Simmons a sizeable down payment on his saw mill and grist mill, and the big Kentuckian invested the proceeds in the purchase of the *Orbit* from Sylvester and his partners. Crosby, the sailor turned mill owner, prospered; Simmons, the mill owner turned sailor didn't do too well. At first the *Orbit* returned handsome profits, hauling timber to San Francisco and supplies back to Puget Sound, Simmons sold much of the cargo through a general store which he opened in partnership with a glib-tongued former California miner named Charles Harte Smith. When he had accumulated sixty thousand dollars, he dispatched his protege to San Francisco aboard the *Orbit* with the money to buy more stock. Young Smith was not seen again on Puget Sound, nor was Mike Simmons' sixty thousand dollars.

The canny Crosby, in the meantime, apparently consulted a frontier lawyer and decided that Mike Simmons' right to the Tum Water claim was doubtful at best, and that he might as well file on it himself under the new homestead laws rather than pay off the balance due to Simmons. Simmons brought suit against Crosby, and the matter dragged on for several years while the mills stood idle.*

In the spring of 1850 the former Smith claim was dedicated as a town. Edmund Sylvester was still the sole proprietor of the new municipality, and he decided to launch it with a new name . . . Olympia.

The name appears to have been suggested by Colonel Isaac N. Ebey, one of the former owners of the pioneer brig *Orbit,* who settled on an upper Puget Sound claim at Whidbey Island. The colonel was down for the dedication ceremony and added his oratory to the occasion. He composed these lines for the little assemblage gathered at the city's birth:

"Afar their crystal summits rise
Like gems against the sunset skies,
While far below, the shadowy mist
In waves of pearl and amethyst,
'Round somber fir and stately pine,
Its dewy, jeweled fingers twine;
Olympia's gods might view with grace,
Nor scorn so fair a dwelling place."

The arrival of the *Orbit* on New Year's day of 1850 inaugurated homeowned merchant shipping on Puget Sound and required the establishment of a customs house. The federal government chose Olympia, despite the fact that it was 160 miles from the entrance to Puget Sound, and the all-encompassing mud flats which made navigation of the harbor impossible except at high tide. Colonel S. P. Moses was the first collector of customs and Ebey was appointed as one of the early customs collectors at this first port of entry for Puget Sound.

Levi Smith's original log cabin had expanded into a crude hotel and store, but only the barest essentials were to be purchased in Olympia until 1852, when George A. Barnes opened a general merchandise store at the west end of First street. This opened a new era, with such luxuries as soap, sperm candles, hoop skirts and patent medicines added to the pioneer necessities of axes, powder, shot, smoked salmon and whiskey.

A hard-drinking physician named David Maynard, finding the pioneers to be distressingly healthy, had opened a small general store, but he soon found it even less profitable than the practice of medicine. As a matter of fact, Doc Maynard's sovereign remedy for most

---

*Another successful business man and well known vocalist, Bing Crosby, is one who can trace his ancestry to the Crosbys of the brig *Grecian.* The old Crosby house still stands at Tumwater, and unlike most historic old landmarks in the Olympia area, has been carefully preserved as an historical shrine.

*The transcripts of these legal proceedings have been lost or removed from the court records.

CHIEF SEATTLE spent more time in Olympia than in the town that was named for him.

T. F. McElroy, co-publisher of the Olympia *Columbian*, Washington's first newspaper.

ills and afflictions, was whiskey. He didn't like to drink alone, so he dispensed his stock to those kindred souls who dropped in at his store. As the level of Doc's medicine jug went down, so did his prices ... until he ended up giving his stock away. This was not only unprofitable; it also made him unpopular with the profit-motivated merchants of the town, and before long Doc Maynard went down to Elliott Bay with Chief Seattle. There the founders of another new town, named after the Duwamish chief, made room for Doc and he and old Seattle went into the salmon salting business.

Other business houses were soon opened by A. J. Moses, J. G. Parker, Sam Coulter, L. Bettman, Goldman and Rosenblatt and Louison and Company, all of them operated more conventionally and successfully than Doc Maynard's hospitable establishment. Soon the big San Francisco shipping and mercantile firm of Kendall & Company opened a store at Olympia and made it the terminus of its line of sailing packets, thus ending forever the shortage of consumer goods on the new frontier.

Olympia soon became a mecca for frontier journalists, and within a few years it had the distinction of supporting nearly as many newspapers as saloons. The first of these were Thornton F. McElroy and J. W. Wiley, who brought a little Ramage hand press to town and, on September 11, 1852, brought forth the first issue of the weekly *Columbian*. The four-page paper was Whig in politics and dedicated to the creation of a new territory north of the Columbia river, to be named Columbia ... thus the name chosen for the region's only newspaper.

Oregon territory was admittedly far too big to be properly administered, embracing as it then did the present states of Oregon, Washington, Idaho and much of Montana, and there was not noticeable opposition to dividing it up. The result was the Monticello Convention, held on the bank of the Cowlitz river in November and December, 1852. The *Columbian* duly recorded its progress in its issue of December 11:

"Pursuant to a resolution adopted at a public meeting of the citizens of Northern Oregon, held on the 26th and 27th days of October last in the court room for Lewis County, a convention of delegates from the different precincts and settlements of Northern Oregon assembled in the town of Monticello on the 25th day of November, 1852. The convention was called to

13

Ramage hand press which printed the first newspaper in Washington.

"Just as we are going to press, a gentleman who came passenger in the steamship Columbia from San Francisco, informs us that Mr. Stevens of Massachusetts, has been appointed Governor of Washington Territory."

The editors didn't even know the first name of the new governor, but that state of affairs didn't last long. Within a few months the name of Isaac I. Stevens was known to every man, woman and child, red and white alike, in Washington territory. Some considered him a blessing and some considered him a catastrophe, but everyone was thoroughly aware of his presence.

Other progress was chronicled in those early issues of the *Columbian.* Postmaster A. W. Moore imported the first commercial vehicle, a dray pulled by a *"long-eared, high-strung, double-bass"* mule, and *"anything in the line of draying will receive prompt attention by leaving orders one door south of the Methodist Church."*

order by William H. Plumb, whereupon G. N. McConaha, Esq., was chosen President by acclamation."

Thurston County's delegates to the convention were Michael Simmons, S. D. Ruddle, S. P. Moses, Adam Whyte, Quincy A. Brooks and C. H. Hale. As a result of the convention, Congress was memorialized to create the Territory of Columbia from that portion of Oregon territory lying north of the Columbia river. The bill was introduced by Joseph Lane, delegate to congress from Oregon territory.

Congress wasted little time in doing so, although it didn't go along with the citizens in their choice of a name. Richard H. Stanton suggested that a District of Columbia and a Territory of Columbia might be confusing, and urged that the name be changed to Washington, thus honoring the father of his country. It apparently did not dawn upon the congressmen that two Washingtons might be just as confusing as two Columbias (perhaps because the national capital was always referred to as Washington City in those days), and they accepted Stanton's amendment. The measure was signed by President Millard Fillmore on March 24, 1853.

News reached Olympia either around Cape Horn or across the plains to San Francisco, thence by coastal sailing ship to Portland, and over the abominable Cowlitz trail, but the *Columbian* was able to proclaim the joyful tidings by late April of 1853. On May 7 it published a late bulletin:

Joseph Tebo respectfully informed his friends and the public generally that he had *"again established a livery stable in Olympia, where good fat horses can be obtained at any time, for a trip to the Cowlitz or for pleasure parties."* The founding father of the town, Edmund Sylvester, also took occasion to *"respectfully inform the public"* that he had just completed a scow named the *Schictwoot* (probably his version of the original Indian name of his claim, Chetwoot) and this vessel was *"in readiness to convey goods from points below to this city, being capable of carrying a large amount of freight, and perfectly water tight."*

It was further reported that *"The Kendall Company's store has become vastly popular*

Olympia's first school was source of pride to pioneers.

Captain and Mrs. Sam Percival, Olympia socialites of the Civil War era.

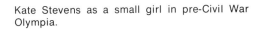

Kate Stevens as a small girl in pre-Civil War Olympia.

under the gentlemanly management of our excellent friend Capt. S. W. Percival." and furthermore, that *"the clipper captain D. J. Gove, in command of the Kendall Company's fast sailing brig G. W. Kendall, arrived in our harbor on Wednesday last, 14 days from San Francisco. She brings fine assortments of provisions to our merchants but not half enough to meet the demand."* The brig also brought a fresh supply of white paper for the *Columbian,* which was often in a state of crisis because its stock of newsprint had dwindled almost to the vanishing point, and none was to be had north of San Francisco.

On the grim side, the paper reported that *"the Indian dogs about town have been playing havoc with our neighbor's poultry."* It recommended draconian measures; *"We would prescribe a little raw beef, seasoned well with arsenic or strychnine . . . Try it. If successful, you will have the proof on table during the summer and fall."*

But there was far more good news than bad in that exciting year of 1853. The Methodists and the Catholics had both built churches during the year, and the Presbyterians were meeting in a cooper shop on the edge of town while they raised a building fund. A public school had been built the previous year, and repaired after it caved in under a heavy snowfall that winter. Edmund Sylvester donated two lots to the Masonic lodge and the first Masonic temple in the territory was built.

Olympia became a steamboat port in 1853, with the arrival of the diminutive side-wheeler *Fairy* from San Francisco on the deck of the bark *Sarah Warren.* She was intended for the Seattle-Olympia route, previously served only by a few small sloops and Indian canoes, but she proved too unseaworthy to navigate lower Sound waters with any degree of safety, and she was soon diverted to the more sheltered run between Olympia and Steilacoom, which she served more or less faithfully for four years. Then her boiler exploded as she was leaving her Steilacoom dock and her career was abruptly ended.

CHAPTER TWO
The First Decade
1853-1863

Such was the infant metropolis of the Puget Sound country when, in 1853, it welcomed the first governor of Washington territory.

The *Columbian,* which had been published during most of the year by McElroy alone, had been sold in September to Matt Smith, who kept it only about long enough to set in type the story of Stevens' arrival:

"Glorious news for Washington! Arrival of Governor Stevens! . . . Governor Stevens arrived at this place on Saturday last, November 25, 1853, through a drenching rain, having completed one of the most arduous and triumphantly successful explorations ever performed since the organization of the federal government."

Stevens made it clear that he was positive he had surveyed the best possible route for a transcontinental railway, and his enthusiasm was catching. The pioneers of Olympia were convinced that in a year or two they would be hearing the whistle of locomotives echoing over the mudflats. Unfortunately, Jefferson Davis, then the secretary of war, was not about to give his blessing to a northern railway route, and the railroad dream was not to become reality for a third of a century.

The little governor also let it be known that he planned to organize the territorial government, extinguish the titles of the Indian tribes to the lands of the territory and get rid of the Hudson's Bay company, whose subsidiary Puget Sound Agricultural company occupied thousands of acres of farm and grazing lands in the Nisqually Valley.

Stevens set out to achieve his manifold goals with a minimum of delay. On the day after his arrival he issued a proclamation dividing the territory into legislative and judicial districts and calling an election for January 30, 1854, for the election of a territorial legislature which was to assemble February 27 of that year.

The *Columbian* had earlier reprinted an item from the Boston *Journal* which stated that *"the Washington letter-writers very generally agree on the statement that Governor Stevens will probably locate the Territorial government of the new Territory of Washington at Olympia, a thriving town at the head of Puget Sound, which, it is thought in the Land Office, is shortly to become the great commercial Capital of our Northern Pacific coast possessions."*

The prediction proved accurate, at least in part. Stevens named Olympia the provisional capital, leaving it up to the legistlature to select a permanent seat of government, an occupation which engrossed legislators' attention periodically for the next half century and more, and kept the loyal citizens of Olympia in a constant state of nerves.

Stevens' efforts to get the wheels of government turning were assisted by the fact that the other territorial officials, appointed by President Franklin Pierce soon after his inauguration, had arrived at Olympia during the summer and had already undertaken much of the routine of administration. Colonel J. P. Anderson, federal marshal, had completed a census of the territory showing a population of 3,965 white citizens, 1,682 of whom were voters. Other territorial officials were Charles H. Mason, secretary, Edward Lander, chief justice, Victor Monroe, associate justice, and John S. Clendenin, federal attorney.

Immediately following Stevens' election proclamation, the Whigs held a convention at Olympia and nominated Colonel William H. Wallace for delegate to congress. The Democrats, meeting at Cowlitz Landing, nominated Columbia Lancaster, judge of the supreme court under the Oregon provisional government, who was defeated by Samuel Thurston in 1849 as Oregon territorial delegate. That rugged individualist, Mike Simmons, entered the fray as an independent candidate on his own "One Horse Ticket"; his campaign cry, "This horse will neither be stabled nor rid." The national administration was Democratic, Governor Stevens was Democratic, and it was a Democratic year in the brand new territory. The pompous and oracular Lancaster won easily and bumbled off to Washington City to spend a year of dignified confusion as Washington's first congressman.

THE FIRST LEGISLATURE

The members of the first territorial legislature duly arrived at Olympia in response to the governor's call, although the trip was not an easy one and several members arrived late. When the session convened on Feburary 27 on the second floor of a wooden frame store building on Main between 3rd and 4th streets, some members still hadn't made it, but the affairs of state were not delayed.

There were 27 members of that historic body, nine in the council (the equivalent of the present senate), and 18 in the house of representatives. The entire council, with two exceptions, was made up of men from the west side of the Cascade Mountains. D. F. Bradford and William H. Tappan of Wishram represented Clarke County*, which then took in all the sparsely populated eastern part of the territory. Other members of the council were Seth Catlin and Henry Miles of Lewis and Pacific, D. R. Bigelow and B. F. Yantis of Thurston, Lafayette Balch (the founder of Steilacoom) and G. N. McConaha of Pierce and King, and W. P. Sayward of Jefferson. McConaha, a brilliant young attorney and one of the most respected men in the territory, was elected president of the council. The legislative staff consisted of M. H. Frost, clerk, and J. L. Mitchell, sergeant at arms. Olympia lawyer Elwood Evans replaced Frost as clerk when the latter's eyes failed him early in the session.

The house members were Arthur A. Denny (leader of the party which founded Seattle), King; Samuel D. Howe and Daniel Brownfield, Island; H. D. Huntington and John P. Jackson,

Elwood Evans, lawyer, politician and historian, was no friend of Governor Stevens.

Lewis; John Scudder of Pacific; J. M. Chapman, Henry Mosely and L. F. Thompson, Pierce; David Shelton (who later founded the town of Shelton), L. G. Durgin, C. H. Hale, and Ira Ward, Jr., Thurston; F. A. Chenowith, Henry R. Crosbie (both later justices of the supreme court), A. J. Bolan, S. D. Biles and A. C. Lewis of Clarke. Judge Chenowith was elected speaker, Benjamin F. Kendall clerk, and Jacob Smith sergeant at arms. Mr. Scudder of Pacific died while preparing for the journey to Olympia, and never attended the session.

Governor Stevens, who had been busy supervising construction of "several small but comfortable buildings to be used as public offices and also a suitable building for the quarters of the Northern Railway exploring party under his charge," returned from a whirlwind visit to the lower Sound settlements in time to deliver his first message to the legislature the day after it convened.

The *Columbian* had been sold the previous month to McElroy's original partner, J. W. Wiley, who changed its name from *Columbian,* which was no longer relevant, to *Washington Pioneer*. Also, having noted that the territory was firmly in the control of the Democrats, he wisely changed the paper's politics from Whig to Democrat. The *Pioneer* forthwith set about the task of reporting the actions of the Democratic governor and legislature in a most laudatory manner. It listed Stevens' priority recommendations to the joint session of February 28 as follows:

---

*This county was named in honor of the co-leader of the Lewis and Clark expedition, which staked America's claim on the Columbia river. A clerical error placed it on the early maps as Clarke county, a mispelling which stuck until well into the twentieth century.

"1. Improved mail service
2. The extinguishing of all Indian land claims
3. A memorial to Congress urging the extension of public surveys to make possible proper title to settlers' claims.
4. Another memorial requesting a road system connecting the Columbia River with Puget Sound via Fort Vancouver, extending north to Bellingham Bay.
5. A request to the federal government to appoint a surveyor-general for Washington Territory.
6. Continuation of the northern railway survey."

The mail service to this outpost of civilization, or rather the lack of it, struck a responsible chord, for it was a sore point with everybody. The interminable delays must have been particularly galling to Stevens, who was nothing if not impatient. The *Pioneer* quoted him as follows on the matter:

"For six weeks has this territory been without communication with the States. Yet, in this interval, sailing vessels reached Seattle from San Francisco, and brought to that port information on the 12th of January which only reached the same place by mail more than six weeks subsequently."

The governor pointed out the need for a line of mail steamers between San Francisco and Puget Sound, and steamboat service on the Sound to augment the slow and cranky meanderings of the *Fairy*.

Stevens closed his message with a strong recommendation to the legislature to provide an educational system *"which shall place within the means of all the full development of the capacities with which he has been endowed."*

Governor Stevens got most of what he asked for from the legislature. House Bill 1, introduced by Representative Hale, provided for a code commission composed of Chief Justice Lander, William Strong, a former associate justice of the Oregon supreme court, and Victor Monroe, Washington territorial associate justice. The bill was quickly passed over the objections of Mr. Mosley of Pierce, who stubbornly insisted that it was the duty of the legislature to enact laws, and that they were creating a "second legislative body to assume their responsibilities."

It was fortunate that the bill was passed, for the organic act creating the new territory limited the first legislative session to 100 days. It would no doubt have bogged down hopelessly in the task of creating a whole new code of laws in that period of time. As it was, the *Pioneer* reported, *"the commission of judges daily furnished legislators with well-digested laws which could be accepted as competent and essential to promote the public welfare. The legislature was thus enabled to adjourn sine die May 1 after a session of only 64 days."*

During that 64-day session the legislature also created eight new counties . . . Cowlitz, Wahkiakum, Chehalis (later renamed Grays Harbor), Clallam, Whatcom, Sawamish (later renamed Mason in honor of the popular young territorial secretary), and Skamania. Later in the session, the eastern region of Skamania County, including much of the present state of Idaho, and Montana west of the Rockies, was removed to create Walla Walla County. County officers were named for Walla Walla County, but they were never qualified and a formal county government was nonexistent for many years.

Few details were overlooked. A territorial seal, designed by Lieutenant J. K. Duncan, was approved, and Mr. Tappan of Clarke, an engraver by trade, cut the die and turned it over to Secretary Mason to be affixed to all official documents.

By March 26 it was evident that things were progressing so well that Governor Stevens, at legislative request, left for Washington City to carry the various memorials to Congress and to lobby for their acceptance. Mason assumed the duties of acting governor, as he was to do frequently during the administration of the peripatetic governor.

During his absence, the legislature forged ahead. Territorial roads were authorized between Olympia and Shoalwater Bay (Willapa Harbor), from Cathlamet to S.S. Ford's place in Lewis County, and from Olympia to Monticello (the present site of Longview). The new code of laws was adopted, provisional officers were appointed for the new counties, and time was found to perform a heartwarming act of legislative kindness.

MIGHTY WHITE OF MR. BUSH

George Bush, the pioneer of the Simmons party, had developed his Bush prairie farm into the richest in the territory. When the wagon trains of 1853 arrived, stricken by drought, cholera and hostile plains Indians,

Bush had opened his barns to the half-starved immigrants and told them to take what they needed to tide them over until their own crops were in. Many of the families had eaten their seed grain to ward off starvation, and Bush's largess was a true godsend to them. He could have cleaned up a fortune as a frontier food profiteer, but he refused payment, telling his new neighbors to return what they took when they could afford to.

Most of the newcomers appreciated the kindness of George Bush, but a few didn't. The old laws of Oregon territory forbade ownership of land by Negroes, or "persons of African descent" and it was contended by some that, since Bush had filed on his claim under those laws, he held no valid title to it; that his rich farm was up for grabs.

Early in that first legislative session, Mr. Bigelow of Thurston, according to the *Pioneer*, *"presented the petition of I. N. Ebey and 54 others asking the Legislative Assembly to memorialize Congress to donate to George Bush, a free mulatto, a section of land under provisions of the Act of 1850."*

The petition was referred to the committee on memorials, which quickly approved it, as did the legislature and, in due time, the Congress of the United States. George Bush and his heirs were given title to the farm they had carved from the wilderness. It should not be inferred, however, that this indicated a spirit of racial tolerance among the frontier legislators. They admired George Bush as an individual, but most of them were strongly anti-abolitionist Democrats, not a few were out and out copperheads, and the majority favored exclusionary land laws similar to those of Oregon. Governor Stevens was among those who wanted to ban nonwhites from the territory, a stand which eventually led to a showdown with Mike Simmons, who was one of Stevens' most loyal early supporters, but who remained even more fiercely loyal to his old friend Bush.

One of the few things the first territorial legislature didn't accomplish was the choosing of a permanent capital. This it held over for the second session to be held in December of the same year. Olympia remained the interim capital. It also failed to pass the governor's militia law . . . an oversight which was to be bitterly regretted . . . and also rejected by one vote, a measure proposed by Arthur Denny to grant the right to vote to the white women of the territory . . . the first round in what was to be a 58-year-long fight.

Although the first legislature had earned the accolade of the *Pioneer* that, during its 64-day session, *"more business was dispatched, with the assistance of the Code Commission, we will venture to say, than has been accomplished by any legislative body within the same length of time on the Pacific Coast,"* it found time for such diversions as the rude frontier capital provided.

A bed of delicious native Olympia oysters had been discovered, and the *Pioneer* observed that *"oyster suppers appear to be the order of the evenings since the commencement of the session of our legislature, and the delegations from the 'fresh drink' on the south appear to have an unusual relish for the clam chowders and oyster stews of our 'salt chuck'."*

Editor Wiley attended "a magnificent entertainment" given by Colonel McConaha on the evening of his election to the presidency of the council, at which the governor, the judiciary, most of the members of the assembly and others participated. Later in the session, Mr. Wiley and his always robust appetite were present at another seafood banquet given by Speaker Chenowith at the Washington hotel. This he reported with equal enthusiasm, concluding with the opinion that *"Mr. Chenowith is one of the most agreeable men living."*

There were several saloons in Olympia by 1854, and the bar of the Washington hotel was conveniently adjacent to the first legislative building, which was located, somewhat fittingly, at the present site of the Washington state liquor store. Arthur Denny and one or two of the other assemblymen were teetotalers, but the majority were not. It was customary in those early sessions of the territorial legislature to keep a demijohn of high-voltage frontier whiskey behind the door of each chamber. As the members entered, they were asked by the sergeant at arms if they had "taken the pledge of allegiance". If not, they were directed to the jug behind the door and took a refreshing swig from the shoulder in true pioneer style.

McConaha, the young president of the council, described by Elwood Evans as *"a thorough parliamentarian, an able debater and a master in invective; a consumate jury lawyer, a successful advocate,"* was one of the rare few who did not take the "pledge of allegiance." An alcoholic, he had come west to find a new life, and he had found it. He stopped drinking and became a devoted husband and father as well as a highly successful frontier lawyer. He was, as Evans wrote in his early history of Washington, *"in the prime of vigorous manhood, and had he lived, a brilliant future awaited him."*

When the first territorial legislature adjourned *sine die* on the evening of May Day, 1854, McConaha intended to go directly to the Indian canoe which was to take him down the Sound to his home in King County. Then, as now, *sine die* was celebrated with much liquid cheer. Some of the celebrants overtook the popular McConaha, dragged him back to the hotel bar and forced a drink down his throat. After the first one the reformed alcoholic didn't have to be forced. When he finally embarked on his return voyage to Seattle, his canoe was swamped between Vashon Island and Alki Point. He and all but one of his Indian crew were drowned.

James W. Wiley of the *Washington Pioneer* was an alcoholic who had never tried to reform. As a matter of fact, it was his boast that he couldn't write until he got so drunk he couldn't walk. His considerable wit, he was convinced, was sharpened with every drink, and he would prop himself up in the back shop and dictate his news stories and pungent editorials to the compositor. He was apparently little concerned with his personal appearance or grooming, editor Charles Prosch of the recently establish-

ed *Puget Sound Courier* at Steilacoom describing him as looking *"wild enough to have made his escape from Barnum's Museum of Curiosities."*

The legislature had established the position of public printer, the act providing that this official was to be elected annually by a joint session of the house and council, and was to "execute all printing ordered by the assembly".

Wiley, having further proved his loyalty to the party in power by changing the name of his paper again, to *Pioneer and Democrat,* was chosen.

The job of public printer was to be a center of controversy and a prime political plum until well into the twentieth century, and Wiley set the ball rolling in fine style. The new territorial laws were turned over to him for printing soon after adjournment. There were 572 pages of them, providing an impossible task for a printing shop with only one compositor, two small hand presses and few fonts of second-hand type from the *Oregonian.* Wiley sent his partner, Alfred Berry, east to have the laws published in New York, but by June numerous public officials and lawyers were getting impatient. Wiley responded with a monumental display of journalistic rage and indignation at this public ingratitude, pointing out that he had devoted almost all of his newspaper to printing the more important laws and advising the malcontents to buy back issues of the

FIRST KNOWN PICTURE OF OLYMPIA, from sketchbook of Army Lieutenant Alden, 1860.

Pioneer and Democrat as a source of reference until the books were printed.

Berry, having placed the printing order in New York, made a visit to his home in New Hampshire, where he died of smallpox at the age of 29. The laws never did appear in Washington territory during Wiley's term as public printer. When they were finally distributed, late in 1855, they bore the imprint of his successor, George Goudy. Not even the journals of the two houses of the legislature ever emerged from the confusion of the *Pioneer and Democrat's* back shop, and Wiley bowed out as gracefully as possible after one term as printer and got himself elected to the legislature.

There was, by 1854, a growing feeling of unrest between settlers and their Indian neighbors, as more of the Indian's choicest land was appropriated. Furthermore, many of the newcomers did not treat the Indians as kindly and fairly as had the first settlers. Isolated cases of Indians murdering white men and white men murdering Indians were on the increase, and it was becoming increasingly apparent to the Indians that murderers of their race were usually hanged, whereas white men who murdered Indians went free.

But it was Governor Stevens, back from Washington City and still vibrating with energy, who managed to goad the naturally indolent and easy-going Sound Indians into active hostility . . . or at any rate, enough of them to throw the white settlers into a state of panic and the territory into a virtual state of suspended animation.

Returning to Olympia in December as the second territorial legislature convened, Stevens met with the members long enough to deliver a message largely devoted to various measures he felt should be taken against the Indians . . . the urgency of immediately organizing the militia and memorializing congress to place upon the Oregon Trail "such force as will inflict summary chastisement on hostile Indians and render it safe for our immigrants moving in small bodies."

Having delivered his message, Stevens set off on a whirlwind series of treaties, aimed at acquiring the Indian's rights to most of the present states of Washington, Idaho and Montana. Before leaving Olympia, however, he met with Michael Simmons, whom he had appointed Indian agent, and other members of his staff to draw up a treaty which would decide the future destiny of "the Nisqually, Puyallup, Steilacoom, Squaxin and other tribes and bands of upper Puget Sound who, for the purposes of this treaty, are to be considered as one nation." There was, of course, no consultation with the Indians involved. Colonel Benjamin Shaw, a glib, baby-faced man who served as interpreter in Stevens' dealing with the Indians, when asked by Steven if he could get them to sign the document, replied, "Yes, I can get them to sign their death warrant."

BURY MY CONSCIENCE
AT MEDICINE CREEK

After writing the treaty and dispatching a crew of advance men to assemble the Indians, Stevens and his retinue left Olympia on a schooner for the twenty-mile voyage to the Nisqually river delta, where the council was held on the banks of McAllister creek, called *She-nah-nam* by the Indians, near its junction with Medicine Creek.

The fiction of Indian "nations" in the Pacific Northwest was most unrealistic. In fact, the so-called tribes generally had no formal government or laws and no chiefs of any real authority. With rare exceptions, the tribal "chiefs" were appointed by Stevens in order to have official signatures, or rather "X's" on the treaties. Ezra Meeker, one of the early settlers and a later historian, wrote:

"The fiction of the nine tribes to deal with in the Medicine Creek Council can readily be seen when the facts are stated. There were less than nine hundred Indians, nearly eight hundred of whom belonged to the Nisqually and Puyallup tribes, leaving but a hundred to comprise the remaining seven so-called tribes, probably fifteen to a tribe."

Assured by his advisors of an easy victory over the simple savages, Stevens' never abundant patience wore thin when he found that only about two-thirds of the Indians had gathered at the treaty ground, and that they were suspicious and in no mood to quickly sign over their heritage to the white man. There had been many frightening rumors circulated among the Indians, including a widely believed one to the effect that the government planned to ship all of them out of the country to a land of perpetual cold and darkness. There was much palaver among the Indians, with Shaw and Simmons circulating among them, backslapping, cracking jokes in the Chinook trade jargon and generally trying to get them in a good humor, but with marked lack of success.

Stevens, angry and scowling, paced back and force in front of his tent with his massive head down and his hands behind his back and there is some reason to believe, as did Meeker, that he occasionally entered the tent for a pull at a jug of his favorite nerve medicine.*

By the next day it was common knowledge among the Nisquallies that Stevens intended to herd the whole tribe onto two sections of heavily timbered and virtually useless table land on top of the bluffs east of the Nisqually delta. The Nisquallies were horse and cattle breeders, and Stevens' proposed reservation would have provided no grazing land whatever, and would have given each member of the tribe only four acres of the unusable land.

The news caused much dismay among the Indians, as well as a major division of opinion. Some influential tribesmen took a defeatist attitude, pointing out that it would be useless to pit their strength against that of the Boston men; that they should sign the treaty and hope for the best.

Leschi, the first Indian friend of the first white settlers was a leader of the opposition. He was not a chief . . . the Nisqually tribe had no formal chief at that time . . . but he was the wealthiest and most influential member of the tribe, running large herds and operating a successful farm. He was the tribe's informal judge, settling disputes and keeping the peace along the Nisqually. For these reasons, Stevens had commissioned him, along with his brother, Quiemuth, as sub-chiefs of the Nisqually tribe.

As the day progressed, Leschi's anger and frustration equaled those of the governor. He was outspoken in his opinion that it would be better to die fighting for his peoples' rights than to starve to death on the miserable reservation which was to be alloted to them.

Nothing was accomplished that day. On the second day, under a weeping sky, some of the less determined chiefs and sub-chiefs signed the treaty. On the third day Stevens felt the time was ripe to woo the rest with the gifts brought along for the occasion, but his plan backfired badly. The gifts consisted of a limited supply of cheap cloth, jewsharps, other tawdry trinkets . . . and jugs of blackstrap molasses. Many of the Indians were under the impression that these constituted the full payment for their land and homes. Even those who knew better were scornful of the white men's *cultus ictas* (useless things).

Stevens and his party insisted that Leschi was among the chiefs who had signed the treaty, and they had his "X" on the document to back up their contention, but the Indians who were present insisted, as long as they lived, that Leschi had demanded bottom land for farming and prairie land for grazing; that Stevens' temper exploded and he shouted that Leschi was not a true Nisqually . . . that his mother had been a Klickitat . . . that he must leave the treaty grounds. Leschi, they said, then tore up his commission as sub-chief and stamped it in the mud. His mark on the white man's paper was forged.*

Among those who witnessed the chiefs' marks was Hazzard Stevens, the governor's 12-year-old son, who insisted just as stoutly throughout his lifetime that Leschi had signed. George Leschi, interviewed a half century later by Ezra Meeker as to whether his uncle, Leschi, had signed the treaty, replied, "I don't know; I was a boy then, about the size of Governor Stevens' *tenas man,* and we were having a good time eating blackstrap and playing jewsharps while the men were talking. We didn't know what they were talking about."

Whether he signed or not, there is no doubt that Leschi went from the treaty grounds in anger, vowing to fight for his peoples' land if need be. The *Pioneer and Democrat* of December 30, 1854, commented blandly that *"On Tuesday, the 26th of this month, a treaty was made with several Indian tribes at the*

---

*Meeker stated flatly that "the reason why this awful blunder was made (the attempt to assign the Indians to a reservation area incapable of supporting life) is not hard to find if we will but search a little and tell what we know. Governor Stevens was intoxicated and unfit for transacting business while making these treaties." (*Pioneer Reminiscences of Puget Sound; the Tragedy of Leschi, Ezra Meeker, 1905, page 258*).

---

*Meeker wrote, "To my mind the fact is abundantly proven that the Indians strenuously objected to having all their land taken from them save a small area of heavily timbered upland, totally unfit for cultivation; that the governor stubbornly refused to give way an inch, but insisted that they must submit to his will, and that not only did Leschi not sign the treaty, but many others whose names are attached as signers did not sign, or give their assent." (*Pioneer Reminiscences,* page 245).

*head of the Sound, whereby they relinquished all their lands * * * * Nearly every member of the several tribes was present, 633 actually ratified, and through their chiefs and delegates signed the treaty; 29 came afterwards, and 20 more were on the way. Great pains were taken to express the provisions of the treaty, and the Indians were entirely satisfied."*

For awhile it appeared that all might pass over as quietly as the *Pioneer and Democrat* seemed to think it would. The treaties had to be sent to Washington City for ratification, and during much of 1855 the Medicine creek treaty was in abeyance. Governor Stevens had dashed on to make more treaties with the Puget Sound tribes to the north and thence back across the Rocky Mountains to treat with the Blackfoot nation. Leschi returned to his home on Muck creek, where he and his brother Quiemuth planted their crops and tended their herds.

Meanwhile, back at Olympia, young Secretary Mason had again assumed the duties of acting governor, and the second territorial legislature continued its deliberations for a full 60 days... in early 1855. It passed a militia law sufficient to entitle the territory to its quota of arms and ammunition, amended the school, road and fence laws, and increased the membership of the house of representatives from 18 to 30 members.

Apparently determined to prove that their tender treatment of George Bush during the previous session hadn't set a precedent of racial tolerance, they amended the marriage laws, *"declaring all marriages void between parties where one of the spouses was a white person and the other more than one-fourth Negro or one-half Indian blood, except that parties within the proscribed classes then unlawfully living together could marry; a penalty of not less than 50 nor more than 500 dollars to be imposed against any clergyman or judicial officer performing such marriage."* The frontier legislators were thus enabled to express both the bigotry and sexual morality of their era in a single bill.

Much of the session was devoted to wrangling over which of the territory's ambitious settlements should receive the political plums of the various territorial institutions. The territorial university was eventually awarded to Seattle, with a branch to be established on Boisfort Prairie in Lewis County. The penitentiary was to be located at Vancouver, and the capitol building on ten acres of land on the hill

"immediately south of the platted townsite of Olympia," which Edmund Sylvester had donated for that purpose from his original donation claim . . . provided clear title could be established. Steilacoom and Vancouver, then major population centers of the territory and both larger than Seattle, were also contenders, and their supporters wanted to be assured that things wouldn't move too rapidly in the matter of capitol construction.

A five-member committee, three from the council and two from the house, was appointed to examine the title to the donated land. Chairman William H. Wallace, Councilman Henry Miles and Representative Timothy Heald reported the title unsatisfactory and recommended repeal of the just-passed capitol location bill. Representative Alexander S. Abernethy and Councilman Benjamin Yantis of Thurston issued a minority report insisting that the title was "as good as any title to lands in the territory could be made." They added a supplementary bill instructing the territorial secretary to file the deeds, and declaring the capitol location law in force "from and after its passage." Their bill was passed by a thin majority, along with a joint resolution asking the federal government to approve the spending of $5,000 to build a "temporary" capitol building. Loyal Olympians breathed a sigh of relief, but they would soon find that the fight to secure this prestigious plum had just begun.

THE LULL BEFORE THE STORM

The capital city of the territory had some reason to feel smug during that spring and summer of 1855. The *Pioneer and Democrat* pointed out with much civic pride that:

"Two years ago we had no school here of any description, and the gospel of Christ was nowhere dispensed. A resident minister, Mr. Whitworth, now administers to the members of the Presbyterian Church and the public, on fixed Sabbaths, and a Sabbath school has sprung into existence under his charge.

"Education, Christianity and general improvement go hand in hand, and under the direction of Mrs. M. A. Hamm, one of the best sacred musical teachers in existence, a class has been organized and will no doubt be adequately sustained. The Classical, Mathematical, Commercial and Training School of Mr. B. Cornelius is filling its office most

successfully with the youth by which we are surrounded."

Samuel Holmes, daguerreotypist, had established studios "over the cabinet shop of D. Beatty" and was prepared "for the taking of Daguerreotype likenesses, and all other matters connected with the art." Colonel William Cock opened up a new hotel, the Pacific House, at the corner of Main and 3rd streets and was *"prepared to accommodate boarders and travelers with private rooms and afford such entertainment as he trusts will be appreciated by a liberal and discriminating public."* A. J. Baldwin completed a *"large and commodious livery stable"* with a capacity of 100 horses and providing service *"night and day."*

Local shipbuilding had progressed from the rude scow *Schictwoot* of Edmund Sylvester to the launching of the schooner *Emilie Parker,* built by D. H. Morgan and chartered to John G. Parker for freight and passenger service on the Sound. Furthermore, the frail and unreliable steamboat *Fairy* was joined by Parker's small iron propeller steamer, the *Traveler,* which ventured to such distant waters as Port Townsend and Whidbey Island. Soon she was joined by the 100-foot propeller *Major Tompkins,* brought up from San Francisco by the firm of Hunt and Scranton to carry mail, freight and passengers between Olympia, Victoria and way ports.

Edward Giddings built a wharf 300 feet out over the mudflats to accommodate this increasing shipping, and legislators from the lower Sound were able to reach the capital in unheard of comfort.

Unfortunately the career of the *Major Tompkins* and the *Traveler* were brief, both being wrecked and sunk on the treacherous waters of the lower Sound and Strait of Juan de Fuca, but the pioneers had demonstrated that they would patronize steamboats in preference to Indian canoes, and these early and ill-fated vessels were soon replaced by larger and more seaworthy craft.

By early fall the *Pioneer and Democrat* was able to report that the county commissioners had appropriated $500 to build a bridge across the west arm of Budd inlet, contingent upon the citizens of Olympia raising another thousand dollars. They did, and the contract for the plank and pile structure was duly let to J. L. Perkins. It was noted that *"its completion will be hailed as a great public convenience."* The

AUNT BECKY HOWARD'S PRIDE, the Pacific House, was a favorite gathering place of territorial politicians.

editor might not have been so enthusiastic had he known the troubles that bridge and its successors would inflict upon the town over the years to come.

Further *"improvements in Olympia and vicinity"* were duly noted by the *Pioneer and Democrat* throughout 1854 and into the autumn of 1855. Politics were going much to Editor Wiley's liking also. President Pierce had appointed General Samual Tilton, a hero of the Mexican war, as territorial surveyor-general, and the settlers were happy that the Democratic administration was in the process of making their land claims valid. Wiley was also able to report that:

"The legislature is largely Democratic in both branches and all the officers are Democrats except one, who owes his election to an unfortunate misunderstanding on the part of some of the members." He was referring to Benjamin Kendall, the clerk, whose political loyalties were frequently in doubt.

The choice of a territorial printer was not subject to misunderstanding. As a replacement for the deceased Berry, Wiley selected a young *Oregonian* printer named George B. Goudy to manage his newspaper's back shop. Goudy was selected by the legislature in January of 1855 to replace the senior partner, and the profits were thus kept in the firm.

To Wiley and the other citizens of pioneer Olympia, the goose may have appeared to hang high, but the storm clouds were gathering.

REAPING THE WHIRLWIND

Isaac Stevens, having completed his whirlwind round of treaty-making in the Puget Sound country, had departed for eastern Washington and then on to the Blackfoot country, leaving a smouldering fire of savage indignation behind him. Gold had been discovered on the Colville river and miners on their way to the diggings were murdered by Indians through whose land they passed. A. J. Bolan, the Indian agent, was killed and cremated when he went to the Yakimas to demand the murderers. Major Haller and a detachment of U.S. dragoons were dispatched from Fort Dalles, and Lieutenant Slaughter with a small force of infantrymen from Fort Steilacoom, to punish the hostile tribesmen. Haller's force was mauled and routed, and Slaughter's troops retreated back across the Cascades.

On October 22, 1855, Leschi was in Olympia, and was pointed out to Acting Governor Mason by James McAllister as a possible source of trouble. "He don't talk right." McAllister told Mason. A week earlier Mason, at the request of Captain Maloney, then in command of the regular troops at Fort Steilacoom, had issued a call for two companies of territorial volunteers, one to be raised at Olympia; the other at Vancouver. The ranks were promptly filled and one of the companies, commanded by Captain Gilmore Hays was sworn into the federal service and assigned to Captain Maloney's force of regulars. On the day Leschi visited the capital, Mason issued another proclamation, calling for four additional companies "In order to make fully secure the lives and property of our inhabitants from any incursions or outbreaks on the part of the Indians, and to be prepared for any emergency." One of these companies, commanded by Captain Charles Eaton and known as Eaton's Rangers, was dispatched by Mason on October 24 to take Leschi into custody and bring him to Olympia as a hostage for the good behavior of his tribe.

Word reached the Nisqually leader on the prairie where he was helping his brother Quiemuth plow for the fall planting. Both men fled on their fastest horses, leaving the plowshare of peace to rust in its uncompleted furrow.

It was a serious mistake on the part of the acting governor, a young man still in his twenties, but one for which he could hardly be blamed. McAllister, whom Leschi had

Indian War blockhouse on Chambers Prairie near Olympia.

befriended from the first, had warned Mason that his old friend showed signs of becoming a "bad Indian," and it is unlikely that Stevens, the haughty little governor, had had many kind words for the big Indian who had outshouted him at Medicine Creek and stalked from the treaty ground.

Eaton's Rangers continued on the track of Leschi and Quiemuth, camping for the night to the east of the Puyallup river. Having set out with only two days supplies, the 19-man company was running short of food, and Quartermaster William Winlock Miller was dispatched to Fort Steilacoom for supplies and pack horses. At the same time, the two second lieutenants were sent to Olympia and Grand Mound to try to recruit more members for Eaton's undermanned unit. The first lieutenant, none other than James McAllister, volunteered to reconnoiter the military road leading to the White river. He left with one soldier and two friendly Indians with orders from Eaton to return that evening.

"I will return if I am alive," McAllister replied.

Soon afterward, Eaton and Editor Wiley, who had enlisted in the ranger company and was serving as both soldier and war correspondent for the *Pioneer and Democrat,* rode off in the same direction to investigate a reported soft spot in the trail that might need repair. As they were returning to the cabin in which the company was spending the night they heard seven shots in the distance.

"My God, our boys are gone!" Captain Eaton told Wiley. Then, galloping ahead to the camp, he ordered his men to saddle their horses, pack their baggage, "and above all things keep cool."

According to Wiley's on-the-spot report, the shots that killed Jim McAllister and began the

Indian war on the west side of the Cascades were fired on the evening of October 27, 1855. There, within a few square miles of the area known as Connell's prairie, between the Puyallup and White rivers, the major battles of the war were to be fought and the small band of Puget Sound Indians who had chosen to fight for their homes . . . probably no more than 200 . . . would make their headquarters for the next five months.

The first of the battles began quickly after the ambush death of McAllister and his companion, Connell, who had died on the claim he had staked and the prairie which was named for him. Hurrying on toward the ranger's camp, the Indians nearly captured Eaton and Wiley, and kept the cabin under siege all night. At dawn they withdrew, taking all the volunteers' horses with them. The rangers, one wounded, made their way back to Olympia on foot.

On October 28, as Governor Stevens began the thousand-mile journey back to his capital from the Blackfoot country, and the day after the death of McAllister and Connell, nine settlers on the White river were attacked by Indians and massacred, men, women and children. Only four small children, shepherded by seven-year-old Johnny King and aided by a friendly Indian, reached Seattle to tell their frightening tale of murder and mutilation.

Later reconstruction of events indicates that the massacre was the work of a band of Klickitats under Chief Nelson; that Leschi was not present and that, indeed, his anger at this slaughter of the peaceful settlers came near to breaking up the coalition of fighting Indians from the Sound tribes. But Leschi's name was becoming a household word on the frontier . . . a word synonymous with terror, death and destruction.

News of the White river massacre spread panic across the Puget Sound country and sent most of the settlers racing toward the nearest settlements, forts and blockhouses. Agriculture, business and trade virtually came to a standstill. At Olympia, workmen putting the last touches on the little wooden capitol building on the hill lay down their tools and joined the volunteers. At a town meeting presided over by Colonel Cock and Elwood Evans, and upon the advice of Surveyor-general Tilton, who was also serving as adjutant-general of militia, the whole town turned out to build a timber stockade along 4th street from one arm of the bay to the other. A

FRIEND IN NEED: Hudson's Bay Company's steamer *Beaver.*
. . . *from painting by Patrick Haskett*

blockhouse was erected at Main street, mounting an old cannon from the revenue cutter *Lane.* The cannon was not destined to be fired in anger, but it would see a great deal of service in happier days to come.

On November 10 the body of McAllister was brought to Olympia, along with those of A. Benton Moses and Joseph Miles who, like McAllister, were shot from ambush on Connell's prairie. They had been returning from the Yakima country with dispatches from Captain Maloney, who with Captain Gilmore Hays' Puget Sound Mounted Volunteers from Olympia, was campaigning against the Yakimas, who were on the warpath in strength. They died on October 31.

Olympia's first military funeral was a sad occasion. The bodies were placed in rough coffins and driven to the cemetery on Chamber's prairie under sable clouds and dismally falling rain. The mourners, including Moses' and McAllister's young widows, followed the wagon through the mud. The town's only musical group, a fifer and a drummer, led the way playing the one tune they knew . . . "The Girl I Left Behind Me".

The general fear and despondency was not dispelled by the arrival in the harbor of the bark *Willimantic* from San Francisco. The vessel's arrival had been eagerly anticipated, as she was expected to have on board the quota of federal arms and ammunition which had been authorized by the secretary of war following the passage of the territorial militia law. Her holds held not a single musket or a grain of powder. Captain Bolan, the brig's master, explained that grafting army officers at

Benicia Arsenal had demanded that he pad his freight charges from the standard $10 a ton to $14, and kick back the difference to them. When the crusty shipmaster told them to go to hell, they decided to let the shipment wait until they met a more amenable and less honest mariner.

Things looked a little better on November 23 when the Hudson's Bay Company's armed side-wheel steamer *Beaver,* dispatched from Victoria by Governor Douglas, arrived at Olympia. Mason had appealed to Douglas for help and he had responded with the arms and ammunition which had been denied the settlers by the United States army, along with the assurance that the *Beaver,* with her battery of brass cannon, would remain on Puget Sound as long as she was needed.

The third territorial legislature assembled at Olympia on the first Monday in December, meeting at the new Masonic Temple on upper Main street. Governor Stevens didn't arrive from his latest treaty-making until January 19, 1856. He was greeted by the entire populace and a 38-gun salute from the blockhouse cannon. He responded with a blood-and-thunder speech in which he promised that *"the war shall be prosecuted until the last hostile Indian is exterminated."**

He went further in his warlike remarks in his address to the legislature, letting his implacable hatred for Leschi and the other Indians who had opposed him spill out to be recorded in the journal of the house of representatives:

"I am opposed to any treaties; I shall oppose any treaty with these hostile bands. I will protest against any and all treaties made with them:—nothing but death is a mete punishment for their perfidy—their lives should pay the forfeit."

Stevens was roundly cheered, while the *Pioneer and Democrat* fiercely attacked the editor of Steilacoom's *Puget Sound Courier,* who had had the temerity to caption one of his editorials *"Governor Stevens' War,"* and further intimate that the little governor's high-speed and arbitrary treaty-making had precipitated the Indian troubles. Wiley of the *Pioneer and Democrat* took time off from his martial duties to compose an editorial of his own, charging that *"the above elegant caption*

heads a miserably untrue, and worse gram-matical, editorial in the HALF-SHEETED COURIER."*

Marshaling further reserves of indignation, Wiley proceeded:

*"The COURIER justifies the Indian perfidy of these misbegotten heathen in murdering innocent and inoffending Americans * * * It is not our business here to inquire how the war began. It now EXISTS and there is but one duty, and that is TO CONQUER A JUST PEACE * * * We have read the treaties already negotiated, and we pronounce it FALSE THAT SUCH TREATIES ARE THE CAUSE OF THIS WAR. There is not an instance in the history of our Indian affairs where so much benevolence and liberality has been extended to the Indian tribes."*

Although no battle of the Indian war was waged within miles of the territorial capital, political orators and jingoistic frontier editors succeeded in whipping war hatred and hysteria to the boiling point. Much was said of the massacre of the nine noncombatants on the White river. There was little or no mention, either then or by future historians, of the equally brutal massacre of four times as many old men, women and children of the Nisqually and Puyallup tribes on the Michel river by Captain H.J.G. Maxon and his mounted volunteers. Maxon, described by Meeker as *"a jolly wit, with a stomach entirely out of proportion to his brain, but of such address as to gain the full confidence of his men,"* also gained the full confidence of his commander-in-chief, Stevens, becoming one of his most trusted lieutenants.

By January of 1856 the hostile Indians in the Puget Sound country were scattered, hungry and almost out of ammunition. Leschi, aware that his cause was lost, visited the Olympia area in secret to sound out the possibility of an honorable peace. He was met by Stevens' cries for total extermination. He and the other war chiefs decided upon a last desperate gamble to gain food, weapons and a victory over the whites.

THE BATTLE OF SEATTLE

As they deployed in preparation for that final effort, Stevens left Olympia on the government steamer *Active* for a tour of the Sound. He arrived at the straggling village of Seattle on Jaunary 24, where the United States sloop-of-war *Decatur,* Captain Gansevoort, lay

*Pioneer and Democrat, January 25, 1856.

at anchor with guns run out. The citizens had been warned by friendly Indians of an impending attack upon their settlement, and they had convinced Captain Gansevoort that they needed the protection of his ship.

Stevens, in one of his more remarkable speeches considering his recent warlike utterances, told the settlers, "I have just returned from the countries of the Nez Perces and of the Coeur dAlenes. I have visited many tribes on the way, both going and coming, and I tell you there are not fifty hostile Indians in the territory, and I believe that the cities of New York and San Francisco will as soon be attacked by Indians as the town of Seattle."

The governor spent the rest of the day trying to convince Captain Gansevoort that he should abandon Seattle and take the *Decatur* on down the Sound with the *Active*. The captain, fortunately for Seattle, declined, and Stevens sailed away in a huff on January 25. Fifteen hours later the Indians attacked Seattle. The battle raged all day and two of the defenders were killed, but when Stevens returned he still insisted that the hostile Indians and, presumably the Battle of Seattle, were figments of the townspeoples' imagination.*

---

*Ezra Meeker ventured the predictable opinion that Stevens' bizarre behavior at Seattle was the result of having been at the *Active's* rum keg on the cruise down the Sound from Olympia.

To William N. Bell, one of Seattle's founding fathers, the battle was real enough, and he described it thus to Arthur Denny in a letter dispatched to him at Olympia, where he was serving as speaker of the house:

"Sebastopol is not taken yet. We had an engagement with the Indians last Saturday (January 26th). It commenced at half past 8 o'clock a.m., and continued until dark, incessantly, and resulted in the death of two 'Bostons' . . . Milton Holgate and Christian White. I have no idea how many Indians were killed, but there were a number. My house was burned on my claim during the action, but the out-houses are still standing around the ruins of the cabin. Your cabin on the point is standing, but your house in town was robbed of flour, and perhaps other things on the night of the attack.

"Please find out and inform me what course I must pursue to obtain remuneration for the loss of my house. But a part of my cattle came in last night. Should this state of things

continue there will not be six families left here in the spring. The Decatur is afloat, and most of our women and children are aboard her."

The Battle of Seattle was, in fact, almost the last skirmish in the war west of the Cascades. Driven off by the guns of the *Decatur* and thwarted in their attempts to capture new supplies and weapons, the Indians knew that they were beaten. After inconclusive engagements in February with the regulars at White river and the volunteers on Connell's prairie, the remnants of Leschi's ragged band made a winter retreat across Natchez pass to seek refuge with the Yakimas.

MARTIAL LAW

By the time the war in the west was really over, Stevens had reversed his previous stand and insisted that it was still raging. He viewed with great suspicion a group of former Hudson's Bay employees who had taken claims in the Nisqually valley. A number of them had Indian wives, and the fact that they were not molested by the hostile bands indicated to Stevens that they must be traitors. He ordered them to leave their claims for a stockade, and when they persisted in returning he ordered them imprisoned.

The imprisoned settlers obtained the services of attorneys William Wallace and Frank Clark (described as "designing lawyers" by the *Pioneer and Democrat*), who applied to Judge Francis A. Chenowith, chief justice of the territorial supreme court, for writs of *habeas corpus*. The judge was confined to his home on Whidbey Island by illness, but he issued the writs, and asked his colleague, Judge Edward M. Lander, to call a special court session at Steilacoom to act upon them. Lander, a former Mexican War officer, was serving at the time as a lieutenant-colonel of territorial volunteers and was encamped with his troops on the Duwamish river at Georgetown. In order to avoid a charge of desertion, he sent his letter of resignation to Stevens and departed for Steilacoom.

The little governor didn't take kindly to being crossed by one of his own militia officers, even if he did happen to be a supreme court justice, and he immediately proclaimed martial law, suspending all civil courts. Aware of the risk he was running, Lander nevertheless opened court on May 7 and was empaneling grand jurors when a detachment of volunteers led by the baby-faced and magnificently epauletted Colonel Shaw entered the courtroom. Shaw waited until the jurors were sworn in; then announced that court was closed by order of the governor. His troops pushed aside the deputy marshal and surrounded the judge. Lawyers rose to their feet in great excitement, and citizens in the room made tentative motions toward the revolvers they carried under their coats. Fearing a shoot-out between settlers and militiamen, Lander adjourned the court.

Shaw and his troopers then quickly hustled the judge outside, where the full company of volunteers was assembled. The judge, his clerk and the court records were escorted to Olympia at a gallop, where Stevens told Lander he was no longer in custody, since martial law had been proclaimed only in Pierce county.

District court was due to convene there on May 12, and Lander opened proceedings right on time in the meeting hall on the second floor of the Washington hotel, next door to the building that had housed the first legislature. There he quickly issued the writs directing the governor to produce the jailed settlers. Stevens responded by extending martial law to Thurston county.

The judge then cited the governor for contempt of court. The governor ignored the order. The marshal, with a posse, was ordered across the street to the governor's office with a warrant for his arrest. They were ejected bodily from the executive office by Stevens and his supporters, and Stevens, his dander now fully up, sent for a company of Oregon volunteers encamped at Tumwater. Judge Lander hastily adjourned court and fled to the law office of Elwood Evans. Captain Bluford Miller of the volunteer company tracked him there, kicked in the door, and marched both Lander and Evans down the muddy street to confront Stevens. Evans was dismissed, and the governor offered the judge his freedom if he would agree not to hold court again until the governor told him he could. Lander refused and was taken to the volunteer Camp Montgomery, where he was locked up with the settlers for whom he had issued the writs.

Evans and Benjamin Kendall proceeded to organize a protest meeting in front of the governor's office but a rival meeting of Stevens supporters soon assembled and drowned them out.

Judge Chenowith, urged on by members of the bar, who were generally appalled at Stevens' high-handed disregard for the law,

arose from his sickbed and opened court again at Steilacoom, having first ordered the sheriff of Pierce county to organize a 50-man posse to protect the court.

Lieutenant Silas B. Curtis duly arrived from Camp Montgomery with 30 armed volunteers, but finding the courtroom well defended and being reluctant to order his Indian fighters to fire upon their fellow settlers, he heeded the advice of Colonel Silas Casey, commander of the regular garrison at Fort Steilacoom, and withdrew his troops. Chenowith continued with routine legal matters. That night Stevens terminated martial law, which he had no legal right to invoke in the first place.

The next day Judge Chenowith issued a new writ, ordering all the prisoners, including Judge Lander, brought into court, but Colonel Shaw, in command of the volunteer post at Camp Montgomery, refused to honor it. Chenowith sent the United States marshal to arrest the colonel.

Stevens had played out his hand. During the period of martial law he had convened a court martial of militia officers to try the troublesome settlers on charges of treason, but even his hand-picked court, which included Maxon and Hurt, decided that it didn't have jurisdiction, that the proceedings "involved the absence of many valuable officers from the command of the troops, and that the prisoners should be turned over to the civil authorities."

Stevens capitulated, approved the findings of his court martial and dispatched a surprisingly meek letter to Judge Chenowith, asking him to fine Shaw, or release him on bail, in order that he might return to his command. Chenowith complied with the governor's request and, except for the contempt warrant outstanding against the governor, the battle to guarantee citizens of Washington territory a trial by a jury of their peers was ended.

Lander subsequently found Stevens guilty of contempt of court and fined him $50. It is said the governor countered by signing his own pardon, but Lander refused to accept a pardon signed by the defendant and ordered the governor arrested. Friends of the embattled chief executive then raised the money and paid the fine.*

---

*Official records of a number of Stevens' most controversial actions have been lost, strayed or stolen, including those relating to his self-pardon, the records of the court martial he appointed to try the Nisqually valley settlers, and even the proceedings of the controversial Medicine creek treaty.

The peppery and self-willed Stevens had thus brought two wars upon himself. The battle over civil rights was to cause him more difficulty than all the battles with the Indians. His martial law proclamation divided the territory and his own political party. Thereafter the legislature wasn't composed of Democrats and Whigs, but of pro-Stevens men and anti-Stevens men. The latter were in control of the 1856-57 legislature, the first to meet in the new $5,000 territorial capitol, and they forced through a severe condemnation of the governor, the resolution concluding that, *"in any attempt to interfere with our courts of justice, or to try citizens before a military tribunal, he acted in direct violation of the Constitution and Laws of the United States, and that any such attempt to exercise unconstitutional power, tends to the subversion of our institutions, and calls at our hands for the strongest condemnation."*

Criticism of the governor's actions wasn't limited to Washington territory. He received a great deal of it from the national capital, where he had been making waves throughout the Indian troubles, largely as a result of a running feud with Major General John Ellis Wool, a crusty veteran of the War of 1812 and the Mexican War, who was in command of the army's department of the Pacific. Stevens had not endeared himself to Wool when they met at a public function in San Francisco shortly before the outbreak of hostilities in Washington. Wool, never an advocate of false modesty, claimed credit for the victory at Buena Vista during the war with Mexico. Stevens broke in to remind Wool that General Zachary Taylor was in command during that battle, and that the credit belonged to him. Ezra Meeker would doubtless have had an explanation for the little governor's tactlessness, but in any event, Wool was not thereafter a fan of Isaac I. Stevens. The outbreak of the Indian troubles did nothing to strengthen their relationship. Wool was convinced that it had been caused by Stevens and the settlers and that the army should protect the Indians from abuse and exploitation by the whites. He roundly condemned Stevens' treaties, and he had no use at all for the governor's ragtag and usually undisciplined militia. Wool's temper reached the boiling point when he received a long and somewhat dictatorial letter from Stevens telling the general exactly how he should conduct the campaign to pacify the Indians. Wool was not hesitant about expressing his opinion of the governor to those in authority at Washington City.

The abortive martial law fiasco was the last straw. Stevens received a strong letter of disapproval from Secretary of State William L. Marcy, which concluded with the ominous sentence, *"your conduct, in that respect, does not therefore meet with favorable regard of the President."*

The United States senate, meeting at Washington City as the territorial legislature was in session in Olympia, condemned Stevens even more severely, and refused further appropriations for the territorial office of Indian affairs unless he was removed as superintendent.

These proceedings did nothing to improve the governor's disposition and, just as Leschi had become the symbol of evil to the settlers, he apparently served as a whipping boy for Stevens' pent-up rage and frustration. The capture and death of the Nisqually chief became an obsession with him.

DEATH OF A CHIEF

With the collapse of the Indian cause east of the Cascades, Leschi gave himself up to Colonel George Wright, whom Wool had placed in command of the regular army forces in the Northwest. Wright considered him a prisoner of a war that was now over, and released him on parole, although Stevens had made it abundantly clear that he considered Leschi, along with Quiemuth, Nelson of the Klickitats and Kitsap, war chief and shaman of the Indians living near Port Madison, to be murderers, and kept up a barrage of correspondence demanding that they be turned over to him for a fair trial and speedy hanging.

Leschi and his brother, homesick for their beloved Nisqually, soon returned to the Puget Sound country. Soon afterward Leschi was betrayed by his nephew, Sluggia, for the reward of 50 blankets offered by Stevens for his capture. The aboriginal Judas was not warmed long by his new blankets, for he was killed by Wahooit, a Nisqually warrior known to the whites as Yelm Jim, and a loyal friend to Leschi.

Leschi's brother, Quiemuth, had gone to Olympia on November 7 and surrendered himself to Stevens. He was locked up under guard in the governor's office and was to have been taken to the Fort Steilacoom blockhouse the next morning. During the night a man named Bunting, a brother-in-law of the slain McAllister, entered the office, and in the presence of the guard, shot Quiemuth. The unarmed and bleeding prisoner pursued Bunting through the office door, where he was stabbed to death. Bunting was arrested for the cold-blooded murder, but the court records show that "there was insufficient evidence to hold the party."

Leschi was betrayed six days later, on November 13, and was taken to the same office where his brother had been murdered. The big Nisqually chief and the little governor stood face to face for the first time since Leschi had hurled his defiance and stalked from the treaty ground on the Nisqually delta two years before. Stevens ordered him to Fort Steilacoom to be imprisoned while awaiting trial.

Colonel Casey, in whose custody he was placed, considered Leschi a prisoner of war and he suggested to Stevens that "the better way would be to consider that we have been at war with these Indians, and now we are at peace."

But the little governor had been flouted by the big red man, and his hatred was implacable. Murder charges were made, based on the death of Moses, ambushed on Connell's prairie early in the war.

The jury disagreed at Leschi's first trial, a telling point when it is considered that it was an all-white jury made up of settlers who had suffered bitterly, and that they were deciding the fate of the man who had been branded by the administration and much of the frontier press as the arch-fiend responsible for it all.

Judge Chenowith instructed the jurors that if they found the death of Colonel Moses to be the result of an act of war, the prisoner could not be found guilty. Four of the jurors, Ezra Meeker among them, held that this was the case. Two of those who were for acquittal finally gave in to the pressure of the majority and the public demand for vengeance, but Meeker and patriarchal William Kincaid held out. A mistrial was declared and Leschi was held over for a second trial at the regular court session of the second judicial district in March of 1857.

Congress had recently ordered that court hearings be limited to three locations in the territory. Seattle and Steilacoom were removed from the list, and all legal business in the second district had to be transacted at Olympia. This was unfortunate for Leschi, for the town was a hotbed of hatred against him, the flames constantly fanned by Stevens and his loyal mouthpiece, Wiley. Furthermore, although the Olympia area had escaped the major devastation of the war, it had not escaped entirely. After Leschi's final defeat and retreat across the mountains, a small band of warriors, determined to get in a few last licks against the whites, waylaid and shot William Northcraft, a teamster for the volunteer forces, on Yelm prairie. The same day they came across William White, his wife and children and another woman returning to their farm near Olympia following church services. White was walking behind the wagon in which the others were riding. At the appearance of the Indians the horses ran away at a gallop. White stood and fought desperately, but the odds were seven to one, and he was soon overcome by weight and numbers. The wagon reached the safety of a blockhouse on the prairie nearby.

A. J. Baldwin, the Olympia livery stable proprietor, was overtaken by four of the Indian band the next day near the scene of White's murder. He had not been in the militia, and Yelm Jim, the leader of the Indians knew him. In more peaceful times Jim had been filling his water bucket at a spring near the corner of 4th and Main streets in Olympia, which served as the town water supply. A white man had jerked the Indian's bucket away and thrown it into a mudhole, of which there were many in Olympia's streets. Baldwin had picked up the belligerent white man and pitched him head first into the mudhole after the Indian's bucket.

Baldwin was spared, and the incident is typical of the Indians' selective manner of waging war. Many of the settlers who had treated them fairly and did not take up arms against them were unmolested throughout the period of hostilities.

At Leschi's second trial in Olympia, defended by Clark and prosecuted by Kendall, he was found guilty of Moses' murder and sentenced to hang on January 22, 1858, at Fort Steilacoom. The case was taken to the supreme court. Lieutenant August Kautz of the Fort Steilacoom garrison had prepared a precise map which proved conclusively that Leschi could not have been at the site of Moses' killing at the time it occurred,* but the supreme court would only review the conduct of the lower tribunal; not accept new evidence. The verdict was upheld.

The Pierce County sheriff, ordered to perform the execution, was conveniently arrested on a charge of selling whiskey to Indians, and a new execution date had to be set. The Thurston county sheriff, Isaac Hays, was to officiate, but he had left the territory and his deputy, William Mitchell, went to Fort Steilacoom with a posse of 12 men and the hangman, Charles Grainger.

Colonel Casey was angry and he made it plain that, in his opinion, murder was being done, but all alternatives had been exhausted. Although Stevens had been replaced as governor by Fayette McMullen of Virginia, who had at first seemed receptive to a pardon, he had been intimidated by the mob spirit in Olympia, led by Maxon and other Stevens supporters, and in the end he refused to act.

Casey refused to let the judicial murder take place on army ground and the scaffold was erected well out on the prairie.

Leschi died without a struggle. It was, said witnesses, like hanging a statue. Charles Grainger, the executioner, said in later years, "I felt that I was executing an innocent man."

Ironically, the Medicine creek treaty was revised before Leschi's death, and the Nisqually leader saw his people given the very land he had requested for them. He had won his fight, although it cost him his life . . . a fight which would never have occurred if the more reasonable treaty provisions had been made two years earlier.

POLITICS AS USUAL

The legislature of 1856-57, having thoroughly castigated the governor, passed an act to incorporate the Northern Pacific Railroad company, with Stevens as one of the incorporators, and prescribing the route he had surveyed and which ultimately became the right-of-way of the Northern Pacific three decades later.

Before the legislators left town, the leading members of the disintegrating Whig party, prominent citizens opposed to the Democratic national and territorial administrations, along with a number of Free Soil Democrats, met at Olympia, approved the principles of the first Republican convention held at Philadelphia in 1856, and organized the Republican party of Washington territory. At their convention they nominated the elder statesman, Alexander Abernethy, as their candidate for delegate to Congress. The Democrats' choice was none other than Governor Isaac I. Stevens.

Columbia Lancaster, the first territorial delegate, had discovered that dignified bulk and a slow and oracular manner of speech were not sufficient to impress his colleagues in Washington City. He proved a singularly ineffective delegate, and was beaten for the Democratic nomination in 1855 by J. Patton Anderson, the territorial marshal, who was an ardent copperhead . . . *a pro-slavery Democrat of the most ultra-Southern school."* He narrowly defeated the Whig candidate, Judge William Strong, and served for two years in Congress with the same lack of effectiveness as Lancaster. He never returned to the territory after his term of office ended.

Stevens, anxious to recoup his recent political losses, campaigned diligently, while Abernethy, one of the territory's oldest and most respected settlers, was described by his friends as "modest and unassuming to a fault". He refused to make any campaign speeches, choosing to stay home and let the voters decide the contest for themselves.

Stevens was ably assisted in his campaign by a glib-tongued newcomer to the territory, Selucius Garfielde, who had been appointed receiver of the United States land office in Olympia, arriving with a national reputation as an orator and stump speaker. He was destined to become a colorful figure in Washington politics.

Garfielde was described by Elwood Evans as *"of admirable personal presence and address, with a rich, round and full voice of which he had singular control"*, but he added, *"He lacked application. His ambitions for office were boundless, but were merely those of the*

---

*The *Pioneer and Democrat* referred to Lieutenant Kautz's testimony as *"a cautious and cunning affidavit,"* and the testimony of Dr. Tolmie, who spoke for Leschi as *"an elaborate and powerful appeal in which he exhibits an artful cunning, ingenious special pleading, worthy the representative of an unlawful, illegitimate foreign corporation."* Mr. Wiley had apparently forgotten that it was this "unlawful, illegitimate foreign corporation" which furnished the settlers arms, ammunition and ships to protect themselves when their own government had failed them.

---

*An *Illustrated History of the State of Washington,* H. K. Hines, 1893.

GOLDEN-TONGUED ORATOR Selucius Garfielde.

place-hunter. With talents that fitted him for any office within the gift of the people or a national administration, he lacked the energy to establish his claim, and forgot what was due himself. He was neither true to himself nor to his friends, nor to any political party, nor consistent in anything."

Garfielde was, however, a practical politician, and it didn't take him long to size up the real issue of the 1857 campaign in Washington territory. The issue was not one of Republican versus Democrat. It boiled down simply to the argument that a vote against Stevens was a vote against the Indian war as carried on by the people of the territory. The territory itself, and a large number of its citizens had gone deeply in debt to carry on the war, and failure of the federal government to assume and pay off these obligations would be truly ruinous.

Garfielde accompanied Stevens on his campaign tour, constantly and eloquently reminding the voters that the defeat of the Democratic candidate would be an admission that the Indian war debt had no claim to recognition and payment by the federal government; that Stevens, as delegate, offered the best hope of getting payment.

Many a settler, facing bankruptcy unless the war debt was taken over by the national government and the worthless territorial scrip issued by Stevens in payment for war supplies redeemed, doubtless voted his pocketbook rather than his political convictions. Stevens received 953 votes; Abernethy 518.

The outgoing delegate, Anderson, was offered the post of governor, but he didn't accept. Second choice was a lanky ex-congressman from Virginia named Fayette McMullen. Rumor had it that he accepted the backwoods governorship as a convenient means of ridding himself of his wife, a southern belle whose maiden name had been Polly Wood. The territorial legislature was in the habit of granting divorces to those with sufficient political clout or lobbying ability. Reform-minded legislators, led by Arthur Denny, were bitterly opposed to the concept of legislative divorces, pointing out that they were grossly unfair, since the women involved were not given their day in court.

McMullen arrived at Olympia in September, in time to prepare his case for the December session of the legislature. Over the opposition of Denny, his divorce from Polly Wood was granted and he promptly married an Olympia girl named Mary Wood. Soon after this marriage in the summer of 1858 he was removed from office and returned with his bride to Virginia, becoming a member of the Confederate Congress during the civil war. The territory's second governor remained less than a year and left little imprint upon its history. Upon his departure Secretary Mason again assumed the duties of acting governor.

In addition to granting McMullen's divorce, the 1857-58 legislature expressed strong opposition to Oregon's efforts to annex all of Washington territory south of the Columbia river, appointed a commission to superintend construction of a territorial penitentiary at Vancouver and, in line with its policy of passing political plums around to the various aspiring settlements, relocated the territorial university at Cowlitz Prairie, Lewis County, thoughtfully failing to grant an appropriation in order that the institution might be moved somewhere else at the next session. The federal government had appropriated $30,000 for a permanent capitol building to replace the $5,000 two-story frame temporary building in which the legislature was meeting, and an additional $20,000 for a penitentiary. Like every legislature since, this one was anxious to spend any available federal funds, and it directed the appointed capitol commission to "superintend the erection of the permanent capitol building at Olympia upon the 10 acres of ground now occupied by the temporary capitol building," but no agreement was forthcoming as to a suitable plan for the

Judge Edward Lander.

building or, for that matter, whether or not it should be located in Olympia.

Local citizens remained nervous, and with good reason. The Indian war had brought progress to a standstill in both the territory and its capital, and if the capricious legislature were to move the seat of the government away, Olympia would very likely revert back to Chief Seattle and his tribesmen as a winter fishing camp. The *Pioneer and Democrat* no longer printed glowing reports of new businesses, new buildings and new plank sidewalks, such as the one from 3rd street to the new Masonic hall on 7th which *"gave the promenade-loving people of Olympia a fine walk at all seasons of the year, when the mud is not more than knee-deep in most places below the hall."*

The lumber for the Marshville bridge across the west arm of the bay had been diverted to the town's defensive stockade, and no more was heard in the columns of the local newspaper of such grandiose projects as that for *"throwing up an embankment around the tide prairie north of and fronting on Olympia, thus effectually to restrain the high tides from encroaching within certain bounds."*

(Euphemisms are not the sole prerogative of 20th century man. Wiley was describing a plan to build a dike on the mudflats to prevent the business district from being flooded when the tide was in.)

Governor McMullen had scampered back to Virginia with his latest bride, and Mason was again occupying the governor's chair by December of 1858. The legislature wasted no time in rescinding the resolution of censure against Stevens, on the grounds that "the resolution passed January 16, 1857, does not now, and did not at that time express the opinion of a majority of the citizens of Washington Territory." It also castigated General Wool and eulogized the territorial militia.

It created Spokane county from a portion of Walla Walla county, incorporated the town of Olympia, and found time to grant the usual number of legislative divorces.

CIVIC IMPROVEMENTS

Finding itself with the status of a municipal corporation, the capital city proceeded to elect its first slate of city officials. George A. Barnes, U. G. Warbass, Edwin Marsh, W. G. Dunlap and Isaac Lightner were chosen as trustees, or councilmen. Dr. Warbass decided he didn't want the job, and Elwood Evans was appointed to fill his place. Barnes was elected president of the board, or mayor. The new officials wasted no time in reviving the civic improvements which had lapsed during the Indian troubles and subsequent depression. Underground cisterns were built at the corners of Main, and, 3rd and 4th streets at a cost of $155. The main source of water had previously been the spring at the northeast corner of 4th and Main next door to Edmund Sylvester's store, where the town founder played checkers with all comers, occasionally leaving the game with great reluctance to wait upon a customer. The stumps which dotted Main street above 4th were removed, and several blocks of wooden sidewalks built alongside the streets, which remained quagmires of mud in winter; dry rivers of dust in the summer.

Drama came to Olympia in time to entertain legislators as well as townspeople, and the *Pioneer and Democrat* proudly reported:

"Are we not becoming quite a community? For the first time in our yet brief history we have been visited by a real, live theatrical company. No runaway Sandwich Island concert seranaders, or 'sleight of hand', or phantazmagora illusion, but the 'Chapman Family' and 'Taylor Brothers' have been dealing out

comedy and farce to crowded houses at the Washington Hotel, and delighting their audiences with songs, dances, duetts, solos, burlesque extravaganzas, & etc. On Tuesday evening we had 'The Young Widow', and 'The Limerick Boy' * * * We will not be many years behind our Portland contemporaries in having a regular BUILT theater of our own to blow about."

Quite fittingly, Olympia's first theatrical troup closed its three day run with productions entitled "The Enraged Politician" and "The Artful Dodger".

Steamboat transportation had grown beyond its infancy as a result of the Fraser river gold rush of 1858, which brought much grander and gaudier packets to the inland waterways of Washington territory than had been seen in the past. The big side-wheelers *Constitution* and *Wilson G. Hunt* were both on the Olympia-Victoria route.

By the Fourth of July the town was so far recovered as to stage its greatest Independence Day celebration yet, a satisfyingly noisy and dangerous event which was to become a tradition for many decades. The festivities attracted, according to the *Pioneer and Democrat*, "a concourse of citizens and strangers estimated at 1,200 to 1,500, by far the largest assemblage ever convened at one time in the Territory."

Almost anything served as an excuse to fire a cannon in those days, and salvos boomed from Tumwater, Olympia, and from the steamer *Constitution*, while "youthful America evinced his patriotism by the explosion of an infinite quantity of fire-crackers."

At 11 o'clock in the morning the Sons of Temperance and the Masons assembled in full regalia in front of the Washington hotel and, preceded by the recently organized Olympia Brass Band and the orchestra of the Chapman theatrical company, which was back in town for the occasion, marched up Main street to a shady grove near the territorial capitol. There assembled, the brass band gave forth with "Hail Columbia" as noisily as any band on the Pacific coast, Reverend G. F. Whitworth gave a lengthy prayer which was both "fervent and patriotic", and Attorney Benjamin Kendall recited the Declaration of Independence in a manner which the *Pioneer and Democrat* described as "peculiar to himself". Elwood Evans then made the oration of the day which, "although lengthy, was listened to with marked attention." Mr. Evans' lengthy oration was punctuated by another fusilade of cannon fire

from the revenue cutter *Shubrick*, which had steamed into port in time to observe the noon hour. Not to be outdone by Evans or the *Shubrick*, Kendall mounted the rostrum again and read George Washington's farewell address. At long last, the *Pioneer and Democrat* reported:

"The assemblage then proceeded to a sumptuous FREE dinner, prepared and set upon tables close by which fairly groaned beneath the weight of roast beef, sheep, shoats, pigs, etc., and no end of pies, cakes, etc."

Wiley reported smugly that "not a single instance of drunken or disorderly conduct has come to our attention, and with much pride we close our article by stating this fact."

Olympia had come a long way in the three years since the entire population had huddled behind the stockade along 4th street waiting for the Indians to attack the town, but progress is not without its problems. Crime on the streets was one of them.

Soon after the memorable Fourth of July celebration the *Pioneer and Democrat* wrathfully reported:

"A few nights since, some graceless scoundrel, unknown to our community, cut the ropes which are used to support the seats in the Pavilion Theater of the Chapman family, while engaged in performance of this place, and the entire structure, with a fearful crash, came to the ground. Strange to say, no one was seriously hurt, although the seats were densely crowded at the time with ladies, gentlemen and children."

Not long afterward the town received the attentions of its first recorded pickpocket, and Wiley was forced to advise his readers to leave their money at home in a safe place if they planned to be abroad after dark or, "in lieu thereof, put a good revolver in your pocket".

Mr. Hefron of the new Capital Saloon took Wiley's advice to good advantage, using his revolver to run "an idle and profligate loafer" out of the back room of his establishment when he caught him there after closing time. When the suspicious character gave indications of breaking into Elwood Evans' law office next door, "he was frustrated by the timely 'whiz' of a bullet sent at his head by Mr. H. from a revolver."

J. C. Rathbun, nineteenth century Olympia newspaper publisher and author of a *History of Thurston County, Washington*, wrote of this lawless period in the town's development:

"In the early part of the winter of '59-60, the town was infested with that class of nomads, *latterly called tramps or hobos. Several fires occurred. * * * On December 24th a meeting was held at the school house to discuss the project of organizing a hook and ladder company. As an outgrowth of the agitation of the question, was formed the Alert Hook & Ladder Company."*

Certainly the town was badly in need of fire protection. It was built entirely of wood, including what sidewalks there were, and if the "tramps and hobos" didn't succeed in burning it down it seemed likely that one of the over-enthusiastic Fourth of July celebrations would. Unfortunately, although the hook and ladder company was formed and duly elected officers, it couldn't raise the money to buy a fire engine and so proved quite ineffective. Editor Wiley constantly agitated for an adequate fire department, as Olympia editors were to do for the next fifty years or so, and some of the young blades tried to shame the city fathers into action by assembling a beer barrel on wheels, painting it bright red, and christening it *Squilgee*. This humorous caricature of a fire engine was dragged to various minor conflagrations to dramatize the lack of adequate equipment, and eventually served its purpose.

One of the structures set on fire by the evilly-disposed was the old Indian war blockhouse on the town square, sometimes referred to grandly by the local press as the Plaza, and now known as Sylvester Park. The blockhouse was used as the town jail and one ingenious inmate set fire to his blanket. A great deal of smoke was produced, and when the populace arrived with buckets of water the inmate walked away amid the shouting and confusion.

GOVERNOR GHOLSON
STIRS THINGS UP

In the midst of all the excitement, the third territorial governor, Richard D. Gholson, arrived in Olympia from San Francisco on the steamer *Northerner*. Gholson has become something of a mystery man. He remained in the territory less than a year, no portrait of him has ever been found and even his birthdate was unknown to earlier historians.

Soon after the new governor arrived Charles Mason died at the age of 29 and Gholson lost the advice and counsel of the man who had certainly done more than any other to keep the territory on an even keel during the comings

and goings of three governors. There is some evidence that Mason, who arrived on the frontier as a rosy-cheeked youth of exemplary habits, had followed the example of Isaac Stevens, and spent the last years of his short life determinedly drinking himself to death.

Governor Gholson stayed in Olympia long enough to address the seventh territorial legislature which convened in December, 1859, and to produce a remarkable document, which if it had been made public, would certainly have given him a more prominent place in history than he attained.

For several years the water boundary between the United States and Canada had been in dispute, the Canadian version of the line placing the San Juan Island group under the British flag. Governor Douglas had insisted that American settlers in the disputed zone were under British law, while American authorities stirred up a hornet's nest by confiscating a number of Hudson's Bay company sheep for nonpayment of taxes to Washington territory. Things reached a climax in 1859 in the celebrated case of the Canadian pig, the property of the Hudson's Bay company agent on San Juan island, shot by an American settler for repeated thefts from his potato patch. In the ensuing furor, General Harney ordered Company D of the 9th Infantry under Captain George E. Pickett from Bellingham Bay to the island. The legendary pig war resulted in numerous confrontations between American and British forces, but no actual bloodshed. Joint occupancy of the islands was finally agreed upon, and the two governments continued to haggle over the boundary for more than a decade.

Governor Gholson, arriving in the midst of warlike alarms and excursions, immediately outdid his predecessor, Stevens, in taking the law into his own hands. He drew up a proclamation authorizing the citizens to arm themselves and fit out armed vessels as privateers for a war between Washington territory and Great Britain. Northern Indians had continued their warlike raids on Puget Sound, one band murdering Colonel Ebey at his claim on Whidbey Island, and this was the issue upon which Gholson based his proposed war.

The governor showed his proclamation to Judge William Strong of the territorial supreme court, a man with a great air of dignity, but an equally powerful sense of humor. The judge told the governor solemnly that his remarkable document would certainly make him the most famous man on the Pacific Coast. Highly pleased, Gholson then showed it to Surveyor-General Tilton, who nearly had a heart attack. He pointed out that England had five warships in the area, and the United States only the ancient steamer *Massachusetts* and a wheezy revenue cutter. Fortunately for world peace, Tilton convinced Gholson that he had better suppress the proclamation.

In his address to the legislature, the governor delivered a long and flowery address in support of the Constitution and the Union, urging that everyone *"firmly set our faces, now and forever, against all who would destroy or jeopardize the palladium of liberty,"* closing with the fervent opinion that this could be accomplished by *"clinging to the Constitution and the Union as the shipwrecked mariner clings to the last plank when night and the tempest close around him, let our motto ever be 'The Union'"*.

Wiley of the *Pioneer and Democrat*, who was capable of equally eloquent prose in support of states rights and slavery . . . (*"Belial and Beelzebub, the foulest fiends that curse the earth, are reveling in hideous orgies around the dome of our national capitol, and the country is full of vampires. * * * Awake ye sons and daughters of liberty-loving, patriotic white men. Shake off the foul nightmares of negrophobicy. Arise in your might and shake off the black demon of destruction ere its fangs poison the heart. If you pursue the mad folly of your abolition party zealots destruction awaits us"*. . . . was among his more outstanding efforts), was doubtless disappointed in the governor, whom he had considered to be as ardent a copperhead as himself, and whom he had predicted would *"'take better' with our people than* SOME*of our governors had done."*

If so, Gholson soon set his doubts at rest. In the spring of 1861 he took a six months leave of absence and returned to Kentucky. When Abraham Lincoln was elected president Gholson resigned his commission as governor the day before the inauguration, declaring that he was "unwilling to hold office, even for a single day, under a Republican president." Henry M. McGill had arrived in November to succeed the late Charles Mason as territorial secretary, and he took over as acting governor until Lincoln got around to appointing a permanent executive.

The year ended with Olympia receiving another legislative blow to its civic paranoia.

In a sudden and unexpected move, the house of representatives passed a bill moving the capital to Vancouver. The vote was 19 to nine. The Puget Sound contingent brought all its power to bear on the council, where the measure lost by a scant five to four vote, but there was evidence of a strong and determined effort to force through a capital relocation bill, and Olympians looked forward to the winter session of 1860-61 with justifiable trepidation. Their suspicions were further aroused by the fact that the legislature had spent part of the $30,000 appropriated by congress for a permanent capitol to clear the ten-acre grounds around the $5,000 temporary capitol, and the rest had reverted to the federal treasury.

Fortunately for the nerves of the citizenry, Isaac Wood opened the town's first brewery in a primitive plant on Columbia street, producing a cream lager beer which old settlers insisted to their dying days was never equaled in deliciousness even by the famed artesian wells of Tumwater.

The year 1860 brought major changes in the press of the capital city. Wiley of the *Pioneer and Democrat* had met defeat at the hands of a coalition of legislative Whigs and his partner, Goudy, lost the post of state printer to William Wallace, a Whig member of the council whom Wiley accused, among other things, of "shameless perfidy, infamy and meditated fraud."

The embattled publisher then began firing off a barrage of letters to the national capital, with the result that the secretary of the treasury informed the legislature that Goudy was still the public printer. Goudy, no doubt fed up with frontier politics and the antics of his eccentric partner, quit as soon as the battle was won. Wiley, still a member of the countil, promptly acquired a new partner, Edward Furste, and succeeded in getting *him* appointed public printer. Soon afterward Furste bought out Wiley, although the latter stayed on for several months as a paid part-time writer.

MURPHY OF THE STANDARD

Perhaps Wiley had observed the activities of a 20-year-old redhead named John Miller Murphy, and realized that the *Pioneer and Democrat* was soon to lose its status as Olympia's only newspaper.

Office and printing plant of the *Washington Standard*.

John Miller Murphy was born in Indiana and was left an orphan while still a toddler. His older sister, Mrs. George A. Barnes, took him to raise, and he crossed the plains with the Barnes family in 1850 at the age of nine. George Barnes opened a store in Portland and John was put to work as a clerk, devoting much of his spare time to the duties of choir boy at the Methodist church, and making the rounds of the town as the first *Oregonian* delivery boy. A love of music and a strong dose of printer's ink remained in his blood throughout his life.

In 1951 Barnes moved his store to Olympia, John riding the Cowlitz trail behind his sister and holding on to her all the way to keep from falling off the horse. At the age of ten he was assigned the job of clearing the block of land where the Barnes family planned to build their house. It was covered with virgin timber and junglelike undergrowth and was partly submerged at high tide, being on the outskirts of town, bounded by 4th and 5th, Adams and Jefferson streets. Thomas Prather, hardy frontiersman, Indian fighter in Gilmore Hays' company of volunteers and mate on Captain Parker's cranky little steamer *Traveler*, admitted in later years that Barnes had offered him $100, which was a great deal of money in those days, to do the clearing, but the job looked too tough to him and he turned it down.

John Miller Murphy, described by Prather as "a fat, red-cheeked lad of probably ten years of age, and a favorite with everybody," took on the job with a single Indian helper, and the wilderness lot became one of the town's beauty spots. He also continued to clerk in the store,

learning to cope with bargain-hunting Indian women who would give the carefully measured calico a quick jerk in order to get a few inches extra for their money.

As a teen-ager he returned to Portland long enough to get a job as printer's devil at the *Oregon Weekly Times,* learn the trade and rise to the position of foreman, all within two years. Back in Olympia, he issued Volume One, Number One of the *Washington Standard* on Novemver 17, 1860. His first editorial stated that *"we enter upon the task of editing and conducting a newspaper with many misgivings as to the future,"* but any fears the youthful publisher might have felt were unfounded. The *Standard* would continue to record the events of Washington's capital city for more than six decades . . . long after the *Pioneer and Democrat* was forgotten.

That first editorial also made it abundantly clear that the *Standard* was a Republican newspaper, dedicated to the preservation of the Union. In the second edition of his paper Murphy recorded with much satisfaction that *"a salute of 100 guns was fired by the Republicans at Tum-Water, in this county, in honor of the election of Abraham Lincoln President of the United States. After the salute a large and enthusiastic delegation marched to Olympia, ringing bells, blowing horns, etc., serenaded the Washington Standard office and adjourned with hearty cheers for 'honest old Abe,' the president elect of the United States."*

John Miller Murphy.

The event demonstrated the courage, as well as the enthusiasm of the Tumwater Republicans, for the previous year the Democrats of the same settlement had tried to fire a similar salute on election night and the cannon had blown up in their faces, injuring several of them.

WHO STOLE THE CAPITAL?

Within a month the *Standard* had evil tidings to report. The legislators of Seattle, Port Townsend and Vancouver, the latter backed by Portland money and influence, had perfected their campaign to reshuffle the territorial institutions . . . and the territorial capital. It was an exercise in log-rolling or vote-trading which would do credit to the most sophisticated legislature of the 20th century.

Port Townsend was to get the territorial penitentiary, the foundations for which were already under construction at Vancouver. Seattle was to get the territorial university back from Lewis County . . . and Vancouver was to get the capital.

Politicians from the areas affected performed prodigious backflips. Arthur Denny, who had stoutly defended Olympia as the best and most logical seat of government at previous sessions, had a plan to nail the university down for his community once the bill was passed, and he adroitly reversed his field. Others followed his lead, and the deed was done. The bill passed both houses, and Governor Gholson signed it shortly before departing on the leave of absence from which he never returned.

Things looked bleak for Olympia in the cold and soggy winter of 1860-61. Although the federal census showed that Thurston County had grown to a population of nearly 1,500 and that more than a third lived in Olympia, making it the territory's largest city, the loss of the capital came in the midst of a general economic recession. The reaction from the post-Indian war boom had set in. The town had spent a lot of money trying to pull itself out of the mud and attain the proper image of a self-respecting territorial capital. Tax assessments were still based on the inflated values of the boom period. Times were hard and the future looked gloomy indeed, but things turned out to be not quite as bad as they seemed.

Soon after the legislature adjourned it was discovered that the capital removal bill had no

Eliza Anderson, legendary steamboat on the Olympia-Victoria mail route.

enacting clause and bore no date. It was rather general knowledge that some inspired lobbyist for the interests of Olympia had bribed a legislative clerk to remove these essential details before delivering the measure to the territorial secretary. Unfortunately, history does not record the name of this civic benefactor. The supreme court later ruled that the act was invalid, and in July the question of the capital location was submitted to the voters . . . a classic method of sidestepping thorny and controversial issues.

Of the total of 2,315 votes cast, Olympia received 1,239, Vancouver 639, Steilacoom 253, Walla Walla 67, Port Madison 72, Seattle 23, Cherbourg (Port Angeles) 3, and one each for Port Ludlow, Forks Touchet, Jefferson and Coveland in Island County. At the same election Olympia found itself in another contest . . . with Tumwater for the location of the county seat. It won this prize also, getting 344 votes to 104 for Tumwater and four for West Olympia. It would seem that this should have settled the capital question for all time, but it didn't; not by a long shot.

STEAMBOAT TO VICTORIA

During the boom times of 1858-60 Olympia had acquired a number of new civic assets. Dr. Warbass opened the first hospital in "a large and commodious building on 3rd street next door to the Pacific Hotel" and was prepared to supply "operations of a surgical character, as well as medical advice." A "lady of color" named Rebecca Howard had taken over the Pacific hotel, and her excellent cuisine was achieving an enviable record all over the Northwest frontier. A foot bridge had been built on 4th street over the tidal slough at the head of the east waterway, connecting with John Swan's claim, which he was in the process of platting as Swantown. Several new saloons had appeared on the business scene. But the most interesting of the new acquisitions was a stout sidewheel steamboat named *Eliza Anderson,* and she added more legends to early Olympiana than any of the others.

Built at Portland as a river boat, she was soon brought to Puget Sound to enter the battle for supremacy on the lucrative Olympia-Victoria mail route. She fought off all competitors, secured the $36,000 a year mail subsidy, and proceeded to make a great deal of money for her owners over a long period of years.

The *Anderson* also succeeded in upsetting a committee of the territorial legislature. Arthur Denny, having returned to Seattle with the territorial university in his pocket, went to work with other founding fathers of that enterprising community to anchor it solidly on the hill above Elliott Bay. A ten-acre site was donated, the land was cleared, and in May of 1861 the cornerstone was laid, containing a Bible and copies of the Declaration of Independence and Constitution of the United States. By the time the next legislature met, the big white wooden building, complete with hand-carved columns and belfry, was an accomplished fact.

Horrified that Seattle had shown the bad taste to take its political plum seriously and thus deprived the legislature of such prime vote-trading stock as the university, that august body dispatched a committee on the *Eliza Anderson* to visit Seattle and see what could be done about it.

The legislators were given a royal welcome, complete with brass band, and taken on a tour of the splendid new institution of learning. Convinced that there was nothing they *could* do about it, they repaired to the Felker House to spend the night. The *Anderson* always left port at ungodly hours, usually before dawn, and in the pre-dawn darkness the befuddled lawmakers arose, scrambled into their clothes and made their way through the rain to Yesler's wharf. There one of them espied a blaze of light as the fireman opened the furnace door and threw in a slab of wood to stoke the boiler. the engine room looked like a welcome refuge from

the chill and rain, so they all clambered in and proceeded to warm themselves.

After a while they began to grow impatient as the advertised departure time came and passed. At last one of the delegation tapped the busy fireman on the shoulder and inquired politely, "When, might I ask, do we leave for Olympia?"

With equal courtesy the fireman wiped his sweaty brow and replied, "I am sorry sir, but this sawmill doesn't run to Olympia."

The legislators had blundered into the engine room of Henry Yesler's steam sawmill instead of that of the steamboat *Eliza Anderson.*

CIVIL WAR DAYS

In the meantime, the faraway cannonade of Fort Sumpter echoed in the Northwest. Acting Governor McGill mustered in the territorial militia in response to a proclamation from President Lincoln. The copperhead press grappled with the Republican and Unionist editors in a battle to the death, although John Miller Murphy took time out to castigate the Portland *Advertiser* (the political organ of Governor Curry of Oregon) for poking fun at the Olympia militia company, which its editor had dubbed "the Noisy Fusileers."*

Washington territory got its first Republican governor, and the first who was already known to its citizens, when Lincoln appointed the colorful William H. Wallace, who had served as both speaker of the house and president of the council in the Iowa legislature, and as council president in the Washington legislature. A resident of the territory since 1853, he had served as a captain of volunteers during the Indian war and . . . briefly . . . as territorial printer.

Soon after his appointment he was selected by the Republicans as their candidate for delegate to congress. The nomination was applauded by the *Standard,* which pointed out that Wallace *"is a* bona fide *citizen. His interests, his sympathies and his home are all here. He came to cast his lot with us for weal or woe. Sink or swim, survive or perish, he is with us."*

Murphy was never an admirer of the territory's silver-tongued orator, Selucius Garfielde, and when the Democrats selected him to oppose Wallace he reported the proceedings in a less than kindly manner:

"THE SECESSION CONVENTION AT VANCOUVER—*The Distracted Democracy met at Vancouver and after four days of whiskey-drinking, log-rolling and wire-pulling, nominated Garfielde, one who would probably never have pressed the soil of our territory had he not been sent here with a Federal Commission in his pocket."*

Wallace had tried for the seat in congress in the first election and had been defeated by Columbia Lancaster. The delegateship was considered a more prestigious position than that of governor. He soundly defeated Garfielde, along with Judge Lander of martial law fame, who ran as an independent. Lincoln appointed William Pickering, a close personal and political friend, to succeed Wallace as governor.

Pickering, although a man of great integrity and character, was a native of England and a graduate of Oxford and, as Wiley would have

put it, he didn't "take well" with the horny-handed pioneers of Washington territory, most of whom had graduated only from the school of hard knocks. He had apparently been thoroughly brain-washed as to the constant rain to be expected in the Pacific Northwest and he insisted on carrying an umbrella and wearing high gaiters, rain or shine; winter or summer. The local citizenry took to calling him "Pickwick" behind his back, and Francis Henry, the town wit, cartoonist and writer of satyrical verse, composed a doggerel verse about him which plagued him throughout his tenure in office. Henry, whose most lasting composition was "The Old Settler" (. . . *"I laugh at the world and its shams, as I think of my happy condition, surrounded by acres of clams"),* first gained fame as a political satyrist in one of the first sessions of the territorial legislature, at the expense of one of Seattle's most distinguished citizens, Hillory Butler.

Butler, one of the early settlers of Arthur Denny's town on Elliott Bay, survived the Battle of Seattle, but his fortunes were at a low ebb in the post-war depression. Denny got him the job of sergeant at arms at the next legislative session, but after the legislature convened the Walla Walla delegation, then a potent political force led by peppery publisher William H. Newell of the Walla Walla *Washington Statesman,* succeeded in ousting Butler and getting one of their constituents the place. To take care of Butler, the first opening for a legislative page was established, and he was given that position. Butler was a dignified Virginian and the sight of him delivering messages and running errands was too much for Francis Henry's easily-aroused sense of humor. He penned a wicked caricature of Mr. Butler's mature face above a child's body in short pants and smock. Butler later became a wealthy man, his posh Butler Hotel a Seattle institution, but he never quite recovered from the humiliation of his menial job in Olympia and Francis Henry's widely-circulated cartoon.

Back in Washington City, Isaac Stevens sniffed the smoke of battle like an old war horse and set out to get a commission in the Union army. In due time he was given command of the 79th Regiment of Highlanders, whose colonel had been killed at the first battle of Bull Run. Before long he was promoted to brigadier general and began achieving a reputation as one of the army's more promising general officers.

---

*Murphy's indignation was nothing compared to that of Washington's assistant adjutant general, who, in a letter to the *Standard* referred to Governor Curry as "an ape-browed, ash-colored abolitionist, a black-hearted, blear-eyed, cheese-faced knave, and a mere remnant of deformed mortality."

While bloody battles raged in the east, equally violent if less deadly skirmishes took place in Washington territory.

Benjamin F. Kendall, the colorful and controversial frontier attorney, succeeded in getting for himself the post of superintendent of Indian affairs despite the efforts of Arthur Denny and William WallAce to secure the job for Captain C. H. Hale, also of Olympia. This post carried with it the dispensing of more patronage than any other federal appointment and so was much sought after.

Kendall, as egotistical and self-willed as Isaac Stevens, succeeded in alienating most of the Indian agents, the missionaries and practically everyone else with whom he came in contact. The *Standard* charged that he was a Democrat in disguise, and in a short time he was removed and replaced by Captain Hale. He did not, however drop into obscurity.

With the Republican party in the ascendancy and the *Pioneer and Democrat* frozen out of the lucrative public printing business, it quietly folded up. The plant was picked up at a bargain by Alonzo Poe, one of the earliest settlers at Tumwater and a member of the legislative council during three of the first four sessions. He began publication of the *Overland Press,** which he described as "non-partisan."

Within a year, Poe was forced to move to California for his health. He turned the paper over to Kendall, his attorney, who immediately took the romantic pen name of "Bion" and focused his abundant energies and talent for invective on journalistic pursuits. The results would prove explosive.

WHO'S GOT THE CAPITAL?

A new territorial secretary, L. Jay S. Turney, arrived in Olympia in the fall of 1861 to find himself also embroiled in controversy . . . including the still unsettled question of exactly where the territorial capital was. Wallace had left for Washington City; Pickering hadn't yet arrived, and Turney found himself in the unenviable position of an acting governor who wasn't sure where his seat of government was located.

---

*The real projectors of this enterprise were the owners of the Victoria *Press*. When the war news arrived by courier from Portland the *Overland Press* printed "extras" and dispatched them to Canada on the *Eliza Anderson*. The Victoria *Press* thus consistently beat its rival *Colonist*.

Vancouverites insisted the legislative removal bill was legal, enacting clause or no enacting clause. Turney's predecessor, McGill, had tried to find out from federal authorities whether the bill locating the capital at Vancouver, or the bill referring the matter to a vote of the people, both passed by the same legislature, had priority, but with little success.

Turney, in a letter to angry citizens of Vancouver, wrote plaintively:

"Before leaving the States, I learned your Capitol had been removed to Vancouver. On reaching the Territory, however, I failed to find it at that place. Consequently I had to come to this place (Olympia) to enter upon the duties of my office. Had I found the Capitol at Vancouver, I certainly should have stopped there, but not finding it there, is it a part of my duty, as Secretary of this Territory, or Acting Governor, to remove hither? This is a big question."

The territorial legislators were apparently equally confused. By December 7, the 1861-62 session still didn't have a quorum. The Clarke County delegation was stubbornly sitting in Vancouver and others were awaiting the supreme court decision on the capital question.

By January 4, however, John Miller Murphy was able to report that *"The Legislative Assembly is now fairly at work, and we think the indications are that the present session will be unusually quiet. Thus far nothing has occurred indicating a division of either House into local cliques, so detrimental to the best interests of the people. We see that the entire delegation from Clarke County are now here."*

Murphy's kind words for the legislature were prompted by the fact that he was firmly convinced they would elect him public printer as a reward for his dedication to the Republican cause. He had, in fact, purchased much of the equipment needed to do the work. Unfortunately for him, however, he had allied himself in his bid for the appointment with another of the abrasive and controversial figures who seemed so prevalent in Olympia at the time . . . Anson Henry, an uncle of Francis and crony of Lincoln, who had been appointed surveyor-general. Autocratic and high-handed, he quickly alienated all the Democrats and a good many of the Republicans in the legislature. As a backhanded slap at Henry they elected Alonzo Poe, and the upstart *Overland Press* got the gravy, *"to the mortification and disappointment of the manager and supporters of the Republican organ,"* as Charles Prosch of the Steilacoom *Courier* put it. Prosch probably felt some personal satisfaction, for Murphy had taken to referring to his journal as "Granny Prosch's paper" and accusing him editorially of being a secessionist who perhaps should be hanged.

It is proverbial that the weather is always bad in Olympia when the legislature is in session, and the winter of 1861-62 outdid itself. By mid-January there was three feet of snow on the ground, but in the spring the town dug itself out and proved that it could generate plenty of controversy without political assistance.

SCANDALOUS BEHAVIOR

In May an itinerant lecturer named Charles Henry De Wolf (or De Wolfe) appeared in town and promptly won the heart of Eliza Hurd, daughter of a respected pioneer family. De Wolf claimed to be a doctor of medicine, phrenology, metaphysics and almost everything else in the book. The suave doctor convinced the frontier belle that conventional forms of marriage were a fraud, and a notice duly appeared in the *Overland Press* announcing that Charles Henry and Eliza had become man and wife in the following manner:

"We, the undersigned, hereby announce to the world that we have contracted a conjugal alliance and entered into matrimonial copartnership, believing in the divine right of souls to dictate their own forms, and the inspiration of Mother Nature and Father God as being above custom and priestly ceremony, however long dignified by legal enactment and Christian dictation. This act we perform, taking upon ourselves the responsibility in the presence of these witnesses."

The happy couple intended to embark for their honeymoon voyage on the next early morning departure of the *Eliza Anderson*, but they were intercepted by a deputy sheriff, who brought them before Squire Plum on a charge of violating the marriage laws. De Wolf delivered an oration, asserting that he would never give in to "sneaking, lying, peddling, begging sons of Ahab; the drunken justices and besotted judges and their blackhearted and villainous supporters." Unimpressed, the justice of the peace bound him over to the district court on $100 bail. He was subsequently rearrested on a charge of "open and notorious conduct" and locked up in the blockhouse-jail.

When he appeared before District Judge McGill with Eliza at his side, the jurist opened the proceedings with a couple of simple questions.

"Do you," he asked De Wolf, "consent to take this woman as your wedded wife?"

The doctor-minister-phrenologist conceded that he did.

In response to the judge's next question, Eliza admitted that she had taken De Wolf as her wedded husband.

"Then," Judge McGill intoned calmly, "by virtue of the authority vested in me, I pronounce you man and wife."

De Wolf, the free thinker, very nearly had a stroke of apoplexy, but the deed was done and he couldn't undo it. Eliza, however, got in a last blow to Olympia's moral sensibilities before the now legally wedded couple left town. As reported by the *Standard*, *"the good people of our town were shocked on Saturday evening last to witness a woman dressed in NEARLY men's apparel, riding ASTRIDE a horse upon the public thoroughfare. We are informed that the woman (who now can claim the name of Mrs. Charles De Wolfe) has heretofore prided herself upon belonging to the 'strong-minded' sect, and that this was to be taken as a demonstration of that fact . . . instead of showing good sense, or any commendable qualities in the exhibition referred to, she showed that she was but a weak, silly woman. We have too good an opinion of the ladies of Olympia to think that such acts will ever be repeated, and cause the blush of shame to mantle even the cheek of manhood."*

Charles, the advocate of free love, and Eliza, a liberated woman, were more than a hundred years ahead of their time, and the sleepy town of Olympia couldn't have been more shocked if Lady Godiva had ridden up Main street on one of Joseph Tebo's good fat livery horses.

DEATH OF A GOVERNOR

In the summer of 1862 Brigadier General Isaac I. Stevens died a hero's death leading his troops at Chantilly during the retreat of General Pope's army from Bull Run. He was 44 years of age.

Benjamin Kendall of the *Overland Press* saw no reason to alter his long-held opinion of the ex-governor just because he was dead. While other newspapers of the territory printed flowery obituaries, Kendall wrote:

"He (Stevens) was a man of education, ambitious of distinction, sometimes false to his friends when by so doing he promoted his own ends, prodigal of his means to advance his political aims; a hard worker wherever he was; and on the whole a man of more than average ability. He accommodated his political views to suit the current of events."

FIGHTING, FEUDING AND FUTILITY

Murphy, who had not taken kindly to the *Press* getting the public printing contract, had already rejected Kendall's sobriquet of "Bion" and referred to him in the *Standard* as "Bazaleel," further castigating the *Press* as Kendall's *"filthy sheet."* He added that when he had occasion to notice either, *"we feel the same nausea and desire to vomit which most men would experience after witnessing the victory of a skunk."*

Kendall's lack of tenderness in the Stevens obituary aroused Murphy to new heights of indignation:

"The public need not be told that the language was penned by the heartless and soulless creature who now owns and controls that infamous sheet, Bazaleel F. Kendall; no one but him would thus have outraged the feelings of the family and friends of the man who has reflected so much honor upon the Territory of his adoption by yielding his life on the field of battle in defense of the Union."

In his next issue Murphy noted that *"the morbid ulcer who edits the* Overland Press, *B. F. Kendall, denies having slandered the late General Stevens,"* but made it clear that in his opinion, and that of all right thinking people, Kendall most certainly had.

By fall the territorial secretary, Turney, was replaced by Olympia's own Elwood Evans, to the delight of Murphy, who, in his November 22 issue proclaimed that *"we had the pleasure yesterday of taking by the hand our 'bran new' Secretary of the Territory, Elwood Evans, Esq. This pleasure was enhanced by the fact that the new appointee does not belong to that much hated class of officials known as 'IMPORTATIONS,' but is, and has been for the past nine years, a respected citizen of our Territory."*

Murphy had blamed Turney for the hated Kendall *"growing fat on the territorial prin-*

ting" instead of himself, and he concluded his announcement of Evans' appointment with a parting blast at the former secretary:

"We are not surprised at Mr. Turney's removal. He has worked hard to bring it about; but it was not until he embarked in Bazaleel's leaky boat that it became apparent he would succeed. It is another proof that Bazaleel's very touch is political destruction."

The citizens of Olympia joined with Murphy in celebrating the appointment of one of their own to high territorial office. Quite predictably, they gave vent to their enthusiasm by repeatedly firing the town's Indian war cannon. Murphy, however, would subsequently lose much of his high regard for his old friend Evans.

In December the legislature came back to town and joined in the spirit of things by engaging in an unprecedentedly bitter fight over the speakership. During the proceedings it occurred to somebody that the members hadn't been sworn in yet, and their actions were probably illegal as well as futile. It was customary for the territorial secretary to swear in the legislators, and a three-man committee was selected to wait upon the secretary. Reaching his office, they found it still occupied by the just ousted Turney. They escorted him back to the capitol and he administered the oath of office, after which the members cast ten more inconclusive ballots for speaker. Mr. Ferguson of Snohomish, in a huff, cast his vote for somebody who wasn't even a member of the house.

The next day a belated member arrived and the sergeant at arms was dispatched to find the territorial secretary to swear him in. A "lengthy discussion" ensued over whether Turney or Evans should perform the ceremony. Finally a compromise was reached and another committee was appointed to ask Chief Justice James E. Wyche of the supreme court to do the job. After a long recess the committee came back and reported that they couldn't find the judge. Finally Squire Head, a member who happened to be a justice of the peace, administered the oath of office to the late-comer. Then, on the 17th ballot, they elected Thomas M. Reed speaker. That gentleman mounted the rostrum and delivered a long patriotic oration, urging his fellow members to *"never lose sight of that glorious banner, the stars and stripes that is now floating from the capitol in which we are assembled"* (cheers in the lobby) *"and so long as time shall last, may it float as in the language of the poet, Forever float that standard sheet, where breathes the foe but falls before it."*

The pioneers appreciated both patriotism and oratory, and Speaker Reed gave them a good dose of both. So did Governor Pickering who, in his inaugural message to the assembly spoke eloquently on the "sad and immoral effects" of legislative divorces. The members listened politely: then proceeded to pass 16 divorce bills.

The squabble began again as to whether or not the whole membership should be sworn in again and if so, by whom. Finally it was decided to let Squire Head do it, but he wasn't sure he had done it right the last time and had wandered off to see if he could find the form of oath used by Turney.

The house gave up and adjourned. Anyway, since nobody was quite sure who was legally the territorial secretary and thus responsible for providing them with stationery, stamps, ink, pay and reimbursement for mileage they had covered in reaching the capital, there wasn't much they could do.

It wasn't until January 5 of the next year that it was established that Evans was, indeed, territorial secretary. Even then there was some doubt about it, as congress didn't confirm the appointment for another month or more.

Thus the tenth legislative assembly of the territory of Washington saw the old year of 1862 out amid fighting, feuding and futility.

All in all, it had been a good year for that sort of thing in Olympia.

CHARLES H. MASON
First Secretary and Acting Governor of the Territory

FAYETTE McMULLIN
1857-1859
Second Governor of Washington Territory

CHAPTER THREE
The Second Decade
1863-1873

The new year of 1863 found the tenth territorial legislature still in session in the little wooden capitol on the hill above the town. It was still engaged in political combat, and a major issue was that perennial one of who was the public printer.

The removal of Alonzo Poe to California had prompted Governor Pickering, in mid-December of 1862, to declare the office vacant and to appoint George A. Barnes, the local merchant, capitalist and mayor as Poe's successor. On the surface it appeared a strange choice, for a printer was one thing George Barnes wasn't. He was, however, the brother-in-law of John Miller Murphy. Murphy and his financial and political backers, Anson Henry and Elwoods Evans, had found a way to get the territorial printing contract for the *Standard* by a somewhat circuitous route.

Belligerent Benjamin Kendall of the *Overland Press* believed the post to be his by right of inheritance from Poe, at least until the legislature held an election to decide the matter, and he was forthright in his denunciation of Murphy, Evans and Henry.

The legislators, for their part, were somewhat miffed at Pickering's usurpation of a political plum which they considered to be their sole prerogative. Besides, they were aware that Barnes had been picked by the autocratic and unpopular Anson Henry, in cahoots with Evans and Murphy. There were strong rumors afloat that Henry was already skimming off more than his share of the available public funds. Kendall had, in fact, recently fired an editorial blast at Henry under the heading, *"Have We a Swindler in Our Midst?"* in which he charged Henry with being able to do *"anything, and everything to suit the occasion"* . . . including the theft of public funds.*

Even after Kendall was removed suddenly and tragically from the fray, it took 20 ballots in the legislative assembly to confirm Barnes' appointment as territorial printer, assuring Murphy and the *Standard* of the work and Henry and Evans a share of the profits.

SUDDEN DEATH

The removal of Kendall was the result of the first sensational murder in the history of the sleepy territorial capital and might have been expected to make headlines, but Murphy "played it down" to a remarkable degree in the *Standard* of January 10, 1863:

"DIED: *Suddenly at this place on Wednesday, January 7, 1863, B. F. Kendall, formerly of Bethel, Maine, aged 34 years, and late editor of the Overland Press."*

Apparently feeling that some explanation should be made of his one-sentence reporting of the most sensational news story of the decade, Murphy noted elsewhere in the same issue that *"we have no desire to add to the excitement now prevailing in the community."*

---

*Surveyor-general Henry, wrongfully ascribing the editorial to Alonza Poe, armed himself with a large bowie knife and went in search of Poe, locating him at Edmund Sylvester's store where he was peacefully smoking a cigar and chatting with the town's gregarious founder. Henry struck Poe with his cane and Poe returned the blow with his light walking stick, whereupon Henry, according to Mr. Prosch of the *Puget Sound Herald, "drew his bowie knife and brandished it with loud words of defiance."* Edmund Sylvester broke up the fight, Poe refused to take Henry's threats seriously, and no blood was shed. Poe was not the last Olympia newspaper man to be attacked in error by an outraged subscriber.

Kendall's murder was, on the surface at least, the result of an article he had printed regarding an attempt made to drive George Roberts, a farmer and agent for the Puget Sound Agricultural Company, off some farm land he was holding for the company on the Cowlitz river. Kendall was the attorney for the company and a close personal friend of Roberts, and he came to the conclusion that a 70-year-old farmer named Horace Howe had set fire to Roberts' barn and outbuildings. He made his suspicions known in the *Overland Press* in no uncertain terms:

"It is the general impression that Horace Howe is the venerable gray bearded villian who attempted to perpetrate this high handed, diabolical deed. This veteran wretch goes on with his work of robbery. We trust the wretch may sooner or later meet his deserts . . . the gallows."

Howe didn't pay much attention to Kendall's tirade against him until a small army of Kendall's enemies, of whom he had no lack, descended upon the old man to explain to him how grievously he had been slandered. After a month of such pressures, Howe arrived in Olympia in December, 1862, but then spent another week deciding what to do.

On the morning of December 20 the rumor spread over the Olympia gossip grapevine that something exciting was about to happen in front of Aunt Becky Howard's Pacific House. Those who heeded the message were not disappointed. At about nine o' lock, Kendall finished his breakfast and left Mrs. Howard's dining room, pausing in front of the hotel to discuss with a friend the efforts of Murphy, Henry and Evans to steal the public printing for the *Standard*. Howe, having at last made up his mind . . . or had it made up for him . . . rounded the corner of 3rd and Main, walked up behind Kendall and brought a hazelwood ox-goad down across the editor-attorney's shoulders. Kendall whirled, drew a revolver and shot the old man in the left side. Then he started running toward his office, emptying his gun over his shoulder at Howe, who continued to pursue him despite his wound. Kendall outdistanced him and escaped inside his office.

Kendall claimed he had fired in self-defense, but his enemies did their best to stir up the prevailing excitement to mob action aimed at lynching the troublesome editor, or at least running him out of town. Their failure to do so was partly attributable to the fact that more fights broke out around town as the merits of the case were argued, thus distracting public attention from the main event. Even the legislators became involved. Two of them, J. D. Bagley and M. S. Griswold sat down in Aunt Becky's dining room for a friendly lunch. The conversation naturally turned to the favorite topic of the day, the shooting of old Mr. Howe by Kendall.

Griswold expressed the opinion that a vigilance committee should be formed to deal with Kendall. Bagley, on the other hand, felt that he had only done what any other red-blooded frontiersman would have done under the circumstances. Their words grew heated and they came to blows, but not for long. Aunt Becky Howard didn't hold with such goings-on in her hotel, and she was not impressed by politicians. (When Governor Pickering, soon after his arrival, had the temerity to address her as "Aunty" she had fixed him with a withering gaze and informed him that, to the best of her knowledge, she was not a sister of either his father or mother.) She promptly embraced Mr. Griswold and raised him from the floor a good two feet, holding him thus suspended until he lost both breath and belligerency. Griswold later confided to Charles Prosch of the *Puget Sound Herald* that *"Becky's grip reminds him of an old fashioned blacksmith's vice."*

No less a distinguished frontier statesman than the silver-tongued orator, Selucius Garfielde, abandoned his griddle cakes to pinion Mr. Bagley and, according to Prosch, *"performed his duties in a most commendable manner, and thus ended the great battle of Becky's dining room."*

With so much excitement going on all of a sudden, Olympians didn't have time to concentrate on a single project like riding Kendall out of town on a rail and, in the meantime, Dr. Warbass let it be known that old Mr. Howe would soon be back on his feet again.

The ring of territorial statesmen led by Anson Henry thought for a while their efforts might pay off anyway. The spectacle of the big, handsome Kendall, who had brought with him a reputation for swash-buckling bravery, running from a gravely wounded old man armed only with a hazelwood switch, had been vividly described by eyewitnesses and the *Washington Standard*. Public opinion was against Kendall, and his enemies hoped he would decide to leave town, or at least stop writing those embarrassing articles about whose fingers were in the public cookie jar.

The next issue of the *Overland Press* blasted any such hopes. After portraying his side of the affair in great detail, Kendall addressed himself to Henry, whom he was convinced had masterminded the Howe offensive:

"Henry in his sheet (the Standard*) says 'we forbear comment.' He is at perfect liberty to comment on this case, prejudice and affect the public mind to the fullest extent of his lying ability. We acted under a conscientious conviction of right; regretting the necessity of inflicting injury upon old or young, enemy or friend * * * We shall shrink from no responsibility by failing to express our views."*

Kendall's brash defiance of both public opinion and the political establishment coalesced the enmity of the people he had alienated, and he had started alienating people even before he got to Olympia.

After graduating from Bowdoin College with honors, he had gone to work as a clerk in the federal land office at Washington City. Within a year his boss recommended him to President Pierce for the job as secretary of the newly-formed territory of Washington . . . the job which eventually went to Charles Mason. Kendall then joined Stevens' railroad survey party as personal secretary and scout, receiving $25 a month. He managed to keep on fairly good terms with the irascible Stevens, but his "sour and harsh viewpoint, sardonic scowl, bulldog voice" and "apparent rudeness and severity of bearing" did not endear him to other members of the party.

With Stevens' support, Kendall was unanimously elected chief clerk of the house of representatives for the first session of the territorial legislature. Soon afterward he defeated Frank Clark, the attorney for the imprisoned settlers during the martial law controversy, for the position of territorial librarian. The victory did not endear him to Clark.

Although Kendall held both positions during two legislative sessions, the pay was even poorer than he had been getting as a member of Stevens' survey party, and he took up the practice of law in order to eat regularly. Although he had little or no formal legal training, he was a natural born frontier lawyer, soon winning the post of U.S. district attorney. A year later he became embroiled in the martial law controversy, joining with Judge Lander in opposition to Stevens. As a result he withdrew from the Stevens-dominated "Olympia Ring" which currently controlled territorial politics, and refused to continue as either legislative clerk or librarian.

Stevens and his supporters placed the name of Kendall high on their list of bad guys when, as prosecutor, he won the contempt of court case against the governor which cost them $50 and a great deal of embarrassment. Thereafter he and Elwood Evans rounded up the mob which marched to Stevens' mansion near the capitol building to demonstrate loudly against the governor.

The following year Kendall headed the prosecution of Leschi, again butting heads with Clark, who was the defense attorney. In subsequent cases, both as prosecutor and private attorney, he consistently defeated Clark, William Wallace and Elwood Evans, rubbing verbal salt in their wounds afterward at every opportunity. Before long his erstwhile friend Evans was describing Kendall in letters to Wallace as *"a man who has no soul; who is as sordid as self can make him."*

Shortly thereafter Kendall learned that the lucrative job of superintendent of Indian affairs would soon be open and he headed for Washington City to nail it down for himself. While he was there the rebels fired on Fort Sumpter and Kendall volunteered to become one of the first Union spies. General Winfield Scott was impressed by his credentials and accepted his offer. The general later reported that *"he has executed a confidential mission for me of great danger and importance (covering) nearly all the seceded states including Louisiana."*[*]

At the urging of General Scott, Kendall received the job he was looking for and returned to Olympia amid the inevitable firing of cannon and "general rejoicing." It wasn't that Kendall was any more beloved to the populace. It was just that times were hard and, as Charles Prosch pointed out in the *Herald*, *"Who wouldn't be the friend of a man who has anything to give in these hard times?"* Kendall

---

*John Miller Murphy, in his *Washington Standard*, conceded that Kendall had performed this service to his country, but took a rather dim view of it, writing that *"Some insist now that no honest, loyal man could have traveled (in Confederate territory), but a man that has the manners so peculiar to a southern negro driver can travel anywhere in the south with perfect impunity."*

now had jobs to distribute, and some of the jobs had traditionally carried the political perquisite of lining the holders' pockets at the expense of the taxpayers and their Indian wards.

Evans, Henry . . . who had just received the job of surveyor-general . . . and Wallace . . . who had been elected delegate to congress, were not among those who cheered and fired off cannon. Their noses were hopelessly out of joint because they hadn't been consulted in regard to this choicest of political patronage plums. Murphy took up their war whoops and duly published them in the *Standard.* Kendall may have been independent, arrogant and extremely hard to get along with, but he was also well educated, brilliant, hard-working and honest, and the Republican political power-brokers could only base their opposition on the charge that the new superintendent was a turncoat Democrat.

Evans, in a letter to Wallace in Washington City, summed up their lacerated feelings against *"such an outrage to Republicans as confirming this best position, most lucrative and most influential from its patronage,"* thus forcing deserving Republicans *"to submit to indignities from a poltroon because bread & butter depend upon it."*

This political infighting among the hungry Republicans didn't greatly impress the general public. Even the *Puget Sound Herald,* which seldom had anything bad to say about Republicans, and which was particularly tender of the feelings of Wallace and Evans, sided with Kendall on this issue.

As usual, Kendall managed to stub his own toe without help from anyone. The obstacle which felled him was a well-fed Methodist preacher named James H. Wilbur, who occupied a spacious residence and drew the then magnificent salary of $3,000 a year as superintendent of Indian education on the Yakima reservation.

A number of Methodist clergymen achieved marked success as arm-twisters and wheeler-dealers on the Northwest frontier. The Reverend John De Vore of Olympia had actually caught the tight-fisted Clanrick Crosby in a weak moment and talked him into pledging all the lumber from his mill that the man of God could load and raft to Olympia in one day. He then proceeded to roll up his sleeves, labor from dawn to dark without even taking time out for lunch, and float off on the tide with enough of Crosby's lumber to build Olympia's first

REV. JOHN F. DE VORE,
PIONEER METHODIST MINISTER
OF PUGET SOUND OF 1853.

Methodist church. The Reverend Daniel Bagley of Seattle was the guiding spirit of his town's successful theft of the university from the territorial legislature, selling off public lands quite illegally to finance the construction, and then getting Arthur Denny to talk congress into retroactively authorizing what he had already done.

The Reverend Wilbur was possessed of similar talents, but what he was interested in building was a comfortable and well-feathered nest for himself, and this he had achieved in the Yakima country. He had virtually taken over the management of the reservation from the superintendent and staffed it with the faithful of his church. He was an ardent exhorter at revivals, had been active in the Northwest missions since 1846 and was said by the *Standard* to be *"better known throughout Oregon and Washington than almost any other man."*

Kendall fired the reverend educator on the grounds that he was a trouble-maker and was costing the taxpayers too much. His few friends tried to point out that he had just committed political suicide, but as usual he refused to listen.

Murphy, in a burst of outraged piety, asserted in the *Standard* that the action demonstrated Kendall's *"fixed determination to dispense with the services of all praying men."*

Anson Henry wrote to Henry Wallace the joyful tidings that *"Kendall has most grossly offended the entire Christian community, and most especially the Methodist Church. There will be almost a universal demand for his removal."*

Public outrage, which had failed to generate as a result of Henry's plaintive outcries against Kendall for not letting him do his hiring and firing for him, was fanned to fever heat by a united pastorate which viewed Wilbur's dismissal as an attack by the forces of the devil upon the very foundations of the Christian church. Denunciations thundered from pulpits all across the territory, and poor Kendall found himself in the position of so many government officials before and since who have tried to save money for the taxpayers.

For good measure, Anson Henry talked the Reverend Wilbur into making a pilgrimage to Washington City to lay the sins of Benjamin before Father Abraham. Henry was one of Lincoln's closest personal friends and the President received Wilbur cordially. Then he consulted with Delegate Wallace and got the kind of answers to be expected.

It was then that Captain Hale replaced Kendall as superintendent of Indian affairs. The *Standard* reported gleefully, *"Kendall went to the wall * * * and Father Wilbur returned to the Yakima reservation."*

The political plums had been returned to the pioneer power-brokers of Olympia.

Soon afterward Kendall took over the editorship of the *Overland Press* and began getting some of his own back, in the process generating the comic opera battle of the Pacific Hotel.

Two days after that engagement, Horace Howe, Jr., appeared at his father's bedside in Olympia, where he was besieged by the same parties who had goaded the old man into his attack. They convinced the younger Howe that family honor demanded a complete retraction of the arson story by Kendall. They knew the embattled editor's stubborn character well enough to know he would rather die first. Young Howe admitted he didn't have much book learning, and Attorney Clark wrote the proposed retraction for him.

The following week Kendall put the current edition of the *Overland Press* to bed. It contained his last, strangely prophetic editorial:

*"Friends prove enemies * * * The recipients of our bounty become ungrateful. Our trusts are betrayed. The free generous confidence of youth is fast giving way to cold, selfish distrust of the existence of all we once regarded as most sacred and holy of human ties * * * It is an unpleasant maxim that we are ever to be suspicious of our fellow men * * * Act as we may, discharge our duties well or ill, be honorable or dishonorable, generous or mean . . . we must all find rest at last 'The End of the Play'."*

On January 1, 1863, the younger Howe met Kendall on the street near his newspaper office. Howe demanded the publication of the retraction and Kendall, with uncharacteristic reasonableness, told him to bring it to the office. It took Howe a week to get around to it. On January 7 he went to the newspaper office twice, but finding a number of other people there, he didn't stay to talk to the editor. On the third call he found only Kendall and his clerk in the office.

He and Kendall went into an inner office. The clerk heard a few minutes of low conversation which he couldn't make out. This was followed by a few seconds of dead silence and then a single pistol shot. Howe dashed from the office, a cocked derringer in his hand.

A moment later Kendall staggered to the outer office, exclaimed that he was shot, "grasps the mantle shelf, reels forward and falls lifeless upon the hearth." He had been shot through the heart.

In a preliminary hearing at the courthouse, Clark acted as Howe's attorney, while Kendall's friend, Judge Lander, led the prosecution. Clark denied repeatedly that he had ever laid eyes on the retraction Howe had submitted to Kendall. He admitted that he owned a derringer just like the one that had killed Kendall, but he refused to say where it was. In any event, he had an excellent alibi for the time of the murder. As representative for Pierce and Sawamish counties, he was up at the capitol attending the deliberations of the tenth territorial legislature. There is no record of Anson Henry's whereabouts that day, but it was pretty generally conceded that he or Clark, or both of them, had provided Howe with the murder weapon.

Murphy of the *Standard* continued his peculiar reticence in regard to the case, avoiding any comment except that *"The crowded state of our columns prevents our publishing the evidence."*

Judge Lander had taken over his late friend's newspaper and in it observed that *"the refusal of the witness to answer questions, gave rise to many unpleasant surmises in regards to Mr. Clark's connection with the melancholy affair."*

The impoverished Howe was subsequently provided with $3,000 bail by unidentified benefactors and returned to Cowlitz Prairie. The *Overland Press* intimated that it intended to *"stir up the Rip Van Winkles of this country,"* and that Howe might be a major factor in the stirring.

Soon thereafter the defendant disappeared. Some said he had left the country, others that he had accidentally drowned, while still others intimated that he had been silenced the same way he had silenced the troublesome Kendall.

The mystery was never solved. Anson Henry died two years later in the wreck of the steamer *Brother Jonathan* off the California coast. There were persistent rumors that a good deal of money went down with him.

Frank Clark became a successful criminal lawyer, prospering for another half century, but his reputation never recovered from the Kendall affair. In 1917, 34 years after his death, Hewbert Hunt, in his book *Washington West of the Cascades,* described him as *"a man whose actions did not at all times conform to the highest ideals of moral philosophy."*

Elwood Evans and John Miller Murphy lived even longer lives, but like Henry and Clark, they remained singularly silent regarding any part they might have had in the celebrated case.

And, as in so many other controversial cases which might embarrass the politically powerful, Case. No. 1304—Washington Territory *vs* Horace Howe—of the 2nd district Court, long since disappeared from the court files of Thurston county.

The death of Kendall and the disappearance of Howe remain surrounded with mystery to this day, but as Willis A. Katz wrote in the *Pacific Northwest Quarterly* of January, 1958:

"Righteously or otherwise, Kendall has been a martyr to the politics and politicians of frontier Washington Territory."

On January 31, shortly after Kendall was safely laid away in his grave, the tenth territorial legislature adjourned, but not before Mr. Bagley, the representative from Clallam and Jefferson counties, having recovered from the state of breathlessness brought on by Aunt Becky's bear hug, introduced a resolution honoring *"the late B. F. Kendall, whose many virtues as a man are deserving of remembrance, whose culture of mind was worthy of imitation, whose energy of character has left its imprint upon the Territory".*

The legislators were willing to spread a few kind words about the deceased on the record, as long as he *was* deceased, and even John Miller Murphy produced a decent obituary.

There was a strange lack of the usual festivities which traditionally took place in Olympia following legislative adjournment *sine die,* but it wasn't the result of sadness over the untimely demise of Benjamin Kendall. It was caused by the fact that the federal government had failed to send so much as a deflated greenback to pay the expenses and mileage of the members. A number of them had to hock their belongings to get home, and even though Secretary Evans pried loose $2,000 from some undisclosed source to succor the more needy and deserving Republicans, few of the legislators had the price of a drink after they bought their tickets home.

Olympia's civic leaders, convinced that it was the lawmakers' love for that "silent and succulent lobbyist, the Olympia oyster" that gave them the best chance of retaining the capital, sent them off with full stomachs to somewhat offset their empty pockets.

PUBLIC PRINTING
FOR FUN AND PROFIT

When the eleventh legislature assembled at Olympia in December, no time was wasted in getting a good, hot fight going over the territorial printing contract. Elwood Evans, still secretary of the territory, had been engaged in a quiet but nonetheless bitter personal feud with his erstwhile partner, John Miller Murphy, for the past year. Even earlier he had broken diplomatic relations with the third member of the triumverate, Anson Henry. Evans had coveted the governorship and was never really satisfied with the secondary position of territorial secretary. He came to the conclusion that Henry, the close friend of Lincoln, had deviously blocked his appointment and secured the job for Pickering.

The reason for his quarrel with Murphy is less clear, although Mr. Prosch of the *Herald* attributed it to the fact that Evans insisted upon writing articles for the *Standard* of a quality *"which Murphy's small brain was incapable of conceiving."* He added that Murphy had flown into a fine rage when he received an article in the mail addressed to Evans as editor of his beloved *Standard,* and had thrown it into the stove instead of printing it.

Be that as it may, on December 7 Evans announced that he, not the legislature, had the right to select the public printer. He summarily removed Mr. Barnes, implying that Olympia's conservative Republican businessman-mayor was a violent copperhead, intent on overthrowing the Union. The U.S. treasury department, he told the legislature, had given him the authority to appoint a public printer "to prevent the public treasury from being plundered by the enemies of the people".

Murphy, well aware that he was one of the unnamed "enemies of the people" whom Evans was charging with plundering the treasury, was outraged; he was even more so when he learned that none other than T. H. McElroy, co-partner in the establishment of the *Columbian,* nee *Pioneer and Democrat,* had been selected to take the printing away from the good Republican *Standard**.

Many of the legislators were as outraged as Murphy. This juicy political plum had traditionally been theirs and they weren't inclined to give it up without a fight. Furthermore, the bizarre charge of Evans that George Barnes was a copperhead was a bit too much for even those who were otherwise favorable to McElroy. The squabble crossed party lines, with F. P. Dugan, Democratic house leader from Walla Walla entering into an alliance with Evans, and ex-Acting Governor McGill leading the anti-Evans, anti-McElroy faction. Ironically, McGill had set the precedent which Evans was following when, back in 1861, he had appointed James Lodge to replace George Gallagher, resigned.

Evans won the battle and the war as well. McElroy kept his job and public printers were henceforth appointed by the territorial secretary until Washington achieved statehood. Evans battered down all efforts to unseat McElroy as long as he was secretary, and Charles Prosch charged flatly that Evans was a silent partner with McElroy in the old Pioneer Job Printing Office, and so was again sharing in the profits of the public printing.

The profits must have been considerable, for McElroy rose from an impecunious printer to one of the wealthiest men in the territory. This was to be the pattern for public printers until well into the twentieth century; most of them started out broke and ended up prosperous.

Backed by Evans, McElroy didn't have to publish a Democratic newspaper to retain his job, although his shop did commercial job printing as well as the territorial publications. Urban E. Hicks, a printer of decidedly copperhead persuasion soon arrived on the scene to fill the void issuing a newspaper called the *Washington Democrat.* The following is typical of his journalistic style and political convictions:

"It is impossible that peace should come again while a fiendish ape is at the head of our affairs. He realizes nothing of the awful destruction of property nor the wasting slaughter of life. Neither does he care. He has none of the instincts or sensibilities of a man, nor the dignity of a respectable tyrant."

John Miller Murphy was a great admirer of Lincoln, and he remained so even after his politics turned Democratic. He was shocked at Hicks' diatribes against the Great Emancipator, and he was boiling mad because he was pretty sure that Hicks was being financed by a pair of his arch enemies. The *Standard* proclaimed that:

"The capital upon which the Democrat *is founded, incredible as it may seem, has been furnished by friends of Mr. Lincoln's administration. The ostensible conductor of this new enterprise are U. E. Hicks & Co., but we have cogent reasons for believing that its real projectors are Evans, McElroy & Hicks . . . Secretary and Public Printers for Washington Territory. That this nondescript firm of professed Union men and Copperheads, were concocting a scheme to secure the Public Printing among themselves, and make the government furnish a club to be used to break its own head, has been known for two years past."*

Apparently young Murphy was unable to vent his Irish temper sufficiently in type, and Hicks claimed in later years that Murphy was

---

*It was growing apparent at this time that Murphy was becoming increasingly disenchanted with his Republican affiliation. He was beginning to refer to the *Standard's* political philosophy as "Union" rather than Republican, and in later years he was known to deny that it ever *had* been Republican.

in the habit of throwing rocks through the windows of the *Democrat* office. Fortunately for the Murphy blood pressure, the *Democrat* lasted only about a year, although the capital city hadn't seen the last of U. E. Hicks.

The journalistic kettle was boiling in Olympia during civil war days, and the *Standard* soon had new competition. Even the much smaller village of Seattle got a newspaper, although it was printed in Olympia on Murphy's press. James R. Watson didn't have a printing plant of his own and talked Murphy into doing the job on credit. The first issue of a newspaper with a Seattle dateline was thus produced at Olympia on August 15, 1863, and carried to Seattle by its enterprising publisher on the *Eliza Anderson.* He did so well that by December he had his own printing plant in Seattle.

PUTTING ON AIRS

The burgeoning crop of territorial newspapers shared in the rewards of progress when, in 1864, the transcontinental telegraph line reached Olympia. No longer were their editors dependent upon weeks-old copies of eastern newspapers brought up the coast by sidewheel mail steamers. The citizens of the territorial capital were assured of news which was not more than a week old.

John Miller Murphy had tried to speed up the journalistic process some years earlier. He was in San Francisco on his honeymoon, and as he and his wife approached the dock to embark on the steamer for the return trip, newsboys were shouting an extra announcing that Fort Sumpter had been fired upon. Murphy bought up all copies, kept them hidden until he reached home, and at once cranked out a small extra edition of the *Standard,* complete with big black headlines. He expected to clean up a tidy profit on his scoop, but he made one serious mistake. The news was all in the headlines, and the headlines were large enough to be read at a distance of 50 feet. So nobody bought his extra.

Henceforth, to the end of his long career, Murphy made it a policy to hide any important news on inside pages and in type so small that the reader often had to go through the paper several times to find it.

On August 27, 1864, the *Standard* reported, *"The telegraph will be completed to Skookumchuck to-day and will probably be finished to this place by next Saturday."*

Governor Pickering wasted no time in utilizing the newly-strung wire to dispatch the first telegraphic message from Olympia . . . a lengthy congratulatory telegram to President Lincoln. The next day the brass key in the Olympia telegraph office chattered into life and this message was copied in the operator's fluent copperplate script:

"Washington, D.C., Sept. 6, 1864.

Gov. Pickering, Olympia, W.T.

Your patriotic dispatch of yesterday received and will be published.

. . . A. Lincoln"

Honest Abe had avoided the tendency of most politicians, including Pickering, to send long, expensive messages on historic occasions. He kept his answer well under ten words.

Despite the hard times brought on by the war, progress in Olympia wasn't limited to the coming of the telegraph. The first home-built steamboat, the *Pioneer,* was launched by Miller and Ethridge, sawmill operators, and made a successful trial voyage up the Deschutes waterway to Tumwater. Although designed primarily for towing logs to her owners' mill she was equipped with "a well arranged cabin 18 feet in length and about 12 feet wide and can carry comfortably 30 or 40 passengers."

The town fathers erected a hand-pump over the spring next door to Edmund Sylvester's store, and it became more of a social gathering place than ever, but its days were numbered. Later in the year a water company was franchised and began laying pipes made of bored logs. It was a primitive affair and for the next sixty years or so it provided the citizenry with more grounds for rage and frustration than drinkable water, but it was viewed as new evidence that Olympia was progressing from frontier village to modern metropolis.

Most heartening of all was the news from Washington City that congress had granted a charter to the reorganized Northern Pacific Railway, and had thrown in a fat land grant to finance its construction. It looked as if Stevens' dream was to become reality, and Olympia was certain to be the western terminus of the transcontinental line. When that happened the boom would be on and everybody would get rich.

The dreams were far more impressive than the reality. Samuel Bowles, editor of the Springfield (Massachusetts) *Republican,* considered one of the great journalists of his day, made the trip from Portland to Puget Sound over the Cowlitz Trail. He included an account of this journey in his book, *Across the Continent; a Summer's Journey to the Rocky Mountains, the Mormons and the Pacific Coast.* The trip took three days by steamboat and stage, and cost $30 for transportation. Regarding the territorial capital and principal settlement he wrote:

"We dined the second day at Skookum Chuck, and came to the head of Puget Sound * * * *and this town, the capital, at night, encountering the usual demonstrations of artillery, brass band and banners and most hospitable greeting from Acting Governor Evans and other officials and citizens.*

"Olympia lies charmingly under the hill by the waterside and counts its inhabitants less than 500, though the largest town in the territory, save the mining center of Wallula down in the southeast corner.

"It numbers more stumps than houses within its limits, but is the social and political center of a large area, puts on airs and holds many of the materials of fine society. We were entertained at a very 'Uncle-Jerry-and-Aunt-Phoebe' little inn, whose presiding genius, a fat and fair African of 50 years and 300 pounds, robed in spotless white, welcomed us with the grace and dignity of a queen and fed us as if we were in training for a cannibal's table."

The great eastern editor was obviously more impressed by Aunt Becky Howard than by anything else in pioneer Olympia, even the remarkable number of stumps in the streets.

MARRY IN HASTE

Weddings were also major social occasions in pioneer Olympia, but once in awhile the participants failed to "hold the materials of fine society", thus depriving their fellow citizens of an excuse for celebrating.

Young Christopher Columbus Simmons was one who staged an unconventional wedding. The son of Michael Simmons, born in a sheep pen on the Cowlitz while the pioneers awaited the spring of 1845 to continue on to Puget Sound, was a strapping lad of 19 in the fall of 1864. His father, Big Mike Simmons, cheated by those he had trusted and driven from the political scene by Stevens, would soon die in poverty on his last land claim, in Lewis county.

Christopher Columbus seems to have inherited his father's lack of business shrewdness. Mrs. George Blankenship, in her *Early History of Thurston County, Washington,* quotes from a personal interview with the younger Simmons in 1914:

"One time when I was working for my uncle, Dr. (David) Maynard, who was one of the first settlers of King County, he made me a present of a deed to 160 acres of what is now West Seattle. I held onto it for awhile and then found it too troublesome to care for the deed and to keep the small amount of taxes paid, so I gave it back to Uncle Maynard, much to his disgust. He thought I must have very little sense not to hang on to what he knew would be very valuable at some not far-off day."

Christopher Columbus Simmons knew he didn't want the responsibilities and anxieties involved in getting rich, and he acted forthrightly to avoid them. He acted just as forthrightly in claiming what he *did* want, and that was a pretty girl named Asaneth Ann Kennedy, who was just 14 years old that fall. Her parents had sent her to Steilacoom to finish school, and they made it plain that Chris Simmons' attentions to their daughter wouldn't be welcomed, at least not until after she had graduated.

One night in late August Christopher decided he couldn't wait that long. He borrowed a boat at Big Skookum, where he was working and rowed to Steilacoom. There he met Asaneth Ann and the two rowed on down Puget Sound to Seattle. Territorial law required that parties to a marriage who were under 18 years of age must have parental consent, and the young lovers were worried. When they arrived at Elliott Bay they proceeded at once to seek the advice and counsel of Doc Maynard. In his interview with Mrs. Blankenship, half a century later, Simmons recalled the solution found for them by the ingenious doctor:

"This good man considered for a moment and then said to Ann, 'Take off your shoes'. She did so and Dr. Maynard wrote the figures 18 on two slips of paper and put them in her shoes. Ann caught on as quick as lightning. A

few minutes later we stood up before Rev. Daniel Bagley, who asked her age. 'Why I'm over eighteen', she said as bland as milk, and so we were married and lived happily together."

The pioneers of Olympia may have missed the wedding festivities, but the event provided them with a cherished legend which, unlike some of the others, appears to be quite authentic. The *Standard* of October 1, 1864, duly recorded the nuptials at Seattle of "Christophur *(sic)* Simmons and Amanthi *(sic)* Ann Kennedy", as performed at Seattle by the Reverend Daniel Bagley.

And Parson Bagley, the father of the University of Washington, certainly wouldn't have done anything illegal unless tricked into it.

Chris and Ann filed on a claim on Eld Inlet, which included tidelands with fine beds of oysters, which grew naturally and provided a good living without undue exertion. In 1914, when he talked to Mrs. Blankenship, Christopher Columbus and Asaneth Ann had just celebrated their golden wedding, surrounded by their nine children, numerous grandchildren and countless oysters. They lived on in peace and contentment, without ulcers, high blood pressure or nervous breakdowns, for many more years.

DEATH OF A PRESIDENT

The most dramatic event of the year 1865 was, of course, the assassination of Abraham Lincoln. The news was flashed to the backwoods territorial capital by the telegraph, bringing the same grief and shock that rocked the rest of the nation.

The territorial Democratic convention was being held in Olympia at the time, and one of its delegates, Major Haller of Seattle, was visiting the office of P. D. Moore, recently appointed collector of internal revenue for Washington and Idaho by President Lincoln, when the news came. Haller was so overcome that he proceeded to the convention and, with tears streaming down his cheeks, moved that it adjourn immediately, without selecting a delegate to congress. The motion very nearly passed.

As a means of relieving his feelings, Moore mounted a drygoods box on the corner opposite U. E. Hicks' copperhead *Washington Democrat* office and delivered himself of a stirring eulogy to the martyred president. His impromptu speech so inflamed the crowd that they decided to burn down the newspaper office and string Hicks up to the nearest shade tree.

Moore was a great orator, but he was also a devout Quaker, and the incipient violence he had stirred up horrified him. He remounted his box and made another impassioned speech on the virtues of tolerance and neighborly love, thus saving the property and health of Mr. Hicks.

The Democrats might as well have followed Major Haller's suggestion and adjourned without nominating a congressional candidate. Arthur Denny, aided on the campaign trail by the silver tongue of Selucius Garfielde, won the election handily and proceeded to Washington City to bail out the Reverend Bagley and his questionable sales of university lands. He had the blessings of Governor Pickering in this endeavor, for the governor was among the many prominent citizens of the territory who had availed themselves of the Reverend Bagley's choice bargains in public land.

HERE COME THE BRIDES

As an aftermath of the civil war, an enterprising young Seattle man named Asa Shinn Mercer, evolved a plan to bring out a shipload of New England ladies of respectable character and marriageable age to help solve the imbalance of the sexes in Washington territory. Men outnumbered women by better than ten to one in Washington, whereas the civil war had decimated the male population in New England and left a surplus of equally restive females.

Mercer had helped to build the territorial university and, upon its completion, had been appointed its first president and dispatched to the villages and logging camps of Puget Sound to try to round up a student body. He found only one individual in the entire territory who was eligible for enrollment at the college level, and the student body had to be filled out with the grammar school children of Seattle. His scheme to import young ladies to the territory seemed based on better logic, but he had the misfortune to run out of money along the way, and spent that entrusted to him by other Seattle citizens for various purchases to get his bevy of damsels to Puget Sound. (Governor Pickering had been an eloquent backer of his project, but when Mercer telegraphed the executive office for help he was rewarded only by an inspiring telegram several hundred words in length . . . and sent to him collect.)

The citizens of Olympia reaped a greater harvest from the Mercer expedition than did those of Seattle, who had involuntarily paid the bill.

The townspeople selected a committee to "cooperate with" the Seattle committee. The Olympia group consisted of such solid and persuasive citizens as Elwood Evans, T. F. McElroy, George Barnes, Francis Henry and Daniel Bigelow . . . and their wives. Homes in the Olympia area were quickly found for 80 of the widows and orphans. The advantages of the capital city and the comfortable respectability of the Thurston county homes were set forth so convincingly that more of the Mercer girls ended up in Olympia than in Seattle, and poor Mercer was more or less gently run out of town.

AND HERE COME THE WHORES

Shortly after Mercer's abortive effort to solve the woman shortage in the Puget Sound country, an equally enterprising, but less idealistic gentleman named John Pinnell, set about to do the same thing in a different way. Described by *American Mercury* magazine in later years as *"Tall saturnine and suave, wearing a flowered waistcoat and a plug hat"*, Pinnell arrived from San Francisco and opened an establishment on the sawdust fill near Henry Yesler's waterfront sawmill. He named it the *Illahee** and stocked it with high-proof whiskey and Indian maidens. Before too long he imported a cargo of genuine white women from San Francisco's Barbary Coast. Unlike Asa Mercer's shipment of widows and orphans from New England, Pinnell's girls did not pride themselves on either their respectability or marriageability (although legend has it that several of them did, indeed, wed Seattle pioneers and that they shared with the Mercer girls the founding of several prosperous and respected families of the town).

*Although Pinnell made a major contribution to Seattle's emergence as the metropolis of the Pacific Northwest, no streets or parks are named after him. Only the name of his brothel, *Illahee* (an Indian word meaning "the place") has been immortalized as the name of a ferryboat in the Washington state ferries fleet.

Several of Seattle's less stuffy historians argue that the coming of John Pinnell was the greatest single factor in Seattle's survival and ultimate supremacy. Most of the 10,000 or so single, virile and lonesome men who toiled in the area's logging camps and mines got in the habit of spending their spare time . . . and their money . . . in Seattle and the Illahee. Besides, Pinnell hadn't spent anybody's money but his own to get his project under way, and he paid more than his share to the town's modest treasury after he got things going. Seattle's total city budget in those days was $5,000, to which Pinnell's license fee contributed $1,200.

Olympia, having capitalized on Mercer's importation of virtuous womanhood, failed to follow through and lure Pinnell's non-virtuous sisterhood to the capital city. The few dozen Mercer girls were very quickly married, thereafter presumably bringing contentment only to their husbands. The Pinnell girls were far more efficient. Each of them could provide solace to hundreds of lonesome bachelors each month, and each pay day more and more of the territory's loggers, miners, seamen and single homesteaders took the steamboats to Seattle and the Illahee.

Olympia was still the biggest town in the territory, but after John Pinnell chose Seattle as the location for his business, the capital city's days of supremacy were numbered.

MR. WILLIAMS' FIRE ENGINE

Not that there wasn't real progress in 1866.

For one thing the town finally got that real fire engine so long advocated by the pioneer newspaper editors, although for a while there was considerable doubt as to whether it was owned by the town or prosperous local merchant Charles E. Williams. Williams learned of a big hand-pumper for sale second-hand in Seneca Falls, New York. At that time he owned Olympic hall, which was later acquired by Captain Finch of the *Eliza Anderson* and given to the Good Templers lodge. Williams decided to stage a "grand engine benefit ball" at his hall, with tickets at $10.00 each, which was a lot of money during the post-civil war era on the Northwest frontier.

PROUD CREW OF OLD COLUMBIA pose with their rig in front of Columbia Hall in 1888. Upper row: John McClellan, foreman; D. S. B. Henry; William Craig; George Allen, chief; Charles Talcott; Ed Robbins, Joe Chilberg. Lower row: Thomas Ford; Clem Johnston; William Schofield; Jose Rizbeck; John Miller Murphy; Sam McClellan; Robert Frost; Dick Wood; E. T. Young.
... *State Capitol Museum Photo*

The townspeople wanted that engine, though, and they responded so generously that the required $900 purchase price was raised and the engine was ordered. When, in due time, it arrived on the ship *Black Hawk* by way of Cape Horn and was landed at the Main street wharf, the whole town was there to celebrate its arrival. It was a handsome thing of gleaming red and shining brass, with long pump rods along each side and a dome bearing the letters in black brass . . . *Columbia.* It was generally agreed that the name was most fitting and should be retained.

Mr. Williams was particularly entranced by the beautiful new fire engine; so much so that he apparently forgot that all the citizens had chipped in to buy it. He had big doors cut in Olympic hall and ordered the *Columbia* to be delivered there.

It was, he claimed, his own private fire engine, although the fire department could borrow it whenever there was a conflagration within the town limits.

Despite great public outrage and indignation, Williams was obdurate.

Finally, to meet this civic crisis, the Squilgee Engine Company was mustered for drill. After a lapse of several years the giant beer barrel on wheels was reassembled by her gallant crew. Other concerned citizens built a fire in the street in front of Williams' store at 4th and Main. The fire alarm was vigorously banged and the dread cry of "Fire! Fire!" echoed through the town. The gallant Squilgees responded, hauling their ridiculous engine with a long hauser from *Eliza Anderson's* wharf. Liveryman A. J. (Jack) Baldwin, the foreman, strode forward and began squirting at the fire with a large horse syringe. The spectators went wild with delight and poor Williams arrived on the scene at a dead run, convinced that his store was doomed.

Williams was no fool and he knew when he was beaten. He went into his store and soon reappeared with the ownership papers for the *Columbia,* which he presented to Baldwin.

The Columbia Engine Company was forthwith organized, with Baldwin as its foreman. the *Squilgee,* having served its final purpose, was seen no more.

The fire company, soon equipped with red shirts and brass helmets, loved to practice with their engine, despite the effort involved in hauling it and working the pumps by muscle-power alone. The citizens, especially the small boys, loved to watch them.

On summer evenings the banging of the fire bell would bring both firemen and citizens running to the performance. The bravely helmeted firemen would wheel the gleaming red and gold *Columbia* from its shed and race with it to 3rd and Main, where a tall flagpole stood. The town character, Jake Summers, a burley pockmarked individual with a whiskey baritone voice of great volume, would mount the engine and start singing soft and low. As he increased his volume, the firemen increased their efforts . . . twenty of them toiling at the primitive hand-brakes . . . and when Jake reached a crescendo the hosemen proudly sent a stream of water arching far above the flagpole. To the applause of the assembled multitude, the firemen would then repair to the old brewery on Columbia street to suck up cream lager as thirstily as their engine sucked up water.

Before long the firemen of the new company put pressure on the town trustees to provide quarters of suitable dignity for their beloved *Columbia.* They also raised enough money to underwrite a good share of the costs, although the town fathers had to borrow $500 from Tom Prather to round out their contribution. The result was a new city hall, named Columbia hall in honor of the town's first fire engine. It was one of the grandest public buildings in the territory, far superior to the territorial capitol, and a fine public meeting room was provided on the top floor. Thereafter theatrical productions, lectures and political rallies were held at Columbia hall instead of the old Washington hotel.

Optimistic newspaper publishers continued to set up shop in the capital city during the immediate post-war years. The *Overland Press,* under the management of a long series of publishers, became the *Pacific Tribune*.* After 1867 Charles Prosch moved down from Steilacoom to take over its editorship, and he and John Miller Murphy were enabled to carry on their cherished feud at close quarters.

FOOLS' PARADISE

The death of Lincoln and the controversial succession of Andrew Johnson had thrown the politics of the nation . . . and of Washington territory into turmoil. Old political affiliations were again severed, and anti-Johnson Republicans formed "bolters'" parties. The *Standard* had changed its politics to Democratic. The *Tribune* was anti-Johnson Republican. J. N. Gale brought his family up from Oregon in 1866 and established the *Union Guard,* which supported the national administration. After a few months he formed a partnership with Elisha T. Gunn and the paper was enlarged and renamed the Olympia *Transcript.*

Gale had decided temperance leanings, and since he wrote the editorials, while Gunn gathered the "locals" and set the type, the *Transcript* tended to emphasize the evils of drink more than the evils of Democrats and "bolters". Gunn was afraid this would have an adverse effect on the paper's revenues. Gale wouldn't compromise his principles, so Gunn eventually bought him out. Gale soon found a perfect spot for himself as editor of a new paper, the *Temperance Echo,* which was supported by local temperance organizations.

Soon after Gale and Gunn launched the *Transcript,* J. R. Watson, founder of the Seattle press, got restless and returned to Olympia to publish the *Territorial Republican.* The village was saturated with partisan newspapers, and Watson soon sold out to a young journalist named Clarence B. Bagley, who changed the paper's name to *Commercial Age.*

By 1870, with a population of 1,200, Olympia had four newspapers, and in the years immediately ahead the field would become even more crowded, prompting John Miller Murphy to refer to the town as a journalistic fools' paradise.

---

*In 1873, with the coming of the Northern Pacific Railroad, it was moved to New Tacoma, becoming a lineal ancestor of the present Tacoma *News-Tribune.* the journalistic history of both Seattle and Tacoma thus had its beginnings in Olympia.

HERE COME THE CARPETBAGGERS

In the meantime, the shifting tides of national politics had deposited new territorial officials on the muddy shores of the capital city. Andrew Johnson, in 1866, had appointed George Cole, the delegate to congress, as governor, but in its vendetta with the former vice president, the senate refused to confirm the appointment. Johnson replaced Cole with Yale graduate Marshall F. Moore, who had been breveted brigadier general for heroism in the war. In the process he had acquired wounds which failed to heal, and he died at Olympia early in 1870 after meeting with only one session of the legislature . . . that of 1867.

Like most territorial governors, Moore brought with him a small retinue of supporters and job seekers. Included was his brother-in-law, Philemon B. Von Trump, who soon gained fame by climbing to the top of Mt. Rainier in company with Isaac Stevens' son, Hazzard . . . the first recorded conquest of the mighty mountain which broods eternally over the Puget Sound country, and can sometimes be seen during the summer months.

Moore also brought along a new territorial secretary, one Ezra L. Smith. Like many of the "carpet-bag" appointees of the period, Smith was not adverse to making a quick dollar or two. Charles Prosch, who had led the chorus of moral indignation over the alleged partnership of Evans and McElroy in the public printing, was quick to take advantage of the new secretary's itching palm to get the job for himself. After his term of office ended, he published the details with surprising frankness in the *Pacific Tribune*:

"We are indebted to Mr. Smith. He appointed us public printer, charged us over $2,000 for the boon, got his pay at the start, and so laid the foundation for his present prosperity. We have not yet been paid for our labor."

This transaction, which can scarcely be termed anything but outright bribery, failed to arouse much moral indignation. Even Murphy, who had devoted columns to lambasting McElroy and his friends, merely observed that Prosch's admission *"has been the subject of much comment. The public expects Mr. Smith to exonerate himself, or plead guilty to the charge. Should he not do this, the Legislature may very properly make it the subject of an investigation."*

This was all that was ever printed in the Olympia papers on the subject and the legislature made no investigation. Presumably the whole thing was considered "just politics".

Anyway, two survey parties were hard at work under General Tilton blazing the right of way for the Pacific division of the Northern Pacific Railroad. Prosperity was just across the mountains, and there was little time for minor scandals.

THE VOICE OF SELUCIUS IS HEARD IN THE LAND

Alvin Flanders, a good conservative Republican, was elected to succeed Arthur Denny as a delegate to congress, serving from 1867 to 1869. Flanders, even less articulate than Denny, was, like his predecessor, elected (over Democrat frank Clark) largely through the oratorical efforts of Selucius Garfielde. The local poet laureate, Francis Henry, was moved to describe the proxy campaign in his inimitable verse:

"Alvin Flanders rode upon
A horse that wouldn't mind him,
And so to act as fugleman,
Selucius rode behind him.

"Selucius was a proper man
And had so good a straddle
That he could ride two horses with
One office for a saddle.

"His classic seat was full of grip,
His brain was scientific,
And large enough to hold a train
Of cars for the Pacific.

"His mouth o'erflowed with oily words,
In fact 'twas even hinted
That he could make an off-hand speech
Just like a book that's printed.

"And thus they rode from place to place,
Where'er their pony bore them;
When Flanders had to speak a piece
Selucius spoke it for him.

*"'Tis mostly thus with those who shriek
    Of Congress orthodoxy,
When called upon to fight or speak
    They do it best by proxy."*

John Miller Murphy didn't think much of the silver-tongued orator, a fact which he made abundantly clear in the columns of the *Washington Standard*. Within a period of little over a month, he composed the following gems of political invective:

"Selucius, the man of words, who, in order to illustrate the force of eloquence, has literally TALKED HIMSELF INTO NOTHING. *The ass, who having been used by Wallace, Denny and Flanders to ride upon to Congress, imagines that he will be carried there in his turn . . . the old man of the islands in politics, who once seated on the neck of a party never lets up as long as it has the strength to carry him. A man whose moral turpitude is the subject of comment wherever he is known."*

This was followed by a couple of even less kindly observations:

"Selucius is always cocked and primed, as our "Devil" inelegantly expresses it, 'to shoot his mouth off'. In this he resembles a turkey cock; you have but to clap your hands and his feathers become at once erect, showing much more than nature intended."*
and:

"Selucius resembles an ass in being most noted for his bray. In some other respects they are quite opposite. One would appear to be well hung, the other wouldn't."

Murphy's contempt for Garfielde reached a climax when, on January 18, 1868, he listed the passengers arriving on the *Eliza Anderson* as *"Mr. Smith and wife, Dr. Ostrander and wife, Mr. Bigelow, one klootchman, two siwashes, Garfielde and three Chinamen."*

---

*The "printer's devil" at the *Standard* during the era was young Sam Crawford, who later became a colorful newspaper man in his own right.

THE LEGISLATURE IS ARMED AND DANGEROUS

The year 1868 was an exciting one for the frontier capital. It got both the legislature and its first circus, and it was difficult for the natives to decide which was the most exciting.

Post-war political bitterness was at its peak, and the struggle to steal the capital from Olympia was on again. Feelings ran high and the legislators were armed and dangerous. Much time on the floor was spent in re-fighting the civil war, and the bitterness overflowed to the local saloons, where fistic encounters were frequent.

Many of the frontier statesmen carried revolvers to the capitol with them and sometimes flourished their weapons, but fortunately nobody was shot.

A bill was introduced to move the capital to Vancouver. William H. Newell, publisher of the Walla Walla *Statesman,* one of the most peppery of the pistol-packing legislators, averred that he had come to Olympia with the determination not to interfere with the location of the capital, but that when meetings were held by the local citizens to "intimidate and overawe the action of the assembly," he was disposed to give the bill his vote. Newell was just letting off steam, for he was dedicated to getting the prize for Walla Walla. The bill languished throughout the session in the committee on corporations.

The assembly did find time, between the feuding and fighting, to create Quillehuyte county (which was never organized), establish a board of regents for the territorial university (presumably in an attempt to keep the Reverend Mr. Bagley under control), dispatch 23 memorials to congress begging for federal funds, and pass an act submitting to the voters of the territory a proposition for calling a convention to frame a state constitution and to apply for the admission of the state of Washington into the Union. When the voters got the opportunity to cast ballots on the latter measure they were less then enthusiastic. It failed 1,109 to 974.

After the legislature adjourned the town fathers had the old Indian war blockhouse in the square torn down, thriftily utilizing the salvaged lumber to plank one of the more swampy sections of Main street. Town

60

Marshal Hawk, left without a jail, informed the *Standard "that he has fitted up a cell in the cow-shed adjoining Grainger's stable for the reception of town prisoners."*

One of the first to occupy the cow-shed jail was one Heo, who was charged with assaulting an Indian girl of his tribe. General T. I. McKenny, the Indian agent, sentenced Heo to 50 lashes, vigorously laid on his bare back by the brawny arm of William Billings, Indian agent. After receiving 15 blows from Billings' five-stranded whip, poor Heo ruined the Indian reputation for stoicism under torture by fainting dead away.

Also, following the adjournment in February of the 1867-68 legislature, the council sergeant at arms, Louis Meyers, froze both his feet while trying to return home to Vancouver over the Cowlitz Trail on foot.

Washington territory might be on the railroad builders' maps, but it was still frontier country, and its citizens needed a certain hardiness to survive.

Olympians proved theirs when the circus came to town. Bartholomew's wagon show pitched its tent on Main street between 4th and 5th. It got in late in the day, and the tent-raising was hurried. No sooner had the audience, comprising the total population with the price of a ticket, assembled, then the seats collapsed. The ensuing pandemonium was finally quelled and the seats reerected. As the grand entry was about to be made the seats went down again.

Mr. Bartholemew, sweating profusely, offered to refund the admittance money and give up, but the hardy pioneers of Olympia wouldn't hear of it. They insisted they would stay there and keep collapsing all night if necessary. Heartened by the loyalty of his audience, Bartholomew finally got the bleachers properly secured and the show went on.

The Olympians, who got little excitement between legislative sessions, expressed themselves as well pleased with the eventual performance.

Having become a Democrat, John Miller Murphy needed a little prompting to assail the members of the Republican party, but his feelings were probably more than usually tender at this time. Having given up hope of reclaiming the public printing, he had embarked in 1967 on a search for other public office. He succeeded in being elected territorial

William Billings, Indian agent and sheriff.

auditor, and also quartermaster-general of the territorial militia. The first job paid little, and the second nothing, but both carried prerequisites of office, which Murphy enjoyed. As quartermaster-general he even got to wear a gold-bedecked uniform and assemble with other members of the governor's military staff on special occasions.

He ran hard for another term as auditor, even going so far as to order the compositors in the *Standard*'s back office to never, under any circumstances, spell the name of his rival candidate correctly. His crew became adept at misspelling the unfortunate man's name in every conceivable way, but despite their best efforts, he succeeded in beating Murphy who, for many years thereafter confined himself to town politics and to making life as miserable as possible for Republicans in territorial office.

By the time the 1869 legislature arrived on the scene, its members found new signs of modest progress at the capital. A fine concord stage was in operation between Olympia and Commencement City, sometimes referred to as Tacoma. George Barnes was in the process of building the state's first brick bank building on Main street, between 3rd and 4th. Just to the north, I. Harris had opened one of the largest drygoods stores in the territory. The splendid

Columbia hall was available for dances and entertainment, and the local termperance organization, the Good Templars, had established a free public library in their Tacoma hall, which had formerly been the Olympia hall, owned by D. B. Finch, owner of the *Eliza Anderson*. The old sidewheeler was said to move slower and make money faster than any other steamboat in history, and she made Finch so wealthy that he could afford to give his building away in an age when income tax decuctions had not yet been invented. Perhaps most startling of the signs of progress was the appearance on the streets of the capital city of two velocipedes, one a store-bought ancestor of the two-wheeled bicycle; the other a three-wheeled contraption of back yard construction.

The town's horses had something to run away from beside the whistle of the *Eliza Anderson* and the frequent firing of cannon.

Selucius Garfielde, having sent Wallace, Denny and Flanders to congress on the wings of his oratory, at last received his reward, the Republican nomination and inevitable victory.

GARFIELDE'S TRUNK

The silver-tongued orator soon found, however, that in achieving his victory, he had made a great many more campaign promises than he could possibly keep. Like many notable politicians to come, Garfielde just couldn't say no. He promised grants of public lands, the repeal of the law against selling liquor to Indians, and the privilege of stealing the choicer reservation lands from the Puyallup Indians. He promised federal mail contracts, jobs, pensions and promotions. According to the *Washington Standard* he even promised John Pinnell, proprietor of that house of ill fame but healthy profits, the Illahee, *"to protect him and his 'nonprofessional dancers' by act of Congress."*

Poor Selucius was less fortunate than earlier delegates from Washington territory. With the advent of the telegraph he couldn't just ignore the increasingly clamorous demands of his political creditors. At last, in desperation, he sent word back from Washington City that he had placed all his campaign promises in a trunk and the trunk had somehow been lost along the way.

This was met with a burst of honest indignation from the delegate's erstwhile supporters, and of hilarity from his political enemies. Francis Henry took pen in hand and brought forth a cartoon picturing a huge trunk with the lid thrown back, disclosing lifelike caricatures of all the well known politicians in Olympia.

Murphy composed some of his more satyrical feature stories, usually captioned "THAT TRUNK", but he didn't limit himself to lampooning Garfielde. He also harpooned him, as for example:

*"A man who has betrayed his party, who has jumped from a devout Southern sympathizer to a sharer in the spoils he did not help to earn, will find but little aid or sympathy * * * so it is fair to presume that Garfielde's political record will balance his eloquence and talent and leave enough duplicity and treachery to condemn him to eternal perdition besides."*

That Selucius Garfielde was, indeed, no ordinary political spellbinder is attested to by the fact that he succeeded in getting himself elected to a second term.

The census of 1870 showed that Thurston county had achieved a population of 2,246 with 1,203 of its citizens residing within the town limits of Olympia. The territory's capital city was still its largest city . . . and there was reason to believe the immediate future would be even brighter.

WORKING ON THE RAILROAD

Early in the year ground was broken at Thomson's Junction near Duluth, Minnesota, for construction of the long-awaited Northern Pacific railroad. Soon afterward construction began at Kalama, near the southwest corner of the territory, of a right of way toward Puget Sound. There were efforts to boom Kalama as a railway terminus, but everyone knew it would be only a way station when the main line was completed from Duluth to the Sound. The results to investors in its town lots were so disastrous that the *Standard* claimed the name of the town should be changed to Kalamity.

Besides, everyone also knew the real terminus could hardly be located anywhere but Olympia, the capital, the head of navigation and the undisputed metropolis of the territory.

Olympia was doing so well that its enemies were accused of trying to burn it down. There was, at any rate, a series of incendiary fires which kept the fire laddies of Columbia Number One breathless and prompted the citizens to organize a vigilance committee to rid the town of arsonists. A second fire company, the Barnes Hook and Ladder Company, was organized, with George Barnes as chief. Barnes was one of the richest men in the territory by that time, and he staked his men to fancier uniforms than those of the Columbia, but his liberality didn't extend to the purchase of a hook and ladder wagon. The firemen had to improvise one of sorts from an old farm wagon, and the Barnes Company was noted for performing better in parades than at fires.

In December the superiority of the capital city seemed to be clinched when Ezra Meeker wandered into town and succeeded in plucking 53 varieties of blooming flowers. These he took east and displayed to the wondering gaze of Horace Greeley, that noted admirer of the west, who advised him to write a book about the marvels of Washington territory. The result was Meeker's first literary effort, a modest pamphlet which caught the eye of Jay Cook, financial wizard of the Northern Pacific. The railroad company bought thousands of copies and distributed them all over the country.

PROFITABLE POLITICS

Governor Moore had, in the meantime, been forced to give up his office as the result of increasingly serious illness. Alvin Flanders, the uncommunicative Wallula business man who had been elected delegate to congress by the oratory of Selucius Garfielde, was appointed to replace Moore. Flanders had planned to run for another term, but he had not been an outstanding success at the national capital. Besides, Garfielde felt it was his turn to elect himself. In a deal with President Grant, Flanders was offered the governorship if he would vacate his seat in congress in favor of Garfielde. He lasted only one year as chief executive, being involved only with the 1869 legislature. It was conceded by most observers of the territorial political scene that a thin, saturnine individual named Elisha P. Ferry, who had received the appointment as surveyor-general, was the real power behind the scenes at the capital.

ALVIN FLANDERS
1869-1870

Soon after Flanders assumed the executive chair, a new territorial secretary arrived on the scene, a lean and hungry individual named James Scott. He came, according to John Miller Murphy, *"with all his belongings in a carpet-bag."* In addition to his carpet bag he brought his nephew, James Rodgers. These two enterprising political appointees were men of purpose and that purpose, Murphy observed with seeming accuracy, was to *"bag the fat of the land."* Their first step was to bag Charles Prosch, the territorial printer, and replace him with Rodgers. All they had to qualify them as public printers was unlimited greed. They needed a newspaper plant and a boss printer.

They solved the first problem by buying J. R. Watson's *Territorial Republican,* which was renamed *Commercial Age* and placed under the nominal ownership of Clarence Bagley. T. F. McElroy was printing foreman. Murphy also claimed that he was one of the undercover owners of the *Commercial Age* under the assumed name of "Mr. Reed". Others were Olympia liveryman "Rice" Tilley, Samuel Coulter, who owned a local butcher shop and livery stable, and Randall Hewitt, who had owned an interest in the old *Territorial Republican.*

This strangely assorted group of old political enemies, acquisitive local business men and carpet-baggers was prepared to cut the fattest hog in the history of the public printing business. John Miller Murphy summed it up fairly well when he write:

*"Coulter is public printer * * * Messrs. Coulter & Tilley expect to realize many fat rounds from the legislative printing. They are the heavy men in the firm, and furnish the main stake, the remainder being spare ribs. They stand a chance to commit an indiscriminant slaughter upon the funds * * * we feel they are more at home with cleavers and sausage stuffers than rounces and shooting sticks."*

They were assured of fat profits for several reasons. McElroy, who had tried to form a printers' union during his absence from the political scene, reduced the wages of the *Commercial* printers to 45 cents per 1,000 ems of type, although the going rate was 60 cents.

Furthermore, the unprecedented sum of $20,000 had been appropriated to print a new set of laws, the *Code of 1869*, which had been described as the *"greatest work ever performed by a legislative body in this territory."** *

And just to keep an anchor out to windward, the gentlemen of the *Commercial Age* made deals with their many and diverse friends in the legislature to introduce a paper blizzard of bills, few of which made much sense, but all of which had to be printed.

It should be recorded to the credit of Governor Flanders that he was aware of what was going on in the public printing office and did his best to hold down the larceny. He vetoed more than fifty bills, all of which were passed for the single purpose of increasing the profits of the public printer, claiming that his action had saved the government at least $10,000 on the printing of the *Code*.

The proprietors of the *Commercial Age,* for rather obvious reasons, didn't agree. Having lost money every time the stubborn governor vetoed a bill, they complained editorially that *"the Governor made a dunce of himself in this veto matter, and made a further dunce of himself by giving publicity to it in his organ"* (The *Transcript).*

The *Commercial Age* floundered about helplessly under the avalanche of printing, while its proprietors demanded still more. Two months after the session convened, the governor's message still hadn't been printed. The

Code didn't appear until the summer of 1870, and the announcement of its belated completion was published in the last issue of the *Commercial Age,* that of June 25, 1870. Rodgers, the official public printer, had been out of the territory during much of the year, returning two weeks before the paper folded to collect his share of the profits, along with the various other partners. Grant's election to the presidency had altered the power structure at Olympia.

In the *Standard* of January 15, 1870, Murphy had announced:

"THE NEW APPOINTMENT.—The telegraph brings the information of the appointment of E. S. Salomon, Governor of Washington Territory, in place of Alvin Flanders, removed. As any information regarding the 'party-hacks' who are foisted upon us is of interest, we publish the following from the Tribune, which paper claims to be posted on the matter of which it speaks."

Edward Salomon, ninth territorial governor of Washington, was actually a man of greater attainments than most of the territorial executives of that era. A Jew, born in Germany, he migrated to Chicago after completing high school. At the age of 24 he was an alderman. At the outbreak of the civil war he entered service as a lieutenant, fought bravely in many of its greatest battles, and rose to brevet brigadier general. After the war he served as clerk of Cook county until appointed governor of Washington territory by Grant. After the 14th legislature of 1867-68, annual sessions gave way to biennial gatherings, so Salomon had only one legislature to deal with during his two-year term of office. He exhibited considerable political courage, vetoing an early-day gerrymandering effort of the Republican majority. Their legislative redistricting measure was returned to them with the comment that "this bill seems to me to be unjust, and would deprive some of the citizens of the territory of the representation they are entitled to."

Despite his abilities, Salomon found his term as territorial governor no bed of roses.

In the first place, he inherited a political hornets' nest. Although the Republicans were solidly in control of the legislature, the glib-tongued congressional delegate, Selucius Garfielde, had by this time managed to split the party as effectively as had Isaac Stevens. The surveyor-general, Ferry, with his penetrating gaze fixed on the governorship, headed the pro-

---

*Compiling the Territorial Codes of Washington, Arthur Beardsley, *Pacific Northwest Quarterly,* Vol. XXVIII (1937).

Garfielde faction, ably assisted by Garfielde's campaign manager, L. P. Beach. During the 1871 session, the anti-Garfielde Republicans "bolted" the party organization and formed a coalition with the minority Democrats, led by the new territorial secretary, J. C. Clements. This group was dedicated to scuttling the ambitions of the Garfielde-Ferry-Beach triumverate, and had the backing of the Republican *Transcript*, in which McElroy had a healthy financial interest along with Gunn, and Prosch's *Tribune*, as well as Murphy's *Standard*, which was against any Republicans who happened to occupy the seats of power.

The pro-Garfielde forces had been supported for a time by the *Message*, which had been established in 1870 by one Harry Sutton with the hope of using the paper as a means of getting the public printing appointment. He, too, was caught in the political crossfire, however. Secretary Clements had a deep and personal hatred for Garfielde, who had tried to block his appointment as territorial secretary, and Sutton was Garfielde's protege. The ubiquitous McElroy was, on the other hand, a close friend of the new secretary. He formed a partnership of convenience with his old enemy, Prosch, who owned the most suitable printing plant for the purpose, and Clements appointed them public printers.

The unfortunate Sutton had to close down his paper and the Ferry-Garfielde faction was forced to establish a political organ of their own, the *Daily Courier*. Clarence Bagley, late of the *Commercial Age*, seemed to be making a career for himself as a journalistic figure-head. He was listed on the masthead as editor and manager, although most of the financial backing for Olympia's first daily newspaper was provided by Ferry.

Amid the din of political infighting at the capitol and the editorial uproar created by four violently partisan newspapers, Governor Salomon had difficulty making himself heard, and when he did succeed, he was frequently laughed at.

Short, plump and sporting a magnificent spiked German mustache and goatee, the governor spoke with a thick German accent. Like the Englishman, Pickering, the natives found him amusing.

Murphy, who showed little mercy toward the physical peculiarities of his political and journalistic enemies, frequently made fun of the governor's accent in the columns of the *Standard*. Judge Orange Jacobs, supreme

Edward S. Salomon
1870–1872

court justice and an ambitious Republican politician, was referred to by Salomon as "Yudge Yawcups". Thereafter, Murphy for many years did likewise in the *Standard*.

Hilarity reached its peak when the governor took the steamboat to Seattle to address the citizens of that town. Disembarking at Yesler's wharf, he proceeded up Mill street (now Yesler Way) to meet the assembled natives. The street was then made of slabwood covered with sawdust from Yesler's mill. The sawdust was partly rotted and well intermixed with the droppings of the dray and coach horses which used Mill street to reach the steamboat landing.

Governor Salomon launched into his speech, eulogizing the territory, its climate, soil and future greatness. In the midst of his oratory he suddenly paused, stooped down and gathered up a handful of the odorous street covering.

"*Mein Gott!*" he exclaimed, "*vot a splendid soil to raise cabbages!*"

65

Despite all the confusion, the legislators of 1871 hewed to the line on at least a couple of issues upon which they felt strongly. Statehood they were sure, would bring new and profitable political plums, which they were anxious to harvest. They passed another resolution calling for a constitutional convention and a request for full membership in the galaxy of sovereign states. Again the citizens turned them down at the polls.

They also knew what they didn't want. If any were in doubt, Elisha Ferry was prepared to straighten them out. Some of the women of the territory were getting uppity ideas about equal suffrage, a concept most repugnant to Ferry. He blamed the agitation on Mrs. Abigail Scott Duniway, who had the bad taste to publish a newspaper devoted to women's rights, and to travel across Oregon and Washington unescorted to advance her radical ideas from the rostrum.

Ferry and the legislature put Mrs. Duniway . . . and any misguided women who might have been listening to her . . . in their places. A law was passed which was brief and to the point:

"Hereafter no female shall have the right to ballot or vote at any poll or election precinct in this Territory until the Congress of the United States of America, shall, by direct legislation upon the same, declare the same to be the supreme law of the land."

ELISHA P. FERRY, two-term territorial governor and first governor of Washington State.

DEMON RUM

There were many who also blamed the women and their growing activism for the increasing enthusiasm for the temperance movement, which was sweeping the territory and was particularly noticeable in Olympia, where Gale's *Temperance Echo* was beating the drums in the war against Demon Rum. The five newspapers of the town had as widely divergent views on this subject as on politics.

John Miller Murphy, who opposed heavy use of hard liquor, but liked his cheese and beer, was annoyed by the sanctimonious and uncompromising stand of the *Echo*. He took great editorial delight in exposing the fact that lager beer had been dispensed and consumed at a temperance party held by the Good Templars at their Tacoma hall. Gale of the *Echo* responded in his columns to the effect that the only lager beer at the party was brought in under Murphy's waistcoat.

Murphy responded with solid evidence to back up his claim and Gale, being more gentlemanly than most frontier editors, published a retraction in his next issue.

Despite Murphy's repeated victories in the battle of wits with Gale, the temperance movement continued to gain ground to such an extent that the supreme political opportunist, Selucius Garfielde, became an ardent disciple of the Good Templars in his bid for a third term in congress. The Thurston county commissioners also responded to the pressure by refusing to grant any saloon licenses on the basis of a forgotten territorial law requiring that anyone applying for such a license must procure the signatures of a majority of the adult inhabitants of the election precinct where the saloon was to be located.

The *Echo,* of course, editorialized that the commissioners *"deserve the thanks of every inhabitant of the county, in having done righteously and fearlessly their duty."*

In the rival town of Steilacoom, the *Herald* chortled gleefully that, *"The county commissioners have refused to grant licenses for the sale of spiritous liquors in Olympia. That's a settler. The town won't last much longer now. That and the terminus (of the Northern Pacific) were the props on which it leaned."*

66

WE WAS ROBBED!

The *Herald* had hit an extremely tender spot for Olympia *had* been leaning heavily on the expectation of becoming the tidewater terminus of the railroad, and with considerable justification. The company had informed the town trustees that it proposed to locate the terminus on Budd Inlet, provided a right of way was obtained from Bush prairie to tidewater. This was quickly provided and the citizens settled down to await the arrival of steel rails and sudden prosperity. Late in November the line reached a tiny settlement called Hodgson's Station in Coal Bank precinct, 15 miles south of Olympia. It never got much closer. Instead, it proceeded on to Commencement Bay and the sawmill village of Commencement City, which had lately taken to calling itself Tacoma.

Olympia was left in a state of shock; so was Seattle, which had been just as sure that it was going to be the terminus. Inflated property values in both towns were punctured, and a rush was on to "New Tacoma".

It appears that Olympia lost the prize as the result of a coronary occlusion which struck down an obscure agent of the Puget Sound Land company, a subsidiary of the Northern Pacific.

The man's name was Ira B. Thomas, and he had been dispatched by the land company to buy up large tracts of land on the east side of Budd Inlet on deep water north of Olympia. The company wanted it done quietly, to keep out other speculators and reserve the forthcoming land boom profits for itself.

After acquiring title to the proposed terminus site, Thomas suffered his heart attack and died. Rather than go through the slow process of probating his estate, the company sent other agents to buy up land on Commencement Bay and plat a substitute boom town.

Had Ira Thomas lived just a little longer, Olympia would probably have gotten the railroad and all the ensuing blessings of over-population, congestion, pollution and odorous smog.

The citizens were heartbroken at their loss, and civic enterprise went into a state of sad decline.

Olympia was still the capital city, however, and the political show had to go on.

Elisha Ferry had, in the meantime, succeeded in getting President Grant to remove Governor Salomon and appoint him in his place. John Miller Murphy and the *Standard* were less than enthusiastic. Titles were important to the politicians of the post-civil war era, especially military titles, and Ferry liked to be addressed as "general", although his only warlike service had been as assistant adjutant-general on the staff of the governor of Illinois. Murphy took a sly dig at Ferry on this subject in May of 1872, after Ferry had received word of his pending appointment, but before he had formally taken office:

"ANTICIPATES HIS GLORY.—*Ferry, in his organ (the Courier), has doffed the title of 'General' and assumed that of Governor, although his trowserloons have not yet pressed the chair of state. This haste to abandon a title fairly earned by many well contested bottles * * * is quite inexplicable.*"

Apparently Murphy's journalistic needle was penetrating painfully, as were those of Prosch of the *Tribune* and Gunn of the *Transcript*. Ferry responded, as have many outraged politicians since, by cancelling his subscriptions. Murphy took note of this in the *Standard*:

"*Our newly appointed Governor, in a fit of rage stopped his STANDARD, Transcript and Tribune. 'Whom the gods would destroy they first make mad'.*" In a lighter mood, he then quipped that "*As 'General' Ferry has stopped his paper, we can indulge in as much 'jocularity' at his expense as we please. Of course he won't see it.*"

The published biographies of Elisha Peyre Ferry indicate that he was a lawyer, having been admitted to the Illinois bar at the tender age of 20. There is no mention of his ever having been connected with the brewing industry, but Murphy insisted that he had somehow been involved in beer-making. Whether he had owned stock in a brewery or whether the whole thing was a figment of Murphy's fertile imagination, the columns of the *Standard* carried numerous unkind comments based on Murphy's assumption. This one is typical:

"'*General' Ferry is said to have been a greater success as a brewer than as a politician. It cannot be said, however, that he has had more experience in brewing malt than brewing mischief, although it may have extended over a greater period of time.*"

THE EXECUTIVE COW

The governor's interest in fresh milk, rather than beer, was the basis for another feud between the executive office and the editorial sanctum of John Miller Murphy.

Every Olympia family that could afford one kept a milch cow in those days, and they were in the habit of letting them wander the streets of the town during the day. The public square was a favorite grazing spot and so, apparently, was Murphy's lawn. He fulminated frequently in his editorials against the plague of unrestrained cows. He felt their infestation of the streets was both unsanitary and undignified for the capital city of a great territory. He also resented their munching on his shrubbery and fruit trees. His one-man crusade finally induced the city fathers (of which he was now one) to pass a mild ordinance forbidding "cattle other than milch cows from running at large within the corporate limits of Olympia," and further directing the "milch cows, if found in the streets or alleys at night shall be impounded."

Murphy felt this was a step in the right direction, but it didn't go far enough. He continued to press the wandering cow issue.

Governor Ferry's daughter, Eliza, had been presented with a cow by her uncle, Seattle Fire Chief Gardner Kellogg, and when the family moved to Olympia she insisted on bringing it with her on the steamboat. The executive cow wandered off one night and fell victim to Murphy's impoundment ordinance. Eliza was heartbroken, her father was outraged, and Murphy printed a highly uncomplimentary account of the whole affair in the *Standard*.

Murphy may have been a match for the governor, but not for the governor's daughter. Eliza, intent on revenge, gathered a number of her young friends. Under cover of darkness, they spread salt all over the Murphy premises. The salt attracted every vagrant cow in town, and there was no way of dispersing them until they had licked up all the salt. The clang of their bells made the night hideous for Murphy and his family, and he wrote no more of Eliza Ferry's cow.

GREAT SEALS OF THE COMMONWEALTH

CHAPTER FOUR
The Third Decade
1873-1883

The year 1872 had closed with twin shocks for the citizens of Olympia. In December the town was jolted by the worst earthquake in its history, damaging buildings, toppling chimneys and splitting trees, as well as causing a great deal of panic among the people, cows and horses of the area. Only one Olympian was apparently unaffected by the quake. He was undergoing the usual rough and tumble initiation into a local fraternal organization at the time, and was blindfolded for the ordeal. When the building began to sway, his brethren departed at high speed, leaving him alone.

Upon their return, they found the new member philosophically waiting for the next step in his initiation.

The shock of the quake was as nothing, however, to the growing realization, as the years passed away, that the Northern Pacific was not going to honor its promise to locate the terminus on Budd Inlet. The property owners along the inlet had pledged half their holdings to the railroad, and others had pledged scarce cash. As late as Christmas day, 1872, General John W. Sprague and Governor John N. Goodwin, agents for the company, had dispatched a telegram to Marshall Blinn, Olympia businessman and railroad promoter, informing him that the construction crews were heading for the capital city. Besides, the town's railroad promoters, Blinn, George Barnes, Clanrick Crosby, Elisha P. Ferry, John Miller Murphy, Edwin Marsh and others, had a written acceptance by the Northern Pacific of the townspeoples' donation and a promise to lay track to Budd Inlet.

But anyone could see that the track, after reaching Plum's Station, a good seven miles east of town, was curving away to the northeast and Commencement Bay.

Amidst their blasted hopes, the citizens of Olympia were even frustrated in finding a target for their rage and indignation, for the Northern Pacific was a corporation and, as such "had no bodies to be kicked; no souls to be damned."[*]

For a while it looked as if the railroad might not get that far. The affairs of its chief promoter, Jay Cooke, were tangled and the bonds of the Northern Pacific were not in great demand. In September, 1873, the Cooke financial empire crashed, triggering the worst national financial panic in 40 years.

The track finally reached Commencement Bay, but there was little holiday spirit to commemorate the long-awaited event. Track gangs had been unpaid for weeks, and they were threatening to burn the bridges and tear up the tracks behind the locomotive which pulled the first cars to Puget Sound. Funds were scraped together to keep the railroad from being demolished by the same men who had built it, but it was no grand transcontinental line, joining east and west together with bands of steel.

The already rusting track began at the village of Kalama and meandered through sparsely settled wilderness to the tent and shanty town of New Tacoma. It had no connection with Portland, except by ferry. In the east, construction was halted on the east bank of the Missouri river, at Bismark, Dakota, 450 miles west of Duluth. The impressively titled "Pacific

---

[*]A History of Thurston County, Washington, Rathbun.

69

Division" was nearly 1,500 miles from the eastern segment. A single "mixed train daily" took care of the total freight and passenger traffic between Kalama and Tacoma. It would be another decade before the golden spike was driven at Gold Creek, Montana . . . and four years more before the first transcontinental train would reach Tacoma over the Cascade division.

The Northern Pacific railroad, a dream of 20 years, proved a nightmare to towns like Olympia and Seattle, whose carefully constructed hopes were demolished by its decision to create a new boom town of its own. To the rest of the territory it was a bad joke, and delegate McFadden was bombarded with demands that congress cancel the company's land grant, which donated to it every other section of land across its projected right of way. Tender feelings toward the railroad company were not restored when the nationwide depression, precipitated by the frenzied financial methods of Jay Cooke, moved westward at a much more rapid rate than had Cooke's steel rails.

Olympia, at this critical period in its history, was still the largest settlement in Washington territory and, despite its miles of mudflats at low tide, the most attractive. As streets were laid out in the 1850's and 60's, maple trees were planted to shade the wooden sidewalks, and by the 1870's these shade trees were the town's greatest visual asset, giving it the appearance of a carefully tended New England village and sparing it from the raw and temporary look of most frontier towns. Every published description of the territorial capital of that era placed heavy emphasis on its maple-shaded streets.

One whose enthusiasm for the bucolic beauties of Olympia was quite unrestrained was Miss Addie L. Ballou, authoress, advocate of women's rights and temperance, who was delivering a series of uplifting lectures at Tacoma hall. She presented the following bit of flowery prose to the *Washington Standard:*

"Olympia, the capital of Washington territory, is one of the most charming small cities in the far west. Taste, culture and finance have combined with art and nature, to complete her beauty. She sits like a queenly diamond sparkling among emerald settings, emblazoned on a disk of retreating and adorning globules of watery fret-work, and when she shall have tied her navigation commerce to the eastward and southward with the iron bands of her nearly prospective railroad, she shall be the queen city of the far western territories."

While impressed by Miss Ballou's *"graceful garlands of poesy,"* John Miller Murphy, loyal Olympian that he was, seemed to feel that she might have gone a little overboard in her pean of praise. He intimated that she might have been influenced by a desire to get more people to her lectures and was operating on the same basis *"as was the politician who went around kissing the babies."*

Murphy also took a realistic view of the railroad situation as it existed in 1873, summing up his feelings with a combination of cynicism and pragmatism:

"Now you see it and now you don't see it! The riggers and cappers of the great Northern Pacific Humbug have passed from our midst, and with them has gone the fond delusion that we had spotted the little joker in the terminus; for, it is said, they fully repudiated the idea that said company was under any obligation to build a branch road into Olympia. Many a good citizen who but yesterday was reveling in visions of wealth to flow from his reserved lots in this vast municipality, has forever abandoned the idea of a coach-and-six from that source, and quietly taken his place in that countless throng which, since Adam, has been marching down the slope of time to the tune of 'Sold and got your money'."

The former Hodgson's Station, renamed Tenino,* was the nearest railroad station . . . 15 miles to the south . . . and two or three competing stage lines quickly went into business, running between downtown Olympia and Tenino twice a day to meet the decrepit train of mixed freight and passenger cars at the Tenino depot.

---

*Considerable disagreement exists as to how Tenino got its name. Some have insisted that it was taken from a box car or surveyor's stake number . . . 10-9-0, but there is no evidence that this was the case. The most likely explanation is that "Tenino" was an Indian word meaning "fork in the trail."

RACES AND RATE WARS

Olympia remained the terminus of the steamboat mail route between Puget Sound and Victoria, although the old *Eliza Anderson* was lying forlorn and neglected at the dock. She had been displaced by faster and fancier sidewheel packets.

Ever since her arrival in 1859, the old *Anderson* had been fighting off rival steamboats, most of them bigger and faster than she. The mail subsidy made it possible for her owners, D. B. Finch and Captain Tom Wright, to cut fares and hold them down until the opposition gave up, but by 1870 the going was getting tough. The well-financed Oregon Steam Navigation Company entered the fray. Finch and Wright had to pay a big subsidy to get rid of them. They had already realized that the *Anderson* was getting too slow and wheezy to hold her own in the increasingly competitive business, and had placed an order in New York for a fine new sidewheeler, the *Olympia.*

The *Olympia,* built of seasoned oak, 180 feet long, brig-rigged, beam-engined, and handsomely appointed, was the finest and fastest steamboat on Puget Sound, but she labored under a serious handicap from the start. Finch and Wright had lost the mail contract to a man named Nash. Nash began constructing a steamer on the beach near Priest Point, ran out of money, and sold out to a couple of Portland business men named E. A. and L. M. Starr. The Starrs completed Nash's boat, the 115-boat sidewheeler *Alida,* and began running her in competition with the *Olympia.*

Although greatly inferior to the New York-built *Olympia* in size, speed and seaworthiness, the *Alida* was the biggest vessel yet built at Olympia, and the *Standard* announced with some pride that *"the neat little steamer* Alida *arrived at Percival's wharf Thursday evening to begin her new mail service."*

Rival Victoria boat *Olympia* in later years as the Canadian *Princess Louise.*

The *Alida* didn't wear well, however, and by 1873, the *Standard* announced the departure from the Olympia maritime scene of *"the old tub* Alida."

The Starrs also found her less than satisfactory. They quicky found that she scared her passengers and crew half to death when she tried to navigate the stormy waters of the Strait of Juan de Fuca. They had to buy another small, but more seaworthy steamer, the *Isabel,* to transfer freight and passengers across the strait to Victoria. Efforts to widen the *Alida* and make her less likely to capsize in a brisk breeze, further retarded her less than breathtaking speed.

The Starrs, like Finch and Wright, gave up and ordered a big new sidewheeler, the *North Pacific.* When she arrived at Olympia from the builder's yard in San Francisco, a new and even more spirited rate war developed. Passenger and freight rates fell to the lowest level yet.

Things culminated in the summer of 1871 with a classic steamboat race between the *Olympia* and *North Pacific* from Victoria to Port Townsend. The *North Pacific* won by three minutes.

---

*Shortly after the close of the civil war, Captain Samuel Percival, who had taken over ownership of the pioneer Kendall and Company store, built a steamboat dock at the foot of Water street. In the 1870's he turned its operation over to his son, John C. Percival, who retained management until his death in 1942. It is currently owned by Puget Sound Freight Lines.

Olympia-Victoria packet *North Pacific.*

OLYMPIA-BUILT STEAMER *Alida* at Seattle;
Territorial University on the hill in background.

The victorious Starrs offered the *Olympia's* owners $7,500 a year to take her off the route. They did, and she paddled down to San Francisco, where her owners were paid another liberal subsidy to keep her off the Sacramento river route. She made more money for them by not running than she could earn in operation, so they collected their profits for several years; then sold her to the Canadian Pacific Navigation Company, which renamed her *Princess Louise* . . . the first of the famous Canadian *Princess* steamers.

The poor little *Alida* became a passenger ferry between Old Tacoma and the Northern Pacific's New Tacoma after the establishing of the terminus on Commencement Bay. She ended her days as a floating "pest house," harboring the victims of small pox, plague and the other contagious illnesses which periodically afflicted the citizens of Washington territory.

The *North Pacific* maintained her home port at Olympia for less than a year after 1873; then the capital city lost even its 20-year-old status as the Sound's major steamboat terminus. The Starrs made Tacoma the southern starting-point of the Victoria route. The little sternwheeler *Zephyr,* operated by Captain Wright, provided a mere feeder service between Olympia and the upstart port of Tacoma.

Olympia's civic ego was thus further bruised, although Captain Wright made a good deal of money with the *Zephyr* and then sold her to Captain W. R. Ballard, who also prospered, investing his profits in a new town just north of Seattle, which he named after himself.

The San Francisco firm of Goodall and Nelson did continue to run its coastwise steamer *Dakota* from that port to Olympia, with stops at Victoria, Port Townsend, Seattle and Tacoma, but with increasing frequency she was eliminating the trip to the tip of the

Type of Pacific Coast Steamship Company side-wheel coastal liner which called at Olympia's Westside wharf in early days.

Percival Dock 100 years later. Historic schooner *Explorer* moored alongside. Deep-sea freighters loading at Port of Olympia piers, background.

Sound in the winter months, when visibility was bad and extreme low tides common.

In a brave effort to do *something* to save civic face, the town fathers ordered signs with the names of the streets erected at each corner of what Murphy referred to grandly as *"our main business thoroughfares."*

The unwillingness of the citizenry to part with what little money they had in this era of blasted hopes also postponed the town's entry into the age of flight. A "Professor" Brown advertised in May that he would make a balloon ascension from the outskirts of town, but the exhibition never took place. In order to finance his flight, Brown erected a tent and proposed to deliver a lecture on the art of aerial navigation. The population of the town assembled to view the free balloon ascension, but few if any were willing to pay to hear the preliminary lecture. The professor folded his tent, and his balloon, and departed, vowing never to give the parsimonious people of Olympia the opportunity to witness the wonders of man in flight.

Summer came, bringing hot weather and making the gracious shade trees welcome, as the streets made the annual transition from mud to dust. The town sprinkling wagon was, according to the *Standard, "in constant use these hot, dusty days."*

With the coming of October the sprinkling wagon was relegated to the town barn and the maples proved less of a blessing. Their leaves began to fall, and the town marshal made his rounds, reminding business men and householders that they were responsible for raking and burning them. With October, too, came the biennial session of the territorial legislature.

THE LEGENDARY BASEBALL GAME

Governor Ferry delivered his first message to the legislature on October 9. He gave priority to matters connected with the recent settlement of the long-standing boundary dispute between the United States and Canada. The matter had been placed in the hands of the emperor of Germany for arbitration, and his decision had given the San Juan islands to the United States.

The feelings of the Olympia baseball team were somewhat hurt by the fact that the governor didn't give them credit for winning the lovely archipelago for Uncle Sam.

Shortly before the decision was to be announced by the German emperor, some practical joker had posted official looking telegrams at strategic locations about the town announcing that Wilhelm had decided to award the islands on the basis of which team won the upcoming baseball game between Olympia and Victoria. The Olympians beat the Canadian team, the award was duly made to the United States, and many were quite convinced that this long and sometimes noisy battle had been won on the playing field of Olympia.

Ferry, who not only considered this highly improbable, but who even had doubts that Emperor Wilhelm was a baseball fan, confined his remarks to "reciting in brief its history down to its arbitration", and informing the legislators that "immediately after receiving notice of this decision, I caused civil authority to be re-established over the islands lying between the two channels, and I am pleased to be able to inform you that these islands now form, undisputably, a part of the county of Whatcom, in the territory of Washington. I suggest the propriety of forming these islands into a new county.

The legislature responded quickly, creating San Juan county.

The usual legislative battle over the appointment of a public printer developed, but it was the final skirmish before a long armistice. This, like most wars, was based on economics. After 1873, as the nation plunged into an ever-deepening depression, congress tightened the purse-strings on the territories. The rate for public printing reached a new low of 75 cents per 1,000 ems of type during the 1873 session, and by the early 1880's it had dropped as low as 30 cents. It was no longer possible to get rich on the public printing, so the politicians lost interest in the matter.

The 1873 legislature refused to abandon the tradition entirely, however. Clarence Bagley had been defending the Ferry-Garfielde-Beach forces against the massed assaults of all the other Olympia papers for some time. He and his partner, John Harned, had recently bought out Ferry's personal interest in the *Courier* and were continuing it on their own as a stout partisan of the administration. Ferry intended to see to it that Clarence got his reward, but the legislature beat him to the punch. Two days before Ferry delivered his message to them, they passed a resolution appointing his bitter enemy, Elisha Gunn of the *Transcript*. Ferry nursed his wounds for two weeks; then, on October 21 he informed the legislature that their action was null and void; that Clarence Bagley was the public printer by order of Henry Struve, the latest territorial secretary and a loyal member of Ferry's well-disciplined political organization.

There was considerable grumbling among the legislators and charges by the *Transcript* that Bagley and Struve were splitting the profits, but when it was discovered that the profits were no longer all that enticing the issue was dropped and Bagley enjoyed an all-time record tenure of 12 years.

RAILROAD TO TENINO

By the spring of 1874 the territory's two biggest towns, Olympia and Seattle, had recovered somewhat from the Northern Pacific's stunning blow in locating its terminus at Tacoma, and both decided to build railroads of their own.

The Seattle effort has gained a larger place in Northwest history, but it was Olympia which actually completed its line to its destination through its own efforts and resources. The Seattle civic leaders promoted a general assembly of the citizens to start grading a right of way toward the Cascade mountains and Walla Walla, but it was largely a showing of good intentions to induce congress to provide a land grant to finance construction by professionals. The collapse of the Northern Pacific had, however, made railroads and land grants unpopular at the national capital. When Seattle's request for federal help was turned down, the ambitious project to tap the wheat fields of the Walla Walla country was abandoned. It wasn't until a Scottish engineer named Colman came to town and took over the moribund railroad that it was actually built as far as the coal mines east of Lake Washington.

The Olympians did much better than that. Following a mass meeting at Columbia hall, during which speeches were made by Hazzard Stevens, Governor Ferry, ex-Governor Salomon and other civic leaders, the entire able-bodied male populace assembled at the town square. The governor, the supreme court justices, the town trustees, the fire department, the baseball team and the Good Templars were all there. John Miller Murphy and the rest of the small army of warring newspaper editors declared an armistice and donned working clothes.

Even the usually indolent Indians were aroused to action, and by mid-April Murphy reported the remarkable news that *"The head chief of the Squaxon Indians, Kettel, with three of his chosen braves reported early yesterday morning to the foreman on the grade of the railroad. 'Nesiki ticki cultus potlatch mamook ict sun copa la-lode'.* They manfully went to work."*

---

*The Chinook jargon, a primitive mixture of Indian, French and English words, was the standard means of communication between whites and Indians during much of the 19th century in the Pacific Northwest. Chinook words became a part of the normal conversation of the day, and were understood by practically everyone. The translation of Murphy's Chinook means, roughly, "We want to give work one day on the railroad."

FIRST BRICK HOUSE in Washington Territory, built in 1874 by William Billings with material from his own brickyard. Mrs. Billings and daughter Blanche in the stylish pony cart of 1895 vintage; Frederick Billings leaning on gate.

Captain Sam Percival's mansion at the west end of Marshville bridge was an Olympia landmark for many years.

Most of the townspeople appeared to be in agreement with Judge McFadden, who wrote from Washington City that, *"without railroad connections, Olympia cannot stand still. She cannot go forward, even slowly. She must retrograde, and in a few years her dilapidated dwellings will become the fit abode for owls."*

The idea was to build a 15-mile line from Olympia to Tenino, where it would connect with the main line of the Northern Pacific. The grading was 15 per cent done by the close of that eventful day. And, unlike the citizens of Seattle, who soon gave up and concentrated on nursing their blisters and strained muscles, the determined Olympians kept right on working, donating one day a week to labor on the railroad.

Not only labor, but equipment, tools, horses, mules and food for the workers were donated by the railroad enthusiasts. At an election the previous fall the voters of Thurston county had authorized the county commissioners to float a modest bond issue to provide some hard cash for the project, but in the prevailing financial gloom the bonds were easier authorized than sold. The clearing of the roadbed over the relatively flat prairie between Olympia and Tenino could be accomplished largely with volunteer labor, but there was some anxiety about the financing of rails and rolling stock.

With the coming of those rains in the fall of 1874, the working parties were abandoned, but the *Standard* pointed out that the grading was just about completed anyway. It also took to task those faint-hearted citizens who were beginning to mutter that the line would never be completed.

Despite the general hard times and the drain of the community's manpower and resources to build its railroad, there were some signs of progress in other areas.

William Billings, the long-time sheriff of Thurston county, was building the first brick mansion in the Puget Sound country, using his own bricks from a plant he had established earlier to build the county's first jail down on the flats on 6th and Adams. Billings' bricks must have had the consistency of peanut brittle, for a parade of prisoners made their way out of the jail through the walls until the structure eventually had more patches than original material.

In addition to the sheriff's unique and impressive home, Captain Sam Percival was building the town's ultimate in gingerbread carpenter-Gothic wooden mansions above the Deschutes waterway at the east end of the Marshville bridge. The structure may have served as balm to the grand groundbreaking for the Olympia-Tenino railroad. Captain Sam was a leading light of the temperance movement, which was becoming a powerful force in town, but charges were brought by some of his brethren of the Good Templars that he had carried his pitcher once too often to the barrel of Columbia street cream lager at Warren's Point. The combination of warm spring weather, hard labor and unaccustomed tippling had, according to his critics, caused the good captain to navigate with difficulty, listing badly from port to starboard, and bringing the rude humor of the unregenerate down upon the forces of temperance.

CARLTON HOUSE, Olympia's leading hotel in the 1880's, became a notorious bootleg joint in prohibition era.

The members of the 1873 legislature were offered the hospitality of a new hotel, the Carlton House, just built by G. W. Carlton, a former printer, and John Van Wormer, who had been the mail carrier between Olympia and Chehalis. John Miller Murphy described the new hostelry as *"new, large and well adapted to the business, with large family rooms, cozy fireplaces and many home comforts not found in ordinary hotels."* He offered the opinion that *"Carlton is a good printer and we therefore think he has sense enough to run a hotel,"* but added a word of caution to his former colleague, pointing out that members of the newspaper fraternity were (and are) confirmed free-loaders and that if he let them establish credit the Carlton would probably become *"the home for indigent printers."*

MORE TRANSPORTATION TROUBLES

The year 1874 drew to a close with public indignation focused upon that corporate monster, the Northern Pacific railroad. A law suit, instigated according to popular belief in Olympia by the big railroad, voided the county bond issue for the narrow-gauge line to Tenino. Good old Judge McFadden got a special act of congress passed authorizing the county commissioners to issue railroad bonds, but that meant the whole proposition had to be submitted to the voters again, causing more delay.

Furthermore, the congressional action, although favorable, resulted in still another blow to the town's faltering civic ego. In reporting the proceedings the *Congressional Record* referred to the capital city and principal metropolis of Washington territory as "Bolivia"!

After the bonds were passed a second time the Olympia Railroad Union, the civic organization formed to build and operate the line, assumed that its major problem was solved. With Hazzard Stevens as its president and its board of trustees including such civic heavyweights as Marshall Blinn, T. I. McKenny, John Miller Murphy, George Barnes, Sam Percival, T. F. McElroy and Oliver Shead, it was predicted the bonds, in the amount of $75,000, would be quickly sold in Portland.

This was not the case, and Hazzard Stevens was dispatched to San Francisco to dispose of them. He met with no better success there. These failures were likewise attributed to the devious machinations of the Northern Pacific, rather than the general state of the economy.

There was no doubt, however, that the railroad company was imposing discriminatory freight rates on Thurston county in an effort to divert as much trade as possible to its own town of New Tacoma.

Indignation reached the boiling point in November when it was learned that P. D. Moore, who was willing to try his hand at anything to make an honest dollar, had underbid the Starrs for the lucrative Victoria mail contract, although he didn't own so much as a rowboat with which to make deliveries. Moore had bid $26,980 to operate the route from Olympia, with an alternate bid of $20,980 if Tacoma were made the southern terminus. In its current economy mood, the federal government accepted the Tacoma proposition, and Moore was authorized to begin the service at once. Since he didn't have a boat, this was easier said than done. The former contractors refused to touch the growing piles of undelivered mail. Finally, in desperation, the government offered Moore $500 a trip on an emergency basis. Moore chartered the ungainly sidewheel tugboat *Favorite* and operated her from Olympia to Victoria until January, 1875, when the mail terminus was officially changed to Tacoma. The Starrs, in the meantime, had abandoned their Olympia wharf in disgust and were running the fine big packet *North Pacific* from Tacoma.

In Olympia, indignation meetings were held to denounce this latest example of Northern Pacific perfidy. Telegrams were sent to Washington City, but to no avail. The glory days of steamboating were over, and the poky little sternwheeler *Zephyr* became the only link with down-Sound ports, except for the sometimes erratic service of the Goodall and Nelson coastwise steamers from San Francisco . . . and there were rumors that this service might also be terminated at the instigation of the Northern Pacific.

The old Westside wharf was in a bad state of repair, and the only means of transferring freight and passengers from it to downtown Olympia was by small boats at high tide. Captain J. G. Parker wrote to the steamship company in San Francisco, asking if they would continue to operate to Olympia on a regular schedule if the town provided an adequate deep water dock and a suitable connecting road. Their reply was in the affirmative, and the townspeople spent most of the year arguing over where the ocean dock should be located. B. F. Brown finally secured the civic improvement for his claim on the west side south of Butler's Cove. A special levy was passed in September and construction was completed early the following year. Goodall and Nelson made good their promise, running their steamers *Dakota* and *Panama* to Brown's wharf on a weekly schedule.

The Olympia Water company, second only to the Northern Pacific as a whipping boy for local frustrations, was probably a major factor in keeping the town on the main line of at least the coastwise steamships. William Horton, who had been the engineer on Captain Parker's little pioneer steamer *Traveler*, and later her owner, had obtained the franchise for the water company and established a small plant at Tumwater to manufacture the wooden water pipe. The product proved popular and, after the Olympia lines were laid, Horton incorporated the Washington Water Pipe company and organized a Pacific coast distribution system for the product. The major part of the cargo lifted at Brown's wharf by the San Francisco steamers was, for many years, wooden water pipe from Tumwater. The company remained in business and expanded fre-

Stern-wheeler *Zephyr* in her later years as a towboat.

quently, in later years as the Washington Pipe Manufacturing Company and Puget Sound Pipe Company, until well into the 20th century.

Despite the increasingly hard times, Olympians were in a mood to fight back against the slings and arrows of outrageous fortune. In addition to financing the railroad and the wharf, they voted another tax on themselves to buy a tract of land south of town for a fair grounds, and spent $100 to erect "the tallest flagpole in the territory" on the town square.

The legislature returned to Olympia in the fall of 1875, grumbling considerably about the ramshackle state of the "temporary" capitol building. The $30,000 made available for a new building during the term of the late unlamented Governor Gholson had been partly spent on clearing the 10-acre capitol grounds and the balance had long since reverted to the federal treasury.

The sad state of the capitol was described in detail in a letter from Secretary Struve to the secretary of the interior, forwarded by Governor Ferry with his full endorsement.

Although Struve's tale of woe reached almost poetic levels in places, it failed to move the bureaucrats of Washington City. The territorial capitol continued to slowly disintegrate and territorial legislators continued to fall through the wooden sidewalk, suffer exposure to the winter winds which blew through the decrepit outhouses . . . and curse the unfortunate secretary, whom they held responsible for the sad state of affairs.

Despite their shabby surroundings, the legislators of 1875 produced a joint resolution calling for a constitutional convention and request for statehood which was finally accepted by the voters the following year.

The legislature was also preoccupied with the creation of more new counties, but Governor Ferry put a stop to this by vetoing the first of the proposed measures, which would have created the "county of Ping"* from Walla Walla county, and letting it be known he would do the same to any others which might pass.

A number of legislators, as well as most of the townspeople, took time off in October to visit the *Standard* office and gaze in awe at the marvelous workings of the steam-powered press which John Miller Murphy had installed to replace the time-honored hand press of the territorial news media.

THE SCHIZOPHRENIC
DAILY OLYMPIAN

Clarence Bagley had found the financial strain of trying to maintain a daily paper too much for him, but the civic leaders of Olympia felt they needed one badly. If the statehood request were granted by congress there would be another vote on the location of the capital, and they wanted both the prestige of the territory's only daily newspaper and the propaganda value it could provide at a rate seven times faster than any of the weeklies.

They prevailed upon Murphy, the ardent anti-Ferry Democrat, to join forces with Bagley, spokesman for the governor and the Republican administration, to produce a daily paper on Murphy's marvelous new steam press. Agreement was reached on the understanding that Murphy and Bagley would dictate the political policy of the new paper on alternate days. As a result, the *Daily Olympian,* as it was christened, had a uniquely schizophrenic editorial personality, being partisan Republican one day and ardently Democratic the next.

---

*This still-born county was to be named after a backwoods statesman named Elisha Ping, who showed up in Olympia for the 1877 session as a member of the council from Columbia, Whitman and Stevens counties.

This arrangement worked fairly well until young Bagley left town and was temporarily replaced at the editorial desk by his father, the Reverend Daniel. The elder Bagley slipped several galleys of the Republican propaganda into the *Olympian's* columns on one of the days it was supposed to be Democratic. Murphy, who was still giving much of his attention to his first love, the weekly *Standard,* felt that he had been taken advantage of and his Irish temper erupted in a monumental explosion. He and Clarence parted company, and the *Daily Olympian* lasted less than a year. Bagley brought the *Daily Courier* back to life, but its days were also numbered.

HARD TIMES

There were few other signs of progress in the depression-plagued year of 1876. W. O. Bush, a son of the pioneer George Bush, carried a display of agricultural products from the family farm to the Philadelphia Centennial Exhibition of 1876, and it won first prize but created no stampede of settlers or investment capital to the Northwest. The narrow-gauge railroad bonds remained unsold, though further efforts were made to dispose of them in San Francisco. The county commissioners had stipulated that construction must be completed before 1876, and Marshall Blinn and Sam Percival of the Railroad Union, backed by the town trustees, had to beg for a year's extension of time which was granted.

The citizens of the community's growing Chinatown on Columbia street financed a Chinese language school for their children, presided over by the Reverend Don Gong, but there was little else at which to point with pride.

The town trustees weren't even in a position to pay off Tom Prather's $500 note on the town hall. They had to give him another I.O.U. instead.

A few hardy souls were not yet ready to throw in the towel, however. The Seattle and Walla Walla Railroad of rival Seattle had been in an even deeper coma than the Olympia and Tenino Railroad, but it now showed signs of coming to life. Its directors entered into a contract with Colman's Seattle Coal and Transportation company to complete the line to the coal mines, and it appeared that he meant business. The more loyal Olympians were determined that Seattle wasn't going to "hear the snort of the iron horse" before they did.

Another community meeting was held at Columbia hall in June. The members of the Olympia Railroad Union reiterated their willingness to bow out in favor of anyone who showed greater promise of getting the job done. The result was the formation of the Thurston County Railroad Construction company and the issuance of $250,000 in capital stock at one dollar a share. The issue was quickly sold, despite the hard times and many previous disappointments.

There ensued some wrangling between the Olympia Railroad Union and the Thurston County Railroad Construction company over when the transfer of assets should take place, but this was worked out, the papers were signed and another grand field day was held to grub out the undergrowth which had sprung up on the right of way.

Legislators converging on the dingy territorial capitol in the fall found a new climate of optimism in the capital city. They found it catching and wasted no time in authorizing the assembly of a constitutional convention of 15 delegates to be elected from the counties of the territory and the "panhandle" counties of Idaho. The proposition for statehood envisioned the inclusion of these Idaho counties in the new state of Washington. The vast majority of the Idaho citizens involved were heartily in favor of the idea, but it was viewed with little enthusiasm in Olympia.

Civic paranoia was still rampant, and the proposed annexation was viewed as a means of shifting the center of population in a plot to move the capital to eastern Washington.

At about the time the legislature was celebrating another adjournment *sine die,* E. N. Ouimette, merchant and secretary of the Thurston County Railroad Construction company, was boarding the trusty sidewheeler *Dakota* for San Francisco. In the March 30, 1879 issue of the *Standard,* Murphy advised the citizens of Olympia and Thurston county that the time had come to make good on past pledges and promises:

"A telegram from Mr. Ouimette, received last Tuesday evening, announced the welcome intelligence that he had completed negotiations for the purchase of iron (rails) for our branch railroad, and was about closing terms for a locomotive and six freight cars. A subsequent dispatch stated that the latter transaction likewise had been consummated and the rolling stock shipped on the* Chester."

The diligent Ouimette was the hero of the hour, the same issue of the *Standard* reporting that *"there is some talk of electing Mr. Ouimette Mayor, as a mark of recognition of his services in managing the railroad negotiations."*

The current state of the local economy was attested to by the fact that nobody was willing to buy gunpowder for the town cannon when the good news arrived from San Francisco, the *Standard* noting that *"our people did not burn any gunpowder over the railroad news, but they rang the bells, which made quite as much noise, without costing anything."*

Even the local boot and shoe maker, Benjamin Vincent, gave vent to the general spirit of jubilation in an advertisement in that same issue of the *Standard:*

*"Now that the railroad's to be built
You surely can't refuse
To treat yourself without ado
To a pair of boots or shoes."*

THE LITTLE ENGINE THAT COULD

The little eight-wheeled narrow-gauge locomotive duly arrived at the new ocean dock on the west side. To modern eyes it would have looked more like a toy than a serious piece of railroad equipment and, like a modern toy, it had to be assembled before it could be used. It was transferred to Percival's dock by scow and the pieces assembled at the foot of 2nd street by Engineer Mason, who would have the honor and glory of handling the throttle once the locomotive was put together and placed in operation.

John Miller Murphy's steam press, and even the marvelous steam sausage-slicer at the butcher shop of D. J. Chambers and Son, were neglected as the population of the town flocked to the waterfront to watch its long-awaited pride and joy take form under the skilled hands of the engineer and his helpers. Meanwhile, the rails were being unloaded from the ship *Tidal Wave* and placed on the roadbed by a crew of 75 men, "one third of whom are Chinamen."

WAITING FOR THE TENINO CANNONBALL at Sheldon's Station on the Olympia-Tenino railroad line.

By late July the rails were in place and the rolling stock transferred to them. August 1 was the great day. The train was assembled, steam was up, and everybody in town was invited for free rides to Tenino and back. Well over half the total population responded enthusiastically. The *Standard,* on the following Saturday, reported the historic event with enthusiasm and in detail:

"We confidently assert that no similar demonstration ever culminated in a more perfect success than did the free ride given last Thursday, by the managers of the Olympia-Tenino Railroad. Foremost, and most important of all the elements of success in such matters, was the fine weather which prevailed. Providence did, indeed, seem to smile upon the undertaking and its happy results.

"The morning train, consisting of six cars, crowded with humanity, left at 8 o'clock. By actual count it was ascertained that 353 per-

sons made the first trip over the road. An equal number left by the 2 o'clock train, and when the cars arrived at Long Bridge, in the evening, it was estimated that fully five hundred people were on board. The road proves, upon its own showing, to be all that the most sanguine ever expected from it . . . a first-class road, devoted to the interests of the people.

"The Olympia Cornet Band accompanied the excursionists, and enlivened the ride with soul-stirring music. At Tenino, during the stay, the time was passed in dancing, in which town and country united with great glee. A special train being in waiting on the track of the Northern Pacific, it was dispatched to Centerville,* for a load of pleasure-seekers, who arrived in time to bask in the smiles of the 'muse of the many twinkling feet'.

---

*Now renamed Centralia.

"But it is unnecessary to refer at greater length on this subject. The railroad is a success, and declared to be so by the people. It now ranks among the living, inspiring and progressive enterprises of the day."

Murphy's enthusiasm was probably accounted for, at least in part, by the fact that he was accorded a place of honor in the locomotive cab, whereas Bagley of the *Courier* was relegated to a flat car which, according to Murphy, *"is about as near 'riding on the rail' as sitting on the cellar door and calling it sliding down hill."*

Following the free excursion, the train began a twice-a-day schedule over the 15-mile route, the conductor, who also acted as station master and flagman, collecting 12¢ for the ride to Tumwater, 50¢ to Bush Station, 75¢ to Spurlock Station and one dollar to Tenino. Regular freight and grain was transported to or from any point on the line for a dollar a ton, with hay going for two dollars a ton. Each of the little freight cars could carry eight tons, and at the end of the first week's operation the *Standard* reported that *"the receipts of the Olympia-Tenino Railroad have been from $40 to $50 per day ever since it was opened to business, and as the expenses of operation do not exceed $12 per day, a very fair margin is left for profit."*

The early operation of the railroad was not without its problems and frustrations, despite the glowing reports in the local press.

Property owners on the west side of the Deschutes waterway had refused to cooperate in the securing of a right of way and it was necessary to build a trestle on the mudflats to carry the line the last couple of miles to the depot at the 4th street "Long bridge." In the rush to get the train rolling, the builders had failed to add sway-braces to the trestle and when the Tenino Express passed over it the trestle groaned and swayed alarmingly, while the cars pitched and rolled and the passengers prayed. The *Standard* was able to report before the end of August that this condition had been corrected, adding the encouraging advice that nobody should *"feel any more trepidation in riding over that part of the road."*

The Thurston county cows presented a problem not so easily solved. They were of an independent and fearless breed, and they caused the railroad even more trouble than they did John Miller Murphy. They refused to be intimidated by the falsetto whistle of the diminutive locomotive and seldom moved off the track. If there was time the train would stop while the fireman and conductor shooed the stubborn beast away, but in darkness or on curves there were frequent collisions, in which the local cows always came out second best. At each meeting of the railroad directors there were delegations of angry farmers demanding restitution for the loss of their choicest cattle.

Engineer Mason's navigation was also hindered by the fact that the locomotive had been delivered without a headlight, as well as by the lack of a turn-table at the north end of the line. The train was forced to back into the Olympia station with the conductor lighting the way with a kerosene lantern, which was not a properly inspiring approach to the capital city.

The directors eventually authorized the construction of a turn-table and the ladies of Olympia held a benefit supper to procure a headlight for the locomotive, but misfortune continued to plague the railroad. In mid-September the *Standard* reported, *"a slight mishap at the turntable last night unfitted the engine for taking the train to Tenino today, and hence no whistle greeted our ears this morning. The mail was sent out on a hand-car."*

Furthermore, when the long-awaited headlight arrived from San Francisco it was discovered that the unscrupulous dealer with whom the ladies' order had been placed had taken their money and shipped a second-hand mine lantern instead of the majectic hand-painted kerosene locomotive headlight everybody had been expecting.

Early passengers on the line also traveled in some discomfort due to another oversight. The line's one passenger car had arrived without seats. By late September, however, the *Standard* was able to impart the glad tidings that the seats had arrived on the *Dakota* from San Francisco.

The citizens of Olympia, used to a less complicated way of life, were confused by the proliferation of transportation facilities. The sternwheeler *Messenger* had joined the *Zephyr* on the down-Sound route, and the *Standard* reported the resulting state of affairs as follows:

"Since the locomotive made its debut, mingling its shrill whistling with that of the steamers, our citizens are often at a loss to know 'which is which', and a few ridiculous mistakes have already occurred in consequence."

While the Olympia-Tenino railroad did not immediately bring miraculous prosperity to Olympia, it was considered a definite civic asset. A real, operating railroad, even though it was neither as long nor as wide as the Northern Pacific, was a fine status symbol, which would doubtless impress the legislature when the next fight over the capital location broke out.

It also engendered a new industry. With the railroad providing connections with the Northern Pacific and relatively speedy freight transport to Portland, a group of enterprising Olympia citizens formed the Olympia Oyster company, gathering and shipping the succulent local bivalves in considerable quantity. Until that time the oysters had mostly been gathered by Indians and hawked from baskets to the limited Olympia market.

The Indian oyster-gatherers now sold their wares direct to the oyster company, which also cultivated beds in the outlying bays, shipping them to town on its own little sternwheel steamer, the *Old Settler*.

Somewhat carried away by all this progress, Murphy even went so far as to let the civic leaders of the town talk him into taking another fling at publishing a daily paper, a project which he described, with some lack of enthusiasm, as follows:

". . . The Daily Experiment, *as the name implies, is an experiment. It will be published, if at all, a week, maybe a month, possibly a year, and if it attains that mature age, will doubtless be continued indefinitely.*

". . . *It will endeavor to note every local event, but in return expects to receive from each of its patrons 25 cents per week.*

"*While it will endeavor to puff town and surrounding country higher than Gilray's kite, it don't propose to laud anything that puts wealth into anybody's pocket, without receiving a small moity of its own. This might as well be understood at the outset . . . Its motto will be . . . You tickle me and I'll tickle you, which, next to the Golden Rule, is the most sensible of proverbs.*

". . . *Advertising will be inserted at reasonable rates by the week. Special notices 5 cents a line each insertion, but none inserted for less than 25 cents. At these rates, those who have insisted that a daily paper would pay can have a chance to demonstrate their faith by their works.*

". . . *Let it be distinctly understood that the present project is not of our own suggestion or seeking, but simply a compliance with the wishes of some very enthusiastic friends.*"

Despite Murphy's highly practical and realistic proclamation, the little four-page tabloid survived only a short time beyond the one year probationary period. Murphy, now a twice burned child in the precarious game of daily newspaper publishing, vowed that he would never again be fast-talked into getting out a paper more often than once a week. He stuck to his guns for well over a decade before he gave in to the pleas of civic boosters and ventured for the third and last time into the field of daily journalism.

ANOTHER TRY FOR STATEHOOD

In mid-June the constitutional convention, authorized by the voters and the last legislature, assembled at Walla Walla to hopefully draw up a state constitution. In addition to 15 delegates from Washington territory, it included a representative of the three Idaho panhandle counties, Shoshone, Nez Perce and Idaho, which wanted to become part of the new state of Washington. The sum of $200 was appropriated to pay the expenses of the Idaho delegate, but he wasn't permitted to vote. Washington territory's elder statesman, Alexander Abernethy of Cowlitz was the convention chairman; Francis Henry represented Thurston and Lewis counties.

In an effort to abolish the politically powerful organizations which had traditionally grown around the territorial governors, the new constitution limited governors to a single four-year term, although they could run again after being out of office for a term.

It fixed the salaries of the governor, secretary of state, state treasurer and superintendent of public instruction at $1,500 per annum, supreme and circuit court judges, $2,000, circuit attorneys, $1,000 and members of the legislature, $4.00 a day per diem while in session and 10¢ per mile in "going to and returning from the seat of Government."

Despite the continued efforts of Mrs. Duniway and her followers of the woman suffrage movement, the delegates made it clear that only *male* persons of the age of 21 or over were to be electors. They did, however, provide for the submission of female suffrage and local option on liquor sales as separate propositions, to be voted on at the same time as the proposed constitution. If they received a majority vote they would be incorporated into the constitution.

The delegates took a swipe at the much disliked Northern Pacific by including a provision that "all railroads in the state shall be deemed public highways, and shall be free to all persons for the transportation of themselves and property, under such regulations as may be prescribed by law." They also struck a blow for thrift in government by providing that "the public debt shall never exceed one hundred thousand dollars unless contracted to repel invasion or suppress insurrection."

The convention also stood firmly for morality, with provisions that the legislature could not grant divorces or authorize lotteries. A proposal to establish "separate but equal" schools for non-white children was voted down by better than two to one, but a memorial to congress was authorized requesting the abolition of all Indian reservations granted under the treaties of 1854-55, thus permitting white homsteaders to grab the last remaining Indian lands.

In regard to the capital question, the constitution provided that:

"The legislature shall have no power to change or locate the seat of goverment; but shall at the first session after admission submit the question of the permanent location of the seat of government to the qualified electors at the next general election, the seat of government to remain at Olympia until permanently located by a majority vote."

The document was approved by a vote of 6,537 to 3,236. It was overwhelmingly favored in the three Idaho counties . . . 742 to 28 . . . but there was much difference of opinion among Washington residents on the desirability of including them in the proposed new state. The official position of the legislature was favorable to their annexation, probably to a large degree from political consideration. The Idaho counties were heavily Democratic, as was congress at that time, and there was a belief among the territorial politicians that congress would take more kindly to the request for statehood if Washington were somewhat less overwhelmingly Republican. Others felt the inclusion of the Idaho counties would complicate and endanger the request for statehood.

Everyone was convinced that statehood would bring increased land and property values, along with a golden flood of federal money, and the majority simply and selfishly wanted statehood, with or without the panhandle counties.

There were a few exceptions. The citizens of Pierce county, the promised land of the Northern Pacific, were opposed to the anti-railroad provisions of the consitution and voted against it. Walla Walla county had come to the conclusion that it would like to be annexed to Oregon; furthermore, Mr. Newell of the Walla Walla *Statesman* had convinced a large segment of the population that the whole thing was a plot by Elisha P. Ferry to get himself elected United States senator. Statehood and the constitution lost there, too.

And four out of five of the electors voted against woman suffrage and local option.

Thomas J. Brent, who was elected as the Republican delegate to congress at the same election that ratified the proposed constitution, introduced no less than three bills providing for the admission of Washington as a state. Similar bills were filed at the succeeding three sessions of congress, but only one of these . . . with the three Idaho counties deleted . . . emerged from committee, and it failed to pass.

Although Thurston county had favored statehood by a fair majority, many Olympians breathed a sigh of relief when congress failed to act. At least the town wouldn't have to go through the traumatic and expensive process of another capital location election for a while.

TINDER TOWN

The summer of 1878 was unusually hot and dry in the Puget Sound country. The *Standard* complained of *"the impalpable dust that so thoroughly invests everything,"* despite the best efforts of the town sprinkling wagon. Forest fires broke out and raged unchecked, as they would each summer for many years. Smoke blotted out the sun and made it difficult to recognize acquaintances on the streets at a distance of half a block. The steamboats groped their way from landing to landing, hooting their whistles dismally, and the

Standard was moved to observe that *"the early Christians walked by faith and not by sight. The Sound steamers run by whistle and not by compass."*

Even the sidewalks of the capital city were not immune from the threat of fire. At two o'clock on a June morning the fire alarm sounded and, according to the *Standard,* *"brought out nearly our whole town population to wage battle against the dread destroyer."*

It was, in fact, a section of the dilapidated wooden sidewalk leading to the equally dilapidated territorial capitol which was on fire. Many had hoped that it *was* the capitol. At this time the *Strandard* was still complaining editorially about another block of sidewalk between 3rd and 4th on Washington street, which had been damaged by a previous fire and still hadn't been replaced.

Shortly thereafter the fire bell clanged again, and this time the citizens and the volunteer fire companies had a real problems on their hands. Fire had broken out in a wooden shed near the drug store and office of Dr. Rufus Willard, and it spread through the frame business stuctures faster than the best efforts of the *Columbia* could cope with it. Before it was over the entire block from 3rd to 4th between Main and Washington streets was in ruins. Only a fortuitous change of wind and the combined efforts of men, women and children prevented the complete destruction of the downtown area.

John Miller Murphy, an ardent fire buff and member of the Columbia engine company, immediately set up a hue and cry for a steam fire engine, both as essential to the safety of the community and as a civic status symbol. Having made up his mind on the matter, Murphy kept up his campaign until he got it, but he did not neglect his traditional crusades against such minor civic problem areas as unruly cows and hazardous streets and sidewalks.* He had unsuccessfully matched wits with the town cows for years, and appeared to view them with a certain grudging awe and admiration, coupled with a deep hatred:

"Olympia has some of the most wonderfully ingenious and persistently intrusive cows that have ever cursed any community. They break into yards, destroy fruit trees and shrubbery, eat the fruit, and guard their retreat and dodge missiles with the extraordinary precision of intelligent beings. Their mode of procedure is as systematic as that of the burglar, and shows

the extent to which dumb beasts can be educated. Their skill in opening gates will, with the constant practice they maintain, soon enable them to pick a McNeal & Urban lock. Still the owners 'comply with the law' keeping them in at night, and consider themselves free from responsibility for depradations committed in the day-time. One or two suits for damages will probably place this matter in a new light."

THE TOWN MAY BE HAZARDOUS TO HEALTH

The year 1879 was ushered in by a period of intense cold. The never very effective town water system gave way entirely beneath the drain of frozen and burst water pipes. The *Daily Experiment* reported on January 11 that *"the water tank on Percival's wharf is empty and the supply pipe fails to discharge into it on account of the immense waste in the upper part of town."* The local steamboats not only had to dodge floating ice from the Deschutes river, but were unable to take on water for their boilers. No mail had been received from California and the east since the first of the month because the Columbia river was frozen solid and no boats were operating.

John Miller Murphy and other respectable citizens fell victims to icy sidewalks made even more hazardous by the boys of the town who used them for sledding, and the *Standard* warned ominously that *"the boys who poured water on the sidewalk to have it freeze and thus facilitate the coasting business had best be wary as their names are already recorded."*

The cold weather did not put an end to the contagious diseases which were, at best, endemic in 19th century Olympia. Diphtheria was sweeping the town, and the white plumes were often in use on the hearse of Rabbeson and Harned. The new East Olympia school was closed because of the epidemic, and doctors disagreed as to what caused the disease and what remedies should be used. Between the obituary notices in the *Standard,* a short

---

*Murphy devoted his columns to a defense of the town's street and sidewalk maintenance program only when he served as a town trustee.

article pointed out that *"diphtheria, as a malady of late appearance in the world, stands without kith or kin; nor have physicians yet agreed upon such a diagnosis of it as is reconcilable with its infinity of symptoms."*

Throughout the year the columns of the *Standard* were well laced with such dismal tidings as *"neuralgia, influenza, diphtheria and a number of kindred diseases are troubling a good many of our citizens."*

There were also comments on the large number of rats displaced by the extreme January tides which inundated the lower town, the strange foreign bodies to be found in the town water supply, and the fact that the heaps of muddy offal scraped from the gutters were used to fill depressions in the streets instead of being more suitably sold to farmers as manure. By late spring it was reported that the flies were back, as they swarmed over the manure piles of the livery stables, the unprotected meat in the butcher shops and the outdoor privies of the residential areas.

Furthermore, reported Murphy, who was not particularly fond of the town's Chinese residents, it was time for the authorities to do something about the *"pool of filthy water standing in the gutter in front of the Chinese wash houses on 4th street between Main and Columbia for a week past, which leaves a slimy stratum of putrid matter to taint the atmosphere we breathe when evaporated under a hot sun."*

The continued economic depression had added a new problem . . . that of abject poverty among a number of the aged citizens whose savings had been wiped out and who were too feeble to harvest the fish, shellfish, birds and game which swarmed in the bay and its surrounding forests.

The county commissioners were forced to pass the first "poor law", authorizing Mary Mann of Tumwater to "keep the paupers of the county." She was provided with five dollars a week to feed, clothe and house each of the unfortunates. J. C. Horr, merchant and wharf owner, had added the manufacture of wooden coffins to his enterprises, and he was awarded the contract to bury those paupers who failed to survive on the bounty of the county. He was paid $3.50 "per corpse", which made it evident that it was much cheaper for the community to bury its indigent citizens permanently than to feed them for a week.

When the smelt began to run in the bay and up the Deschutes waterway the impoverished citizens of Olympia scooped them up and salted them down by the barrelfull and when the tide was out they dug clams.

The *Dakota*, which had been stopping only at Port Townsend during the winter months, resumed her calls at the west side wharf. Merchants restocked their depleted shelves from her capacious holds and piles of merchandise blocked the wooden sidewalks along Main street. Only one major business, the store of W. H. Clark at 3rd and Columbia, was located elsewhere, and the *Standard* consistently bewailed *"the provincial idea that Main street constitutes the whole of the city of Olympia."*

Included in the *Dakota's* consignment to the City of Paris store was a clothing dummy of lifelike appearance, which the proprietor, Mr. Toklas, dressed in a style described by Murphy as that of a "Broadway swell." This splendid effigy stood at the store's entrance, to the subsequent confusion of a number of the townspeople. One gentleman was observed to rush up to the dummy with extended hand and a loud, "Good morning, Mr. Toklas!" He seemed quite offended for several moments when the dummy failed to respond to his hearty greeting. Murphy claimed in a *Standard* "local" that *"an inebriated individual spent some time on election day trying to ascertain if the dummy was registered so as to vote him for the whiskey ticket,"* but Murphy didn't always let the truth interfere with a good story.

A WAGON-LOAD OF VOTERS

The reference to the whiskey ticket was in relation to the annual spring town election, which attracted the usual widespread and general apathy of the citizens. Only the temperance crusaders and the saloon men took much interest in such matters. It was a matter of principal with the wearers of the blue ribbon and a matter of survival for the liquor vendors. If reform-minded candidates should be elected and enforce the Sunday closing laws, the license regulations and other such bothersome rules and regulations it would be extremely bad for business. The saloon men invested in a form of business insurance by rounding up itinerant loggers, town loafers and any drifters

M. Glover, Portland, Oregon.

Entered according to Act of C...

IWATER.

REFERENCES:

1. Capitol Building.   5. Masonic Hall.
2. Public School.   6. Baptist Church.
3. Congregational Church. 7. Unitarian Church.
4. Catholic Church.   8. Presbyterian Church.

BIR

CITY O

EAST OLYM

Puget Sou

in the Office of the Librarian of Congress.

A. L. Bancroft & Co., Lithographers

OF THE

LYMPIA,

D TUMWATER,

 gton Territory.

BUDD'S IN

REFERENCES:

9. Episcopal Church.
10. Court House.
11. Odd Fellows' Hall.
12. Town Hall.

13. Methodist Church.
14. Champion Hill.
15. Good Templar's Hall.

who happened to be in the neighborhood, plying them with bad liquor, worse cigars and a little spending money, and transporting them to the polls to participate in the democratic process.

Both the *Echo* and the temporarily enlightened *Standard* editorialized against this form of organized mass voting, and even Elisha Gunn of the *Transcript* didn't entirely deny that it existed, but as the spokesman for the town's more sporting business community, he denied that it was as widespread as Murphy and Gale claimed. Murphy self-righteously put him properly in his place when the *Transcript* attempted to mimimize the problem with the statement that only one wagon-load of voters had been hauled to the polls by the saloon men. *"We know how difficult it is,"* the *Standard* philosophized, *"for a man who eats his principal sustenance from a bottle to tell the truth."*

WOMEN ARE PEOPLE?

By late September the territorial legislators were gathering in the capital city for another biennial session. They found the pioneer Washington Hotel at 2nd and Main rejuvenated and back in business as the New England under the proprietorship of William and E. T. Young. A handsome coach met all trains and steamboats and conveyed guests to the New England House in style and comfort, free of charge. William Young died at the hotel soon after its reopening . . . from "paralysis of the lungs," according to the coroner's jury, but his brother, E. T., remained for many years and became one of the town's most respected civic leaders.

The legislature no sooner convened than it threw John Miller Murphy into a fit of indignation by adjourning for six days to attend a reception in Portland for President U. S. Grant. Warming up with charges of *"legislative junketing"* and *"pompous recreation,"* Murphy concluded that *"by this freak of toadyism our honorable legislators will cause an expenditure of the peoples' money amounting to above $1,000, for which the territory receives no value."*

By early October the junketing lawmakers were back in town, in time to visit the territorial fair, which was being held at the new fairgrounds south of town near Tumwater. It featured such varied attractions as a fine display of beets, a notable exhibition of Berkshire pigs, a 28-inch oyster shell from Scow Bay, a case of stuffed birds and, as reported by Murphy, *"a splendid exhibit of cheeses,"* one of which, he later reported joyfully, *"found its way to our table."*

There were also numerous medicine shows, displays of revolving patent flour-sifters and fancy articles made by the ladies aid society of the Episcopal church. There was also horse racing and gambling, but the fall rains had come to greet the legislature, and the fairgrounds were nearly two miles from town on the muddy Tumwater road. The livery stables charged 50 cents for the ride out in a hack, four-bit pieces, along with other varieties of legal tender, were in short supply and the turnout was disappointing.

Governor Ferry addressed the assembled legislators, modestly proclaiming that, under his admininstration, health had prevailed, the seasons had been propitious, the fisheries productive, agricultural interests prosperous and commerce and industry thriving.

He delivered himself of a complaint which was to be voiced by many future governors. The legislature of 1877 had dallied until the last few days of the session and "important measures were then crowded to passage with undue haste." More than two-thirds of the bills passed had descended upon the governor in a paper blizzard within 12 hours after adjournment, many of them "interlined so imperfectly that their meaning was obscure and the provisions incongruous."

He expressed the wistful hope that the members this time would "confine legislation to the more important subjects, and mature the same, rather than embrace all objects in a crude jumble of conflicting and inconsistent laws."

Ferry further reported that the territorial treasury had collected $112,365.30 in taxes during the past year, had disbursed $109,-487.98, leaving a balance of $2,878.32. There was no public debt.

No sooner had the governor departed than the legislators began their response to his plea to stifle trivial legislation by introducing bills to amend an act prohibiting hogs from running at large in Stevens county, to prevent the sale of intoxicating liquor to half breed Indians, defining lawful fences in Columbia county, establishing a minimum length of skirts for female children in the public schools and to dissolve the bonds of matrimony between D. C. Belshea and Zutoda Belshea, as well as a resolution inviting General U.S Grant to visit the territorial capital.

The year drew to a close with modest reports of progress recorded in the columns of the *Standard.*

"The new sidewalks and crossings recently put down were not a whit too soon," Murphy editorialized as the gentle rains of October became the chilling downpour of November. *"While our gutters are filled to the brim by the late rains, and the streets like mortar beds, it is pleasant to be able to perambulate the town dry shod."*

Mr. Munson, the local agent for the McKennon Stylograph, a primitive version of the fountain pen, presented Murphy with one of these latest marvels of American inventive genius. The publisher, who dearly loved gadgets, recommended it highly, informing his readers that they could purchase various models from Mr. Munson at prices ranging from $3.50 to $5.50.

Another scientific wonder which attracted the attention and admiration of the *Standard*'s editor was the marvelous hot air furnace installed in the cellar of T. F. McElroy's elegant new mansion.

But there were not noticeable improvements in public health, Murphy sadly reporting:

"We believe not until the present reign of diphtheria have the ears of our people been so often pained by the sad and measured tolling of the funeral bell. Seven children have been snatched away in about ten days."

The town's newspapers carried recommendations for fumigation of homes and hopes that cold weather might end the epidemic, but there were no suggestions as to the control of raw sewage, promiscuously strewn garbage, rats and flies.

ENTER THE 1880's

The census of 1880 made it clear that Olympia was no longer the metropolis of Washington territory. The capital city had gained only a few hundred citizens in the decade since the last census, and could now boast a population of 1,532, but Seattle, aided by John Pinnell, the territorial university and aggressive civic boosterism, had more than doubled that, attaining a population of 3,533. Tacoma, hit hard by the bankruptcy of the Northern Pacific and the subsequent hard times, was trying to catch up, but was able to muster only 1,098 citizens for the census-takers to count.

The decade of the 80's was ushered into the Puget Sound country in January with "the great snow storm," which was recalled to their dying days by those who had to cope with it. At Olympia the snowfall reached six feet on the level, with mountainous drifts. Young trees bent over under its weight and remained hunchbacked as they grew to maturity. A huge tree in front of Reynold's livery stable on lower Main street threatened to fall and was cut down and sawed into cordwood. Improvident householders whose woodsheds were empty bought it all within an hour at the unheard-of price of $12 a cord.

Intervals of heavy rain between blizzards soaked the accumulated snow and multiplied its weight. Wooden awnings collapsed onto the snow-blocked streets. The old *Pioneer and Democrat* building, built on piles over the bay at the upper end of Main street and in use as the surveyor-general's office, was completely demolished. The roof of the Ward and Mitchell sawmill near the Swantown bridge collapsed and the machinery was engulfed in snow. A two-story building on Third street, "occupied by Chinamen," went down beneath the accumulated weight of wet snow, and there were major landslides along the steep banks of Capitol Hill above the Deschutes waterway.

Southwest gales swept the rain in from the Pacific, causing heavy swells in the shallow harbor. The rickety wharfs swayed so badly that prospective steamboat passengers sometimes got seasick while waiting for the boat. The *Messenger* clawed her way out from Percival's dock just as J. C. Percival's big new warehouse suddenly collapsed, the wreckage crashing into the bay where the steamer had been tied up.

The town had no equipment capable of making even a dent on the thick white blanket. Town fathers and citizens alike simply stoked their stoves, counted their firewood, and waited philosophically for the warm Chinook wind which was sure to come eventually.

A THIRD TERM? NEVER!

By March things were back to normal and Murphy of the *Standard* was able to concentrate on the rascality of Republican politicians rather than the unusual nature of the weather.

His ire was focused on the determined campaign of Elisha P. Ferry to get himself appointed to an unprecedented third term as governor. The *Standard* reported the *"strong pressure on* (Congressional Delegate) *T. H. Brents by 'the territorial ring of office-holders' for the appointment of Ferry to another term."* The leader of the drive, he said, was Francis Tarbell, the territorial treasurer, who like the rest of the official family, owed his job to Ferry's influence and would probably be among the unemployed if his patron were replaced.

Murphy was not in favor of a third term for anybody, and especially not for Ferry. *"The mere suggestion of a third-term governor should be as much condemned as the proposition for a third-term president,"* he insisted. *"Rotation in office is as essential to the purity of the civil service as a succession of crops is necessary to maintain the integrity of the soil."*

Ferry and his cohorts apparently overreached themselves in their grab for another term of office. The resulting furor in the Republican party prompted Hays to appoint a new territorial governor and Ferry, his family and their cow returned to Seattle, where the ex-governor took up the practice of law and bided his time.

William Augustus Newell, M.D., former congressmen and the first Republican governor of New Jersey, was appointed the eleventh territorial governor of Washington.

Murphy would have much preferred a Democrat, of course, but he rejoiced nevertheless in the downfall of "Elisha the Prophet" by resorting to the Biblical prose of Francis Henry:

"The federal clique sorroweth and will not be comforted. It pulleth its hair, it putteth ashes on its head, its lamentations are heard far and near, for Elisha that was is not, and the place which knew him will know him no more forever. Amen and amen."

Within the decade, Murphy would find that he had been premature in publishing Ferry's obituary as a political corpse.

W. A. NEWELL
1880–1884

Dr. Newell, who was 63 years of age when he arrived in Olympia, had behind him a distinguished career, both professionally and politically. He had been Abraham Lincoln's personal physician for a time and, as a congressman from New Jersey, had attended John Quincy Adams when that great orator and statesman fell to the floor of the house with a fatal stroke in 1848. He was instrumental in establishing the original bureau of agriculture and the federal lifesaving service.

Unfortunately, the good doctor was always financially hard up. Between terms in public office he was forced to rely on the practice of medicine, and few doctors in those days got rich. Newell seems to have been even less of a financial success than most of his colleagues, and the dignity of his position as territorial governor was somewhat tarnished by the expedients he resorted to to avoid spending money and his tendency to put the arm on people for small loans.

GOD BLESS THE OLYMPIA OYSTER

Perhaps the most important event to befall the capital city in 1880 was the result of an ex-steamboat man named Woodbury Doane taking note of the abundance of delicious oysters to be had for the taking from the mudflats which surrounded Olympia in just about every direction.

Captain Doane, a big, handsome, good-natured adventurer had come west from Maine during the California gold rush of 1849. He piloted the first steamer up the Fraser river during the later gold rush in British Columbia. He explored the interior of British Columbia, followed the course of the Mackenzie river and Great Slave lakes to the headwaters of the Mackenzie, crossed the mountains between Alaska and the Northwest territories, and followed the Stikeen river to its mouth. He later settled down to steamboating on the more placid waters of Puget Sound and was widely known and liked in Olympia as mate of the old *Eliza Anderson.*

After retiring from maritime pursuits he served for a while as night watchman on the two-man Olympia police force, and in 1880 he rented a tiny stall on 5th street between Main and Columbia, erected a hand-lettered sign and opened Doane's Oyster House. Somewhere in his wanderings he had acquired the recipe for an oyster pan roast which has frequently been described as fit for the gods.

At first the captain and his two sons gathered the little Olympia oysters on the early morning low tide, took them to the stand on 5th street, cleaned and shelled them, and were ready to prepare the succulent Doane's oyster pan roasts for the lunch trade. As the fame of this delicacy spread far and wide the oyster house expanded, Indians were employed to gather the principal ingredient, Chinese chefs were trained to prepare the specialty of the house, sworn to secrecy as to the recipe, and Captain Doane prospered. Long after his death in 1903 Doane's Oyster House remained as the center of epicurean delight in the capital city, and the famous pan roast is still a favorite of seafood gourmets who patronize its lineal descendant, the Olympia Oyster House.

Cap. Doane made the Olympia Oyster famous.

Another seafaring man who was destined to have a long and prominent part in the community's affairs, Captain Samuel Willey, arrived on the scene in 1880 from the woods of Mason county, where he had operated a logging camp. He bought the little propeller steamer *Susie* and placed her on the run between Olympia, Arcadia (where a clam cannery had recently been placed in operation) and Oakland, then the Mason county seat. His three sons, La Fayette, George and Philander, made up the crew of the *Susie.* Since the profits were all kept in the family, the Willeys prospered and, three years later, replaced the *Susie* with the larger, although still diminutive, sternwheeler *Willie.* They continued to dominate that route for many years and later took over control of the steamboat trade to Tacoma and Seattle.

The ocean steamer *Dakota* was still paddling regularly to the west side wharf, bringing general cargo, merchandise for the local stores and a scattering of passengers, and departing with water pipe, wool and hides. In August she brought a party of 25 men, women and children intent on establishing an agricultural colony near Olympia. The group was, for some unexplained reason, referred to as the "Newell

Colony," and it has been widely assumed that they were brought west by Governor Newell. The new chief executive was, in fact, barely able to finance his own journey and, as far as is known, had nothing to do with their arrival. He was on hand to welcome them, however, along with a delegation from the recently organized Olympia Board of Trade. Quarters were found for them until they located a site for their colony, and when they took claims west of town near Black Lake the town trustees even contributed toward building a road to provide access for them.

Despite this auspicious welcome, and the opinion of the *Standard* that the Lindquists, the Frisches and the other members of the party were *"hardy-looking people, apparently well adapted to constitute the cornerstone of the great social and political fabric which is in time to be erected,"* the colony, like the statesman whose name it bore, failed to prosper. Like many settlers before them, they found the task of clearing the thick stands of virgin timber a hopeless one for men without machinery, and all but a family or two drifted away to other pursuits.

Generally, however, times were better in 1880 than at any time since the panic of 1873 had set in. The local papers were fond of boasting that all of the seven local churches and most of the remarkably large number of fraternal organizations owned their own buildings, as did five of the six drygoods merchants and three of the five hotel proprietors.

For the first time, local merchants began using dimes and "half-dimes," or nickels, in making change. Hitherto the smallest coin available had been the "two-bit" piece and if a customer bought a 15-cent item the storekeeper took his quarter and returned nothing except a friendly farewell. As with most new-fangled ideas, especially in Olympia, the small change was at first received with a good deal of contempt by those who were benefitted, but it soon became an accepted part of everyday transactions.

The first militia company since Indian war days was formed during the year by Captain R. G. O'Brien, an Irish immigrant who had become an officer of Illinois volunteers in the civil war following an undistinguished career as a farmhand and drygoods clerk. His military service and title opened the way to

political appointment, and he was brought to Olympia in 1870 by Governor Salomon as assistant assessor of internal revenue. He later became clerk of the U. S. district court, but, like Francis Henry, he longed for the romance and glory of brass buttons, epaulettes and sword. He had gotten himself elected to the honorary position of territorial quartermaster-general in 1878. Aided by the prestige of commanding an actual militia company, he was named adjutant-general in the 1882 election, continuing in that office for many years and going down in the state's military history as the "father of the Washington National Guard."

MY WIFE HAS FLEAS!

In October the first presidential visit was made to the territorial capital by President Hays, who was making a western tour. The reason for this, according to the *Standard,* was his wish to escape for a while from the terrible mess his administration had made of things at Washington, D.C.

One might have expected such an historic event to be heralded in bold type in all three of the town's remaining weekly newspapers, the *Standard, Courier* and *Transcript* (the *Tribune* had been moved to Tacoma by the Prosches in 1873 and the *Echo,* after trying to become a daily had folded in 1877, along with the *Daily Courier*). Bagley and Gunn did, indeed, devote much space to the arrival of the Republican president, but it was necessary to read the *Standard* very carefully to get the word. A single short paragraph buried on an inside page reported that the chief executive and his party had arrived by stage coach, *Mister* Hays had made a speech from the balcony of the Pacific Hotel, and had then departed on the steamer *Geo. E. Starr,* "chartered to carry them over the Sound."

Murphy would have devoted more space to anyone who presented him with a cheese.

Although one might not know it by reading the *Standard,* the town made the visit quite an occasion, firing the inevitable cannon, ringing the church bells and marshaling the fire and militia companies as a guard of honor.

Most of the territorial officials accompanied the presidential party on its tour of the lower Puget Sound settlements, among them the current territorial secretary, Colonel N. H. Owings. At Port Townsend, the gallant colonel was delegated to escort Mrs. Hays while the president went on ahead to address the citizenry. From the dock the first lady saw a Clallam Indian camp on the beach and became possessed with the urge to inspect it at close range.

Owings, who had been in the territory long enough to know something about Indian camps, tried to dissuade her, but to no avail. He took her to the camp, ceremoniously introduced her to the chief, and waited outside while she inspected the interior of the mat and driftwood shelters, which were inhabited by numerous dogs and fleas as well as Indians.

The secretary noted that Mrs. Hays appeared to be extremely uneasy during the meeting they attended later, but he maintained a tactful silence.

Not so the president. The next morning he drew Owings aside and said, "Mr. Secretary, hereafter when you take my wife to visit an Indian tepee kindly inform me of the fact; then being forewarned I shall sleep alone."

SUMMER SICKNESS

The spring of 1881 brought the first major infestation of tent caterpillars, the town's famous shade trees providing an inviting habitat for them. Ladies strolling the wooden sidewalks were forced to keep one eye on protruding nailheads and the other peeled for the nasty creatures dropping from leaves overhead. The descendants of those 19th century pests still periodically infest the vacant lots and orchards of the area, although the majestic maples have long since vanished.

There were other problems as well. As the weather warmed the accumulating sewage of the town obtruded upon the olifactory senses of even the least fastidious citizens. Most of the overflow eventually made its way to the mudflats, which became increasingly malodorous at low tide. Diphtheria and croup continued to take their toll of the juvenile population, and there was fear that a smallpox epidemic which had broken out in Tacoma would extend itself to Olympia.

The town water system remained a source of much irritation. Under the best of conditions it was subject to frequent breakdowns. During heavy rains it delivered muddy ground water well laced with the flotsam and jetsam of flooded Moxlie creek. When the weather got hot the pressure dropped as the thermometer went up and all water was frequently shut off after nine or ten o'clock at night, when the water company apparently felt all decent citizens should be in bed anyway. In August the *Standard* began an editorial campaign urging the town trustees to buy the water system, pointing out that the water company's pump had been out of commission for months and that *"the upper portions of the town are almost at the mercy of fire"*.

Furthermore, there was increasing evidence that the little wooden town was very likely to be wiped out by a major conflagration. As early as April the *Standard* had reported eight minor fires within the past two weeks, although there had been no general alarm for a year prior to that time.

During the long rainy season, heavy accumulations of moss grew on the shingle roofs of the wooden buildings and during the shorter periods of sunshine the moss dried and provided a natural tinder box for the reception of sparks. For many years Murphy and the fire department heralded the coming of spring with pleas to property owners to please scrape the moss off their roofs, but they seldom responded. Murphy was somewhat embarrassed during one hot spell when dry moss on the *Standard* office caught fire, an unfortunate incident which his rival editors were a long time letting him forget.

Despite the *Standard's* continuing editorial campaign for a new steam pumper, the old *Columbia* hand-pumper and the converted farm wagon of the Barnes Hook and Ladder Company remained the only fire protection equipment. Forest and brush fires continued to ring the town periodically in the summer and wood-burning kitchen stoves continued to emit sparks from hundreds of chimneys in even the hottest weather. There was good reason to be nervous about the threat of fire.

The shooting of President Garfield by an assassin cast something of a cloud over the town's annual Fourth of July celebration, although early reassuring bulletins on his improved condition avoided its cancellation.

The *Zephyr* and *Messenger* brought excursionists from Seattle, as did the *Annie Stewart,* which brought along the Pacific Cornet band to add to the festivities. The *Daisy* and *Phantom* hauled capacity loads of excursionists from Tacoma and the mill ports. The revenue cutter *Oliver Wolcott* was also in the harbor to add its noisy salutes to those of the town cannon. The festivities included the usual parade, including a "liberty car" bearing the local belle chosen as the year's goddess of liberty and drawn by 50 brawny loggers. There was a clambake in the public square, along with the usual oratory and band music from both the Olympia and Seattle cornet bands. There were rowing races and Indian canoe races in the harbor when the tide came in, and local youths splashed noisily into the bay from the greased pole protuding from Percival's dock. Jimmy Dofflemeyer made it to the end and back and won the prize, a five dollar gold piece.

In October there was more excitement, as the fair opened on the remote grounds south of town and the legislature assembled at the not quite so remote territorial capitol.

Murphy was critical of the fair's management, sounding almost as sanctimonious as had the late *Daily Echo* when he reported in the *Standard* that, in addition to betting on the horse races at the fairgrounds, *"other gambling devices are notoriously conspicuous, while liquors are sold on the grounds for the first time."*

"Is this progress?" Murphy's editorial asked plaintively. *"If so, in what direction?"*

Despite the liberalized policy of the Washington Industrial Association, which managed the fair, it had difficulty competing with the legislative assembly in entertainment value and again failed to meet expenses.

A TORRENT OF TRIVIA

The 1881 legislature was, as the *Standard* had indicated earlier, strongly Republican. The council was made up of eight Republicans, three Democrats and one independent, while the house of representatives was 15 to nine Republican.

Henry Villard, who had picked up the pieces of the bankrupt Northern Pacific and was putting it back together, came to Puget Sound in his own splendid new ocean steamship, the *Queen of the Pacific,* and was invited to address the legislature. In an aside to the eager townspeople of Olympia he informed them that, in his opinion, the maple-shaded capital city was "already so pretty a town that more railroads would spoil it".

The loyal Olympians didn't know whether to feel flattered or put down.

Despite its Republican majority, Murphy and the *Standard* viewed the legislature with some optimism:

"Our law-makers, this session, are, by common consent, pronounced as promising a class of men as ever graced legislative halls. If physiognomy and brain indications warrant anything like favorable conclusions, then have the people of the Territory a just right to expect good results from their deliberations."

The editorial opinion of the *Standard* was revised downward considerably as what turned out to be the longest session in territorial history droned on, grinding out a record number of bills on almost every subject imaginable.

Governor Newell, his hair and whiskers freshly dyed in his continuing and much laughed at efforts to look younger than he was, delivered his message to the legislators and was followed by ex-Governor Ferry, who delivered what he termed a retiring message. As might be expected, Murphy composed a less than flattering summary of Ferry's remarks:

"He congratulated the people upon the healthful condition of the Territorial finances and divided the credit for it between himself and the previous Legislatures. The people, who have groaned under heavy taxation, like the soldier who does the hard fighting in the field while the officers receive all the glory, were not mentioned in his panegyric. He then told the people what a serious loss they had sustained in his removal from office."

Despite the alleged healthy condition of the territorial treasury, the federal government had cut the legislative funds so sharply that there wasn't money for Public Printer Bagley to produce journals of both houses or of the governor's message. Only a house journal was printed. The days of the public printing gravy train were indeed past, for a while at any rate.

Early in December a special session was called by Governor Newell, who wanted more time to consider the bills already passed. As a result, about 300 measures were ground out, including such vital legislation as acts to prohibit fowl from running at large in Pacific county, hogs from running at large on Fidalgo island and goats from running at large in Klickitat county; to regulate rates of toll for grinding corn, and a true classic which placed the legislature squarely on the record as opposed to even a vague hint of incest.

This remarkable set of marriage laws not only prohibited bigamy, but banned marriages between "persons of kinship nearer than second cousins" and prescribed a one to 10 year penitentiary sentence for marrying one's "father's sister, father's widow, wife's mother, daughter, wife's daughter, son's widow, sister, son's daughter, daughter's daughter, son's son's widow, daughter's son's widow, brother's daughter or sister's daughter, and for any woman to marry her father's brother, mother's brother, mother's husband, husband's father, son, husband's son" . . . and so on to the outermost twigs of the family tree.

Another stout blow was struck in defense of morality when an even tougher (and less frequently enforced) Sunday closing law was passed making it illegal to operate almost any kind of business on the Sabbath.

The solons did, however, approve gambling, if conducted by churches or recognized charities . . . a dispensation which has a modern ring to it.

A bill granting woman suffrage passed the house amid much falsetto cheering from the galleries, but, despite an impassioned oration by Elwood Evans, it didn't make it through the council. Murphy, who supported women's rights if they weren't too loud about them, took considerable pride in the fact that the measure was introduced by George Comegys, a prosperous Whitman county rancher, who had crossed the plains with him as a small boy in 1851.

Its failure to enfranchise women caused the council some minor embarrassment later in the session when the *Standard* pointed out that Governor Newell, in addition to having one daughter on the public payroll as his private secretary, had appointed the other to the post of territorial librarian, which was a public office and thus barred to women along with the right to vote. (An 1877 law had modified the all-male code slightly, making "women the equal of men in all matters affecting school interests, and no further"). Murphy pointed to the confir-

mation of Miss Newell to her post by the council, including the seven members who had voted against women's right to hold other than school offices, as *"one of the inconsistencies peculiar to the present assembly."*

The councilmen tried to push through as quietly as possible a bill permitting women to serve as librarians, but unexpected opposition arose and it was defeated twice. It was then left to cool for a time, while a number of its opponents were delegated to inspect the territorial penitentiary and hospital for the insane, about which scandalous rumors were being circulated.

In the absence of seven of the obstructionists, the bill was finally passed, and Governor Newell returned the kindness of the legislators by refraining from vetoing a single one of their bills.

Previous governors had been accustomed to rent office space for themselves in downtown Olympia, but the always financially embarrassed Newell took over the territorial library rooms in the capitol building to save that expense. When his daughter was out he frequently ambled from his inner sanctum to check out books for clients of the library, a charming example of territorial informality which Murphy found as amusing as the governor's use of hair and beard dye. When the seemingly endless session finally adjourned, the *Standard* described how *"the Governor from his seat in the Library room of the Capitol, like an eagle from his aerie, looks down with complacency on the lesser birds taking their flight."*

The capitol itself Murphy described as standing *"like some 'banquet hall deserted'. And this quotation calls to mind that the last banquet dispensed within its revered precincts was neither carved with a knife or eaten with a spoon."*

Murphy was doubtless referring to the traditional liquid refreshments of *sine die*. If there was any doubt in his readers' minds, he settled it with this additional comment:

"Nobody would have the rashness to assert that any of the honorable legislators were drunk when the session closed, but we can bring ample proof to show that many of them were not sober by a jug-full."

The town lost an institution in 1881 when Aunt Becky Howard had a stroke and died. Her obituary in all the local papers referred to her respectfully as Mrs. Rebecca Howard, as she would have wished, and the respectability she had gained during her years at the Pacific House is further attested to by the fact that her funeral was conducted from the Episcopal church.

Among the multifarious bills passed by the last laglisature was a third charter for the capital city. This one made Olympia a third class city, providing for a mayor and two councilmen from each of three wards. Mr. Ouimette, former mayor and moving spirit of the Olympia-Tenino railroad, had decided that the financial pastures were, after all, greener in Tacoma. With Villard at the head of the rejuvenated Northern Pacific, the gap in the track between Dakota and the Pacific was rapidly being filled and there was talk of a Cascades division over the mountains to tidewater on Commencement Bay. Mr. Ouimette sold out the stock of his Olympia store, moved to Tacoma at just the right time and subsequently cashed in on his foresight. He was succeeded as mayor by Dr. Ostrander.

Olympia was deeply hurt at Ouimette's desertion to the enemy and his name was removed from the locomotive of the narrow guage line, which had been renamed the Olympia and Chehalis Valley Railroad. It became just *Number 1* again.

MAY WAS A HELL OF A MONTH

In May the staid capital city was badly shaken up by one of the worst earthquakes in its brief history. The *Standard* classed it as *"major,"* reporting that *"buildings creaked like ships at sea, while the tall shade trees were violently agitated, their branches thrashing together in a manner produced by no other natural means."*

The panic into which the tremor threw the populace was attested to by the fact that *"half-clad women and crying children poured forth into the streets like bees from a hive, to be reinforced by stalwart men who showed scarcely less trepidation."*

It took something special to get an Olympia housewife of 1882 out on the street without all her clothes on.

The quake prompted Murphy to provide a bit of editorial advice as to how to cope with such situations. It is probably as valid today as it was then:

"Our advice to all is: cultivate amicable relation with your neighbors; keep the conscience clear and trust in Him who holds the waters of the Earth in the hollow of his hand, and who has promised that not a swallow shall fall to the ground without His knowledge, and all will be well in time and eternity.."

Since the town was made up almost entirely of low and limber wood frame buildings, the damage was limited to shattered nerves and crockery and toppled chimneys, but worse was yet to come.

At two o'clock on the morning of May 18, *"our people were."* as the *Standard* put it, *"aroused by the dread sound of the alarm bell, and even before clothing could be hastily donned, a ruddy glare indicated unmistakably the serious nature of the misfortune to occur to our beautiful town."*

The wood-burning cookstove of the Vienna Restaurant, located between Joseph Chilberg's grocery store and Cap Doane's oyster stand on Main street between 4th and 5th, had set fire to the wooden wall behind it. The fire was discovered by a night watchman, who first tried to put it out with a bucket of water. When that didn't work he dashed down Main street and up 4th to Columbia to sound the alarm.

By the time the old hand-pumper *Columbia* arrived on the scene the flames had spread through the restaurant and were rapidly attacking Doane's oyster stand, Chilberg's grocery, the post office and the drygoods store of Toklas and Goldstein on the northeast corner of 4th and Main.

Unfortunately, while the *Columbia* arrived on the scene in good time, the firemen had forgotten to bring along the cart which carried all the hose. It took them about 15 minutes to go back and get it, during which time the flames continued to spread and the rival Barnes Hook and Ladder men distinguished themselves by rescuing two young women and several children who had been asleep above Chilberg's store and hadn't awakened until the outside stairway was on fire.

When the gallant laddies of the Columbia Engine Company finally got it all together, they concentrated on the buildings at the north end of the block. The fire, in the meantime, crept less spectacularly south and soon broke forth in the Olympia Beer Hall, Robert Frost's hardware store, a stove and tinware emporium, Charles Talcott's jewelry, grocery and ice

CITIZEN PARTICIPATION was evident in this photo of the big fire at 4th and Main.

cream soda store and other buildings. A brisk wind sent flaming brands all over the downtown area, which had been drying out under several days of sunshine. It looked for a while as if the whole town was done for.

But, as the saying goes, it's an ill wind that blows nobody any good. A plump German named Phillip Hiltz proved the truth of that adage.

Hiltz had come to Olympia in 1870 in the retinue of Governor Salomon, and had stayed on to become the proprietor of a high-class family beer garden and restaurant. Having assured himself that his own premises were out of the immediate path of the fire, he observed that the printing plant of the weekly, *Courier* and a couple of other buildings owned by Clarence Bagley at the southeast corner of 5th and Washington were about the only structures in the entire square block area not yet on fire.

The enterprising Hiltz ambled down to the *Courier* office, where Bagley was frenziedly trying to move his printing equipment to safety. It seemed certain that his buildings would be the next to go.

Hiltz offered Bagley a riduculously small sum for his buildings. Bagley, convinced that they were going to be reduced to ashes in the next few minutes anyway, decided that he might as well salvage all he could. He paused from his labors long enough to sign the deed and hand it to Hiltz, whom he decided must have gone crazy from all the excitement.

The fat German was not crazy, however. No sooner was the deed in his pocket than he trotted off to where the men of the *columbia* were puffing at the hand-brakes. There, in stentorian tones, he annonced to firemen and volunteer citizens alike that if they saved the Bagley buildings he would open his beer garden to all for a full day of unlimited refreshments on the house.

The entire firefighting effort was immediately transferred to these three buildings and they alone survived the holocaust.

To make the whole thing more improbable, a heavy rain shower doused the town at this strategic moment, although the skies had been clear for days and remained so for some time thereafter.

As a result the remainder of the town was saved, along with Mr. Hiltz's new acquisitions.

And, for once in the history of Washington territory, a citizen made a profit at the expense of the public printer.

John Miller Murphy was somewhat ambivalent in his reaction to the big fire. While he viewed the sudden rain shower as an act of divine providence, proving that God was on Olympia's side, he also considered the fire something of a blessing, since it was likely to result in fireproof buildings for the business district and that long-awaited steam pumper to help keep them that way.

In this he was correct. The citizens were frightened badly enough to approve a fire protection bond issue and the city fathers eventually placed an order for a brand new Silsby steam fire engine.

Thus reassured, the burned-out property owners did, indeed, replace many of their former wooden buildings with structures of brick and stone. William Billings, although running for sheriff again, reopened his brickyard on the east side and began turning out 14,000 bricks a day. Among the rebuilders was Charles Talcott, who had come to town in 1872 with his entire stock of watches and jewelry in a satchel, which he packed up and took home with him every night for safekeeping. He had prospered by branching out into any area which looked profitable, including the town's first soda fountain, and he didn't stop making an honest dollar while his new brick building was being built. He erected a stand in front of the construction site and dispensed lemonade and soft drinks throughout the summer.

The entire press of the town, led by the *Transcript,* was united in its outrage at the water company, the pressure having been at its usual low point when it was needed. The company bowed to this barrage of indignation and sent for a new steam water pump, another move which was hailed by Murphy as a major step in the right direction.

"Hitherto," he commented scathingly, *"there has been nothing more uncertain under Heaven than when the water supply would serve you, and nothing more certain than that the bill would be presented promptly at the end of each month."*

TALCOTT'S brick building was one of the early non-wooden structures in Olympia. The seal of the state was designed here in 1889.

Despite all these forced improvements at the territorial capital, the Democratic congress turned down the second plea for statehood made by Washington's Republican Delegate Brents. The opposition claimed that Washington's 1880 census population of only 75,000 couldn't afford the burdens of statehood. It just wouldn't be good for them.

The citizens of Olympiá, having grown somewhat cynical after observing the activities of politicians at close quarters for nearly thirty years, suspected a less altruistic motive for the refusal.

The way Washingtonians were voting in those days, statehood for them would mean two new Republicans senators and a Republican congressman in Washington, D.C. And that could upset the whole precarious power structure in congress.

It wasn't the number of citizens that was keeping Washington territory from the sisterhood of states. It was the way those citizens were voting.

CHAPTER FIVE
The Fourth Decade
1883-1893

In the decade since 1873 the Pacific Northwest had recovered considerably from the Jay Cooke-inspired panic and subsequent nationwide depression. The long-delayed filling of the gap in the Northern Pacific's transcontinental line was bringing an influx of new settlers, by train rather than covered wagon. Since the Cascade division to Puget Sound was still four years in the future, many of the newcomers stayed in eastern Washington, although a good many reached Tacoma and Seattle via the Kalama branch and the steamboats of the Oregon Railway and Navigation company.

Few if any were diverted from the main stream of transportation to the narrow-gauge, bob-tailed Olympia-Tenino train. The maple-shaded territorial capital, preoccupied with hanging onto the seat of government, still a navigable seaport only at high tide and too moralistic to lure its share of loggers and millworkers away from the increasingly glamorous flesh pots of Seattle and Tacoma, failed to garner its share of the expanding population. In fact, a census taken by the county assessor in 1883 indicated that Thurston county's population had dropped by 520 since the previous year. There were loud complaints from civic boosters that the figures were inaccurate, but even the most indignant were unable to locate those 520 missing people.

Olympians were especially sensitive to their town's lagging position in the population race. The rapid growth of eastern Washington was reviving the effort to remove the capital to a more centrally located and dynamic town. The fact that statehood appeared to be inevitable in the near future made the prize more desirable than ever. Another major battle was shaping up and it was no time to be exhibiting signs of civic weakness.

UP BY THE BOOT-STRAPS

The city council did its best to make it look as if Olympia was growing, even if it wasn't. They invested $600 a year with the water company to install and maintain 10 fireplugs on the principal corners of the business district and it was generally agreed that they gave the town an increasingly metropolitan air. The improvement also provided an interesting variation from maple trees for the large numbers of wandering dogs who shared the streets and sidewalks with the milch cows.

The municipal government also embarked on the largest street project in history, grading east 4th street through Swantown to the foot of Ayer's hill. The surplus earth was used to fill in under the east end of the Swantown bridge, creating according to civic booster John Miller Murphy, *"a magnificent causeway."*

A number of householders along the route of the regrade were less enthusiastic than Murphy when they found their houses perched high above the new thoroughfare.

Captain Tom Wright, who was trying valiantly to run the old *Eliza Anderson* between Olympia and New Westminster, B.C., in opposition to Villard's OR&N was attempting to restore the old Main Street wharf to a condition of stability and extend it toward deep water as a terminus for his Olympia and Puget Sound Steamship company.

Captain Tom's efforts to again put Olympia on the international steamboat route were appreciated by the citizenry, but that steam calliope of the old *Anderson* got him into trouble, just as it had Captain Fleming at Victoria back in the 1860's.

The calliope had been exhumed and restored by Captain Tom, who felt it might still serve as a trade stimulant for his steamboat. When the engineer got it working on a quiet Sunday evening the skipper decided to favor the *Anderson's* home port with an impromptu concert. The resulting din, according to the *Standard, "woke up the welkin and forest for miles around."*

So enchanted was the captain with the powerful voice of his ancient steamboat that he kept the welkin and forest, as well as the town, wide awake until well into the night. Murphy, the lover of good music, was not enchanted at all.

"Like the practice of a new band," he commented sourly, *"it was prized chiefly for its novelty, some of the notes being sadly out of tune. It is suggested that Capt. Wright employ an organ-sharp the next time he comes whistling into our harbor."*

Reconstruction following the big fire of 1882 was still going on, with solid masonry buildings rising from the ashes. The *Standard* expressed the opinion that *"the magnificent new store of Toklas and Kaufman, the 'stone front' of L. Bettman's second store, the brick and iron hardware emporium of S. Williams, and Talcott's new brick building would do credit to any city."*

A second brickyard had been placed in operation on the east side of the bay near Gull Harbor and the local sawmills were straining to meet the demand for building material as lesser structures and new houses were constructed, partly as a result of better times and partly because the First National Bank of Olympia had taken over the pioneer brick bank of George Barnes and was extending somewhat more liberal credit.

Although after effects of the depression forced the local school directors to charge tuition until tax collections caught up with costs,* the Sisters of Charity were erecting a big frame building on upper Main street to house their Providence Academy for girls. It would when completed, wrote Murphy, *"be an architectural ornament to our city."* Also on the educational scene, the Puget Sound conference of the Methodist Episcopal church purchased the buildings of the Union Academy, which hadn't survived the depression. The Olympia Collegiate Institute was opened on the grounds above the bay on the east side of town, and for some years operated as a more prestigious institution of higher education than the territorial university.

FOR WHOM THE FIRE BELL TOLLS

The warm, dry weather of August and September brought new alarms of the fire bell and excursions by the volunteer fire companies. In late August the Carlton House was totally destroyed by a midnight blaze, creating a housing crisis for the upcoming legislature. The hotel's original proprietor had long since returned to the publishing business,* but its new owner, Mrs. L. M. Clark, wasted no time in beginning construction of a new hotel on the site of the old one. The Barnes Hook and Ladder Company was even less effective than usual during the Carlton House fire. Its rickety ladders had been stored in the town pound for safekeeping and nobody could find the key.

In mid-September the wooden office of Surveyor-General McMicken caught on fire. The new steam pumper hadn't been ordered yet, so the old *Columbia* responded as fast as the legs of her crew would take her.

---

*Many property owners were years in arrears in their tax payments and were never able to bail themselves out. The fairgrounds and buildings were sold to George Barnes on a $4,000 tax lien, while a Mr. Ford purchased the original depot building of the Olympia-Tenino line for $99.25 in delinquent taxes. He converted it to a hay barn.

---

*Mr. Carlton moved to California and established a newspaper. As the result of the customary feud with a rival editor, he shot and killed his opponent and went to jail for a while.

The wooden building, built hastily to replace the old *Pioneer and Democrat* office which had collapsed under the last big snow, was located on Main street between 7th and 8th. The nearest cistern was at 5th, and the closest of the town's new fire plugs even further away. The fire department didn't have enough hose to reach the full two blocks, so it concentrated on saving General McKenny's residence to the north of the burning building. A bucket brigade was formed to fight the blaze in the office building and the Unitarian church next to it, which soon caught fire as well. Both buildings were destroyed, although most of the surveyor-general's records and the church furnishings were saved.

Meanwhile, back at General McKenny's smouldering residence, the crew of the *Columbia* were horrified, after 15 minutes of vigorous pumping, to find that they had pumped the reservoir dry.

In those days the western arm of the bay lapped the western edge of Main street when the tide was in, as it fortunately was at the time of the fire. The pumper was hastily wheeled down to the beach and the general's home was saturated with salt water and a few startled smelt. It thus survived this latest conflagration.

Murphy, having carried on the agitation for a steam fire engine for years, now reversed his course, pointing out that, without an adequate supply of water, no pumper was much good. Also, he had decided, a hand-pumper could get into operation as soon as it arrived on the scene of a fire, whereas it took some time to get up steam in a more modern rig. Besides, he wrote, *"without any water as at the last two fires after twenty minutes of pumping, a squirt-gun would be quite as effective as either."*

To be as efficient as the *Columbia,* he insisted, a steamer would require a paid engineer and a constant head of steam. *"Is it not plain that we have bitten off more than we can chew?"* he wondered editorially.

Murphy's sudden reversal of course on the steam fire engine question may have been an instinctive reaction to the fact that the *Transcript* and *Courier* had taken up the cry in favor of it and had been poking editorial fun at the old-fashioned *Columbia* and her brawny crew. In addition to being opposed to almost everything Bagley and Gunn favored, Murphy was loyal to his old engine company and nostalgically fond of the *Columbia.*

The city council responded to the *Standard's* cautiously negative advice by immediately placing the order for a 5th class Silsby rotary steam pumper at a factory cost of $4,500. By the time the freight, commission, hose, boiler heater and other accessories were paid for, a lot on Columbia street purchased and a new fire station built, the town was out nearly $10,000 and there were numerous taxpayers who felt that Murphy had been right.

The Silsby steamer eventually justified its cost, if for no other reason than that it did, indeed, contribute toward the retention of the state capital, as will be shown later in this chapter.

Its arrival precipitated a bitter controversy between the Columbia Engine company and Barnes Hook and Ladder company over which should be given the prestige and glory of operating this gleaming status symbol. From its brightly polished brass smokestack to its ornamental silver wheels, the Silsby was a thing of beauty and the firemen were prepared to fight for its possession.

The city fathers solved the dilemma by authorizing an entirely new fire company, Olympia No. 2, to take charge of the steamer. A paid engineer was hired to get up steam and tend the complicated array of dials and valves, but this exhausted the available fire protection funds and it was impossible to provide a team of horses to pull the heavy rig to the scene of action. Instead, local teamsters were offered a five dollar reward for being first to hitch up to the Silsby when the fire alarm was sounded.

Thereafter the usual confusion attendant upon the sounding of the bell was compounded by teamsters lashing their horses and competing drivers through the muddy or dusty streets like Roman chariot drivers in a life-or-death race. If the race resulted in a tie by two or more prospective drivers, they sometimes settled it with their fists at the firehouse door.

Such delays, plus the time involved in getting up steam, resulted in frequent vindication for Murphy and the *Columbia,* with the old hand-pumper from Seneca Falls often getting streams of water on fires five or ten minutes sooner than the steamer.

WOMEN ARE LIBERATED . . . BRIEFLY

Early in October the ninth biennial session of the territorial legislature assembled. Although the Republican majority was smaller than it had been in years . . . 13 to 11 in the house and eight to four in the council . . . the *Standard* greeted it with little enthusiasm. When Bagley and the *Courier* pronounced it, even before it convened, *"superior to any that has preceded it,"* Murphy snorted editorially that the public printer undoubtedly had *"dull axes to grind."* He did concede one improvement over past legislatures. It contained many new faces in place of the "old settlers," as he termed the long-time politicians.

Although Republicans Sewall Truax of Walla Walla and E. C. Ferguson of Snohomish were elected president of the council and speaker of the house respectively, the Democrats carried enough weight in the house to be accorded a number of patronage jobs, with the result that a few deserving party members got on the payroll after years of famine. One of them was Hillory Butler, now 58 years of age and a prosperous landlord of Seattle, who finally made it as sergeant at arms, thus regaining the dignity that had been lost to him as the legislature's first page.

The marked increase in the population of the territory now justified the creation of new counties, and this session created more of them than any other in history. Douglas and Lincoln were carved from Spokane. Others established in 1883 were Asotin, Skagit, Adams, Franklin and Kittitas.

Vancouver, Yakima, Chehalis, Seattle and Ainsworth* were provided with charters as full-fledged cities, Tumwater became an incorporated town and the name of Centerville was officially changed to Centralia.

But the 1883 session is best remembered as the one which gave equal suffrage to the women of Washington territory.

The amendment to section 3050, chapter 238, Washington Code, provided that "wherever the word 'his' occurs in the chapter aforesaid, it

---

*The long-since vanished city of Ainsworth, on the north bank of the Snake river just above the Columbia, was created when the transcontinental line of the Northern Pacific made this its junction point with the Oregon Railway and Navigation line to Portland.

---

shall be construed to mean 'his' or 'her' as the case may be."

The amendment passed the house of representatives with surprisingly little opposition on October 8 and Speaker Ferguson was directed to send congratulations to the American Female Suffrage Association, "now in session in Brooklyn, New York."

The council, like its successor, the state senate, was more conservative and set in its ways than the house, and the measure faced strong opposition there. Abigail Scott Duniway, sensing a potential victory at last, marshaled her cohorts at Olympia for an unprecedented lobbying effort. The twelve councilmen were coerced, charmed, flattered and threatened throughout their waking hours. Eventually even those who insisted they were going to vote against it agreed not to speak against it on the floor.

As a result, one of the most controversial measures ever to confront the Washington legislature was acted upon amid a complete lack of verbiage.

It passed the council seven to five and was quickly signed by the obliging Governor Newell.

The forces of women's liberation immediately staged a grand jubilee at Columbia hall. There was standing room only, according to the *Standard.*

The ninth biennial session also produced one of the legendary practical jokes in legislative history.

Judge J. R. Lewis of Seattle, a chivalrous, opinionated and courtly member of the house of representatives, was one of the most eloquent of the defenders of feminine rights. When the overwhelmingly favorable vote was taken in alphabetical order, led by J. W. Arrasmith of Whitman and Adams, Judge Lewis was unable to restrain his enthusiasm and insisted on making a long congratulatory speech after the fact.

"Would that my name were Arrasmith," he enthused in the course of his oration, "that mine might be the honor of casting the first vote for the enfranchisement of the fair womanhood of our territory."

Then, overcome by emotion, he departed from the chambers.

His colleagues immediately introduced and passed a bill changing his name to J. W.

Arrasmith. They sent it to the council and that august body gave it priority attention.

When a friend of Judge Lewis located him and told him what was going on the judge allowed as how it was all just a joke. The boys were trying to "get his goat," but he would just ignore the foolishness.

"You better *not* ignore it, judge," his friend warned. "When I left the capitol it was on third reading in the council."

Horrified, the judge sped up the hill and burst into the council chambers.

"Sorry," President Truax informed him solumnly. "We passed it and sent it to the governor to sign."

Poor Lewis whirled, dashed up to the territorial library rooms and found Governor Newell checking out a book to a customer. Sweating profusely, the unfortunate legislator implored the chief executive not to sign the bill.

"Sorry, judge," said the kindly governor. "They told me you *wanted* your name changed to Arrasmith. I signed it immediately as a favor to you, and I'm afraid your legal name is now J. W. Arrasmith."

It was several days before the unhappy Lewis was informed that the whole thing had, indeed, been a joke. Much relieved, he in turn conceded that the elaborate hoax had been successful. The boys had "gotten his goat."

The newly enfranchised women of Olympia turned out in considerable force at the January, 1884, municipal election in Olympia, inaugurating the new year with a blow for civic purity and badly shaking up the town's business establishment.

THE LADIES MAKE WAVES

That good, gray community leader George Barnes was the Republican candidate for mayor, opposed by a councilman, J. S. Dobbins, on the "Peoples' Ticket." Although Dobbins had not achieved much of a record as an anti-saloon reformer on the council, he was smart enough to sniff the changing winds of feminized politics and loudly proclaimed his purity, abstinence and church membership. Barnes, although not a drinking man, did not parade his virtue and, like many of the territorial legislators, classed himself as a "liberal" in regard to church affiliation . . . which meant he didn't belong to one.

As a result of Dobbins' self-proclaimed piety and promises to put the saloons out of business if elected, he received the endorsement of the local WCTU chapter. Clarence Bagley, running for 2nd ward councilman, followed in Dobbins' tracks and likewise received the accolade of the lady temperance crusaders although, according to Murphy, Bagley "frequented saloons," while his opponent, a Mr. Rawson, was a teetotaler although a follower of the free-thinking Robert Ingersoll.

When enough lady voters turned out to offset the usual "wagon-load" of male voters hauled to the polls by the saloon-keepers, making Dobbins and Bagley victorious, Murphy lost much of his enthusiasm for woman suffrage.

He proclaimed in the *Standard* that the town's fair electorate had shown they could be taken in by any candidate who put on a properly "goody-goody" campaign and walked around with a Bible in his hand; that Barnes and Rawson hadn't been blacklisted because they favored Demon Rum, but because they didn't belong to any of the town's many Protestant churches; in short, that there was more Christian than Temperance in the selection-making process of the Women's Christian Temperance Union. Finally, he predicted, the saloon business would go on just as it always had.

In the latter opinion, at least, he was correct. The new administration did raise the price of saloon licenses from $300 to $500 a year, but thoughtfully arranged the dates so that all proprietors could buy licenses for another year at the old price. By then there would have been another annual city election.

THE SOUNDS OF PROGRESS

In lieu of demolishing the saloons, the new town fathers set out on a compulsive campaign to regrade the streets. As soon as the soggy ground dried out sufficiently in the spring they put a crew of pick and shovel men to start hacking away at the bluff west of Long bridge in an effort to extend 4th street by a negotiable grade to Marshville, or West Olympia as it was now called. In the past year the population of that area had quadrupled . . . to about 200 . . . and it had its own school, a brickyard and a logging camp. The dirt and clay removed by the workmen was hauled away to fill in the series of dips and gulleys in Washington street, which had been a favorite locale for raft regattas among small boys during the rainy seasons.

A contractor was hired to grade various streets east of the Swantown bridge and he, in turn, hired a crew of 30 Chinese laborers to do the work at the lowest possible wages. Times had improved somewhat, but there were still lots of white Anglo-Saxon protestants out of work and the influx of cheap Chinese labor was not viewed favorably. The *Standard* made it perfectly clear whose fault it was:

"At one time it looked as if the heathen crew would be mobbed, but better counsels prevailed. The fact is that the 'City' Council in this matter, as almost everything else, blundered, and the sequel was a natural result."

The completion of the Northern Pacific, largely built by Chinese labor, had released thousands of these hardworking and frugal people on the general labor market and there was increasing hostility toward them all across the Pacific Northwest. The minor episode at Olympia would soon be magnified into riots and forced expulsion of the Chinese in other Puget Sound towns.

A number of citizens were further incensed when the grading project on Cherry street left the houses on one side high in the air and those on the other well below street level. Many of the fine old shade trees were destroyed by the grading operations also, a pattern which was to be followed in future years until the town lost much of its original placid charm.

Outrage became general among the tax-payers by the end of the year when it was discovered that the "improvements" had used up all the funds in the treasury and the town was nearly $10,000 in debt.

The tranquility of the capital city was further shattered by more locomotive and steamboat whistles as the propeller steamer *Wildwood* entered into competition with the O R & N steamer *Emma Hayward* and the smaller sternwheelers *Zephyr* and *Messenger* on the Seattle-Tacoma run, and loggers Ike Ellis and Ben Turner completed short logging railroads terminating at log-dumps on the bay. Ellis ran his line three miles from the direction of Plum's Station to the headwaters of the east waterway at Moxlie creek . . . the principal source of the town's water supply. Turner's four-mile line ran from Black lake to a dump on

the west waterway. As the dinky logging locomotives converged on the town from both sides their shrill shrieks mingled with those of the steamboats, the sawmills, the water pipe works and the "big" new engine just acquired to haul the ever-8ncreasing loads of logs on the Olympia-Tenino narrow-gauge.

The heavier loads also forced the railroad directors to abandon the old trestle between Tumwater and Olympia and relocate the right of way on the shore as originally planned a decade earlier. The depot was moved north to a small cove on the opposite side of Long bridge.

The steam calliope of the old *Anderson* was heard no more, however, for Captain Tom Wright failed to prosper in his war against the Oregon Railway and Navigation Company. The big corporation had placed the faster sidewheeler *Geo. E. Starr* on the *Anderson's* route to race ahead and garner her passengers and freight at cut rates, but the tough old pioneer caught the *Starr* in the fog and butted the newer boat half to pieces. At this point the collector of customs was prevailed upon to arrest Captain Tom and impound the *Anderson* on a charge of smuggling Chinese from Canada. The resulting litigation bankrupted Wright, leaving the long-awaited "long wharf" in limbo and the *Anderson* on the mudflats, from which she was resurrected years later to make a final and fatal voyage to Alaska during the Klondike gold rush of 1898.

By 1884 the deeper bellow of the coastwise San Francisco steamers was no longer heard on Budd Inlet. The old firm of Goodall and Perkins had become the PACIFIC Coast Steamship Company. Stiff competition with the newly-arrived railroads put an end to leisurely schedules and meandering voyages to the less profitable Puget Sound ports. Freight and passengers for Olympia were transferred at Seattle or Tacoma to the big OR&N sternwheeler *Emma Hayward*.

Along with the expensive and controversial street improvements on shore, the local business men and property owners continued to replace the pioneer wood frame buildings of downtown Olympia with ornate Victorian structures of brick and stone, some with the added sophistication of fancy cast-iron false fronts. The two-story Burmeister building at 3rd and Main was described by the *Standard* as *"the finest building in the territory,"* while the Horr Block, a little further south on Main street was also considered to be *"a splendid addition to our business community."* A second franchise was granted . . . to the Olympia Gas and Electric Company . . . to manufacture and distribute hydrogen gas and "electrical fluid." The projectors of the new enterprise wisely decided that the citizens of the sleepy territorial capital weren't quite ready for such a newfangled lighting source as electricity. They concluded that the natives should be broken in gently, and concentrated on the gas plant first. A large structure, complete with elevated storage tank, was constructed on the east side between 5th and 6th streets and gas mains were shipped up from San Francisco.

All this progress took further toll of the maple trees. The excavations for the gas mains uprooted some, while the proprietors of the new masonry business blocks didn't want their architectural glories hidden. They hacked down the trees to give the citizens a better view of their storefronts.

Long bridge had again fallen victim to the omnivorous marine borers and was again rebuilt. No sooner was the job completed than wooden business structures were erected along both sides, supported on piling and fronting on the thoroughfare. This gave the structure the appearance of a medieval bridge and made it almost impossible for strangers to find it. It had something in common with its predecessors, however. It was still almost impossible to open the draw-span.

A new brewery was built on the east side, Isaac Wood having closed his legendary 5th and Columbia establishment when the city and territory imposed various taxes and record-keeping requirements on the brewing industry. That rugged individualist simply said, "To hell with it," and went back to farming. The new brewery was located over one of the town's finest springs, but the product never achieved the popularity of the old cream lager made with the brackish water of the shallow downtown well. The new enterprise failed to flourish and was soon closed.

To help the wave of construction retain its momentum . . . at a highly profitable rate of interest . . . the Olympia Building and Loan Association was organized; the only 19th century financial institution to survive to the present day.

THE WAR OF WORDS CONTINUES

Another hopeful new daily paper, the *Daily Critic,* had appeared on the Olympia jour-nalistic scene, published by W. A. Roberts and F. A. Dunham. Murphy of the *Standard* wasted no time in entering into a running battle with the newcomer, along with the *Transcript* and *Courier.* When Mr. Roberts ventured to observe that the territorial capital could stand a good cleaning, Murphy put him properly in his place:

"The Critic *says the inside of the Capitol needs cleaning. Why, pray tell us? It stands empty nearly two years at a time, is never visited by our towns-people and is not an object of special inquiry to tourists. This is not required by the owls and bats which are now its only tenants."*

Bagley of the *Courier* incurred the greater wrath of the *Standard* when he fell victim to the civic boosterism of Tacoma, which was trying to get the name of majestic Mt. Rainier changed to Mt. Tacoma. Murphy felt that capital punishment for the *Courier* was the only proper penalty:

"The Courier *refers to an ascent of 'Mt. Tacoma.' Any newspaper outside the terminal city which would tolerate such a name for our grand old Rainier ought to die a natural death, and the sooner the better!"*

On July 4, 1884, the telegraph announced the appointment of Watson C. Squire to succeed Governor Newell, whose term had expired. Squire, the 12th territorial governor, was appointed in the last year of the term of Republican President Chester A. Arthur. Except for Wallace and Ferry he was the only chief executive to be appointed from among the citizens of the territory. Loud and repeated howling from the territories regarding the carpetbag politicians inflicted upon them from Washington, D.C., had resulted in the last Republican convention adopting a platform urging the appointment of home-grown politicians whenever possible. If President Arthur accomplished nothing else to achieve a place in history, he should be honored as perhaps the only president to remember the party platform three years after his election.

Squire, who was 46 at the time of his appointment, was a native of New York, a lawyer and educator who rose to the rank of colonel during the civil war. At the end of the war he went to work for the Remington Arms Company, wisely married the granddaughter of its founder, and in due time became its treasurer, secretary and manager. As an officer of the company he signed the first contract for the manufacture of typewriters in the United

States. In 1876 he invested in Seattle property and moved west to become a leading capitalist of that enterprising city.

Dr. Newell was not immediately forced to return to the unprofitable practice of medicine. He was appointed United States Indian inspector until 1886, after which he served for a time as health officer for the city of Olympia before getting an appointment in 1898 as resident physician at the state Veterans' home.

Governor Squire was soon to face major problems of violence and wholesale insurrection, which he dealt with in a steadfast and courageous manner, establishing a reputation for himself as one of the more competent of the territorial governors.

In the November election of 1884, the faith of John Miller Murphy in female voters was somewhat restored when Democrat Grover Cleveland carried Olympia and the nation, despite the fact that 312 women voted in the Olympia precinct. That Cleveland kept Republican Governor Squire in office for three years after his inauguration . . . and that Murphy didn't complain much about it . . . is further indication that he performed his duties admirably.

The seemingly inevitable boom and bust cycle of 19th century economics caught up with Olympia in 1885. Over-optimism had prevailed as the transcontinental railroad reached the Northwest. Government and private enterprise alike had, as Murphy would say, "bitten off more than they could chew." Credit was over-extended, taxes had risen again to the inflated valuations set by land speculators and jobs were scarce. For those that were available it was necessary to compete with the Chinese, who would work longer, harder and for less pay than anyone else.

At the January election the voters of Olympia turned out Mayor Dobbins, Councilman Bagley and all the rest of the city administration in retaliation for having raised their taxes and messed up their front yards with the street-grading operations. A. A. Phillips, a solid business candidate, was elected mayor. He and the council immediately reduced the saloon license fee back to $300.

A Taxpayers' Protective Association was formed, its membership limited to those who owned property valued at $1,000 or more, and met regularly to make speeches to each other about the awful burden they were forced to

WATSON C. SQUIRE
1884–1887

bear and write angry letters to the city council and the newspapers. George Barnes was president; Francis Henry treasurer. The lawyers of the town also formed a protective association of their own known as the Olympia Bar Association.

The organizational fever extended to the women, nine of whom met at the Edmund Sylvester home on Main street . . . the first of the fine mansions to be built by the pioneers . . . and formed the first Women's Club on the Pacific coast, the primary purpose being "literary pursuits and home improvement."

The new city council stopped letting contracts to grade the streets, but some of the previous contracts carried over into 1885, causing a continuation of the civic squabbling. The lowering of the grade on 8th street between Main and Washington caused the Masonic Temple to show signs of collapsing and it had to be moved to the center of the block. The gas company wrought similar havoc with citizens' property and the town's shade trees and the

Sylvester house, built by the town's founder to replace his original log cabin, served in later years as communal home for unemployed legislators.

sounds of contention and strife assaulted the tranquility of the capital city.

What little tranquility that had existed in the town's newspaper fraternity was likewise disturbed by major upheavals in the established media. Clarence Bagley had been making something of a career out of selling the *Courier* to unsuspecting publishers by accepting any funds they had as a down payment. When they discovered the paper couldn't provide both a living to them and monthly payments to Bagley, they gave up, gave the key back and Bagley sold it to the next comer. In 1885 one Thomas H. Cavanaugh bought it, kept it and renamed it the *Partisan,* carrying on the good fight for the Republican office-holders. In this he was assisted by P. P. Carroll, who started the *Republican.* Cavanaugh proved the better propagandist, and the *Republican* suspended publication after a year's losing struggle. The death of E. T. Gunn during the year resulted in the suspension of Murphy's old antagonist, the *Transcript,* but he was left with plenty of targets for his editorial shafts.

UNDER A BLACK CLOUD

Even as Henry Villard drove the golden spike linking the transcontinental rails of the Northern Pacific, he and the railroad were in deep financial trouble. The stock market was falling again, with Northern Pacific shares leading the way. Villard was forced out and the succeeding company management repudiated his policy of fairness to communities other than Portland and Tacoma. Even loyal Tacomans became somewhat disenchanted when the hook-up was made with the OR & N at Ainsworth, making Portland the western terminus and leaving the Kalama-Tacoma section a mere branch line, separated from the cross-country trackage by the broad Columbia River.

Bitterness against the Northern Pacific reached the boiling point and became the main political issue in the territory. Although another Republican legislature was elected for the 1885 session, a Democrat, Charles S. Voorhees, won the seat as congressional delegate on an anti-railroad campaign.

A map of the territory was prepared by the anit-railroad partisans. Labelled "Under a Black Cloud," it showed the huge areas . . . nearly half of all the available land in the territory . . . claimed by the railroad under its very liberal grant from the federal government. Hundreds of the maps were sent to the national political conventions and thousands more were circulated within the territory. Increasingly vociferous demands were made that the railroad either make good its contract and extend the main line to Puget Sound, or forfeit its granted lands from the Columbia to the Sound.

Appalled by this possibility, the new directors began a leisurely construction of the long-awaited Cascade division by way of Stampede Pass.

By the time the tenth biennial session of the legislature convened in December, 1885, it had an even more bitter controversy on its hands; one which would result in the most serious threat to the peace and good order of the territory since the Indian wars.

THE CHINESE MUST GO!

The long smouldering hostility of the working people toward the highly competitive Chinese exploded into violence on the night of September 7, 1885, when five white men and two Indians* climbed the fence of Wold brothers ranch in the Squawk (Sammamish) Valley of King county and began firing into the tents in which 37 Chinese hop pickers were sleeping. Three of the Chinese were killed, three were wounded and the survivors beat a hasty retreat from the valley.

Four days later the white employees of the Coal Creek mine in King county attacked the Chinese quarters there and burned them to the ground. On November 3 a blast of mill whistles in Tacoma summoned a mob of several hundred men. The Chinese section of the town was raided and about two hundred of the oc-

---

*The annual hop picking season was a traditional opportunity for the Indians to earn substantial wages as migratory farm workers, and was the chief source of cash income for many of them. Their bitterness against the Chinese equalled or exceeded that of the white workers.

cupants, including women, children and sick old people, were marched to a railroad siding outside the town and left there in the cold rain.

At Olympia, Governor Squire received word of the forced exodus and began firing off telegrams to Sheriff Lewis Byrd of Pierce county, offering to send troops if he couldn't keep order. The sheriff replied that all but a few of the Chinese had already been removed beyond the city limits, that no lives had been lost, no property destroyed and that it would be impossible for federal troops to arrive in time to prevent the final clean-up the next day.

On November 4 the governor issued a proclamation calling upon the sheriffs to preserve the peace and calling upon the people to "array yourselves on the side of the law."

The Tacoma mob responded by running the remaining Chinese out of town and setting fire to their homes and stores.

The violence was spreading to Seattle, and on November 8 troops were sent there from Fort Vancouver. The soldiers diverted themselves by beating and further terrorizing the Chinese residents of Seattle, in addition to shaking them down for "protection." In Tacoma the maYor and much of the business establishment supported the attacks on the Chinese, but the civic leaders of Seattle heeded Governor Squire and "arrayed themselves on the side of the law." Some of them suggested that the citizens might have to mobilize to protect the Chinese from the troops.

Members of the Seattle anti-Chinese forces apparently felt the army was doing their work for them and things quieted down to such an extent that the troops were returned to Fort Vancouver on November 17.

With the convening of the legislature in December, a resolution was passed commending Governor Squire for his handling of the situation. The legislators felt that continued insurrection and mob violence would endanger the efforts to achieve statehood and the political plums which would come with it.

As an alternative to the kind of private enterprise tactics employed by the King and Pierce county mobs, a strong effort was made to run the Chinese out of the territory by legal means. Bills passed the house of representatives denying ownership of lands to aliens ineligible for citizenship and providing that land so held would escheat to the territorial school fund upon the death of the owner;

giving cities and towns the authority to regulate laundries; prohibiting the employment of Chinese on any public works, and their employment by private industry after July 1, 1886.

The council rejected all but the first of these and the anti-Chinese forces, angered at the failure of the legislature to solve their problem for them, resumed their agitation in Seattle.

The legislature was also much preoccupied with the continuing story of the capital location. Governor Squire had painstakingly compiled a complete and glowing report on the territory's flora, fauna, natural resources and potential greatness. His facts and figures were accurate and impressive (the secretary of the interior called it the best report ever made by a territorial governor) and it was widely circulated by both the federal government and the Northern Pacific. It claimed that the population of 75,000 shown by the 1880 census had at least doubled and it strengthened the conviction that congress couldn't delay statehood much longer.

With the increased prospect of statehood the fight for the capital took on new vigor. Eastern Washington was particularly anxious to have the seat of government moved. Olympia was too far away and too difficult to get to. It was argued that the territorial capitol building was about ready to fall down and that a new state capitol should be built in a new location.

Yakima, now on the right of way of the Northern Pacific's Cascade divison and feeling its oats, made a strong bid, placing a deed to 50 acres of land in escrow and offering $12,000 to relocate the capital there. But neighboring Ellensburg had also heard the "snort of the iron horse" and it made an equally determined bid. The eastern Washington forces were divided and the two ambitious towns killed each other off. Olympia kept the capital, but its grasp appeared to be weakening. Almost everybody agreed it should be moved; they just couldn't agree on where it should be moved *to*.

The women of the territory had helped to elect the members of the 1885 legislature and they responded by passing a local option law which permitted voters in the various towns and rural precincts to decide whether or not the sale of liquor would be permitted. They thoughtfully included so many loopholes that any thirsty citizen would be assured of a source of supply in any event, which was a waste of time as the territorial supreme court quickly declared it unconstitutional anyway. Further social reform legislation included authorization for a territorial penitentiary at Walla Walla to replace the infamous private prison at Seatco, and appropriations for a permanent hospital building for the insane to replace the old wooden barracks of Fort Steilacoom.

There was no argument over the appointment of Secretary Owings of Thomas Cavanaugh to replace Bagley as public printer by right of inheritance, Cavanaugh having purchased Bagley's Republican newspaper. Not even the *Washington Standard* bothered to comment, and Cavanaugh remained as the last of the territorial printers.

Three days after the legislature adjourned, the anti-Chinese forces in Seattle set out to run the Oriental population out of town. Mayor Yesler called out the two companies of local militia, but confided to governor Squire that he didn't think the mob could be controlled. Most of the Chinese were terrified and anxious to leave town voluntarily. A collection was taken up to pay their steerage fares to San Francisco on the *Queen of the Pacific,* but there was room for only 212. When the militia tried to escort the remaining hundred back to Chinatown the mob rushed them. The militia fired, killing one of the ringleaders. The other company came up from the waterfront to reinforce the first and the mob was dispersed. The federal troops requested by Governor Squire soon arrived on the scene, most of the remaining Chinese departed on the next San Francisco steamer, and martial law was revoked on February 22. The furor which followed Squire's declaration of martial law for a time promised to rival that of Stevens 30 years earlier.

Seattle civic boosters . . . and subsequent historians . . . proclaimed loudly that law and order had prevailed there, although the Chinese, whose only crimes were working hard, living frugally and looking different, lost almost everything they owned, while none of the arrested leaders of the mobs were ever convicted.

A number of Chinese from Seattle and Tacoma chose to escape to Olympia, which had a reputation for greater tolerance and devotion to law and order than most of the frontier communities.* The capital city already had a Chinese population of more than 200, and the new arrivals were not welcomed by a major segment of the white and Indian population.

On the morning of February 8 some thirty of the more militant gathered for the avowed purpose of driving the Chinese out of Olympia. This time there was no nonsense on the part of the civil authorities. A force of 150 citizen deputies was sworn in by Sheriff Billings and organized as a military company to guard the rights and property of the local Chinese. They remained on duty for several weeks and there was no violence of any kind. Five of the mob leaders were arrested, tried and sentenced to six months in prison plus fines of $500 each and court costs.

In Seattle, 15 persons were indicted after the 1885 disturbances, charged with conspiracy to deprive the Chinese of the equal protection of the law. These, along with a number of the ringleaders of the 1886 riot, were all declared perfectly innocent by juries of their peers.

And far away in France, the artist Bartholdi embarked for New York to superintend the erection of the Statue of Liberty with its inspiring message of welcome to the poor and huddled masses of the world.

Washington's bid for statehood, presented this time by Senator Dolph of Oregon, was finally passed by congress in 1886. It called for the annexation of the three Idaho panhandle counties, which had been approved by the legislatures of both Washington and Idaho and overwhelmingly favored by the residents of the three counties involved. (The vote was 1,216 to seven).

Grover Cleveland, the Democratic president, looking toward a second term and not entranced by the prospect of a new batch of presumably Republican presidential electors from a new state of Washington, quietly did the measure in by means of a "pocket veto". It was pointed out by the politically knowledgeable that final approval would certainly be forthcoming as soon as Cleveland either

secured his second term or was defeated by a Republican. Presidents were limited to two terms in those days, so he would have nothing to lose by signing an admission bill for Washington.

This made Olympia's civic leaders nervous, for there was increasing truth in the charges of those who wanted to move the capital that the one-time metropolis of the territory had degenerated to a backwater village well off the established lines of transportation.

YOU CAN'T GET THERE FROM HERE

The San Francisco steamers had long since stopped calling at the old Brown's wharf, the *Standard* gloomily conceding that *"our once lively Westside wharf has at last succumbed to the humble service of being a wooding and watering station for passing steamers."*

With the reorganization of the Northern Pacific, the big sternwheeler *Emma Hayward* had been withdrawn to the Seattle-Tacoma route and the *Zephyr* had gone with her. The *Otter* no longer shuttled passengers from the west side wharf to Percival's dock. She was sold and became a floating general store, jobbing around the upper Sound selling or trading for her wares. Among her ports of call was Oyster Bay where, it was bitterly charged by the Olympia Oyster Company, the workers swapped the company's oysters for red-eye whiskey and other goodies from the *Otter's* cargo.

The abandoned remains of the old Main street wharf, the departure point of the legendary *Eliza Anderson,* were sold at auction by the sheriff for a few dollars in back taxes, which the bankrupt Captain Tom Wright couldn't pay, and purchased by the First National Bank.

The maritime trade of the capital city was at a low ebb, and civic leaders were delighted when an enterprising steamboat man named Z. J. Hatch arrived on the scene with the fast and fancy propeller *Fleetwood,* which had come around from the Columbia river to run on Puget Sound. She had been built for the Portland-Astoria route and she ran the paddlewheels off the big OR & N boats with which she competed. She did so well, in fact, that her owner had to build an even bigger and faster boat, the *Telephone,* to replace her on the Columbia.

---

*The Tacoma *News,* in October, 1885, noted that *"This morning 13 Chinamen from the establishment of Yee Lee & Co., embarked on the steamer Messenger with their baggage for Olympia, where they say, 'that white man, him no killee Chinaman'."*

STEAMER FLEETWOOD.

FAST TIME
—FOR—

Seattle, Tacoma, Steilacoom, McNeil's Island, Puget City and Olympia.

SUMMER TIME TABLE.
—GOING—

Leave OLYMPIA, daily except Monday,			6.00 a. m.
Leave PUGET CITY, daily except Monday,			7.00 a. m.
Leave STEILACOOM, " " "			8.00 a. m.
Arrive TACOMA, " " "			9.30 a. m.
Leave TACOMA, " " "			10.00 a. m.
Arrive SEATTLE, " " "			12.00 m.

—RETURNING—

Leave SEATTLE, daily except Monday,			1.00 p. m.
Arrive TACOMA, " " "			3.00 p. m.
Leave TACOMA, " " "			3.30 p. m.
Leave STEILACOOM, " " "			4.15 p. m.
Leave PUGET CITY, " " "			5.15 p. m.
Arrive Olympia, " " "			7.00 p. m.

LANDINGS—Seattle, Yesler's Wharf; Tacoma, N. P. R. R. Wharf; Olympia, Horr's Wharf.

ONLY BOAT MAKING THE ROUND TRIP ON SUNDAYS.
MEALS ON BOARD.

Z. J. HATCH, President.

The *Fleetwood* was slim and fine-lined, and her high-pressure compound engine drove her plenty fast enough to make a daily round trip between Olympia and Seattle with stops at Steilacoom, McNeil Island and other outports along the way. Her loyal Olympia passengers were especially delighted when she would catch up with the big *Emma Hayward* between Tacoma and Seattle and leave the OR & N packet rolling in her wake.

THOSE DAMNED MUDFLATS

The coming of the *Fleetwood* was a step in the right direction, but much more remained to be done. For years there had been heated arguments among the movers and doers of the town as to whether the mudflat problem could best be solved by building the much-discussed "long wharf" to deep water, or by dredging the mud from the bay and placing it behind bulkheads to extend the limited downtown area. In 1886 steps were taken in both directions.

The Main street wharf was purchased from the bank by the city fathers for $150 as the starting-point for the mile-long pier to relatively deep water, but the dredging advocates kept insisting it would be better to dredge a channel from the existing dock than to extend the dock itself.

Later in the year the council contracted with the Oregon Improvement company to bring its dredge *Umatilla* to Budd Inlet to clear a 100-foot channel, twelve feet deep at low tide, to a point one mile below the foot of Main street. The company estimated the job could be done in three days at the rate of $400 a day.

Another round of civic bickering set in at this point over whether the channel shouldn't be dredged further west, from Percival's dock, which seemed less likely to fall into the bay than the Main street wharf. In desperation, the council called for a vote of the people, and the Main street channel was approved. The *Umatilla* then failed to put in its promised appearance. When it finally arrived there was a further argument between its owners and the town council. he Oregon Improvement company wouldn't let the dredge start dredging unless the council waived all claims for damages that might result from the long delay in getting *Umatilla* to Puget Sound. City government finally gave in, but still the *Umatilla* didn't get her pipes out and go to work.

Perhaps her crew, having seen the Olympia mudflats at first hand, felt that it would take the rest of their lives to make a dent in them.

Finally, after much public indignation, the dredge set halfheartedly to work, but after a couple of days it was apparent that it was just nibbling around the edges and killing time. Alarmed at the shrinking treasury and apparently shrink-proof mudflats, the city fathers gave up, paid the *Umatilla* $800 for accomplishing nothing, and sent it away.

Olympia's first efforts to achieve the status of a deepwater port were an expensive fiasco.

The fact that Olympia had been moving backward, despite its spasmodic efforts to achieve growth and progress, was dramatized when a newcomer named E. Martinsen bought a 20-acre tract on Ayer's Hill on the east side of town. When he cleared it of the second-growth fir trees which covered it he found the ruins of houses and an orchard of full grown fruit trees which had been planted 30 years earlier.

About the only thing that continued to grow was the number of newspapers. The old warhorse of temperance, J. N. Gale, started publishing the *New Transcript* to replace the vanished *Echo,* while Professor L. E. Follansbee, president of the Olympia Collegiate Institute inaugurated an educational journal which he called the *Northwest Teacher.*

The local business community started off the year by reorganizing the Olympia Board of Trade, with George Barnes as president and such civic leaders as Dr. Ostrander, General McKenny, N. H. Owings, A. A. Phillips and A. H. Chambers as officers and trustees. They got Chambers elected mayor and set out on a program of enlightened progress.

The mudflat problem was high on the agenda, and there were almost as many proposals for solving it as there were civic leaders. There was much talk of the town buying its own dredger to gnaw away at the gooey barriers to commerce on a continuing basis. There was also talk of interesting "eastern capital" in financing a dam and lock across the bay at Priest Point to provide the capital city with a tideless fresh water harbor. The fresh water, it was pointed out, would kill the teredos and other marine borers and prevent the town's docks and bridges from continually collapsing. It was believed the job could be done for $120,000, but no eastern capitalist stepped forward to donate even that modest sum.

The city council donned hipboots and floundered around at low tide wondering if it wouldn't be possible to put a crew of men to work on the ebb tides, stirring up the mud with long-handled rakes. The outgoing tide, it was thought, might carry the stirred-up mud somewhere else. Mayor Gates of Portland, a noted waterway engineer, came to town, looked the situation over and concluded that the town should charter a large seagoing tugboat to do the same thing with its propeller. Forty men with forty rakes, he pointed out, might well rake the mud for forty years without accomplishing much.

The Board of Trade and city council finally threw up their collective hands and awarded a contract to extend the Main street wharf. The result was an imposing structure extending 4,798 feet down the bay from the foot of Main

street, supported on 927 piles, which the local teredos viewed as the finest banquet in the history of the species.

The long wharf not only served as a charming summer promenade for local citizens; it brought the OR & N back with the *Emma Hayward* and the old *North Pacific* alternating on a daily service to Olympia, with the *Fleetwood* outrunning them both.

POINTING WITH PRIDE

Up in the business district, Mayor Chambers set an example for his colleagues by building a handsome two-story brick business block over the site of the old town pump on the northeast corner of 4th and Main, one of the few structures of that era to survive to the present time. Sam Woodruff, who had recently purchased the old Marsh donation claim on the west side and opened up Woodruff's addition, followed suit with another substantial two-story brick building on Main between 3rd and 4th streets. C. H. Springer built a big sawmill on the east waterway on the edge of Swantown, and the enterprising Sisters of Charity, having been given a block of land near the territorial capitol at 11th and Columbia, erected a big three-story wooden hospital, St. Peters, which was duly blessed by the Right Reverend Janger, bishop of Nisqually, and dedicated to the health and welfare of the general public.

The hospital was a blessing, indeed, to both townspeople and the working men of the hinterlands. Industrial safety was a term that hadn't even been coined yet and the workers in the highball logging camps and sawmills were frequent victims of appalling accidents.

After St. Peters hospital was completed, injured timber beasts were brought in from miles around by steamboat, train and buckboard. Often their injuries were beyond help from the primitive medical technology of the day and civic boosters were disturbed because their high mortality rate was adversely affecting Olympia's claim to being the healthiest town on Puget Sound.

Some effort was even made toward improving the general health from a preventive standpoint when the first piped sewer was constructed along 4th street to drain the

FIRST ST. PETERS HOSPITAL was built by Sisters of Charity at a cost of $20,000; served as health care center for upper Puget Sound area for four decades.

sewage of the business district onto the mudflats instead of the city streets. During the excavation some of Mr. Horton's original bored-log water pipes were removed, the bark still on the outside and the interior as sound as when they were first laid.

The gas company was purveying its fluid to about 75 of the town's more affluent and enlightened households, while the city council made funds available for about 15 gas street lights. The hydrogen gas produced had an unfortunate tendency to emit a horrible sulphur-dioxidelike odor which prompted some of the customers to return to kerosene and candles, and the company decided to go ahead and produce "electrical fluid" as well. They succeeded in time to string a line to the territorial capitol and install a total of eight incandescent bulbs in the chambers of the two houses, so the 1887 legislature was the first to deliberate and orate under electric light rather than the tin sconces of the past.

There were still grander hopes for the little 15-mile narrow-gauge line during the year when it was purchased by the Oregon Improvement company, one of the Villard-created corporations. The company was constructing its Port Townsend Southern Railway south from Port Townsend toward Olympia. The Olympia-Tenino line became the Puget Sound end of the Port Townsend Southern. Unfortunately the Oregon Improvement company collapsed by the time its rails got to Quilcene and the long gap between the two sections was never completed.

Still, there were definite signs of progress in the capital city at which its boosters could point with pride when the 1887 legislature arrived on the scene in December.

VIEWING WITH ALARM

The legislators doubtless appreciated the improved transportation facilities and the electric lights which illuminated the dingy capitol and lighted their way up the rickety wooden sidewalk, but they were preoccupied with the outraged cries of their feminine constituents, who had just lost their hard-won right to vote through the machinations of Tacoma's "boss gambler," Harry Morgan.

The territory's saloon men, gamblers and pimps were already feeling badly threatened by the reforms being pushed by women activists in politics. So many undesirables were departing for the greener and less restrictive fields of British Columbia that the provincial parliament was forced to give women the vote there, as the member who sponsored the bill said, "in self-protection."

Morgan was especially upset when one of his henchmen, Harlan, was convicted of felony charges and sent to prison by a jury which contained a number of women. The wily Morgan saw an opportunity to get his associate out of jail and put women back in the kitchen where they belonged by a single legal action. The result was Harlan *vs.* Washington Territory, which was lost in the lower court and appealed to the territorial supreme court. Judge George Turner was assigned to write an opinion and he was a noted curmudgeon on the subject of women's rights. Morgan figured that, if Judge Turner wrote the opinion the way he was sure he would, it would solve a great many problems. Since the right of women to serve on juries depended upon their right to vote, it would both create a mistrial, thus releasing the estimable Mr. Harlan from the new territorial prison at Walla Walla, and bar women from the polls at future elections.

Judge Turner duly ruled that women had no right to serve on juries because the law granting them the right to vote hadn't been given a proper title. The law required that titles specify the intent of the bill, and the woman suffrage measure was simply entitled "An act to amend Section 3050 of Chapter 238 of the Code of Washington."

The judge ignored the fact that 19 other laws passed at the 1883 session had been headed the same way, one of them being the bill authorizing the sitting of the court which made the decision. The court was divided on the matter. Chief Justice Roger Greene and Judge John P. Hoyt both held the suffrage law to be valid, but Judge Hoyt was disqualified because he had been the trial judge in the lower court. There were four judges and one of them, William Langford, joined with Turner to nullify the bill by a vote of two to one.

The leaders of the suffrage movement weren't too distressed by the ruling, which was made in February, 1887. The legislature would be meeting in a few months and they had assurances from members of both political parties that the bill would be passed again, this time with a clear and concise title.

The ladies underestimated the political cunning and determination of their adversaries, however, and their troubles were far from over, even though the legislature of 1887-88 made good its promise.

The tradition that the weather is always bad in Olympia when the legislature is in session was strengthened when it began convening in December. The members straggled into town in the midst of a series of wind and rain storms which threw steamboat schedules into confusion and put the narrow-gauge railroad out of commission as a result of a series of landslides which buried the track. When they got back from the usual holiday interlude in early January of 1888, it was in the midst of a blizzard. The wooden sidewalk from downtown to the capitol was covered with drifting snow and the only livery stable proprietor who owned a suitably large horse-drawn sled charged them 50¢ each for the seven or eight block trip.

There were loud screams from the freezing solons that Olympians were engaged in their usual commercial activity of "gouging" the legislature, which was unfortunate, because a bill was in the hopper to move the territorial capital to North Yakima. Another was being drawn up to move it to Ellensburg. If a fortuitous Chinook wind hadn't arrived in time to melt the snow a profit-hungry Olympia liveryman might have succeeded in getting one or the other of them passed. As it was, the Yakima bill lost in the house of representatives by one vote. The disappointed Yakima forces then joined with the southwest

Washingtonians to keep the Ellensburg measure bottled up in committee.

Grateful Olympians agreed to chip in for a grand banquet and ball to show their appreciation to the legislators. The ball was held, but the chairman, hardware merchant Robert Frost, complained bitterly that many of the local citizens who had gorged themselves at the feast failed to make good their pledges, leaving him with a deficit of $100; furthermore, he charged in a letter to the *Standard,* some of these free-loaders had arrived early, taken over seats at the head table and refused to move for the distinguished guests who had been invited to sit there.

Controversy seemed to be the keynote of territorial politics in 1887.

THE DEAD DONKEY SHOWS SIGNS OF LIFE

Grover Cleveland had finally gotten around to appointing a Democratic governor that year; a Vancouver sawmill operator named Eugene Semple. Semple, a scholarly, neatly bearded and bespectacled man of 47, had been a lawyer in his younger days, after graduating from Cincinnati College and moving to Oregon. Later he became editor of the *Daily Oregon Herald,* the leading Democratic newspaper of that state. After serving as state printer, clerk of the circuit court and commissioner of police in Portland, he moved to Vancouver in 1882 and entered the lumber business.

He arrived on the scene at an unfortunate time, immediately inheriting the still red-hot Chinese issue and the almost equally controversial woman suffrage fight. Feelings were high on both sides of both issues and it was apparent he would be "damned if he did and damned if he didn't."

In the anti-Chinese matter he maintained the same firm law and order stance as his predecessor, Squire, but there were far more bigots than liberals involved in this controversy. Their voting strength had blasted the political careers of a number of respected citizens at the last election and those who survived were wary of supporting the governor in his determination to uphold the rights of what the anti-Chinese leaders were fond of calling "slant-eyed, opium-eating heathens."

A great many male citizens besides the saloon and underworld types were already disenchanted with woman suffrage. A number of the more vociferous feminists had shown undue haste to use their political clout in efforts to dictate the morals and personal habits of everyone else. John Miller Murphy, a long-time advocate of both equal suffrage and temperance, was among the disenchanted. He still loved his beer and cheese, and there was a good chance the women would deprive him of at least half of his favorite refreshment.

When Semple indicated that he would support a revised bill to return voting rights to women he acquired another large army of enemies from among the male population.

The general hatred of the Northern Pacific Railroad, which had swept Delegate Voorhees into two terms of office as a Democrat, was waning as a major issue and source of Democratic strength. However the issue did result in six Democrats getting elected to the 12-man legislative council . . . the first time the Republicans hadn't enjoyed a healthy majority since civil war days.

This resulted in further wrangling at the capitol. The Democrats, with some logic, argued that the officers and employees of the council should also be evenly divided. The Republicans, long used to absolute power and unwilling to part with any of it, countered with the charge that two of the Democratic members had been elected as "Independents" and therefore didn't count.

After many recriminations a compromise was reached. The Reverend J. R. Thompson, Republican of Clarke, was elected president, but the Democrats got to name the sergeant at arms and seven other employees. Francis Henry was appointed chief clerk of the council and, when the session ended, nimbly landed in the chair of supreme court clerk.

The Republicans had a smaller-than-usual majority of three in the house of representatives, but this time they refused to give anything in the way of patronage to the Democrats. All officers, "from the Speaker to the Page," as the *Standard* put it, were Republicans. The speaker, T. J. V. Clark of Walla Walla, was noted for his modesty, timidity and lack of parliamentary knowledge and before the session was over he doubtless felt like the man being ridden out of town on a sharp rail who observed that if it wasn't for the honor he would just as soon have walked.

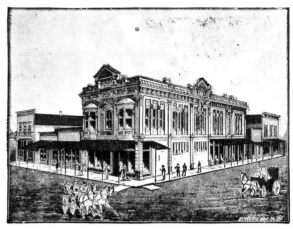

CHAMBERS BLOCK, OLYMPIA.

The legislators did get together to make a gala excursion to Steilacoom with Governor Semple on the *Emma Hayward* to participate in the dedication of the handsome new hospital for the insane. While they were entertained by Dr. Waughop, the superintendent, the guards and matrons kept the inmates on their good behavior in the wards. (Most of these uniformed therapists could work wonders with a bar of soap wrapped in a towel.)

They also gathered amicably together at Sam Percival's mansion at the end of Long bridge for a reception held by Governor and Mrs. Semple, which was described by the *Standard* as "the crowning social event of the season."

They also passed bills removing various tax loopholes and other preferential treatment granted the railroads by earlier legislatures, produced what they hoped would be a legally acceptable woman's suffrage bill and approved a record biennial budget of $513,970.

Taxpayers and press were alike outraged by this display of profligacy. The Tacoma *News* began referring to the 11th biennial (and last territorial) session as *"the Washington Territorial Liability,"* charging that *"this enormous expenditure"* would result in a $450,000 deficit, including a $120,000 shortage inherited from the 1885 session.

With the departure of the legislature, the capital city went right on with its wave of progress aimed at qualifying it to continue in that role when Washington became a state, as now appeared inevitable in the very near future.

The Port Townsend Southern provided the local narrow-gauge line with a couple of new passenger coaches to match the "big" 30-ton locomotive already on the run. Railroad buff Murphy proclaimed them to be *"equal in elegance and comfort to those of any first-class road."*

Mr. Chambers had a "patent stone" sidewalk constructed around his new building at 4th and Main, giving, as Murphy reported proudly, *"a decidedly city-like ring to passing footsteps."*

Sam Williams built another handsome brick block across Main street from the Chambers Building, the two-story Olympic block, which he rented to the prospering mercantile firm of Toklas and Kaufman. These structures were topped by the new Odd Fellows building on the southwest corner of 5th and Main, which rose a tall three stories, topped by an ornate tower. Charles Talcott, who had been joined by his brother Grant in the watch, clock, jewelry and general merchandise business, started a successful campaign to raise funds for a "town clock" to be placed in the tower.

The OR & N was more than doing justice to the town's water transportation needs, now that the long wharf had eliminated the worst of the harbor's navigational hazards. The fast sternwheeler *Hassalo* joined the *Hayward* on the Seattle-Tacoma passenger run, while the sidewheeler *Idaho* ran on a freight-only service, thus speeding up the schedules of the passenger steamers. The fast propeller *Fleetwood* remained highly competitive, keeping passenger and freight rates down.

In the fall the OR & N replaced the *Hassalo* with the legendary racing sidewheeler *T. J. Potter,* the most elegant steamboat ever to run on upper Puget Sound. From her ornately decorated paddle-boxes to her damask hangings, clusters of incandescent electric

Odd Fellows Hall was tallest building in town in 1880's.

lights, carved paneling and gilt-framed plate glass mirrors, she was the epitome of steamboat-gothic splendor. Her officers, from

GAUDY SIDE-WHEELER T. J. POTTER, was most splendid of the Olympia-Seattle boats.

ORNATE INTERIOR shows passenger salon on *T. J. Potter.*

Captain Gil Parker to the freight clerk, were garbed in blue broadcloth uniforms glittering with brass buttons and gold braid. Gourmet meals were served in the grand dining room salon and the aristrocratic traveler who didn't want to rub elbows with the common folk had a choice of 39 luxurious staterooms.

Olympians felt they had come a long way from the steamboat *Fairy*, the *Old Settler*, the *Capital* and even the *Zephyr*, which had been reduced to towing booms of logs from the harbor for the Tacoma Mill Company.

SIN CITY

Another development was never mentioned in the records of the Board of Trade or the columns of the loyal Olympia press, although it was probably appreciated at least as much as any of the others by the legislators during their biennial visits to the capital city.

With the movement of the town's business district from the foot of Main street to above 4th street, the old wooden false-fronted buildings of the lower town were abandoned by the reputable business establishments, which moved to the new brick buildings "up town."

The old buildings were taken over by working-class saloons, cardrooms and an ever-increasing number of brothels. None of the latter were in a class with the more glamorous and gaudy joints of Seattle and Tacoma, but staid Olympia was developing its own "restricted district," where a certain amount of vice was tolerated by the civic authorities.

A big rambling wooden theater, the Brunswick, was built on piling at the muddy lower end of Main street and booked the kind of daring burlesque entertainment that was never seen in the respectable confines of Columbia hall.

All this livened up the town considerably, the noisy revelry of the restricted district drowning out the traditional night sounds of snipe on the mudflats, cows on the town square and frogs croaking on the swampy outskirts. The town fathers, engaged in the life-and-death struggle for the state capital, were doubtless aware that the restricted district provided them with useful ammunition, but respectability was still the watchword. The churches and the WCTU might run another successful reform ticket if things got too garish, so the establishment just sort of pretended the girls, the pimps, the

tinhorn gamblers and the burlesque shows weren't there and the madams kept the red lights dim.

The local papers took the hint and mentioned the existence of the shabby square block of sin only obliquely, usually when one of the girls, always referred to as "one of Olympia's unfortunates" or "a woman of the half-world," drowned herself in the bay, was murdered by her pimp or a client, or died in Chinatown from an overdose of opium.

The future of all the territory's sin cities became much more secure when a carefully-laid plot by the proponents of male supremacy again wrested the ballot from feminine hands.

THE BARTENDER'S BRIDE

The legislature having restored the vote to them early in 1888, women voted in the spring elections and returned to jury duty. In the Spokane municipal election, the vote of one woman, a Mrs. Nevada Bloomer, was challenged, while the votes of all the others were accepted without question. Mrs. Bloomer just happened to be the wife of a bartender in one of the local sporting establishments, and her subsequent adventures were as improbable as her name.

Mrs. Bloomer became the heroine of the territory's embattled women when she brought suit against Spokane election officials for $5,-000 damages, for they were innocently unaware that she was really helping to do them in.

Good old Judge Turner resigned from the supreme court to defend the election officials. Somehow the case was given the highest judicial priority and placed at the top of the supereme court docket, although that august body was a year behind in its work and usually proceeded at a slow and stately pace. Four of the five judges who then constituted the court agreed that Nevada had suffered no injury because she hadn't been entitled to the vote in the first place. Chief Justice Richard Jones personally wrote the majority opinion, which had a remarkable resemblance to ex-Judge Turner's brief to the court.

The territory's highest court reached its decision through a refreshingly original line of judicial reasoning.

While congress had, in the organic act creating Washington territory, authorized the enfranchisement of all citizens, the judges came to the conclusion that it *should* have put the word "male" before the word "citizen." Since congress had failed to do so, the territorial justices did it for them by amending the 1853 act of congress!

Since the judicially amended act of 1853 now specified that only *male* citizens could vote, Mrs. Bloomer and all the rest of the territory's feminine population did not now have, and never had been entitled to voting rights. Although *they* could retroactively *amend* an act of congress, the judges said, the territorial legislature couldn't pass bills in conflict with acts of congress.

There seemed little doubt that the United States supreme court would quickly overrule the unique action of the territorial court. Friends of equal suffrage raised $5,000 and offered it to Mrs. Bloomer to defray the costs of appealing the case.

Nevada flatly refused to fight the case any further, even with all her expenses paid.

During that same winter the statehood bill finally passed congress. There was not time for the suffragists to start a new action and gain a reversal before a constitutional convention was elected to set the guidelines for the new state. Thanks to Nevada Bloomer, women would be unable to vote for delegates to the convention or have any effective influence on its deliberations.

History does not record whether her husband the bartender got a raise in pay, but there is no doubt that he and Nevada had earned one. Women suffrage had been effectively killed for nearly another quarter of a century.

STATEHOOD AT LAST!
There were still a good many of the wagon train pioneers of the 1840's and 50's on hand to greet the new year of 1889 and to join in the jubilation that attended achievement of victory in the long battle for statehood.

The omnibus bill granting statehood to Washington, Montana and the Dakotas, passed both houses of congress late in 1888, surviving much contention, caucusing, filibustering and a wide range of delaying tactics.

Grover Cleveland, having been safely returned to office in the 1888 elections, signed the measure with a quill from an American bald eagle on Washington's birthday, 1889.

Joy was unrestrained throughout the territory. Every town and village that possessed a cannon charged it to the muzzle and fired unlimited salutes. Church bells rang, mill and steamboat whistles shrilled, crowds cheered and everybody but the ladies, who weren't allowed in saloons, and some of the temperance men, got drunk. There was a general conviction that the magic of statehood would somehow create instant and unlimited prosperity; that everybody lucky enough to own a plot of land in Washington territory would become a wealthy citizen of Washington state.

Nowhere was the enthusiasm less restrained than in Olympia. An overnight real estate boom developed. The prices of town property increased daily and a half dozen new subdivisions were staked out. The north Olympia Land Company was organized to acquire the long idle acreage northeast of town which had been purchased nearly twenty years earlier by Ira Bradley on behalf of the Northern Pacific Railroad.

Unfortunately, every other town in the territory was also embarked on a speculative land boom and their weren't enough prospective buyers to go around. By May the ambitious property owners of Olympia had priced themselves out of the market and the real estate business went into a state of decline.

Everything else was proceeding full speed ahead, however, as the citizens girded themselves for what they hoped would be the final battle to retain the capital of the Great State of Washington.

At the dawn of the statehood the town boasted five weekly newspapers, the *Standard,* the *Partisan,* the *New Transcript,* the *Review* and the *Republican Partisan.* Even Professor Follansbee's *Northwest Teacher* had competition from the *Northwest Journal of Education,* established by B. W. Brintnall. Jessie Ferney began publishing the Bucoda *Enterprise* at the site of the abandoned Seatco prison, and was soon followed by C. E. Berry, with the Tenino *Herald.*

It would seem that the town and county were abundantly supplied with news media, but Olympia had no daily newspaper. The eager members of the Board of Trade felt that a daily was an essential status symbol as well as a

GRAND OLD OPERA HOUSE was the pride of publisher John Miller Murphy in 1892. The street in front is being replanked and one of George Savage's bobtailed horsecars appear to be lining up for a race down 4th Street with the delivery wagon of the City Steam Laundry.

valuable propaganda tool in the capital fight. They approached John Miller Murphy, proprietor of the town's only steam press, who told them emphatically that he wasn't going to "get stung" a third time. When he remained adamant the business community, in utter desperation, actually signed contracts to buy enough advertising to underwrite costs for the first year of publication. Murphy relented, and the *Evening Olympian* took its place in Olympia's long and complicated journalistic history.

The city council, for its part, began a new program of street and bridge improvements, replaced the evil smelling gas street lights with electric arcs and embarked on a round of franchise-granting.

The Sunset Telephone company was authorized to erect poles and string wire along the streets. So was the Olympia and Grays Harbor Electric company, which proposed to establish telephone communication between Olympia and the towns of Grays Harbor. The Western Union Telegraph company began adding its poles and wires to those of Postal Telegraph, which were already in place. The Olympia Water company was permitted to extend its mains and install 20 modern fire hydrants, for which the city would pay $100 a year each, and E. T. Young was franchised to distribute electric light and power.

GRAND AND GAUDY Hotel Olympia, built by public subscription to provide legislators with the comforts they demanded . . . and thus help to retain the capital . . . A "state ball" was held there on March 28, 1890, the closing night of the first state legislative session, although it wasn't quite completed and didn't open to the public for almost another month.

HORSE CARS AND A HOTEL

Two street railway franchises were granted, one to the Olympia and Tumwater Railway, Light and Power company, which proposed to lay track from 4th and Main to Tumwater Falls, and the Olympia Railway company of George M. Savage, which was to operate on 4th street to the east side. The former company never raised enough money to take advantage of its franchise, but Savage took advantage of his in every sense of the word.

The town fathers and the citizenry in general had envisioned splendid electric streetcars, such as Seattle had recently placed in service, conveying delighted legislators smoothly and comfortably up the hill to the capitol.

Savage and his investors had other and less expensive ideas. The franchise was rather loosely written and didn't specify the type of motive power to be used. Savage wisely felt that if the Olympia boom continued he could sell his street railway franchise for a tidy profit regardless of whether he invested in track and rolling stock or not. It would be good business to keep present expenditures to the minimum needed to meet the requirements of his contract with the city.

The original bob-tailed horse cars of the Seattle street railway were now surplus and on the market at modest prices. Savage bought two of them, No. 1 and No. 4, and had them transported to Olympia. He then picked up a couple of reject teams of underfed and overworked livery stable horses and a few thousand feet of second-hand ironrail, and he was in business. So set was he on economy that he even vetoed the suggestion of Adjutant-General O'Brien, one of the principal stockholders, that the drivers be provided with blue uniforms and brass buttons.

Those who complained that the street railway wasn't quite what they had hoped for were assured by Savage that two "pneumonia boxes," as the *Transcript* scathingly referred to the ex-Seattle horse cars, were only temporary expedients in the interests of getting the system in operation as quickly as possible, and that they would soon be replaced by the most modern and luxurious of electric cars.

Another shortcoming of the hopeful state capital was corrected in a much grander manner. For years the legislators had been complaining that Olympia didn't have a really first class hotel. Most of them took the cheapest available quarters in third-rate rooming houses and private homes, but they felt they should have a hostelry befitting their dignity in which to congregate, caucus and consume free drinks set up by the lobbyists.

General McKenny became a prime mover in a project to erect a truly palatial hotel with which the community could bedazzle the legislators. With such other civic leaders as Colonel Owings, George Shannon, J. F. Gowey (who was the current mayor), T. M. Reed, Mrs. P. C. Hale and Mrs. A. H. Stuart, he formed the Olympia Hotel Corporation, a community stock company in which scores of loyal citizens became stockholders. About $80,000 of the $110,000 needed to build and furnish a suitably elegant hotel was subscribed. The directors then floated a $30,000 mortgage loan with a Boston firm and construction was started. It wasn't quite ready for business when the first state legislature convened, but its ornate Victorian bulk loomed over the lesser buildings of the town and gave promise of great things to come.

Fronting on Main street between 7th and 8th, it extended back almost to the salt water of the Deschutes waterway. Built of wood, the Hotel Olympia was four stories high, surmounted by a taller and gaudier tower than that of the new Odd Fellows building. It was festooned with verandas and decorated with a profusion of gingerbread carvings. It was lighted by both gas and electricity and had central heating. Its amenities included a huge lobby, an elevator, a luxurious dining room, ballroom, bar, laundry, club rooms and bellboys in uniforms so fancy that they might have been designed by General O'Brien himself.

The town was going for broke in its efforts to retain the capital, feeling that it had too much invested now to quit. In addition to everything else the city council donated $2,500 to enlarge and renovate the territorial capitol building to house the constitutional convention, which would convene on the Fourth of July. They also threw another $1,000 of city funds into the capital campaign war chest of the Board of Trade.

The delegates to the convention, 75 of them from all the counties, were selected at a special election in May. J. F. Gowey, T. M. Reed and Francis Henry were elected from Thurston county.

THE MIDNIGHT RIDE
OF OLYMPIA NO. 2

Shortly afterward, on June 7, most of the city of Seattle was wiped out by a fire which started when a gluepot overturned in a cabinet shop. Nobody was killed and the conflagration turned out to be a blessing in disguise for the town. Its business leaders were even closer with a dollar than their counterparts in Olympia, and as long as their old wooden buildings were producing good rents few were willing to replace them with brick and stone. The great fire of 1889 forced them to do so.

It was also something of a blessing in disguise for Olympia.

The news of the Seattle fire reached Olympia in the evening and the town fathers called an emergency meeting. They knew they needed all the friends they could get, so they authorized the fire department to take the town's pride and joy, the silver-wheeled Silsby steam pumper to Seattle by the fastest possible means of transportation. That, obviously, was Captain Hatch's racing steamboat *Fleetwood*. The *Olympia No. 2* was wheeled down to Percival's dock and loaded on the forward deck, the slim-hulled *Fleetwood* listing alarmingly as she took the weight of the heavy fire engine. Placed carefully amidships, the engine was chocked and tied down, the *Fleetwood's* whistle blasted the evening quiet of the waterfront and, with surplus steam in a white plume at her funnel, she swung away from the dock and began the fifty-mile run to Seattle.

As Captain Hatch swung the wheel hard to starboard to round Dofflemeyer's Point, seven miles north of town, the little steamer listed over sickeningly and the pumper strained at its restraints. The skipper ordered all passengers to seats below with instructions to sit still and confine their activities to silent prayer.

Down below the firemen were tossing hoarded pitch slabs into the furnace with wild abandon and the engineer hung his cap over the steam gauge. Shoreside witnesses claimed the *Fleetwood* was throwing sticks of firewood out her smokestacks as she foamed past Johnson's Point and Devil's Head. Presumably Captain Hatch was adding his prayers to those of the passengers as his topheavy craft sent her wake crashing on the beach below the federal penitentiary on McNeil Island and squared away to run the Narrows . . . the half-mile-wide passage south of Tacoma where the

SEAGOING FIRE ENGINE: Steam pumper *Olympia No. 2*, pride and joy of the Olympia Fire Department in 1889, voyaged to Seattle on the fast steamer *Fleetwood* to help battle the great fire. Barnes Hook & Ladder Company, at the right, had nattier uniforms but less efficient equipment. Among the firemen posing for the photographer were John Stewart, Alex Wright, L. Grant Talcott, William Weller, Joseph McCarogher, William Henry and Sam McClelland.
. . . State Capitol Museum Photo

constricted tides of Puget Sound form great whirlpools as they race through at five to seven knots.   As she rounded Point Defiance at the north end of the Narrows the *Fleetwood* was caught in a wild tiderip and lay over on her side. For seconds it appeared that she could never right herself, but she did, and by midnight *Olympia No. 2* was on the Seattle waterfront with steam up, sucking salt water from Elliott Bay, a feat of strength which the Gould steamers of the Seattle fire department hadn't been able to accomplish, and played her streams on what was left of Seattle.

In the election that fall, when the voters were given the opportunity to select a state capital, approve the state constitution and select the first slate of state officers, many Seattle voters doubtless remembered the heroic voyage of *Olympia No. 2* to help them in their hour of need and showed their appreciation at the polls.

Olympia got 25,490 votes; North Yakima, 14,711; Ellensburg, 12,883; Centralia, 607; Yakima, 314*; Pasco, 130, and a long list of other hopeful cities, towns and villages, 1,088.

But it was a moral victory only; since no town received a majority of the total votes cast, Olympia would have to go through the whole thing again in 1890, this time with the competition limited to the two runners-up, North Yakima and Ellensburg.

*In line with its policy of creating and cashing in on its own boom towns, the Northern Pacific had located its Cascade division tracks and depot a couple of miles north of the established town of Yakima. Just as there was for some years, a New Tacoma and an Old Tacoma, there was a Yakima and a North Yakima until the towns merged by natural growth.

The new state constitution was approved by a vote of 40,152 to 11,789. Politically, the Republicans swept the state. Of the 35 state senators, one was a Democrat. There were eight Democrats and one Independent among the 70 representatives. That old political warhorse, Elisha P. Ferry, got his third term as governor. John L. Wilson of Spokane was elected the state's first congressman. Other Republican victors were Charles E. Laughton, lieutenant governor; Allen Weir, secretary of state; O. A. Bowen, treasurer; Thomas M. Reed, auditor; Wesley C. Jones, attorney general; R. B. Bryan, superintendent of public instruction, and W. T. Forest, commissioner of public lands.

The change in the national administration from that of Democrat Grover Cleveland to Republican Benjamin Harrison had also brought a Republican, Miles C. Moore of Walla Walla, to take his place in history as the last of the territorial governors. The prosperous grain merchant and banker held office for only seven months, keeping the gubernatorial chair warm during the transition to statehood.

The voters also had an opportunity to decide a couple of issues which had proven too hot for the constitutional convention delegates to handle . . . woman suffrage and local option in regard to the sale of liquor.

The court-disenfranchised women of the territory had been urged not to make too much of a fuss after the Nevada Bloomer fiasco, on the grounds that a suffrage squabble might endanger statehood. They were assured that they could depend upon the chivalry of the male electorate to restore their rights in the new state constitution. However, only about half a dozen of the 75 delegates proved to be friends of woman suffrage and the result was not exactly what the ladies had hoped for.

Leaving as little as possible to chance, the organized opposition to woman suffrage, led by the saloon and liquor industry, offered to furnish ballots for the 1889 election to the Republican party at no cost. In territorial days the voter was required to ask for a ballot of the party of his choice. These carried only the names of the candidates chosen at the territorial party conventions. A disenchanted voter could cross out a name, but he couldn't vote for anyone not on the printed ticket. Measures to be voted on could be crossed out to register a negative vote. If the elector failed to draw a line through any measure on the ballot he was presumed to have voted for it.

The champions of male supremacy decided to make it easy for the voters. They rented a small printing plant in Seattle . . . ironically that of a temperance publication which was strongly in favor of woman suffrage . . . and moved in their own crew. After carefully locking the doors, they then proceeded to run off thousands of Republican ballots with local option and woman suffrage *already crossed out!*

Nobody knows how many of the pre-marked ballots were dropped in the boxes on election day, but there were no doubt a lot of them. The counter on the temperance press indicated a run of 180,000.

So much for the chivalry of the male electorate. . . . although Mrs. Duniway stated forthrightly that the ladies had brought disaster on themselves by joining in the strident chorus of the WCTU. (She was immediately banned from the state's Protestant churches.)

Despite the disappointment of the feminists and militant teetotalers, most people looked forward eagerly to formal ceremonies of statehood; none more eagerly than the citizens of Olympia, where it was going to happen. The scene at the capital city in the days immediately prior to the great event were described well by an eye-witness, Charles Miles, a nephew of one of the first state senators, Henry Miles, who made the journey from Portland to watch the festivities:

"November 10—This finds me in Olympia, the territorial capital, the city where the state will soon be born. The ride from Chehalis was uneventful, the change from the main line to a narrow-gauge at Tenino being the chief feature. When our train stopped we found the Olympia train of two cars and an engine waiting. At Olympia the depot is across the bay to the west in a cove between a bridge crossing and the mouth of a creek.

"I found the citizens bustling about preparing for the big doings to celebrate statehood, but wondering what has gone awry in Washington, D.C. that the President has not yet signed the proclamation.

"November 11—I awakened this morning to the damp smell of the Sound, which is at Olympia's front door. The weather is mild, but a fresh breeze comes in off the water. I was presented with raspberries at breakfast, a scattered crop so late being due, I am told, to the springlike weather.

"In a morning stroll I saw a number of signs of progress, though at one point I was treated to some doubts about the desirability of progress. On 4th street of the city a new street railway grade is progressing eastward and three graybeards were eyeing the proceedings.*

"'Wonder who'll pay for the hoss's legs that git busted stumbling over them T-rails,' said one.

"'And there'll be plenty of bashed-in hub caps,' asserted another.

"The third 'reckoned' it might be all right, 'but why in thunder don't they run the cars over here by the sidewalk so's passengers won't have to wade up to their knees getting on?'

"Later I saw the same three examining the new Hotel Olympia. This is a fine building indeed with broad verandas, cozy alcoves and sightly porticos. It is to be lighted by both gas and electricity and heated by steam.

"I have mailed a picture of Olympia's shoreline to the home paper. It was carved by Mister A. J. Weston, a local engraver. He was just taking the print of a man's portrait when I went in, and from the fact the subject was present, I was able to see that Mr. Weston is a competent artist.

"The social life is provided with amply dramatic diversion. At Columbia Hall last Saturday there was a showing of Jules Verne's "Around the World in 80 Days." It required two railway cars to carry the scenery and cast. Next Thursday a musical and instrumental concert is billed for the hall."

The new state legislature had already convened at the enlarged and renovated capitol, but it was still only a territorial legislature until the president signed the proclamation of statehood. The members could hardly wait to pry open the pork barrel and there was mounting irritation as the days passed without word from the national capital. Territorial Governor Moore was still the top man, much to the annoyance of Governor-elect Ferry. Finally he

---

*Young Mr. Miles had happened upon a trio of what were known to the press of the territory as "Olympia moss-backs." Even the loyal John Miller Murphy conceded that the town had more than its share of the species. It still does. The modern version can be seen at its best eyeing the new breed of college students rather than horse car rails, but their general philosophy has changed little with the years.

and Moore fired off a joint telegram to President Harrison requesting action.

They were informed by return wire that Governor Moore, who hadn't thought he was supposed to do anything but wait for Ferry to take over, was supposed to have certified the constitutional election. The president couldn't do a thing until he got the territorial governor's signature, which he had forgotten to place on the document.

Under the accusing gaze of Elisha P. Ferry, the unfortunate Moore wasted no time in getting a new certificate on its way to Washington, D.C.

The legislature droned through most of November 11 on details of organization when the presiding officer of the senate was interrupted by a page with a message from Governor Moore. It was announced that President Harrison had signed the statehood proclamation at 5:20 that evening.

There was a moment of dead silence, followed by a roar which shook the ancient wooden capitol. Jubilation spread from the senate to the house and then down Main street to the town. The cannon, which had been charged for days awaiting the great event, fired unceasing salvos and the male populace rushed to the town's 14 saloons.

It took a week to prepare for the formal celebration. Four companies of national guard infantry and three cavalry troops were brought to Olympia for the event and encamped in a vacant lot across Main street from the capitol. Typical November weather prevailed . . . continuous cold rain and gusty winds . . . and the territorial legislature had not appropriated much money for militia equipment. Each trooper was furnished one thin blanket. Fortunately for them, the street railway construction crew had piled wooden ties along Main street and the militiamen quickly used them to build bonfires, innocently unaware that their leader, Adjutant-General O'Brien, was one of the principal owners of the diverted street railway ties.

When the grand parade formed up on the morning of November 18 the sun broke through the black rain clouds and cast its welcome blessing upon the scene of jubilation. With T. C. Van Epps as grand marshal, the parade was the largest in the town's history. It was led by Mayor Gowey and the town council, followed by Governors Moore and Ferry and

Percival's dock with all flags flying for Statehood Day, 1889; the *T. J. Potter* and *Fleetwood* bringing in excursionists.

the outgoing territorial and incoming state officials, all in shiny carriages.

The last of the territorial officials were Secretary O. C. White, Surveyor-general T. H. Cavanaugh, District Attorney William H. White, Marshal T. J. Hamilton, Treasurer F. I. Blodgett and Auditor John Miller Murphy, who had managed to get himself appointed to a third term in that office for a brief period from 1888 to 1889. Most of them were Democrats, and there was something symbolic about their carriage ride to political oblivion. It would be a long time before any more democratic officeholders would make it to the capitol.

Wagner's First Regimental Band followed the dignitaries. Then came the Pioneers of Washington, including old Edmund Sylvester, who had lived to see his Smithfield cabin replaced by the capital of a new state; the Seattle drum corps led the militia troops, followed by the Knights of Pythias in full regalia, the Tacoma band, the Mason Rifles, and citizens in carriages, on horses and afoot.

The parade moved up Adams street to 13th and onto the capitol grounds, accompanied on each side by cheering crowds. *"—t was,"* wrote Murphy, *"simply three living streams of humanity, one as long as the other, marching toward the capitol."*

The legislature had met at ten o'clock that morning, but adjourned at 11:55 when the crowd arrived and marched in a body to the front of the capitol to join the festivities.

The old frame building was festooned with evergreens and bunting and the balcony over the entrance was fitted out for the more distinguished political figures of the day. Another American eagle had been sacrificed to the formalities of statehood and stood stuffed behind the speakers' platform. Banners across the building proclaimed *"Isaac I. Stevens, First in the Hearts of the People of Washington Territory; E. P. Ferry, First in the Hearts of the People of Washington State,"* and, in the Chinook jargon so cherished by the pioneers, *"Quanisum Ancutty Alki; Che Chaco Alki"* which, more or less literally translated meant "Long time ago it was bye and bye; come to stay now." Murphy used a somewhat more literary version in the *Standard* . . . *"Living*

NOVEMBER 18, 1899: The little territorial capitol in the woods was decked out bravely for the proclamation of statehood and the inauguration of Elisha P. Ferry as first governor of the state of Washington.

. . . State Capitol Museum Photo (Dr. P. H. Carlyon Collection)

hitherto in the past, we now begin to live in the future.”

At noon the Tacoma band struck up "America" and Mayor Gowey, in high collar and stovepipe hat, delivered his address of welcome. After the invocation Governor Moore introduced Governor Ferry, who advanced to the platform to the strains of "Hail to the Chief." His remarks were punctuated by people firing 42-gun salutes with the town cannon. When he finished somebody unfurled a flag with a new star, although the 42-star flag wouldn't be official until the next Fourth of July.

In the evening Governor Ferry reviewed the militia from a balcony of the Woodruff block, one of the fancy new commercial buildings of downtown Olympia. That was followed by a reception for the new state officials at Colum-

WOODRUFF BLOCK was another imposing structure of territorial days. The balcony was a favorite spot for governors and other dignitaries to review downtown parades.

CHARLES E. LAUGHTON,
LIEUTENANT-GOVERNOR.

ALLEN WEIR, Secretary of State.

A. A. LINDSLEY, State Treasurer.

THOMAS M. REED, State Auditor.

ROBT B. BRYAN, Sup't of Public Instruction.

bia hall and the first inaugural ball for the governor in the town's tallest building, Odd Fellows hall.

The observant Charles Miles, having made a brief journey to Grays Harbor and caught a bad cold while waiting for Governor Miles to get the show on the road, was back in time to join the crowd of 3,000 at the capitol and to prowl the streets of Olympia recording local color:

"The civic spirit is inspiring. A window display put up by the firm of Toklas & Kaufman is typical of current spirit. In their middle window is a picture of our first President, after whom the state was named, and around it are skillfully arranged military decorations. The military figure of a soldier supports a frame of flowers, while around his feet are articles of warfare. The corner displays tents and the arms and accoutrements of a military camp. A boy in blue is coming from the canvas. Truly a clever and inspiring display!"

Patriotism was the theme of the day and "articles of warfare" were recognized symbols of patriotism. If any were so un-American as to be in favor of peace they had the good sense to keep their opinions to themselves in those days.

That young Miles had a sense of history as well as an observant eye is indicated by his notation that *"while I was dining today in the Gold Bar Restaurant I learned that it is in the building in which the first territorial legislature assembled in 1853-54."*

FOR A FIRST-RATE STATE . . . APPROPRIATE!

After the tumult and the shouting died and the crowds of visitors departed, the first legislative assembly of the sovereign state of Washington set out to harvest the crop of plums. They had unlimited time in which to accomplish this . . . the new constitution limited sessions to 60 days, but placed no restrictions on the first one . . . but they were eager to get going. Like most of the citizens in general, they were under the misapprehension that they had been handed the key to the U.S. mint along with membership in the sisterhood of states. Washington was riding the dizzy crest of the boom which started with the coming of the transcontinental railway. Nearly 100,000 new settlers had arrived between 1887 and 1889. Land values had skyrocketed, new capital was being invested and the sky appeared to be the limit.

GENTLEMEN OF THE PRESS: These dignified journalists covered the first session of the Washington State Legislature in 1889. Front row: Morris J. Hartnett, Seattle *Budget*; C. Gower, Tacoma *Ledger*; Henry E. Reed, Portland *Oregonian*; second row: Edgar Piper, Seattle *Post-Intelligencer*; F. S. Musseyer, Seattle *Times*; Charles H. Hailes, Tacoma *Ledger*; Thomas Henderson Boyd, Tacoma *Globe*; Maj. C. M. Barton, "Journalist", Tacoma; Fred Puhler, Portland *Oregonian*.

Governor Ferry, who couldn't be accused of being a spendthrift with either his own money or the public's, delivered a cautiously optimistic message to the legislators, urging them to concentrate on setting up mechanics of government and go easy on the spending.

The solons listened politely to the governor and even gave lip service to his homily on thrift by noisily voting down a bill to provide each member with five dollars worth of postage stamps. (A little later in the session they reconsidered the bill and passed it with no fanfare whatever.)

And unlike most subsequent sessions, the first bills introduced were not legislative appropriations. The first three senate bills had to do with appointments and fees of notaries public, price fixing and organization of the supreme court. House Bill 1 provided for payment of a deficiency incurred by the hospital for the insane. The payment of legislative

expenses was taken care of in house bills 4 and 38, which passed quickly and without noticeable opposition.

Before the end of November the press of the state was expressing alarm at the lavish spending of the legislature. There were 13 accredited newsmen covering the session and, just as at the 42 subsequent sessions, they made the legislators nervous. The reporter for the Seattle *Morning Journal* achieved a journalistic first when a resolution was introduced to expel him. He had informed his readers that a minority of the law-makers were forming an "anti-boodle society." Boodle was the current colloquialism for political bribes, payoffs and kickbacks, and the incensed legislators felt his story inferred that the majority of them were *pro*-boodle. The resolution was eventually tabled.

The Seattle *Post-Intelligencer* was one of the state's first journals to start viewing with alarm the proceedings at Olympia. By mid-November it was firing away at the "extravagance of the present Assembly":

"Both houses have attached to themselves a small army of employes and clerks, many of whom are entirely useless and might better have never been named. For instance there are in the Senate sergeant-at-arms and assistant sergeant-at-arms, and door-keeper and assistant. Neither assistant was necessary. Then the President (of the senate) *is cumbered by a private secretary and a messenger, and there are watchmen, clerks and pages almost without number. In the House it is almost as bad."*

When the legislature took a 16-day recess with pay for the Christmas and New Year holidays the journalistic cries of outrage increased. Even that Republican stalwart, the Olympia *Partisan,* took a left-handed swipe at the legislature late in December. Thomas Cavanaugh, the last territorial printer, had formed the State Printing and Publishing company with Oliver Cromwell White, newspaperman and former Republican legislator and constitutional convention delegate, and White had been appointed the first state printer. When the legislature was criticized for heavy printing expenditures, the *Partisan* responded defensively:

"There has been a good deal of carping criticism about the printing expenses of the session of the Legislature up to date. Do you know how much it amounts to? It amounts to about three days pay of the legislators who are off on a turkey junketing trip for sixteen days at the expense of the state."

This may help to explain why the legislature decided that in the future the public printer should be elected by the voters of the state. It also prompted Murphy of the *Standard* to observe that, with the defection of the *Partisan, "the disposition to find fault with the present Legislature now seems general."*

One of the new duties of the legislature was the naming of two United States senators, one for a two-year and one for a four-year term. This involved considerable bickering and political in-fighting in the early days of the session, although the Republican party was well organized and its nominees, ex-Governor Squire and ex-Delegate John B. Allen, had smooth sailing compared to later candidates. The biennial selection of a U.S. senator would thereafter form a major stumbling block to other legislative action and a focal point for bribery, corruption and political warfare.

Another thorny problem (which still plagues legislatures every 10 years) was that of setting up legislative districts. The first session never did get that accomplished.

More time was consumed in an inter-house squabble over a bill to abolish the office of lieutenant governor. The constitution provided that this could be done by legislative action, and little time was wasted in making an effort to do so. Charles Laughton was a newcomer to Washington and its politics. The veteran politician of the senate didn't like his committee appointments and the representatives didn't like his treatment of some of their pet bills in the senate. He finally mustered enough support to table the bill, but the legislative urge to abolish the lieutenant governor kept cropping up in future sessions as a further bone of contention.

The first session established a land commission, to dispose of the timber lands which would be a major source of income to the state, a mining bureau and state geologist to promote development of the state's natural resources, a commissioner of labor, a board of equalization and boards to pass on the professional qualifications of doctors, dentists and pharmacists. The office of insurance commissioner was created under the secretary of state. They established a system of common schools, outlawed private armies, prohibited discrimination by tug boats and protected lobsters (of which there are none in Washington waters). They passed a tax bill which included a poll tax to be paid by all male citizens from 21 to 50 years of age, except paupers, idiots, lunatics and members of volunteer fire departments and the militia.

The representatives considered the complaint of sergeant at arms John Leiter against the insubordinate and generally loutish behavior of the four $2.50-a-day pages, who apparently felt their political backing exempted them from giving heed to Leiter, who reported that he had "remonstrated with the boys, but have been met by a spirit of insubordination that is, to say the least annoying." A Mr. Fox, committee clerk, was discharged for drunkenness, but the next day he was appointed to a similar position in the senate.

The senators gave heed to their sergeant at arms, who sadly reported that he couldn't comply with his standing orders to keep Old

Glory flying from the capitol flagstaff. The winter winds had nearly ripped it to pieces. The senate gravely authorized the purchase of a new flag.

But those first legislators had the most fun dividing up the contents of the newly-opened pork barrel.

They gave the state soldiers' home to Orting, in Pierce county, a state normal school to Ellensburg, whose chances of getting the capital in the next election didn't look too bright. They gave another normal school to Cheney, an agricultural college to Pullman, a state museum to Tacoma, and they transformed the territorial university into the University of the State of Washington, increasing the appropriations accordingly. Senator Henry Long of Chehalis was pushing a bill for a third normal school for his town, but it was amended to *Reform* school and Long voted against it. It passed anyway.

A total of 587 bills was introduced during the 143-day session and only 175 were enacted into law. It was inevitable that a lot of pet projects were plowed under, but a fair crop of plums was plucked and distributed to the grateful constituents of the more powerful legislative blocs.

The total appropriations came to $985,-639.45, compared to the half million of the last territorial legislature which had created such a howl from press and public.

The legislature finally adjourned on March 28.

Before the members dispersed to their various homes they had an apportunity to ride the horse cars of the Olympia Railway company from the town square to the edge of the capitol grounds on 12th street, in company with the small boys of the town, who spent all their available pocket money being noisily conveyed up and down Main street. Murphy reported in the *Standard* that he had interviewed one prosperous urchin who told him that he was on his seventh trip that day and planned to take several more if his nickels held out. Murphy also reported with some pride that the trip from 4th to 12th streets was made in the breathtaking time of eight minutes, or one minute per block.

RIDING HIGH

As for the capital city, it was riding the heady crest of the biggest boom in its history as it ushered in the decade of the gay nineties.

In addition to the street railway, it was about to open one of the grandest and gaudiest hotels in the state. Although it had fallen far behind in the population race . . . the 1890 census showed Seattle with 42,837 (up 20,000 since the great fire), Tacoma, 36,000 and Spokane Falls 20,000 . . . it had achieved a modest but record-setting gain of more than 3,000, to 4,698, during the past decade. Walla Walla was slightly larger, making Olympia now only the fifth largest city in the state.

Its boosters just ignored the census figures, by general agreement claiming that their town had a population of "nearly 10,000," which they probably felt was justified; after all, they were almost half way there.

Anyway, the glory days were just dawning. The optimistic figure might well be accurate by the time the booster material was set in type and delivered to the reader.

Early in 1890 the courts ruled that the city had the right to assess abutting property owners for the costs of street grading. The result was another wave of regrading. Whenever a few residents asked for a new street they got it, since the council reasoned it cost the town nothing. They ordered it done, paid the bills with warrants drawn on the city treasury and hopefully assessed the costs on a pro-rata basis against the improved property.

It took them some time to become aware that practically none of the property owners were paying their assessments.

In April the voters demonstrated their optimism by authorizing a municipal indebtedness of up to five percent of the total assessed valuation for a continuation of other civic improvements, and that was only the beginning. A little later the school board was authorized to issue $59,000 in bonds to construct two splendid brick schools, one on the east side and one in the south end. Only one negative vote was cast in that election. And in the fall election another bond issue, this one for $100,000, was approved to allow the Thurston county commissioners to erect a towered stone courthouse facing the town square.

And that was still only the beginning.

During the spring of 1890 the railroads, which had for so long rejected the advances of the fair Olympia, suddenly began to woo her ardently. At a town meeting in April two of them made their formal proposals.

The Union Pacific, through its subsidiary Portland and Puget Sound Railroad company offered to build a line from Portland to Seattle via Olympia, provided the citizens would grant the line a franchise on city streets, 15 acres of land for yards and a station, 1,000 feet of waterfront and $50,000 cash.

The Port Townsend Southern of the Oregon Improvement company, which was still operating the narrow-gauge to Tenino, proposed to extend its line from Port Townsend to Portland, also by way of Olympia, in return for right of way along the west side to deep water, yard and depot area and $50,000.

To prove they meant business the Union Pacific promised to begin construction before June 1 and to have trains running as far as Tacoma by December 31, 1891. The Port Townsend Southern agreed to have the line to Portland completed by January 1, 1891.

Both propositions were accepted and the money pledged within the month.

No sooner had the financial miracle been accomplished than the representatives of the Tacoma, Olympia and Grays Harbor Railroad arrived in town smiling brightly and promising to build a line from Tacoma to Grays Harbor by way of Olympia in return for a right of way through town, 200 by 2,000 feet of property for yards and station . . . and $50,000 in cash or land.

These suitors were met with some hostility, for everyone recognized beneath the friendly facade of the O.T. & G.H. the black hat and mustache of that arch-villian, the Northern Pacific.

For a while the streets resounded with the war cry, *"We ain't gonna give the Northern Pacific a damned thing!"* The broken promises of the 1870's hadn't been forgotten.

Cooler heads prevailed, however, pointing out that a Northern Pacific line from the terminus of the Cascade division would provide a transportation link with eastern Washington and end once and for all the charges of rival aspirants for the capital that it was impossible to reach Olympia by any civilized means of transportation.

Again the citizens dug deep and pledged the additional $50,000, but they refused to make things *too* easy for their old enemy. The town fathers vacated several streets west of Main for a railroad yard and depot, but they were mostly under water; the Northern Pacific would have to bring in a dredge and pump its own land out of the bay, thereby somewhat reducing the mudflats. The citizens owning property along 7th street also dug in their heels and protested bitterly against a railroad running down the

street in front of their homes. The Northern Pacific would have to build an expensive tunnel under 7th street.

The terms were accepted by the railroad and within a short time work was under way on all three lines. The first visible signs of progress were those of the Port Townsend Southern, which widened the tracks from Tenino to standard gauge and extended them north along the bay to deep water.

There could be no doubt now that Olympia was destined to become a major metropolis at last. Progress was the watchword of the day and the costs be damned.

During 1890 and 1891 things were happening so fast that the local "mossbacks" had difficulty deciding what to watch.

John percival built a splendid new steamboat dock along Water street. (His father, Captain Sam, didn't live to see it completed. He died in his ornate mansion at the end of Long bridge early in 1891.)

The Olympia Water company, taken over by Cincinnati capitalists, extended its mains, built a huge reservoir on Ayer's hill and installed powerful pumps at Moxlie creek to "insure an adequate supply of water at high pressure the year around."

General McKenny, who knew something of the process of bureaucracy, wisely decided that proliferating state government would soon overflow the very limited quarters available to it and make a first class downtown office building profitable. He began construction of the four-story brick and stone McKenny building on the southwest corner of 4th and Main. Since its ceilings were twice as high as those of 20th century structures, its carved stone cornice soon rose as high as a modern seven or eight story building.

The number of banks was tripled with the opening of the Capital National and Olympia State, the latter financed by the same eastern capitalists who had taken over the water company.

The Olympia Iron Works was established, the *Standard* reporting that *"large crowds gathered to watch the dazzling flow of molten iron."*

The Congregational church was grading land on the bay north of Butlers Cove for a major institution of higher education, Athens University, and the Westside Railway company was organized to build an electric streetcar line to the campus. The enterprising Professor Follansebee resigned his post at the

Olympia Collegiate Institute and established Calathea College. Over 800 children were enrolled in the public schools and the board was forced to rent space for the overflow pending the completion of the new brick buildings. Teachers were receiving the tidy salary of $50 a month; principals got $75.

The Olympia Light and Power company, organized in Boston by Hazzard Stevens and managed locally by L. B. Faulkner, took over the primitive plant of the old gas and electric company, installed generators at Tumwater Falls and began replacing the old sputtering arc lights with a modern incandescent system.

A new post office was opened with the elegant nicety of separate windows for male and female patrons.

The Keeley Institute for the cure of the drug and liquor habits was established on the west side and a number of prominent local citizens promptly enrolled.

John Miller Murphy, the lover of good music and drama, invested the profits of thirty years of publishing the *Washington Standard* in the Olympia Opera House, a fancy three-story wooden building erected on piling at the edge of the Swantown slough at 4th and Plum. All the gilt and glamour of the nineties was incorporated in its design, from its barouque stage and hand-painted scenery to its maroon plush opera chairs from Grand Rapids. On opening night box seats were auctioned to the affluent for over $100 each. General admission was $10 and the prevailing prosperity was dramatized by the fact that all 1,000 seats were filled for the premier production of "Little Lord Fauntleroy."

A new baseball park was established at 17th and Main and the street railway company was urged to extend its tracks four blocks south to the grounds. In the interim, Mr. Young established an omnibus line from the horse car terminus on 13th street clear out to Tumwater.

The local brickyards installed steam brick-pressing machines, which diverted the town's sidewalk superintendents from the iron foundry, but they still couldn't keep up with the demand. A new wharf was built just to handle the scowloads of brick, stone and structural steel being brought in from Seattle and Tacoma. The sawmills were working around the clock to meet the demand for lumber, and still they couldn't keep up. In March of 1891 the *Standard* reported that at least 300 buildings

were going up within the city limits and that jobs were available for anyone who wanted to work. Those who didn't want to were encouraged to change their minds by being arrested for vagrancy and put to work on the streets as members of the local chain gang.

Both downtown bridges were rebuilt again and the *Standard* claimed that *"one man power suffices to revolve the new draw,"* which was a great improvement over the last one. That one, according to Murphy, *"required the services of the entire police force, several white men and a sternwheel steamboat."*

City crews were planking 4th street and blasting out the hardpan at the top of Ayer's hill in another major regrading operation. Murphy was soon able to report that *"4th street is now nicely planked in front of the opera house. The numerous vehicles which congregate on nights of performances awaiting custom will not be compelled hereafter to stand axle-deep in mud, nor will the sidewalk be plastered with splashings from the many teams constantly passing on that important thoroughfare."*

As for the east side grading project, he informed his readers that *"the grade up Ayer's Hill is now so slight and uniform that a carriage horse need not break a trot in going from the bottom to the summit."*

As both an editor and member of the city council, Murphy was less pleased with the dilatory tactics of Mr. Savage, who was dickering with the Olympia Light and Power company to buy out his franchise at a good plump profit. Even so, under the urgings of city officials and the public, the horse car rails had reached Eastside street by mid-July. The Westside line had tracks laid across Long bridge and a third company, the Olympia and Tumwater Electric Railroad, was planning to run a line along the west side of the inlet to Tumwater.

The town even invested in a new animal pound and began vigorously enforcing the stray cow ordinance, which delighted Murphy as much as any of the other signs of progress.

"There is no greater evidence that Olympia is growing into metropolitan significance," he rejoiced, *"than the fact that the bell-cow is no longer heard in the land."*

Land values were booming again, the local papers frequently publishing three or four full columns of real estate transfers each week. The land office, which had been stolen some years earlier by aggressive Seattle, was forced to establish a southwest Washington branch in Olympia.

Subdivisions sprang up in all directions. A new company was formed to develop one on the old Oblat mission grounds at Priest Point and the Olympia Railway company promised to extend its rails to that lovely forested headland above the bay.

Kind-hearted citizens watched teamsters whip overloaded dray-horses through the streets with vast loads of building materials and machinery and organized a humane society with George Barnes as president. The more convivial formed a local lodge of the Benevolent and Protective Order of Elks, organized by Charles Vivian, who had been well known in Olympia in earlier days as a strolling theatrical producer.*

Polk and Company had accorded Olympia the dignity of a city directory of its own in 1890. It contained just under a thousand individual listings, not including business firms. The latter included 14 saloons (not counting bars in hotels and restaurants), five newspapers, three banks and one public school. There were six churches, but within the year the number had increased to 12, while the saloons proliferated at an equal rate, and the number of public schools tripled.

The leading occupation of Olympia residents was that of clerk, which included retail, hotel and office varieties; there were 60 listed. There were also 43 laborers, 38 carpenters, 27 teamsters (including draymen, truckmen, cab, hack and horse car drivers), 22 bartenders, 15 printers, nine doctors, seven teachers, six capitalists and one "spectulator."

The number of bartenders and printers indicates that the town still had more than its share of saloons and newspapers. Among the latter was a new daily, the *Tribune,* established by J. W. Robinson, who purchased the old *Republican Partisan* plant and installed C. M. Barton as managing editor. Murphy thankful-

ly suspended the *Evening Olympian,* but the *Tribune* had competition for a while from still another hopeful daily when B. M. Price bought the *Review* and published it during 1890 and 91 as the *Daily Capital.* Early in 1891 a group of local printers including George Blankenship established a Democratic daily, the *Morning Olympian,* which was soon purchased by Thomas Henderson Boyd and its politics changed to Republican.

The fire department, convinced that it wasn't getting its share of the civic improvments, supported J. C. Horr, feed, fuel and building material merchant, as the first successful independent candidate for mayor. Sam McClelland, the first paid chief of the volunteer department headed his campaign, and Horr did all he could for the firemen during his 1891 term.

The construction of the new east side reservoir and resulting adequate water supply at high pressure made the two pumpers less essential, although a farm team was purchased and equipped with drop-harness to pull the Silsby steamer. A new chemical and hose wagon and two hose carts were added to the roster to take advantage of the 10 new fire hydrants added to the city system under Mayor Horr, and the ultimate sophistication of a telegraphic fire alarm was installed. Charles Peterson, engineer of the steamer, was promoted to superintendent of the alarm system and got a pay raise from $70 to $80 a month. Fire Chief McClelland received only $25 a month, but he made his living as a blacksmith when he wasn't directing the city's firefighting forces.

The Northern Pacific line reached the city limits in time to qualify for its subsidy and by early April the sidewalk superintendents were congregated on Jefferson street watching the crew of the first work train lay track toward the 7th street tunnel, which formed a giant unroofed chasm across Main street. A Bowers dredger was hard at work disgorging mud behind the bulkheads of the new yard and depot area. Regular passenger trains were running to a temporary depot east of the cut by mid-April.

All this progress was not without its inconveniences, of course.

The uncompleted railroad tunnel blocked vehicular traffic on Main street, while pedestrians clambered across by way of a shaky temporary foot bridge. The J. N. Murray family, residing in a house near the new depot site, were inconvenienced more than most. The

---

*Vivian was a dapper dresser and made a great impression on the simple belles of fronter Olympia. Upon one occasion when he appeared in town in lavender waistcoast, doeskin trousers, ruffled shirt and high hat, a native decided he had better buy a clean shirt before he called upon his girl. "It's no use," a friend told him. "I took one look at that dude and bought every new shirt in town . . . and I've got 'em on now."

railroad work crew was blasting stumps in the area and one of the largest of them crashed through the Murrays' dining room ceiling just as they were sitting down to dinner. None of them were injured, but Mrs. Murray declared the cheese souffle a total loss.

An unidentified transient found the new city reservoir a convenient place to end it all and when his decomposed body was discovered floating in it the sale of beer and soda pop boomed along with everything else.*

The multi-storied Victorian-towered Washington and Lincoln schools added a fine touch to the city's growing skyline, but the damp climate and defective heating systems prevented the plaster from curing and teachers complained that they were getting rheumatism from the cold and damp. A storm struck the Lincoln school building in the south end before all the winows were installed; the tower became waterlogged and collapsed, taking a sizeable section of the building with it.

Saddest of all was the sacrifice of the maple shade trees to the gods of progress. Between the street graders, the layers of water mains and the erectors of telephone, telegraph and electric light poles and wires, almost all of the leafy giants along the principle streets were gone by the end of 1891.

No longer would visitors write of Olympia's likeness to a green and goodly Olympian bower or, at the very least, a neat New England village.

One of the last who did was a W. W. Hartley, whose peans of praise were published in the St. Paul *Pioneer-Press* following his visit to Olympia in the summer of 1889. Mr. Hartley had waxed poetic over *"this amphi-theater, commanding, as it does, an unobstructed view of this charming, everlasting panorama, * * * a city nestled in overhanging fruit and ornamental shade trees, and studded with luxuriant vineyards and grassy glades and terraces, one of which latter we might almost imagine to have been the scene of the temptation of Hassen Ban Kahled."*

So charmed had Mr. Hartley been that he offered the rather naive conclusion that Olympia should certainly be retained as the state capital because *"Legislatures could never enact mischievous or wicked laws in such a place as Olympia, calculated as it is to bring*

out men's best impulses and promote their better natures."

Perhaps he was right, but by the time the second state legislature convened in December of 1891, the trees had been chopped down and the terraces had been regraded into raw earth. The swaying maples were replaced by a wooden jungle of utility poles and the overhanging fruit by glaring wooden signboards.

The lovely little territorial capital had vanished and in its place was a bustling, noisy, frontier town trying to look as much as possible like its larger and uglier contemporaries, Seattle and Tacoma.

But nobody was much concerned. Progress was far too exciting and profitable to mourn over shade trees chopped into firewood.

In July, according to the *Standard*, *"the first passenger train from Tacoma dashed through the 7th street tunnel for the first time and pulled up at the new depot building at the rear of the Hotel Olympia."*

And a month later the Northern Pacific began routing its transcontinental trains through Olympia, bringing the excitement and glamour of the main line limiteds to the long-neglected state capital. Murphy was clearly elated when he recorded the development:

"Olympia is now on the main transcontinental line of the Northern Pacific Railroad Company. Thursday, the 10th, was the day that, unheralded and unexpected, the first overland trains passed through our city. The eastbound train crossed the trestle and arrived at the depot, direct from Portland at 12:30, and about half an hour later the westbound train, direct from St. Paul, came thundering through the 7th street tunnel."

The legislature had returned to town in August for its first special session to tackle the thorny problem of legislative districting. Having accomplished this, it adjourned thankfully. Like the homosexual who fathered a child, it vowed that it never wanted to go through *that* again, and it didn't; not for many years.

It was obvious that state legislatures were going to spend more time and more money in the capital city than had the territorial assemblies, and at the November election of 1890 the voters had overwhelmingly selected Olympia as their state capital. Out of 51,413 votes cast, Olympia got 37,413, Ellensburg 7,722 and North Yakima 6,276.

The golden goose still hung high, but there were increasing indications to the more obser-

---

*Not to be outdone, Tacoma immediately claimed that it had snakes in *its* municipal water system.

vant that Washington's boom might be inflating itself for the inevitable bust. In the same issue of the *Standard* which recorded the arrival of the first transcontinental train, Murphy included the single, ominous line . . . *"'Hard times' being mentioned."*

There was no space for further warnings of a possible economic decline after December when the second state legislature convened. The columns of the press were full of accounts of political battles, bribery, scandal and blackmail.

A LITTLE BRIBERY NOW AND THEN ..

It began in the early days of the session with Squire, the two-year senate appointee, lobbying for another term. There was no doubt a Republican would get the appointment . . . There were only 17 Democrats in the house and four in the senate, giving a Republican majority of 70 on the joint ballot for U.S. senator . . . but a number of prominent Republicans were cutting each other up to win the prize. The legislature remained deadlocked for days while the battle raged and the bitterness engendered within the party would result in a complete stalemate when Senator Allen's term expired two years later.

Five hundred dollars appeared to be the going price for a legislator's vote in the senatorial contest and none of them seemed to question the policy except a freshman representative from Stevens county, John Metcalfe.

When a lobbyist for W. H. Calkins, one of the leading contenders, approached young Metcalfe with the usual inducement in cash, the innocent legislator from Thetis, Washington, yelled bloody murder and rushed to the speaker of the house. He turned the money over to the speaker and pointed the finger at the lobbyist, one Harry Clark.

A legislative committee was forthwith appointed to look into Metcalfe's charge of bribery. In due time it made public its findings, which included these highlights:

"That Harry A. Clark has hitherto borne a good reputation for truth and veracity, for honesty and integrity, but that in his zeal to accomplish his ends in the state senatorial contest, he offered and gave to said John L. Metcalfe, the sum of $500 for and in consideration of Metcalfe's voting for Hon. W. H. Calkins for U. S. Senator, and that the said $500 is the same $500 turned over by Metcalfe to the Speaker of the House."

Having reached these conclusions, the committee then made it clear that the honorable Mr. Calkins had no knowledge of the attempted bribery of the miserable Mr. Metcalfe, the snitch.

It also found that Metcalfe had *"accepted and exposed said bribe under the false delusion that the same would tend to prevent corruption in politics and elevate him in the minds of the people,"* concluding with the recommendation that *"Metcalfe deserves at least the severest censure."*

A resolution was then introduced on the floor of the house to expel the unfortunate gentleman from Stevens from the legislature. It failed to pass by only eight votes.

There was no suggestion from anyone that Clark, the dispenser of banknotes, be either censured or run out of the capitol.

At the close of the session Metcalfe returned to tranquil Thetis, a sadder and wiser man. He did not again become involved in state politics.

Even before the legislative committee issued its report suggesting Metcalfe's proper reward for having a big mouth, new scandal was making the rounds. The *Washington Standard* took note of it in the issue of February 6, 1891:

"A sensational story is going the rounds, set afloat by some Olympia correspondent, that a very pretty young woman has been enacting the part of a blackmailer. Her plan, according to the report, was to send her card to a victim and invite him to call at her room (at the new Hotel Olympia). *As soon as a man was seated she locked the door and withdrew the key and threatened to summon the bell boy and cry for help unless the money was forthcoming. It is said that a prominent Chehalis county lawyer was blackmailed out of $125 a few nights since. The police learned that the woman picked up about $600 last week. An effort was made to induce one or two of her victims to prosecute, but they were not anxious to make public fools of themselves and Emma Holman was told to go. She went."*

The staid state capital, hitherto so noted for its innocence and high moral tone, was indeed becoming citified.

The tight-fisted and strong-minded Governor Ferry was not present to keep a restraining hand on the legislature in 1891. He wasn't feeling well and had been granted a leave of absence to travel for his health. Acting Governor Laughton, in his message to the legislators, had little to say about economy in government. He did make numerous suggestions on how to spend money. He urged appropriations for state fish hatcheries and a state forestry commission; for construction of a state office building in downtown Olympia pending construction of a permanent capitol; for emergency appropriations to make up the deficiencies caused by overspending in various state departments, including the military and the public printer.

Adjutant General O'Brien, he said, had been forced into deficit spending because the militia had been called out to guard Seattle and Spokane after the great fires which had struck both cities in 1889.

He made no mention of the last militia summer camp, during which the gallant general had made it clear that nothing the taxpayers could provide was too good for his men. When it was time for the weekend warriors to return home a force of carpenters was still busy laying matched hardwood flooring in the tents. And when Governor Ferry returned from his leave of absence, he nearly had apoplexy when, in checking over O'Brien's accounts, he found a bill for a ton of radishes delivered on the last day of the encampment.

The legislature had directed the secretary of state to supervise the state printer, but neglected to vest power in him or anyone else to control the amount of printing done. Departments and institutions ordered tons of stationery, brochures, pamphlets and publications, running up deficits which it took years to pay off. The state printer provided his own plant and pocketed the profits of the work done, so he prospered as no public printer had since the early 1870's.

Despite the growing evidence that the boom was about to bust, the legislature failed to take heed. Prosperity and spending remained the watchword even as the early months of 1892 brought louder cries of alarm from those whose fingers were on the economic pulse of the state. This time the total expenditures zoomed to over two and a half million dollars.

Edmond S. Meany, who served in the second and third legislative sessions wrote that, as chairman of the house education committee, he bore the brunt of the demands of practically

every town in the state for another new normal school. *"Overwhelmed with the surprising number, he sought advice from 'Uncle Joe' Megler, an older member, who said: 'Pigeonhole them all. We are trying to make it so ridiculous that these fellows will let up'."*

The second legislature did take heed of the increasing public outcry against the numerous corporations which had moved in with the railroads and were in the process of exploiting the new state for all it was worth. Timber barons who had raped the northeast and midwestern forests, grabbed for the huge land grants of the Northern Pacific, outbidding settlers and small local operators. For years the bribing of federal and territorial land officials by speculators had been an endemic scandal, and the greed of the railroad promoters had aroused the active hostility of a large segment of the population.

The legislators responded with a number of bills mildly curbing corporate powers and regulating to some extent their right to exploit the land, their customers and their workers.

As soon as they adjourned Acting Governor Laughton vetoed every one of the corporation bills.

The storm of public indignation which followed caused even the most conservative Republicans to wash their hands of the never very popular Laughton. Even Murphy indicated some sympathy for the Republican party in a post-legislative editorial:

"The Republican party of Washington, through its public leaders, through the newspapers that speak on its behalf and by the general acclamation of its membership, disclaims and repudiates the act of Lt. Gov. Laughton in vetoing the corporation laws passed by the Legislature. By universal judgement the acting governor is condemned and censured not only as a traitor to the interests of the state but to the party through whose agency he was elevated to public office."

Murphy seemed to believe that, with friends like Laughton, the Republicans didn't need the attention of avowed enemies such as himself.

Laughton was generally acknowledged to be an excellent fiddler, however, and he played rollicking tunes at the *sine die* banquet in the luxurious Hotel Olympia, which the town fathers financed with $500 of the local taxpayers' money to show their appreciation for the capital remaining in Olympia.

PAYING THE PIPER

The year of 1892 was not very gay. The city council awoke from its spending spree to a hangover of red ink and public indignation. The ledger showed that it had spent $143,-619.30 on street improvements, including the grading of Ayer's hill, the new bridges and the macadam paving of lower Main street. The property owners, who had been expected to foot the bill, had come through with only about $11,000 and those 10 percent treasury warrants were costing the city over $13,000 a year.

The entire city council resigned in January. Murphy commented on his own departure from city hall as follows:

"With all reverence, let me say that had the Messiah appeared and filled the high and honorable position of mayor, and his disciples taken the humbler places of councilmen, and with wisdom ineffable have guided the bark through these tumultuous times, a sect might have arisen that would have nailed them to the cross without any compunctions or conscience."

The dissension at city hall prompted both Democrats and Independents to enter candidates in the municipal election against the Republican incumbent, General O'Brien. The Democrats nominated C. J. Lord, cashier of the Capital National Bank, which wasn't a very good choice. With increasingly hard times he had been foreclosing a lot of mortgages and discounting the pay warrants of working men at the highest possible rate of interest. Judge J. W. Robinson, the Independent candidate, won the election.

As the year progressed things got worse. Working men, attracted to town by the big boom, departed for more likely job markets. Businesses closed and business buildings stood empty and neglected. The price of logs dropped to five dollars a thousand as building ground to a halt throughout the state. The Oregon Railway and Navigation company gave up and sold its Puget Sound steamers and the *Fleetwood* was on the Seattle-Tacoma route. The long wharf, which was already being gnawed to destruction by the teredos, was used only by Captain Willey's sternwheeler *Multnomah,* which he had purchased on the Columbia river to take over the remaining trade between Olympia, Tacoma and Seattle. And even without any serious competition, the *Multnomah* was forced to cut freight and

PADDLING SEDATELY THROUGH A PUGET SOUND MIST, the old stern-wheeler *Multnomah* churns down Budd Inlet toward Seattle on the run she maintained for two decades, carrying thousands of politicians and lobbyists to and from the capital city.

One of the original Pullman-built trolley cars at the Tumwater station on a summer day in 1895.

passenger rates to a dollar a head and a dollar a ton to either Seattle or Tacoma.

By late summer the new city administration ordered most of the incandescent street lights turned off in the interests of economy and the county commissioners were looking for a suitable location for a poor farm. The care of the indigent was costing almost as much as the construction and maintenance of county roads.

When smallpox broke out to join what the *Standard* delicately referred to as "the usual summer complaint," the empty warehouse at the end of the long wharf was converted to a pest house.

Dr. William A. Newell, who had retrogressed politically to city health officer after running for congress on the Prohibition ticket with a marked lack of success, stated forthrightly that the town should either install a real sewer system or provide itself with a regular pest house, becoming quite oratorical in this references to "the wooden sidewalks under which a festering fermentation has continued for years."

The town fathers gave up and appropriated the last of the dwindling treasury funds for a sewer survey.

They also encouraged those who didn't have anything better to do to entertain themselves shooting rats. Several thousand were slaughtered, but the rat population continued to steadily increase while the human population just as steadily declined.

There were a few highlights during the year. The new county courthouse of Chuckanut sandstone was completed, to the tune of another deficit, and its eight-sided Gothic clock tower dominated the town's modest skyline. The townspeoples' pride in the great gargoyled stone structure was increased when an expert on such matters pointed out that it boasted one of the only three octagonal clock towers in the world.

Hazzard Stevens had succeeded in floating the bonds necessary to buy out Savage's horse car line and replace it with the long-awaited electric street railway, and work proceeded despite the growing depression. The other two aspiring street railway companies had quietly gone bankrupt.

On July 18 the *Daily Tribune* announced the arrival of the first of the new electric streetcars:

"The morning freight today brought in two flat cars on which were two of the five handsome palace cars for use by the Olympia Light and Power company on its new line. The cars were covered with an awning bearing the imprint of the Pullman Palace Car company, Pullman, Ill. The cars will be unloaded this afternoon and taken down Columbia street to Fourth, and thence to the depot.

"The cars are Nos. 1 and 3. Another car left four or five days in advance of the two which came this morning, but has not yet arrived. The other two are open cars and are being manufactured in Philadelphia. They are painted white picked with gold, and bear the inscription "Olympia and Tumwater". Below is a handsome monogram of the Olympia Light and Power company. The interior of the cars is a handsome sample of superior and modern workmanship. The seats are upholstered with moquette carpet, and the woodwork is handsomely finished and polished in panelled maple, cherry and ash. The cars are wide and roomy, and at each window is an electric button by which the passengers can signal the conductor and brakeman (sic). Electricity supplies both light and heat, and guard gates on the outside protect passengers from cars coming from the opposite direction.

"As soon as the tracks are cleared, which will be by Wednesday or Thursday, the cars will be given their trial trip. Everything is now in readiness for operation and the last turn-out is completed. On the first day the company proposed that everybody shall be given one free ride.

"Superintendent Shock says the cars are, without exception, the handsomest on the coast."

The *Tribune* then noted with editorial pride that *"Olympia will have its electric line in operation this week and the great city of Philadelphia with over a million inhabitants, still has the horse cars jogging along its cobblestone streets."*

John Miller Murphy was, of course, invited to go along for the ride on the first of the electric palace cars, and he described the experience in the *Standard* of July 22:

"The inauguration of the electric street railway system of Olympia marks another epoch in the progress of the capital city. Thus it is that the good work goes steadily on. The completion of an efficient sewer system will mark another epoch of no less importance. Olympia is fast outgrowing its swathing (sic) clothes.

"The first car passed over the track of the Olympia Light and Power company yesterday afternoon at 4:30 p.m. with Superintendent Shock at the electric lever. The passengers on that memorable occasion were, besides the writer: George D. Shannon, Robert Frost, George L. Sickels, Thomas Henderson Boyd, C. T. Whitney, A. S. Gillis and L. B. Faulkner.

"The cars will run to Tumwater at least once an hour, and will give seven-minute service in the city. The fare will probably be 5¢ to all points, although a 10¢ fare to Tumwater has been discussed.

"The cars are engaged in finishing and ballasting the road bed, and regular service is to start in about ten days."

Things didn't go quite so smoothly when the first of the open cars from Brill and Company arrived at about the same time as the autumn rains. The results were disturbing to Superintendent Shock and shocking to the patrons, according to the *Standard's* account:

"When the interior woodwork became wet, the electric current played like the aurora borealis among the passengers and converted the whole vehicle into immense Leyden jars, ready to discharge a current whenever a proper connection was made."

Olympians were learning again that progress is not without its painful side, and the open "wind-scoopers" were henceforth used only during fair weather.

Probably the second most exciting event of that rather drab year was the arrival in town of the heavyweight boxing champion of the world, the great John L. Sullivan, who was playing the lead in the traveling melodrama "Honest Hearts and Willing Hands" on a one-night stand at Murphy's Olympia Opera House. Most of the population assembled at the Northern Pacific depot to see the great John L., who liked to be referred to as "the Champion of Creation," make his grand entry. Enough were able to pay admission to see his bad acting and better boxing exhibition to fill most of the seats at the opera house.

After that the state capital was preoccupied for a number of weary years with mortgage foreclosures, bankruptcy proceedings, delinquent taxes and expensive subdivision lots that couldn't be given away.

And when people went to the depot it was to wave a sad farewell to somebody else who had given up and was *leaving* town.

CHAPTER SIX
The Fifth Decade
1893-1903

The third state legislature assembled on January 9, 1893. The general gloom prevailing at the state capital as a result of the steadily declining economy was enhanced by the terrible weather which traditionally greets state legislatures. The town was covered with over a foot of unmelted snow during much of January. The new electric streetcars gave up and service was suspended indefinitely.

The thaw came in February on the wings of a Chinook wind from the Pacific and it rained drearily during most of that month.

Both houses got down to business promptly and organized themselves in record time, giving hope that this was going to be a no nonsense session. Even John Miller Murphy was impressed:

"There has scarcely been a precedent in our legislative history when both houses fully organized on the first day and with so little apparent friction between the parties"

The Democrats in the house of representatives might well congratulate themselves upon having anything to say about the selection of a speaker. They had increased their membership by only two . . . to a total of 19 . . . but 10 Populists had been elected, reducing Republican strength from 59 - 18 to 49 - 29.

The senate likewise moved rapidly, selecting T. P. Dyer, Seattle lawyer, as president pro-tem, Allen Weir as secretary and authorizing the employment of an assistant secretary, minute clerk, journal clerk, enrolling clerk, engrossing clerk, sergeant at arms and assistant, bill clerk, messenger and postmaster, doorkeeper, watchman, janitor and two pages. Salaries ranged from $7.00 a day for the secretary and chief clerk to $2.00 for pages.

Women were given six clerkships in the house and four in the senate. Two of them were ex-governors' daughters . . . Miss Bernice Newell and Miss Josie Ferry. A rising young

Seattle lawyer, Hiram Gill, was clerk of the senate Judiciary committee and Hill Harmon, former state asylum superintendent, was night watchman.

One Thomas Beedy, not satisfied with his $2.00 a day remuneration as a page, took up moonlighting as a purse-snatcher and pickpocket. His legislative career came to an abrupt end when he was arrested and convicted of having "abstracted a pocket-book containing money from the coat pocket of a member and stolen the purse of Miss L. E. Yeomans."

Young Mr. Beedy had violated the first rule of legislative conduct. He had gotten caught in the act.

On the second day the senate appropriated $60,000 for the expenses of the legislature and the army of still unemployed political hangers-on in the wings licked their chops and rubbed their hands. It was the same preliminary appropriation that had been made for the 1891 session and it was comforting to note that the senators apparently hadn't heard about the approach of hard times. The senators eventually hired 41 employees; the representatives 31, and quietly appropriated an additional $12,000 to help pay their salaries.

In the afternoon a joint session was convened and Speaker Arrasmith formally announced the results of the previous fall's election. Republican John Harte McGraw, having amassed 38,228 votes, was named the second governor of the state of Washington. Democrat Snively had trailed badly with 29,948 votes. The surprise of the election . . . and a portent of things to come . . . was the impressive showing of Populist party candidate C. W. Young, who was close behind Snively with 23,780.

McGraw, who claimed to be a graduate of the University of Hard Knocks, had made it the hard way. Born on an unprofitable Maine farm in 1850, he left home at 14 to make his way in the world. At the age of 17 he was manager of a New England general store. After going broke in a business partnership with his brother, he headed west, landing at Seattle in the winter of 1876 without a penny to his name. He got a job as clerk in the Occidental hotel and soon became proprieter of a small hotel of his own near Yesler's wharf. When it was destroyed by fire he joined the police force and became city marshal and chief of police. Then he was

He ended up as one of the only two Washington governors to have a statue erected in his honor.

The sun broke through on Governor McGraw's inauguration day, which his family and friends, with some justification, considered a minor miracle. The inaugural ball, preceded by a parade of state and local dignitaries escorted by seven companies of militia, was held in the grand ball room of the new Hotel Olympia. Music was provided by the opera house orchestra led by Professor Cross. The grand march was led by the McGraws' daughter Kate, wearing a white dress made by Mrs. McGraw for the occasion, and escorted by General O'Brien in full and glittering uniform. They were followed by the governor and his wife, which was considered a major breach of protocol, which dictated that the chief executive should escort the wife of some other dignitary. May Kelley McGraw wanted to share the occasion with her husband, however, and she did.

Mrs. McGraw was different in other ways, too. After moving her family into the rented house at Maple Park and Main street vacated by the Ferrys, she became a no nonsense housekeeper, doing her own marketing and soon becoming a friend of store clerks and delivery boys. Mrs. McGraw had no interest in politics or "society" and hadn't wanted her husband to run for governor in the first place, but she liked people and people liked her, which made her a major political asset in spite of herself. When she died, 14 years after her husband's inauguration, a long-time Olympia postmistress wrote to Kate. It was a long letter, but the thing that impressed the postmistress most was the fact that Mrs. McGraw was *the only governor's wife (territorial or state) she could recall who bought her own postage*

Hon. John H. McGraw.

stamps instead of having the state pay her postage."

The inaugural ball was preceded by ceremonies at the capitol, during which Ferry, as the outgoing governor delivered a long farewell message to the legislature. His financial report showed the treasury in the black. He strongly recommended laws regulating railroads and other common carriers and the establishment of a railroad and transportation commission to enforce them. He also favored passage of the "Pinkerton law" making it illegal for corporations to employ armed bodies of men. Attempts to organize miners in the state into the union had prompted operators to hire armed Pinkerton guards as strike-breakers and their clubbing and shooting of working men had created widespread anger throughout the state.

*"The Light in the Mansion," Mary Lou Hanify, Seattle, 1971.

Ferry emphasized the need for a new capitol building with the opinion that "no citizen who has the slightest concern for the dignity of our state, or who would view with pride the substantial manifestations of our prosperity, but must feel chagrined and impatient at the delay in beginning the construction of suitable capitol buildings."

Since the sad state of the timber market made it unwise to try to dispose of the capitol grant timber lands, he suggested 10-year state bonds to finance construction to be paid off when times got better and the price of logs went up.

Ferry also made the first recommendation for a state highway commission . . . "a commission of elected or appointed members should assume control of maintenance and construction of all roads in the state, with an annual state tax for road purposes, thus establishing a system of highways constructed on a common design."

Mr. Laughton wound up his brief political career in the state of Washington with a farewell address to the senate. According to the *Standard, "his remarks were mostly a complaint for the manner in which he had been criticized for his acts as Executive."*

By mid-January the polite ceremonials were over and the legislators were locked in the biennial battle to select a United States senator from among four competing candidates including Allen, the incumbent. Allen was well in the lead on the first ballot, with 49 votes to 26 for Turner, 27 for Griggs and nine for Teats, but he didn't have a majority of all votes cast. As the balloting went on interminably he began to lose support. On the fourth ballot Representative Roscoe of Snohomish rose to announce that he had decided to "vote his honest convictions" and switched from Allen to Turner "amidst great applause."

Murphy dipped into his fonts of bold-faced type to report the antics of the Republican legislature:

"NOW THE STORM BEGINS TO LOWER: HASTE! THE LOOM OF HELL PREPARE. FIRST VOTE ON SENATOR . . . ALLEN'S GOOSE COOKED . . . HIS STRENGTH DAILY GROWING LESS . . . BOTH HOUSES CREATING A MULTITUDE OF NEW OFFICERS TO REWARD DEPENDENTS."

At the close of the fifth ballot Senator Rutter of King county offered a resolution "that the joint convention adjourn for the day out of respect to the memory of ex-President Rutherford B. Hayes."

Senator Frink of King wanted the assembly to rule that 10 more ballots must be taken before adjournment, but Senator Easterday pointed out that if one of the candidates got a majority before the 10 ballot had been taken "the convention would be in an awful dilemma." Senator Frink's amendment was tabled and a heated discussion followed.

Senator Forrest of King thought it rather late for the convention to start showing its respect for the late Rutherford B. Hayes after having already taken five ballots. Representative Baker, Pierce county Populist, shouted that the people had sent their representatives to Olympia to work and some respect was due to the living, but the assembly voted 70 to 41 to call it quits for the day.

The next day, according to the *Standard, "the house resumed its favorite occupation of appointing clerks."*

There was also more balloting. On the sixth roll call Senator Rutter announced that he had decided to join the gentleman from Snohomish and vote *his* honest convictions. He too switched from Allen to Turner. Then Senator Sargent of Buckley, who had just returned to the capitol after his mill burned down, threw the Allen supporters into a complete tizzy by nominating a fifth candidate, Eugene T. Wilson. In the voting which followed Allen got 47, Turner 28, Griggs 27, Teats nine and Wilson one. A total of 57 votes was needed for election.

As January drew to a close amid frustration anf fulminations, Murphy observed that *"the creation of a few more employees is the only progress made as the session is one-third over."*

Allen had gained four votes, giving him a total of 51, six short of election, but that appeared to be all he was going to get. Senator Claypool of Pierce, pointing to the continued deadlock, offered a resolution limiting the senatorial voting to one ballot a day in order that the legislature might get something else accomplished. Representative Meany offered an amendment to make it *two* ballots per day. Representative Mays said he thought one ballot was enough. "If there is any trading or trafficking still to be done it can be attended to in the lobby of the hotel and need not be brought here at all," he thundered. This prompted a good deal of appreciative laughter, but Meany's amendment was adopted.

Following the next futile vote, the body adjourned for the day to honor the memory of James G. Blaine.

After more than a hundred inconclusive votes, the legislators admitted they were hopelessly deadlocked and gave the whole thing up as a bad job after dispatching a resolution to Washington, D.C., instructing the state's congressional delegation to work for a constitutional amendment permitting a direct senatorial vote of the people. The state of mind of the frustrated solons is indicated by the fact that the resolution passed by a 103 to eight vote.

Senator Allen, who had been strongly criticized for remaining in Olympia to lobby his cause while drawing the munificent salary of $14 a day, was appointed by Governor McGraw to succeed himself, but that was declared unconstitutional. For the next two years the state of Washington was represented by only one United States senator, Watson C. Squire.

Allen wasn't the only lobbyist who was buttonholing legislators at the capitol and in the lobby of the Hotel Olympia.

The legislative committee of the Washington State Teachers' Association, the state's first education lobby, was out in force pushing bills on truancy, school libraries, certification and school taxes. A group of Garfield county citizens presented a petition demanding a 50 percent reduction in state officers' salaries and a reduction in the supreme court from five members to three. Ezra Meeker preferred charges of extravagance, dishonesty and neglect against the state's Columbian Exposition commission. A legislative investigating committee agreed that there had ben extravagant and excessive expenditures, but felt it was the result of inexperience rather than dishonesty and the commissioners shouldn't be replaced.

The railroad lobby was out in force, seeing to it that all the legislators had free passes over all the lines in the state; the liquor lobby was setting up the drinks and gently twisting arms to defeat Senator Frink's bill giving county commissioners the power to regulate liquor

sales and making the possession of cigarettes a crime.

No less than five bills were in the hopper to appropriate funds for a new capitol building and Olympia's civic leaders had to redouble their already intense lobbying efforts when a Pierce county group led, according to the *Standard,* by that "ancient fraud," Ezra Meeker, began a campaign to move the state capital to Puyallup.

Despite the complications caused by the Pierce county boosters, Senator T. F. Mentzer's bill for a new capitol at Olympia was passed, after the appropriation was reduced by amendment from two million dollars to one million.

Olympia Mayor Robinson called a mass meeting at the opera house "to rejoice over the passage of the capitol appropriation bill." After having a complete abstract of title made on the capitol site which finally established the legality of the Sylvester land gift, Governor McGraw signed the bill and joy was unrestrained in the capital city.

Despite these major issues, the legislators found time to argue less important matters. The *Standard* described a typical minor skirmish:

"Mr. Sallee wanted to provide revolving easy chairs for the members, but as nobody would second his motion he will not be afforded the oriental luxury that he imagined belonged to the office of law-maker. Instead of securing the privilege of sitting on a costly divan, the House sat down on him with vigor."

There were no less than 23 newspaper correspondents covering the 1893 session and, as usual, a number of the legislators resented their presence. Senator Van De Vanter rose to express his opinion that the newspapers were continuously making trouble and that he strongly favored throwing "the whole outfit" out of the senate chamber. Senator Horr responded to say he didn't think the newspapers were "worth heeding". He had, he reported plaintively, been "hounded by them for two years" and had "never said yea or nay."

There were also moments of tranquility, as when the senate extended its thanks to Miss Bush for the painting of a rhododendron which she presented to that body. Then, "at the urging of the ladies," the senate approved the rhododendron as the state flower and "Evergreen State" as its official title.

The members found time to attend the Elks "grand social session" held at Columbia hall in their honor. The entertainment included vocal selections by General O'Brien, fiddling by ex-Lieutenant Governor Laughton and "comicalities" by Sam Woodruff. Refreshments "liquid and solid" were served in profusion.

They also found time to make total appropriations from all funds of $2,941,321.42 . . . up more than a million dollars over the 1891-93 biennium. The state printing bill alone was up to $115,000 a year and was described by Murphy as *a big leak that should be stopped.* The 1893 session showed little inclination to stop the leak, however. Its *Legislative Hand-Book and Manual* even included a complete reprint of Francis Henry's "Old Settler."

Despite the passage of the capitol construction bill, Murphy took a more than usually dim view of the legislature, which he described at some lengh in the *Standard* of March 31:

"When the Seattle Telegraph *agrees with the* Olympian-Tribune* *that the legislative term of 60 days is too short, with our late experience so prominently in view, it is time to protest . . . The fact is that if the sessions were prolonged to 100 days or for six months, the business would be no nearer completion when the last day came than it is now. There would be more time for junketing excursions, dress parade and posing as Solons of State, and more time for display of party spleen in voting for U.S. Senator, but there would be just as much conflict in the laws enacted, just as much legislation left undone, and just as many sinecure officers employed.*

" * * When the tax payer sees able-bodied men and women dawdling away an hour or two each day in the service of the state, either as legislators or employes, and receive from $4 to $8 for it, while labor toils persistently, rain or shine, nine or ten hours for one-half or a quarter of that pay he cannot but become imbued with one of the true and fundamental principles of reform . . . Oh no! Give us no more of the last two Legislatures."*

This Murphy editorial of 80 years ago differs only in technicalities from a number of modern day press commentaries on the accomplishments of the legislature.

---

*The daily *Tribune* was absorbed in 1893 by the *Olympian* and the merged papers were published for a short time as the *Olympian-Tribune.*

MORE HARD TIMES

As the year progressed it became increasingly evident that Washington wasn't just undergoing a leveling-off period following the railroad boom of the 1880's. The nation was descending into another of its seemingly inevitable depressions, and this one was going to be a lot worse than usual. Bank failures became almost routine events. Within three years the total number of banks in the state had been reduced by half, partly as the result of mergers, but mostly by bankruptcy. In Tacoma, 21 of the city's 28 banks failed, along with five of the six in the rival towns of Whatcom and Fairhaven on Bellingham Bay.

Early rains in the fall rotted the wheat in the fields of eastern Washington, resulting in the first crop failure in the state's history and much hardship to the farmers. who weren't yet being paid by the government for not producing crops.

The depression hit hardest in those Washington cities which had enjoyed the biggest booms . . . Seattle which grew from 3,500 people to nearly 43,000 in ten years, Tacoma, up from 1,100 to 36,000 and Spokane, which had increased its population from 350 in 1880 to nearly 20,000 in 1890.

In Olympia the signs of progress continued for some time. The city council reported that more than five miles of new sewers with 19 syphons were completed and neatly depositing their contents in the bay. However, many citizens and some public agencies were slow to take advantage of the new sanitary system. The Washington school sewer emptied into the street at 5th and Pear, while that of the Lincoln school poured its contents onto the Northern Pacific right of way. The council ordered the school board to make connectiohs with the city system immediately.

The federal government had at last appropriated $35,000 to dredge a channel from 3rd street to deep water; and none too soon. The long wharf, so recently the town's pride, had been gnawed so badly by the teredos that it had been declared unsafe for all but pedestrian traffic. When the dredger completed its first project in the long battle to remove the mudflats, the council issued warrants on the depleted treasury to fill in land at the east end of Long bridge, creating several acres of new business area and decreasing the number of bridge pilings vulnerable to attack by hungry marine borers.

145

A third fancy brick schoolhouse was erected on the west side and named in honor of the martyred President Garfield. There was some citizen discontent when it was learned that County Treasurer C. B. Mann had awarded himself a commission of $1,169 for selling the $59,000 in school building bonds, but he eventually paid back a small percentage of it and the citizens of Olympia showed their appreciation by electing him mayor at the next election.

The public square was graded, landscaped and, to the delight of Murphy, enclosed by an ornamental wrought-iron fence which kept even the most wily of cows away from the new shrubbery.

The federal government had established a door-to-door mail delivery service by postmen in handsome gray uniforms with brass buttons. A few of the more ardent members of the G.A.R. complained that the new postal outfits reminded them of rebel uniforms, but most citizens felt that the postmen . . . and the new street numbers required by postal regulations . . . added a further metropolitan touch to the capital city. They were particularly impressed by Postman Clark Savidge, who made the rounds on the east side in "a trim looking mail cart drawn by the well trained horse he has ridden on his rounds the past year."

Hazzard Stevens was selling lots in his Maple Park addition, advertising the proximity of the electric railway. His father the governor had purchased the area when it was a howling wilderness and in 1877 Hazzard had deeded a part of it to the town as a park in return for a contract to plant it with maple trees. The southward movement of the residential section which followed the coming of the street car line also engulfed the baseball park at 17th and Main. The Olympia Light and Power company leased the former fairgrounds from George Barnes for a new ballpark to stimulate traffic on its street cars, which passed the grounds on their way to Tumwater.

All this progress, of course, continued to take a toll on the nerves and well-being of some citizens. The first recorded accident involving the new street cars occurred early in the year when one of them clanged noisily into Bigelow's milk wagon, according to the Standard, "damaging the vehicle considerably and bruising some of the milk cans."

A little later, when the Northern Pacific train came "dashing through the 7th street tunnel" it so affected the nerves of "the large gray team drawing the Olympia Hotel bus" that they screamed in unison and set off on a mad dash down Main street all the way to the end of long wharf, which swayed alarmingly, around the pest house - warehouse on the far end and back toward town before they were stopped. *"The gurney,"* according to the *Standard, "was slightly damaged."*

Aside from such scientific and technological problems, things were relatively quiet in the capital city after the legislature adjourned.

The *Olympia-Tribune* reported that W. J. Ogden, while on his way from his job at the Westside mill to his home at Butler's Cove, was attacked by an eagle, resulting in *"a furious battle which ended in a draw."*

Presumably the angry eagle was retaliating for his kin which had sacrificed their lives and tail feathers to the ceremonies of statehood.

A couple of the local Indians made news; some good and some bad.

Leschi, the son of the murdered Quiemuth and nephew of the first Leschi, distinguished himself when the *Olympia-Tribune* reported that he was *"the first Indian known to have ascended to the summit of a volcanic mountain,"* having accompanied members of the Tacoma Academy of Science and the Tacoma Alpine Club on the first exploration of the north slope of Mt. St. Helens.

On the bad side, that "dangerous savage," Heo, who had been whipped by George Billings 25 years earlier for his assault on an Indian girl, came to the bad end which General McKenny had predicted for him. Despite his advancing years, Heo still had an eye for a handsome woman. During a visit to one Slekman on the Chehalis reservation, Heo won the heart of Mrs. Slekman, who ran away from her husband and came to Olympia to live with her lover. Slekman and a tribal friend named George Williams came to Olympia later to see how Heo and Mrs. Slekman were getting along. They were greeted cordially and a bottle of high-proof whiskey was passed around. As Slekman got drunk a sense of his wrongs overcame him and he and his friend took their host for a staggering stroll to the end of Long bridge. There they hit Heo on the head with a

OLYMPIA COLLEGIATE INSTITUTE brought higher education to southwest Washington.

large rock, knocked him down and cut his throat from ear to ear.

There were few to mourn the dissolute Heo, but selling whiskey to Indians was against the law. A local character named John Foley was found to have supplied the fatal liquor and was subsequently sentenced to a term in jail. Slekman and Williams were also jailed, but they tunnelled through Sheriff Billings's bricks and disappeared into the tall timber.

THE NOT GAY NINETIES

J. C. Rathbun, who established another Republican weekly, the *Palladium,* in 1894, began publication of his "history of Thurston County," which was later released in book form. His account of conditions in Olympia during his first year in business was not enthusiastic:

"The year 1894 will be a memorable one in the history of the county not so much on account of what was accomplished of truly historic importance as being characterized by the absence of important data. It was a year of business inactivity. The inaction that followed the collapse of the Western Washington boom was increased by the financial panic that hung like an incubus on the business prosperity of the nation. Indeed, were it not for the latter the former would have been temporary and insignificant. It was a year of stagnations; the agricultural and manufacturing interests both languished. Logging operations were suspended and saw mills operated at irregular intervals. Public finances were embarrassed during the year. County, city and school district warrants were begging for buyers. Owing to the business depression property owners were unable to pay their taxes."

The right of way grade of the Union Pacific, which had reached town from the north along what is now East Bay drive, was abandoned. The Oregon Improvement company went under and the long gap in the Port Townsend Southern was never filled. The Methodists, tightening their financial belt, merged the Olympia Collegiate Institute with the College of Puget Sound at Tacoma and the buildings were abandoned. The Congregationalists abandoned their ambitious plans for Athens University, and the clearing between Budd and Eld Inlets was soon reclaimed by trees and underbrush. It would be almost 80 years before a college would rise on the peninsula west of town. Professor Follansbee's Calathea College and his educational journal both suspended and the professor mysteriously disappeared from the scene.

The splendid Hotel Olympia was losing money at an alarming rate and both city and county officials agreed to declare a moratorium on its tax payments. George Barnes reactivated the Citizens' Tax Relief Association with Charles Ayer as secretary and C. J. Lord as treasurer. Pressure was applied to city and county governments to reduce the salaries of public employees and teachers.

About the only bright spot in the economic gloom was the beginning of construction on a massive foundation for the new capitol on the hill. This not only provided work for carpenters, laborers, stone-masons and teamsters in Olympia, but kept the sandstone quarry at neighboring Tenino humming with activity.

In many other areas of the state there were no bright spots at all. Northern Pacific workers went on strike, tearing up tracks and demolishing bridges to emphasize their demands. Spokane was without rail service for 10 days, Tacoma for five days.

"General" Jumbo Cantwell, an ex-prize fighter and Tacoma saloon and brothel bouncer, organized a Washington contingent of Coxey's Army to march on Washington, D.C., to demand relief for the unemployed. About 2,000 idle loggers, sailors and fishermen rallied to his cause and took possession of an uncompleted hotel building in Puyallup as their headquarters. They terrorized the inhabitants into providing them with food and demanded a Northern Pacific passenger train to convey them to the national capital free of charge.

Tough John McGraw, accustomed to forthright action against breaches of the peace, went to Puyallup with a single companion, mounted a box car and addressed the unruly mob. He singled out individual members by name and shamed them for their bad behavior. Then he told them to either disband or face the bayonets of the militia, which he had placed on the alert.

Jumbo's brigade of Coxey's Army quickly melted away. A few made it to Washington, but too late to join forces with Coxey. Most of them just went home.

Discontent continued to increase among the hard-hit farmers who had for years been squeezed between high freight rates and low prices for agricultural products. Previous efforts to organize through the Patrons of Husbandry in the 70's and the Farmers' Alliance of the 80's had failed, but in the 90's they flocked to the banner of the new Peoples' or Populist party, adding to its surprising strength in the 1892 elections. In the fall of 1894 21 Populists were elected to the lower house of the legislature; two to the senate. Strangely enough, the Republican majority was larger than it had been two years earlier, most of the Populist gains having been made at the cost of Democratic candidates.

The Seattle *Sun*, on January 1, 1895, published a word of advice to the fourth legislature which seemed to pretty well sum up the mood of the times:

"Born during a boom, the state was set going on a high-pressure system. Too many offices and commissions were created, and salaries were made too high. Public institutions were created in advance of need. Liberal expenditure was the order. We tickled our ears with a welcome acclaim of the greatness of Washington. We proclaimed it the most wonderful state in the Union. 'We are the people; nothing is too good for us,' we shouted. 'Give us the best there is to be got and darn the expense!' A jag of that sort may be exhilerating for a time, but it comes high, and the awakening in the morning is not at all pleasant. The state has awakened, and is very headachy and remorseful. A new year is at hand and it is a good time to turn over a new leaf."

Governor McGraw had his back up and his message to the 1895 legislature was clear and to the point. He suggested that the lawmakers take a good look at "the effects that have resulted from an over confidence in our great resources during a protracted season of business depression." He reminded them that, instead of the $227,000 surplus which the previous legislature had estimated would be on hand, there was a treasury deficit of $750,000; that only a fourth of the 1893 state taxes had been paid.

He spoke with some pride of having vetoed funds for normal schools at Cheney and Whatcom (Bellingham) and intimated strongly that he would veto any unnecessary expenditures by the current legislature.

The cost of supporting state institutions had increased by $128,000 during the past biennium and the state's first prison scandal had broken. The warden of the penitentiary at Walla Walla had pocketed the proceeds of the sale of grain bags from the prison jute mill to the tune of several thousand dollars. When apprehended he committed suicide. McGraw recommended a separate department of institutions headed by a director responsible to the governor to replace the commissions which administered each institution separately.

McGraw departed from a line of strict economy to urge the need for continuation of work on the new capitol. "No more eloquent argument could be invoked," he said, "than the protests of your own pride and dignity against the shabbiness and meanness of your legislative surroundings." He also pointed out that this project didn't constitute a tax burden, since it was funded by capitol land grants which couldn't be used for any other purpose. Furthermore, 80 percent of the materials would "come from our own virgin resources."

The Republicans, still dominant, had already caucused and selected their officers and employees, so organization of the two houses proceeded at the brisk pace of an express train. Ellis Morrison of King was named speaker of the house and B. C. Van Houten of Spokane president pro-tem of the senate.

The house then moved to increase its staff somewhat over that of the previous session, including three general pages and one for the speaker, committee clerks, and day and night watchmen. One of the latter was the legislature's first minority employee, listed in the *Standard* as *"Joe Hagan (Colored) of Spokane."*

The amount appropriated for expenses of the legislature was loudly reduced to $45,000 prompting Murphy, who should have known better, to predict that *"the extravagant expenditure of $1,000 a day of last session will not be repeated."*

By early February he was having great doubts as he noted *"the political henchmen in the wings with spoons extended like Oliver Twist"* and the *"frequent efforts to slip in more clerks, etc., which are frequently successful."*

At adjournment in March he conceded bitterly that *"one by one the party henchmen were admitted to the charmed circle where big pay for little labor was placed within their covetous grasp, and $20,000 more quietly appropriated, making the cost an even $1,000 a day . . . same as last session."*

The *Olympian-Tribune,* its name now shortened to *Olympian,* tried its hand at predicting, with equally bad results. Early in February it boldly prophesized the *"the capitol building will be completed by May 1, although the foundation has not yet risen to the surface of the ground."*

The legislators of 1895 had more than the gloomy state of the economy and the tough attitude of the governor to depress them. They arrived in the midst of another major snow storm which deposited 1,100 pounds of grimy slush on McBratney's 8 by 21-foot hay scale on Columbia street and proportionate amounts on the rest of the capitol city.

The Olympia Light and Power company, undergoing bankruptcy proceedings with Hazzard Stevens as managing receiver, was in no condition to clear its line and keep the street cars operating on a dependable schedule. Consequently the lawmakers again had to frequently plow their way through drifted snow on the wooden sidewalk to the drafty capitol. To add to their miseries, the city fathers ordered all the street lights turned off just as they arrived in town. This was just one of many stringent economy measures forced upon them by the deepening depression. The *Standard* pointed out that the county's delinquent tax roll, which had been 25 percent in 1893, had reached 50 percent in 1893 and was still rising, *"proving only too well that the limit of endurance has been passed; the means of the people have been exhausted and a complete financial breakdown involving taxes, bonds and warrants in common bankruptcy and the community in lasting disgrace is imminent."*

The high winter tides seeped into the gas lines in the lower part of town and that essential winter utility was denied the saloons and lodging houses which depended upon it. Despite the cold weather, malaria had broken out in the Black Lake area just west of town, according to the *Standard* *"attributed by Dr. Newell to settling of meadows causing malarial exhalations to arise and impregnate the atmosphere in the area from Black Lake to*

Little Rock, the prevailing southwest winds having carried the deleterious influence to that side."

POLITICKING AND PANDEMONIUM

Despite the myriad problems facing them, the legislators found time for the usual amount of bickering and more than the usual number of trivial bills.

The big battles were the usual ones . . . the selection of a U.S. senator to fill the remaining two-year term left vacant by the failure of the last session to reach agreement, and the latest efforts to move the state capital somewhere else.

At the close of the second week, Murphy harrumphed editorially that *"time is still being frittered away on what Republican Senate candidate will fill out the fractional term."*

The leading contenders were Levi Ankeny and State Senator John R. Rogers who, in the balloting of late January each had 23 votes. John L. Wilson, who had served two terms as congressman and was rapidly emerging as the state's dominant Republican political boss, was third with 18. Three lesser candidates trailed with a total of 33 votes. Things seemed to be as badly deadlocked as they had been in 1893.

The astute Wilson apparently convinced his principal Republican rival, Ankeny, that his time would come if he played ball (it did, a few years later) and on January 31 a letter was received from Ankeny announcing his withdrawal from the race. This released most of the Republican votes to Wilson and insured his victory over Populist Rogers. The *Standard* sourly reported the proceedings when the announcement was made:

*"Pandemonium for a time reigned. Members jumped on tables, screeched and howled. For fully ten minutes the Representatives' hall resembled a lunatic asylum with all the dangerous patients lose. * * * In succeeding speeches many of Wilson's most violent opponents became his staunchest supporters."*

Having placed Wilson in the United States senate, the house spent the rest of the day squabbling over Representative W. H. Ham's bill to abolish the office of lieutenant governor.

The senate concurrently became involved in a teapot tempest of its own when Senator Sargeant of Pierce, on a point of personal privilege, read an article from a Tacoma paper which intimated that a part of the Pierce county delegation had sold out Wilson in favor of Ankeny "for a consideration." The article was signed by Senator E. W. Taylor, a colleague of Sargeant's from Pierce county and contained the charge that Ankeny *"is maintained by his proselytes for a consideration."*

When Sargeant waved the offending paper under Senator Taylor's nose and demanded to know what he meant by "proselytes" the latter claimed it was a typographical error . . . it should have read "parasites." Then, warming to his own defense, he arose to shout that many members had borrowed money from Ankeny and "are here for a consideration. Yes, paupers and parasites. Men who cannot pay for their desk room or office rent, living here at a first class hotel!"

Turning purple in the face, Senator Sargeant then thundered, "If it is my colleague's intention to impugn my motive or character, I say he is a contemptible liar!"

It appeared that fisticuffs were imminent. The president rapped his gavel vigorously and sent his page for the sergeant at arms, but Taylor backed down as gracefully as possible, claiming that he hadn't been referring to legislators at all . . . just to lobbyists.

Sargeant then calmed down and announced that "if my colleague says on his honor that he does not refer to me I will cheerfully withdraw my remarks."

Peace was restored for the time being.

Populist members of both houses kept demanding that the leadership stop hiring highly paid and underworked employees, one prominent Populist representative claiming that he could supply a hundred competent clerks from all sections of the state who were prefectly willing to work for room and board. A number of the big spenders were further outraged when it was ruled that they couldn't travel to sessions on free railroad and steamboat passes and still collect their travel claims at 10 cents a mile.

Late in February Senator Taylor added new fuel to the legislative fire by proposing annulment of the contract for building the capitol foundation and the repeal of some $500,000 already appropriated from the capitol land fund.

Murphy, sensing further machinations of Ezra Meeker and the Pierce county delegation to rob Olympia of the capital, responded irascibly in the next issue of the *Standard*:

"A few owners of land in a hop-yard (Puyallup) actuated purely by selfishness, have seen in the delay of the Capitol Commission an

opportunity to misrepresent facts and secure further delay, and fancy an opportunity to again place the capitol 'on wheels' leading to a possible land speculation boom."

On March 14 the fears of Murphy and other loyal Olympians were allayed, for the time being, when the legislature appropriated $500,000 for the completion of the state capitol on the massive foundation which was nearing completion.

The "barefoot schoolboy" bill being pushed hard by Populist Senator Rogers was another well-chewed bone of contention. This measure was designed to give reality to Governor Stevens' recommendation to the first territorial legislature that every child should have an equal opportunity for an education. It provided for state support of public schools on a per-pupil basis and was bitterly opposed by the three largest cities, Seattle, Tacoma and Spokane, whose citizens were already carrying a heavy load of school taxes and were much opposed to making further contributions toward the support of rural and small town schools. The barefoot schoolboy bill was voted down several times, but the determined Rogers kept it alive and it finally passed in the closing days of the session, appropriating six dollars a year in state funds for every child of school age.

Its passage would sweep Rogers into the governorship at the next election and insure him a degree of immortality as the second and last governor to have a statue erected in his honor.

Not all the bills considered were as significant as this. There was the usual assortment of trivia, including measures to prohibit the display of any but the American flag in parades and on public buildings; to reduce the salaries of all state officers (including legislators), which predictably got nowhere; to require all saloons to close at midnight (it failed by three votes); requiring Pullman car porters to keep upper berths folded up when not in use; requiring all judicial instructions to juries to be typewritten; prohibiting lewdness; protecting song birds and requiring all businesses to close on Sundays.

A bill prohibiting boxing and sparring matches passed, but the presiding officers forgot to sign it and it was voided. The obstruction of railroad or street car tracks was declared a felony punishable by five to 20 years in prison. Women were authorized to serve on school boards, state board of education and as school superintendents. Legislative committees were given the power of subpoena, gripmen, motormen, drivers and conductors of street railways were limited to 10 hours work a day and all persons were granted "full and equal enjoyment of all rights and public accommodations." Saloon keepers were promised $500 fines if any females were found working on their premises, but another local option bill failed to pass.

Representative A. S. Bush of Pacific county, spokesman for the oyster growers' lobby, enjoyed a most successful session, getting bills passed allowing the planting of oysters on state tide and shore lands pending sale by the state, allowing oyster growers to purchase up to 40 acres of tidelands at extremely low prices and prescribing large fines and long imprisonment for oyster poachers.

The grateful oystermen financed a gala oyster banquet for the legislators, presided over by Mr. Bush who, as the *Standard* pointed out, had *"represented their interests so well that they received all the legislation they asked, and the banquet was in acknowledgement of the service."*

The legislators also participated in what Murphy described as *"a unique 'roast' of Adjutant-General R. G. O'Brien,"* the general having requested a deficiency appropriation of $44,000 in addition to the $80,000 already alloted the militia for the 1893-95 biennium. The senate committee on appropriations, while recommending passage of the request, expressed itself as "appalled by an exhibition of recklessness, extravagance and incapacity on the part of the Adjutant General, who occupies a palatial official headquarters with a large force of assistants, consisting of a clerk, stenographer, quartermaster's clerk and storekeeper-armorer." (O'Brien himself held the additional titles of quartermaster general, commissary general, inspector general, chief of ordnance and chief of staff.)

Murphy responded editorially to this official chastisement of the jolly general with the opinion that *"General O'Brien belongs to that class of men who have never learned the important lesson that the well has a bottom."*

The legislature was not about to let him off so easily, however. They passed a new law making department heads personally liable for any funds spent above their authorized appropriation. Seven infantry companies and two cavalry troops were disbanded, annual encampments and dress parades were abolished and all the militia officers who had voted for the unfortunate O'Brien were stripped of their commissions.

All in all it was a bad session for General O'Brien, who had started things off so bravely with the governor's daughter on his arm at the head of the inaugural grand march.

The pace of social life in the capital city was increasing with the dignity of statehood and despite the hard times. There was even some confusion generated by the holding of two state balls for the legislators, both advertised as "Grand." One was held at the Hotel Olympia by the ladies of local society, with an admission charge of $2.50. The Populists showed their disdain for such hifalutin' affairs by staging theirs at the old Tacoma hall of the Good Templars and charging only 50 cents.

The state's first lady, Mrs. McGraw, held a party for the legislative wives, serving excellent refreshments which she had personally selected and prepared, and the Reverend and Mrs. T. J. Lamont held a "fagot social," which wasn't at all what you might be led to suspect. Each guest was given a small stick of wood to be cast upon the fire and was required to tell a story while his fagot burned.

And the ladies of St. John's Episcopal church further enlivened things by staging the first of a long series of "beautiful baby" contests. Among the winners were such exquisite Olympia infants as Ellis Ayer, Selwyn Harris and Mildred Lemon.

As usual, the legislators procrastinated until the last minute and had to stop the capitol clocks and pretend their alloted 60 days weren't used up, a device which Murphy derided as *"boys' play."*

Although the 1895 legislature reduced general fund appropriations from over two million to somewhat over a million and a half dollars (the grand total from all funds was $2,581,920.08 compared to $2,934,374.76 two years earlier) and had appropriated money to complete the capitol, Murphy still wasn't very pleased with it. At its close he wrote:

"The record of the Legislature just past absolutely banishes all hope of reformation of abuses from a party machine like that which controls the destiny of this state * * * When the Legislature met it was exultantly claimed that Economy should be the watchword; but there came with the membership a long train of hungry camp followers who pitched their tents and drove their tethers with a confidence that indicated a perfect knowledge of the vacillating nature of their local statesmen."

The Republican-oriented *Olympian* took a more charitable view of things, although it was not overwhelmed with enthusiasm:

"Another session of the Legislature has passed into history and time will demonstrate the wisdom or unwisdom of its various acts. One thing is certain; the personnel of the fourth Legislature embraced as hard-working, conscientious and withal as able a body of men as is likely to assemble in a similar capacity at any future time.

"It is highly improbable there has been any truly vicious legislation. Many of the measures passed will not respond to the anticipations of the people and the men who enacted them, as hope had led them to believe, but they will not make conditions worse than they are at present."

With the departure of the legislators for another two years, Olympia settled down to muddle through the hard times as best it could. The dredge *Anaconda,* having reclaimed new acreage for downtown Olympia and so shortened the length of Long bridge that it was given its third name . . . the 4th street bridge . . . departed for LaConner. Work on the massive capitol foundation continued. Barefooted Indian women vended baskets of clams from door to door and on downtown streets and pigtailed Chinese truck gardeners trotted about making deliveries from huge bundles on long poles.

The Willeys had added the sternwheeler *City of Aberdeen* to the *Multnomah* and were providing adequate if not spectacular service on the Seattle and Tacoma route. Captain Thomas Tew, who had taken over the Willey's Shelton run, placed the new sternwheeler *City of Shelton* in the trade to Oakland Bay, replacing the little *Willie* and proudly advertising that his new steamer "now makes the run between this city and Shelton in one hour and 45 minutes". The little propellor steamer *Seaside* carried mail, freight and passengers to Harstene Island twice a week. The recent dredging made it possible for the steamers to utilize Percival's dock at all stages of the tide and the remains of the long wharf were left to the seagulls and teredos. Even the warehouse was unused, the city having procured a float house on logs at the urging of Dr. Newell for the purpose of a pest house.

Land transportation was less satisfactory, however, the *Standard* reporting that

"Northern Pacific passenger service has degenerated into a local train from Tacoma, arriving at 10:30 A.M. and departing at 4:30 P.M. Passengers for through service must take the Port Townsend Southern to Tenino.

"What in Hades inspired the suspension of the Northern Pacific train, just at this time, is beyond ordinary comprehension to fathom," Murphy concluded in obvious frustration.

Out on the east side of town at a rural crossroads called Woodland, the Benedictine order established a college called St. Martins which, unlike all the other hopeful institutions of higher education projected for Olympia, was destined to stay a while. And downtown a short, rotund German immigrant named George Mottman, who had been instrumental in the donation of 40 acres for the college campus, abandoned the real estate business and established a cash and carry drygoods store in the Stuart Block at 526 Main street, advertising lavishly in the local press that he had a resident buyer in New York and could undersell everybody in town. Every penny counted to the housewives of Olympia in 1895 and George Mottman prospered. He too would be around for a long time, and he probably had more impact on the community than the quiet Benedictine college out at Woodland, which he had the principal hand in bringing to the area.

1896

The depression-ridden year of 1896 was one in which the people of Washington and the whole nation sought panaceas in political action. The national issues were free silver and protective tariffs. Washington farmers strongly favored the unlimited coinage of silver, which they were convinced would increase the flow of money, and low tariffs, which would reduce the costs of farm machinery and implements. On the national scene, McKinley, an advocate of high tariffs and the gold standard, won the Republican nomination and proceeded to campaign on the slogans of "the full dinner pail" and "the advance agent for prosperity". The Democratic convention had also leaned toward the gold standard and "sound currency" until an astonishing burst of eloquence from a young congressman named William Jennings Bryan swept him into the nomination on a platform of free silver and tariff reduction.

The platform split the party and a third party of "Gold Democrats" entered the field. Business and financial interests backed McKinley with massive transfusions of campaign funds and he won the presidency by 602,000 popular votes, but things had changed radically in Washington, that long-time stronghold of rugged pioneer individualism; the reform platform of Bryan struck a responsive chord. He carried the state by more than 12,000 votes.

Within the state the Populists, who had been gaining strength steadily during the past four years, joined forces with the Democrats and free silver Republicans to form the Fusion party. These rather divergent groups met at Ellensburg in three separate conventions, but formed a working alliance to wrest political control from the long dominant Republicans. The joining of hands was not easily accomplished. There were plenty of political prima donnas in all three segments and there were bitter quarrels and recriminations over whose names should appear on the common ticket of the new Fusionist or Peoples' Party.

The final compromise gave the Populists the candidates for governor, lieutenant governor, secretary of state, auditor, treasurer and commissioner of public lands. The Democrats selected one congressional candidate, judge of the supreme court and state printer, while the Silver Republicans were allowed to name the other congressional candidate, state attorney general and superintendent of public instruction.

The Fusion platform called for free silver, lower tariffs, reduction of excessive salaries for state officials, lower railroad and telephone rates, free public school textbooks, the prohibition of free transportation passes to officials . . . and woman suffrage. It also provided for property tax relief through adoption of the single tax concept and greater protection for those whose property was foreclosed for debt.

The platform contained something for every discontented segment of the state, with the exception of the prohibitionists who had fallen into some disrepute as a result of their increasing fanaticism.

The Fusionist ticket, led by John Rogers, who had become a popular political hero through his barefoot schoolboy law, swept every state office and elected a majority in both houses of the legislature.

The Republicans, who were either unaware of the massive shift in public opinion, or had decided their cause was hopeless anyway, nominated an old-line, cigar-chewing politician named P. C. Sullivan, who was the current political boss of Pierce county.

The colorful J. Hamilton Lewis, who had remained behind the political scenes except for his one term in the last territorial legislature*, was elected to congress, along with Silver Republican Wesley L. Jones.

Governor McGraw and his family returned to Seattle and for a time he was employed as receiver for the defunct Bank of Everett. Unlike the governors of later years, he left office poorer than he had entered it, and real financial disaster soon descended upon him. Major shortages were discovered in the King county sheriff's office and were attributed to defalcations during his terms as sheriff. There was apparently little or no evidence that he had participated in the theft of public funds, but he assumed responsibility and eventually paid off the entire amount.

IT'S THE WATER

The outgoing governor's rented home at Maple Park was taken over by a newcomer to Olympia who was welcomed by both permanent residents and politicians. His name was Leopold Schmidt and, upon his arrival in the capital city from Montana he had refreshed himself from the pioneer artesian well recently bored by the Talcott brothers to avoid paying monthly bills to that "grasping monopoly", the Olympia Water company. Impressed by the crystal purity of the water, he had wandered

---

*The pink-whiskered and sartorially elegant Lewis, said to be so courtly that he always removed his hat when talking to a lady on the telephone, had been the Democratic favorite to run against McGraw for governor in 1892. Both he and McGraw, being from King county, strongly favored state aid for the current pet project of Seattle's civic leaders, who unlike their more naive Olympia counterparts, usually managed to get *their* major civic improvements financed by the taxpayers of the state and nation as a whole. (They still do very well in this regard). A ship canal between Puget Sound and Lake Washington was what they wanted at the moment, and when the "cow county" delegates, along with a number from Pierce, refused to support "the ditch" as a platform plank, Lewis bowed out and J. M. Frink was chosen to replace him.

The gallant J. Hamilton Lewis.

about the area, located springs of similarly potable water at Tumwater and stayed to establish a brewery there.

John Miller Murphy, who had long since severed his brief association with the sons of

POPULIST GOVERNOR John Rogers, author of the Barefoot Schoolboy bill, was one of two Washington governors to have a statue erected in his honor. Financed by the contributions of school children, it stands in Sylvester Park opposite the entrance of the old statehouse.

POPULIST

The arrival of Governor Rogers, along with the host of new legislators and elective officials in early January of 1897 brought many changes in the established order of political ceremony. Rogers, the man of the people, refused to head an inaugural parade riding in a shiny carriage and wearing a silk hat; furthermore he demanded that the ordinary folks, not just the political and social bigwigs of the community, be invited to the inaugural ceremonies. The civic dignitaries in charge of arrangements winced, but opened the public reception and inaugural ball at the Hotel Olympia to all comers without charge. The banquet which followed was served at cost . . . one dollar a plate.

Rogers then holed up in his modest lodgings in Mrs. Patterson's boarding house at 4th and Franklin and, with the assistance of his private secretary, John E. Ballaine, went to work on his inaugural address to the legislature. He had a lot to tell them.

The legislators and lobbyists, in the meantime, set about getting acquainted. Seldom before had so many strangers come to town to take their places in the halls of state and, according to Murphy:

"The principal business of legislators this week is introducing themselves to each other. These social amenities occur on street corners, hotel lobbies, restaurants and saloons. Such overtures are in marked contrast to the free and easy courtesies of the good old Territorial days when everybody was acquainted with his colleague, even to his aunts, uncles, sisters and cousins".

John Miller Murphy, the stripling editor of 1860 was a portly, graying gentleman of 57 in 1897 and he was growing nostalgic. He even observed that it seemed to rain more on Washington state than it used to do on Washington territory.

The weather which greeted the Fusionist politicians was, in fact, more propitious than anyone had expected, the *Standard* noting in mid-January that the pleasant days were resulting in *"bulbous garden plants springing out of the ground"* and that *"family cows, tethered in front lawns, are feeding on lush green grass".*

The combination of warm weather, victory and on-schedule street cars to the capitol should have made the Fusionist legislature of 1897 a happy and amicable one, but it did not. The coalition of radical reformists and more

temperance and was once again washing down his cheese with a little beer, was one of the first to take public note of the new industry and its product:

"One of the most helpful enterprises for our community, one that brings the most money from abroad, to place it in circulation in our midst, is the Capital Brewery. Its trade is extended wherever the merits of its products become known. It is unqualifiedly the best beer made on the Pacific Coast and that is saying much. In the estimation of many it fairly rivals the famous Milwaukee product."

Once Mr. Schmidt had the new brewery fairly in operation he made it a custom to hold open house periodically in its taproom for the members of the legislature and Olympia beer soon took its place with the Olympia oyster as a "succulent lobbyist" in the cause of keeping the state capital where it was.

conservative Democrats and Silver Republicans was precarious at best. Most of the legislators were political novices and unaware, or unwilling to concede, that compromise is the lubricant essential to the turning of the wheels of the ponderous legislative machinery. They were also subject to the same temptations as their predecessors, and in increased volume, for the railroads, liquor interests, fish-packers, timber barons and other corporate fat cats were in a state of considerable alarm. The new crop of wild-eyed liberals at Olympia might actually enact some of the reforms upon which they had campaigned. A record number of lobbyists was dispatched with bulging wallets to the capital city to woo the Fusionists with Olympia oyster suppers, whiskey, big cigars and, if necessary, cash.

And most of the legislators were hungrier than usual, having been the victims of political drought for many years.

Governor Rogers, soon to observe his sixtieth birthday; tall, thin, balding, with neatly trimmed mustache and pointed beard, delivered his message to the legislators like a stern father, reminding them of their duty and of the grim realities they faced.

He spoke of the low pay of labor, the depreciation of property values and of men vainly seeking employment "which, if found, is not adequately remunerative." He reminded them that "times are hard. Wives and mothers look with fear to the daily diminishing family stores. Mortgages cover much of the real estate." But, he pointed out, "want and poverty is not the result of wastefulness or lack of industry, but forced by the constantly appreciating value of money caused by the demonitization of silver and the establishment of the gold standard."

He urged them to forego factionalism in electing a United States senator and cautioned "enthusiasts and dreamers" not to expect miracles as the result of the election upset. He spoke strongly for fair revenue laws. Corporations and men of great wealth, he said, refused to pay their taxes; then lobbied relief measures through the legislature evading penalties and interest; that "to a large extent the great properties of the state escape just taxation, while the poor property owner is taxed to the limit of endurance."

Among his specific recommendations were state-financed free school books, preferably published at the state penitentiary to provide vocational training to the inmates and to escape the high prices of the monopoly publishers; the exclusion of fish traps, wheels and other stationery gear from the fisheries of the state; the creation of a state bank examiner to "prevent frequent and most grievous losses through bank failure."*

He urged passage of a law to prevent coercion and intimidation of voters at the polls and asked that penalties be prescribed for violation of the constitutional provision against acceptance of free transportation passes by state officials. Previous legislatures had scrupulously avoided doing so and everyone from governors to representatives had consistently violated the law.

Rogers was the first to take note of the proliferating bureaucracy since statehood, assailing the trend toward a myriad of minor commissions and officials . . . arid lands commissioner, and dairy commissioner were special targets of his disapproval. "The dairy commissioner," he pointed out, "hasn't been able to produce a pound of butter more than would have been produced if his office had not been created, nor raised the price or quality."

The solemnity of his address was varied with a touch of irony when he asked, "Why not a hen commissioner who will see that the grocers properly count the eggs and might, by way of diversion, undertake the instruction of our farmers in the highly important art of properly and scientifically setting a hen?"*

Rogers, like McGraw, urged a single department of instructions to replace the several independent boards, and recommended a legislative committee with full authority to investigate the penitentiary where scandals and rumors suggested to him that "all the criminals are not on the inside."

---

*Within the month the new state treasurer, C. W. Young, withdrew a large deposit of public funds from the First National Bank of Olympia, sparking a run on the bank and the first failure of an Olympia financial institution.

---

*The irony of Rogers' remarks would probably be lost to today's legislators who make regular appropriations for a corps of "state egg inspectors" who presumably perform the functions of Rogers' mythical "hen commissioner," each at a salary approximately five times that which the governor was collecting in 1897.

ROGERS—An investigation of the affairs at the penitentiary leads to the belief that all the criminals are not on the inside.

HENCHMEN—We must choke the old man off—he is getting altogether too personal.

Post-Intelligencer political cartoon of 1900 hints at chicanery on the part of Populist John Rogers' Fusionist henchmen.

The lack of proper state mine inspection, he charged, had resulted in three recent major disasters at Roslyn, Franklin and Blue Canyon mines, "with more than one hundred killed and 200 orphans made."

The sombre tone of the governor's remarks was not in keeping with the jubilant optimism of the newly empowered legislators and they were greeted with only modest applause, but they were, to some degree at least, taken to heart. The number of employees was reduced somewhat and the total expenditures of the session reduced to $56,000 from the $68,000 of the previous one. Salaries were also reduced, to $4.50 a day for secretary, chief clerk and reading clerks, $4.00 for sergeants at arms and $1.00 for pages.

Rogers took the lead in practicing the spending reform he advocated, reducing the operating costs of his office from $35,000 a year to less than $14,000. His example seemed to have impact on several subsequent governors. Expenditures by the executive office didn't reach the old level for another 10 years.

HOW DO YOU REFORM THE REFORMERS?

A number of Fusionist politicians were competing for the senatorship, including the newly-inaugurated lieutenant governor, Thurston Daniels, but the legislators succeeded in electing Judge Turner, the former supreme court justice who had quashed woman suffrage, before the end of January. This wasn't bad, compared to the record of previous sessions, but Murphy editorialized crankily in the *Standard* that *"this farcial 'Legislature' has cost the taxpayers considerably more than $10,000 to elect a U.S. Senator."*

The reform legislators of 1897-98 did not long escape the usual charges of bribery and corruption in connection with the senatorial contest. On the same day that Turner garnered 68 votes and was declared the winner, the Seattle *Post-Intelligencer* published charges by Dr. G. V. Calhoun, one of Watson Squire's campaign managers, regarding *"the venality of some members of the legislature."*

Dr. Calhoun claimed that he knew personally the six or seven who had offered to sell their votes to the highest bidder. One, he said, was Senator W. H. Plummer of Spokane, president pro-tem of the senate, who offered to vote for Squire for $500. Representative A. D. Warner, Snohomish county Republican, was more ambitious according to the doctor, who said Warner had approached him with an offer to vote a 20-member "pool" solidly for Squire in return for a $1,000 down payment and an additional $5,000 when he was elected.

The *Post-Intelligencer,* according to Murphy, *"created quite a breeze in the Legislature"* for, as he pointed out, *"The well known probity of the accuser and his high standing socially and politically, makes the charges bear almost the force of a Grand Jury indictment."*

Both Warner and Plummer loudly declared their innocence and demanded a full-scale legislative investigation, but their cries of outrage were for a time lost amid the hubbub of further recriminations.

A retaliatory rumor, allegedly set afloat by Populist Representative Witt, had it that Judge Turner had personally offered the Populist senatorial candidate $5,000 to withdraw in his favor.

The bitterness of the senatorial campaign and its aftermath spilled over from the halls of state to the Hotel Olympia, which was the after-hours gathering place for both politicians and lobbyists. The *Standard* reported gravely that the dignity of the plush hostelry was being consistently violated:

"Some one with a grotesque sense of humor has christened our leading hotel the 'Olympia Prize Ring'. This is doubtless owing to the exciting gladatorial display made by the rival candidates in the Senatorial fight, as well as the numerous fistic combats that have taken place within its walls since it has been turned into an arena for pugilism."

Legislators, being immune from arrest for ordinary crimes and misdeameanors during sessions, were free to battle over the Brussels carpets and amid the potted rubber plants without fear of serious interference from the Olympia police, who probably couldn't have controlled things anyway. Municipal economies had reduced the force to two.

The senatorial combat achieved heights of melodrama not being equalled by the cast of "Little Lord Fauntleroy," which was playing again at the opera house, when, during a night session, Representative Conine arose to shock and titillate his colleagues with a tale of sexy intrigue which was duly recorded by the *Standard:*

"Representative Conine told of his experience with a beautiful woman lobbyist who, he alleged, had offered to pay him a 'consideration' to vote for Turner, that he had repelled the suggestion, even as Samson thrice repelled Delilah."

Judge Turner's supporters cried that the beautiful mystery woman was really a "private detective," hired by a rival candidate to frame Conine and make the judge look bad.

The senate and house eventually staged the investigations demanded by Plummer and Warner. The statements of the two committees indicated that the inexperienced Fusionists were fast learning the legislative ropes.

The senate committee found that "no money was used to bribe any member of the legislature." Senator Plummer had simply been told that if he worked for Squire his legitimate expenses would be paid by Squire's friends. Senator Plummer, they decided, "should be and hereby is fully exonerated from all rumors and charges."

The committee had proven its efficiency and almost clairvoyant powers by reaching its conclusions after one brief meeting at which no witnesses were heard. One of those barred from the proceedings was C. H. Hagan, private secretary to Senator Squire, who had made an affadavit, which was reproduced in the *Standard* as follows:

"That on or about the 13th day of January, 1897, one W. H. Plummer, State Senator from Spokane, said to me in the lobby of the Hotel Olympia, 'I have made a proposition to Dr. Calhoun and if it is not accepted by 5 o'clock it's off with me'. I asked him what he meant, and he replied that he had told Dr. Calhoun that he must have $500 by 5 o'clock or it was off with him. He further said, 'I don't propose to have any more God-damned monkey business about it'. The foregoing conversation occurred near the staircase of the lobby of the Hotel Olympia."

The house committee deliberating the charges against Representative Warner listened to the sworn statement of the respected Dr. Calhoun that Warner had, indeed, approached him with a proposition to deliver 20 votes for

Squire, $1,000 down and $5,000 if elected, and that he had even recited the names of the "club"members. Senator Squire then took the stand and swore to the same facts, throwing in for good measure the testimony that Plummer had demanded his $500.

The committee was subsequently discharged with thanks after making a long, rambling and inconclusive report on the affair. No further action was taken.

By early March the lawmakers had accomplished little to make good the campaign promises of the Peoples' Party and Governor Rogers took the street car up from his offices in the McKenny Building to deliver an unusual mid-session scolding. He reminded them of the "assurances given to the people during the late campaign that relief would be afforded them from unjust railroad charges; that any failure rests on the members of the legislature." He lashed out unmercifully at the railroads and their agents. "Never before," he thundered, "has such a formidable railroad lobby assembled at the state capital," and it was aided and abetted by "the newspapers in the service of the railroad companies which teem with arguments from the pens of railroad attorneys."

He concluded grimly, "I most earnestly hope it will not be necessary for me to call an extra session of the legislature because of failure upon your part to do your duty."

Thus whipped into line, the chastened legislators set about to make good on at least some of their promises, although the proceedings continued to be interrupted regularly by squabbling and acrimonious debate, frequently over trivialities.

The standard was set on the opening day when outgoing Lieutenant Governor F. H. Luce called upon Senator Van Patton, a minister, to open the session with prayer. Senator Rinehart of Whatcom, a crusty agnostic, objected, claiming it was "nonsense to have prayers in such a body." Warming to the attack, he shouted, "It will do no good to pray for us! It is a farce! If these people desire prayer let them pray for themselves. I want to object to such nonsense."

"The president," according to Murphy's account of this religious controversy, *"was compelled to rap for order on account of the confusion which followed, and again asked Senator Van Patten to lead in prayer."*

The intransigent Rinehart broke in upon the reverend senator's opening words to shout, "Well, pray if you will, but do not include me in it." He then remained stubbornly in his seat while his more pious or discreet colleagues stood with bowed heads.

At the close of the lengthy prayer, Senator Taylor of Pierce, determined to strike a strong blow for Christianity, called upon the secretary of the senate, Dudley Eshelman, to sing "Nearer My God to Thee," which he did in fine tenor voice.

Senator Rinehart was rendered speechless with indignation, but not for long. When the hymn ended he arose majestically and intoned, *"Mister* President, I now move that the Salvation Army be invited to come in."

The senate thereupon adjourned for the day.

Soon afterward the senate spent an hour in bitter debate over a proposal to hire Charles Ryan, a "colored boy of Spokane," as a doorkeeper. a vocal segment of the august body felt that their dignity would be adversely affected by having "a man of color" in such a prominent post, and that Ryan was pretty "uppity" to ask for the job in the first place. The last black legislative employee had been a night watchman and he could hardly be seen while performing his duties.

Downstairs in the house of representatives speaker Charles E. Cline of Whatcom was doing his share of gavel-banging as the members argued bitterly over whether or not soap and towels should be provided in their legislative outhouse. In the interest of economy (and perhaps to placate the governor) it was finally concluded that "all ablutions should be performed before coming to the capitol."

Several members then became infuriated at the reading clerk, who couldn't decipher the handwriting of many of the legislators and was having a great deal of trouble trying to read their bills. A motion was made that, in the future, all bills submitted to the clerk should be typewritten. Mr. Smith of Whatcom arose in a fine fury to say that he had no money to pay type-writers (stenographers) and that all members were *supposed* to know how to read and write before they came to Olympia.

A bill was then introduced to abolish "that fifth wheel," the lieutenant governor, and the tumult and shouting reached new heights.

159

And that's the way it went as the Fusionists (or *triple-alliance,* as Murphy was fond of calling the Populist political potpourri) floundered through the 60-day session trying to maintain a semblance of cohesiveness in the face of their divided opinions.

In the end they succeeded in instituting a number of minor reforms, although many of the governor's major recommendations were partially or completely ignored.

They slapped the railroads lightly on the wrist by setting a maximum freight rate of $4.25 a ton within the state, but they failed to establish a railroad commission with the power to fully regulate the companies.

They established a state labor board "to protect the health and lives of employees," but failed to set up any very effective controls over corporate operations.

There was considerable legislation passed to protect debtors from foreclosure and garnishment, to encourage agriculture and to give laborers priority in liens against employers for nonpayment of wages. Prison reform occupied their attention and bills were passed authorizing reduced sentences for good behavior and establishing a board of pardons consisting of the secretary of state, state auditor and attorney general. And perhaps as a means of keeping legislators out of jail, a bill providing penalties for accepting railroad passes was quietly killed in committee.

An inspector of coal mines was authorized and a board of institutions commissioners was established. The state land laws were codified, leases of land at lower rates were authorized and a land commission established, composed of the land commissioner, secretary of state and superintendent of public instruction. An insurance committee was also created to regulate insurance companies and a number of regulations were prescribed for insurance companies doing business in the state.

A new revenue law was produced, providing new and somewhat more liberal methods of assessment and collection of taxes and remitting the penalty on delinquent taxes except six percent interest from the date of delinquencies.

They made good on their promises to the women of the state, allowing married women to act as administratix or executrix of estates and passing another resolution for a constitutional amendment granting woman suffrage (which was subsequently turned down by the all-male electorate). The first girl page, 13-year-old Ina Forrest, was hired by Speaker Cline, and was described by male chauvinist Murphy as " *'too cute for words' . . . with her short skirts and sailor blouse."*

The bicycle craze was sweeping the Northwest in the nineties, and means were provided for "the reservation and improvement of cycle paths and fixing a penalty of $50 for willful obstruction or damage," and Senator Plummer got through a bill "protecting manufacturers, bottlers and other dealers in ale, porter, lager beer and other beverages from loss of their casks, barrels, kegs, bottles, etc."

The session drew to a close in March amid flurries of snow outside the capitol and storms of debate within. A motion by Senator Deckebach for a concurrent resolution noting the inauguration of President McKinley, extending him the "hearty congratulations" of the legislature and expressing the wish that "his administration might be crowned with the blessings of the Almighty", aroused the deep suspicions of the Populist senators. The resolution had to be read to them three times before they were satisfied that it was not some sort of cleverly veiled Republican propaganda. It finally passed with only one dissenting vote . . . that of Senator Rinehart, who objected strongly to such official legislative recognition of the Almighty.

CLUTCHING THE
SEAT OF GOVERNMENT

A controversy which had simmered throughout the session drew more attention from the anxious citizens of Olympia. This was the matter of whether or not funds should be appropriated to continue work on the new capitol building.

The capitol commission had reported in January that the stone foundation had been completed at a cost of $48,029, which was well below the original estimates. Economies had been made possible by the hard times, which cut the cost of materials and reduced the pay of laborers to $1.25 a day, although the contractor claimed that he had lost $12,500 on the job. The report also pointed out that, because of the collapsed state of the money market, it was impossible to float the authorized bonds to complete the structure.

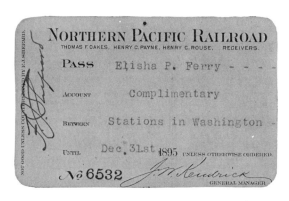

Even the sanctimonious Governor Ferry was willing to accept free transportation from railroads . . . although passes like this one were technically illegal.

The Pierce county forces, still bent on stealing the capital for Tacoma or Puyallup, saw in this another opportunity to delay matters and gain time to strengthen their plot. Many inducements were offered legislators to vote against a proposal to authorize a general fund loan to guarantee the interest on the construction warrants. The *Standard* observed darkly that it wondered *"if some of those wise Solons of the House would like for the reasons to be given why they voted against an effective capitol bill, as stated by them while under the influence of booze?"*, adding that *" 'When wine is in wit is out', you know, and sometimes that truth which shouldn't be told at all times, bobs up"*.

A compromise was finally agreed to grudgingly and, in the final hours of the session, a bill was passed guaranteeing four percent interest on only half of the $500,000 construction appropriation. The amount of interest was too low and the fact that it didn't cover the full obligation made the bill acceptable to the advocates of delay, while the passage of the emasculated measure made the ploy less obvious.

Murphy, outraged at this *"shabby treatment of Olympia"*, composed a bitter editorial:

"When Thurston county had the largest population and representation, it generously gave the plums to other towns, including the opportunity for Seattle to squander a munificent land grant upon a Seattle high-school, yclept a University."

He attributed this latest legislative low blow not only to the machinations of the Pierce

county conspirators, but to the fact that *"Olympia, from the stress of circumstances, was not able to entertain as lavishly as in the past, nor have the money to 'loan' the impecunious legislator when his wants become disproportionate to his per diem"*.

The University of Washington had achieved the magnificent new campus envisioned by Professor Meany and the legislature had increased its appropriation from $65,000 to $100,000 amid enthusiasm generated by much oratory regarding the glorious victories of the university football team over the Seattle Athletic Club and Y.M.C.A.

"Now", Murphy sourly suggested, *"let us have a review of the literary and scientific work done at the University during the past year, with honorable mention to those students who have distinguished themselves."*

But worse was yet to come.

Olympia civic leaders, already nervous because of Governor Rogers' Pierce county residence and loyalties, appointed a committee of leading citizens, including Murphy of the *Standard*, J. C. Rathbun of the *Palladium* and J.O'B. Scobey of the *Olympian,* to call upon the chief executive and urge him to sign the guarantee bill on the grounds that it was better than nothing at all. Rogers was not encouraging. He doubted, in the first place, that the bill had actually passed the house. He had been told that the vote for final passage of the conference committee-amended version was one short of the "constitutional majority required for final passage of an act."

When Olympia attorney James A. Haight quoted several chapters of law to support the validity of the vote, the governor expressed fear that the interest guarantee might somehow make the state responsible for the principal as well. Mr. Haight, according to Murphy, *"in a few words so plainly showed the legal principle involved that it must have settled that doubt"*.

Rogers, however, had plenty of doubts left. He couldn't see much point in selling half the capitol warrants and ending up with a still incomplete building.

The results of this confrontation were, at best, inconclusive and Murphy viewed them as ominous:

"The committee left the executive presence at 9:30 without the slightest intimation of what the result will be, and so far their hopes and

fears are typified, in more ways than mere suspension between heaven and earth, by Mohammed's coffin, which cannot under any circumstances be regarded as a very cheerful object of contemplation."

Murphy's fears were justified. When the committee returned to the offensive with the plea that continuation of capitol construction was needed to support the sagging local economy, Rogers lost his temper and thundered, "Do you expect the state to help you out from bankruptcy?"

Olympians, convinced that the current civic bankruptcy had been brought on by their efforts to provide the amenities of a state capital in response to the demands of legislators and governors, were completely outraged. In Murphy's opinion, *"The people of this city deserve great credit for the forbearance manifested toward John R. Rogers. Many were determined to hold an indignation meeting, pass resolutions denouncing his perfidy, hang him in effigy etc., but better counsels prevailed".*

For some time thereafter the *Standard* refused to mention Rogers by either name or proper title, referring to him as "his accidency", a term which apparently came to Murphy as he was composing an article to express his indignation regarding a trip home to Puyallup made by Rogers after the legislature adjourned and he had vetoed house bill 620, the capitol guarantee measure:

"His accidency hied himself to Puyallup Saturday after vetoing the capitol bill to receive the plaudits of an admiring constituency. He was received with open arms by that antiquated fraud Ezra Meeker."

BITTERNESS AND BANKRUPTCIES

Eggs were selling for 10¢ a dozen, fresh butter for 35¢ a roll. Mottman's was advertising children's heavy school shoes for 58¢, men's spring underwear for 43¢ and high quality suits for $9.00. E. C. Bickford offered complete bedroom suites for $7.00 and up, good chairs for 25¢ and heating stoves for 50¢. The City Bakery remained open all night to serve "the best 15¢ meal in town". The *Multnomah* was able to handle the Tacoma and Seattle trade alone and the *City of Aberdeen* was laid up forlornly at Percival's dock.

Even the town's once wealthiest citizens were often unable to pay their taxes and before the year was over the *Standard* was publishing such melancholy accounts as this:

"All the property of E. T. Young and wife have been sold by Sheriff Billings on account of the Land Mortgage Bank of Northwestern America, including the historic Young's Hotel at 2nd and Main (the former Washington and New England of territorial days) *and also Young's addition on the west side of the bay. * * * Mr. Young lost his property through his public spirited endeavor to advance the interests of this community."*

The Boston capitalists foreclosed their mortgage on the grand and gaudy Hotel Olympia. Its local backers lost their entire investment and for a time it stood locked and empty.

The efforts to build a suitable capital city had been costly indeed to many Olympians, and the efforts to retain the seat of government equally so. Even the unfortunate minute clerk of the house of representatives, J. M. Page, was caught in the bitter aftermath of the latest struggle. Speaker Cline charged Page had erased a penciled notation "The Bill Did Not Pass" from the capitol guarantee measure. Charges of forgery were brought against him, but the county prosecutor understandably refused to take the case. The hot potato was then tossed to the state attorney general's office, which also declined to take action until Rogers applied personal pressure. Page was subsequently cleared of all charges by a Thurston county jury.

Journalistic infighting was also stimulated during the bitter period of disappointment. When the *Olympian* and *Palladium* editorialized for kindness and understanding toward "his accidency" in articles such as this one in the *Olympian* . . . *"We must not withhold from the Governor our most courteous civility and our most generous hospitality, for he is sincere in his objections and believes he is acting for the best interests of the state"* . . . Murphy lost his remaining scant supply of patience. He had been fighting with practically all the other editors in the state, who were against spending any money during the hard times, and when his own colleagues in Olympia began to champion the governor's action it was too much. He led off by publishing a long and angry letter from loyal Olympian Daniel Gabey blasting the editorial policies of the two disloyal papers. This he followed up with blistering personal attacks on Scobey of the *Olympian* and Rathbun of the *Palladium*. They responded with charges that Murphy was a shyster, a quack, a hypocrite, a bushwacker and a pirate, and that the *Standard* was "pandering to the low and uncultured".

Murphy counter-attacked with a broadside aimed at his colleagues and the governor: *"The executive (His Accidency) has put Scobey and Rathbun in the same little bed and they now snooze quietly together, two good little cookoos, and chirp in unison that the* Standard *is 'mediocre in kind and degraded in journalism'."*

"Now when," he asked his readers, *"did the* Palladium *scintillate and how often has the* Olympian *transgressed the proprieties in its efforts to be vulgar if it failed to be funny?"*

Murphy's disposition was probably worse than usual in these trying times, for he, too, had fallen victim to an excess of enthusiasm for the glowing future of the capital city. The mortgage on his splendid new opera house was in the process of being foreclosed.

GOLD RUSH

The latest capital squabble was snowed under in mid-July with the arrival in San Francisco of the steamship *Excelsior* from the mouth of the Yukon river with what the Associated Press referred to grandly as "a ton of gold". A week later the *Portland* pulled into the Schwabacher wharf at Seattle with another ton or more of gold from the Klondike. It was apparent overnight that a new gold rush was about to begin; one that would eclipse the California stampede of 1849. Practically every port city from San Francisco north leaped into the battle to become the port of embarkation for the new El Dorado. Seattle civic leaders gathered together a modest purse and hired a former *Post-Intelligencer* editor, Erastus Brainerd, to beat the drums of publicity for Seattle. Brainerd preempted the "ton of gold" phrase which had originated in San Francisco and utilized it so effectively that Seattle got the prize and became the undisputed metropolis of the Pacific Northwest as a result.

The frenzied scenes of gold rush Seattle were not evident in the sleepy state capital, but things did begin to pick up somewhat. The *Standard* captioned a cautious word of advice on July 23, "DON'T GET EXCITED", urging its readers to *"look at the glowing reports from the Klondyke as we would any other business proposition. It is a venture about as sure of results as a lottery. There must be an occasional spider sitting at the border of the web who has grubstakes for sale".* But the whole world was getting excited about the Klondike. Murphy might as well have tried to put out a forest fire with the *Squilgee.*

A week later the *Standard* reported that *"Seattle and Tacoma have the Klondyke gold fever bad, while a few Olympians are coming down with the unmistakable symptoms of the epidemic".* But Murphy was bowing to the inevitable. The front page carried three columns of *"Information on the Klondyke"* and only two and a half columns devoted to *"The Perils of the Trip".*

The same issue reported that "Olympia zealots", unable to personally join the rush, had formed the O. K. Mining company with 60 shareholders at $75 each to grubstake somebody who could, and that *"piles of goods stacked in our stores with Alaskan addresses indicate many of our prospectors are outfitting at home".* George Mottman, a strong believer in advertising, was soon running front page broadsides advising would-be miners that they could "do better at Mottman's", the price of outfits there being far less than was being extorted by the greedy merchants of Seattle.

Phil Vincent, local boatbuilder, swept the cobwebs from his shop and began producing light boats to be taken to the Klondike by local treasure seekers, including a company scheduled to leave Seattle immediately, headed by Fred Carlyon, brother of a prospering Olympia dentist, Dr. P. H. Carlyon. The little schooner *Atlanta,* launched a year earlier but never completed, was quickly rigged for Klondike service, and Captain Pierce's little steamer *The Doctor* was dispatched to Skagway with a barge of lumber. A big scow was built and fitted with housed upperworks for use as a lighter at Dyea and the *Multnomah* was hauling capacity loads of horses to Seattle for transshipment to the north. The little steamer *City of Olympia* was built as quickly as possible and sent to Skagway, while a brisk market in dogs developed for shipment north to pull sleds. The going price was such that the local canine population was greatly depleted.

So great was the excitement that Murphy's efforts to revive the sagging fortunes of his opera house with the showing of the first motion pictures ever seen in Olympia were lost in the tumult, although the *Standard* gave the event top billing over the Klondike gold rush with such enthusiastic reviews as this one, which appeared on August 6:

"LATEST FAD OF PROGRESSIVE SCIENCE AT OLYMPIA THEATER.—*The wonderful Lumiere Cinematographe; the perfection of animated life on canvas. Those who have never seen the wonderful devices for cheating the eye and deluding the imagination in portrayal of passing events by lifelike moving pictures should see the effect of this wonder. The pictures are plain, distinct and true to life and are exhibited without that 'shimmer' which affects most other instruments for projection of moving pictures.*"

The Cinematographe views, according to the *Standard*, "*include scenes in foreign lands as well as at home, serious and comic, by land and sea, all taken from actual occurrences, and only wanting the various noises which usually attend motion to make them veritable realities.*"

Unfortunately for Murphy, the citizens of Olympia, along with everyone else in the Pacific Northwest, were, with few exceptions, engaged in a love affair with the Klondike and would not bestow their affections on the movies for another decade or so.

Among the few who turned their backs on the gold fields of the far north was Speaker Cline of the house of representatives, who headed a party which included Charles Giles and R. A. McNair of Olympia to "develop a new Klondike in the Olympics." They failed to do so, but came back no poorer than most of those who made it to the Yukon.

The great Alaska gold rush brought a dramatic end to hard times in the Northwest, but the new prosperity came too late for many of the old settlers who, like Young, lost everything or were forced to sell most of their holdings on the rejuvenated market to pay the back taxes on the little that was left.

It has been said that there was no panic in Washington by the close of 1897, but its aftermath was to be felt for a long time in Olympia.

REMEMBER THE MAINE . . .
AND THE OLYMPIA

Olympia suffered additional civic humiliation in 1898 when Miss Hanford of Seattle

FLAGSHIP OLYMPIA.

made public the answer to a letter of inquiry which she had written to Admiral George Dewey. The brief war with Spain had been ushered in amid an almost hysterical atmosphere of jingoistic patriotism. The 1st Regiment of Washington National Guard was mobilized and sent to the Philippines and the armored cruiser *Olympia* gained undying fame as Dewey's flagship at Manila Bay. From her bridge came Dewey's immortal words, "You may fire when ready, Gridley" as the prologue to the destruction of the pitifully inferior Spanish fleet.

Olympia citizens had been proud when she was launched at San Francisco in 1893 as the fastest and most modern warship of the navy and paintings and photographs of the U.S.S. *Olympia* were widely displayed in downtown show windows, but there had been too many other irons in the fire and too few unencumbered funds available to present the ship with a suitable token of appreciation.

When the *Olympia* became famous Miss Hanford queried Dewey and received this reply:

"*As regards the matter of a testimonial to the flagship* Olympia *I must confess to having felt that the city of Olympia has not done its duty by its namesake. Inasmuch as all the other vessels in the squadron have been in some way honored by the cities from whom they took their names, it was an invidious comparison that the largest and best should be under-*

valued. I have no personal interest in the matter, however, as should any testimonial be sent hereafter to the Olympia, *I will probably not be on board."*

Olympia citizens felt that insult had been added to many injuries when the popular hero of the hour singled their community out for such unkind comments. Murphy and the *Standard,* unawed by Admiral Dewey as by other critics of Olympia, chided the great man for *"arrogance and lack of modesty."* The *Olympian,* with more restraint but obviously hurt feelings, pointed out that the community had staged a successful carnival to raise funds and that Dewey had been advised that the great American sculptor, Dan C. French, had been commissioned to design and execute a heroic bronze plaque to be presented to the *Olympia.* It added that it had been impossible to present a suitable testimonial at her launching because everybody in town was broke.

The silver tablet bore the "Figure of Fame" and on one side the words: "Presented to the Cruiser *Olympia* by the People of the State of Washington"; on the other, "We Honor the Ship Bearing the Honored Name Olympia. *Anno Domini* 1898."

The *Olympian* urged the Cruiser Olympia Memorial Committee to change the wording from "People of the State of Washington" to "Citizens of Olympia," on the grounds that no other Washingtonians had contributed so much as a thin dime to the memorial fund and were now pointing their fingers at the citizens of the capital city and castigating them as cheap skates.

For once the *Standard* was in agreement with the *Olympian.*

Subsequently the entire state did chip in and raise more funds for a magnificent silver service for the *Olympia's* wardroom. The honor of both the state and its capital was fully restored when Leopold Schmidt dispatched a large consignment of Olympia beer as a gift to the men of Dewey's squadron, who weren't allowed to use the wardroom silver service.

During the summer of 1898 Olympia suffered still another disaster, this one almost as serious as that which befell the Spanish fleet at Manila. The electric street car fleet, in which so much pride was taken, was utterly destroyed.

Fire broke out in the car barn off 4th street on Chestnut at a little after three o'clock on the morning of July 12. The beautiful white and gold trolleys were resting for the night over grease-soaked repair pits and the whole barn was in flames by the time the alarm sounded. All six passenger cars were consumed at a loss of $15,000, only partially covered by insurance. The only survivors were a freight trolley and a few motorless flat cars used for hauling beer from tumwater to the freight yards and steamboat dock.

Since the Olympia Light and Power company was still in receivership there were fears that service might not be restored or, if it were, it would be on a less grand scale. After all, as Murphy pointed out in the *Standard, "the cars destroyed were built to order before the gold standard had disturbed property values and bankrupted men of modest means, and their specifications were prepared by the late George Shannon, whose esthetic taste and pride in everything he undertook called for the very best."*

Public confidence was not restored when Leopold Schmidt procured horses to tow the beer cars with the result that, for a time, the lowly horse car was again seen on the streets of the capital city. Things didn't improve a great deal when Superintendent Faulkner was able to obtain the first replacement car. This was an ancient and dilapidated relic of the Portland car line know as "Old 49" which was greeted with little enthusiasm. Faulkner hadn't had much choice, since most of the street car lines of the region were narrow-gauge, while the Olympia-Tumwater line boasted standard railroad gauge.

An order was quickly placed with J. G. Brill Company of Philadelphia for five new cars which, Murphy assured his readers, *"will be of modern style and first class in all respects and furnished with westinghouse motors."* Delivery was promised in plenty of time to serve legislators of the 1899 session.

Murphy expressed the fervent hope that this would prove to be the case, for the infirmities of "Old 49" were such that he predicted it would collapse spectacularly like the "wonderful one-hoss shay" unless it was quickly relieved of its duties.

Leopold Schmidt's Capital Brewing company continued to lead the parade of economic recovery in the Olympia area, its market expanding to the booming gold rush towns of Alaska. A wharf was constructed at the

INFANT INDUSTRY: Leopold Schmidt's original Capital Brewing company plant at lower Tumwater Falls, about 1898.

Tumwater brewery and *"Olympian Standard beer"** was transshipped to the Olympia docks by both street railway cars and barges. The increasing competition among Pacific coast and other breweries with the development of the refrigerated railway car had prompted brewers to either subsidize saloons for the exclusive distribution of their products, or establish their own. The former method created many of the abuses which would lead eventually to the abolition of the saloon. The saloon keepers were always in debt and under obligation to their sponsoring breweries and were usually required to support the "wet" lobby which had such a remarkable influence on the state legislature, both financially and by "lining up the vote" in their neighborhoods. They were also under constant pressure to increase sales and many resorted to such "trade stimulants" as prostitution, high-stakes gambling and box house burlesque.

Schmidt preferred to expand his business by establishing his own saloons and requiring high standards in their operation. The first of

these was a saloon and oyster house at Tacoma, the kitchen being managed by none other than the legendary Cap Doane, who had sold his now large and prospering oyster house in Olympia, but was unwilling to withdraw entirely from the culinary world of which he was an acknowledged and highly respected leader.

This and subsequent dispensaries of Olympian Standard beer relied upon genteel surroundings, good service and good food rather than girls, gambling and primitive gogo dancers to attract business. Had the same standards been maintained in all the saloons of the state the advocates of prohibition would have been deprived of most of the ammunition they used so successfully in the years just ahead.*

In selecting this early trade name for his product, Schmidt was doubtless moved by his good public relations sense, since it was a combination of the names of the capital city's two most influential newspapers. Murphy, in particular, frequently alluded with pride to the fact that the name of his beloved Standard *appeared on every bottle of Schmidt's beer.*

---

*Efforts of the Prohibition party to gain political power in Washington had been markedly unsuccessful, their two candidates for congress, Dr. Newell and Judge Greene having been able to attract only fractional votes. In 1898 a state chapter of the three-year-old national Anti-Saloon League was formed to coordinate the militant evangelism of the WCTU and other existing temperance societies with the Protestant evangelical churches and focus that power on the politicians of existing parties. Although the Washington Anti-Saloon League was not very effective during the first few years of its existence, it eventually exerted as much control over state legislatures as the "liquor lobby" ever had.

PALE EXPORT: Leopold Schmidt and other dignitaries ride the platform of electric freight trolley carrying first load of Olympia beer for export, 1896. Buildings, left to right, are First National Bank, I. Harris & Sons drygoods store, Kneeland Hotel, Mottman's.

POLITICS AS USUAL

The fall elections of 1898 were a testing ground for the question of whether or not the Fusionists were to remain a cohesive force in the politics of the state. The results indicated that their strength was already waning. Although they widely publicized such accomplishments of the past 18 months as the reduction of the state debt from $2,309,763 to $1,722,492, the cutting of the biennial budget almost in half, and the fact that the Fusionist legislature had spent $10,000 less than the last Republican session,* they lost control of the house of representatives and retained a diminished majority in the senate only because of the fact that the Fusionist senators elected in 1896 wouldn't have to run for reelection until

*Although a $10,000 legislative saving may have appeared significant in 1898, it is probable that present day legislators *spill* more than that during a normal session.

1900. Two Republican congressmen, F. W. Cushman and Wesley L. Jones, were sent to Washington, D.C., both retaining their seats for the next 10 years and Jones later moving up to the U.S. Senate.

The People's party was not only made up of diverse political factions, but had been born as a party of discontent, seeking solutions to the problems of a depression economy through governmental action. The remarkable response of the voters in 1896 was in answer to the Fusionist promises of "better times," rather than to such reform planks as woman suffrage, local option, direct elections and direct government. The voters had previously, and would in the future, prove at the polls that there was not yet any mass enthusiasm for the Populist reforms.

The great Klondike gold rush, now shifting to Nome, had dramatically ended the hard times which had swept the Fusionist into office and their days were numbered.

The members of the sixth legislature began straggling into town in early January of 1899 and with them came the usual retinue of lobbyists and patronage job-seekers, the *Standard* taking note of the *"unusually large number of women in the city seeking legislative clerical positions."*

The weather was, as usual, at its worst in January and February, alternating between snow and cold rain. The town authorities had the sidewalk to the capitol cleared of snow by the opening day of the session and the *Standard* reported that *"everybody is rejoicing over the arrival of the new street cars,"* which it described as larger and twice as powerful as those which had fallen victim to the fire of the previous summer. The affairs of the power company had so improved that a snow plow was available to put the line in service from 4th and Main to the capitol. The bankrupt Hotel Olympia was kept open through the heroic efforts of banker C. J. Lord, who was serving as president, treasurer and a director of the company. The Carlton, although relegated to second rank, was modernized with "electric lights from first floor to attic" and a free public telephone, and the historic Washington (Young's) Hotel at 2nd and Main had again been "thoroughly renovated, repaired, improved and modernized at heavy expense" by George E. Huggins and was being operated under its fourth name, Hotel Huggins, by his daughter, Georgia.

Despite these efforts to make them welcome, the legislators of 1899 seemed even crankier than usual, perhaps because the miseries of "la grippe," or influenza, were added to those of the weather and the drafty, tumble-down territorial capitol building which afforded them doubtful shelter. The *Standard* reported earlier in March that only 21 of the 34 senators had returned from a week-end recess, *"due to late trains and la grippe,"* and that Lieutenant Governor Thurston Daniels was unable to preside over the senate because he, too, was suffering from achy joints and running nose. Murphy thoughtfully appended his favorite remedy for the unpleasant malady . . . *"Good sharp apple cider, raw onions and woolen underwear."* To further cheer and entertain the legislators and citizens he booked the great John Philip Sousa and his band for concerts at the opera house.

The opening address of Governor Rogers did little to cheer the sniffling solons and it left the citizens of Olympia in a state of ambiguity, uncertain whether to curse or praise him.

Rogers scolded the legislators for failing to reduce the costs of government to the bare minimum. He opposed the maintenance of more than one normal school and advocated the consolidation of the University of Washington and the agricultural college, to the dismay of those whose districts had received these educational prizes in past political deals. He complained that the $337,000 which had been appropriated to sustain the public printer since statehood was quite outrageous. Pointing out that the four states of North and South Dakota, Idaho and Montana combined spent less per year on printing than did Washington, he suggested that abolition of the position of state printer and substitution of a contract system would result in a 50 percent saving.

Old line legislators were aghast at the thought of abolishing this lucrative office and so was the current elective state printer, Gwin Hicks, the son of old Urban Hicks who had tried unsuccessfully for the post in territorial days. The younger Hicks was in the process of becoming a very wealthy man and he was lobbying against Rogers' proposal almost as soon as it was made.

The governor rubbed the legislative noses in the fact that they had done very little to protect the public from the greed of the railroads and demanded a railroad commissionion to be selected by, and serve at the pleasure of the governor.

The railroad lobbyists, who were accustomed to wander freely through the legislative halls and frequently shared desks with members during sessions, began their lobbying even quicker than State Printer Hicks.

Rogers rather plaintively reminded the assembly that no teeth had yet been put in the law against free transportation passes, and that the telephone and telegraph companies were now compounding the evil by handing out passes of their own.

Nobody had to lobby against that. The legislators were well aware of how much money they were saving through use of these freeloading permits.

As the father of adequate public education for all, the governor dwelt at length on the necessity of raising the standard of common school education and increasing the school tax nearer to the four-mill constitutional limit. Legislators who tend to squirm at the suggestion of any tax increase, grew more uncomfortable when Rogers urged increased corporation and inheritance taxes and the imposition of an income tax on

Like all governors, he boasted a bit regarding the accomplishment of his administration, pointing with particular pride to $50,000 savings in the operations of the state institutions through his new board of control. He particularly praised the efficiency of its young chairman-auditor, Ernest Lister who, he said, deserved a raise from $1,500 to $2,000 a year. He confessed, however, that he couldn't understand why it cost more per "inmate" to maintain the state school for the feeble minded at Vancouver than the state reform school at Chehalis.

The biggest surprise in the governor's message . . . particularly to the citizens of the capital city . . . was the suggestion that the state abandon the massive stone foundation next door to the territorial capitol and buy the Thurston county courthouse in downtown Olympia as a state capitol building. He insisted that capitol grant lands were currently worth only a dollar an acre and couldn't possibly finance an adequate new structure. He felt that $150,000 would be a fair price for the courthouse, which could be enlarged to fill the needs of state government "for the next 50 years."

Murphy, sensing another ploy in the Pierce county plot, sprang at once to the attack. Regarding the governor's claims that the capitol lands were worth only a dollar an acre, the *Standard* proclaimed, *"He seems to assume that a falsehood, slanderous though it may be, stoutly adhered to, is as good as the truth . . . so long as it serves well his purpose."* Furthermore, he demanded editorially, *"Who authorized Governor Rogers to offer to the state Thurston county's courthouse for $150,-000? Certainly not the people of Thurston county."*

The *Olympian,* along with a segment of the town's population, was inclined to think that half a loaf might be better than none and that the capital would be better anchored by an enlarged and renovated sandstone courthouse than by the tottering territorial "dog kennel," as Murphy was fond of calling it. But the doughty publisher of the *Standard* wasn't having any of that. He had cast Rogers in the role of villain and his prose warmed up progressively to make his feelings known in such pointed editorials as this:

OLYMPIA LIGHT & POWER COMPANY'S NUMBER 3, proudly piloted by Motorman Bush Baker

*"It is said by spectators that his accidency betrayed the animus which controlled him in the tone and inflection of every sentence he uttered regarding capitol construction, in the delivery of his message. * * * It was plain to everybody that he was juggling with his subject. This is nothing new in the presumptuous freak who disgraces the executive position."*

No sooner had Governor Rogers departed from the capitol than the two houses began their usual opening bouts of bitter bickering.

The religious issue again arose in the senate, the *Olympian* noting that *"Reinhart, the venerable senator from Whatcom county, protested the invocation at the opening session, feebly got to his feet and protested that the rules contain no provision for prayer."*

Senator Van Patton went right ahead and prayed anyway, while the old gentleman from Whatcom remained stubbornly seated.

The senators then succeeded in passing a resolution of respect for the memory of Seattle's founding father, Arthur Denny, who had died that week in his city, full of years and honors and . . . unlike most of the true pioneers . . . quite wealthy.

No sooner was that accomplished, however, than a new fight was precipitated by Senator Miller of Walla Walla who had the bad taste to introduce a railroad commission bill before a legislative appropriation measure could be placed before the membership. He was efficiently stifled and the body quickly resolved itself into a committee of the whole to pass the $50,000 appropriation. President pro-tem Plummer banged the gavel and said with delight, "Now we'll get our mileage."

The members then engaged in a series of minor quarrels. When the sergeant at arms was instructed to buy five dollars worth of postage stamps for each member, Senator Warburton demanded that they be purchased from the Olympia post office. After considerable debate Plummer said he guessed it would be all right, if there were that many stamps *in* the Olympia post office.

The sergeant at arms was then instructed to procure an umbrella rack to prevent staining of the new brussels carpet which had been placed in the senate chamber. A number of members who had no umbrellas bitterly opposed this expenditure. When they were finally overruled Senator Cole said the rack should be requested by requisition from the secretary of state.

This threw Senator Megler into a high dudgeon. He proclaimed loudly that he did not propose to have the senate "running to state officers for every little article needed by the legislature" and that, if such were to be the case, "the senate had better give way and let the state officers run things."

Rinehart, who had been dozing lightly, was startled by the vehemence of Megler's remarks and seemed to believe that the religious issue was still being debated. He rose shakily to make the somewhat disconcerting statement that "If any idols or gods are to be set up, a throne should be erected for that purpose."

Although the house of representatives managed to get through the opening prayer amicably enough, the reading clerk mispronounced so many names in calling the roll that the chamber erupted into confusion with nearly all the members on their feet hurling maledictions at the unfortunate clerk and angrily demanding corrections.

The Republicans again had control of the lower house and asserted their prerogatives by naming all officers and employees, but the senate was so evenly balanced that a compromise had to be worked out. The leadership and top staff positions went to Fusionists and such lesser posts as assistant secretary and assistant sergeant at arms to the Republicans.

There was less time and vituperation than usual expended in selecting Addison G. Foster to replace veteran Republican party leader Watson C. Squire as U.S. senator, but that did not prevent the usual charges of political hankypanky. The *Standard,* in a burst of sarcasm, proclaimed that *"$120,000 is the size of one stake in the Senatorial election. But then, Washington's legislators are honest, incorruptible men and not one of them would be mean enough to take a bribe, say $5,000 or $10,000* or so; oh no, especially if he were a Republican."*

Murphy, who was a confirmed freeloader himself, looked with increasing irascibility upon the lawmakers as they happily accepted the largess of the lobbyists, giving way again to sarcasm:

"It is splendid to be a legislator. Only think of the free cigars, champagne, brandy cocktails and just bar'ls of money!"

Rogers' opinion of the legislature was probably little higher than Murphy's for it refused to enact any of the major legislation he had proposed. The only effort made to control the railroads was a new law requiring them to carry bicycles as baggage, and that was offset by another, urged by the rail lobby, making it a crime to steal a ride on a train. Although no additional tax revenues were provided for the public schools, a bill was passed making attendance compulsory in cities of over 10,000 population. The reform bills that were passed had little tendency to shake the state. In the area of tax relief the revenue law was amended to permit the exemption of $300 in personal property from taxation, exempting from taxation ships engaged exclusively in offshore trade, and "exempting as personal property of householders necessary wearing apparel, one bed and bedding for each member of his family, all necessary household and kitchen furniture and all necessary tools of his trade."

City water supplies were protected by "prohibiting the maintenance of slaughter houses, stock yards, hog pens and the like about the springs, streams or other sources of supply." The state dairy inspector was given the additional duties of food inspector and penalties were provided for anyone he might catch adulterating food, and provision was made for the official measurement of milk cans.

In the field of conservation, 16 new fish hatcheries were authorized on the various

---

*If Murphy's figures were at all accurate, the price of a legislator's vote in the senatorial election had increased at least 1,000 percent since earlier sessions. He was probably indulging in considerable literary license.

rivers, lakes and bays of the state and fishing gear other than lines were banned from rivers and river mouths.

All three normal schools were funded, contrary to Rogers' wishes, two additonal appropriations were made for legislative expenses, raising the total to $62,000 and an agricultural experiment station was established at Puyallup. A state traveling library was created to provide books to isolated communities without library facilities of their own.

The eight-hour day was mandated for state, county or municipal public works and Senator Megler, who had taken over from Represenative Bush as the voice of the oyster growers, succeeded in getting through a couple of more bills for their protection.

The lawmakers also ignored the governor's suggestion regarding the purchase of the Thurston county courthouse as a second-hand state capitol. They appropriated $600,000 from the capitol fund to complete a new building on the now aging foundation and created a new capitol commission to see the job done. The three-man body included A. A. Phillips, a leading Olympia business man and booster.

GOOD TIMES A'COMIN'

Although Olympia was in a relatively quiet backwater of the gold rush economic flood, some of the new affluence was reflected in an increased tempo of both business and social life. The brewery was operating at full capacity, making big shipments to Alaska and expanding its market to Hawaii and Japan. At Tumwater it was constructing a big new bottling plant with the most modern machinery and an ice-making plant on the site of the pioneer Biles tannery. A number of electrically-powered freight cars were placed in operation on the street car tracks to speed up delivery to railyard and docks.

The local lumber and shingle mills were back on double shifts and, for the first time in many years, ocean ships were coming to Olympia to load cargoes. In mid-February of 1899 the *Standard* reported that four vessels were en route to load lumber; the brig *Courtney Ford* and schooner Ethel Zen for San Pedro; the bark *Vidette* and schooner *Ory* for San Fran-

cisco. By April the mills had sawed 15,000,000 feet of lumber and 4,000 cords of shingle bolts. By mid-summer the *Standard* was regularly printing such good tidings as these:

"The Eastside and Westside sawmills, the Olympia Sash & Door Co., the Richardson shingle mill and other shingle mills adjacent to the city are running full time. Hardly a day passes but locomotives are seen hauling away carloads of lumber and shingles from the Eastside mills and three ships are loading at the Westside mill. All logging camps are running full blast and dumping carloads of logs into the west side of the bay daily. Vacant houses are rapidly filling and rents are going up. No idle men are loafing about the streets and business men are doing a flourishing business."

In November it was reported that *"the Westside mill dock is full and the schooner* Premier *is lying in the stream loading from scows from the Eastside mill."*

Furthermore, the army engineers, having at last made up their minds to do something about the Olympia mudflats, seemed determined to maintain the battle. By 1899 a second dredging project had been completed and it was proudly reported in the local press that the ocean tug *Tacoma*, drawing 14 feet of water, was able to remain afloat at Percival's dock at dead low tide.

Municipal finances were further augmented when the council took note of the popularity of a newfangled gambling device, the "nickel-in-the-slot machine," which was appearing increasingly in local saloons and pool halls. A $25 license fee was imposed on each of the primitive one-armed bandits.

The new affluence was prompting other forms of leisure-time activities than playing the slots. More and more families were spending their summers at cottages or camps at such bayside retreats as Butler's Cove, Oyster Bay, Priest Point and Hartstene island. The fleet of small pleasure boats was increasing. Ernest Lister's new steam launch *Tussler* was one of the more pretentious, along with Billy Phillips' sailing yacht *Daphne*, which won second prize in the Seattle Yacht Club regatta that year, and Ren Patterson's *Evelyn G.*, which beat the *Daphne* in a subsequent race on Budd Inlet.

But it was the bicycle which had captured the hearts of more Olympians than anything else. Talcotts' could provide the prospective wheelsman with a shiny Imperial, Phoenix, Rambler or Golden Eagle for from $20 to $55. M. O'Connor was advising "Do not buy a bicycle until you examine the Victor," and the Mead Cycle Company was advertising its mail order special, the Iroquois, postpaid for $16.75. It was reported by the *Standard* that bicycle sales were averaging a half dozen a week during the summer of 1899 and that sometimes that many were sold in a single day. Merchants took to erecting bicycle racks for the convenience of their customers, the more thoughtful providing awnings to keep the rubber tires from melting when the sun was hot. An indoor wooden bicycle track called a "Velodrome" was erected on the old fairgrounds, the financially ailing street car company having abandoned its plans for a first class baseball park there.

The urge to become a speed demon, once possessed of a fleet two-wheeler, created new problems in the quiet capital city, whose "mossbacks," children, dogs and cows were used to a slower tempo. The city fathers levied a one dollar license fee on bicycles, earmarking the proceeds for a new "Board of Special Bicycle Police." Dr. Carlyon, Robert Blankenship and H. Cowles were appointed bicycle police by Mayor C. S. Reinhart, who was also clerk of the supreme court and captain of the local militia company. These officials were charged with enforcing a set of new bicycle ordinances and expending fines on the bicycle road fund. The first to fall into their clutches was P. Stixrud, who was convicted of riding his bicycle on the sidewalk at night without a license. He was soon joined by others, including Ed Henderson, who was charged with running over the little daughter of Conrad Schneider. Ray Rogers and Clyde Berry, zooming across Long bridge on a tandem, were suddenly confronted by a horse which emerged from an abutting warehouse. They flew gracefully over the amazed horse, their tandem was demolished and it was generally agreed that "it was a miracle the riders escaped serious injury."

Perhaps the saddest plight of any cyclist that year was that of one Daniel Lively, a Tenino "sport," who rode his bicycle to Olympia, accompanied by a deaf-mute friend, for a night of revelry on lower Main street. Returning erratically home in the early morning hours, Daniel fell off his bicycle at the south edge of town and broke three ribs. His deaf friend, unaware of the disaster, wobbled on toward Tenino. The unfortunate Daniel lay abandoned in the ditch for a long time before his howls of anguish awakened neighboring householders and brought them to his aid.

LAMENTABLE BEHAVIOR

The new prosperity brought other problems with it, too. Although the police department made only 53 arrests during the first quarter of the year, there were growing indications that the law-abiding placidity of the capital city was endangered.

John Riley was arrested for robbing the blackjack table of a gambler named L. Troth, who was better known in sporting circles as "South Before the War," while Constable Safely had his pistol taken away form him by a hobo named Tracy, who was later arrested in Portland for a series of armed robberies for which he was sentenced to the Oregon state prison. Admitting to having disarmed Constable Safely at Olympia, Tracy said, "I could have killed the constable, but I didn't want to. It is not pleasant work."

The local lawman had, indeed, experienced a narrower escape than he would realize for some time. A few years later Tracy, no longer an unknown hobo, but the most feared outlaw in Northwest history, would leave a trail of death and terror behind him from Salem to an eastern Washington wheatfield by way of Olympia.

It also appeared, to Murphy at least, that the old virtues were no longer being instilled in the youth of the town and that juvenile delinquency was rampant. In the fall the *Standard* gave editorial vent to his fears: *"It is a lamentable fact that quite a number of young girls paraded the streets on Halloween night and indulged in quite as lawless pranks as the hoodlum boys. It may be that something more than the curfew regulations will be necessary to curb the lawless disposition which seems to be spreading like a plague over the rising generation."*

Scandal and dishonesty were revealed in state government also when, in June, it was discovered that Deputy State Auditor George Evans had been living a double life, financed by the illegal sale of several thousand dollars worth of state warrants. Evans confessed his sins, but claimed that he had been entirely honest during his four years under former Auditor L. R. Grimes; it was only during the administration of the current auditor, Neal Cheatham, that his defalcations had taken place. (Perhaps the new auditor's name had given him the idea.)

The *Olympian* recorded the affair sensationally and with relish, observing that Evans had *"enacted a Jekyll-Hyde role; industrious and a seemingly faithful accountant by day . . . at night a virtual 'Coal-oil Johnny' on Swiftwater Bill in the magnitude of his dissipations and the profligacy of his expenditures."*

Demonstrating that there is no honor among thieves, Evans complained bitterly that he had been "rolled" and relieved of a large wad of the taxpayers' money while disporting himself in Portland's red light district. Sheriff Billings returned him to Olympia and lodged him in the county jail to await trial.

Environmental pollution was another problem spawned by prosperity. Local fishermen claimed that sawdust, dumped into the bay in huge quantities by the local mills, was depleting the salmon in the bay. Cedar dust from the shingle mills was the most deadly, they said, and they exhibited deceased salmon, their gills stuffed with cedar dust, to prove their point. Game laws were rudimentary and "sportsmen" slaughtered water fowl by the thousands on the surrounding beaches and mudflats. Deer and other game were slaughtered in the same profusion by the use of bright lights and packs of hounds.

But it was good to be able to buy beefsteaks again . . . even at the outrageous price of 15¢ a pound . . . to vary the monotony of the clams, oysters and tom cod which could be had for the taking. It was good to have a little silver rattling in pockets to enjoy the other good things in life. The *Multnomah* was crowded again when she made the gala excursion to Seattle with the newly organized and uniformed Olympia Military Band to welcome back the Washington regiment of volunteers, returning from war service on the *Queen,* which was Henry Villard's old *Queen of the Pacific* with her name shortened to fit a less expansive age.

It was good to participate in another all-out Independence Day celebration, which began with a balloon ascension over Tumwater falls on July 2, an exhibition of Mlle. Pianka's trained lions at Main and Union on the 3rd and

band concerts every evening in the town square. On the great day itself there was a grand parade of Rough Riders and of bicyclists in costumes with liberal prizes from local merchants for the best decorated child's bicycle, the best Negro character rider, the best tandem character team and the best character tricycle rider. There were foot races, bicycle races, tub races, log rolling and greased pole contests. There were lemonade stands, pickpockets, cheap Chinese firecrackers and stirring patriotic orations.

It was just like the good old days, except that the capital city's new sophistication was showing. No windows were shattered by the firing of cannon. *"That,"* Murphy explained loftily, *"is 'too chestnutty' for repetition at this original function."*

NEW CENTURY

All in all, Olympia was in a mood to welcome in the 20th century with a feeling of general well-being and renewed optimism. The one bank which had closed during the hard times had paid off its obligations and had been replaced by a newer and stronger one, with C. H. Kegley, an experienced banker from Iowa as president and such solid citizens as Capt. Reinhart, George H. Funk and Millard Lemon as directors.

In January of 1900 the harbor was a scene of purposeful activity as the Puget Sound Bridge and Dredging company's *San Diego* (the old *Anaconda,* which had pioneered the first port improvements six years earlier), gnawing away at the still plentiful mudflats on behalf of the army engineers. The Westside mill had contracted with the company to dredge a deeper basin off its enlarged export dock when the government job was finished and coastwise sailing vessels were still flocking to Olympia to load cargoes of lumber as fast as the straining mills could saw it. The *Standard* reported that *"Messrs. Brenner, oystermen, are building an oyster repository for their Mud Bay product near the site of the old draw on Long Bridge."*

The little brig *Tanner* was a unit of the 1900 lumber fleet, bringing back stirring memories to old-timers. She had carried a contingent of the legendary Mercer girls from San Francisco to Puget Sound back in the 1860's.

And an almost forgotten monument to earlier days marked the division between the

FUNERAL CORTEGE for Spanish War casualties of Washington Volunteer Regiment passing Hotel Olympia on the way to the cemetery in Tumwater.

cast and west waterways, the *Standard* noting that *"Long wharf if now only marked by decayed piles extending nearly a mile into the bay."* Most of the remaining planks had been stolen for firewood during the hard times and the old warehouse had long since fallen into the bay and been reduced to driftwood. Even the floathouse which had replaced it as the town pesthouse had drifted away from its moorings, which was unfortunate because another smallpox epidemic was sweeping the Puget Sound country. The chief of police was assigned to meet all trains and steamboats and "turn back anyone who looks as if he has smallpox." Since police chiefs were chosen for their brawn and political connections rather than for their medical background, it may have been difficult for anyone suffering from acne or other skin disorders to enter the capital city.

Memories of the Spanish American war were revived in February when the *Multnomah* steamed solemnly in to Percival's dock bearing the unclaimed bodies of nine soldiers of the Washington volunteer regiment who had died in the Philippines. The body of Regimental Chaplain Thompson had arrived earlier in the week for private funeral services.

The state provided full honors for Corporal Henry Leinbacher and Privates Fred Bushman, Frank Lovejoy, John Smith, Damian Grossman, Edward Perry, Albert Ruppert, Frank Smith and Daniel Campbell Companies of national guard troops accompanied the bodies as an escort of honor. Steamers from Seattle, Tacoma and Shelton brought 1,500 visitors to join Olympians and state officials at the funeral services in the opera house. Dad Wagner's First Regimental Band played mournful dirges, followed by the regimental quartette and a choir. Governor Rogers, accompanied by the adjutant general and staff officers of the militia in full dress uniform, paid tribute to the nine young men who had given their lives to their country, the Philippine fevers and the poisonous food provided them by patriotic suppliers of the army quartermaster corps.

Some 3,000 people accompanied the funeral cortege to the Masonic cemetery south of town through streets draped with black crepe and muddied by a sadly falling rain. The battle flag and pennant from the flagship *Olympia* were prominently on display, having been presented to the citizens of Olympia by the ship's gunners . . . probably more in appreciation of Leopold Schmidt's gift of Olympian Standard beer than the silver plaque and table service.

In the business community, hard-driving George Mottman, who had started as a clerk at the Toklas and Kaufman store upon his arrival in the early 1880's, bought out that leading establishment and moved his stock to its impressive building at 4th and Main. Sol G. Simpson, wealthy Shelton logging operator, bought out C. J. Lord's majority interest in the Capital National bank and installed his prospective son-in-law, Mark Reed, as manager. Lord, who had taken over the moribund Tacoma *Ledger* and didn't quite know what to do with it, saw an opportunity to profit further from his association with the charmingly wealthy Simpson family, Murphy reporting in June that *"C. J. Lord has unloaded the poor old Tacoma Ledger upon Mark E. Reed, manager of the Capital National Bank. The animus which prompted the act is known only to the Man With the Marble Heart."** Olympia also got a second daily newspaper, George Blankenship and several other local printers launching the evening *Recorder* to compete with the morning *Olympian*. Within five years both dailies would be owned by Tacoma capitalist Sam Perkins.

P. J. O'Brien, blacksmith and implement dealer, was introducing the 20th century refinement of rubber tires for buggies and carriages.

---

*It may be conjectured that Mr. Lord was given that grim title because he refused to bail out the financially distressed Murphy from the bankruptcy of his beloved opera house.

The sale of bicycles remained brisk, the *Standard* noting that 10 years earlier there had been only 14 "wheelmen" in the city, most of them riding "High-wheelers," while there were now hundreds and their numbers were increasing daily. The Olympia Bicycle club was one of the most active social organizations in town.

By far the most noteworthy event of the year in Olympia was the arrival on April 3 of that perennial Democratic candidate for president, William Jennings Bryan, described by Murphy as *"The Great Commoner and People's Idol."*

The *Standard* chronicled the great man's visit with headlines, to which Murphy had been allergic ever since he lost money on his Fort Sumpter extra back in 1861:

"Mr. Bryan and party arrived at an early hour Tuesday morning, by special steamer, under escort of the committee sent from here to accompany him to town. At 8 o'clock he was taken to the Olympia for breakfast, and at 9:30 was escorted to the stand erected over the court-house steps, fronting Sylvester Park.* An audience of from 3,000 to 4,000 people had assembled, notwithstanding the early hour, to listen to a man whose name has become a household word and whose reputation for honesty and sincerity is worldwide."

The entire text of Bryan's speech was carried in six full columns of the paper, its gist being that "the Republican party has outgrown its usefulness and become a refuge for the Trusts."

The Republican *Olympian* was much less enthusiastic than the still staunchly Democratic *Standard*. It branded the Bryan visit a failure, while conceding that *"the weather was fine, the oratory excellent and the crowd large."* Bryan *"spoke silly rot,"* it claimed, and his *"reception was cold."*

Murphy dismissed this carping with the observation that *"The fact is, the Olympian's criticism comes from a torpid liver instead of a sound heart and an active brain."*

It was a political year. The Republicans launched an all-out effort to eliminate Populist Rogers from the political scene, their chorus led by the Seattle *Post-Intelligencer,* currently

owned by party mogul John L. Wilson. The *P.I.* engaged in a rising campaign of villification against Rogers which reached a crescendo just before the general election in November. Screaming five-bank headings called attention to stories charging that he was the most extravagant governor in the state's history (although his stern warnings and forthright vetoes had reduced legislative appropriations for 1897-1899 to less than a million and a quarter dollars from the nearly three million of the previous biennium), that his appointive dairy commissioner, E. A. McDonald, had extorted payoffs from the state's dairy farmers, that scandal and bribery were rampant in state institutions, that he had suppressed legislative investigations of bribery by his appointees, sent the Washington volunteers to war in "condemned uniforms," endorsed the plunder of the state fair fund, participated in the sale of pardons to convicts, formed "an unlawful and corrupt political partnership" with George Turner and secured his renomination by "most corrupt methods of politics." He was branded as an enemy of education (although he was the father of the state's public school system) because he had vetoed normal school appropriations, and an enemy of labor because he had proposed a school textbook printing plant at the penitentiary.

Despite such all-out efforts, the solid record and personal popularity of Rogers returned him to the governor's chair, but it was a lonely seat. All the remaining Fusionists were swept out of office from lieutenant governor (Republican Henry McBride) to land commissioner (Republican S. A. Calvert).

1901

The 1901 legislative session convened amid a new campaign to strip Olympia of the capital. The few remaining Democratic legislators had previously caucused in Spokane and unanimously adopted a resolution to move the seat of government to Tacoma because of Olympia's "disagreeable climate, its inaccessibility, its poor hotel and restaurant accommodations and its miserable mail service."

The Seattle *Weekly Review* responded that *"the proposition discussed by Democratic members of the State Legislature to pass an act establishing the State Capitol at Tacoma will receive the hearty endorsement of every taxpayer in King county. * * * By all means, take*

---

*Pioneers such as Murphy were advocating that the erstwhile "plaza" and "town square" be named for its donor and the town's founder, Edmund Sylvester. It wasn't made official for several years, but the *Standard* began using the name still born by the charming square block of shady green in the city center.

the capital away from the 'Mud Flats of Despondency' and give it to the 'Bay of Hope.'" Murphy was predictably outraged, pointing out that the weather is the same in Tacoma as in Olympia, that the sadly reduced railroad service was *"due to Northern Pacific retaliation for the boom failure of 1891 which made it impossible for Olympia citizens to pay the company its promised subsidy,"* and the town had built one of the finest hotels in the state, but that *"the Legislature, in the majority, refuse to patronize good hotels; even Rogers, when in the Legislature lived in a 'two-bit' lodging house on the bridge."*

Nor was he mollified when Governor Rogers again urged the legislature to appropriate funds to purchase the courthouse for a capitol building, a suggestion which was quickly acted upon by Thurston county Senator A. S. Ruth, an organization Republican who had replaced Fusionist Warburton. Murphy was still highly suspicious of Rogers' motives, suspecting him of being a participant in the plot to get the capital for Pierce county, and he observed sourly that Ruth's bill *"will probably pass and then it will be interesting to see what the freak in the executive chair will do about it."*

John Miller Murphy might be getting old, but he hadn't lost his talent for invective in a good cause.

He was further angered when he learned that *"the Legislature is on a junketing expedition as guests of Tacoma to view Wright Park as a possible capital site . . . a mild form of bribery."*

He concluded with a few lines of bitter verse:

"T'is an old maxim in the schools
That flattery's the food of fools;
Yet now and then your men of wit
Will condescend to take a bit."

When "Colonel" Blethen of the then Democratic Seattle *Times* used the inaugural ball and reception at the Hotel Olympia, described by the *Olympian* as *"the greatest social event in the history of the Capital City,"* as further propaganda for the capital removal it was considered a low blow by the daily as well as the *Standard.* The *Times* correspondent wrote of the ball and its aftermath:

"The festivities were so extensive, so brilliant, so fascinating that the capital city was asleep until 9 o'clock this morning and when the train arrived, which furnishes a single opportunity to get out of town in each twenty-four hours exclusive of Sunday, the management was compelled to delay the train and the actual departure did not occur until high noon * * * but when the train did go it was loaded with members of the Legislature and their employes on their way to Seattle to spend Sunday and get in touch with the spirit of an up-to-date civilization."*

The *Standard* suggested that the Northern Pacific had catered to the hung-over legislators as a means of preventing them from doing their duty and demanding decent rail service to the capital, while the *Olympian* mildly pointed out that *"Besides the Northern Pacific train there are two boats daily leaving Olympia, one in the morning and one in the afternoon, and a train over the Port Townsend Southern shortly after noon, and arrival of trains and boats are as many in number."*

The editors of both papers were either too polite or too innocent to point out that Blethen's vaunted "spirit of an up-to-date civilization" consisted mostly of a host of harlots, box house theaters, gambling joints, thieves, pimps, strongarm men, wide-open saloons and hospitable whorehouses which were giving Seattle's "tenderloin" the proud reputation of being wickeder than San Francisco's Barbary coast.

The Seattle spirit was still the spirit of John Pinnell, and it was still paying off.

And while legislators, lobbyists and employees were enjoying the civilized fleshpots of Seattle, Thurston county's new sherriff, Jesse T. Mills, urged on by the local WCTU and Anti-Saloon League, was raiding the capital city's modest saloons and hauling away blackjack layouts, roulette wheels and poker tables, which were later publicly burned before a large crowd. It was, according to Murphy, *"the first case of public destruction of property used in illicit business in the city's history."*

Having returned to the capital, the legislators made the usual motions in the direction of fiscal responsibility and moral probity. The house voted to limit its employees to 15, the senate talked a great deal about getting the legislative business done in 40 days, and both houses spoke fiercely of firing any state bureaucrats who dared to lobby them for increased salaries or appropriations.

The usual results followed. The number of employees was gradually increased, the legislators had to stop the clocks to extend the sixtieth day and, as for the tax-paid lobbyists, the Tacoma *News* soon commented as follows on the resurgence of the "state brigade":

"It is to be regretted that the legislature did not have the moral stamina to stand by its

actions to banish the official brigade from the lobby. Olympia is simply over-run with salaried officials of the state institutions who are offensively persistent in offering uncalled-for advice and who have formed a third house combine for the purpose of securing excessive appropriations."

The total biennial appropriation was also increased by about $700,000 and legislative appropriations increased from $62,000 in 1899 to $71,000 in 1901.

The capital removal controversy accelerated, the loyal citizens of Everett chipping in to provide the legislators with another all-expense tour of *their* city with a view to making a bid for the prize, and the *Olympian* claimed that no less than 50 Tacoma lobbyists were constantly attached to the buttonholes of the lawmakers.

Even the out-of-town papers which opposed the move tended to write scathingly of Olympia. The Yakima *Democrat*, for example, defended *"poor old Olympia, made to suffer the tortures of the damned by the threat of depriving her of the State Capital, which now seems to be all that she has to live for. At each and every session of the Legislature her delegates have been hung up by grafting politicians on this question and made to stand in, either on the threat of removal or of not building a capitol."*

Yakima, which had tried and failed to gain the plum, was obviously less concerned for Olympia than angry at Tacoma, which was described by the *Democrat* as *"standing with all her four feet in the trough as usual and (with remarkable agility) now down on her knees begging for the capital."*

When Murphy denounced the attitude of the *Democrat* as "patronizing," the Yakima editor denied it with the snide comment that *"Her age, if nothing else, entitles Olympia to some respect."*

When the Ruth bill to purchase and enlarge the Thurston county courthouse as a capitol was finally approved in February the Tacoma *Ledger,* which had been sold by Mark Reed to an enterprising newspaper publisher named Sam Perkins, was so angered that it immediately abandoned its Olympia society column.

The 1901 session had its share of verbal and fistic combat, the *Standard* reporting in early March the details of one of the more sensational encounters:

A. S. RUTH, CANDIDATE FOR STATE SENATOR

Olympia's Senator Ruth was the hero of the town's battle to retain the capitol, as portrayed in this 1908 *Recorder* cartoon.

"Representative Easterday became so enraged when his bill to repeal the libel law was defeated in the Senate by indefinite postponement, that he made a vicious assault on Senator Ruth immediately after the vote was taken, by word and act. Mr. Ruth was a match for his antagonist and got in a few blows on the Easterday knowledge-box before bystanders could interfere. Easterday later patched things up with the Senate by apology, a privilege he was not willing to accord the poor newspaper man, if he ran up against a libel suit, to square himself with the injured party."

The *Olympian* also took note of the affray, claiming with a complete lack of historical perspective, that it was *"unprecedented in the history of Washington."*

Pioneer Murphy, an observer of the legislative scene since the 1850's, set the record straight:

"Our neighbor is mistaken. Such scenes were not unusual in Territorial days. Many older residents remember when Bradshaw shied an inkstand at an opposing member and 'Ned' Barrington wiped the floor with an opponent whose conduct justified such extreme measures, and when Editor Newell of the

Walla Walla Statesman *drew a pistol to settle a dispute.*" He added that *"if the* Olympian's *editor will examine the record he will find that the precedent was established on more than one occasion."*

Governor Rogers did not live to see his second-hand capitol acquired by the state. He died late in December of 1901. Even before his funeral, the Republican lieutenant governor announced that the remaining Populist and Democratic appointive officials would immediately be required to "walk the plank."

As the old year of 1901 was ushered out in a pall of cold rain, the body of the governor lay in state at his home on Main street. A simple service followed, attended only by his family, intimate friends and state officials and the body, escorted by militia troops and state officials including McBride and the supreme court justices, was carried by special funeral train to Tacoma, where it again lay in state at the Pierce county courthouse.

The body of John Rankin Rogers was buried in his home town of Puyallup, but the school children of the state donated their pennies and nickels to pay for a very bad statue of a good man and the lifesized figure of a frock-coated Rogers stands to this day in Sylvester park, its back to the old gray sandstone statehouse and its face toward a high-rise luxury hotel across from what used to be Main street. Carved in the granite base is the creed of the old Populist . . . *"I would prevent the poor from being utterly impoverished by the greedy and avaricious . . . the rich can take care of themselves."*

First building at St. Martin's College, 1895.

CHAPTER SEVEN
The Sixth Decade
1903-1913

In the half century since Isaac Stevens had trudged through the rain and mud to the town's one hotel to proclaim Washington a territory and Olympia its capital, changes had occurred which would doubtless have seemed marvelous indeed to the little governor.

The muddy lanes dotted with stumps, which then served as downtown streets, had been straightened, graded and planned or, in a few locations, paved. Wooden or "patent stone" sidewalks, lined with electrical, telephone and telegraph poles, fronted impressive three and four story business and office buildings lighted by electricity or gas. From six in the morning to seven in the evening, the bright yellow street cars of the Olympia Light and Power company rattled merrily up and down Main and 4th streets and, four times a day, trains of the Northern Pacific and Port Townsend Southern whistled their way in and out of the downtown yards.

The Indian wickiups were gone, the south Sound tribesmen living at their island reservation or in the community which had grown up around the church of their new Shaker religion on Mud Bay, and their dugout canoes had given way to the steamers *Multnomah, City of Aberdeen* and *Capital City* of the S. Willey Steam Navigation company.

The old Washington Hotel was still at the corner of 2nd and Main, as it had been when a hungry Stevens came seeking food and shelter, but it was no longer fashionable. The business district had moved south and the old frame hotel was an oasis of shabby gentility amid a raucous desert of saloons and brothels housed in the ramshackle wood frame buildings of old Olympia. The Gold Bar restaurant building, where the first teritorial legislature had met, was still there, too, and so was the little wooden territorial capitol on the hill, but the tall eight-sided clock tower of the new statehouse, its huge addition still under construction, rose above the trees of the old town square.

Neat homes, set in green lawns and shaded by elm and maple trees bordered upper Main and 4th streets, where there had been only virgin forests, although many of the intersecting side streets still existed only on the city plats.

In actual area, the town had not changed much from Stevens' time. Although dredging operations had provided a channel to deep water, most of the mudflats were still much in evidence at low tide. Bulkheads and filling had created a few acres of new land at the Northern Pacific Yards on Water street, at the east end of the old Long bridge and at the edges of some private property where owners had been willing to erect bulkheads to retain the dredgers' spoil, but downtown Olympia was still the short and ragged peninsula which the Indians had called *Chetwoot*. The Deschutes waterway, which covered Water and Columbia streets (except at the Northern Pacific fill) and lapped the edges of Main street at high tide, carried tidewater to the foot of Tumwater falls. The east waterway, its muddy course obstructed but not blocked by the old Swantown bridge, still extended all the way through town to Moxlie creek and there was 10 feet of water under the pilings of the opera house at high tides. At abnormally high tides the lower town was still likely to be flooded as far south as 4th street.

Despite the changes which had been made, Isaac Stevens would probably have recognized his old capital city more easily, had he returned from his hero's grave in 1903, than would a citizen of today warped backward in time.

LEGISLATING IN THE BARN

The legislators made their biennial pilgrimage to Olympia in 1903 under the usual mid-winter difficulties, although this time it was not snow which hindered their travel. Relatively warm, but extremely violent southwest winds were sweeping in from the Pacific, bringing with them deluges of rain. The high winds raised havoc with steamboat schedules and when the sternwheelers did venture out on the stormy waters of the Sound their passengers could do little but hang on and either pray or throw up. Mud slides likewise made train service erratic and even the street cars of Olympia had a new reason for failing to meet their schedules. Their overhead trolley wires kept blowing down. That became a secondary problem, however, when the Deschutes river flooded, inundating the power house and putting not only the street cars, but all the electric lights in town, out of commission again. A massive landslide at Tumwater even knocked the brewery's new bottling house off its foundations and temporarily interrupted the supply of beer.

There was one ray of brightness amidst the general dreariness. The ancient "temporary" territorial capitol of 1856 had finally been condemned as totally unfit for human . . . or legislative . . . habitation, and the lawmakers had temporary new quarters while they awaited the completion of the renovating and enlarging of the former courthouse.

The new legislative hall was no palace, but it was roomier than the termite-ridden territorial capitol, it was somewhat less drafty, its roof didn't leak, it had indoor plumbing and it was closer to downtown, making the legislators less vulnerable to "la grippe" and the wintertime eccentricities of the street cars.

The building was constructed in 1890 by A. Farquhar on land at 7th and Adams which he had purchased from Michael Simmons 30 years earlier. The rambling two-story wooden structure, operated for some years as a general store, was said to be the largest building in town when it was built. In more recent years it had been rented by the state military department for the storage of arms and ammunition and, as temporary capitol, was soon designated "the barn" by the lawmakers, who found their way to their desks, or "stalls," by means of large white identification cards, which only slightly alleviated the confusion attendant upon their strange surroundings.

Governor McBride*, in his address to the legislature, referred to the untimely death of Rogers and urged an appropriation of $589.55 to defray his burial expense, which were "a heavy burden to the widow." He then recommended the usual reforms . . . creation of a railroad commission, elimination of free passes, better means of controlling corporations and banks and a more efficient means of making appropriations for the biennial budget.

The railroad commission proposal was being bitterly fought at this time by King as well as Pierce county, for James J. Hill had built his Great Northern Railway to its terminus at Seattle and was promising to make that the transportation center to the Orient if he were given a free hand to derail the competition by his own methods.

The railroad lobbyists were also out in force and the combined pressure was apparently too much for even dedicated reformers. Representative Harold Preston of King county, who insisted loudly for 10 days that he had been elected solely on his promise to support a commission bill, then caved in completely and agreed to vote against it.

After protracted debate, the senate voted to indefinitely postpone the bothersome measure, but not until the members, along with a "tremendous crowd of spectators," listened to inspired oratory from Senator Hamilton of King, who advised one and all that *it would be better for those who feel they are imposed upon by the railroad companies to appeal to them for fair treatment, than to listen to the idle vaporings and promises of either disappointed or ambitious politicians.*

The house later passed a modified commission bill, but it, too, was done to death in the senate. A bill controlling foreign banks doing business in the state was likewise postponed to a quiet grave. A measure requiring Puget Sound pilots to navigate offshore vessels in the waters of Puget Sound was defeated, and those free passes continued to add bulk to legislators' wallets.

---

*The Seattle *Times* refused to concede that McBride was, in fact the governor, claiming that the constitution merely authorized the lieutenant governor to perform the functions of a deceased or incapacitated governor. Throughout his three years in office, McBride was consistently referred to as the "acting governor."

The 1903 session made up for its negative attitude toward all measures opposed by big business by showing a remarkably tender regard for the morals of the common folk. Another local option bill was passed, this one requiring that a majority of the voters in any city must sign a petition for an anti-saloon election. Another permitted search and seizure of liquors kept in "blind pigs," and still another made it a felony for a male to live off the earnings of a prostitute.

A felony gambling law was passed, but only after its opponents, having exhausted all the delaying tactics known to the legislative mind, resorted to a practice known in the halls of state as "trimming the Christmas tree." This procedure involved the tacking on of so many weird and wonderful amendments to the original bill that it either becomes unpalatable even to its supporters, can't be enforced or is declared unconstitutional by the courts.

The gambling bill, as finally passed, laboriously spelled out an almost infinite number of games of chance, including such esoteric ones as lansguenette, rondo, rouge et noir, brag, bluff, throw and tan, which were banned; provided up to three years in the penitentiary for possession of a slot machine and even made the holding of a church raffle a pentitentiary offense.

And, as a final salute to law, order and public morals, a cumulative felony law was passed requiring judges, passing sentences for second offenses, to double the previous sentence if the culprit pled guilty and impose a mandatory life sentence if he claimed he was innocent!

The railroad fight entered the biennial senatorial selection process when the Tacoma *Ledger* claimed that Levi Ankeny's campaign was being financed by the Southern Pacific railroad on his pledge to work against the Great Northern. There were, of course, the usual charges that votes were being purchased, the *Olympian* reporting even before the legislators assembled, that "*Ankeny henchmen are touring the state, 'closing out cash deals' for the necessary votes for U.S. senator.*"

Ankeny, described by Norman H. Clark* as "*a Walla Walla banker who smelled of cigars, whiskey, privilege and corruption and who,*

The Dry Years: Prohibition and Social Change in Washington; University of Washington Press, Seattle, 1965.

according to the most credible story, had laid down $49,000 of his own money to buy the votes of the state legislature," must have had the wheels well greased with something, for he was elected over five opponents, at least three of whom were political heavyweights, before the end of January.

Although old Senator Rinehart was no longer present, the traditional religious wars were fought in the senate, sparked this time by a resolution to employ a chaplain at four dollars a day to open all sessions with prayers. Senator Graves of Spokane took up Rinehart's sword and charged into the fray, declaiming that "this senate has no business incurring expense for the purpose of opening its business with prayer any more than the supreme court. We are here for business, not for prayers!"

Senator Welty responded that, while he questioned four dollars for 15 minutes work, he felt that ministers had a good field for missionary work in the senate.

Senator Ruth, perhaps feeling that his colleague shouldn't have uttered such an obvious truth even in jest, moved that the resolution be tabled, which it was.

Olympia tried hard to counteract the discomforts of the temporary capitol with a series of social events to keep the legislators' minds off their troubles. The legislative ball, the last to be held in the grand and gaudy Hotel Olympia, was attended by guests from other Puget Sound cities and from as far away as Spokane and Walla Walla. The reception room was, according to the *Olympian,* "*decorated in evergreens and Chinese lanterns*" (a dangerous combination in the highly combustible wooden building) and the grand ball room "*in pink with dainty festoons of wild tea vine hanging from the chandeliers.*"

The menu at the midnight banquet consisted of "Consumme en Tasse, olives, Olympia oyster patties, sandwiches, chicken and shrimp salad, Curacao punch, assorted cakes and mixed fruit." Thereafter a series of "legislative hops" was staged weekly for the entertainment of the town's distinguished guests.

McBride turned out to be something of a shock to the legislators. Under the convention system of selecting candidates it had been customary to toss the dry bone of the lieutenant governorship to loyal but not necessarily very bright party hacks. The job paid little and entailed even less reponsibility and, after all,

181

no governor had died in office until John Rogers came down with pneumonia.

Henry McBride, a 47-year-old native of Utah, who had been a country school teacher on Whidbey island; later a lawyer and superior court judge, was an exception to the rule. He was possessed of a strong mind and a strong will and he proved it by wielding his pruning knife selectively on the fruits of the legislature's 60 days' labor.

He vetoed the local option bill on the grounds that it was merely a fatuous gesture in the direction of morality, being impossible to apply or to enforce. He used his veto pen to trim more than $400,000 from the appropriation bill, which was still the largest in the state's history . . . over two million dollars from general fund revenues and a total from all sources of nearly five and a half million dollars. As subsequent legislators have been known to do, those of 1903 simply ignored the dire forecast of the state auditor that general fund revenues for the biennium would be less than two million dollars.

McBride spanked the legislators unmercifully in his veto of a tax commission bill, which he had asked for, on the grounds that the legislative version was not designed "to cure existing evils, but to postpone the inevitable day when a legislature will be elected that will prove true to the people." The bill called for an unsalaried board of equalization to also act as a state tax commission and, in McBride's opinion, the expenditure of the $15,000 appropriation for such a purpose would be "little short of a criminal waste of public funds," which would do nothing to stop the political tax-dodging activities of the state's wealthier individuals and corporations.

The governor also infuriated a number of the newspaper-hating lawmakers by vetoing a new and highly punitive libel law which they had finally succeeded in getting passed to replace the existing one, which was far too mild for their tastes.

EXIT LAUGHING

The eighth state legislature adjourned *sine die* in the early morning hours of March 13, 1903. It had become a custom for legislators, employees and the general public to descend upon the chambers and strip them of everything movable as part of the *sine die*

revelry, and the *Olympian* commented favorably on the restraint shown this time:

"There was much revelry, but no vandalism such as marked the 1897 and 1899 sessions, although three oil stoves were stolen and the sergeant at arms lost his inkstand."

At all sessions, much of the work in the final hours was accomplished in committee rooms as compromises were worked out on the more important and controversial measures. It was customary to fill the interlude on the floor with entertainment, clowning and friendly badinage which probably served to heal some of the wounds of the session as well as providing relief from the boredom of the final hours. The custom, which was later formalized for some twenty years as the "third house," was described by the *Olympian* as it was practiced in 1903:

"Senator Van De Vanter occupied the chair in the upper house and fined Dr. Thoms, head of the state anti-saloon league, the price of lemonade for all the ladies present. Representative Easterday presided in the House and with his dry humor kept the House roaring. There was no limit to the jokes perpetrated on the members during the wait for business which would close the session."

And so another legislature exited laughing.

With them went the last of the Rogers-appointed Democratic office-holders in Olympia, bright young Ernest Lister, who was replaced by H. T. (Deep Creek) Jones on the state board of control. McBride had to appoint one Democrat to the three-man board, but Lister had been too close to Rogers to please the new Republican governor, although Lister had the endorsement of 67 of the legislators of both parties. Deep Creek had also been a Rogers appointee, but he had been given the job reluctantly as a grudging reward for his efforts, as state Democratic chairman in 1896, to engineer the successful Fusion party. He wanted to be warden of the state penitentiary, but Rogers came to suspect that he might be better qualified as an inmate and appointed somebody else. Deep Creek had stormed into Olympia and after a shouting match with Rogers was given the job of deputy grain inspector, which he later left to join the Klondike stampede. After going broke in the north, he had gotten a job as a court bailiff in Spokane through the influence of Democratic Senator Warren D. Tolman of Spokane. His appointment to the commission was described by the *Olympian* as a political pay-off by McBride to Tolman, who had introduced and fought hard though unsuccessfully for the governor's railroad commission bill.

PROGRESS RESUMES

For the first time in years, no serious effort had been made to move the capital, the impressive addition to the former courthouse apparently discouraging the advocates of change. There was some panic among Olympians in May when the capitol commission, after advertising the current series of construction bonds for a month, announced that it had found no takers. C. J. Lord came to the rescue, his bank took the whole block at par and work continued, including the installation of a monstrous hydraulic elevator and a steam-powered electric plant.

But there are always problems with a second-hand capitol building. By September the local press was reporting that the street cars were running on Western Union rather than statehouse clock tower time. Each of the eight clocks was showing a slightly different time of day, which was confusing to the conductors and motormen as well as their patrons.

Under a solid business-oriented city government, Olympia was getting out of debt in 1903. The restricted district south of 3rd street was prospering and paying more than its share to the municipal treasury in license fees and "fines." More streets were being planked in the business district, but it was a continuing and frustrating process. The soft wood streets were quickly ground into splinters and people kept falling through the wooden sidewalks, which suffered from dry rot. In the fall the *Olympian* reported that a hack and team fell through the street planking in front of the opera house and C. B. Guiberson's grocery team suffered a similar mishap on the old bridge which spanned a gully near 12th and Eastside streets. The ultimate solution to collapsing streets and sidewalks was believed to have been found when Main street, from 4th to 7th, was paved with macadam. The big iron roller which had been used to smooth the asphalt surface was then hauled out to the old fairgrounds by four of William Weller's biggest draft horses to finish off the long-delayed ball park.

So far, however, no suitable answer had been found to the problem of the town's constantly collapsing bridges. The 4th street bridge to the west side had fallen into the bay again and the council was forced to appropriate $9,600 for a new lift bridge with a center section which lifted like an elevator on cables attached to a high steel tower and operated by an electric motor.

The sophisticated mechanism was not authorized voluntarily by the city council. It was forced upon it by Leopold Schmidt and the Olympia Brewing company. The town fathers had tried a compromise solution earlier in the year, raising the center span of the bridge a few feet to permit scows and small craft to squeeze under . . . if the tide wasn't too high . . . but Schmidt was adamant, demanding that both the city and the Northern Pacific cease and desist from blocking the navigability of the Deschutes waterway and install full draw spans in their bridges. He brought suit against both and, since the law was clearly on his side, both the railroad and the town decided to comply.

The matter was further taken out of the hands of the civic officials when a big gravel scow owned by the brewery and being poled toward Tumwater on the flood tide by three men, went out of control, crashed into the bridge, and wedged under it, converting the rickety structure into a drawbridge the hard way. As the tide continued to rise the scow dumped its cargo . . . a heavy concrete mixer . . . and began inexorably pushing the bridge superstructure upward from the piling. When the tide ebbed a large section of the bridge collapsed upon the scow and all traffic to the west side was halted until an enterprising small boy with a row boat began a ferry service at 5¢ a head.

ENTER THE MOTOR VEHICLE

The local "moss-backs", having marvelled at the ponderous operations of the street roller and the electric bridge lift, were treated to an even more thrilling spectacle when W. G. Ashley roared over the newly paved street on his Yale California motorcycle, for which he had taken the local agency. The internal combustion engine had come to the quiet streets of the capital city and they would never be the same again. By August Dr. G. W. Ingham had taken delivery of a new red Indian, capable of going 40 miles an hour, the *Olympian* reporting with awe that the daring physician had negotiated the former Ayer's hill (now referred to as the east 4th street hill) at a steady and breath-taking 30 miles an hour.

An even more remarkable spectacle was revealed to the wondering natives when, in August, the *Olympian* reported that *"the big Haynes-Apperson automobile of Dr. and Mrs. L. Lawbaugh of Portland stopped at Mills & Cowles hardware store for gasoline en route to Victoria."*

Old Chief Seattle's prediction was well on its way to being fulfilled. Soon, indeed, there would be no place dedicated to solitude.

Nor were these the only scientific marvels to appear in Olympia in 1903. Dr. Ingham, having entered the 20th century with a whole series of bangs from his primitive motorcycle, also became, according to the *Olympian*, *"the proud possessor of an X-ray coil, the first in the city, and has been putting on displays for the press and public. By attaching regulating handles and electrodes it can be used for the treatment of rheumatism and other diseases."*

There is no record of Dr. Ingham's patients glowing in the dark, but it seems likely that another 20th century blessing, overdoses of radiation, arrived the same year as carbon monoxide.

... AND THE MOVIES

And in November the Edison theater, advertised as "a suitable place for ladies and children to spend an hour," opened its doors with a show which the *Olympian* proclaimed to be *"both novel and entertaining, consisting of steroptican views, ending with pictures of principal men and pioneers of Olympia; G. C. Barr, champion paper tearer of the world; Morris Jones, baritone; Raymond and Stevens, acrobats, singers and dancers; and the moving picture 'Bluebeard and his wives', which is a thousand feet long."*

Thereafter the Edison provided regular movies, along with vaudeville and illustrated songs. General admission was 10¢; children's matinees 5¢.

The Port Townsend Southern railroad, under the superintendency of Ed Kevin, who sometimes doubled as conductor on the "Tenino Cannonball," abandoned its west side terminal and moved its operations to the Northern Pacific depot, that company having taken over control from the Oregon Improvement company. Its advent made the still popular pastime

of watching the trains come in more exciting, for the *Olympian* reported:

"The days of poking fun at the Port Townsend Southern Railroad passes with its purchase by the Northern Pacific Railroad. A standard locomotive has arrived to replace the little dinkey that has pulled the train back and forth to Tenino so many years. The big engine could almost accommodate the dinkey in its fire box. What the natives along the line of the Port Townsend Southern will think when they hear the new bell and whistle and see the monster tearing down the track cannot be imagined by people in a big city like Olympia where large engines and swift steamboats are as common as four-horse wood wagons." *

PROGRESS BRINGS POLLUTION

Although nobody in town had ever heard of "ecology", it was becoming evident that progress and prosperity bring pollution as well as change. The U.S. army engineers threatened to stop projected harbor improvements unless the seven sawmills at Olympia stopped dumping their debris into the bay. The threat

---

*A few days later the "monster", which was in fact a second-hand 42-ton switcher from the main line, broke both her forward connecting rods and was forced to operate for some time with only two drive wheels, thus limping rather than tearing down the track until repairs could be made.

"**THE BIG LOCOMOTIVE**" of the Port Townsend Southern, Number 858, prepares to leave Tenino for Olympia in the 1890's.

of losing the services of the government dredges worked, as the display of sawdust-choked salmon hadn't, and the mills were ordered to burn their waste, or confine it behind booms. The smoke from the mill burners did not add noticeably to the usual air pollution from unchecked forest fires which blotted out the sky every summer and frequently made it necessary to turn on the street lights at high noon.

For good measure, the city authorities banned the time-honored custom of dumping garbage into the bay at the foot of Main street, but the local draymen, used to this convenient depository, continued to use it when members of the four-man police force weren't looking.

BOSS SPORT: Big Bill McGowan.

TENDERLOIN

The restricted district was running full blast under the tolerant policies of a business-oriented city administration which seemed to have come to the belated conclusion, long recognized by the civic leaders of Seattle and Tacoma, that a little sin is mighty good for the economy. Periodically the madams were escorted to Judge Milton Giles' police court by a bright young lawyer named Gordon Mackay, paid their monthly license fees in the form of "fines," and returned to their housekeeping duties.

It did slow things down a bit when, at midnight on June 10, the new felony gambling law went into effect and everybody lined up at the bars and drank to "the good old days." The farewell to gambling proved premature, for although the supreme court upheld the constitutionality of the law, it was rather quickly forgotten and the card tables, roulette wheels and slot machines soon found their way back to the saloons.

To overcome the temporary lull in the reacreational offerings of the restricted district, the city council was petitioned by "55

185

taxpayers and business men" to permit continued operation of the dance hall adjacent to the Green Tree saloon of William McGowan.

Every Puget Sound city with pretentions toward metropolitan stature had a restricted district in 1903, and every restricted district was dominated by a "Boss Sport." In Olympia the Boss Sport was one William (Big Bill) McGowan, a huge baby-faced man with an impressive bartender's mustache and jaunty derby, who fancied himself to be a potential heavyweight boxing champion of the world. His Green Tree saloon on lower Main street was where the action was, particularly when his dance hall girls were permitted to ply their trade. To further enliven the scene, McGowan also refurbished the old theater at the foot of Main street as the Variety, a box house patterned after the type which had brought fame and fortune to Seattle's Boss Sport, John Considine.

Big Bill and his restricted district enterprises were a constant thorn in the side of Olympia's clergy, the WCTU, Good Templars and the Anti-Saloon League, who felt that a lawless and undesirable element was being attracted to the respectable state capital. The less godly members of the establishment felt that while some of Big Bill's customers might be undesirable, their money, which they spent freely, was as good as anybody's.

The result of this controversy was the same kind of civic schizophrenia that has traditionally afflicted Seattle. When the town's moralistic personality was temporarily dominant Big Bill's more lurid operations were shut down; when things cooled off and the forces of decency weren't looking they opened up again. City elections, which had long been exercises of apathy, were enlivened during this period by the underlying issue of open restricted district vs. a closed town.

There was considerable evidence during the year that the open town critics had a point. On January 21 the *Olympian* sent a shudder up the collective spines of its respectable readers with this glaring front page tale of sex, sin and violence:

"Leila Page, alias Maud Richards, a woman of the half world and keeper of a house of ill fame known as the Jewel was murdered yesterday morning and her paramour, his own throat cut in an ineffective attempt at suicide, is charged with the crime. Insane jealousy is assigned as the cause for the terrible deed. The wound of Charles Clarke, the slayer, is reported to be superficial. The woman was brained with an axe, and her throat cut with a pen-knife, which Clarke used ineffectively on himself. Leila Page was generally a favorite among the sporting class, while Clarke is a local young man, not of evil disposition, but who has drifted from bad to worse. He is a former employe of the Olympia Door Company."

HANKY PANKY AT THE JAIL

The town was further shocked and titillated when, during the course of Clarke's trial in August, it was revealed that Deputy Sheriff John McClelland had been fired by Sheriff E. A. McClarty for locking another "woman of the half world" in the cell with the young prisoner for the night. Deputy McClelland claimed that it had always been the custom to provide such solace to prisoners who could afford the fee before Sheriffs Billings and Mills retired and he hadn't realized he was doing anything improper.

The unfortunate Clarke was subsequently convicted of first degree murder and became one of the first to mount the scaffold at the state penitentiary in Walla Walla after the 1903 legislature ordered executions to take place there rather than at the various county seats. The black sheep son of a prominent Olympia family, a bartender in a local saloon, disappeared the night of Leila's murder and was not seen again. On his deathbed, many years later in another state, he confessed that he had killed the woman and cut young Clarke's throat.

There is little doubt in the minds of the few old timers who remember the bizarre tragedy that, at least upon this occasion, the state of Washington hanged the wrong man.

There were also less sensational forms of excitement in the usually dull capital city in 1903. The baseball park had finally been completed and a grandstand erected from the lumber of the velodrome, which failed to prosper and was torn down. Local business men, perhaps seeking to divert attention from the crime wave, subscribed $250 to place an Olympia team in the southwest Washington minor league and a grand ball was held to raise funds for uniforms. Throughout the summer the breezy open trolley cars hauled masses of fans to the ball park to see the Olympia Maroons take on such rivals as Aberdeen and Centralia, or the Olympia high school sluggers in their gaudy red, yellow, green and white uniforms perform against neighboring high schools. Peoples' University and St. Martins College also fielded teams. Most of the population joined the ranks of baseball fans and the *Olympian* noted that a large crowd had accompanied the high school team on the Northern Pacific train to Woodland to cheer them on to a 6 to 4 victory over St. Martins. Apparently Woodland was in the process of becoming Lacey, for the *Olympian's* sports story located the college at Woodland, but also referred to the St. Martins team as "the Lacey lads."

GOLDEN ANNIVERSARY

Another major spring event was the semi-centennial celebration of the formation of Washington territory. Pioneers arrived by train and steamboat from all over the state to gather with legislators and Olympians for the banquet at the Hotel Olympia and the ceremonies at the opera house, which included the inevitable remarks in Chinook and singing of "The Old Settler." John Miller Murphy, who was celebrating the 51st anniversary of his arrival in town, told tall tales of pioneer hardships and no doubt enjoyed himself immensely.

Murphy was also a member, along with such other local dignitaries as Senator Ruth, Allen Weir, George Mills and Mitchell Harris (proprietor of the Mottman Mercantile Company's major competitor, the Harris Drygoods Company), of the arrangements committee for Olympia's second presidential visitation.

Teddy Roosevelt arrived, grinning jovially, on May 22. The town had gone all out to give him a fitting welcome. The statehouse, schools and depot were festooned with $300 worth of new red, white and blue bunting, and more was looped from the trolley wire stays to set off large framed pictures of T.R. in action which were suspended from the middle of the streets. The bandstand in Sylvester park had been freshly painted, although there hadn't been time to replace its termite-gnawed foundation.

And now that I'm used to the climate,
I think that if man ever found
A spot to live easy and happy,
That Eden is on Puget Sound,
        Cho.—
That Eden is on, &c

From "The Old Settler," by Hon. Francis Henry.
By kind permission of Miss Mary V. O'Niel, owner of Copyright.

Its slight list to starboard and gay paint gave it something of the raffish look of a well-dressed drunk, adding to the general jollity of the scene.

Special trains and steamers brought holiday crowds and uniformed militiamen to swell the crowd of 10,000 which met the president's special train when it whistled in at 1:18 p.m. behind the pilot engine carrying President Mellen of the Northern Pacific and a secret service guard. As mill and steamboats whistles shrilled and the crowd cheered, Mayor Lord advanced to meet the president, wincing only slightly at the legendary Rooseveltian grip. Accompanied, in that age of innocence, by only two relatively relaxed secret service agents, T. R. briskly strode to the presidential carriage, proudly driven by liveryman George Reynolds, shaking hands along the way with the military escort.

187

The procession, led by Wagner's regimental band, the George H. Thomas post of the Grand Army of the Republic and the militia, made its way to the 7th street entrance to the capitol, the president standing, grinning and bowing right and left. At a brief reception in the governor's office he recognized and effusively greeted P. J. O'Brien, who had shoed horses for him in earlier days in Dakota and was introduced to E. A. McClarty, a veteran of San Juan hill. T. R. insisted that McClarty accompany him to the speaker's platform and the ensuing reflected glory no doubt helped get him the appointment as sheriff when Jesse Mills quit.

With the military band blaring "Hail to the Chief," Roosevelt mounted a flag-draped platform at the main entrance to the sandstone statehouse and briefly addressed the assembled multitude. The secret service men kept looking at their watches. Things were running behind schedule and when the president concluded his remarks the carriages were whipped to a gallop and the troops double-timed all the way back to the depot, by-passing the Masonic Temple where the brethren had been waiting in full regalia to greet the chief executive. The troops deployed down both sides of the 7th street tunnel, the locomotive whistled and the train disappeared underground with T. R. waving and grinning from the rear platform.

He had been in town exactly 70 minutes. The Masons were inconsolable, but everybody else was, to quote the president, "de-lighted."

The president had announced publicly, from the steps of the capitol, that Olympia was the prettiest western town he had ever visited. Let the smart-aleck visitors from Seattle and Tacoma put that in their pipes and smoke it!

1904: THE YEAR OF THE BENZINE BUGGY

The horseless carriage had made its noisy appearance in Washington by the turn of the century, but few had disturbed the still generally sedate streets of the capital city. Neither the state of the automotive art nor the primitive roads of the era encouraged long-distance touring, and no Olympia citizen had fallen under the spell of the new mechanical monster.

All that changed in 1904. That was the year the more venturesome citizens began a love affair with the automobile which was to prove both long-lasting and passionate. Available sources disagree as to who was the very first Olympian to astound the local citizenry by the purchase of what the local press quickly began to refer to as a "benzine buggy." The first newspaper account of the coming of the motorcar appeared in the *Olympian* of July 20:

"The advent of the first automobile owned in Olympia, that of Dr. G. W. Ingham, which has been flying about the streets for several days, was followed yesterday by another, the property of Hewitt and Ashley of Tumwater. Dr. Ingham has a Rambler*, a pretty, well finished car chosen as best adapted to the roads of this locality after examining numerous makes. The doctor and his friends have enjoyed the new prize very much. Hewitt and Ashley have one of the famous Oldsmobiles and last night Wilbur Ashley toured about the city like a veteran chaffeur (sic). Several other machines are expected in the city very soon."

Ashley, who pioneered the Olympia transportation evolution with the first modern bicycle and the first motorcycle, later claimed that his single-cylinder, two-horsepower curved-dash Olsdmobile arrived in town before Dr. Ingham's Rambler, and H. W. Crowell, a mill operator, was sure he had taken delivery of another Olds from Ashley's firm before Wilbur began touring about the city in his. It would appear that all three burst upon the scene within a week or so of each other, and the fever spread through town faster than membraneous croup or "the summer complaint."

The sudden appearance of the automobile was hard on the nerves of the equine as well as the human population of Olympia. The same month that it chronicled the arrival of the first of the horseless carriages, the *Olympian* carried this typical account of the reactions of a typical Olympia horse:

"Charlie, the popular old horse belonging to D. C. Bates (furniture dealer) *saw his first auto last night and it certainly threw a scare into*

---

*The Rambler of the early 20th century should not be confused with the later vehicle, which can be seen in such remarkable numbers being perambulated cautiously about the city, usually by little old ladies. Those pre-world war 1 Ramblers were great, primitive, hairy brass-bound beasts with three-foot gearshift levers mounted on the running boards. It took a strong and determined man to shift gears, let alone crank the monster to get it started.

Olympia automobilists on old Tacoma highway
near Sherlock station, 1913.

Charlie. He was attached to the U.S. Mail wagon at the depot when a red automobile flashed by and Charlie forgot all about his 22 years. The way Charlie scratched gravel over the Northern Pacific flats put the automobile to shame. The mail wagon crashed into a telephone pole and was nearly demolished."

The arrival of the automobile did not decrease the popularity of the motorcycle among the younger and more adventurous blades. Dr. Bridgford was establishing something of a reputation as a speed demon on his new Indian. In July he roared all the way to Albany, Oregon, in two days, making the return trip sitting gingerly on the cushions of a Pullman car, his motorcycle in the baggage car ahead. By early August the doctor was sufficiently recovered to make the run, with Ashley, from 4th and Main to the Donnelly hotel in Tacoma in the record-breaking time of one hour and 20 minutes. They returned by way of Yelm and Rainier, arriving back in town before dark, to the admiration and amazement of all.

The demand for better roads was heard almost concurrently with the rattling, banging and belching of the first motor vehicles. By August a subscriber signing himself "an automobilist" had written an angry letter to the *Olympian* demanding to know what had happened to the promised *"80-foot-wide*

boulevard to Tumwater, graded, graveled and bordered by shade trees." The road, he complained bitterly, *"remains a dust pile in summer and a mud hole in winter . . . a disgrace to the town."*

The cry of the eager automobilist would echo across the state and the nation, bring a smoggy concrete revolution to change the face of the land and the whole way of life of its people, but in 1904 the benzine buggy was just a fascinating toy. Probably even such bold pioneers as Ashley and Ingham could not have visualized a day when there would be no horses left to be frightened and the cost of state highways for a biennium would be ten times the total costs of operating the entire state government from 1903 to 1905.

THE PROLIFIC PROMOTERS

Glib promoters and grandiose schemes were as prolific as flies around a livery stable in this period of continued good times and Olympia was getting its share of them. The most ambitious of these in 1904 was that pioneer newspaperman, P. P. (Judge) Carroll, who had become a Seattle lawyer, but abandoned the legal profession and now had bigger irons in the fire.

In mid-May he descended upon the Olympia Chamber of Commerce with the dazzling an-

189

nouncement that he represented the Washington State Improvement company, a corporation allegedly financed to the tune of a million dollars by those ubiquitous "eastern capitalists." After casually announcing that he had purchased the Olympia Water company and was soon to take over the light and power company, and dropping such glittering names as Harriman, Villard, the Goulds and Astors and J. Pierpont Morgan, all of whom he inferred broadly, were or had been close friends of his, he informed the fascinated business leaders that he was going to construct a metropolitan seaport at Boston Harbor, just east of Dofflemeyer's point seven miles north of town. Streets would be graded and paved with concrete blocks, which would be manufactured on the site. No wooden buildings would be allowed. Great ocean piers would front the magnificent boulevards and in a year or two his new city would engulf Olympia to create the greatest metropolis on the Pacific coast.

Mr. Carroll's flow of golden oratory hit its first snag when he said that a million dollars a year couldn't make a real seaport out of the Olympia mudflats. There he ran afoul of old Elias Payn, a building contractor and a doughty champion of the port of Olympia who, according to the *Olympian, "knows every sounding from the narrows to Tumwater falls."* It took the best diplomatic efforts of Chairman John Byrne to quiet the enraged Payn and let Carroll proceed with his marvelous tale.

It was a wasted effort, however, for the promoter blundered into even more dangerous shoals when he blandly informed the assembled civic leaders that they were expected to buy $20,000 worth of stock in the cement factory which was going to pave the new city, as a modest gesture of cooperation and good faith. It also dawned upon his audience that the parent company's million dollars hadn't actually been paid in by the eastern capitalists. It consisted mostly of blank stock certificates and Mr. Carroll, in a burst of generosity, offered to let the Olympians buy some of them. He made it clear, however, that they mustn't be greedy. They were strictly limited to a quarter of a million dollars' worth.

According to the *Olympian, "the invitation to purchase stock depopulated the room quicker than a fire alarm and so a motion to adjourn followed."*

The enthusiasm of Carroll was not squelched. A couple of weeks later stakes were appearing beneath the tall firs of Priest Point, designating the route of an electric railway to connect Olympia with the new townsite, which Carroll let it be known was to be called Harriman City, in honor of the president of the Southern Pacific railroad. That transportation tycoon, he said, had promised to extend his railroad from Portland to a new terminus at Boston Harbor.

Some discord was interjected at about this time when Fred Schneider started yelling that Carroll was building a dock on his property. Grave doubts were added when, four days after Carroll's announcement that the Southern Pacific was coming, all work stopped at Boston Harbor and the men laid off, except the project engineer, who remained amid "a small forest of piles" on Mr. Schneider's beach and surrounded by angry laborers demanding their pay. The engineer hadn't been paid either, and all he had to show for his efforts were a lot of maps and sketches showing the locations of federal buildings, grand opera house, railroad terminal, ocean piers and other imaginary edifices.

Immediately thereafter James Dofflemeyer began suit to reclaim his point. Judge Carroll's impressively titled investment company didn't own a square foot of "Harriman City." All it had ever had were options to buy.

Harriman City was dead at conception, but local boosters still had hopes for Robert Ball, the dapper president of "Ball's Great American Marble company" (capital stock a modest $70 million), who had pledged to locate a subsidiary at Olympia to produce breakfast cereals under the frightful brand names of "Nervulous" and "Coffeeno." Backers of Ball became nervulous indeed when they learned in September that he had been ejected from his Seattle offices for non-payment of rent following an altercation with a director of the company who kicked President Ball in the stomach and beat him about the head with a stapling machine upon learning that his life savings had gone down the drain. It was subsequently learned that Ball was really a disbarred lawyer from Battle Creek named Charles R. Maines, who had been tried for murder and indicted for perjury before coming west.

More high hopes were dashed when the *Recorder*, with its usual flair for accuracy, headlined the news that gold had been discovered on the hillside above the old Olympia Collegiate Institute on East Bay. When the paper hit the street, excited townspeople with picks and shovels began racing up 4th street toward East Bay to stake their claims. Edward Cheadle, a carpenter who lived on the scene of the "gold strike" was horrified to find his lawn and shrubbery trampled by shouting treasure-seekers and his property completely surrounded by claim stakes.

When an old Klondiker declared the *Recorder's* gold to be mica, the crowd quickly and sheepishly dispersed. It was probably the shortest-lived gold rush in history.

TINDER TOWN

The state fire chiefs held a convention in Olympia that year, the event being properly ushered in by a fire on the roof of the *Chronicle* office, caused by an accumulation of dried moss. Gardner Kellogg, the Seattle fire chief who had presented the cow to Governor Ferry's daughter, predicted ominously that the capital city was about due for a major conflagration. Shaking his head, he pointed to the wooden streets, and sidewalks, the ancient wooden buildings on lower Main street, the lack of fire escapes . . . and the moss on the roofs. He so alarmed the city fathers that they immediately enacted a fire escape ordinance, proscribed a $25 fine for failing to scrape the moss off roofs and made an appropriation to put the Silsby steam pumper back on its wheels.

Chief Kellogg proved to be an excellent prognosticator as well as a knowledgable fire chief. Civic disaster descended upon Olympia at 10:30 on the night of November 16, 1904. Although everybody for miles around was aware of it, the next day's *Recorder* emblazoned the news with glaring headlines . . . "BEAUTIFUL OLYMPIA HOTEL IS NOW A HEAP OF SMOKING EMBERS."

The fire, which was thought to have started in an unused bathroom behind the club rooms of the Olympia Athletic club in the basement, swept up a rear stairway in a matter of minutes and gnawed through the roof to send sheets of flame and burning embers sweeping toward the business district before a strong south wind. Within an hour the outer walls had fallen inward "with the roar of a volcano." The paint on the historic Masonic temple across the street was blistered and smoking, and the home of General McKenny just to the south appeared to be doomed for certain this time. The north walls of Providence Academy were scorching brown.

Live electrical wires fell to the street and the power had to be cut at the power house. The town was lighted only by the conflagration and the flaming embers that spiraled from it to land on roofs and wooden sidewalks. The hotel's steam boiler exploded at the height of the blaze, sending a new eruption of firebrands high into the night sky.

The fire department knew a hopeless situation when it saw one and concentrated its efforts on trying to keep the flames from spreading. Fire Chief E. D. Raymond collapsed from exhaustion and smoke inhalation in the midst of the battle and was sent home to bed by Grant Talcott, an old-time member of the Columbia engine company, who took command of the firefighters. These included just about every able-bodied man in town. Governor McBride, with his clothing smoking, held the nozzle of a hose playing a stream on the McKenny residence to the south. O. C. White, the former state printer, trapped on a rear stairway, groped his way to the front entrance and out to join the volunteers. E. P. Kingsbury, the U.S. surveyor general, made it to safety, but he lost all his belongings; so did Louise Ayer, the supreme court stenographer and Josephine Holgate, assistant state librarian, who shared an apartment in the hotel. Ed Kevin of the Port Townsend Southern salvaged only his work clothes, which he was wearing when the fire broke out. Grant Neal of the state board of control also made it with only the clothes he was wearing, as did most of the 25 transient guests, including ex-Senator George Turner, who was campaigning for governor on the Democratic ticket.

County Auditor George McKenzie and two other volunteers were hauled from the basement unconscious from smoke inhalation and Chief of Police R. W. Faylor streamed blood from numerous gashes caused by an exploding window as he led a hose crew.

At dawn the city's pride and joy, built at such financial sacrifice by its citizens, was a dreary heap of smoking ashes, but it is surprising that things weren't much worse than they were. The great wooden structure had been built for ostentation, not safety and, as power company Superintendent Faulkner observed, "The hotel was so constructed that a boy with a newspaper and a match could have started such a fire in a few minutes that the New York fire department could not have saved the building". That no one was killed was nearly miraculous, and the fact that no other building was lost, despite the fire-bombing the town received, would seem to speak well for the firefighters, although the fact that a heavy downpour of rain soaked the town all that night was the ultimate factor. Had the blaze occurred in the midst of a summer dry spell there is no doubt that Olympia would have had its "great fire", along with Seattle, Spokane and Ellensburg.

The citizens of the capital city were in no mood to count their remaining blessings, however. The legislators would be arriving in a couple of months with renewed outcries against the lack of decent hotel facilities. The loss of the grand hotel could further endanger the precarious grasp on the state capital, and somebody had to be blamed. The fire department was the obvious whipping boy. After all, the chief had gone home to bed in the middle of the fire and an embarrassing oversight had occurred. The firemen had forgotten that the city had just paid $800 to have the steam pumper overhauled. Nobody thought to bring it to the fire.

The *Recorder,* which was currently attacking the establishment city government, headed this term by Lord's hand-picked successor, lumberman H. G. Richardson, used the hotel fire as a means of attacking it, whipping up public indignation with charges that *"more whiskey than good for them was used by the firemen to keep warm . . . Councilman Ingham told the firemen to stop drinking to get warm and get closer to the fire . . . Chief of Police Faylor, on his own initiative, got a team of horses and tried to get the steamer out of the barn, but there was only enough coal for 20 minutes on hand".*

When Councilman R. G. Shore, chairman of the committee on fire, light and water, called a special meeting to investigate the alleged inefficiency of the fire department, the *Recorder* responded scathingly that *"It needs no official investigation to elicit the information that the steam fire engine, overhauled and refitted at a cost of $800, stood cold and forgotten in the fire barn while the entire business district of the city was threatened with destruction. That it is not a heap of smoking ruins is due to the heroic work of the volunteers, and to a kindly providence that sent a downpour of rain".*

The *Olympian,* which was supporting city government, carried Mayor Richardson's stirring defense of his fire department and his expressions of resentment against the *Recorder's* slurs, but the latter journal only sniffed editorially that *"the ruins of the Olympia Hotel, still smoking, tell a mute story of what a 'gang' council can do in the way of providing political favorites with jobs at the expense of efficiency and public safety".*

Most of the town's leading citizens attended Councilman Shore's meeting to defend the fire department and the uproar was soon forgotten in efforts to provide emergency facilities for the coming legislators.

Fortunately, W. H. Mitchell had recently completed a three-story brick hotel at the northwest corner of 7th and Main and, although its roof had caught fire from the flaming brands of the Hotel Olympia fire, it was equipped with its own firefighting equipment and the blaze was extinguished with little damage. Mitchell announced that he would immediately begin construction of a large addition to include the banquet, bar and meeting facilities the legislators would demand. The city fathers offered Columbia hall for legislative dances, and committees were appointed to provide a housing service and to "attempt to devise some way of providing a suitable lobby for the congregating of the legislators and on-lookers during the evening".

After much discussion, the old armory building, which had been the meeting place of the last legislature, was rented, renovated and converted from a barnlike warehouse to a comfortably furnished "lobby", complete with lounges, bar, meeting rooms and dance floor.

It was expensive, but this seemed no time to pinch pennies. Both Seattle and Tacoma had kindly offered to host the 1905 legislature on the grounds that the loss of the Hotel Olympia would leave the solons without the luxurious surroundings to which they would like to become accustomed. There were strong suspicions among Olympians that if the legislature were lured away to either metropolitan setting it would be extremely difficult to ever get it back again. Even the opinion of Judge J. W. Robinson, a prominent local attorney, that such a move would be illegal and unconstitutional did not completely relieve Olympia's feelings of insecurity. Subsequent events would prove that if the town hadn't been paranoid it would have been crazy.

LEGISLATIVE LUXURY

Some comfort was taken in the fact that the former county courthouse, with its addition which was considerably larger than the original structure, had been accepted by the state and would be ready for legislative occupancy, although a few "bugs" had shown up. To celebrate its completion, the new steam lighting plant was fired up and the incandescent bulbs turned on to present the completed state house to the public in a "blaze of glory." The blaze was sensational, but brief. The boiler in the basement couldn't keep its steam up and the lights faded to a dull glow after a few minutes. A pre-heater was ordered for the boiler.

Another problem was created by the fact that the original building had been constructed of Chuckanut sandstone, while the massive addition was of Tenino sandstone. The two didn't quite match, although the contractor persistently tried various chemical and acid solutions which produced almost every shade except the right one and dripped on the windows, making it difficult to see through them.*

In general, however, the new capitol was a vast improvement over the past meeting places of the state lawmakers. The great baroque wrought-iron elevator, which rose and descended in awful majesty and in full view of all, provided a unique touch of modern luxury. Another source of wonderment to the natives was the thermostatically-controlled central

heating system, each thermostat enshrined in a fancy wrought-iron cage. There was an abundance of restrooms, all supplied with hot and cold running water. No longer would Washington's statesmen have to brave the January blasts to reach a drafty "convenience" out back, as had been the case at the territorial capitol.

The total cost of the building, including the addition, was $405,141.56, not counting interest.

There would be numerous new faces in the new building. Henry McBride, whose penchant for reform had convinced the more reactionary that he was a Populist in disguise, had incurred the enmity of the railroad operators in particular, and their powerful lobby, led by the state's leading political wheeler-dealer, George C. Stevenson, was sicked on the delegates to the Republican state convention at Tacoma. They quickly succeeded in rendering McBride a political corpse, after which the convention proceeded to select its slate of candidates on the parochial basis peculiar to the era. The governor was to be named* by the delegates from King and Pierce, where most of the votes were. The northwestern counties got the lieutenant governor, auditor and secretary of state, the southwest the treasurer, superintendent of public instruction and land commissioner, and eastern Washington the attorney general.

A 43-year-old Kansas-born lawyer from Bellingham named Albert E. Mead was selected as the Republican candidate for governor. George Turner, the Democratic nominee, did his best to brand Mead and the Republican candidate for lieutenant governor, Charles E. Coon, as "prisoners of the railroad lobby," while pointing to his own "anti-corporation" record as a delegate to the constitutional convention. The Republican press cried loudly that Turner had, in fact, scuttled efforts to get a

---

*The right solution was never found and if one looks closely beneath the grime of 70 years it will be seen that the two parts of the old statehouse still don't quite match.

*That's what the Republican convention did in those days; name, rather than merely nominate the state elective officials. The state was so overwhelmingly Republican that nomination was tantamount to election. Van R. Pierson, Democratic candidate for state land commissioner in 1904 summed up the situation pretty well when he called at Rogers' photographic studio in Olympia to have publicity pictures taken. When asked to smile, Pierson replied, "How do you expect a Democratic candidate to look pleasant in the face of a Republican majority of 20,000 votes?"

Governor Albert E. Mead

railroad commission plank in the state constitution and that *"the railroads, through George Stevenson, the greatest lobbyist in the Northwest, are supporting Turner."*

The voters were either confused on the issue or simply imbued with the Pavlovian reflex to vote Republican. Mead received 74,278 votes to Turner's 59,119, leading the ticket even over the popular Theodore Roosevelt, who won his first full term in a landslide over obscure "Gold Democrat" Alton B. Parker.

If the railroads had believed the Democratic charge that Mead was their slave, they were in for a terrible shock and so were a great many of the other 19th century primitives in the political and financial power structure of the state. Governor Mead proved to be an enigma they couldn't understand. Although basically conservative, he was aware of the tide to reform that was sweeping the state and the nation in the first decade of the 20th century and he rode with it instead of trying to dam it. A good deal of reform legislation was passed during the two sessions he occupied the chief

executive's chair and he refused to wield his veto pen against it.

A railroad commission and a tax commission were established in 1905, after being talked to death in every session since 1889. Also among the 186 bills passed were measures to prohibit public employees from accepting gifts from those doing business with the state, to provide sanitary regulations for hotels and restaurants and making adulteration of milk a felony, establishing a system of juvenile courts and appropriating funds for a new "home for the feeble minded" at Medical Lake near Spokane.

Hunting license fees were established to finance an office of state game warden and put an end to the indiscriminate slaughter of birds and animals. A closed season was proscribed for clams, Green Lake and shorelands were dedicated to park purposes and the Megler fishing bill provided the first closed season and effective control of gear used in the state's commercial fishery.

A direct primary bill, to do away with the old political convention system for selecting candidates for state office passed the house, but died in the senate, while a local option bill, being pushed by the anti-saloon forces, was killed in the house. The temperance people were not yet politically potent, and the legislature added insult to injury by passing a bill relieving saloon keepers of liability for injuries caused by their drunken customers. This was apparently the final blow to Dr. Thoms, the Anti-Saloon League's not very effective superintendent. He quietly departed to Alaska, taking the league's treasury with him.

THEY'VE STOLEN
THE CAPITAL AGAIN!

Any indignation and outrage that might have been felt by the enemies of Demon Rum were as nothing to that of loyal Olympians, however. As far as they were concerned, the legislature of 1905 would not be remembered for its reforms; rather, it would live in infamy for having turned, like a rabid monster, upon the hand that had been feeding it Olympia oysters and good bourbon for 50 years.

George Stevenson, the railroad lobbyist, proved that he knew his business. He railroaded the state capital right out of Olympia and to Tacoma before the bemused local citizenry was fully aware of what was going on.

FAT ENOUGH TO KILL.

This *Morning Olympian* front page cartoon of 1905 hinted at capital city's feelings toward lobbyist Stevenson and the hoggish city of Tacoma as a result of the Great Capitol Grab of the year.

Stevenson, who was also a professional campaign manager for U.S. senatorial candidates, including Levi Ankeny, was financed in 1905 by Charles Sweeny to maintain "oil rooms" at Olympia to dispense cigars and whiskey to legislators who might be willing to vote Sweeny, Tacoma's favorite son, into the senate. When Republican Samual H. Piles was overwhelmingly elected on the 13th ballot, Stevenson had to find somebody to get mad at. He selected Senator Ruth and the rest of the Thurston county delegation, which had strongly supported Piles.

Stevenson wanted to get even, but it was against his principles to engage in political maneuvering for purely emotional reasons. There had to be a cash profit.

He wasted no time in convincing a large timber combine that it would be in their interests to have a new capital located at Tacoma. The capitol land grant funds were already in debt for construction of the abandoned foundation on the hill and the purchase and renovation of the downtown statehouse. Now, if the capital were moved and a whole new construction program started, state timber

THE CAPITOLS
OF WASHINGTON TERRITORY . . .

1854 Territorial Legislature met on second floor of this building at present location of Washington State liquor store.

Territorial Capitol, 1867-1903.

Old Masonic Temple (first in the territory), completed in 1855, housed legislatures of 1855-56.

... AND WASHINGTON STATE

Thurston County Courthouse, was purchased by state; served as capitol from 1905 to 1929.

Old Farquhar General store building was remodeled to house 1903 Legislature.

Present Legislative Building housed its first full legislative session in 1929.

197

could be had at distress prices. It would be like taking candy away from a bankrupt baby.

Stevenson then used his persuasive abilities on a group of Tacoma land developers, pointing out that the transfer of the seat of government to the City of Destiny would bring on the biggest land boom since the arrival of the Northern Pacific.

With two tidy retainers thus assured, the super-lobbyist went to work in earnest.

On February 1 the bill to move the capital to Tacoma was introduced in the senate, printed, read three times and put at the top of the calendar for the next day. By 11 o'clock on the morning of February 2 it had been passed 26-12, the enthusiastic voice vote drowning out the outraged cries of "railroading" by Senator Ruth, who claimed that Stevenson had let a majority of the legislators into the pool to profit in the forced sale of capitol land grants.

The press of the state was in general agreement that a swindle was being perpetrated upon the taxpayers. Even "Colonel" Blethen of the *Times* editorialized that the move was *"Unwise and Unnecessary,"* using the argument that if the center of government remained in a place as dull as Olympia the state's public servants would have little to divert their attention from their duties, adding gratuitously that *"aside from Boston and St. Paul, most state capitals are in unimportant cities."*

The *Post-Intelligencer* charged that Stevenson, *"having failed to control the U.S. senate election and the Republican state ticket,"* was engaged in a power play that was *"simply a hold-up game."* The Hoquiam *Washingtonian* termed the move *"not only unwise and unnecessary, but ruinous."* The Aberdeen *Herald* used stronger words . . . *"Tacoma dotes on thriving on the misfortunes of others * * *. An opportunity was seen in the burning of the Olympia Hotel, thus gratifying a jealous spite against Olympia * * * The swinish proclivities of Tacoma were not in need of further proof; its disposition to strike below the belt and kick a rival when it is down have now become matters of record."* The Snohomish *Tribune* observed that *"it looks as if Tacoma, having lost the senator, wanted to get even by stealing the capital."*

The *Spokesman-Review* felt that Stevenson had *"inspired the fight to punish Senator A. S. Ruth for refusing to vote for Charles Sweeny for U.S. senator,"* while the Leavenworth *Echo*

observed cynically that *"a lot of legislative grafters, in order to worry or punish some of the members who declined to fall into line on some scheme to graft somebody, sprung that wormy chestnut of capital removal."* The Yakima *Democrat* agreed with the *P.I.* that *"the capital removal bill is a scheme for revenge against Olympia hatched by that loathsome and irresponsible lobbyist, George Stevenson, aided by his loyal henchman, Baker of Klickitat."*

One country weekly, the Lincoln County *Times,* expressed the belief that too much time was squandered by the legislators adjourning every week end to whoop it up in Tacoma or Seattle, and that it might save money in the long run to change the capital, but the Whitman County *Commoner* took a dim view of the argument *"that in a larger city the members of the legislature can have a better time. They should remember that they are elected to do something besides having a good time."*

The *Recorder* embellished its editorials with a front page cartoon of a villianous Stevenson emptying a bucket of swill into a trough before a monstrously fat hog labeled "Tacoma." The caption read, *"Fat Enough to Kill."*

Stevenson did, indeed, appear to have cast a spell of some kind over the legislature. The majority simply ignored the protests of the press and the flood of mail which their constituents unleashed when it dawned upon them that moving the state capital at this stage of the game would be extremely expensive. Despite every parliamentary maneuver by the bill's opponents, the senate consistently refused to reconsider it.

On the night of February 15 the house judicial committee held an executive session, with six members voting for removal, four against and three absent. The Stevenson forces later got the signatures of two of the absentees on the "do pass" recommendation, making the vote eight to five for removal. Mayor George P. Wright of Tacoma was permitted to attend the meeting to offer Wright Park as the new capitol grounds, immediate quarters for the supreme court and library at city hall, construction of a $50,000 capitol building at no cost to the state, and defrayment of all moving costs. Neither Mayor Wright nor anyone else would subsequently agree to put this lucrative offer into writing and the principal argument of the Tacoma forces remained similar to that of the ancient Greek athletes who wanted the Olympic games moved on the grounds that "Olympia is impossible to reach and, if reached, is impossible to live in."

Two days later the house passed the capital removal bill, 56 to 37.

Most of the loyal Olympians in the galleries were too stunned to give vent to their feelings, but a few did, giving the opportunity to Pierce county representatives to make several speeches to the effect that Olympia deserved to lose the capital if for no other reason than the bad manners of its inhabitants.

Every effort to bring the bill back for reconsideration was beaten down, according to the Olympian, "so overwhelmingly that neither division or roll call vote was called for." On February 20 it went to Governor Mead for his signature. The chief executive, who had made clear his aversion to government by lobbyists in his opening remarks to the legislature, accepted it without comment. He held it for a full week, retaining the same enigmatic silence. It seemed even longer to the Olympia Chamber of Commerce, which had been holding its collective breath the whole time.

On February 27 Governor Mead returned the vetoed bill to the legislature with as stinging a rebuke as any governor had yet flung at the state's assembled lawmakers.

The legislature could not, of course, have moved the capital on its own authority, even had the governor signed the bill; under the state constitution it would have required another vote of the people. But the citizens of Olympia had been playing Russian roulette on the matter off and on for half a century and they were getting tired of the dangerous game. This time they were also good and mad.

The original pretext for the latest effort to "put the capital on wheels" was the loss of the Hotel Olympia, which the citizens of the town had nearly bankrupted themselves to build and keep in operation as a place of entertainment for legislators 60 days every two years. When it was destroyed, through no fault of theirs, they had again dug deep to rush the Lobby to completion and placed the former manager of the Olympia in charge to provide interim hospitality until the new brick Mitchell Hotel was completed.

They felt, with considerable justification, that they had more than done their part and had been repaid with a low blow to their tenderest civic sensibilities. Tacoma, which had stolen the Northern Pacific, was trying to steal Mt. Rainier and had come dangerously close to stealing the capital, was the principal target for the collective wrath of the community.

The day after the removal bill was passed it was reported by the Olympian that "a largely attended meeting of every class of business men was held in the superior court room last evening, the same having been called to discuss the question of future trade relations with Tacoma. The meeting was organized by the election of George A. Mottman as chairman and T. N. Henry (principal of the Tumwater school) as secretary."

The result of this and subsequent councils of war was the declaration of a complete trade boycott against Tacoma. The action took on the flavor of a civic crusade, with canvassers doorbelling every ward to get signatures on the boycott pledges and the local papers running columns of warlike statements from outraged civic leaders.

The boycott was to last two years, every Olympia citizen to "refrain absolutely from any purchase, direct or indirect, in Pierce county." Chairman Mottman, for perhaps ob-

SENATORIAL SEAT THE PARAMOUNT ISSUE

Picking a United States Senator preoccupied legislators for many years, as this *Recorder* cartoon of 1905 suggests.

199

vious reasons, had called for a *perpetual* boycott, to be observed by the descendants of loyal Olympians in perpetuity. L. B. Faulkner, the vice chairman, whose street cars and electric power were in less direct competition than Mottman's department store, issued a minority report recommending a more moderate one year ostracism of the grasping neighbor. Chamber of Commerce arbitrators decided on the two year compromise.

Olympia's united front must have hurt Tacoma, at least a little bit, for by early August the Tacoma Booster Club had chartered the *Multnomah* and *Capital City* to carry a thousand Tacomans, headed by Schmidt's Booster Band, on a goodwill excursion to the capital city. The U.S. revenue cutter *Grant* followed the two sternwheelers with Senator Piles, Congressmen Cushman and Humphrey and other dignitaries, but the *Grant* had a notoriously leaky boiler and got in late. More than 3,000 Olympians, along with the local brass band, were at Percival's dock to welcome the erstwhile enemies. The Tacoma boosters promised they would stop trying to take the state capital away from Olympia; their hosts said they would stop boycotting Tacoma and the citizens of the two communities fell into each other's arms in what the *Recorder* happily termed *"a wonderful reconciliation."*

The end of the internecine warfare must have been a great relief to Sam Perkins, who was publishing the Tacoma *Ledger* as well as the *Recorder* and *Olympian* and had been having trouble keeping his editorial policies straight. One mention of "Mt. Tacoma" in the Olympia dailies during the period of active hostilities could have cost him a lot of subscriptions.

Governor Mead, needless to say, became one of Olympia's favorite citizens after February 27, 1905. The local press treated him tenderly, even the *Standard* refraining from poking

undue fun at him when, on a post-legislative tour of state institutions, he went hunting with the superintendent of the reform school and shot the prize cow of rancher Arthur Bennett near Chehalis.*

As a matter of fact, the big capital removal scare of 1905 was of considerable benefit to Olympia. Public opinion in the state was overwhelmingly against both the proposal itself, which would have been expensive, and the steam-roller tactics of its promoters, which seemed to typify the kind of open and unabashed public-be-damned politics that was fast going out of style.

Political reform was in the air and, after 1905, it was given powerful impetus by the hitherto ineffective Anti-Saloon League of Washington. The vanished Dr. Thoms was replaced that year by Ernest Cherrington, a professional saloon fighter from national headquarters who was also a talented writer, speaker and organizer.

Cherrington rejuvenated the ailing league, raised funds and began publication of a statewide newspaper, the *Citizen*. The nucleus was thus provided for a united political front by the league, the WCTU, Good Templars and other anti-saloon forces, together with Protestant churches and the Grange, which was almost superhumanly moralistic in that era, having taken on the task of defending all the rural virtues against the forces of citified sin. (In 1905 the Grange voted to expel any member who had ever been involved in any way with the sale of liquor.)

The combined temperance group, led by Cherrington and the *Citizen,* quickly made its weight felt in political affairs. Church pulpits became political forums as "wet" politicians were denounced and "dry" ones praised. The districts of legislators who had interests in saloon ownership were soon flooded with photographs of the erring politician *and* his saloon. Voting records were recorded with computerlike accuracy and distributed to the voters with dreadful efficiency. Within a year reactionary legislators were falling victims of the reform wave, and the next legislature would be stacked with first-term insurgents.

While Olympia and Thurston county quite consistently voted against local option and prohibition, even when the state as a whole was overwhelmingly in favor of such reform, Cherrington and his cohorts also championed all the other popular reforms . . . the direct primary, initiative and referendum, recall of

---

*That wasn't Mead's only embarrassing experience on his institutional tour. At Walla Walla the warden took him to the prison barber shop for a morning shave. The barber was a large Negro convict (the term "resident" had not yet been coined) who, having lathered the governor's face thoroughly and honed his razor to a fine edge, inquired as to whether or not the governor proposed to act favorably on his parole application. Mead, his adam's apple bobbing up and down nervously, assured him that he was going to sign it the very first thing when he got back to Olympia.

Olympia from the west side about 1905. Old
4th Street drawbridge in foreground.

public officials by popular mandate and, concurrently, curtailment of the power of the party
bosses and political power brokers such as
George C. Stevenson.

The capital city, having recovered somewhat
from the shock of the 1905 session, continued
as it always had, to expend its available
resources in civic improvements which might
someday satisfy its many critics that it was a
suitable place for the biennial gatherings of the
state legislature.

Early in 1905 the new steel lift-span on the
4th street bridge was given its official trials.
The gearing from the 45-horsepower electric
motor quickly overheated, smoking and grinding horribly, while the city's lights dimmed
and the street cars slowed to a crawl. A major
traffic jam ensued while repairs were made and
there were further complications when the first
tugboat whistled for passage up the waterway
to Tumwater. The city fathers had forgotten to
designate anyone to act as bridge tender. In
view of the electronic problems involved, the
city electrician was quickly given the assign-
ment . . . without increase in pay.

Dr. P. H. Carlyon, who had been elected
mayor that year, formed a task force with City
Attorney P. M. Troy and Police Chief Otto
Braeger to bring abatement proceedings
against the abandoned and ramshackle
wooden buildings which still infested the lower
part of town. The fear of being burned out of
existence was second only to the fear of having

the capital stolen and a recent fire protection
ordinance established an area in the business
district where dilapidated wooden structures
were to be removed at the owners' expense and
only stone, brick or concrete buildings could be
erected. The old original school building of
early territorial days was one of the first to fall
victim to the cleanup campaign. The Gold Bar
building, site of the first territorial legislative
assembly had a narrow escape. It was slated
for demolition, but Allen Weir, in a burst of
nostalgia, bought it and had it moved outside
the "fire limits," thus giving it a temporary
reprieve.

Despite the efforts of the mayor's abatement
team, Olympia had good reason to be nervous
about fires. Soon after the legislators left town
in March the Carlton hotel, already once
destroyed and rebuilt, was gutted by what the
Recorder described as *"the most stubborn fire
the Olympia Fire Department has ever been
called upon to handle."*

It took two hours, "using every foot of good
hose owned by the city" to control the blaze,
which was confined to the interior of the
building by a heavy tin roof installed a couple
of years earlier when a third floor was added.
The Silsby steam pumper was fired up this
time, but it couldn't be used because all the
available hose was already coupled to the
hydrants. The fancy new third story, which
was known as "the texas" because of its
resemblance to the upperworks of a steamboat,

201

was destroyed; the lower floors badly damaged by smoke and water, but its current owner, Attorney Gordon Mackay, promised to have it rebuilt by the time the next legislature arrived.

In the meantime, the big addition to the brick Mitchell hotel was going up and the McKenny building was sold to W. H. Kneeland of Shelton for conversion from an office building to a first-class hotel. (Since the completion of the capitol building, the state offices which had rented most of its space had moved out.)

A few days after the Carlton hotel fire, the ancient flour mill of Clanrick Crosby, currently the property of Leopold Schmidt, was wiped out in a more spectacular blaze. The four-story white structure, for years an empty landmark at the foot of lower Tumwater falls, was a pillar of fire from eight o'clock until midnight, when it collapsed in a great explosion of sparks. The steam fire engine, with a hose cart attached, was dispatched to the neighboring community, drawn by four big draft horses. Unfortunately, Tumwater, like Olympia, had lots of trouble with its bridges. The lower bridge across the head of the Deschutes waterway was teredo-gnawed and so tottery that it was unsafe to take the heavy load across. The fire rigs had to turn around and detour over the upper bridge

across the river. As the smoking Silsby started down the hill to Tumwater the old mill collapsed.

Built of huge timbers, hand-picked from Crosby's sawmill, the ancient structure had been a center of commerce in early days, equipped with its own wharf and basin for loading ships. Although unused for decades, it had been in a remarkable state of preservation, even to the whitewash which coated its exterior. Schmidt, who felt the Olympia Light and Power company was overcharging him for power and street railway services, had taken over the property to obtain the water rights that went with it and had been threatening to generate his own power, with enough left over to sell on the open market. He obviously suspected foul play and offered a sizeable reward for the arrest and conviction of the culprits who put the torch to his flour mill, but there were apparently no takers.

These latest conflagrations prompted the old Barnes Hook and Ladder company, dormant for several years, to reactivate itself. The city council found funds to add the latest model LaFrance chemical wagon, complete with hose, ladders and emergency gear, to the fire department's roster. It was soon found that the

CROSBY FLOUR MILL on lower Tumwater Falls; pioneer Crosby House in the background. Street railway roadbed in foreground led down the hill to the original Olympia Brewing Company plant.

two fire horses were unable to pull the heavy new rig at much above a slow crawl, and a third horse had to be purchased, badly straining the fire department's budget.

Among their many complaints, legislators had been lamenting that their bourbon and water was made unpalatable by wiggly things which kept coming out of the local water taps. Mayor Carlyon, a direct actionist if there ever was one, made the water company drain its reservoir on Ayer's hill in his presence and that of Dr. N. J. Redpath, the city health officer, and members of the council's committee on light and water. The *Recorder* sent a reporter along, too, and he reported that what was revealed *"was not conducive to a good appetite. The water was covered with green scum and thick and decayed vegetable matter, silt and other stuff that would have to be strained through the teeth before drinking. The odor was somewhat worse than that from the downtown pipes . . . like that of a stagnant lake in summer. The bottom and sides of the 2,500,000-gallon reservoir were covered with black mud and slime and was declared by Mayor Carlyon to be unfit for use. It is the home of creepy, crawling creatures; a natural aquarium. Boil the water and you have a morgue."*

Mayor Carlyon procured a bottle full of the liquid, which he displayed to one and all while castigating the water company. According to the *Recorder* man, who was obviously awed by what he was finding in the city water supply, the contents of the mayor's bottle *"contained a miscellaneous and repelling collection at the bottom which would require a post-mortem and botanical analysis to classify."*

The mayor urged the city to condemn and take over operation of the water system, a proposal which was applauded by most of the citizens who attended a mass protest meeting. The committee on light and water, despite the appalling spectacle that had been revealed to its members at the draining of the reservoir, cautiously recommended the use of moral 'suasion on the water company. The company, somewhat alarmed at the furor, agreed to make alterations to the system and reduce rates. Like the legislators who began each session with a pledge to cut down the number of employees, the company's intentions were no doubt good at the time, but it soon got mixed up and *raised* the rates for the same flora and fauna-infested water. The cries for public ownership of the waterworks would be heard periodically for several years to come.

SLOW BOAT TO THE PARK: The launch *Comet* carried picnickers and campers to Priest Point Park from city float in pre-World War I days.

The town did make an acquisition in 1905 which remains to this day one of Olympia's greatest civic assets. The development company which had purchased the old Oblat mission site at Priest Point for a housing development, had fortunately gone under in the last depression and the 240 forested tidewater acres had reverted to the county for taxes. Cap Reinhart, then a councilman, introduced the proposal to buy it from the county for $1,200 as a city park. George Mottman underwrote the payment, the plan was approved, City Attorney P. M. Troy did a masterful job of clearing the legal obstacles, and in the spring the citizens were embarked on a series of field day picnics reminiscent of the Olympia-Tenino railroad efforts of 30 years earlier. William Billings, who had helped to clear the right of way to Tenino, was the first to volunteer. A huge clambake was directed by T. J. Kegley and Theodore Brown and everybody had fun as the forested park began to take form. The work parties were held regularly throughout the summer and early fall, with carriages, automobiles, bicycles and launches conveying overalled citizens to the site. Leopold Schmidt donated the Swiss chalet, erected by the Olympia Brewing company at the Portland Lewis and Clark exposition, and it was re-erected at the park by the volunteer workers.

Priest Point has survived the neglect and occasional outright vandalism of later city administrations to remain as one of the nation's loveliest natural parks. Its great trees filtering the sunlight as through the nave of a cathedral, as solemnly hushed in its more remote sections as when the French fathers established the Mission of St. Joseph of New Market a century and a quarter ago, it remains a refuge against the prophecy of Chief Seattle that, with the coming of the white man, "there will be no place dedicated to solitude."

No less than three interurban schemes were announced during the year, the grandest of them promising express service all the way from Portland to Vancouver via Olympia. There was no doubt in anyone's mind that the interurban was the high-speed transportation development of the 20th century. Certainly the unreliable and expensive automobiles . . . even such advanced models as C. J. Lord's new 40-horsepower Pope-Toledo, which cost an astounding $3,500 and was described by the *Recorder* as *"the first high-power touring car in town"* . . . could never hope to compete with the big electric cars on their smooth steel rights of way.

1906

Olympians, in 1906, had reason to feel that they were living in the best of times and in the best of worlds. The post-statehood depression was all but forgotten. The sawmills along Budd Inlet were singing their raucous accompaniment to prosperity, punctuated by the crash and splash of unending trainloads of logs dumped into the bay. Olympia beer was increasingly popular with its new horseshoe label proclaiming "It's the Water." The steam schooner *Santa Barbara* hustled back and forth loading Olympia beer and Olympia lumber for San Francisco and the *Multnomah* and *Greyhound* carried so much of the barreled brew on their freight decks that they gurgled.

The most concerted effort yet to steal the capital had been successfully beaten off and statewide public opinion was clearly aligned with Olympia on the matter. The great utilities firm of Stone and Webster was repeating its assurances that the electric interurbans would be running from Tacoma to Olympia within the year, and the Union Pacific, having recovered from its financial paralysis of the 1890s was surveying a new line to Budd Inlet. It was freely predicted that a whole new era of prosperity would arrive with the Union Pacific, assuring a population of 30,000 within the next three years. Property values were going up and if one needed bottled optimism, the Olympia Wine and Liquor company was dispensing its rare old Kentucky whiskey for $3.00 a gallon.

On the national scene, Teddy Roosevelt, walking softly and carrying a big stick, was building a navy designed to carry the message, known to all Americans, that the United States could lick the rest of the world any time it wanted to . . . with one arm tied behind its back. There was some shock to the more cultured when Enrico Caruso was fined $10 in New York for pinching ladies at the Central Park zoo but there was comfort in the thought that he was, after all, an Italian.

The great San Francisco earthquake was shocking news, too, but when the rebuilding began it made the mills hum at an increased tempo, while coastwise ships waited in harbor for loading space at the west side wharf. And Olympia was prosperous enough to send a $5,000 relief shipment to the stricken Bay City.

The unions were making a bit of a fuss, trying to sign up the millworkers, but the owners just posted signs warning that anybody with a union card would be fired and the symphony of the saws didn't slacken.

AUTOMANIA BECOMES ACUTE

The new prosperity was also making commonplace the smell and sound of the internal combustion engine. Henry Ford, having met with a success he hadn't contemplated, was nearly a year in filling the back orders of Olympians, but in the fall the first of the soon-to-be legendary Tin Lizzies arrived in town, consigned to Dr. Redpath, Mayor Carlyon, W. A. Weller and Fire Chief Raymond. Dr. Ingham had also ordered a Ford, but when Henry dispatched letters giving customers the alternatives of waiting many months for delivery, taking Ford Motor company stock in the amount of their payment, or getting a refund, the doctor demanded his money back. For years afterward he tormented himself figuring out how rich he would have been if he had taken up that stock option.

The arrival of the automobile in ever increasing numbers was bringing new problems not only to citizens who were forced to dodge the speeding monsters on the streets, but to state government. The insurance commissioner was forced to ask the attorney general for a ruling as to what type of insurance should properly cover horseless carriages. The opinion was that "floating marine" was the most adaptable. The *Recorder* agreed, pointing out that *"gasoline buzz-wagons have many points in common with floating marine, even to the expense of operation. Like steamers, autos are liable to break down, to have collisions and even to pile up on the rocks."*

The last legislature had established the office of state highway commissioner and the new official lost little time in laying the groundwork for the present bureaucracy which has developed over the years into what Clayton Fox, the humorous political writer of the *Daily Olympian* has referred to as *"the state's sacred hog, which feeds on tax dollars and excretes concrete."* Commissioner J. M. Snow announced that he would ask the next legislature for the unprecedented sum of $108,-000 for the construction of state highways. Further, he demanded a private office of his own. He had been given a cubbyhole in the land commissioner's office. Thus Snow also inaugurated the chambered nautilus syndrome which has carried the highway department from the lonely desk of Mr. Snow through a series of ever larger and more expensive buildings to its present concrete monolith which cost more than the state's entire main capitol group.

The sound and smell of the internal combustion engine was not limited to the roads and streets of the community. An increasing number of the more affluent were having gasoline launches built and there was talk of forming a motorboat club. The gas boat was also becoming a popular commercial carrier between the outlying villages and rural landings and Olympia's city float. The small craft came and went daily, bringing a few passengers, milk, butter, berries, clams and oysters, and departing with bales of hay, sacks of feed and boxes of groceries.

The hazards of the new and wondrous fluid which gave them such mobility were not always understood by early day motorists and boatmen. Many seemed unaware that gasoline would explode and that its fumes could be lethal. Numerous tragedies resulted, as in the case of the launch *Traveller,* which exploded spectacularly in the harbor after leaving Percival dock. The skipper, Charles Cheadle, was drowned, two of the passengers were fished out of the water by a boat crew from the *City of Shelton* and a third swam to the mudflats at the foot of Main street and staggered uptown under his own power.

Seattle was promoting a great regional exposition to portray to the world the progress of the Pacific Northwest which had been sparked by the Alaska gold rush. It proposed to call it the Alaska-Yukon-Pacific Exposition and Godfrey Chealander, a special exposition commissioner, took up quarters at the Mitchell hotel to form the Capital City AYP club . . . the first in the state . . . with Dr. Carlyon, mayor and legislator-elect as president.

Mrs. William Winlock Miller, the widow of Isaac Stevens' Indian war quartermaster, donated a block of land just north of the territorial capitol grounds for the site of a new high school, on the understanding that it would be named in honor of her late husband. Olympia had had a high school of sorts since the 1890s, but the voters had consistently refused to bond themselves for a building. Classes had been held in the Washington school and Peoples' University building, but Mrs. Miller's gift prompted them to relent and plans were soon being drawn for an imposing structure of Tenino sandstone.

To further enhance the metropolitan aspect of the capital city, the town fathers appropriated $700 for the purchase of a modern horse-drawn ambulance, the neighboring mill and logging companies putting up an additional $450. Thereafter, when a maimed timber beast arrived in town, the ambulance went clanging to the depot or steamboat dock to transport him to St. Peters hospital.

One of its first passengers was a 16-year-old boy named Ernest Barrett who went to work for one of the town's non-union shingle mills. In a spirit of good-natured fun he was placed on one of the most potentially deadly assignments and his career in the lumber industry began and ended on the same day. One of his hands was cut off. The mill owner was greatly upset when a court subsequently awarded the boy $3,000 damages. It was not customary for industry to be held accountable for the clumsiness or bad luck of its employees.

Subscribers to the local telephone service received all new instruments when a "central energy system" was installed, placing all the electrical batteries in the central station instead of in the hand-crank telephones. It thus became possible to just pick up the phone and hear the reassuring tones of the lady operator asking for "Number pul-eez."

The Olympia Maroons had become the Olympia Senators and the baseball grounds were increasingly patronized as the team gained stature under the guidance of Guy Winstanley, a Canadian printer who had gone into the tobacco and confectionery business with George Blankenship's younger brother Robert.

In 1906 Winstanley and Blankenship moved into new quarters on Main street between 4th and 5th. Their establishment, the Smokehouse, was described by the *Recorder as "resplendent with plate glass windows, brilliant electric lights and handsome fixtures."* In addition to a fine stock of cigars, tobaccos and sundries and the most complete newsstand in town, it had a comfortable and spacious back room with card tables where the members of the downtown establishment could gather in the evenings for a friendly game and political talk, free from the taint of the saloons.

The outspoken George Mottman, though by this time a wealthy merchant, was never a member of the establishment. He felt that the town's political destinies were formed in the back room of the Smokehouse rather than at the polling booth, and he soon coined the term "Smokehouse gang" to denounce the local bigwigs who gathered there to plot strategy. The term became a household word in Olympia for many years.

INSURGENCY AT THE CAPITOL

The members of the 10th state legislature (the 38th since the organization of the territory) arrived in unaccustomed style and comfort. The Northern Pacific had replaced its decrepit branch line train with sleek, all steel vestibuled flyers, complete with parlor and grill cars. The railroad's change of tactics was no doubt motivated at least in part by its anxiety lest the legislators put additional teeth in the railroad commission bill of 1905. That one had been watered down by so many amendments that one of its supporters had sarcastically moved that the word "railroad" be removed wherever it appeared, but a new breed of legislator was going to Olympia in 1907 and it behooved the Northern Pacific to treat him tenderly. The improved service was not just a legislative ploy, however, Moclips, on the Grays Harbor ocean beach, had developed into a major resort area. Although its huge wooden hotel had burned during the winter, it was rebuilt on an even more grandiose scale and 10,000 passengers a year were riding the trains to the ocean beach by 1907.

The lawmakers not only arrived in grand style, but amid bright sunshine and blue skies, with the Olympics forming a magnificent snowy backdrop to the sparkling waters of the bay. Few of the legislative visitors could remember the capital city having looked so inspiring. Of course, when the sun shines and the skies are clear over Puget Sound in January it's cold. New low temperature records were being set and few tarried outdoors to admire the view.

Comfortable havens of refuge were plentiful. The new Kneeland hotel at 4th and Main had formally opened on New Years day, displaying its "elegant lobby in mission style" and its adjoining bar, restaurant, grille and house barber shop operated by the town's leading tonsorial artists, Baude and Klambush. The Kneeland's 34 high-ceilinged rooms were all outside, "many with bath." Telephones were being installed in all of them, an elevator conveyed the occupants smoothly up and down and a handsome new bus was on hand at the depot and dock to provide free transportation to the lobby. The Kneeland was the first hotel in town to operate on the European plan, the price of rooms not including meals.

The enlarged Mitchell hotel, just across Sylvester park from the capitol, was in full operation, the new four-story brick addition having been opened a week after the Kneeland with an open house, complete with chamber music by, believe it or not, McNamara's band.* The Carlton had also been renovated and reopened, its new third floor increasing its former capacity by one third.

By mid-January the record-breaking cold spell ended, the wind switched from north to south, and things returned to normal amid blizzard-like snow and freezing rain.

On January 14 the *Recorder* observed that *"a new political day dawned for Washington with the convening today of the 10th Legislature. The old gang politicians have yielded their domination of the state to men who proclaim themselves advocates of the square deal and*

---

*Actually it was the Harmony orchestra, of which Daniel W. McNamara, proprietor of the Olympia Soda works was director.

who proceed to prove it by breaking up the close corporation methods that have hitherto prevailed in the Senate."

Although the membership of the legislature had changed radically, it was not the result of any party's victory. There were still so few Democrats that they could have caucused in a telephone booth, but most of the newly-elected Republicans had campaigned on the same kind of conservative-reform platform that was being espoused by Governor Mead. Twenty of the 42 senators were freshmen, while only slightly more than a third of the representatives had past legislative experience. There were three Democrats in the senate (the "minority leader," George F. Cotterill, an ardent prohibitionist and reformer, had defeated his Republican opponent, a Seattle barber, by one vote), and nine in the house. A number of the more senior members, either sensing the public demand for political reform or anxious to get on the majority bandwagon, joined the "insurgents" in their successful bid to take over control of the legislature. The remaining old-time politicians of both parties resigned themselves to a minority position and hoped the new-fangled foolishness would prove to be a flash in the political pan. The two caucuses in each house were not formed along party lines, but were composed of "insurgents" and "regulars."

Blethen of the Seattle *Times,* who tended to be paranoid regarding the motives of Republican politicians, and particularly of John Wilson, who had taken over his principal competition, the *Post-Intelligencer,* after losing his senate seat, viewed the whole insurgent movement as a political plot hatched by Wilson.

Blethen considered it to be a devious conspiracy by Wilson to humiliate Lieutenant Governor Coon, who was an anti-Wilson backer of Senator Piles, and to jockey himself into a position to be selected four years hence.

Whatever the motives, the insurgent legislature of 1907 permanently changed the political complexion of the state of Washington.

LET HIM DIG CLAMS!

In the senate J. S. Jones, a 45-year-old Tacoma blacksmith and freshman legislator, was quickly elected president pro-tem, the old guard sitting silently when it was moved that

Inclined to Soar

The state budget has increased approximately 100,000 percent since this 1907 political cartoon viewed bureaucratic spending with alarm.

the election be made unanimous. But the real mover in the senate was another newcomer, William H. Paulhamus, a 41-year-old Puyallup berry grower and power in state Republican politics, who accepted appointment to fill a Pierce county vacancy with the comment that he would try it for one session, but wouldn't run again unless real reform was accomplished. Paulhamus was an innovator and a natural leader. Having observed the progress of anti-saloon sentiment, he had pulled up the hops at his Puyallup valley ranch and pioneered the berry industry. When too many farmers followed suit and glutted the fruit market, he inaugurated the commercial canning of jams and jellies. He was the moving spirit behind the Puyallup Fair and served as its unpaid president for a quarter of a century. A Christian Scientist and a strict moralist, he saw the insurgent movement as an opportunity to bring about major political reform. His remarkable strength is indicated by the fact

Madison, King.
Hanson, King.
Beebe, King.
Lung, King.
Peddycord, Whitman.
Hogan, Chehalis.
Ulsh, Lewis.
Taylo
Sherfey, Whitman.
Erickson, Pierce.
Kirkpatrick, King.
Blackmore, Clarke.
Lambert, Whatcom.
Carlyon, Thurston.
Rice, T
Sayre, Pierce.
McDonald, Walla Walla.
Newitt, Chehalis.
E.P.Gilbert, Spokane.
McCoy, Lewis.
Morse, Island.
Morborg, Pierce.
J. J. King, Chelan.
Coles, King.
D.W.Thompson, Spokane.
Smalley, Okanogan.
Gregg, Spokane.
J. A. Falconer, Spo
Romaine, Whatcom.
Godman, Columbia.
Oleson, Kittitas.
Cameron, Yakima.
Congleton, Spokane.
Stevenson, Skamania.
Weber, Walla Walla.
D. J. Davis, Kitsap.
Connele
Ranch, Clarke.
Renick, King.
Kornberger, Spokane.
Henderson, Walla Walla.
Schultz, San Juan.
Bradsberry, Skagit.
G. T. Reid, Pierce.
McRae, Stevens.
H.J. Jacke
Rhodes, Spokane.
Cloes, Pierce.
Quinlan, Franklin.
Armstrong, Snohomish.

19

Kaliaman, Ferry.
Huxtable, Spokane.
Vergone

Pierce.

Hutchinson, Spokane.

Ramsay, King.

Troy, Jefferson.

Bassett, Adams.

Adams, Whatcom.

Kittitas.

Megler, Wahkiakum.

Tibbetts, King.

Sheets, Pierce.

Caches, Skagit.

Glen, Pierce.

E.C. Davis, Douglas.

King.

Neil, King.

J.B. Gilbert, Spokane.

T.D. Stevens, Lincoln.

Strobridge, Snohomish.

Griffin, King.

Slayden, Pierce.

nson.

Byerley, Conlitz.

McMorran, Stevens.

McMaster, King.

F.C. Jackson, King.

Reeves, Whatcom.

Govan, Clallam.

Pacific.

Sewall, Jefferson.

Lee Johnson, Yakima.

N.K. Thompson, Lincoln.

Hamilton, Benton.

Miller, Lewis.

g, King.

Fulton, Asotin.

F.M. Stephens, Snohomish.

Whiton, Whitman.

Tong, Garfield.

Huntsman, Skagit.

Kayser, Klickitat.

Fauchet, Spokane.

Chehalis.

07

ING TON.

Olympia.

that, as a first-term senator, he was named chairman of the railroad and transportation committee and a member of the appropriations, banks and banking, revenue and taxation and roads and bridges committees ... the most powerful committees in the senate.

The insurgents had quickly stripped the lieutenant governor of his absolute power over committee appointments, all his selections being made subject to floor approval. Since the fate of legislation was decided largely by the committee chairman, who could simply carry a bill around in his pocket throughout a session, the old line senate bosses automatically lost their last hope for a power base. For good measure, a rule was passed permitting any bill to be pulled out of committee by majority vote, a political heresy that must have brought a number of the traditionalists close to apoplexy. The employment committee, dominated by insurgents, reduced both the number of employees and their salaries, cutting staff costs from the $268 a day of the previous session to $128. Another committee was appointed to replace the sergeant at arms in making purchases and paying bills, thus stripping that functionary of his time-honored privilege of extracting a little "cumshaw" from legislative suppliers.

The reformers moved with equal ruthlessness in the house. J. A. Falconer, a one-term representative, was elected speaker, but it was George T. Reid, the floor leader, who ruled with an iron hand. Economy was his watchword. The staff was reduced from 71 to 35 and the pay scale reduced almost as radically. When veteran legislators asked for the customary 1,000 envelopes and letterheads from the state printer, Reid informed them grimly that "There will be no such wasteful extravagance this time."

At the close of the previous session the legislators had discovered a sizeable balance in their appropriation which would revert back to the general fund if they didn't spend it. The representatives had voted to bestow upon themselves complete copies of *Pierce's Code of Washington,* a rather expensive set of law books. When the senators discovered this, they chose fountain pens as their individual status symbols. The press had made quite an issue of this as an example of runaway legislative extravagance and Reid wasn't going to let the members of the 1907 session get any expensive ideas. He clamped the financial lid on from the start, leading to a good deal of grumbling from those who had looked forward to more liberal prerogatives of office.

Four days after the session convened, the *Times* predicted that *"insurrection is likely to come at any time"* as representatives *"chafe under rule of Reid in house."* The front page story led off with a boxed poem entitled *"Who Else But Reid?"*

"Who's the autocrat from Pierce,
Whose dictatorial manner fierce,
Ultra-despotic seems to pierce
The hearts of all from page to Mead,
And leave them palsied, atrophied?
Who Else but Reid?

"Who voiced the slogan: 'T'ell with all
This utter, arrant waste! Let's call
A halt, by hec! and take a fall
Out of those yaps who seek to bleed
The coffers of the state?' Indeed,
Who else but Reid?

"The fear of whom caused Meigs, chief clerk,
(Lest it should ruction tend to work),
Off Falconer's desk a filligreed,
Cut glass decanter? The simple life decreed?
Who Else but Reid?"

The poem went on at some length and the *Times'* prediction was as faulty as its verse. No junta was formed to unseat the terrible Reid.

W. A. Halteman, a freshman representative from Ferry county did have the bad judgment to make a speech demanding restoration of the old pay scale, on the grounds that wages in general and the cost of living were up. Reid fixed him with a steely eye and demanded, "Will the gentleman from Ferry say that the man who stands there at the door and does nothing but open and shut it is worth more than four dollars a day?"

While the unfortunate doorkeeper shuffled his feet nervously, Halteman replied, "Well, he could make more than that digging clams."

"Then let him dig clams!" the floor leader thundered.*

The King county delegation, accustomed to being catered to, found Reid equally adamant when 16 of them approached him with a demand that A. C. Rundle of their county be appointed chief clerk in place of L. O. Meigs of Yakima. The answer was a rare thing in legislative halls ... a simple, direct "no."

---

*This was the *Recorder's* version. The Seattle *Times* correspondent heard it as "Then let him dig *stumps!"* The reader may take his choice. Both have an authentic regional flavor.

When they then suggested that, as a reasonable compromise, Rundle be appointed assistant chief clerk, they got exactly the same answer. They departed, muttering, and sought out the speaker to complain bitterly that Reid had set himself up as a dictator. Falconer listened to their tale of woe and then told them, "If Reid said so, I guess that's about all there is to it."

And that's the way it was. Exactly $75,000 was appropriated for legislative expenses and exactly $75,000 was spent. At the previous session the appropriation had been $87,199; the expenditures $86,267.

Governor Mead, Washington's first clean-shaven governor since Fayette McMullen, delivered his second message to the legislature, urging it to "begin actual labors at once and not crowd the work into the last days of the session." He reminded the members that most of them had been elected on a platform which called for direct primary elections and suggesting that "it should be so framed as to secure the nomination of United States senators, congressmen, all state, county and municipal officers by direct vote of the people." He added, somewhat naively, that the direct primary would insure that "the humblest citizen (will) have an equal chance with the aspiring millionaire in his ambition to serve the people in public office."

He asked that funds be made available to convert the state hospitals for the insane from places of custody to therapy-oriented institutions, recommended a tough law regulating working hours of railroad employees as a means of protecting the public, asked for an independent insurance department and spoke strongly for additional prison reforms including expanded prison industries and the construction of a reformatory for young first offenders.

The legislators listened to him this time. Within the first week bills had been introduced in both houses to establish the direct primary. The senate was moving to make the railroad commission elective rather than appointive and to reduce the $4,000 annual salaries of the commissioners. Highway-minded legislators were arguing for a concentration of funds on trunk cross-state highways rather than the short "farm to market" roads advocated by the Grange.

Even John Miller Murphy, who had learned to view legislatures with an increasingly jaun-

diced eye after having observed the comings and goings of 38 of them, was impressed with the businesslike attitude of the "square deal" lawmakers, observing that many of them were accompanied by their families and that there was a notable reduction in legislative boozing, partying and out-of-town junketing.

Not that the local citizens didn't provide plenty of good, clean entertainment for their guests. The legislative ball, held in the Lobby, was described by the *Recorder* as *"a scene of rare beauty,"* and a long series of parties, dances and receptions was arranged for the duration of the session. These strangely serious young men who had taken control at the capitol didn't seem to be the type to involve themselves in a new conspiracy to steal the seat of government as padding to the profits of timber barons or land speculators, but there was no use taking any chances. It was wise to feed them, dance with them and make them feel welcome.

The citizens of the state capital were not the only ones courting the members of the 10th state legislature. The various corporate interests were in a state of nerves and were represented by an even larger contingent of lobbyists. An effort was made by the house to require lobbyists to register, but the senate was not ready to go quite *that* far. In commenting on the demise of the bill in the upper house, the *Recorder* observed somewhat cynically that it was in accord with the legislative policy of economy since, had it passed, *"several books and a quantity of writing fluid would have been consumed this session."*

The first victim of the "square deal" legislature was a stiff-backed millionaire named John S. McMillan, who owned the Roche Harbor Lime company on San Juan island and ruled his company town with an iron hand. As a member of the railroad commission, it was charged that he had collected $6,000 in salary and $682.40 in travel expenses while putting in a total of 16 days on the job. His vociferous critics also claimed that his only contribution to reduced rail rates had been in his own favor; the Roche Harbor Lime company enjoyed the lowest preferential freight rate of any firm in the state.

McMillan appeared before the joint legislative railroad committee to defend himself. The small army of reporters was first thrown out; then invited back in to hear the industrialist-commissioner haughtily inform the legislators that he "had never sought and

The Great Commoner came to town in 1907.

never desired the position, had accepted it only because the governor insisted, and did not propose to neglect his business for the work of the commission."

The committee conceded that his company's preferential freight rate had been in effect for eight years . . . long before he was appointed to the railroad commission . . . but demanded that he return $3,000 of the pay and expense money he had collected. The lime magnate did return a part of the pay, also turning in his resignation to Mead, who had undoubtedly asked him for it.

Paulhamus and his railroad committee made an investigation of the railroad commission in general, but found nothing very objectionable once McMillan had departed from the scene. The bill to make the commission elective, which had been aimed directly at McMillan, was quietly placed in the committee archives.

E. W. Ross, state land commissioner since 1905, was the next to undergo legislative scrutiny. Rumors and charges of land office swindles had been almost routine since early territorial days, but amid the new demand for reform in government it was no longer quite so easy to ignore them.

One specific incident given wide publicity was the sale of a large tract of state land around Meydenbauer bay on Lake Washington. It was claimed that the land commissioner had, in 1906, appraised the property at $100 an acre, although Seattle real estate men valued it then at $800 to $1,000 an acre and within the year it had increased in value to $2,500 an acre. The motions of a public auction were gone through, it was said, but a fake initial bid of $14,000 drove out other prospective buyers, leaving only one J. I. Croft, who had a former state assistant attorney general as his legal counsel. The lawyer negotiated with his land office friends for the $100 an acre valuation and his client, Croft, got Meydenbauer bay for $6,000 and immediately resold for $14,453.

Another case much discussed during the legislative investigation involved state timber land in Mason county which was cruised in 1904 under the direction of Ross's predecessor, S. A. Calvert at the request of a prospective buyer who was not of the land commissioner's inner circle. The state cruisers listed 29,000,000 feet of timber worth $23,254. The prospective bidder withdrew and soon afterward Mark Reed evinced an interest on behalf of his father-in-law, Sol G. Simpson. Ross obligingly sent the cruisers out again and this time they could find only 21,000,000 feet of marketable timber and, although the price of logs had been steadily advancing, they valued it at only $15,106. Reed suggested that the state should accept $12,000 "to save advertising costs" and that's exactly what the Simpson Timber company ended up paying for the land.

The investigating committee concluded that the appraisal board, which was supposed to pass on Ross's recommendations, performed its duties in a "perfunctory" manner, usually rubber-stamping whatever the land commissioner placed before them. It was recommended that land commission procedures be tightened up, but Ross recovered from his ordeal with only superficial abrasions and proceeded to be reelected land commissioner every election until 1912.

Direct primary bills were introduced in both houses at the opening of the session. The senate hotly debated its version all day on March 2, with much filibustering by its old-line opponents; then passed it with only one dissen-

ting vote. There was less debate but equally affirmative action in the house.

Although unable to redistrict itself, the legislature had little trouble passing a congressional reapportionment bill which provided three districts . . . northwest, southwest and east side.

A state food commission was established to control the sale of contaminated or adulterated foods and a state department of banking was authorized to take its place with the two-year-old railroad and tax commissions among the state's regulatory agencies.

Bills providing "direct legislation" by referendum and initiative failed to pass, as did still another local option measure pushed by the Anti-Saloon League, Grange and other temperance organizations. The house, in a burst of morality, passed a bill making it a crime to sell, purchase or possess cigarettes, cigarette papers or tobacco, but the senate removed the penalties for "possession."

The King county delegation achieved its objective with the passage of bills authorizing the sale of a million dollars worth of state tidelands to help finance Seattle's Alaska-Yukon-Pacific exposition, although they were placed over the political barrel by their eastern Washington colleagues until they agreed to vote funds for an "open river" project to provide navigational dams on the Columbia and Snake rivers.

Loyal Olympians were as delighted as the Seattle boosters when Senator Ruth pushed through a bill appropriating $35,000 in capitol lant funds to build a governor's mansion on the hill west of the decaying territorial capitol and the vast unfinished capitol foundation.

In a final burst of generosity, the legislature raised the governor's salary from $4,000 to $6,000 a year, the lieutenant governor from $1,000 to $1,200, secretary of state from $2,500 to $3,000, land commissioner, auditor and attorney general from $2,000 to $3,000, superintendent of public instruction from $2,-000 to $2,500, and supreme court judges from $4,000 to $6,000.

A number of the legislators were horrified to find that their liberality had blasted their ambitious hopes for the 1908 election. They had forgotten that the state constitution forbade their running for a position paying a salary which they had increased. Alex Polson, a veteran logger-senator, had been considered a strong contender for the Republican guber-

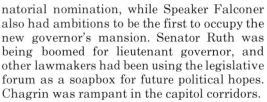

Pioneer merchant George A. Barnes built this imposing home on land cleared by John Miller Murphy and an Indian helper.

Genteel 19th century residence of banker and civic leader A. A. Phillips.

natorial nomination, while Speaker Falconer also had ambitions to be the first to occupy the new governor's mansion. Senator Ruth was being boomed for lieutenant governor, and other lawmakers had been using the legislative forum as a soapbox for future political hopes. Chagrin was rampant in the capitol corridors.

The reformatory for first offenders, urged by Mead, was funded, and by early fall the building commission had purchased a site at Monroe in Snohomish county, and a contingent of young inmates from Walla Walla was put to work manufacturing bricks and building their own new cells. Special quarters for the criminally insane were authorized at the penitentiary and the board of control, at Mead's insistence, ruled that the mentally deranged inmates were not to have their heads shaved or made to wear the striped uniforms of ordinary convicts.

Political history of a more informal nature was made by the 10th legislature when it formalized the final hours fun session prior to *sine die* adjournment. The formerly spontaneous shedding of dignity was organized by George Mueller, a senate journal clerk who had worked for the Montana legislature, which had held such fun sessions for several years. In 1907 it was called the "House of Lords," with Insurance Commissioner John Schively as "Grand Chancellor" and presiding officer. One of its first actions was the assessment of a $20 fine on sober Senator Polson "for occupying his proper seat in the senate during the highjinks." At the next session it was renamed the "Third House" and, under that title, remained a traditional part of every legislature for nearly forty years.

When all the appropriations were totaled up it was evident that progressive reform is expensive, despite the best intentions of legislatures. General fund appropriations were up from less than three million dollars the previous biennium to over four and a half million; total appropriations up from slightly over nine million to exactly $11,418,341.98.

THINKING BIG

But the state could afford a little costly coddling of convicts and lunatics and a few more bureaucracies at Olympia to protect the interests of their appointees and the public (in that order). The population was increasing by leaps and bounds and almost everybody could afford to pay his taxes. Polk's 1907 directory stated fearlessly that Olympia could claim at least 15,000 citizens and the capital city had not been noted in recent years as a fast grower.

Optimism and progress were still rampant, although it would be another 40 years before the city directory's population figures would be achieved. Despite every effort of the Anti-Saloon League and its allies to stem the tide, an ocean of Olympia beer was flowing via railway, steamer and horseshoe-embellished refrigerator cars from Nome to San Francisco. Three new buildings were under construction at the plant, the first in the area to make major use of reinforced concrete. The largest of them was the big five story brick-faced stock house which is still a major landmark at the foot of lower Tumwater falls. Malt extract was also being produced in 1907 and vigorously merchandised as an aid to health, digestion and general well-being. Another new industry, the Buckeye Extract company, opened modestly by J. B. Stentz, was also prospering, its label on spices and flavorings becoming increasingly familiar on Puget Sound area grocery store shelves.

Street and sidewalk improvements continued at a brisk pace. Third street, from Main to Percival's dock on Water street, frequently flooded by high winter tides and described by Grant Angle, legislator and publisher of the Shelton *Journal* as "reason enough in itself to move the capital," was bulkheaded, graveled and flanked by new sidewalks, placing it well above tidewater and putting the street car tracks on the same level as the rest of the street. Fifth between Pear and Jefferson was ordered improved by "grading the uplands and bridging the slough or tidelands," Swantown slough still forming a muddy barrier between the central town and the east side. Cement sidewalks replaced the rickety wooden structures in the business district from 3rd to 7th and from Columbia to Jefferson streets.

Unfortunately, by October the town fathers were facing the sad fact that their new $12,000 steel lift span on the 4th street bridge was listing badly to the west, the electric motor was wearing out, and a virtual citywide blackout was created when a high lift was required. The *Recorder,* commenting on the new safety fenders installed on the street cars, sourly observed that *"there should be special rules for their use in the summer, when the falls are down and the power weak. It's allright to have the fenders in front in going down hill to keep from running over people, but they should be in back going up hill to keep people from running over the cars."* The arrival of the concrete age offered hope for a solution to the ancient problem of "The Marshville Bridge is Falling Down," but the council street committee hesitated to ask for estimates on the cost of a new concrete bridge. They feared the figures might cause them to have heart attacks unless the taxpayers strung them up to the leaning tower of the Deschutes first.

Other civic leaders were not hesitating to think big, however. Gordon Mackay, the legal eagle of the restricted district, who had won a place on the city council,* was beating the drums for a major dredging project to fill the Swantown slough and create commercial property to replace the unsightly and odiferous tideflats. The dredging of the east waterway to

fill in the slough would also make that arm of Budd Inlet navigable at All stages of the tide, but another contingent of property owners petitioned the council to sluice Ayer's hill dirt into the slough by the hydraulic technique being utilized in the great Seattle regrade operations of that era. Enthusiasm for the fill project was such that almost all the owners of property along the slough pledged $300 per lot toward the costs, but second thoughts were engendered when President Hedges of the Puget Sound Bridge and dredging company came to town with his superintendent, Gus Linderman, and announced that the dredge and fill operation would cost from $480 to $600 a lot, which was about the current total market value of the property.

Mackay had, in the meantime, applied to the state land commissioner, on behalf of undisclosed clients, for the purchase of all the unleased tidelands from Priest Point to Tumwater. There were rumors that another great dredging project was in the works to create many acres of new commercial and industrial land in downtown Olympia and to clear the harbor once and for all of those unsightly mudflats, which no longer served even the useful purpose of providing clams and oysters at low tide. Budd Inlet had become so thoroughly polluted that its shellfish were no longer edible.

The long-standing and olfactorially obvious problem of garbage disposal was also tackled by Mackay, who urged the purchase of an incinerator. A tideflat dump at 6th and Columbia was full and teamsters were still stubbornly dumping their loads of refuse at the old site at the foot of Main street. Unwilling to spend money on what the *Olympian* and *Recorder* referred to scathingly as "a garbage crematorium," the council decided to bow to the inevitable and build a bulkhead at the foot of Main street to receive the town's garbage.

The papers were confidently reporting that Tacoma Railway and Power company crews

*Mackay's presence on the city council was reminiscent of that of Hiram C. Gill on the Seattle council. Gill's clientele also leaned heavily toward saloon keepers, prostitutes and other denizens of the restricted district and both were known to occasionally excuse themselves from governmental matters to go down to the police station and bail out those who had violated the ordinances they had helped to frame.

were about to begin laying track from American Lake to Olympia and that the interurbans would be rumbling through the downtown streets within 18 months. Stone and Webster's Pacific Traction company, it was said, was also projecting a cross-state line from the Canadian border via Bellingham, Everett, Seattle, Tacoma and Olympia to Chehalis . . . and eventually on to Portland.

A new gas plant had been completed at 1st and Columbia and the downtown streets were being dug up again, the problem this time complicated by the rising cost of living and the growing militancy of labor. Work came to a halt when the gas line gangs struck for an eight-hour day at $2.50 a day instead of the going $2.25 for nine hours work. Progress resumed when the gas company hired new gangs of "scabs."

The town's doctors had recently formed a trade union of their own, agreeing on increased and standardized medical fees . . . $2.50 for a house call during daylight hours, $4.00 for night calls, $25.00 for complete pediatric service and $10.00 for anesthetics. This prompted Perkins' two daily papers, not hitherto noted for their support of organized labor, to criticize the gas company's strike-breaking methods on the grounds that *"when physicians can boost their prices like they did in this city last night it is nothing but fair to at least give common labor the going wage."**

Things were moving in educational and cultural as well as commercial affairs. The handsome new William Winlock Miller high schoolomposite wood and Tenino sandstone construction, was completed, surrounded by concrete sidewalks and landscaped grounds, and the first student body marched from the old Peoples' University to the new building. Although it cost all of $35,000, the new high school dt have such frills as an auditorium and its first graduating class of 23 received diplomas amid the aging splendour of the opera house. The Washington synod of the Evangelical Lutheran church bought the old Olympia Collegiate Institute buildings and dedicated its new Pacific Lutheran Seminary in time to receive its first class in September. And up at 23rd and Main, a talented local musician named Elmore Rice, who had achiev-

---

*The fact that any Olympia M.D. was willing to make a house call at any price was not considered particularly newsworthy in 1907.

The author helping his father repair a high-wheeled Overland touring car of pre-World War I vintage.

ed some success in the east as a concert violinist, completed a new building for his Olympia Conservatory of Music, which he had incorporated with Frederick Schmidt, Frank W. Stocking and J. B. Stentz.

There were Olympians who were convinced by this time that the proliferating automobile would soon constitute a greater menace to health than any dread disease. Nobody had been killed yet . . . and amazingly nobody would for another eight years . . . but close calls were numerous. In May the big Rambler touring car of Reynolds' livery stable, with Billy Duby at the wheel and the seats full of tourists, broke its steering rod while burning up the road between Tacoma and Olympia. Young Duby, according to the *Recorder's* automotive writer who was still using maritime terminology, *"reversed the engines"* and got the vehicle slowed down somewhat before it left the road, crashed through a fence and scared the daylights out of the tourists.

During the summer the same livery stable Rambler "slipped its gear" while climbing the steep Beaver creek hill nine miles from town on the Centralia road, raced backward down the grade, leaped a three-foot embankment, hurdled a log and crashed into a tree. othe passengers, Mr. and Mrs. Horace Percival and Mr. and Mrs. Laurence McBratney, along with driver Ernest Winchell and co-pilot Floyd Mc-

PROVIDENCE ACADEMY was select boarding school for young ladies of Washington Territory.

Bratney, were all thrown headfirst over the windshield. The flight of L. McBratney was stopped by another tree and he was knocked out. One of the ladies landed on top of Mr. Percival and broke three of his ribs. A neighboring farmer hauled the battered automobilists back to Olympia and William Powe went out the next day with his horse and towed the Rambler ignominiously to town. Reynolds' Rambler was becoming notorious, having made another sensational backward dash down the 4th street hill a couple of weeks earlier when the driver tried to strongarm the outside gearshift lever into second and couldn't.

Another Rambler, described by the *Recorder* as a *"big $3,000, 40-horsepower touring car,"* came to truly spectacular end near American Lake when its gasoline line broke. The driver crawled under to repair the line, becoming well saturated with gasoline in the process. At that point the hot exhaust pipe ignited the leaking gas, the driver rolled out from under, started the car and tried to outrace the flames to Olympia. They caught up with him before he had gotten very far. He wisely abandoned the vehicle, which was completely consumed.

The county assessor proclaimed that the number of automobiles had, in September, increased to 22 from the total of five listed in 1906. As citizen complaints of "speed demons" flooded the courthouse, the commissioners issued orders to the prosecuting attorney and sheriff to "strictly enforce the speed laws." Nobody paid much attention, though, because neither the police department nor the sheriff's force had automobiles and about all the law officers could do when they saw a "speed

demon" roar by was jump up and down and shout.

Motorists continued to become exhilerated by speed and carbon monoxide and get themselves into spectacular trouble. Even city officialdom was not immune from the perils of automobiling, as Fire Chief Raymond proved when, "while skimming down 7th street after dark in his auto," he rammed full speed into a huge pile of sand which had been dumped in the street at the construction site of Dr. Redpath's new house* and left casually without lights or barricades.

When Chief Raymond's Ford runabout imbedded itself suddenly in the sandpile, he sailed majestically over the radiator, landing headfirst in the soft and yielding obstacle. He was pulled out, unhurt according to the *Recorder "except a bad strain to his temper."* The same delighted and helpful bystanders helped the chief extricate his Ford and he proceeded on his way.

One of the few speed demons to get his just reward was a well known Seattle automobilist, Ralph Hopkins, who roared up 4th street trying to get a good run at the Ayer's hill grade. He narrowly missed the cart of South Bay rancher Louis Osborne, causing Mr. Osborne's horse to bolt, strewing garden truck along the street and hurling the driver out on his head. The enraged rancher recovered his wits in time to get the automobile's number (43), and telephone the deputy sheriff at Lacey to set up a road block. Mr. Hopkins was duly apprehended and presumably settled with Mr. Osborne out of court.

Since the early Olympia automobiles seemed to have a knack for staging exciting spectacles without killing or maiming anyone, most people enjoyed their performances. Olympia had been known for many years as a dull town where nothing exciting happened, except when the legislature was in session.

That charge could not be made against it now that the horseless carriage had arrived.

Besides, the general public was becoming increasingly charmed by the shining beauty and marvelous speed of the motor car. Even the owners of the county's 2,750 horses, who fre-

---

*Old house buffs may be interested to know that the Redpath house of 1907 was later moved to the southeast corner of 17th and Water, where it still stands in company with numerous other stately survivors of a more gracious age.

quently cursed the 22 noisy monsters, secretly hoped that some day they could afford to join the glamorously dustered and begoggled elite of the automobile set, and large numbers paid the 25¢ admission charge to view the first "great horse and auto show," held at the baseball grounds and billed as the largest in the state. Dealers from the Puget Sound area brought 25 cars to be admired or entered in the racing events. There would have been more, but demand was exceeding supply and a number of cars scheduled to appear at the show had been sold. Fords were most abundant with, according to the *Recorder, "seven runabouts and a car."* A monstrous 75-horsepower National was the largest and most powerful, while C. J. Lord's Pope-Toledo won the prize as the best Thurston county car. A Ford runabout won the obstacle race over an electric runabout, but no drivers were found who cared to risk their precious machines in the advertised "backward race."

A little later in the year a road race was staged between Tacoma and Olympia. The touring cars started at 1:35 p.m., the first of them, a 20-horsepower Reo, roaring across the finish line at 4th and Main at 3:02. It was followed at 3:16 by a Franklin, which had gotten started five minutes late, and a Rambler. None of the other entrants finished. Doctors Bridgford and Redpath accompanied the racers in a Ford runabout with full medical kits but their professional services weren't needed. Arriving in town to find the streets lined with excited citizens and Rice's orchestra playing on the Mitchell Hotel balcony, they joined the festivities with stopwatches to time the arrival of the next heat at the finish line. The runabouts roared out of Tacoma at 2:30, and the only finishers, a Reo and a Rambler, arriving almost neck and neck an hour and eight minutes later. The state speed limit of 24 miles an hour had obviously been badly fractured, a fact which occurred to Pierce county officials just before a second race was about to start a month later. They threatened to arrest any driver who responded to the starter's gun and the event had to be cancelled.

It seemed that officialdom was determined to prevent life in Olympia from becoming more exciting.

OPEN TOWN

A solid businessmen's ticket had been elected to govern the town in 1907. Mayor Thomas

McLarty was agent for the Mason County Logging company and the council was composed of fuel dealer-contractor W. A. Weller, J. H. Meays, vice president of the Olympia Manufacturing and Building company, C. J. Swayne, piledriver operator, C. D. King and Gordon Mackay, lawyers, F. M. Kenny, secretary of the Olympia Brewing company and James Swan, logging operator. Saloons operated around the clock on a seven day a week basis. Big Bill McGowan's dancehall and boxhouse theater were going full blast and the girls of lower Main street hustling aggressively.

Then, in mid-July, the ministerial association or somebody got to the mayor. He announced that the police department had orders to "put the lid on." Saloons would have to remain closed on Sundays and restaurants were not to serve so much as a glass of beer with Sunday meals. All gambling was out, including "trade" slot machines. A month later the state's generally ignored Sunday closing law was placed in full effect. *All* businesses except hotels, restaurants, undertaking parlors and livery stables, must lock their doors on the Sabbath.

The outcry was loud and immediate as the customary Sunday quiet of the capital city degenerated to a graveyard hush and businesses from theaters to grocery stores saw their income suddenly diminished by one-seventh. The open vs. closed town issue became the basis of the winter election, a 4th street tobacconist named W. A. Hagemeyer opposing McLarty for the Republican nomination. The lonely Democrats of Olympia didn't bother to nominate a ticket in those days, but the *Olympian* and *Recorder* warned prospective voters that the Citizens' ticket, headed by A. H. Chambers, "represents *a disguised Democratic party."*

Gordon Mackay, announcing That he wasn't going to run for another term as councilman, collected a war chest from the saloon owners and other open town advocates and began publishing a new daily newspaper, the *Morning News.* The "Perkins twins," *Recorder* and *Olympian,* joined in a strident attack on the *News* as *"a subsidized exponent of a well organized movement to secure a municipal government that will grant saloon men and their open town following the privileges they once enjoyed."*

When the *News* frontpaged Hagemeyer's campaign statement, including a pledge to establish "a business administration of city affairs" and to work toward repeal of the town's Sunday closing ordinance, and ending with the bland statement, *"I do not consider the question of an open or closed town as an issue,"* the *Olympian* claimed that he was *"sidestepping the issue,"* pointing out that *"he refused to deliver the down-Sound papers, of which he was local agent, on the first 'closed' Sunday."* It concluded sourly that *"if this young man doesn't believe Sunday closing is an issue he shouldn't be in the campaign."*

As the battle warmed up, Perkins' writers developed a flair for invective which must have made John Miller Murphy professionally jealous. From time to time they referred to Mackay's morning paper as *"the Morning Can't-Light-the-Fire-Without It," "The Morning Snooze," "the Little News," "the Mushroom newspaper in an early stage of decadence,"* and *"the morning liquor sheet."*

The *News* responded by throwing the town's garbage in the face of Mayor McLarty and the Perkins press, charging the mayor with *"maintaining a garbage dump near the heart of the city which is bound to prove a disease-breeding hole . . . a veritable plague spot."* It claimed further that the city's chief executive had established the garbage dump at the foot of Main street over the protests of the health officer, Dr. Robert Kincaid, in a spiteful effort to ruin the property interests of Mackay and other respectable, tax-paying citizens.

The Perkins papers counter-attacked in a burst of moral indignation, claiming that Dr. Kincaid hadn't said it and if he had the *News* had misquoted him; that furthermore, the only property in the vicinity of the town dump consisted of *"low houses known as 'the Castle', 'the Red light', 'Green Tree Saloon', 'May Howard's', 'Mary Wright's' and 'the Harem'."*

Mayor McLarty was quoted as insisting stoutly that the dump presented not even the slightest danger of so much as a bad smell. *"Boxes and burnable stuff are burned up,"* it was explained. Although conceding that *"it is unsightly,"* the *Olympian* allayed any possible anxiety by adding that *"where salt water flows over it constantly it rapidly loses its unwholesomeness and becomes simply an unattractive scrap heap."*

No attempt was made to explain where the "unwholesomeness" lost by the tidewater garbage dump went. Instead the *Olympian* changed its editorial course, concluding indignantly that *"the municipal garbage of Olympia has no such reeking unwholesomeness as some of the stuff that has disgraced the pages of the* News *of late."*

The Perkins papers charged further that Mackay and the *News* were responsible for the retention in Olympia of a human garbage heap far more malodorous than the town dump:

*"Gamblers and hangers-on were ready to move to greener pastures until the Councilman from the 2nd ward, who had successfully represented them in the past, gave added hope that with a newspaper behind him he could successfully hoodwink the people and secure a resumption of the wide open town policy along lines that would satisfy even the keeper of dives such as the Green Tree was in its worst days * * * The first consideration was that the saloon interests should support the newspaper."*

The combined political campaign and journalistic feud was fiery but brief. After charges that every sleezy rooming house in the downtown wards was being filled with transients recruited to vote the liquor ticket and that *"nearly every suitable livery rig in town has been secured by the liquor element to take voters to the polls,"* Hagemeyer won the nomination over McLarty and went on to beat Chambers by 449-352. A straw in the wind which may well have given the sporting element something to worry about was the rather impressive 125 votes garnered by James McDowell, who ran as a sticker candidate on the Prohibition ticket. McDowell was a fellow executive of McLarty on the staff of the Olympia Manufacturing and Building company. John M. Overhulse, a plasterer who ran as the Socialist sticker candidate, got 49 votes. Only one "closed town" councilman was elected.

With its battle won, the *Morning News* soon folded, leaving no lasting imprint on the journalistic history of the capital city except that it prompted the last known horsewhipping of a newspaperman. A Colonel L. Weatherby of Seattle, described by the *Recorder* as *"intensely angered by an article in the* Morning News *Saturday considered as reflecting on his horsemanship and in other ways offensive,"* came to town one Sunday and made a charge on the Mackay residence. Bursting into the room of Charles M. Hartwell, business manager of the *News,* who boarded with the Mackays, the slandered colonel *"administered a furious lashing with his riding whip upon Mr. Hartwell."* The unfortunate business manager had been putting on his coat when the colonel crashed in and his arms were pinioned by his coatsleeves. When he finally got his coat off and swung on the colonel, that warrior ran away at high speed.

The colonel was embarrassed to discover that he had horsewhipped the wrong man. He had been looking for Mackay. He was even more embarrassed when the police locked him up, charged with assault and battery and desecrating the Sabbath day. Judge Giles subsequently fined him $100 and costs and the lacerated Hartwell sued him for damages.

The year was further enlivened by the visits of two political celebrities, William Jennings Bryan, who was received politely if not enthusiastically by the Republican legislature, and Roosevelt's secretary of war, the portly William Howard Taft, who arrived by special train on September 6 and was conveyed by automobile to the capitol, where he delivered a brief speech explaining how T. R. had brought unprecedented prosperity to the nation. He was behind schedule and in a terrible hurry to get back to his train, but C. S. Eaton, manager of the Olympia Lumber company and a former neighbor of the Tafts in Ohio, had taken the secretary's wife on an automobile tour of the town and its environs. The *Olympian* reported that *"Mrs. Taft was in raptures over the beauties of Olympia,"* apparently becoming so enthralled that she lost track of time. Her husband fumed and the locomotive whistle *"began a lively tooting."* Soon afterward Mr. Eaton's auto *"whizzed into view,"* Mrs. Taft hurriedly boarded the train under the stern eye of her husband and the special rolled through the 7th street tunnel on the way to Tacoma.

BUSINESS AS USUAL

Within a month of the delivery of Taft's "prosperity speech" to the crows in Sylvester park, financial institutions began toppling like disturbed dominos in the usual east to west direction of national economic collapse. On Tuesday, October 29, the governor of Oregon declared a statewide banking holiday. Governor Mead immediately declared Wednesday and Thursday legal holidays in Washington. It was said that the large banks in clearing house cities were able to get currency, but with the turkey-like panic which tends to afflict bankers

in a financial emergency, they cut off all shipments to their small town correspondents and braced themselves for possible runs on their own institutions. C. J. Lord of the Capital National and H. W. Smith, cashier of the Olympia National, announced that they had plenty of funds and wouldn't even close their doors for the legal holidays.

Mead decided there was no necessity to extend the holidays and the banks which had been closed reopened for business on Friday, November 1, but they were dispensing clearing house certificates instead of cash, all inter-city shipment of cash or currency having been halted. It became popular, in Olympia as in other Northwest cities, to board a street car, give the conductor five dollars in scrip and demand $4.95 in legal tender as change . . . or to hand the bartender a $20 piece of paper for a glass of beer and get back $19.95 in cash. This didn't last long. The conductors demanded exact change and the bartenders made change by check, but it was fun while it lasted.

The first major Northwest bank to go under, the Merchants' National of Portland, closed its doors in mid-November and its troubles spread like ripples in a puddle to its numerous small correspondent banks. A few days later it was reported that the tight money market had reduced construction in the east by 50 percent, reducing carpenters' wages from $5 to $4.50 a day.

The depression of 1907 would have less effect on the forward momentum of the Pacific Northwest than previous panics had, but it provided sobering second thoughts to many promoters of expensive projects. It was some time before anyone in Olympia mentioned the imminent arrival of the interurban line from Tacoma.

At least one financial wheeler-dealer did not lose his optimism, however. In the late summer it was noted that Swayne's piledriver was puffing and thumping at Dofflemeyer's point completing P. P. Carroll's abandoned wharf and that the *Greyhound* had paused there to unload a full contingent of construction workers and building supplies. The *Recorder* let it be known that Olympia was full of *"persistent rumors of something doing on a big scale."* The doings at Boston Harbor were surrounded by mystery until well into October, when C. D. Hillman bounced into town to inform the business leaders of the community that the quiet cove north of Olympia was shortly going to be the biggest city on the Pacific coast.

Hillman, who had specialized in Seattle area real estate developments (a part of the Rainier valley is still known locally as Hillman City), was a man who thought big. He told his entranced listeners that he was about to start construction of a steam or electric railway from Boston Harbor to Centralia via Olympia, that two transcontinental railroads were about to locate terminals at Boston Harbor and that a gleaming metropolis of at least a million people would rise from the forested shoreline.

By October Hillman was running the huge sidewheel steamer *Yosemite* with Captain Mike Edwards in command on free excursions from Seattle to his new city. On the first voyage the 1,700 prospective purchasers from the *Yosemite* were joined by another 300 from the Olympia area who had joined the land rush by wagon, automobile, bicycle and launch. There was a near stampede when Hillman's corps of salesmen appeared with purchase contracts in hand. The salesmen soon became as confused as the buyers and lots . . . some of them under water . . . were sold to several different purchasers by several different salesmen, resulting in a scattering of minor battles. The 2,000 lots placed on the market for the opening were gobbled up within a week, hopeful Olympians having acquired some $30,-000 worth on Hillman's popular 10 percent down contracts. An enterprising young Olympia man named Tom Taylor, who had the foresight to open an outdoor lunch stand near the steamboat dock, made a profit of over $150 on opening day, and a saloon was quickly established in a tent. The *Multnomah* was chartered by Hillman to carry free excursions from Olympia and Shelton and the Boston Harbor land boom roared on, unaffected by the gloomy news in the financial pages.

1908
The hard times of 1907 continued into the following year, but the impact was still not disastrous in Olympia or the Pacific Northwest. Money merchants in a few towns of the state took advantage of the tight money situation to "shave" or discount state warrants at from one to five percent, jobs were scarcer than they had been in several years and there was rather widespread anxiety among working people. Dr. Edwin J. Brown of Seattle lectured at Rabeck's hall in January on "What Caused the Panic" and "Why Are Wage Earners Poor?" and drew a standing room only audience. He predicted that the current depression would be of shorter duration than most and he was right. By the first of the year the Olympia banks were back on a cash basis and were making plans to burn $30,000 in clearing house scrip.

According to the state "booster book," published by Secretary of State Sam H. Nichols, Washington's population had doubled in the past seven years and had, by 1908, reached over a million and a half. The state was embarked on a boom which a national depression could slow a bit, but not bring to a halt.

In Olympia the brewery continued to expand and the Buckeye Extract company, started in 1903 in the basement of the Stentz home on Fremont street, was erecting a concrete manufacturing plant and office building on Main street between 2nd and 3rd. Mrs. J. D. Knox was having a modern apartment hotel, the Knox, constructed on Washington street just north of the new county court house. The new gas works was in operation, bringing the first petroleum tank barges into port. The tankers were brought alongside the gas plant at high tide to discharge crude oil, which was sprayed on super heated brick oven surfaces to produce gas. Peter Schmidt, a son of Leopold, was applying somewhat the same principal to convert coal to gas and was testing the first of his gas-converter engines to furnish 250 additional horsepower to the brewery's power plant. He already had a contract to provide another as auxiliary power for McMillan's lime-carrying sailing ship *Archer** and there were hopes that the Schmidt converter might revolutionize the internal combustion engine.

---

*The gas-converter on the *Archer* had a tendency to backfire, belching out huge clouds of black smoke which, upon several occasions, nearly asphixiated the engine room crew. Schmidt must have been unable to get that particular bug out of his invention, for only the two original models were manufactured.

Things had slowed down at the Hillman boom town of Boston Harbor, but the ebullient C. D. was as full of confidence as ever. He was still running newspaper ads picturing his gigantic metropolis with its gleaming boulevards extending almost to Tacoma and entirely engulfing Olympia. Late in the year he let it be known that he was buying another $45,000 worth of land between Olympia and Boston Harbor, including the old William Billings donation claim east of Gull Harbor. He also "leaked" word to the press of an alleged contract with a major eastern corporation to build a huge steel plant at Boston Harbor, and predicted that the land boom there would be greater than ever in the spring.

The Olympia Brewing company built a big multi-story wooden structure, the Tumwater Club, to serve as a social and recreational center for its employees and their guests, and the Woman's Club, which had been organized 20 years earlier in the old Sylvester house, was putting the finishing touches to its comfortable new clubhouse on upper Washington street.

That people had money to spend is indicated by the fact that crowds of 1,500 were common at the horse races conducted by Captain George Huggins at his Lacey track, and that his adjacent Huggins Hotel entertained capacity crowds. However, Governor Mead and the reformers were campaigning vigorously against race track gambling, and Captain Huggins may have sensed the strength of the reform movement. He borrowed $12,000 with his stable of race horses as security. By the time the lenders had the horses appraised and discovered they were worth only half that amount, the enterprising captain had departed to unknown and presumably greener pastures.

Crowds still flocked to the 10¢ movie houses . . . the Novelty, the Lyric, the Acme and the Capital . . . and live theater continued to flourish at the opera house.

Banks might still be closing their doors in the east, but in Olympia and the Northwest most of the people were simply ignoring the prophets of gloom and proceeding to enjoy themselves.

THOSE DARING YOUNG MEN IN THEIR JAUNTY JALLOPIES

The distant echo of crashing banks certainly had little or no effect on Olympia's continuing love affair with the automobile, although as the number of motor vehicles on the town streets continued to increase a number of the more thoughtful citizens were viewing the poliferation with growing alarm. Even the most enthusiastic automobilists were, in fact, learning that problems as well as pleasure came with their Reos, Ramblers and Fords.

The *Recorder,* commenting editorially on the claim of a New York doctor that *"the fumes from the gasoline used is highly injurious, and to one much in the presence of these fumes they are capable of shortening his life fully ten years,"* conceded that *"this new menace"* was probably real enough, but *"even at that the chances for a long life in view point of the auto are much better from a rear view than a front one."*

The city council, obviously in agreement with the *Recorder,* passed a new motor vehicle ordinance, setting the maximum speed limit at 12 miles an hour, requiring automobiles to be equipped with two white headlights and one red tail light and prohibiting the operation of motorcycles on the sidewalks. Fines of up to $100 were authorized for violators, but the police department wasn't provided with so much as a bicycle for traffic law enforcement. The guardians of the law, traditionally chosen for brawn rather than fleetness of foot, were simply not equipped to outrun a speeding automobile or motorcycle, and the 12 mile speed limit appears to have been largely ignored. The results became increasingly spectacular.

J. Ross Karr, a local motorist with a bent for mechanical experimentation, was the proud owner of a stripped-down "spider runabout" which somewhat resembled a motorized buckboard. On a late spring day he was moved by some impulse known only to himself to, as the *Recorder* put it, *"reverse the steering gear to see how it would work."* Following this novel modification it was necessary to turn the steering wheel to the right to make a left turn and to the left to make a right turn.

Mr. Karr set forth on a test run up Columbia street, making excellent progress until he came upon Tom Hinchcliffe's express wagon parked between 6th and 7th streets awaiting the arrival of the morning train at the Northern Pacific depot. The bulky baggage wagon and two-horse team took up a large part of the street. Karr, forgetting about his modified steering gear, turned the wheel the wrong way and crashed into the wagon tongue between the amazed Mr. Hinchcliffe and his dozing horses. Karr and his passenger were projected from the runabout to the street and the rudely awakened horses fell on them. The two motorists scrambled away on all fours, suffering only minor abrasions. The horses regained their feet, found themselves freed from the wagon by the broken tongue and proceeded to run away, circling the depot amid flying gravel and heading back up the hill toward Main street with Hinchcliffe in hot pursuit. Karr was, in the meantime, viewing the remains of his "spider runabout." It had broken neatly in two in the middle.

Later in the day a wagon was dispatched to the scene. It made two trips to Duby's garage, first with the front end; then with the rear end. The two sections were welded back together, the steering gear was unreversed and Mr. Karr's spider runabout returned to the fray.

An even more sensational contest between horseless carriage and horse was staged a few days later when E. P. Kingsbury took his big touring car on a trip to Mt. Rainier, accompanied by C. E. Grigg, manager of the Mitchell hotel, Bush Baker, the hotel clerk and an unnamed *Recorder* reporter.

On the return trip the Kingsbury automobile overtook a farm wagon loaded with hay near the top of the long hill out of Eatonville. The farm horses screamed and stood on their hind legs. The farmer swore, his wife screamed as loudly as the horses and the gallant Griggs leaped from the automobile and grabbed the horses' heads. They shook him off and headed down the switchbacks at a full gallop. Kingsbury looked over his shoulder and saw the loaded hay wagon thundering toward his one red tail light. The *Recorder* reporter provided a graphic account of succeeding events:

"With the engines in the big car speeding up to the limit of their power, muffler cut out and the big car roaring like a locomotive, the auto dashed down the straight stretches of the road and skidded around the sharp curves on two wheels. The team was outdistanced on the straight sections, but regained on the curves and there was no room to pass."

Events were further complicated when, on one of the first curves, the automobile overtook a rural character jogging placidly along on a mare and leading a colt. The horseman took one horrified glance back and, in the words of the *Recorder's* eye-witness, *"joined the breakneck brigade."*

At this point the race for life was led by the man on the mare, followed by the colt, the automobile, the hay wagon and, far behind and on foot, Mr. Griggs. Midway down the hill the horseman spied a wider place in the road and pulled over against the bank. The automobile shot by, followed by the hay wagon, which soon hit a rock and toppled over against the bank, spilling what was left of its load.

The *Recorder* editorial writer took considerable delight in the fact that the Eatonville farm team had *"turned the tables on the auto"* and chased it down the mountainside in a panic. For some time, he pointed out, automobiles had been frightening horses and it seems to him ironic justice that horses had at last succeeded in frightening an automobile.

Another party of Olympia motorists met humiliation at Mt. Rainier that season. Ralph Hopkins and his guests were planning an early morning start from Longmire in an effort to drive all the way to the ocean beach in a single day. As they were about to depart they were approached by a ranger who pointed out to them that automobiles were allowed on national park roads only between the hours of 3:30 and 5 p.m. They would have to wait. The impatient tourists waited until the ranger's attention was focused elsewhere and tried to make their escape, but their automobile wasn't properly warmed up. As it bucked and backfired the ranger sprinted in pursuit, caught up with it after a 50 yard chase and ordered the party back to the hotel. There he chained the vehicle to a tree.

A bright bellhop suggested that the frustrated tourists hire a team of horses and attach them to the automobile, thus converting it to a carriage. They approached the ranger with this novel suggestion. He scratched his head, consulted his rule book and finally conceded that horse-drawn vehicles could traverse federal roads without restriction. The team was duly produced and hitched up to the Hopkins touring car, which proceeded down the mountain road with stately dignity. Along the way the no longer horseless carriage was stopped by the chief ranger, who had some difficulty believing what he was seeing.

When the situation was explained to him he sighed deeply, wrote out a special permit, helped unhitch the horses and waved the automobile on its way ... under its own power at last.

John Miller Murphy, who was editorially bewailing the fact that people who couldn't afford automobiles were buying them anyway, saw growing evidence that the original cost was only the beginning of the financial drain upon those who abandoned thrift and frugality for the call of the open road. The increased demand for gasoline had skyrocketed the cost to 20¢ a gallon. The skinny high-pressure tires were unable to cope with the primitive roads and a trip to Tacoma without at least one blow-out was considered a major accomplishment. Few motorists were willing to let their expensive vehicles stand outside in the rain and carpenters were kept busy building garages. Bill Weller set a new standard of sophistication when he had his new garage equipped with a turn-table so that he wouldn't have to subject his automobile to the hazards of backing out into the street.

MANSION ON THE HILL

A major event of the summer was the laying of the cornerstone for the new governors' mansion on Capitol hill. Most local businesses proclaimed a half-day holiday and a big crowd turned out to watch the Masonic ceremony. A copper receptacle was placed in the stone containing such memorabilia as copies of the *Olympian* and *Recorder,* along with the Tacoma *Ledger* (Sam Perkins was an increasingly powerful force behind Republican party scenes), a copy of the mansion appropriation bill, a one dollar clearing house certificate, a copy of the new Olympia booster book and rosters of various state, city and fraternal dignitaries.

Olympians were happy to see the first signs of real progress on the hill since the construction of the territorial capitol in 1856, but the building of the mansion created a major panic in mid-September when a group of south end children discovered a box of dynamite caps under a stump at the construction site. Each of the finders took a handful of the deadly devices, dug at them with their pocket knives, blew on them in the hope that they might be whistles, carried them to school in their pockets and took them home to their mothers, who handled them with equal innocence. When William Shroeder returned home from work and found his children tossing dynamite caps at each other he turned pale and sounded the alarm. Word spread rapidly through the neighborhood, but none too rapidly. At one house a lady was prevented in the nick of time from tossing a handful of the caps into her parlor stove and the alarm didn't reach Willie Ellis's house until after he had succeeded in blowing off two fingers and the thumb from his left hand.

The mansion was completed without further incident and accepted by the state in December, in plenty me to receive the sixth governor of the state of Washington upon his inauguration in January, 1909. Fate had ordained, however, that he would never occupy it.

Samuel Cosgrove would certainly never have been elected governor of Washington had it not been for two recent legislative actions. The public officials' pay raises granted by the 1907 session had disqualified many better known politicians from seeking the governorship. The direct primary law had removed the candidate selection process from the back rooms of political conventions to the voting booth.

Cosgrove, 61 years old, had been a 16-year-old soldier in the Union army and a school teacher in Ohio. As principal of Columbus high school in 1878, he handed a diploma to Zepphora Edgerton on graduation day; then called a minister to the stage and was married to her. After a couple of years of prospecting in California and Idaho he had moved to the eastern Washington town of Pomeroy in 1882. He prospered as a lawyer and farmer and served five terms as mayor of his town, but that was the highest office he would accept short of the governorship. The old-line politicians laughed when he went to the Republican conventions, frankly admitting his ambition. His political power base was limited to a tiny Garfield county farming community.

But the direct primary was something else again. Cosgrove had a boyish warmth and charm that belied his years. He loved a good joke and knew how to tell one. Christmas at his farm was a tradition that illustrated his character well. Even the humblest itinerant farmhand was made a member of the family circle for the occasion, his stocking was hung on the mantle and the portly Cosgrove himself, dressed in a Santa Claus suit, delivered the

SAMUEL G. COSGROVE, Governor January-March 1909

gifts to his own delight and that of everyone around him.

Cosgrove even laughed at his own ambition to be governor. When a more serious politician chided him for this levity he replied that he hoped the Grim Reaper would find him laughing when he came to get him. There was more irony than he realized in his graveyard humor.

The coming of the direct primary brought with it the custom of candidates' representatives lining up in front of the secretary of state's office well in advance of filing time to insure their man a top place on the ballot listings. Some 25 men and boys were encamped before the door of Sam H. Nichols the night before the books opened and numerous onlookers appeared on the scene when rumors were circulated of "strong-arm plots to rush the line." No such violence developed, although there was much hooting and catcalling in the morning when Nichols kept his office door locked until he had filed himself for reelection as secretary of state and his deputy, J. H. Schively, for the newly created elective office of

insurance commissioner. Linck Davis of Tacoma was first in line to file for Senator Ankeny, who still held his senatorial seat in somewhat senile dignity.* Although federal law still called for the election of U.S. senators by the state legislatures, their names were included on the new preferential primary ballots and most members of the Washington legislature were pledged to vote for the nominees with the most votes. Of course, since there were only nine Democrats in the entire legislature, the Republican nominee was as good as elected.

The principal Republican candidates for governor (nomination for that office also being tantamount to election), former governors Mead and McBride and Cosgrove, didn't file the first day, but there was enough excitement in front of Nichols' office to prompt the Tacoma *Ledger* to refer to the scene as *"an unseemly scramble."*

The 1908 election was another Republican landslide in Washington. William Howard Taft, the portly hand-picked successor to Teddy Roosevelt, easily beat the ubiquitous William Jennings Bryan, who was making his third try. Republican congressional candidates Francis W. Cushman, William E. Humphrey and Miles Poindexter were also successful, while Cosgrove beat his Democratic gubernatorial opponent, John Pattison, by almost two to one. Marion E. Hay, a 43-year-old farmer-merchant from the eastern Washington town of Wilbur, who had won the nomination for lieutenant governor from incumbent Charles Coon, defeated Democrat A. C. Edwards with equal ease.

---

*The *Recorder* published a report from United Press Washington correspondent Kenneth C. Beaton in which he observed that *"Ankeny looks as much like a U.S. Senator as Candidate Taft looks like a sprinter."* He reported that he had observed the old gentleman dozing all day in a hotel lobby; that he had awakened him and introduced himself, but that the next time the old gentleman awakened he didn't have the vaguest idea who the U.P. man was. According to Beaton, it was a standing joke among capital correspondents that the state of Washington could save money by giving Senator Piles two votes and keeping Senator Ankeny home.

GOVERNOR FOR A DAY

Cosgrove, who suffered from Bright's disease, had overtaxed himself in the strenuous campaign and soon after the general election it was reported that he had spent the night in a Portland hospital, en route to Paso Robles, California, for treatment. Rumors were rife that he would not live to be inaugurated or that he would certainly not survive long thereafter. These led to more backroom politicking than the state had seen in a long time.

If Cosgrove died before taking the oath of office, Mead would continue as governor until another election could be held and a successor elected and qualified. If Cosgrove died *after* taking office, Lieutenant Governor Hay would succeed him. If, on the other hand, incumbent Lieutenant Governor Coon could somehow disqualify Hay's election, *he* would be the new governor.

Coon wasted no time in trying. In fact, he had filed a protest with the secretary of state between the primary and general elections, claiming the new direct primary law was unconstitutional, particularly a rather peculiar aspect of it which the legislature had hoped would prevent the election of a governor who did not have the support of a majority of his own party. It permitted each primary voter to cast two ballots for governor . . . one for his first choice; one for his second. The candidate with the highest combined total of first and second choice votes was declared the nominee. The well-meaning reform faction which had pushed the primary law through had felt that, from a large field of candidates, a nominee would thus be assured who had more votes for him than against him.

When this appeal was turned down, Coon brought another suit early in January of 1909, charging that Hay had violated provisions of the primary law which prohibited a candidate from paying a newspaper publisher for favorable election publicity. By the time this latest suit was placed in the mill in 1909 legislature had convened at Olympia.

Reform as well as uncertainty was in the air. The Anti-Saloon League had gained powerful influence on both political parties, the Republicans endorsing local option, along with such Roosevelt reforms as child labor laws and employers' liability. George Cotterill, the Seattle reformer and one of the three Democrats in the state senate, asked the Democratic convention to also endorse local option and got more than he asked for. The Democratic plank emerged as a demand for a state referendum for complete prohibition. All three Republican contenders for the governorship had wooed the temperance vote. Mead, who had been first to shout for local option, was given the ASL endorsement over Cosgrove, presumably because he was considered more likely to win the election. McBride, who had said less than the others about the evils of drink, had to be content with the endorsement of the Knights of the Royal Arch, who represented the liquor interests and considered him the lesser of three evils.*

The legislature convened at noon on January 11 amid the usual snow and slush and proceeded to organize itself. A. S. Ruth of Olympia, an old-guard senator who was then the senior member of that body, was elected president pro tem. Former Chief Clerk L. O. Meigs of Yakima, who had been elected a representative in 1908, called the house to order and was quickly elected speaker. It was apparently a good choice, for Meigs was obviously a born diplomat. He enjoyed the support of both church and temperance groups and the saloon industry in his home district. Within the week a United States senator had been elected with a strange absence of lobbying, politicking and recriminations. Welsey L. Jones, who had won the advisory vote for the Republican nomination, didn't even bother to come to Olympia. He got 89 votes. George Cotterill got five.

Lieutenant Governor Hay was presiding over the senate, Cosgrove remaining at the California health spa, but his son, Howard, was at Olympia, relaying hopeful medical bulletins to the legislators and press and preparing to take over as his father's private secretary. The legislators offered daily prayers for the early recovery of the stricken chief executive.

---

*It is interesting to note that, despite the growing power of the Anti-Saloon League, McBride won the largest number of popular votes for nomination . . . 33,507. Mead got 32,357 and Cosgrove only 25,519, while winning the nomination on his large number of second place votes. On the other hand, only 15 of 44 legislators blacklisted and campaigned against by the ASL after the 1907 session were returned in 1909. It would appear that the mood of Washington voters was as ambivalent, if not downright illogical, as it often is today.

Legislative ball at Tumwater was featured in this *Recorder* carton of 1909.

The weather is usually bad when the Legislature is in session. It was even worse than usual in 1909, as this *Recorder* cartoon indicates.

No inaugural ball was held that year, but the opening legislative ball was held at the Tumwater Clubhouse on January 26, with free street car service provided for the 600 guests.

The next afternoon, amid dreary rain and flooded str, Governor Cosgrove arrived from California in a private railroad car which had been switched to the Port Townsend Southern at Tenino.

He was driven to the capitol and assisted to the house chamber. The senate journal for January 27, 1909, records that, *"upon the motion of Senator Cotterill, the senate adjourned at 3 o'clock to the house chamber for the purpose of witnessing the inauguration of Samuel G. Cosgrove as governor of the state of Washington."*

The governor's friends were shocked at the emaciated shadow of the stout, hearty man they had known. He spoke only briefly, but it was apparent that even that effort taxed his strength to the limit and that the hand of death was upon the man who had tried for 30 years to become the governor of Washington.

He asked that the Republican legislature honor its party's pledge and enact a strong local option law, that a constitutional amend-

ment be passed to make the railroad commission effective, and that the primary election law be simplified and strengthened. Finally, he asked for a leave of absence until he had regained his health and could "be governor in deed and in truth."

Legislators wiped tears from their faces and there were catches in many voices as Speaker Meigs called the roll for the unanimous vote to grant Governor Cosgrove leave of absence until such time as his health was restored.

The governor's schoolgirl bride of 31 years before was taken to the new mansion on the hill and voiced her delight at the prospect of being the first to live there.

Then the Tenino train, drawing the private car, jolted across the Deschutes trestle and toward the main line for California. Its melancholy whistle, muted by the evening rain, echoed from the forested shore of the inlet, and Samuel Cosgrove, sixth governor of the state of Washington, was gone.

He had served one day as "governor in truth and in deed."

He died at Paso Robles on March 28 and three days later a full military funeral was held for him in the house chamber of the capitol, where he had lain in state in the rotunda since the night before when his funeral train had arrived after being delayed by a wreck on the main line. Honest sentiment wasn't considered corny in those days and the chambers were filled with elaborate floral displays. A huge floral replica of the governor's chair with a white dove perched on the back, holding in its bill a purple streamer with the gold inscription, "from the state officers of Washington," was the most elaborate, but it was rivaled by a multitude of broken pillars, gates ajar and other symbolic funeral offerings of the era.

A long cortege moved solemnly through the rain to the Masonic cemetery, where the militia troops fired three volleys, the buglers sounded taps, and Governor Samuel Cosgrove was laid to rest in company with the pioneers who had helped make the history of Washington territory and state, and of its capital city.

Having paid proper tribute to the dead governor, the legislators turned their attention to making good his last recommendations for reform and to accomplishing a good many of their own.

LOBBYIST FOR THE LORD

The dying Cosgrove had spoken most strongly in his address to the legislature on the matter of local option . . . "I would like to see a good, strong local option law enacted in this state . . . and I want no foolishness about it either."

Outgoing Governor Mead had also urged the legislators to make good on the Republican pledge to enact such a law, and Hay, who was a card-carrying member of the Anti-Saloon League, kept the pressure on from the executive office. ASL Superintendent Cherrington, who had led the state temperance forces from a position of ineffectiveness to one of overwhelming political power, had been recalled to national headquarters as publications director and was succeeded in Washington by Boyd P. Doty, who was given the run of the acting governor's office. After Cosgrove's death the dry leader was consulted on appointments to state offices and Hay advised him politically on methods of defeating wet legislators and getting a 1911 legislature that would pass an even stronger local option law.

Doty was soon enthroned as the state's most powerful lobbyist. Even in its heyday the railroad lobby had never had it *this* good.

Legislators were flooded with petitions from church groups demanding local option and they responded by racing each other to be the first to introduce the desired measure. Early in the session, J. A. Falconer of Everett and W. C. McMaster of Kenmore introduced "county unit" bills which would permit rural areas where Grange and ASL sentiments were strongest, to put the city saloons out of business.

Senator Cotterill, true to his party's platform, introduced a resolution for a total prohibition amendment, although even the ASL wasn't prepared to go that far at that time. Its strategy called for a gradual attack on Demon Rum and its current propaganda line stressed that it was against saloons; not liquor or those who wished to consume it in the privacy of their homes.

Factionalism was rife as the temperance battle grew even more bitter than the fights over the Populist reforms of 1897. Many city legislators opposed the bills which would permit the rural Grangers to close the urban saloons, although they were willing to vote for a more flexible measure. The ASL, WCTU and Grange arrayed themselves for an all-out attack on the saloon lobby headed by ex-Senator Andrew Hemrick, president of the Seattle Brewing and Malting company who had been known as "the beer king of the senate" until his defeat in 1905.

Debate started in January and continued on a 12-hour-a-day basis for more than a month. On February 1 the world famous evangelist, Billy Sunday, with 110 Spokane temperance crusaders arrived in Olympia on a special train to join the local option fight. He was introduced to a giant evening meeting at the opera house by Hay and was described the next day by the *Recorder* as "a geyser of temperance eloquence." Sunday led a march of rum-fighters to the capitol; Hemrick, not to be outdone, organized a march of his own to defend the saloon as the workingman's club and a place of temperate relaxation.

Apparently moved by the evangelical fervor of Billy Sunday, Hay early in February broke precedent and appeared on the floor of the house to lobby for the Falconer bill. The acting governor had been ousted from his long-time mayor's office in his home town of Wilbur by the local saloon forces and he was still good and mad at them.

Opponents of the county unit bill attacked it as not the "reasonable" local option measure called for by the Republican platform. They called it anti-saloon, anti-hotel, anti-drugstore and anti-people. Even the ardent anti-saloon Hay agreed with one legislator who declared on the floor that he was in favor of local option, but not prohibition in the guise of local option.

The ASL-sponsored bill passed the house on February 11 by a 56 to 38 vote after an acrimonious two-hour debate, during which Representative Beach referred to the league leaders and preachers of the anti-saloon lobby as "ecclesiastical tramps and vampires" and charged that their local option bill was, in fact, total prohibition in disguise. The financial impact of saloon closure was emphasized, with figures showing that counties were receiving more than $1,650,000 from the saloon industry, which represented a business investment in the state of $28,000,000. The partisan crowd in the galleries joined the shouting and the speaker was unable to control the prevailing chaos.

The bill faced tougher going in the senate, where it appeared that it could only muster 18 or 19 votes . . . since senators stand for election only every four years, the upper chamber had not been as thoroughly washed by the reform wave as had the house. Senator Paulhamus, the rather liberal Republican from Pierce county and Senator Ralph Nichols of Seattle, an ultra conservative and rather wet King county Republican, were both drafting modified bills.

When oratory began to appear futile, the opponents of the tight option bill resorted to the old legislative trick known as "trimming the Christmas tree." They began amending the bill to death, demanding a full roll-call vote on every amendment. Many of the amendments were, to say the least, fatuous . . . including one to add water to the long list of banned beverages.

The Nichols bill was eventually passed by the senate 24 to 18 and accepted by the house by an overwhelming 91 to two vote. The old-line chairmen of the house and senate appropriations committees used their financial clout to whip the reformers into line, making clear that if they voted against the liberalized local option measure their districts wouldn't see a penny of state money during the next biennium.

The Nichols bill treated the saloon interests rather tenderly. All incorporated towns and cities were separate voting units, independent of their supposedly more virtuous country cousins. Thirty per cent of all registered voters must sign each petition for a local option election, and the process had to be repeated every two years. Breweries could continue to operate, druggists in dry areas could sell liquor for "medical or sacramental purposes" and thirsty citizens visiting anti-saloon territory were allowed to carry a gallon of liquor and case of beer with them to wet their whistles.

The prohibition forces, headed by Senator Cotterill, were less than satisfied with the final version of local option produced by the legislature. Cotterill, who had worked for the Nichols version until he was sure it would pass, then voted against it, calling it "temperance legislation with brewery modifications." The Grange denounced the Republican legislators for having "betrayed their pledge."

As a means of salvaging as much as possible from the session, the anti-saloon lobbyists set to work to get a long list of restrictive saloon bills passed. They succeeded in pushing through measures to keep women and young people out, increasing penalties for Sunday operation, prohibiting liquor and beer wholesalers from having any interest in saloon ownership, and requiring elimination of any obstacles which would interfere with a clear view of the interior of saloons from the street. Cotterill even managed to get a bill passed making it a felony to sell liquor to anyone with so much as one-eighth Indian blood.

For good measure, the more convivial lawmakers managed to get a couple of bills through to protect drinkers; one banning artificial flavorings in whiskey and another barring the sale of any whiskey less than four years old.

The anti-saloon forces were not the only reformers who were busy in Olympia in 1909. Emma DeVoe of Seattle and May Hutton of Spokane, leaders of the woman suffrage movement of that era, were equally determined to secure the vote for their sisters in bondage and the legislators got little respite. Mrs. DeVoe and her cohorts established their headquarters in the ballroom of the J. C. Horr mansion just south of the capitol. The grim ladies of the WCTU operated from the Hale block, just to the north. The two arms of Budd Inlet still formed watery (or muddy) barriers a couple of blocks

SAFE!

"Holy Ole" Hanson saved his anti-race track gambling bill of 1909, but it was a close call, as dramatized by this *Recorder* cartoon.

east and west of the capitol, so it was almost impossible for the embattled solons to dodge the determined ladies.

Ole Hanson, a highly vocal and politically ambitious legislator from King county, had brought forth an anti-gambling bill which brought competing lobbies to the capital. The various reform factions were scarcely speaking to each other, let alone the advocates of gambling, drinking and other forms of sin. The *Recorder* observed early in the session that *"friction, personal jealousies and antagonism between leaders of the anti-gambling and local option forces endanger both reforms. There is open hostility between the leaders as to precedence and procedure."*

As for the suffragists, they wisely remained aloof from the other strident reform groups. Mrs. Hutton, a wealthy Spokane matron, was convinced that it was the prohibition overtones of past women's right campaigns that had defeated them, and since she was one of the major financial contributors to the cause, she was listened to.

Ole Hanson also produced a prison reform bill which had been drafted for him by the Sociological Society of Seattle and Dr. Mark Matthews of the First Presbyterian church, and the gaunt figure of Matthews, backed by his deacons and virtuous lady parishioners, added additional weight to the forces of godliness encamped at the capital city.

It was probably more in a spirit of self-defense than reform that the legislature passed strict rules barring lobbyists from the chambers while in session.

Playing it cool, the woman suffragists did better than the fiery crusaders of the ASL and WCTU. By February 25 both houses had passed an amendment to be placed on the statewide ballot to provide equal voting rights for women. Governor Hay* returned from Seattle, where he had addressed the Pilgrim Congregational church on the sins of the senators who had voted against the strong local option bill (he branded the entire King county delegation, with the exception of Cotterill as bad guys), in time to sign it on that date. The ceremony was held at high noon, with Mrs. DeVoe presenting the measure for the gubernatorial signature. The pen was then presented to Mrs. DeVoe, the ladies of the suffrage movement all packed up and went home . . . and the legislators breathed a sigh of relief. Their escape route to the south was open again.

THE LEGISLATURE IS AGAINST SIN

As if to apologize for having passed a moderate and democratic local option bill, the legislators of 1909 "blue laws" approved a new criminal code which made almost everything that was fun a felony.

Efforts to amend the anti-cigarette law so that it would apply only to minors were beaten down. It was reported that Olympia attorneys who were "cigarette fiends" were smoking up a fog in the Thurston county courthouse in the hope of being arrested and bringing a test suit on the constitutionality of the law. They were

---

*As in the case of McBride, "Colonel" Blethen of the Seattle *Times* held forth stoutly throughout Hay's term in office that *"Hay is not governor; merely acting governor,"* proclaiming that *"from the start it has been impertinence on the part of Lieut.-Gov. Hay to sign his name as 'Governor' of the State of Washington."* The *Times* continued to refer to Hay as either "His Accidency" or as "Lieutenant Governor and Acting Governor," which was a bit clumsy. Blethen was not one to sacrifice his opinions to journalistic grace, however.

disappointed, but an Olympia musician named Fred Reed was arrested by John Meays, who was of all things a deputy fire warden, for allegedly smoking a cigarette in the Kneeland hotel bar. Judge Giles, apparently influenced by the current drive for godliness over personal rights, constitutional and otherwise, made the interesting judicial ruling that what appeared to be nicotine stains on Reed's fingers were sufficient evidence that he had been violating the law. The musician was fined $20 and costs and a crowd of supporters quickly chipped in the total amount.

The ban on boxing was made complete with new legislation making it illegal to box in athletic clubs for exercise or to hold six-round exhibition bouts. A rigid anti-gambling bill was passed, although the almost superhumanly sanctimonious Cotterill voted against it. He was outraged because it permitted card games in private homes. The Sunday closure laws were given additional teeth, particularly when Hay vetoed an exception which would have permitted hotels with 40 or more rooms to serve drinks with meals on the Sabbath. It was delcared illegal to buy a drink for everyone except oneself, illegal to tip anyone for services rendered and illegal to buy a beefsteak or a newspaper on Sunday. "Washington Beloved," with words by Professor Meany and lyrics by Reginald de Koven, was made the official state anthem. The secretary of state furnished copies to all schools and it was heard frequently at the Alaska-Yukon-Pacific exposition. As far as can be determined, it hasn't been heard since.

The emphasis in 1909 was on petty moralistic measures aimed at regulating the personal habits and morals of people and a number of more significant reform measures fell by the wayside. A bill to set a"maximum eight-hour working day for women was scuttled when the cannery operators descended on the capitol. A resolution to adopt the initiative and referendum, thus giving the citizens the opportunity for direct legislation, failed to pass. So did one granting citizens the right to recall public officials.

... BUT A LITTLE FRAUD CAN BE TOLERATED

Ironically, the need for the latter measure was illustrated more dramatically at the 1909 session than at any time before or since in the

DELAYED FOR REPAIRS

TRIMMING THE CHRISTMAS TREE: Amending a bill to death has long been a favorite device of legislators, as portrayed in this 1905 *Recorder* cartoon.

state's history. Fraud, larceny and malfeasance, which had been festering below the surface of state government for years, burst forth malodorously despite efforts of old-line politicians in the legislature to keep the lid on.

The opening skirmish took place late in January, when Senator Alex Polson introduced a concurrent resolution calling for a legislative investigation of the insurance commissioner and the supreme court, as well as the continued use of travel, telephone and telegraph passes by legislators. After heated debate the proposal was voted down 28 to 12. Senator Ruth, spokesman for the senate reactionaries,* denounced Polson's proposal as an "outrage."

---

*The old-guard senators were Ruth, Eastham, Nichols, Roberts, Rydstrom, Smithson, Stewart and Whitney. They had an unblemished record of voting and working against all reform measures, including woman suffrage, local option, the eight-hour law for women, initiative, referendum and recall. Since their seniority gave them control of powerful committees, they wielded legislative clout much greater than their numbers might indicate.

Rumors of scandal in high places persisted despite the outraged bellowings of Senator Ruth. On March 8 Senator Paulhamus brought forth a bill of particulars bringing direct charges of malfeasance in office and misappropriation of funds against the state insurance commissioner John H. Schively, a former Republican state chairman and long-time occupant of the public trough in Olympia. Schively, as deputy to octegenarian Secretary of State Sam Nichols, had performed the functions of insurance commissioner when that office was an appendage of Nichols' domain. When the previous legislature established the separate office of insurance commissioner, Schively had gotten the job.

Paulhamus proposed an investigation of *all* state departments, but it was apparent to everybody that it was aimed primarily at Schively. After what the *Recorder* described as *"one of the most bitter senatorial debates in many a session,"* the Palhamus resolution was defeated on a 21 to 21 tie vote. During the course of the floor battle, Ruth left the president's chair and descended to the floor to defend Schively, charging that the whole thing was "a newspaper plot" to ruin a virtuous public servant.

Senator Booth of King county, chairman of the insurance committee, countered with the solemn warning that *"this scandal is the worst the state has ever known,"* further pointing out that pressures for a thorough investigation was coming from insurance companies and the public as well as the press of the state. He offered a compromise resolution limiting the investigation to the offices of Schively and Nichols, but it too was voted down.

Paulhamus's charges were specific enough; that Schively and Nichols, in 1907, had received $400 for an examination of the Walla Walla Fire Insurance company, although the statutory fee was $50, and that no accounting had been made for the payment; that the same year Schively had demanded $200 from the Washington Hardware and Implement Dealers' Mutual Fire Insurance association for making a similar examination, and had finally settled for $100; that from July to October, 1906, he had drawn his salary as deputy secretary of state while collecting $2,597.35 in additional salary as president and trustee of the Pacific Livestock association; and that he and Nichols had collected from at least eight insurance companies for examinations never made, collecting $25,000 in excess examination fees.

"The insurance department is rotten from A to Z," Paulhamus concluded.

Still the senate refused to authorize any investigation. Although Hay threatened to call a special session unless action was taken, it turned down Paulhamus's motion to reconsider by a 20 to 22 vote on March 10. The next day a similar resolution was introduced in the house as the *Recorder* came forth with a bitter editorial which was typical of the feelings of the state press. It concluded, *"The odor of the rotten mess will follow them* (the senate majority) *to their home communities."*

On March 12, the last day of the session, the house resolution was conveyed to the senate. It had passed, according to the *Recorder, "after two hours of bitter debate in which pandemonium reigned at times in the house,"* by a 76 to 17 vote. In the course of these proceedings the representatives had again broadened its scope to include all state departments, including the supreme court . . . a process known in legislative circles as "loving a bill to death."

In the closing hours, under a call of the senate, the upper house listened to President Ruth solemnly declare that only appropriations measures could, under the rules of the senate, be considered after noon of the closing day . . . that the Paulhamus resolution could not be acted upon. It required 22 votes to overrule the chair and the proponents of the measure were able to muster exactly 22. The investigation was authorized by one vote.

An investigating committee was appointed, headed by Pliny Allen, one of the more progressive legislators, and Hay indicated that he would call a special session to consider impeachment proceedings against Schively and Nichols. Senator Allen let it be known that his committee would investigate all offices, with special attention to the 22 officials who had overspent their budgets and asked for deficiency appropriations. Representative W. M. Beach of Mason county, a member of the committee, insisted that all 22 should be impeached and tried, since all had violated the law.

The sandstone statehouse hummed like a disturbed beehive as the legislature adjourned *sine die* in a greater state of confusion than usual, with the galleries packed and the crowd overflowing onto the floor and crowding some of the members out of their seats.

It had been quite a session. The *Recorder,* reporting the *"third personal encounter in the corridor of the capitol"* on February 16, observed that this one was *"acquiring the title of the 'Fighting Legislature'."*

Red-headed Ole Hanson of Seattle had been one of the participants in the February 16 fray. He had accused a colleague, F. C. Jackson, of "taking a walk" and failing to vote on one of Hanson's pet reform bills ... the eight-hour day for women. Jackson had then taken a firm grip on the coat lapels of the diminutive Hanson, lifted him on tiptoe and declared, *"I am not moved by the same scurrulous motives as you."* He followed this up with a vigorous punch.

Ole Hanson seemed to have a knack for inciting violence. He had become involved in a bitter altercation with the house reading clerk, who persisted in proncouncing his first name as either Ol' (as in ol' folks at home) or Ole' (as in the traditional cheer of bullfighting afficinados), and also tangled with Speaker Meigs, which was a mistake. Meigs was strictly a no-nonsense presiding officer. He summoned the sergeant at arms, who was less vocal than Ole, but much larger, and directed him to "take charge" of the errant member until he had cooled down. The Neanderthal Senator Ruth, in the heat of debate, conferred the ultimate insult upon Governor Hay ... he called him "a Populist in disguise."

Amid the tumult and shouting of the session, Dr. Carlyon, Olympia's dentist-capitalist and Thurston county representative, succeeded in steering a bill through both houses calling for construction of the long-delayed new capitol building on the abandoned foundation on Capitol hill. Governor Hay signed it, but insisted that this was no time to be selling capitol timber lands. His influence with the capitol commission was sufficient to keep the state timber off the market and the ornate domed capitol building on the drawing board.

Hay didn't sign the appropriation bill, which became law without his signature. The reform wave hadn't stopped pork barrel politics and the 1909-1911 budget called for total expenditures of over $13 million . . . the first state budget to reach eight figures. The legislature had appropriated an unprecedented $125,000 for its own expenses compared to $75,000 for

ANOTHER OF THE BUSY BUILDERS OF "GREATER OLYMPIA."

Doc Carlyon was Olympia's top political figure in 1908.

the 1907 session. Most of the state's newspaper editors viewed this profligacy with alarm. Those outside Seattle were particularly enraged at the quarter million dollars appropriated for the Lake Union ship canal, condemning it as *"shoreland grab"* similar to that which had financed the Alaska-Yukon-Pacific exposition and *"the opening wedge in a $7 million boondoggle."*

The editorial outrage was futile. The civic leaders of Seattle had perfected the art of getting what they wanted without dipping into their own pockets. They were represented by much the largest and most powerful delegation in the legislature, so it was becoming increasingly easy to finance "world's fairs," canals, sports arenas and other civic goodies from the state treasury.

It is a knack they haven't lost in the succeeding years.

The departure of the legislature didn't end the rumors of scandal at the state capital. Not even the dignity of the supreme court was proof against the finger of calumny. When M. J. Gordon, a former supreme court justice and later counsel for the Great Northern railway was charged with embezzlement of $9,200 from the railroad, it was made public that he had been in the habit of writing opinions in cases affecting the Great Northern. These he mailed to Justice Milo A. Root, who offered them to the court as his own. Judge Root admitted the charge was true, but said it was "only an indiscretion of friendship."

Soon afterward a Tacoma attorney named Herbert De Wolfe filed sensational charges with the legislative judiciary committee against the entire court, with the exception of Judge Emmett N. Parker. De Wolfe claimed that the last four cases decided against his clients had been ruled upon unconstitutionally.

"Whether the cases were decided erroneously for a monetary consideration or for political prestige I am unable to state," the attorney said, "but that they were intentionally decided contrary to the law and the facts is patent. Behind the first three cases stood Stone and Webster (the electric utility and traction combine), and behind the last stood the Mutual Life Insurance company of New York, represented by attorneys interested in (ex-Senator John Wilson's) Seattle *Post-Intelligencer.*"

The citizens of the commonwealth had some reason to question the integrity of their political system, but worse was yet to come.

Early in April a Spokane grand jury began to investigate Commissioner Schively's role in the affairs of the Pacific Livestock association, the defunct insurance company whose president he had been while still collecting his salary as insurance commissioner. One of those subpoenaed was a former secretary of the Inland Fire Insurance company of Spokane, who testified Schively had licensed the company when it was already insolvent and that it filed for bankruptcy two weeks later.

On April 22 the commissioner was indicted for embezzlement while president of Pacific Livestock. Sheriff Gaston served the warrant on Schively at a hearing of the legislative investigating committee and delivered him to the Spokane authorities. Before leaving, Schively told the investigators that he had "made a clean divvy" with Secretary of State Nichols of all excess fees collected from insurance companies. No records of either expenses or payments had been kept, but with

tearful eyes and much sniffling, he promised that he "would try to do better in the future."

Two days later the grand jury issued a second indictment . . . for perjury . . . against the lugubrious commissioner.

Much pressure was put on both Schively and Nichols to resign. They were a great embarrassment to Hay and the whole state Republican organization, causing the sweet smell of reform at the capitol to be replaced by the unpleasant stink of graft and corruption. The aged Nichols delayed for awhile, issuing the plaintive statement that "if I was young and had my life to live over again I would never go into politics. There is nothing to be gained by holding office," but he gave up and delivered his resignation to Hay on the afternoon of May 4.

Although it was general knowledge that Schively had been promised intercession from on high with the Spokane prosecutor and a well-paid state job for his daughter if he would resign, he asserted that he wasn't going to do it . . . "not in a million years." Thereafter he distinguished himself by becoming the first Washington politician to take the Fifth Amendment. He refused to talk to the legislative investigating committee on the grounds that, in his naive innocence, he might incriminate himself.

Hay decided to call the special session to consider impeachment proceedings on June 23. That was Washington State day at the AYP and he figured most of the politicians would be in the area anyway. After a brief skirmish over whether or not Meigs was still the speaker, the house quickly got down to business and filed impeachment proceedings on the grounds that the state insurance commissioner was "guilty of high crimes, misdemeanors and malfeasance in office." Speaker Meigs appointed a committee of 12 to draft the specific impeachment charges . . . a job expected to take from 40 to 60 days. The legislature adjourned again on July 2 after appropriating $40,000 for the expenses of the impeachment court (the senate) and $30,000 to finance the activities of the investigating committee. This took place, according to the *Recorder, "after a day of details and bickering, joint conferences and back-tracking in which many members lost the thread of events themselves. Many house members were not sure if they are to come back for the special impeachment session."*

A new scandal had broken out even before the special legislative session convened. Early in May Governor Hay had summoned his adjutant general. Oris Hamilton, to Olympia and confronted him with an auditor's report of very large shortages in the funds of the state militia. The general, unable to come up with any plausible explanation for the absence of $38,994.02 from his accounts, was charged with embezzlement, forgery and perjury and led off to the Thurston county jail to sit it out in lieu of $10.000 bail.

Sheriff Gaston got into trouble when it was found that he was taking the general to the Kneeland hotel once a week for a bath and to the Knox hotel twice a week for a taste of Mrs. Knox's excellent home cooking. The sheriff defended himself with the explanation that the unfortunate commanding general of state militia would either die or go crazy if he remained in his cell without a bath or a decent meal until the September term of court.

The whole sad story eventually came out. The gallant general had met a charming inhabitant of one of Seattle's better brothels and had been smitten by her charms. He moved her from the red light district to Capitol hill and a rented mansion. He then introduced her to polite Seattle society under a new name and proceeded to support her in the style to which she had always wanted to become accustomed. It was all done at the taxpayers' expense with forged state warrants. The general had even kited a warrant for $463.65 intended to pay the funeral expenses of the late Governor Cosgrove. The special legislative session had to pass a bill to repay the Olympia National bank, which had been left holding the bag.

A Thurston county superior court jury found the general guilty on one of the several counts against him, he was sentenced to from one to 10 years in the state penitentiary at Walla Walla and the remaining charges were dismissed.

Back at the capitol, in the meantime, the state's senators had shown a marked reluctance to attend the August 11 special session for Schively's impeachment trial. Several begged to be excused on various pretexts, but were roundly castigated and ordered to appear "like men." Nevertheless, a quorum couldn't be mustered until August 18. Then Governor Hay delivered a message giving priority to a proposed direct primary law for the selection of congressional candidates and a measure to shuffle the various state institutions around to different locations. This provided an opportunity to avoid the main issue and the legislators spent the next week passing a variety of bills (but not the requested direct congressional primary measure) and appropriating an additional quarter of a million dollars. They did act on such vital bills as an act forbidding drunken men to appear in public. They also approved a bill permitting women to enter rathskellers, which served beer but weren't considered saloons, but were prevented by innate male chivalry from enacting any law against drunken *women* appearing in public. They shortened the hunting season, provided another $10,000 in bonuses to veterans of the Indian war and squabbled over proposed amendments to the anti-cigarette bill. The latter activity was strictly a waste of time, for the state supreme court shortly declared the entire measure unconstitutional.

THE UPPER HOUSE IS A DOWNER

Finally, on August 26, Olympia attorney George C. Israel presented a stirring defense of Commissioner Schively on the floor of the senate before a crowd estimated at over a thousand. Israel's address was melodramatic:

"Here I see the hidden hand behind this prosecution, there I see it, but never clutchable . . . discernible but yet unseen. Its constant presence is seen about the witness. We almost see its slimy fingers on the door now of the grand jury room in Spokane. It brings this villainous, damnable, corrupt indictment."

Attorney Israel never did identify the "hidden hand," but his client did his best to add pathos to the appeal on his behalf by weeping copiously. Apparently even his tears failed to make him look honest, for Israel was later quoted by the *Recorder* as admitting that Schively was *"the worst witness I ever had. He looks like he doesn't seem to be telling the truth when he is telling the truth."*

Unable to postpone the evil day any longer, the senate convened in evening session on August 27 to render its decision. Richard Hutchinson, a Spokane senator who had a perfect voting record on all reform legislation, but had earned the name of "Slippery Dick"* as a result of his ability to evade voting on bills that might compromise him, was absent when the body was called to order at 7:30 p.m. There was much outrage among his colleagues. Amid threats to declare his seat vacant, a call of the senate was demanded. Senator Booth observed that "it is a serious matter when one man can make a monkey out of the state of Washington."

Under the call of the senate the doors were locked to prevent the escape of other members, while the sergeant at arms was dispatched to ferret out the hiding place of the elusive Hutchinson. He returned after a while to report that he couldn't find him anywhere. There were more angry declarations from the floor and President Ruth ordered the sergeant at arms to enlist the aid of the Olympia police department and engage up to 20 assistants, but under no circumstances to return without getting his man.

Slippery Dick was finally apprehended just as he was entering one of the 10-cent movie houses downtown. By the time he was led back to the capitol it was 9:30 and his fellow statesmen had exhausted their store of expletives. According to the *Recorder's* political reporter, *"an eloquent silence greeted his appearance."*

After a whispered conversation with some of his remaining friends, Hutchinson rose on a point of personal privilege. "I am told," he sputtered, "that someone called me a cur. I want to say I was sick and had a very bad headache from listening to all the hot air here today and took a walk of several miles to get rid of it. No one dare call me a cur to my face! I am not shrinking my duty and never have! I am ready to vote!"

A senator observed mildly that he didn't think anybody had called the gentleman from Spokane a cur and Hutchinson was about to subside when another senator arose to shout accusingly, "I heard it! It was Senator Allen!"

Trembling with rage, Hutchinson yelled, "No one dare call me that to my face! I would beat him until he couldn't walk!"

No sooner had he let off a full head of steam and again seated himself, than another of his friends whispered that Allen had also referred to him publicly as "Slippery Dick." This set off another crescendo of rage from the embattled senator, after which it was voted to "strike

---
*Historical note: This was several years before Richard M. Nixon was born.
---

from the record all frivolous remarks made during the absence of Senator Hutchinson."

Finally the senators got down to voting on the impeachment charges. The final vote was 26 to 14 against Schively, but that was less than the two-thirds majority required to convict him. Throughout the voting 21 (including Hutchinson) remained solid for conviction, while 14, led by the "gentlemen of the old guard" were just as solid for acquittal. Five of the more timorous kept changing their votes on every roll call to square themselves with everyone, but eventually sided with the majority.

Commissioner Schively stopped weeping, returned to his office and continued to occupy it throughout the remainder of his term.

The press virtually united in indignation. The Tacoma *News* observed with sarcasm that *"the $20,000 worth of whitewash was worth that much to find out how far we can trust the state senate,"* adding that *"Schively's lachrymose confession added largely to the value of the investment."* The Everett *Journal* used strong words to tell its readers that *"the impeachment fiasco not only shows that we have a grafter in office, but that we have more than a dozen senators who ought to be kicked out of the legislative body."* The rival Everett *Herald* called the impeachment proceedings *"a spectacle of triumphant intrigue and deception which points up the need for a recall law."*

AFFLUENT SOCIETY

Citizens of the capital city, who had been living with political shenanigans for 55 years, didn't let the sensational revelations of the year bother them. The capitol and the migratory birds of prey who inhabited it were in the town, but not really of it. Politicians came and went, but the solid citizens were still occupied with the affairs of their home town rather than those of the state capitol.

The boosters were still optimistic, although the aftermath of the 1907 depression threw such solid enterprises as the gas company, the Olympia Manufacturing and Building company . . . and even Big Bill McGowan's lower Main street enterprises . . . into receivership.

On the bright side, real estate tycoon Hillman had the steamer *Yosemite* chartered for another season and Boston Harbor was

Olympia's Efficient Police Force

CHIEF ROGERS.

PATROLMAN GANSFIELD.

PATROLMAN HERNDON.

PATROLMAN TRACY.

booming again. At least three interurban lines were announced as certainties for 1909, one of them to connect Olympia with Grays Harbor. More downtown streets were being paved with brick or wood blocks and crowds gathered to watch Bill Weller's top bricklayer slap 75 bricks into place every minute on upper Main street.

Contracts were being negotiated with the International Construction company to dredge more mud from the harbor to fill in acres of new ground over the Swantown slough and along the east shore of the Deschutes waterway to the west. A new industry, the Olympia Knitting Mills, was incorporated with such capitalists as George Mottman, C. H. Springer and Mitchel Harris on the board of trustees. New buildings continued to replace the old wooden structures of pioneer Olympia; George H. Funk and his sister, Mrs. Addie S. Volland, built a handsomely decorated two-story concrete office building on the northwest corner of 5th and Main, the federal government announced that it would erect a fine stone post office building on the scorched site of the old Hotel Olympia, and George Mottman was in the process of building a $10,000 mansion at the site of his old home at 9th and Washington.

At least 100 Olympians owned pleasure launches and in December they organized the Olympia Motor Boat Club, with W. J. Foster as commodore, Frank McKinney vice-commodore, Robert Mallen rear-commodore, Frank Schmidt secretary and Albert Darling treasurer. Trustees were Cap Reinhart, Peter G. Schmidt, Robert Blankenship and George Naden.

The number of automobile owners also continued to increase and 40 of them organized the Olympia Auto Club, with C. J. Lord as chairman and Dr. Redpath as secretary. That same evening the *Multnomah* brought in 30-horsepower Fords for Fred Stocking, Robert Blankenship and P. M. Troy; and Frank Kenny and Judge R. O. Dunbar took delivery of Studebakers from the local dealer.

The complexities of automobile ownership were likewise increasing. The legislature had imposed a $2.00 license fee on all motor vehicles and the local police were adamant that the proper license numbers must be displayed. The force had been issued its first official uniforms . . . long blue coats, striped trousers and helmets . . . and the minions of the law were feeling their oats. Automotive pioneer Ashley was dragged off to Judge

Frost's court and fined for speeding when he narrowly missed the mail cart of letter carrier Clark Savidge. A little later a local urchin, Randy Wilder, aged seven, jumped off the rear of a dray, upon which he had been stealing a ride, and was run over by Mr. Ashley's Ford runabout. After examining him, Doctors Bridgford and Ingham sent the resilient tot home, apparently undamaged.

And signs of the 20th century progress continued to proliferate. Early in 1909 the United Wireless Telegraph company opened an office on Percival's dock. Two 120-foot antenna towers were erected on the mudflats, held up by clusters of piling, and Washington's capital city was suddenly in communication with the world and all the ships at sea via the air waves. The year closed with the Standard Oil company tanker *Col. E. L. Drake* cleaning her tanks off the Nisqually delta, en route from Olympia and Tacoma, creating upper Puget Sound's first major oil spill and causing the untimely demise of a large number of sea birds.

Yes, sir! Signs of progess were showing up everywhere in 1909.

As usual, old landmarks were threatened or done in by that progress or the simple passage of the malicious years. The old Westside mill dock, property of the financially distressed Olympia Manufacturing and Building company, fell victim to the omnivorous teredo and collapsed into the bay, providing beachcombers with a treasure trove of floating lumber which had been stored upon it. The last reminder of the town's earliest maritime commerce drifted away on the ebb tide. Old timers mourned when the old Wood building behind the new Funk-Volland building was demolished to make way for a concrete garage. The old hand-hewn red cedar beams and clapboards were as sound as when Isaac Wood put them in place back in the 1850's.

That was the site of Olympia's first brewery and John Miller Murphy, in his last year at the helm of the venerable *Washington Standard,* observed nostalgically that the remaining pioneers *"would give five dollars for a glass of that cream ale."*

The ladies Civic Improvement club was embarked on another of its periodic cleanup campaigns aimed at getting rid of the town's more objectionable eyesores. Even such a historic structure as the Gold Bar building, where Isaac Stevens had assembled the first territorial legislature, was threatened. The Perkins press was enthusiastically backing the civic-minded ladies and asked in big type, *"Why preserve old Legislative shack?"* The

termite-gnawed territorial capitol on the hill was sufficient reminder of Washington's political past in the opinion of the *Recorder* and *Olympian.*

Other prominent structures fell victim to fire, including a popular lower Main street resort operated by a black madam who was heftier, although less virtuous, than the late Becky Howard. Her establishment, known as Big Lil's, was totally destroyed, but according to Hollis B. Fultz, newspaper man, author, detective and political figure, *"a prominent business man of the the city stumbled out of the house, waving a bunch of towels over his head and shouting, 'I saved the books boys, and you'll have to pay up.' "**

Another conflagration on the evening before the Fourth of July had more serious impact on the economy of the community. The wood pipe and tank works, which had its small beginnings in the 1860's and had developed into a major manufacturing plant at the foot of Jefferson street, was totally destroyed. Much of the town's east side was threatened for some time with a similar fate. A brisk wind carried burning embers for nearly a mile and three buildings on east 4th street were destroyed before the fire department began to get things under control. Trainmen on the railway spur which served the industrial area didn't help the firemen when they backed a string of freight cars over the hoses and put them all out of action. Observers felt the department had done a creditable job in saving the Springer and Richardson mills, which closely abutted the pipe works.

It was a long day for Chief Raymond, who got back from a trip to Seattle just in time to relieve Assistant Chief Barner at the height of the fire. He had made a 3:00 a.m. run with the Seattle fire department to a burning lodging house. The hose team he was working with was buried by a falling wall and an aged woman was burned to death by the fire.

To add to his many problems, word was received at the height of the fire that the tug *Olympian* was caught above the 4th street bridge on an ebb tide and would heel over and sink unless rescued. Raymond, who was the only person in town who could make the draw span work, had to abandon the firefight and open the bridge.

**Elkdom in Olympia . . . A History,* Hollis B. Fultz, Olympia, 1966.

Less than a third of the loss was covered by insurance. The day of the wooden water pipe and storage tank was ending, and that pioneer industry was finished.

The Alaska-Yukon-Pacific exposition opened on June 1 and Olympians flocked to see its wonders, the *Recorder* advising them to *"go and see it, but spend your money at home."*

Even the great exposition was unable to escape the breath of scandal. In October all the gatemen were fired because they were operating on that old street car conductors maxim, "one nickel for the company and one nickel for me."

ficient;" that the state had, over the years, been defrauded out of millions of dollars through the sale of state timber lands for "grossly and ridiculously inadequate considerations." The state school fund had been mulcted of at least $11 million by the land commissioner's office, according to Chairman Pliny Allen, who hazarded the opinion that the same pattern would have been found in the handling of state agricultural and tide lands if his committee had had the time and funds to check in those areas.

At about the same time the state oil inspector, F. A. Clark, was removed by Hay as the result of the investigating committee's report. The legislators said Clark's accounts were in state of fiscal chaos, but they had been unable to establish criminal intent.

1910

The state government scandals of 1909 continued to keep the headline writers busy in 1910. Late in the previous year the state board of accountancy was asked by Hay to check the financial affairs of the state's first highway engineer, J. M. Snow, who had resigned at the request of the governor and state highway advisory board. It was said that Snow had expended $10,000 without legislative authority or appropriation and he had refused to turn his voucher books over to his successor, H. L. Bowlby.

Snow had obtained the $10,000 by selling a state highway right of way along Lake Keechelus to the Milwaukee railroad. He explained that the money had been expended to survey another highway route, but when he finally surrendered his books it was found that over $2,000 of the railroad money was in his personal bank account. He explained that he hadn't wanted to turn it in to the state general fund.

Faced with an embezzlement charge filed in Thurston county superior court at the urging of state Attorney General W. P. Bell, Snow was released from jail on the ingenious legal ruling that, since he hadn't been authorized to sell the state's right of way in the first place, he couldn't have embezzled the proceeds.

The wide-ranging legislative investigating committee had, in the meantime, issued a charge that state timber cruisers were, in general, "dishonest, incompetent and inef-

CIVIC RIGHTEOUSNESS

The capital city, in 1910, appeared to be intent on counteracting the shenanigans at the statehouse with a wave of civic reform, although it was in fact, merely reflecting the national and statewide swing toward reform which had been motivated by the progressive policies of the Roosevelt administration.

The newly organized Humane Society dragged pioneer business man A. H. Chambers off to court for leasing an ancient roan horse to a Chinese pig farmer who used the antique steed to pull a swill wagon around town. Harry L. Parr, who was attorney for the society, claimed that the horse had no teeth and consisted mostly of skin and bones.

A sensational sermon by the Rev. J. M. Orrick on "civic righteousness" brought a standing room only crowd to the Christian church. The minister flailed away at Mayor Harris, Prosecuting Attorney John M. Wilson, the sheriff, chief of police, constable and all three patrolmen of the Olympia police department. Denouncing Olympia as "the only city in the state where fallen women are allowed to parade the downtown streets in the afternoon," he charged that a notorious house of ill-repute was operating outside the restricted district on one of the main corners of the city and that "a local girl had been enticed to that house, drugged and forced to enter a life of shame."

Only about a quarter of those present stood up when the minister asked for a vote on a recall petition, but the boys at city hall and in the back room of the Smokehouse were nervous.

The saloon keepers became even more jittery when Mrs. C. W. White, the wife of a local carpenter, apparently moved to direct action by Mr. Orrick's sermon, took a wooden potato masher to the windows of the White Front saloon on 4th street. Emulating Carrie Nation, Mrs. White succeeded in smashing all the glass before she was pinioned by the bartender and held for Officer Dan McGreavy. The saloon's owner, J. McIntosh, decided not to press charges, although the embattled lady had attacked the wrong saloon. She was under the impression that it was the White Front where her husband and sons were spending most of their time and money; actually it was one of the less respectable establishments on lower Main street.

Eventually Mrs. White was sent home, still clutching her potato masher.

In a further skirmish in the war against sin, the Kneeland Investment company, on the same day brought suit to oust the lessees of the Kneeland hotel at 4th and Main. It was charged that the town's once most prestigious hotel had been converted into a "disorderly house," with beer and liquor served in the rooms all night and the halls frequented by women of the restricted district.

This was followed by a civic reform mass meeting at the opera house. Anti-Saloon League speakers exhorted those present to vote only for "morally upright, righteous men" in local elections without regard to party politics.

The same day the *Recorder* front-paged the list of "fallen women" who had paid their monthly "fines" in police court. It was a virtual roster of the town's two dozen officially recognized whores.

The evening paper also reported that the *"inmates of said houses have been and now are in the habit of exhibiting themselves at the windows and doors and upon the sidewalks in front of the buildings wherein they reside;"* furthermore, the *Recorder* informed its readers in shocked tones, *"they go from house to house in flimsy, immodest and indecent clothing."*

Mayor Harris was in California when these latest exposes shook the town. Councilman Mackey, as acting mayor, announced that he was going to have the police department "clean out the restricted district" . . . as soon as they could find the time.

THE RED LIGHTS ARE EXTINGUISHED

By the time Mayor Harris got back the fall elections had been held and 10 of the state senate's wets had been defeated. The number of avowed drys outnumbered the wets in the house by a considerable margin and woman suffrage had been approved by a large majority.

The mayor decided there was no use bucking the tide of reform any further. He took direct action and on December 2, 1910, the morning *Olympian* reported the following dramatic and historic event:

"For the first time in many years Olympia is without a restricted district and the denizens of the lower end of Main street have quietly gathered their belongings and slipped away, leaving that end of town with a few exceptions, vacant. The word was passed around the town early Wednesday afternoon that the tenderloin district of Olympia was a thing of the past and that a grand orgie would wind up the affairs of the residents of the district. The orgie failed to materialize, but the houses have closed, the inmates seeking newer fields.

"A trip through the district last evening showed that the former hilarious times which have marked that end of town have ceased, the houses are dark, and the rattle and bang of the piano, accompanied by the shuffling of the dancers' feet and the clink of the glasses, is to be heard no more.

"It is stated that the tenderloin was doomed when the suit was started to enjoin the property owners from leasing to disorderly persons, and on and after that date the disorderly persons started to slip away from the city one at a time until yesterday morning found all of them gone from their usual haunts.

"While a great majority have left the city, many have been trying to seek locations elsewhere, but without avail. The police have been asked by certain property owners to see that none of the girls from the redlight district attempt to secure rooms any place in the city.

"With the closing of the houses on lower Main street the restricted district in Olympia is something of the past. Slowly but surely the growth of the business section of the city has forced the district from the corner of Third and Main streets to below Second street, and now the progress of the city, and the moral atmosphere that is sweeping the country, has forced the district from the city.

"The restricted district in Olympia has occupied one of the districts of the city about which historical reminiscenses abound. Originally the business center of the city, the old territorial legislative hall was situated in the heart of the district. The principal business houses of early Olympia were on lower Main street. The first theater of any size was constructed below First street on Main. The steamers, and in early days almost the entire travel to the city came by steamer, landed at the old dock on the end of the long wharf, the remains of which are now pointed out to the new comers, a few stubs of the old piling that are left, almost a mile down the bay.

"The old state house of territorial days and the structure made famous by the passage of many of the earliest laws, was situated in this section of the city.

"The growth of the town being toward the south, the business of the section constructed out over the tidelands and on the low waterfront lands, gradually moved to the present center at Fourth and Main streets. With the moving of the business center, the houses on lower Main street gradually fell into the hands of the denizens of the redlight district and by mutual consent the tenderloin was allowed to remain in that portion of the city.

"Attempts to move the restricted district have failed. Property owners did not want it on or near their holdings. The district has been closed in upon until now it has been found necessary to close it entirely. The location is first class for business property. Improvements are being carried on in all parts of the city except this. With the closing of the district, property will be improved as the demands increase, and the old shack town, the tenderloin, where laws have been made, special privilege bills fathered and lobbied through the legislature, where legislators received their rake-off for some measure they supported, and where many have gone to ruin, is no more."

The passage of time would reveal that the Perkins press and the forces of decency had been highly over-optimistic. As in most efforts to establish morality by legal edict, the abolition of Olympia's restricted district didn't put an end to its evils; it just drove them underground. Before long, citizens in respectable neighborhoods were wondering about the sounds of revelry from various rented houses. First class hotels became the new stamping grounds of the denizens of the vanished tenderloin and life became much more complicated for the town's helmeted and frock-coated minions of the law.

Big Bill McGowan, who was as usual out on bail on gambling charges, vented his frustrations by issuing a challenge to Jack Johnson, the new heavyweight boxing champion of the world, but the champ didn't respond. That was no doubt fortunate for Olympia's Boss Sport, who had already been backed into a corner for a knockout blow by the reformers.

Even the Indian Shaker church, incorporated that year with the assistance of Judge Giles, was embarked on a temperance campaign among its Indian converts.

THINGS WILL NEVER BE THE SAME

Material progress wasn't slowed down by the increasing emphasis on civic reform. The citizens of the west side raised $15,000 to help underwrite an extension of the street car line to their part of town. The first inter-city auto stage, a seven-passenger Winton touring car, was placed in service between Olympia and Tenino and an enterprising used furniture dealer named George Wagner began operating the first city bus. He had acquired an old sightseeing bus and converted it to a delivery wagon and, noting the continued interest in the summer "improvement days" at Priest Point park, he returned it to passenger service on those occasions, collecting 10¢ a ride from downtown to the park. Groceryman A. J. Benson, noting the profitable crowds being carried by Wagner, quickly installed seats in his auto delivery wagon and established a competing service.

There was even talk of adding an "auto fire truck" to the equipment of the fire department. Councilman Mackay made a trip to Tacoma to inspect one of that city's mechanized engines in action, stating that "I am not fully convinced that efficiency can be obtained from an auto fire apparatus and I will not advise the city to invest in one until I am satisfied that they are efficient." Mayor Harris refused to go along. He said he was already convinced Olympia needed an auto fire truck.

The Olympia Auto club, striking a blow for ecology and against blowouts, began a campaign urging "joy riders" to "desist from throwing their bottles on the road where they break and puncture the tires of the next machine that comes along." In the interests of carefree motoring, they were asked to "throw them into the tall and uncut as far from the road as possible."

The only segment of the transportation field which seemed to show signs of regression in 1910 was the Olympia-Tenino railroad. Trainmen on the evening flyer for Olympia were humiliated on September 1 to find that a house mover had left a house parked on the tracks south of town. After a long delay a second train was made up on the Olympia side and proceeded toward the depot, but it was derailed before it got there and the weary passengers had to walk the rest of the way.

Perhaps this was a portent of the present state of railroading when it is almost humanly impossible to get in or out of Washington's capital city by train.

JOHN MILLER MURPHY WRITES "30"

To further enhance the new moral tone of the town the citizens in 1910 dedicated a new concrete YMCA building, complete with swimming pool, gymnasium and auditorium. One of the first major functions held there was the retirement party for John Miller Murphy, who had sold the *Washington Standard* to Eagle Freshwater. Scores of pioneers and prominent citizens from all over the Northwest gathered at the Y to honor the state's oldest active newspaper man. Many were prominent journalists and publishers who had learned to set type in the old wooden *Standard* building on 2nd street. Those who stopped there before the ceremonies found Murphy on his ancient stool setting by hand his speech for the evening.

Governor Hay was toastmaster, introducing frontier newsmen Thomas Prosch, Clarence Bagley, Grant Angle, Beriah Brown and Sam Crawford. Old enmities were forgotten and in their reminiscences they recalled only the good and the humorous. A quartet sang a song composed especially for the occasion:
"John Miller Murphy, John Miller Murphy
John Miller Murphy, bright and gay,
Among his old-time devils
He has come tonight to revel
On the Standard's golden day."
The head table was decorated with a huge bouquet from the women of Olympia, honoring

Murphy as a veteran champion of women's rights and the state press association presented him with a silver loving cup of similarly striking size.

Edwin Eels, Washington's oldest native son, made a speech in Chinook, to the delight of the pioneers, who responded with exclamations in the legendary jargon. Gus Rosenthal, Olympia's oldest merchant, rose to his feet and congratulated Eels in Chinook for his "kloshe hyas wawa" . . . (good big talk.)

Murphy, white haired and mustached, spoke of the span of time during which he had chronicled the events of the town, the region and the nation. The columns of the *Standard* had recorded the appointments of 11 territorial governors and the inauguration of seven governors of the state. James Buchanan was president when the *Standard* was born and it had proclaimed, not always joyfully, the elections of Lincoln, Johnson, Grant, Hayes, Garfield, Arthur, Cleveland, Harrison, McKinley, Roosevelt and Taft.

Throughout its 50 years, the appearance of the *Standard* had never changed. Whole Number 2,636 of December 9, 1910, looked very much like Volume One, Number One of November 17, 1860. The news was carefully hidden on the inside pages with the patent medicine advertisements, while the front page carried a lead article on color in plant life. Other front page items included an account of the tattooing by Dr. Fox of Philadelphia of "the perfect semblance of an eye on the blind eyeball of a girl" and the claim of a Boston medical professor that tea cakes are indigestible. Marie Antionette's favorite musical clock was described in detail and housewives were advised to soak tarnished silver in sour milk.

Perhaps the most dramatic illustration of the change in the town of Murphy's youth and that of his retirement occurred outside the YMCA as the banquet was ending. A horse cab from Reynolds' livery stable, waiting on the street to pick up departing guests, was hit by an out-of-control auto driven by the son of Railroad Commissioner Muir Fairchild. Both the horse and the automobile suffered grievous damage. The horse had to be shot and the vehicle was towed off to a garage.

THE MUDFLATS VANISH

And down on the waterfront, two big dredges of the Puget Sound Bridge and Dredging company were gnawing away at the mudflats to fill the Swantown slough and extend the city's north central area many blocks out into Budd inlet. The very shape of the town was changing; the ragged outlines of the stubby peninsula the Indians had called *Chetwoot* were lost under acres of neatly bulkheaded spoil from the harbor floor.

The creation of the central downtown fill, generally known as the Carlyon fill, provided new sport for the town's canine population. Old buildings near the foot of Main street had to be raised to higher foundations as the level of the grades were raised. This wrought havoc with the generation-old breeding places of the rats and the dogs gathered each morning, when the dredge began operations, chasing and killing hundreds of the displaced rodents. Workmen of the fill said they had never in their lives seen so many huge rats.

Some of the more cynical residents compared the running for cover of the Carlyon fill rats to that of the state officials uptown, who were equally disturbed by the dredging up of bureaucratic graft and inefficiency by Senator Pliny Allen's legislative investigating committee.

1911

The year 1911 brought a new shape to the legislature as well as to the capital city. The wave of nationwide disenchantment with Teddy Roosevelt's hand-picked successor, the fat and reactionary William Howard Taft (a disenchantment which was amply shared by Roosevelt himself), had given the Democrats control of congress and added impetus to the Progressive movement, but the trend toward the Democratic party hadn't pricked the surface of Washington's hard-core Republicanism . . . all three Republican congressional candidates, W. E. Humphrey, Stanton Warburton and W. L. LaFollette, were elected and only 16 Democrats found places in the two houses of the legislature . . . but Progressive reform was in the air.

In 70 municipal local option elections held in 1910, 35 cities including Everett and Bellingham had voted themselves dry. Thus encouraged, Governor Hay had moved toward the Anti-Saloon League county unit local option and had promised ASL Superintendent

Doty that he would request such a bill from the 1911 legislature. He advised Doty on the political art of handling legislators, campaigned actively for dry candidates and helped the temperance forces unseat wets. Together, Hay and Doty hand-picked the 12th legislature as carefully as the railroads had ever done in previous years.

As a rule of thumb, those legislators who voted for anti-saloon legislation also voted for other social reform measures, so the stage was set for sweeping changes in the political and social structure of the state.

As usual, the weather in Olympia was abominable when the lawmakers convened in early January. It was snowing and it continued to snow until there was a foot of it on the streets and sidewalks. The police gave up their efforts to stop the town's small boys from sledding on the steeper streets and legislators joined townspeople in dodging youthful daredevils.

The usual coterie of legislative job-seekers joined the lawmakers and lobbyists, jamming the rooms, bars and lobbies of the Mitchell, Carlton and Kneeland hotels. The Spokane delegation brought five young men as committee clerks, along with a noisy gaggle of youngsters who wanted to be pages. The *Recorder* noted that *"Maynard Duxbury and a half dozen other live young Olympia lads have had cards printed and prepared to collar legislators for jobs as pages."* Three of the enterprising Olympia lads were successful in their bids for employment, prompting Senator Ruth to demand that the patronage committee fire one of the "city boys" and replace him with a "farmer boy."

At the other edge of the job-seeking spectrum was 75-year-old John H. Leiter, who lived with his wife at the Port Orchard veterans' home. Leiter had been sergeant at arms for the constitutional convention of 1889 and the first state legislature and had run up the 42-star flag on the territorial capital flagpole when the notification of statehood was relayed to the hill from the telegraph office downtown.

On January 9 Howard Taylor was elected speaker, Paulhamus president pro-tem of the senate, the new members were sworn in by Chief Justice Ralph Oregon Dunbar and a $75,000 appropriation was passed to finance the session.

The next day Governor Hay addressed a joint session, recommending the abolishment of the railroad, tax and insurance com-

WOMAN'S PLACE IS IN THE HOME: Females were noticeably absent when the employees of the House of Representatives lined up on the front steps of the statehouse to have their picture taken in 1911.

missioners' offices and the substitution of a public service commission and public revenue commission. He wanted an industrial insurance system established and a bureau of labor and industry to replace the labor commissioner. He also wanted a county-unit local option bill and he reported the state's bonded indebtedness down from $1,200,000 in January, 1909, to $700,000 in October, 1910.

Members of the house, with vivid recollections of the ruckus stirred up by the local option battles of 1909, responded by inserting a new section in the house rules banning con-

sideration of any liquor measures that session.

The legislators also appeared to be affected by a male chauvinist backlash on the matter of women's rights. When Senator Piper of King county introduced a resolution instructing the secretary not to discriminate against women for legislative jobs, it was quickly laid on the table by an overwhelming vote. Across the hall, the representatives unanimously passed a recommendation to the patronage committee that *no* women be hired. The same day, Mrs. DeVoe, president of the Washington Equal Suffrage association, was denied an invitation

STATESMANSHIP IS SERIOUS BUSINESS, judging from the demeanor of the state representatives of 1911, whose expressions match those of the stone faces of the statehouse entrance. The youthful types in front were the pages of that session.

to appear at the legislature to invite members to the state convention at Tacoma.*

That the opposition to feminine legislative employees may have been prompted by chivalry rather than chauvinism in some cases, is indicated by one of Senator Paulhamus' letters to Mrs. DeVoe, in which he wrote:

"I am very glad to acknowledge receipt of your note added to the letter of Mrs. F. W. McKinney. I will this day write Mrs. McKinney that I hope her daughter will not receive a position at the legislature as I honestly believe it is not a good place for her to be. I would not care to have a daughter of mine around with such a crowd as usually makes headquarters at the capitol during a session of the legislature. I hope the day is not far distant when these conditions will be changed."

*Even those enlightened legislators who voted for woman suffrage seemed reluctant to be closely identified in public with the militant ladies. A file of Senator Paulhamus' correspondence at the Washington State Library contains a number of his letters to Mrs. DeVoe artfully dodging public appearances at suffragist functions. His excuses were ingenious, varying from a conflicting meeting of the Puyallup Fruit Growers' Association to "a little accident" caused by Mrs. Paulhamus, who sent the wrong suit to him at Tacoma where a banquet was being held in honor of Mrs. DeVoe.

The once time-consuming task of choosing a United States senator was accomplished in just seven minutes on January 17. Miles C. Poindexter had defeated Judge Thomas Burke in the preferential election, although Burke was said to have expended an astonishing and unprecedented $18,000 on his campaign. The joint session of the legislature quickly ratified the popular vote for Poindexter.

The usual preliminary social events were staged, including the governor's ball at the Tumwater clubhouse with the new adjutant general, Fred Llewellyn, and his full staff in glittering regimentals guarding the chief executive. Special street cars and all the automobiles in town were pressed into service to convey the guests through the slush and snow to the scene of festivities. A much smaller group gathered at Doane's Oyster House for a party held by Olympia Democrats P. M. Troy, Harry L. Parr and James E. Dailey for the 16 lonely Democratic legislators. During the festivities Senator H. M. White of Whatcom and Representative F. A. Garrecht of Walla Walla were accorded the purely honorary titles of minority leaders in the two houses.

REFORM AT LAST

After that the legislators got down to business and succeeded in accomplishing a great deal. The businesslike atmosphere at the capitol was probably enhanced by the fact that Olympia's restricted district had been scattered and that Tacoma had followed suit by closing its tenderloin. Seattle was the nearest community still running wide open, under the administration of its colorful mayor, Hiram C. Gill.

The initiative, referendum and recall measures, strongly lobbied by labor and the Grange, were all passed. An industrial insurance program was established, becoming a prototype for the nation. Authorization for the creation of port districts was approved, as well as commission form of government for cities of over 2,500 population. A public service commission was established, with authority over all public utilities and transportation companies. Free passes for politicians were finally abolished and Ole Hanson's eight-hour law for women was passed over the vociferous protests of laundry, hotel and retail store operators, who claimed it would "injure business and work a hardship on women."

They were challenged by Mrs. Edward McMahon, wife of a University of Washington professor, who told the business lobbyists, "If girls were horses you'd be more careful of their health."*

Olympians were delighted when a plan for a complete capitol group was approved and $350,000 appropriated to buy additional land adjoining the old Sylvester gift tract on the hill, which was officially designated Capitol Place, and to begin construction of the first building, to be known as the Temple of Justice. Everett boosters had been engaged in a last-minute plot to steal the capital for their city and a bill had been introduced to move the supreme court and library to Seattle.

The capitol construction bill didn't pass without the usual impassioned opposition.

Representative H. E. Foster of King county led the opposition with the traditional charge that Olympia was a sleepy village inhabited by mossbacks. "What has Olympia ever done for the state?" he wanted to know. "Although it's been the seat of government for 50 years it has been at a standstill, progressing very little. Olympia is asleep and does not deserve any consideration from us."

Dr. Carlyon, representative for Thurston county, having just put together the great downtown dredge and fill project, was speechless with indignation, but Speaker Taylor of King county left the chair to lend his support to Carlyon's measure. William Ray, also of King county, added his voice to the defenders of the capital city, explaining that "the reason Olympia hasn't been going ahead with other cities in the Northwest is simply this: every legislative session some cranks come down here with the idea of moving the capital and agitate the question during the session. No business man or eastern capital is going to invest here until the question is settled once and for all, and I for one am going to vote to settle it by passing this bill."

---

*A statewide survey just made by the "female deputy" of Labor Commissioner Charles F. Hubbard and covering 723 firms, showed that the average factory girl was earning $1.57 per nine-hour day and that 218 of the establishments inspected "had very poor sanitary conditions." Of the 15 companies visited in Thurston county, employing 106 women, it was reported that 30 retail stores were on the nine-hour day, 24 laundries on a 10-hour day, and 16 factories on an eight-hour day. Shop girls averaged $1.51 a day, factory workers $1.33 and laundry workers, despite the 10-hour day they were required to work, $1.25 a day. The commissioner advocated the mandatory eight-hour law and increased funds for factory inspections.

The Pierce county delegation joined the pro-Olympia forces, followed by the Snohomish county delegation, which disclaimed any serious attempt by Everett to steal the capital. The bill passed 72 to 19, with five absent, and was subsequently approved by the senate with only minor opposition. By July the capitol commission had condemned and purchased three blocks of land just north of the original capitol grounds and the following month it accepted the plans of Wilder and White of New York for the Temple of Justice and the various office buildings which, with the magnificent domed Legislative building, comprise the present main capitol group.

The legislators revoked the anti-cigarette and anti-tipping laws, refused to pass a measure to tax automobiles at the rate of 50 cents per horsepower, turned down the proposal to abolish the office of state land commissioner, passed a record budget totaling more than $15,700,000 and adjourned *sine die* at 4:20 a.m. on the morning of March 10 after several hours of hopeless deadlock on redistricting based on the 1910 census and on an omnibus state highway bill. All road construction was left to the counties, subject only to the approval of the highway commissioner, whose salary was doubled . . . from $2,500 a year to $5,000. The highly controversial bill to abolish capital punishment turned down by many previous sessions, was passed before the deadlock developed.*

---

*The legislators of 1911 were doubtless influenced by an extremely unpleasant hanging which had taken place at the state penitentiary on May 13 of the previous year. Richard Quinn of Everett, convicted of killing his wife, was taken to the scaffold protesting his innocence and claiming that the shooting was an accident. The subsequent events were reported in that evening's *Recorder* as follows:
"A horrible scene followed. The drop apparently had no effect on Quinn. He swayed from side ot side moaning: "For God's sake take me up and drop me again, boys." "Boys, this is awful." His brain was so clear that he was able to unbuckle the straps which bound his arms. Finally, after a terrible scene lasting many minutes, during which spectators and officials stood horror stricken and unable to aid in hastening death, unconsciousness came. After 22½ minutes of the sickening scene life was pronounced extinct and the body was cut down."
The gruesome story was front-paged by every daily paper in the state, causing widespread public revulsion against the death penalty as inflicted in Washington.

SCRAPING OFF THE MOSS

Despite the unkind remarks about Olympia in the capitol construction debate, it was evident in 1911 that the capital city was embarked upon an era of community progress, although Representative Foster was correct in his claim that it hadn't kept up with the rest of the state . . . in the population race, at any rate. The 1910 census had shown Washington with a 10-year population gain of 120.4 percent, to 1,141,990. Olympia had gone from 3,863 in 1900 to 6,996 in 1910. That was a healthy gain of 81 percent, but it was well below the statewide average and it was particularly disappointing to the Perkins papers, which had been proudly carrying the Polk directory estimated population of 13,500 on their mastheads.

There was great confidence that the long somnolent town was picking up momentum, however, and considerable visible evidence to support the belief. By April 1 the *Recorder* was able to report nearly a million dollars in current building permits . . . and a million dollars would do a lot of constructing in 1911. The dredging and industrial tideland fills had cost $250,000, all but $58,000 in federal funds provided by local property owners. Reynolds livery stable at the 3rd and Main site of the pioneer Rice Tilly stables, was torn down to make way for a new $20,000 city hall (now the central fire station), and a new concrete building was going up at 6th and Water to house Reynolds' establishment. The cornerstone was laid for a handsome new Masonic Temple on Main street between 7th and 8th. The appropriation was on hand for the new federal building across the street and George Mottman was adding a third story to the old Toklas and Kaufman building at 4th and Main. The enlarged department store would be the first mercantile establishment in town equipped with a passenger elevator for the convenience of its customers. It was also equipped with marvelous overhead tramways upon which mesh baskets flew like miniature monorails to carry cash and merchandise to the cahsier's control tower on the mezzanine and returned with wrapped packages and change for customers. Several generations of Olympia children craned their necks at Mottman's to view with delight the airy flight of the baskets, secretly hoping there would be a collision as the complex tramlines converged on the cashier's booth, which was always tastefully decorated with a spreadeagled suit of old-fashioned long john underwear.

J. B. Stentz, founder of the Buckeye Extract company, was busy installing machinery in his new factory on the the the just completed Carlyon fill, the Heimbach Truck and Manufacturing company, which would produce hand-trucks and stepladders. Carlyon and his associates had constructed a belt line railway to connect the newly created 29 blocks of waterfront industrial land with the Northern Pacific yards, and there was no doubt that other industries would soon locate there to swell payrolls and population. There was even talk of creating a port district under the newly passed legislation and building ocean docks along part of the fill to return deep sea maritime trade to Olympia.

FIRST FLYING MACHINE

The new fill brought another 20th century marvel to town. Still unoccupied except for Stentz's modest hand-truck factory, it was as flat as a billiard table and provided a perfect landing field for aircraft. On May 20, an "intrepid birdman" named Fred J. Wiseman took advantage of it and landed the first heavier than air flying machine at Olympia. It was supposed to be a profit-making exhibition flight. A part of the fill was roped off and admission was charged, but only about 350 bought tickets. Another 1,500 stood thriftily outside the ropes and watched the daring exhibition for nothing.

Unlike the pioneer balloonist, who became enraged at the parsimony of Olympians and refused to go aloft, the indomitable Wiseman went on with the show although, according to the *Recorder's* aviation expert, *"the flanges on the propeller were overheated and in a dangerous condition when he started out."* To

the amazement of the crowd and the disappointment of *"the many knockers who came only to see him fall,"* he coaxed his flimsy biplane off the fill, zoomed out over the bay and came back to circle the landing area twice at a speed of about 40 miles an hour.

He made a couple of subsequent flights, carrying a cameraman of the Western State Illustrating company on one of them. The photographer ground out 600 feet of film on his movie camera thus producing the first air photos of the capital city. His footage was spliced to scenic shots of the Sound and Olympics taken with a telescopic lens from the *Greyhound* and shown the next day at the Rex theater. Viewers were delighted to find that

Olympia — Tacoma steamer *Greyhound.*

FAST STEAMER *NISQUALLY* provided the ultimate in civilized transportation between Olympia and Tacoma in the sunset years of the Puget Sound "mosquito fleet." Naval Militia monitor *Cheyenne* at left.

they could identify friends in the crowd at the improvised airport and the event was a social and scientific success, even though its promoters hadn't made any money.

The participation of the 19th century sternwheeler *Greyhound* provided interesting contrast and she got into the act just in time. Automobiles and interurbans were cutting into the revenues of the Sound steamboats and their days were numbered, particularly the sternwheelers, which were viewed by the increasingly sophisticated traveling public as rather comical anachronisms from another age. The *Greyhound's* faithful running-mate, *Multnomah,* was cut in two a few months later in a midnight collision with the big steel steamer *Iroquios* during a dense fog on Elliot bay. The old paddler sank in deep water in minutes, carring nine head of cattle with her. She had been relegated to freight service and was carrying only two passengers. They and the crew escaped, but Olympians, who had set their clocks by the melodious whistle of the *Multnomah* for 20 years, felt that they had lost an old friend, even though she was old fashioned and a little arthritic.

THE SUN SETS ON THE STEAMBOATS

The *Greyhound* was soon to be replaced by a 20th century steamboat, the slim propeller *Nisqually,* built at Gig Harbor for the Olympia - Tacoma Navigation company. *Nisqually* was 140 feet long and 23 feet wide, powered by a triple-expansion engine, water-tube boiler and oil burners which developed 1,000 horsepower. Her two raked funnels and sharp hull gave her a look of speed which was justified. On her trial run from Seattle to Tacoma she came within five minutes of the record for that much raced course. She arrived in her home port for the first time on June 22 at half past five in the evening, bravely arrayed in flags and bunting. A large crowd greeted her at Percival's dock and she carried a full load of passengers the next evening when she steamed down the bay on a moonlight excursion sponsored by the Woodmen of the World.

The local papers carried advertisements urging one and all, *"whether on business or pleasure bent"* to *"enjoy the beauties of the Sound by patronizing the steamers of the Olympia - Tacoma Navigation Co. plying between Olympia, Tacoma and*

PERCIVAL'S DOCK in 1910, with the Shelton steamer *S. G. Simpson* coming in to join the *Greyhound* and *Multnomah*. The little tug *Sand Man*, brand new that year, is still active on the Olympia waterfront.

Seattle" . . . particularly *"the new steamer Nisqually, fast-going and equipped with every modern convenience."*

Unfortunately, the same papers carried announcements that the new auto stage was making twice daily round trips between Olympia and Tacoma at the modest fare of one dollar . . . and in considerable less time than the *Nisqually,* even when the tide happened to be with her.

In a few years the people would be surprised and somewhat saddened to find that the steamboats had vanished from Puget Sound, but they had helped to end the era of gracious travel the first time they decided to forego the "beauties of the Sound" to take the evil-smelling and new-fangled auto stage, which promised to save them a half hour or so on the trip to Tacoma.

Progress caused old friends to vanish on shore as well as afloat. All three buildings that had housed the territorial legislatures bit the dust in 1911. The ancient Gold Bar building was finally torn down, with only enough of its remains kept to build a small replica of Washington's first legislative hall. The old Masonic Temple, which had also served briefly as legislative chambers, was replaced by the new one, and the little wooden capitol building on the hill was ordered demolished. The *Recorder* of April 22 mentioned casually that the capitol commission was to open bids for its removal, adding that *"it will be good riddance"* because *"it has no historical value."*

A brass plaque was later set in the new concrete sidewalk at the original site of the Gold Bar building (Washington state liquor store customers step on it but seldom see it), but nothing was left to mark the location of the white clapboard capitol building where so much political history had been made.

The sandstone statehouse downtown was the scene of another presidential visit on October 11 when Taft, on a fence-mending western tour, came to town on a special train just ahead of the regular morning local from Tacoma. He was met by the chamber of commerce reception committee and several hundred citizens, who clapped politely as the overweight chief executive squeezed down the car steps, bowing and smiling and the local brass band "discoursed stirring airs."

Taft was escorted to an automobile along with his secret service and press escort. With Governor Hay, Republican National Committeeman Sam Perkins, Major Archibald Butts, his military aide,* C. D. Hilles and Secret Service Agent Sloane, he was whisked to the east entrance of the capitol, preceded in another automobile by Police Chief Alex Wright, resplendent in his new uniform.

Some 800 Olympia school children had been assembled to greet the great man, each provided with a small American flag. As the automobile shuddered to a halt they took up a shrill rendition of "My Country 'Tis of Thee." Taft mounted the steps and quickly addressed a patriotic catechism to them . . . before they could start singing again. The *Recorder* faithfully transcribed this dialogue as follows:

"What was that song you were singing?"
"Our Country 'Tis of Thee."
"Do you love that song?"
"Yes."
"What is that you are all carrying?"
"A flag."
"What flag?"
"An American flag."
"Do you love that flag?"
"Yes."
"Who was the gentleman who introduced me?"
"Governor Hay."
"Now do you love and are you loyal to both your state and the nation?"
"Again came the shrill cry, 'Yes!'"

It speaks well for the discipline and patriotism of the town's school children of that era that not a single one gave a disconcerting answer to any of President Taft's rather inane questions.

Having disposed of the small fry, the president was conducted to the front entrance facing Sylvester park, where he spoke to a crowd of 4,000 adults, praising the state's record of progressive legislation, including the workmen's compensation law, which he called "a model for congress."

A clumsier than usual pickpocket was caught in the act by an elderly gentleman in the crowd and the president's closing remarks were punctuated with cries of "Stop, thief!" but the pickpocket got away. Taft was entertained at luncheon in the governor's mansion, where

Hay told a select group of Republican guests that Taft was one of the nation's greatest humanitarian statesmen, after which the president was taken back to his special train, having spent 80 minutes in town. For a man of his build he had moved pretty fast.

Equal excitement was created when the city's first motorized fire truck, a Seagrave combination chemical and hose wagon, was delivered and put through its paces. The city fathers decided that it must not only meet its specified speed of 15 miles an hour up the westside hill, but prove its superiority to the horse-drawn engine as well. The Seagrave and the horse rig would race to all alarms for a week. The first test came on the early morning of February 26 when the house of R. R. Streets, across West Bay drive from the Westside mill, caught fire. The fire horses ran neck and neck with the mechanical monster for several blocks down 4th street, but when the pavement ended west of the bridge and the grade increased, the racing horses fell behind, arriving about five minutes after the Seagrave, which had experienced troubles of its own. West Bay was mostly ruts and potholes and the solid rubber tires of the truck transmitted every bump and shock to the arms of the driver, which were still jerking spasmodically for some time after the engine was returned to the firehouse. The fire in the Streets house had already been put out by fire extinguishers from the mill before either rig got there.

It was a costly defeat for the gallant fire horses. Thereafter they were put to work with the street department every day, although returned to the firehouse at night to be available for overtime labors in case of a two-alarm fire.

It was a bad year for others, too. C. D. Hillman, the flambouyant real estate promoter, was found guilty on 13 counts of fraud and sentenced to two and a half years in a federal penitentiary. He had already served 20 days in the King county jail for jury tampering. He left the courtroom as jaunty as ever, talking grandly of his plans for a huge fruit and vegetable cannery at Boston Harbor and dismissing his sentence with the assertion that "I won't serve a day of it."

But Hillman did go to jail for a while and his dream city of a million people at Boston Harbor reverted to a quiet cove inhabited by a lightkeeper and a few fishermen.

One of the most popular of Olympia's 10 physicians, Dr. Henry S. Strickland, died of cancer in a Seattle hospital in September. He

*Major Butts was destined to die gallantly in the sinking of the White Star liner *Titanic* off the Grand Banks of Newfoundland less than a year later.

had arrived in Olympia from Missouri in 1896 and established bachelor quarters and an office in the Byrne black at 4th and Main. A doctor of the old school, he hadn't entered the medical profession to get rich. The poor of the area found him to be a sort of one-man free clinic. He never pressed for payment of a bill and frequently handed out a dollar or two along with his pills and powders when he suspected that a patient was hungry. The old doctor was an institution, puttering sedately along the streets and byways in his high-wheeled horseless buggy on his rounds of the bedridden. His practice was sold by his best friend and executor, L. B. Faulkner, the proceeds going to his divorced wife and married daughter in Missouri.

Fortunately for Dr. Strickland's patients, his office was taken over by a successor who operated in much the same manner. Dr. E. C. Story, an 1879 graduate of the University of Michigan school of homeopathic medicine, came to town in mid-October from Montesano and inherited Dr. Strickland's office, equipment and long list of impecunious patients.

Dr. E. C. Story.

1912

By 1912 Olympia's health needs were being met by 10 M.D.'s, four osteopaths, five dentists and a couple of veterinarians. It is an interesting commentary on the declining health or increased hypochondria of Olympians that, while the population has increased about 500 percent since 1912, the number of doctors has increased 900 percent and the number of dentists 1,000 percent. Yet, despite the primitive

The Olympia Fire Department's last horse-drawn rig, left, and first motorized engine, right, raced each other on city streets to determine if the automobile was here to stay.

sewers, swarming flies and rats and periodic epidemics, those 10 physicians of 1912 could usually be found in their offices waiting to greet patients who seldom bothered to make appointments. Today, as in other communities which enjoy the marvels of space age medicine, it is of course necessary to make arrangements well in advance if one is planning to get sick.

For the statistically minded, it might be added that Olympia, in 1912, had more saloons than doctors and dentists put together, which may have helped to account for the limited number of patients in the doctors' waiting rooms. Self-medication was obviously popular. Olympia had 17 saloons, Tumwater one, Tenino four and Bucoda two.

Local politics were neither unique nor exciting until well into the fall. Dr. Wayne Bridgford had been elected mayor on a good, solid Republican-Smokehouse ticket and things proceeded placidly until September, when the ladies of the local WCTU began circulating a petition for a local option election to be held in November. The women of the town flocked to sign the petition, which was to be

expected. No decent woman could enter a saloon in 1912 and the men were having all the fun.

The gentlemen of the business establishment . . . or the Smokehouse gang . . . depending on your point of view, formed an Executive Committee of the Business Men's Pro-License League. Its members, Guy Winstanley, W. J. Doane, E. H. Martensen, A. C. Baker, George Draham, Dr. Ingham, J. J. Brenner, C. J. Lord and a number of other chamber of commerce types, affixed their prestigious names to full-page advertisements in the local papers pointing out the disastrous results to be expected from a closure of the town's saloons.

Mark Reed, mayor of Shelton, testified that he had worked for local option there, but when it passed he was horrified to find taxes doubled, general trade in a state of stagnation and the town just as wet as ever.

H. B. Lamont, a former Anti-Saloon League worker who had seen the error of his ways, pointed to the dreadful results of the saloon closures in his home town of Everett:

"Has public morality and sobriety improved? Visit the toilets in the public buildings and look in the dark places of the alleyways and count the whiskey and beer bottles."

He was now engaged, with other Everett civic leaders, in a public campaign to raise $50,000 to repeal local option and save the city from imminent bankruptcy.

The wet business men proclaimed that a similar catastrophe in Olympia would result in no moral gain and great financial loss, causing a deficit in city revenues of $14,000. They had a point there. Liquor licenses were currently providing $13,600 a year to the town's coffers compared to $1,000 for all other licenses, $550 for rental of stalls at the public market and $400 in police court fines. The only larger source of income was the general tax levy, which raised $31,841.

To counteract the propaganda of the wets, the temperance ladies prevailed upon several of the more straight-laced business leaders to form an Anti-Saloon Executive Committee. Drys Millar Lemon, Fred Stocking, George Bigelow, C. A. Marshal and Charles Bowen charged that the added costs of law enforcement, jail maintenance, insane asylums and poor farms far offset the revenues from Demon Rum. They challenged the spokesmen of the Smokehouse gang to debate with them at the opera house, but they were not taken up on their invitation.

Despite a heavy turnout of determined female voters, local option failed to pass.

NO BLACK SPOTS ON MOTTMAN

No sooner did this furor die down than the usually placid local political scene was thrown into turmoil by George Mottman, who filed against Mayor Bridgford on the Citizens' ticket. The short-fused Mottman was hopping mad about the current Olympia tax rate of 47.95 mills and he proposed to do something about it in his usual forthright manner.

The "Republican City Committee," composed largely of the same establishment stalwarts who had fought off local option, came up with a campaign of smear advertising which would have done credit to a 1972 political campaign. One of their gems read as follows:

"Please stand up Mr. Mottman and let us measure the length of the shadow you cast. In the late afternoon even a small man will cast a long shadow, but in the noon-day glare, where men must stand who volunteer to lead, there is not much difference between the shadow of a small man and that of a dry-goods box."

Candidate Mottman wasn't one to take that kind of attack lying down. He bought full page ads to respond with a combination of invective and a sort of simple dignity:

"The Republican City Committee, ably assisted by the Elks, a delegation from the Smokehouse, Dr. Bridgford as coroner and Mr. Foshay and Mr. Heerman as chief mourners, who have held protracted services over my political remains, have checked the record for nearly 30 years and have been forced to the conclusion that **THERE ARE NO BLACK SPOTS ON MOTTMAN_**

*"If I wanted to be as little as you have shown yourselves to be in your uncalled for attack upon me by trying to make fun of my size and positive make-up * * * I could point out enough black spots to hide your beautiful looks and figures for all time to come.*

"I have realized early in life that I am not as beautiful or as perfectly shaped as the members of the Republican Committee are, and for that reason I have never wasted my time loafing or admiring myself. All my efforts have been to overcome my physical shortcomings in other directions, by leading an honest existence and trying to do as much good as I could."

He followed this up with a final burst of rugged individualism addressed to the voters:

"YOU WILL ALL HAVE TO WALK *if you vote for Mottman. There will be no carriages or autos to take you to the polls. My 'Christian' friends, headed by ex-Mayor Harris, have placed their fine autos at Mr. Bridgford's disposition, and if you agree to vote for Mr. Bridgford you can have a fine auto ride."*

The citizens, either responding to Mottman's forthrightness or resenting the personal attacks against him, gave him 1,075 votes to Bridgford's 806. The new mayor closed the year by firing all the appointive city department heads and replacing them with his own slate . . . Bert H. Barnes, fire chief; William Vance, police chief; John B. Weddell, city engineer and Clem Johnson, street commissioner.

City hall was aware that Mottman had arrived, and the whole town would continue to be reminded of that fact for some time to come.

State politics were even more unsettling in 1912. At the national level the Progressive faction of the Republican party had selected Senator Robert LaFollette as their candidate for the presidential nomination. Seven Republican governors, fearing LaFollette couldn't wrest the nomination from Taft, urged Teddy Roosevelt to enter the race. T. R. responded with the battle cry, "My hat's in the ring!"

Taft got the Republican nomination and Roosevelt's delegates bolted and named their leader candidate of the Progressive or "Bull Moose" party. His running mate was Hiram Johnson. The Democrats nominated New Jersey Governor Woodrow Wilson and Governor Marshall of Indiana. All three parties included progressive measures in their platforms and their campaign oratory was similar in many respects. Wilson came out with some 6,000,000 votes, Roosevelt 4,000,000 and Taft 3,000,000.

THE MOOSE AND THE DONKEY

In Washington Judge W. W. Black won the Democratic nomination for governor, but the supreme court ruled that it was unconstitutional for a judge who was occupying the bench to run for a partisan office. The second place candidate, Ernest Lister, was declared the nominee three weeks before the general election. In a whirlwind campaign he won a photo finish victory over Republican incumbent Hay . . . the results so close that the winner was in doubt for several days after the election.

The maverick nature of Washington voters was illustrated by other results of the 1912 election. All other state elective officials were Republicans, but the state house of representatives ended up without a Republican majority for the first time in the 20th century. Its membership included 30 Bull Moosers, 18 Democrats, one Socialist and 48 Republicans. The senate, with its holdover members, retained a Republican majority of 25 members to eight Democrats, eight Progressives and one Socialist.

The Bull Moose won the state's presidential electors and two congressmen at large, while Republicans returned to the three districted congressional seats.

GOVERNOR LISTER and his adjutant general, Fred Llewellyn at National Guard summer camp, 1913.

To further upset the political traditionalists, two women were elected to the house; Nena Jolidon Croake, a 40-year-old doctor of osteopathy from Tacoma, on the Bull (Cow?) Moose ticket, and Frances C. Axtell, a 47-year-old Bellingham housewife and a Republican.

The Seattle *Times,* which was still referring to Hay as "the lieutenant governor" after almost four years, declared jubilantly that Lister had 97,179 votes to 96,598, making him the first Democratic governor in the history of the state.

CHAPTER EIGHT
The Seventh Decade
1913-1923

The 13th legislature convened at Olympia on January 13, 1913, proving that whatever other faults they might have, its members were not superstitious. They gathered amid a dreary downpour of rain, but the capital city was doing its best to present a festive air. The Chamber of Commerce urged merchants to "keep their show windows in full brilliancy" at night and Manager Faulkner of the light and power company agreed to keep the street lights on until one o'clock in the morning.

On the morning of the 15th a special train from Tacoma and the regular train from Seattle and Tacoma disgorged 700 visitors at the Northern Pacific depot. The steamers *Magnolia* and *Verona,* on special excursion trips from Tacoma, got in late, but the *Nisqually* brought in 352 Seattle passengers, who formed ranks at Percival's dock and marched gaily through the Main street mud puddles behind a big silk banner of the Women's Wilson-Marshall League of Seattle.

At 1:30 in the afternoon the brass band met Governor Lister at the Mitchell hotel and serenaded him as he entered an automobile with his wife and two children. Another parade formed up behind the governor's automobile and the band, which led the way to the statehouse for the inaugural ceremonies. A crowd described by the *Recorder* as *"the largest gathering ever assembled in the capitol building"* looked on as Chief Justice H. D. Crow administered the oath of office to Ernest Lister as the eighth governor of the state of Washington. Immediately thereafter the new governor addressed the joint session of the house and senate, which had listened to Marion Hay's retiring message the same morning.

Hay had confined his message largely to a resume' of the state's flourishing condition under his administration, concluding that *"at no other time in the history of our commonwealth have the people been so happy, prosperous and contented."* He also urged a policy of frugality in government, warning that *"the state should never again incur the burden of a bonded debt."* He recommended a separate institution for delinquent juvenile girls, various changes in the myriad departments and commissions and election reforms including the abolition of the complicated second-choice vote and the authorization of absentee ballots.

The incoming governor led off with a strong warning against the progressive tendency of going to far too fast, cautioning the legislators to *"follow safe and sane lines; to follow public opinion rather than to rush in advance of it."*

He urged passage of the preferential presidential primary law, direct election of United States senators and asked for a nonpartisan election law for city and county offices. He also favored abolition of the straight party ballot, which required voters to select a partisan ballot at the polls.

In the interests of economy he recommended closure of two of the three normal schools, with education courses added to the curricula of the state university and college and seconded his predecessor's request for a girls' training school separate from the old reform school at Chehalis. He declared himself in favor of good roads, but felt that money already accumulated in the state fund and to be received during the coming biennium should be expended before any bond issues or increased taxes were considered to meet the demands of the new but highly vocal good roads lobby.

By evening the two late steamers had docked with an additional 500 visitors and the *Nisqually* was back with another full load of passengers on her second trip from Seattle and Tacoma.

Nearly 2,000 guests splashed their way to the new Temple of Justice for the inaugural ball honoring Governor Lister. There were more Democrats than the capital city had ever seen. The new building wasn't finished. The appropriation had run out and the stone facing hadn't been put in place. For several years the Temple of Justice would present a remarkably ugly facade of red brick and protruding structural steel. Temporary wooden floors and partitions had been built inside and it was brilliantly lighted and amply decorated with flags, bunting, flowers and greenery. Three orchestras played for dancers on all three floors. Mayor Mottman, who had insisted that he was going to appoint a surrogate to lead the grand march, gave in to tradition at the last moment and bravely escorted Mrs. Lister onto the floor, doing his best to ignore the fact that she towered over him by several inches. The parade, inauguration and grand ball were recorded on the celluloid newsreel film of Pathe weekly and subsequently viewed by moviegoers across the state.

It turned out so well that six more legislative dances were planned for the same location over the 60 days of the session.

WOMAN'S PLACE IS IN THE HOUSE

Everyone agreed that the legislature would never be the same again. The political activism of the forces of purity had eliminated most of the old-time politicians. There were more new faces in the chambers than had been seen in years . . . and two of them were feminine. After 70 years the Washington legislature had ceased to be a club for men only.

Neither Dr. Croaken or Mrs. Axtell made much impact on the legislature and both apparently agreed, by the time the session was over, that Senator Paulhamus was right when he said the capitol was no place for respectable ladies during the biennial gatherings of lawmakers and lobbyists.

The press poked a good deal of more or less gentle fun at the two lady politicians, the *Recorder* leading off with the comment that *"when Mrs. Dr. N. Jolidon Croake from Pierce county announced she voted for 'Taylor' (the speaker) after seconding the nomination of*

Corkery, only to switch suddenly, the house members and galleries ungallantly laughed at her confusion and declared it was 'just like a woman'."

Women liberationists will note that, while Mrs. Croake was certainly not the first confused legislator in the state's history, there is no record of press comment to the affect that "it was just like a man."

In organizing the two houses the Bull Moose members voted with the Republicans to keep Democrats in their usual state of ineffective frustration. The senate also confirmed the appointments of some 30 Republican officeholders made by Hay before his retirement . . . an obvious slap in the face for Democrat Lister as he took office. Howard D. Taylor, the King county lumberman, was reelected speaker of the house and Pliny Allen president pro-tem of the senate. This was becoming increasingly an honorary title. In earlier days it had been customary for lieutenant governors to step aside frequently and let the elected president pro-tem preside, but with the coming of the direct primary came a new breed of lieutenant governor. Louis F. Hart, the Republican elected to the number two spot, kept a firm grip on the senatorial gavel.

The power behind the scenes in the house of representatives was a short, tough political wheeler-dealer who preferred to operate behind the scenes rather than in the public gaze. His influence was felt throughout the state political framework and was still growing. This was Representative Ed Sims of Port Townsend. Sims, who was serving his third term, was listed in the legislative directory as a fish packer, which he was, but his fortune and power were based on a less respectable trade. His firm of Sims and Levy had for many years operated the most successful crimping operation in the Pacific Northwest. Maintaining a large sailors' boarding house on Port Townsend's wide-open waterfront, the firm specialized in selling crews to the captains of outward-bound sailing ships, collecting a sizeable fee . . . the seamen called it blood money . . . for every body delivered aboard. Sims and Levy's "runners" were expert at the use of knockout drops and knockout punches in coaxing reluctant seamen aboard the more notorious hell ships. This less than respectable background didn't prevent Sims from being a civic leader in Port Townsend, where crimping was the town's leading industry, but it

257

prevented him from seeking statewide office and prompted him to remain in the shadows of the legislative chambers, from whence he directed the action and dispensed power, patronage and perquisites. First elected in 1909, Sims, as a third-termer, had considerable seniority to add to his dominant personality and political cunning. There were only 14 representatives who had served more than one term and two of these hadn't been in Olympia for years,* so there were, in effect, 70 freshmen among the 97 house members.

Ed Sims handled legislators much as his waterfront runners handled prospective sailors. First he offered them a drink and a bonus. If they didn't accept they usually ended up feeling as if they had been hit over the head by a belaying pin.

The members of the lower house were still suffering from an anti-feminist backlash, it would seem. Of the 73 house employees, only seven were women, while the senate, with a staff of 39, had 12 women on the payroll. Among the male house employees were Chief Clerk Charles R. Maybury and Reading Clerk W. J. (Wee) Coyle, a recent star quarterback on the University of Washington football team, both appointed for the first time. Maybury and Coyle would soon emerge as major political figures in their own right.

RUM, ROADBUILDING AND REFORM

The Anti-Saloon League — WCTU — Grange lobby was as determined as ever to get its program of graduated progress toward prohibition back in motion. The watered-down local option law of the previous session had been viewed as a defeat by the forces of purity and ASL Superintendent Doty had been recalled, succeeded by trained temperance promoter George C. Conger. Conger's cohorts were still ardent crusaders, but the shift in command had slowed their momentum somewhat. The state . . . and its politicians . . . seemed to be having second thoughts on the wet vs. dry issue. Everett, the largest city in the state to vote itself dry under the 1911 local option law,

*N. B. Brooks of Klickitat county, a 54-year-old attorney, had served a single term in the territorial legislature of 1883. George McCoy, Clarke county lumberman, had last served in 1899.

had voted itself wet again . . . this time with the woman vote. The electors were in apparent agreement with the *Labor Journal* that *"the speakeasy, blind pig and bootlegger have replaced saloons * * * Women are drinking * * * You can't have a dry island in a sea of booze."*

On the other hand, the number of dry rural counties had increased, the ASL claiming that 42 percent of the state's population inhabited saloonless territory.

George Cotterill, that stalwart champion of enforced purity and the most prominent prohibitionist in the state, was out of the senate, serving a term as mayor of Seattle. Hi Gill, colorful proponent of the open town policy, had been one of the first to fall victim to the new recall law. A campaign led by the gaunt, spellbinding Mark Matthews and the embattled women of his congregation had resulted in Gill's recall. (He claimed he had been "diselected") and Cotterill had been chosen as his replacement on the ensuing wave of short-lived civic purity.

The general ambivalence toward the anti-saloon issue in 1913 was demonstrated by the fact that neither outgoing Governor Hay nor incoming Governor Lister had mentioned the matter of local option in their addresses to the legislature. The legislature carefully followed their lead and avoided the subject almost completely.

There was plenty to keep the lawmakers occupied anyway.

They moved fast to make Washington one of the first states to ratify the amendment to the United States constitution providing for the direct election of U. S. senators. (The Wyoming legislature had already provided the majority ratification needed to make the federal income tax a part of the constitution, but nobody worried about it. It was only designed to raise an extra $100 million and citizens were assured that the tax on the average taxpayer would never exceed one percent of net income.)

They considered a minimum wage law for women, pondering an Illinois legislative survey which showed that starvation pay was forcing many women and girls into prostitution, but they were reassured by the calming words of Julius Rosenwald, president of Sears, Roebuck and company, which paid its 4,732 female employees an average of $9.12 a week. Mr. Rosenwald, after notifying the stockholders of a net profit of seven million dollars for 1911 and a surplus of $17 million, issued a further statement that "there is practically no connection between low wages and immorality in women" although "a girl earning small wages might use that as a subterfuge to account for her dereliction." He issued further assurance that "five dollars a week is enough for any woman living at home and eight dollars enough for one who supports herself." Since he was a millionaire, the legislators decided he must know what he was talking about and placed the proposed bill in the pending file along with the tougher anti-saloon measure.

They passed a version of the Iowa red light abatement law, which permitted buildings used for immoral purposes to be condemned and padlocked for six months.

They appropriated a record-breaking $22 million budget from all sources, including $92,000 for their own expenses, $200,000 for participation in the Panama-Pacific and San Diego expositions, four million dollars in capitol construction bonds secured by the capitol grant timber lands, and funds for separate deaf and blind schools and a separate girls' training school, but they killed a bill to raise their own pay from five to ten dollars a day while in session.

They authorized the use of voting machines in elections and wrangled long and bitterly over legislative redistricting. The rural delegations, which enjoyed a most disproportionate share of the seats, succeeded in killing King county Representative Victor Zednick's redistricting resolution by indefinite postponement. They salved their consciences by passing a congressional redistricting measure setting up five districts and eliminating the former at-large positions.

They created a department of agriculture and abolished the offices of horticultural commissioner, oil inspector, state veterinarian and food and dairy commissioner . . . and soberly pondered a bill on the sanitary and humane treatment of chickens.

They wasted the usual time over an unusual number of other trivial bills, 1,162 measures having been introduced . . . a record which stood until 1935. Of these, 208 were actually passed and sent to the governor, who had a large bottle of red ink waiting on his desk. There was a rambling debate over the adoption of a state flag, Representative Le Sourd of Island county, a civil war veteran, entered the fray against Representative Chamberlain, who

feared that a state flag would "detract from the Stars and Stripes." Le Sourd delivered an oration, concluding with the stirring assurance that "every regiment, every corps, every division had its own flag, but above them all, with undimmed brightness waved 'Old Glory'."

The 1913 legislative session was viewed by its Republican leadership as a unique opportunity to distribute the contents of the pork barrel without having to assume the blame for increased taxes. It is axiomatic among statehouse politicians that six weeks after the legislature adjourns the voters forget all about it and focus their outrage on the governor . . . and the governor was a Democrat. Furthermore, the large number of Bull Moosers and Democrats in the legislative chambers provided an additional smokescreen for the regular Republicans.

The result was a 60-day running battle between the governor and the legislature on spending and taxes. Lister vetoed a $300,000 appropriation to rebuild Cheney normal school, which has been destroyed by fire in April of 1912. Both houses promptly overrode the veto. Lister retaliated by vetoing the $195,000 maintenance appropriation for the school and it was likewise overriden.

The legislature, urged on by the Good Roads Association, the automobile clubs and the rest of the burgeoning young highway lobby, was determined to put the state in the road building business in a big way. The highway tax levy was raised from a half mill to 1½ mills, which would raise an estimated million and a half dollars a year. Lister promptly vetoed it, saying he favored good roads but didn't think "present conditions justify such large expenditure at this time."

In a vote-swapping coalition, the good roads proponents joined forces with the champions of education to beat the Cheney normal veto, but it proved impossible to muster the full two-thirds needed to void the highway tax veto.

The good roads people viewed this as a double-cross and bitterness was rampant during the ensuing floor discussions. The next day the representatives employed a unique means to declare that the rhubarb in the house had never occurred. In a step unprecedented in the history of the legislature, they voted 56 to 40 to expunge from the record all reference to the previous actions on both the normal school and highway vetoes. This novel approach to the problem, advanced by the wily Sims, was a masterpiece of political strategy. It would have required a two-thirds vote to suspend the rules for reconsideration of the effort to override the highway veto. The Republican leadership couldn't muster that kind of majority, but it could round up the simple majority needed to declare that none of the events of the previous day had really transpired.

Lister was understandably furious. *"By expunging from the record any action that has been taken by the legislature,"* he declared with considerable logic, *"they might go to the extent of expunging from the record action taken two or three weeks ago, so that until the last day of the session no one would be able to figure out what they have done or what they intend to do."*

Senator Henry M. White of Whatcom, a lawyer, agreed with Lister that a somewhat dangerous precedent had been set. He introduced a resolution to place the expunged house proceedings on the senate record. Democrats and some Bull Moose senators joined with him to make a fight of it, but after considerable debate the resolution lost by a vote of 24 to 14. For good measure, the senate majority then voted to expunge all reference to White's efforts from the senate record.

MRS. LISTER'S
TWO MILLION DOLLAR DROP-KICK

Precedent continued to be shattered in the highway battle. By early March the good road forces had regrouped and produced a highway tax levy bill to provide more than $2 million for state highways and an appropriations bill to divide up the contents of the newly created pork barrel. Lister could not contain himself with a mere written veto message of the highway tax bill, which was the first of the two to reach his office. The *Recorder,* on March 8, chronicled the succeeding action as follows:

"Governor Ernest Lister was the central figure in one of the most dramatic scenes this forenoon ever enacted in the halls of the Washington legislature when he presented in person his veto of the public highways levy bill and hurled denunciations right and left. The senate was packed with its members and the members of the house which had adjourned in a body to attend the senate, while the galleries were filled with spectators. Interest had been brought to a high tension by the controversies of the past week or more and by the sensational

incidents of last night when the officials of the house spent hours in trying to deliver the road appropriation bill passed yesterday, into the hands of the governor, only to have the $2,000,-000 document, when finally left at the executive mansion kicked from the door and across the porch where it is still supposed to repose."

The latter reference was to the even more colorful reception of the appropriations bill, which had taken longer to draft than the tax measure. By the time all the horse trading and pork barrel politicking was concluding and the bill drafted, its sponsors faced a time crisis. If it were delivered to the governor on March 7 there would still be time to override his expected veto. If he didn't get it until the following morning he could just hold on to it, veto it after adjournment and there would be nothing the legislature could do about it for another two years.

When the bill passed the house late in the afternoon of March 7, Speaker Taylor detailed Chief Clerk Charles R. Maybury and Representative L. D. McArdle of the roads committee to deliver it to the governor at all costs.

Despite the thunder of the bill's railroading through house and senate, all the details weren't completed until well after the five o'clock closing hour for state offices. Evidently warned in advance, Lister and his secretary, C. C. Dill, locked up the executive offices at 5:20 after tacking up a new sign which read, *"Office hours, 9 a.m. to 5 p.m."* They then vanished from human ken. Maybury and McArdle were confronted by the locked door and the sign when they arrived, breathing heavily, at 6:20 p.m.

Maybury made frenzied calls to the mansion and got something of a runaround. The legislators were holding a return ball for the citizens of Olympia in the Temple of Justice that night and Maybury hurried there to seek out the opinion of an assistant attorney general as to the legal requirements for delivering a bill to the governor. He was given the curbstone opinion that all he had to do was get the bill inside the mansion.

He and McArdle raced back to the mansion, to which they had already been denied admission two or three times. The fatal hour of midnight was growing closer all the time and they were determined not to take no for an answer.

After repeated thunderous knocking on the front door, the two were confronted by Mrs.

Lister, a determined lady with quick reflexes. When she opened the door Maybury tossed the bill inside, but like a skilled soccer player, the first lady drop-kicked it back across the porch. Maybury and McArdle fled.

It was this episode which had constituted the last straw for the embattled chief executive. In the course of his veto message of the companion bill the next day he spoke heatedly of the affair, including the verbal blast transcribed by the *Recorder's* political writer:

"I want to say this right now; that if any gang of ruffians, hoodlums or window-tommies can go to the residence of the governor because it is a public building, any time of the day or night to compel him to be seen I am ready to leave that residence and move to a private house where I can at least during the nights have a few hours of privacy that every public citizen is entitled to. This is all I have to say about the matter."

The term "window-tommy" apparently piqued the curiosity of Speaker Taylor, who dropped in at the state library to look it up in the unabridged dictionary. When he had satisfied his curiosity he rose on a point of personal privilege and remarked that, although he had spent his youth on the range and in logging camps and though he had heard all the bad words known to man, he had never heard of window-tommy. Upon looking up its meaning he found that it "applied to prostitutes who entered rooms through windows for clandestine meetings and such rewards as might be." He felt that it was beneath the dignity of a governor to so refer to a member of the house of representatives and the chief clerk of that honorable body.

After the tumult and shouting died, it was apparent that Lister had achieved at least a partial victory in the dramatic episode of what became known in political circles as "the slipper bill." The *Standard,* still defiantly Democratic and with John Miller Murphy covering his last legislative session for it, reported on March 14:

"The Taylor-Sims-McArdle-Nichols machine in the house and senate 'backed down' entirely in their program of extravagance advanced under the shield of good roads construction and behaved like 'good dogs' after Governor Lister's memorable attack upon the unwarranted expenditures they proposed, and last Monday and Tuesday passed a compromise road measure providing a 1¼ mill (first year) and 1 mill (second year) levy for state roads, which was immediately signed by the governor. This constituted a personal triumph for the governor and a saving to taxpayers of $2½ million."

Although the Republicans did their best to brand Lister as "the most extravagant governor in the state's history," the fact remained that his successful vetoes cut nearly five million dollars from the legislature's record budget and pruned 4¼ mills from the total state tax levy, which was still more than three mills over the previous levy. As a former member of the state board of control, Lister knew the inside workings of the bureaucracy as few governors have, either before or since, and there was additional belt-tightening in the departments under his control. The board of control itself hurriedly pruned $732,000 from its budget after Lister got through checking it out with a sharp pencil.

The half million dollar appropriation for completion of the Temple of Justice was among the bills vetoed. This so enraged the citizens of the capital city that the city council was urged to bring legal action against the Lister Construction company for allegedly having done an inferior job of paving several of the town's streets. Other communities were equally annoyed by Lister's efforts at economy, especially Vancouver, which had been counting on a state-financed bridge across the Columbia. That, too, had been redlined.

By March 13, the next to the last day of the session, the legislators were as tired of it all as the governor. They had paper screens placed over the chamber clocks and stayed in session until three o'clock in the morning in an effort to avoid the last-minute rush. Their good intentions were thwarted by Senator Hutchinson, who was miffed at the failure of his pet bills to pass and demanded reading in full of all bills being considered. He had brought a brown bag dinner and settled down stubbornly at his desk to enjoy his proxy filibuster. President Hart ordered three clerks to read bills simultaneously and, amid a verbal tempest, the members slipped out for dinner and failed to return. The house continued doggedly to the bitter end, the *Recorder* noting that *"the two women members remained on duty until the last."*

The issue of March 14 reported that *"with a final burst of good spirits and cheer, singing, marching and merriment, the 13th legislature of the state of Washington adjourned sine die at 4:47 this morning."*

Sidetracked

In the Wee Small Hours of the Morn

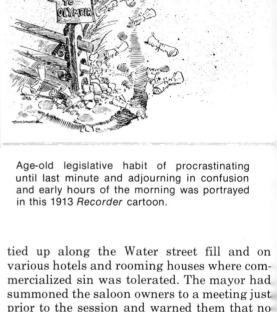

Republicans, Democrats and Bull Moosers were alike taken to task in this 1913 *Recorder* cartoon critical of the bi-partisan legislative proclivity for junketing about the state instead of staying in Olympia and tending to business.

Age-old legislative habit of procrastinating until last minute and adjourning in confusion and early hours of the morning was portrayed in this 1913 *Recorder* cartoon.

The house, which had stuck to business the previous night, had time on its hands and staged an impromptu third house session. The *Recorder* noted that *"there were a number of ladies on the floor,"* adding that, *"whether from this reason or because the custom is dying out, there was lack of the exuberance and rough and tumble scenes usually marking the final hours of the session."*

A piano was wheeled into the chambers. Governor and Mrs. Lister and their children, Florence and John, visited the house, joined the community singing and somewhat healed the rift between the executive and legislative branches of state government.

MAYOR MOTTMAN MAKES WAVES

The city administration of Mayor Mottman did not relax its policy of civic purity while the legislators were in town. The police force, expanded to five patrolmen and a chief since the restricted district had been closed, carried on periodic raids on "flat houses of ill repute"

tied up along the Water street fill and on various hotels and rooming houses where commercialized sin was tolerated. The mayor had summoned the saloon owners to a meeting just prior to the session and warned them that no "hanky-panky" would be permitted and, before the year was over, they were presented with a new ordinance requiring the closure of all saloons and pool halls by 11 p.m. As the new law went into effect, Governor Lister was issuing a proclamation establishing "Purity Sunday" in honor of the International Purity Conference then meeting in Minneapolis. The conference was dedicated to fighting "the white slave traffic" and to a "higher and better standard of morality among the masses."

The sudden shift in the moral climate of the town and the region in general was apparently too much for the stout defender of the restricted district and its denizens, Gordon Mackay. Late in the year he was charged by Ed Henderson with having raised a $4.70 check to $470. Mrs. Mackay requested a sanity hearing for her husband, which was held before John R

262

Mitchell, now a superior court judge, and four local physicians. Dr. Thomas Peppard who was, strangely enough, a veterinarian, testified that he had had a terrible time trying to dress a cut over Mackay's eye caused by a fall. The attorney had refused to sit still and had finally dashed to the bathroom and grabbed a bottle of carbolic acid. Other witnesses said Mackay frequently fell asleep while they were talking to him in his office and Mrs. Mackay testified rather vaguely that he was "taking pills." The board declared that while the former council-man editor was undoubtedly behaving in a peculiar manner he wasn't legally insane. Soon afterward he was convicted of forgery and given a one-year jail sentence. He thereafter disappeared from the annals of the town in which he had been such a prominent and controversial figure.

An added metropolitan touch was given the town when Bronson and LaGue Motor company took delivery of the first of a small fleet of real taxis, complete with meter and outside compartment for the driver. These were considered to be much more "high-toned" than the ordinary touring cars operated as for-hire autos by the livery stables and garages.

Both the county sheriff and police department had been equipped with motorcycles and peace officers were no longer entirely helpless against the speed demons of the motorized set. The *Washington Standard* reported in its issue of April 11 that nine Olympia auto owners, including Judge Emmet N. Parker of the supreme court, had been arrested for speeding by Special Officer Taliferro. Judge Giles fined each $9.80 (including costs) and was not sympathetic to their angry complaints that if they stayed within the 12 mile an hour speed limit they lost momentum on the Main and 4th street hills and couldn't make it over the top.

Governor Lister was equally unsympathetic. At a speech in Seattle the *Recorder* quoted him regarding *"the danger of the automobile and the joy ride. It is a curse and should be stopped. More delinquents result from joy rides and the roadhouse evil, I believe, than from any other source. I will do anything possible to help local authorities in closing roadhouses and suppressing the joy riding evil."*

City government, which usually operated blandly with its major decisions made in advance in the Elks Club or the back room of the Smokehouse, burst upon the public eye in 1913 with Mayor Mottman at the helm. Mott-man, a civic gadfly for progress linked with economy, provided continuing copy for the local reporters. If they failed to take advantage of it he purchased large display advertisements to make his views known.

The mayor was particularly critical of anything he considered to be false economy. He pointed out that the city had, in recent months, paid $20,000 in damage suits, mostly to people who had fallen from or through the many still unmodernized wooden widewalks. "That," he concluded, "would build a long sidewalk."

Mottman's major project for 1913 was municipal ownership of the long controversial city water works and he personally introduced an ordinance authorizing a $150,000 municipal bond election to finance the change. The downtown establishment and the local press . . . even the *Standard,* which had failed Mottman's election as a badly needed stimulant to life in the capital city . . . were unanimous in their violent opposition to the proposal. The mayor countered the journalistic hostility by having printed at his own expense a lengthy circular which he distributed all over town. Ignoring the old political adage that nobody ever won a fight with a newspaper, he devoted a full paragraph to a double broadside against the *Olympian* and *Recorder:*

"I am sorry the Perkins press has not enough patriotism for Olympia to supprt this meritorious proposition, but I am not surprised that the Olympian *and* Recorder *are knocking municipal ownership. They have never supported anything for the real benefit of Olympia because they are owned in Tacoma. The fact that the* Olympian, Recorder *and* Standard *are against me ought to remove all doubt that I am on the right track."*

The Perkins twins charged that Mayor Mottman had hired Ed Henderson, Bush Baker, Eugene Horton and Sidney Rankin to circulate his waterworks petition at the outrageous cost to the city of $76.50. A counter-petition was drawn up by the business men, bearing the signatures of such establishment leaders as C. J. Lord, C. H. Springer, Guy Winstanley, W. A. Weller, George Draham, Dr. Ingham, A. H. Christopher, Frank Kenney, Millar Lemon, George Mills, Charles Dufault and H. B. McElroy.

Despite the furor downtown, the voters of the community proved once again that they had plenty of apathy to go around. Only 1,036 electors bothered to go to the polls and the majority of them favored the Mottman plan. His triumph was marred by the fact that the water company filed a $50,000 libel suit against him for statements he had made about the quality of their product during the campaign. These had included a charge that the city water supply "courses through an open ditch past the China gardens and every time it rains we drink drainage surface water." The mayor had further claimed that the Chinese market gardeners' pigs and ducks used the municipal water supply to wade and wallow in, that the water mains were full of dead ends which served as collecting points for stagnant and evil smelling liquid, and that worms and maggots kept flowing from the taps with the water.

Although the mayor's attorney, P. M. Troy, flourished a bottle of bug-filled city water under the noses of the jury, they declared the chief executive guilty after deliberating for 10 hours. They awarded the company damages of one dollar.

In a classic example of Mayor Mottman's determined character, he eventually fought the case all the way to the state supreme court, which upheld the one dollar judgment. The legal costs exceeded the amount of the damages by several hundred times at that point.

Things remained otherwise placid in the capital city until the 14th legislature got down to business on the first Tuesday of January, 1915, faced with an initiative to the legislature passed by the voters the previous fall.

In other areas of the community's intellectual pursuits, the Benedictine fathers at St. Martins College were having a huge brick main building constructed to replace that institution's original wood frame building. This was fortunate for Olympia's future as a center of higher education, for in December the old Olympia Collegiate Institute building, occupied by Pacific Lutheran Seminary was badly damaged by a fire. The church subsequently merged the Olympia school with its new Pacific Lutheran College in Tacoma and abandoned the East Bay site.

A tightening money market and indications of another of the periodic economic slumps made it impossible to dispose of the municipal water bonds and, despite the mayor's efforts to interest local capital in their purchase . . . he pledged $5,000 worth himself . . . the project was shelved. Unfortunately, the same problem plagued efforts to sell the bonds authorized by the legislature to begin construction of a long-awaited new capitol building on the hill. Those blueprints were also filed away for the future.

More active Olympians continued to enjoy their leisure time with railroad excursions to Moclips, launch parties on the bay, clambakes at Priest Point park and automobile trips over the expanding network of passable gravel roads.

There was something for even the youngest citizens. The Perkins papers staged a subscription contest for the small fry with a Shetland pony and handsome pony cart as first prize. Dr. Redpath's little daughter Catherine became the envy of her contemporaries when she drove off with the pony and cart. Beautiful baby contests had become a popular part of most civic celebrations. At the big baby show of the previous year Theodore Bordeaux had been named the prettiest three-year-old boy and Louise Schmidt the prettiest girl. John Lynch and Louise Hollopeter took the honors as prettiest two-year-olds, Carl Reder and Vernice Churchill prettiest six-month-olds and Catherine and Beverly Ritner prettiest twins.

There was an old-fashioned impromptu celebration at 11 a.m. on October 10 when two taps on the fire bell signaled the joining of the Atlantic and Pacific oceans in the Panama canal as the Gamboa dam was blown up to complete the cut. The street cars stopped and rang their gongs, the various factories tied down their whistles, automobilists sounded their horns, school and church bells rang, firemen ran their apparatus from the barn and clanged the gongs, adults and children cheered and the local dogs, excited by all the commotion, barked and howled. Delivery wagon horses caught the spirit of the hour and ran away in all directions. It was all very exciting and satisfying and boosters predicted that Olympia would once again become a seaport of more than local importance.

1914

The year 1914 was marked by growing threat of war in Europe, increasingly hard times at home and political warfare waged over the first major crop of initiatives from the seed of direct legislation authorized by the 1911 legislature.

THE SEVEN SISTERS

Seven initiatives, which were promptly labeled "the seven sisters" were filed with Secretary of State I. M. Howell on January 30 by Miss Lucy Case of Seattle and state Grange Master C. B. Kegley on behalf of the Grange and Anti-Saloon League. The initiatives would abolish the state bureau of inspection and tax commission, incorporating their functions in the public service commission, establish a "blue sky" law to regulate stock sales, amend the industrial insurance law to provide up to $100 for immediate "first aid" treatment for injured workers, abolish all commercial employment agencies, set up a fish code, eliminate pork barrel road legislation by requiring that all funds be distributed by a highway director and commission rather than the legislature and setting up a standing ½ mill highway levy and, finally, a statewide dry law drawn up by Superintendent Conger of the Anti-Saloon League.

Two other initiatives were filed separately, one establishing the eight-hour day for all workers of both sexes; the other permitting convicts to live in minimum security honor camps and work on road construction at a modest wage. Two referenda were filed, to establish a teachers' pension fund and authorize an irrigation project in the Quincy valley of eastern Washington. An amendment to the constitution was proposed permitting aliens to own land in the state.

A well-financed and highly vocal combination of business and industrial leaders was quickly organized to fight all nine initiatives, apparently on the theory that any change was bad. The "Stop-Look-Listen League," assigned to defeat the eight-hour law, published an interesting article by Ed Sims which claimed that the proposed measure would constitute *"unjust discrimination against workers."* He based this conclusion on the argument that workers were, in fact, enterpreneurs who sold their time and skills on the open market. Since the new law would prohibit them from selling more than eight hours labor per day it was, in Mr. Sims' opinion, *"the most tyrannical legislation ever suggested in this state"* and would, if passed, *"make the working man a slave."* The tender feelings of Representative Sims, who had become wealthy selling human beings to shipmasters for the purpose of working a 24-hour day at $20 a month, was touching to those who knew him. The fish packing industry presented equally cogent reasons for

voting against the fish bill, which would have controlled its looting of the state's marine resources and the liquor interests pointed out the economic disaster which would follow passage of the strengthened dry law.

Initiative 3, the anti-saloon measure, was just as ardently promoted by the godly, who viewed it as the next step toward total prohibition although their official party line was still "We're against saloons; not drinkers." The new law would permit sale of liquor by druggists if prescribed by a doctor or requested by a clergyman, "or in case of extreme illness where delay might be dangerous to the patient." It also permitted individuals to place out-of-state mail orders for rather generous quantities of potables if accompanied by monthly authorization slips issued by county auditors, but it would outlaw all saloons everywhere in the state.

UNEMPLOYMENT, INFLATION AND WAR

Olympians of 1914, in common with Americans in general, were faced with problems remarkably similar of those of today . . . growing unemployment coupled with wartime inflation and high cost of living, a tight money market and high interest rates. Mayor Mottman's administration re-established the town woodpile at Priest Point park and offered unemployed heads of families $1.25 a day as woodcutters. The product of their labor was sold to more affluent citizens for $4.50 a cord.

By July the papers were full of examples of skyrocketing prices resulting from the outbreak of the war in Europe. Automobile tires were up 20 percent and flour up 45¢ a barrel. By early August it was reported in the *Olympian* that sugar prices had advanced 50¢ that day after a rise of 70¢ the day before . . . to $8.50 for a hundred-pound sack. Canned salmon was up $1.40 a case and no end appeared to be in sight.

By October, at the instigation of the Women's Club, Women's Educational Club and Eenati, Mayor Mottman had issued an appeal for contributions to the Red Cross "for the relief of the wounded on the European battlefields and Belgium refugees." Contribution points were established at 11 retail stores.

East 4th Street, circa 1913, with "benzine buggies" beginning to compete with the Olympia-Tumwater trolley.

Even as a gala "subway dance" was being filmed for the Acme theater on newly paved 7th street above the Northern Pacific's completed concrete tunnel, the Oregon Washington Railway and Navigation company was completing its new branch line grade into town to link up with Dr. Carlyon's industrial belt line railroad on Jefferson street.

Fred Stocking and P. M. Troy were completing a handsome new two-story office building on the site of the pioneer Columbia hall and, with a fine sense of history, named it the Columbia building. A new apartment hotel was going up beside it and up at 14th and Main, R. M. Fouts, a Seattle builder, had completed the city's first "completely modern apartment house." The last of the gleaming white gas kitchen ranges were connected up early in November and soon thereafter the Capital Apartments were opened for public inspection. An orchestra played in the basement ballroom and old-timers marveled at the 20th century efficiency of the adjoining underground garage for the convenience of automobile-owning tenants. The populace had hardly accustomed itself to the presence of such a sophisticated and luxurious apartment house when Fouts announced that he was planning "a fine modern fire-proof Class A six-story 120-room hotel at the corner of 6th and Franklin," which would be a 20th century improvement on the vanished Hotel Olympia. By the end of the year Fouts had acquired the proposed hotel site in the swap with Millard Lemon, who took over the Capital Apartments as part of the deal. The hotel had in the meantime grown to seven stories and 126 rooms; the cost of its construction from $100,-000 to $125,000.

The handsome new yellow brick Carnegie public library was dedicated in ceremonies attended by more than 300 citizens. Joseph Wohleb, the rising young architect who had designed the structure, handed the key to the Reverend D. A. Thompson, chairman of the library board, who passed it to Mayor Mottman. His Honor passed it, like a political hot potato, to Miss Janet Moore, president of the library board, who kept it. Only a few years before the city library had been an adjunct to the public comfort station, the toilet attendant doubling as librarian. The presence of the state library had made the city fathers reluctant to spend money on another facility, but the new state librarian, J. M. Hitt, tired of having his premises overrun by noisy school children and dozing vagrants, had blasted the capital city for having the worst library of any town in the state. His challenge to civic pride had been nobly responded to.

TIME TO RETRENCH

Members, lobbyists, employees and would-be employees of the 14th legislature of 1915 arrived at the capital city amid rain and gusty winds and splashed their way to various bars for something to ward off the chill. The usual cheer was lacking, however, for unless the courts reversed the dry law of 1914, every saloon and bar would close its doors on December 31 and succeeding legislatures would presumably convene in an atmosphere of cold and arid morality.

Die-hard wets arrived determined to somehow avert such a tragedy. A so-called "hotel men's initiative" to the legislature was drawn up in advance, ready to be presented to the lawmakers. It would permit the sale of liquor in the larger hotels and the continued operation of breweries to supply the out-of-state trade. Another would authorize operation of saloons during daylight hours and under more stringent regulation. Senator William Ray was clutching a bill which would repeal the dry initiative entirely.

Governor Lister, in his message to the legislature, dampened the hopes of the wets by announcing that he would veto any efforts to change the dry initiative. He further urged a constitutional convention to revise the judicial districts and eliminate at least 10 superior court judges. He advocated a unicameral legislature of 25 members . . . five from each congressional district . . . with biennial sessions extended to 90 days. He urged the establishment of tuition fees at the university, retrenchment in all taxing districts and a firm

check on any additional bond issues. He also reiterated his proposals for non-partisan county and city elections, the abolishment of the party preference requirements in voting, the direct election of U.S. senators, preferential primaries and the abolition of the tax commission. And he asked for funds to enforce the prohibition law, which would become effective at midnight on December 31.

"In recent years there has been an alarming increase in the cost of government," he concluded. "It is time to retrench."

Both houses had convened the previous day and quickly organized, thereafter passing senate bills 1 and 2 appropriating $90,000 for legislative expenses and $15,000 for printing. Former Speaker Taylor had been elected to the senate and was replaced by W. W. Conner, Skagit county Republican. Charles Maybury was reelected chief clerk and ordered to provide each member with $5.00 worth of stamps and issue their pay warrants on a weekly basis. Edward L. French, a Republican from Clarke county, was elected president pro-tem of the senate; Frank M. Dallam secretary.

The most powerful freshman legislator to arrive on the scene and, indeed, one of the most powerful regardless of seniority, was Mark Reed, scion of the wealthy Mason county Simpson Timber company empire and second generation Washington political figure. Reed had cut his teeth on politics and knew how to wheel and deal around the capitol. He was Ed Sims' kind of man and the two joined forces to plot the course of government for the coming biennium. In later years, capitol newsman Bob Cummings asked Reed if it were true that he and Sims controlled the 1915 legislature.

"Hell, no," Reed answered. "Ed and I didn't *control* the legislature. We *were* the legislature."

Another freshman representative who would be much heard from over the next two decades was 50-year-old "Colonel" Roland H. Hartley, Everett mill owner and hard-nosed conservative Republican.

After listening to the pleas of wet lobbyists to heed the tremendous financial loss which would result from the closure of the state's saloons, breweries and hop farms, the legislators placed their initiative in cold storage in commmittee. They also turned down a request for a special election, which meant that the measures wouldn't appear on the

TRANQUIL TUMWATER and the old Olympia brewery just before prohibition put it out of business. Lower Tumwater Falls, at the right, flowed into the salt tide-water of Deschutes inlet.

ballot until November, 1916 . . . almost a year after the dry law went into effect.

The ASL and Grange lobbyists had shouted that the wet initiative "would make every hotel a saloon, a den of vice and a brothel." As customary when an issue became too emotionally hot to handle, the lawmakers decided upon a course of caution, passing the buck to the voters at a future election.

As a last resort the Olympia Brewing company began preparing a legal suit to invalidate the prohibition initiative on the grounds that the original initiative and referendum amendment proposal had been unconstitutional because people had been required to vote on both together and weren't allowed to choose between the initiative and the referendum; that improper notification of the election had been given, the initiative was discriminatory, the prohibition against Washington breweries manufacturing their product for sale outside

the state was an illegal interference with interstate commerce, etc.

The State Federation of Labor, County Assessors' association, Sheriff's association, Purebred Livestock association and Parent Teachers association were all having their state conventions in Olympia and the town was overrun with beer and liquor lobbyists, WCTU ladies, ASL and Grange zealots and Methodists and Presbyterian preachers. In desperation the house revived the ancient battle to keep lobbyists from taking over their chambers, passing a rule that any lobbyist caught plying his trade on the house floor would be stripped of his admission card. For good measure, the speaker ordered house employees not to lobby on pain of instant dismissal. Representative Clark G. Black of Garfield county, a crusty fiscal conservative, complained, "It's unfair. There are so many of them. Let them get busy at *something.*"

The *Olympian* takes an informal look at the
Legislature of 1915.

The house observed another historic tradition by becoming embroiled in a battle with the press. The Seattle *Post-Intelligencer* legislative reporter, J. W. Gilbert, had picked up an interesting rumor in the halls of the state. The report duly appeared on the *P. I.*'s front page, charging that the efforts of Representative McArdle and Zednick to abolish the tax commission and reorganize the land and equalization boards were prompted by promised jobs in the land commissioner's expanded office.*

McArdle, in high dudgeon, demanded that Gilbert take the floor and "explain his untruthful and baseless statement." He said he had noticed that some members of the press had been taken on the Democratic payroll after the last session, and concluded with the righteous cry, "I came here as a *Republican*; not to play cheap politics!"

Gilbert replied that "It was something of common report" and pointed out that the *P. I.* was only one of several morning papers which had carried the story. Democrat Ben Hill rose to ask why the representatives of the other papers hadn't been put on the legislative carpet, but was quickly stifled by Ed Sims, who told him, "Republicans don't need any suggestions for reforms from Democrats."

The McArdle-Zednick bill promptly passed both house and senate, with amendments including an emergency clause to place the changes in effect immediately. Lister just as promptly line vetoed the abolition of the tax commission on the grounds that the proposed sharing of tax responsibilities by the secretary of state and public service commission would confuse the county assessors, who were strongly opposed to the change.

Both houses then passed the bill in its entirety over the governor's veto and within two days the new land board, composed of Land Commissioner Clark Savage, Treasurer Edward Meath and Secretary of State Howell, had held its first meeting.

The traditional bugaboo of legislative redistricting kept the legislators locked in combat until the cow county delegations succeeded in knocking down a King county bill which would have given the three largest counties,

*McArdle landed a state job within the year and remained on the public payroll for many years, but his initial employment was as a deputy to the state auditor rather than the land commissioner.

King, Spokane and Pierce 25 of the 42 senate seats and 47 of the 97 in the house. The battle ended with the constitutional requirement for periodic reapportionment again ignored.

The plaintive cries of the railroad against automobile competition were joined by the state's street railway lines, which were reeling under the onslaught of a new automotive phenomenon, the jitney. Owners of cars, many of whom had been thrown out of work by the prevailing recession, took to operating along the street car routes picking up passengers at five cents a head. Jitney was a popular slang term for a nickel, hence the name of the street cars' new competition. The jitney operators were unlicensed, unregulated and untaxed, which put them in an enviable position compared to the traction companies. Passengers who were injured had little chance of collecting damages.

A bill proposing a requirement that jitney operators be required to post a $5,000 bond prompted Thurston county's bewhiskered J. Sox Brown to his only burst of oratory that session. White beard quivering with indignation, the ancient warrior proclaimed that the measure was "unfair to the common people and backed by corporate interests." The Ford owners in his community "do a little cross-country business," he said, closing with the ominous warning that "Rochester will rise up in righteous indignation if you pass this bill."

Apparently appalled at the thought, the legislators compromised on a $2,500 bond and made the law applicable only to first class cities, which Rochester certainly was not. Lister vetoed the watered-down bill; it was passed over his veto on the last day of the session.

Most of the governor's veto attempts suffered the same fate, although they got a legislative version of the defeated first aid initiative to him too late and he had the satisfaction of redlining it after the session ended, on the grounds that it was too costly and impractical for small employers. The last bill signed before his ten day limit expired was a $12,000 appropriation for additional expenses of the legislature. He took advantage of the occasion to point out "the undue extravagance of the legislature." It had actually spent $94,382, which was second only to the $116,000 cost of the 1909 session. Its total biennial budget

270

An Open and Closed Proposition

Olympia *Recorder* cartoon fostered myth that
Republican legislators of 1915 would protect the
state treasury from Democratic Governor Lister.

appropriation from all sources, somewhat over
$26 million, was the highest so far in the state's
history. This included a new capitol fund
appropriation to complete the Temple of
Justice and to purchase land between the
capitol grounds and Main street to provide a
suitable entrance. Lister let this one become
law without his signature.

Superintendent Conger utilized a campaign
tactic employed with great success by certain
candidates for major statewide office in later
years. He branded all those opposed to his
cause as agents of the devil . . . himself and his
supporters as soldiers of the Lord. A favorite
tactic was to trumpet loudly from time to time
that he had been offered magnificent bribes to
get the initiative withdrawn, although, like the
self-proclaimed political good guys of today, he
offered no documentary evidence to back his
charges of corruption among his opponents.

Conger's campaign was a model of efficiency. The Presbyterians raised $15,000 for the
cause in the three coast states and Idaho. The
Methodists put 700 preachers in the field to
orate against the evils of drink. The Anti-
Saloon League organized the state into

271

precincts of 150 families each, assigning a captain and 10 canvassers to register and propagandize the voters in each precinct. In October, with the campaign reaching a crescendo, the national headquarters sent out a flying squad to organize parades, band concerts, torchlight rallies and billboard advertising.

The Anti-Prohibition Association countered by hiring that ace propagandist and former *Post-Intelligencer* editor, Erastus Brainerd as their chief flak. The state's breweries financed full-page advertisements in most of the newspapers proclaiming *"Moderation but not Prohibition."*

The Reverend Matthews, who had been engaged in noisy hand-to-hand combat with the devil for years, trumpeted that Satan would be at the polls and claimed that fraudulent registrations were being made and people who had been occupants of cemeteries for years would be voting wet in November. The ASL hired Burns detectives to check the registration lists and the indominatable ladies of the WCTU posted signs in every precinct warning that a $5.00 bribe to cast an illegal vote would probably result in "a trip to the pen."

There was considerable evidence that the forces of decency weren't too particular about choosing their supporters either. Of the 112,182 signatures collected on their petitions, 42,000 were thrown out by the secretary of state's checkers and the supreme court heard testimony regarding forged names. But only 32,000 valid signatures were required in those days, and Initiative 3 was certified for the ballot.

A further hassle arose when the secretary of state announced that he was going to have to charge $200 a page to those who wished to place their views in the state's first voters' pamphlet, commonly referred to in 1914 as "the argument book." There were angished cries that some of the interested parties couldn't afford such an exhorbitant fee, but the supreme court ruled that Secretary Howell was required by the legislature to make the charge. The court also threw out two of the initiatives . . . and the fish bill . . . on the grounds that they didn't have enough valid signatures. Of the survivors, only the anti-saloon law and the measure abolishing employment agencies survived at the polls. The massively financed campaign of business and industry had con-

vinced workers that long hours weren't a hardship but a privilege, that they didn't really need immediate medical attention if they were smashed up on the job and that control of fly-by-night stock promoters would be an infringement on the American way of life. They were also sure they didn't want convicts competing with honest laborers for jobs on the state highways. The teachers' retirement fund, Quincy irrigation and alien land measures were all resoundingly defeated.

The statewide vote on the dry initiative was 174,748 to 160,000, a majority of slightly over 14,000. This was the largest total vote cast for any candidate or issue in the state's history, although it appeared on an off-year election ballot. The strong feelings of the electorate were further illustrated by the fact that 40,000 more people voted on the dry initiative than cast their votes for governor. Only six counties, Thurston, King, Pierce, Jefferson, Garfield and Mason, voted wet, although the state's three largest cities, Seattle, Spokane and Tacoma were against the measure by rather substantial percentages. Everett did another flipflop and voted dry, along with Bellingham. The new dry law would take effect on January 1, 1916.

NOW, ABOUT THAT FORKED TONGUE

And, as if Governor Lister didn't have enough problems already, the Northwest Indians chose his administration to start demanding that at least one portion of Governor Stevens' treaties be honored . . . the part about their right to hunt and fish in all their usual and accustomed places.

Jack James and Joe Peters of the Nisqually tribe, arrested for killing a deer out of season, were hailed before Olympia justice of the peace Walter Crosby. They asked for conviction in order to appeal the case to the supreme court. U. S. District Attorney Clay Allen was sympathetic, declaring that he would fight the case all the way to the United States supreme court if necessary. Two of the participants in the Medicine creek treaty testified in the case, Hazzard Stevens and Jim Yelout, Nisqually chief, whose father had been one of the signers of the treaty.

Stevens said it was his understanding and that of the Indians that they were given unlimited rights to hunt and fish. *"I don't think the whites, now that the Indians are rapidly dwindling and unable to put up a fight, should back up on the agreement made more than sixty years ago,"* Stevens declared. *"It is a matter of right and wrong. The treaty is specific in giving the Indians the right to hunt and fish wherever they want to."**

Chief Yelout's testimony was similar in context if not in language: *"Governor Stevens he say Injuns give white man all their lands; the timber. Injun say can have lands and timber, all they want is the* muck-a-muck (food). *Governor Stevens he say that all right. Injuns can have all fish, all clams, all deer and bear and grouse and elk; all game they want any time. No have to pay license like man from Europe."***

It was the opening skirmish in a resumption of the fight for survival led by Leschi in 1856 and continuing to the present day.

WHAT'S GOOD FOR THE
LIGHT AND POWER COMPANY . . .

There had, of course, been less sensational developments in Olympia in 1915.

The Olympia Light and Power company, locked in its periodic conflict with the city council and mayor regarding the paving of the car tracks on the newly-paved streets, which now extended to the city limits, found time to be innovative. Early in the year it became a pioneer in traction company street car-bus service when it announced an auto feeder service from the end of the car line on the east side to Lacey and the Boulevard road. At first the operation was maintained by ordinary touring cars, but by April the *Olympian* was able to announce that *"one of the finest little auto busses will make its initial run for the Olympia Light and Power company on the Lacey extension route tomorrow morning. The ten-passenger body is on an Overland chassis and has a 35-horsepower engine. 'O. L. & P. Co.' is neatly painted along both sides of the body."*

The company also offered to provide all local businesses with electric display signs free of charge, amortizing the costs entirely through the increased use of power. A considerable

number of them took advantage of this bargain and the downtown section was brightened if not beautified by the latest electronic advancement. It was probably a fortunate development at the time, for Mayor Mottman, still an ardent partisan of frugality in government, had come to the conclusion that the power company was charging too much to keep the street lights on until the customary hour of 11 p.m. C. B. Mann, who was planning to run for mayor in the December election, called Mottman's economy move "a suicidal course . . . an insult to the state which has established its capital here."

The council eventually mustered its courage and overrode the mayor's blackout order. Mottman countered with the charge that power company Superintendent Faulkner "has carried the city council or mayor . . . or both . . . around in his pocket like a watch charm for 25 years." Faulkner, in a concilatory mood, offered to turn the street lights back on until September without charge, but it didn't do much good. A shingle mill upstream from the power house built a dam and the flow over Tumwater falls temporarily diminished to a trickle. Lights dimmed to a flicker and street cars couldn't make it up the hill until the mill pond filled up and the waters of the Deschutes again flowed over the falls. By that time the power company had agreed to a new street lighting contract at a nearly 50 percent reduction over the old rate, but Mottman was not lulled into a false sense of security. He announced that he was going to run for another term because "to withdraw now would be cowardly. I must straighten up the city's water and light proposition." He charged that the power company planned to back candidates for all city offices on both tickets in order to defeat him. Faulkner described the mayor's expose' as "malicious misstatement," but Mottman didn't bother to reply. He was busy addressing the PTA and setting them straight on the role of parents and teachers alike. "High schools are a failure if they don't teach a trade," he told them. "Fifty percent of the parents don't govern their children. Children should obey. You ought to use the stick when it's needed."

LAND SAKES! WHAT NEXT?

While its chief executive preached the old-fashioned virtues of frugality, hard work and discipline, Olympia took a further step toward the age of flight and jet set frivolity. Aviator G. W. Stromer had come to town in February to

---

* *Morning Olympian*, July 28 and August 1, 1915.

273

lobby for an aviation corps in the state militia. He had arrived in his "hydro-airplane," which he moored at the city float and offered to place at the service of state officials for trial flights. Governor Lister passed up the chance to be the state's first flying governor, explaining that "the legislature keeps me up in the air enough as it is."

Representative Reuben Fleet of Montesano, who later became a pioneer of the airline industry, made a flight, as did several of the other more daring legislators. Between official flights, Stromer offered cut-rate sightseeing flights to Olympia citizens. Mrs. C. Nommensen, wife of a local jeweler, became the first Olympia woman to make an aerial flight. Mrs. Mowell and Mrs. Ingham were waiting in line, but by the time Mrs. Nommensen's flight ended it was getting dark and the aviator had to head back for Tacoma. He had gotten lost on the way down and been forced to land at the shoreside village of Vaughan to ask directions. He didn't want to take any chances on getting back.

Mrs. Nommensen declared herself as delighted with her experience, but it was felt that she had suffered some sort of temporary brain damage from the altitude when she added that she hoped some day to ride in an airplane all the way to San Francisco.

The wireless telephone was also declared a success when a message was flashed to the Olympia office of the Pacific Telephone and Telegraph company from the east coast by way of San Francisco and Seattle. Many thought that the company's Olympia manager, Robert Daragh, was suffering from the same kind of delusions as Mrs. Nommensen when he declared that "it will soon be possible to talk around the world by a system of relays."

The home radio was still far enough in the future that wireless enthusiast Daragh hadn't yet envisioned it. Olympia baseball fans flocked to the *Olympian-Recorder* building at 3rd and Main to hear the telegraph reports on the world series between the Boston Red Sox and Philadelphia Nationals shouted by megaphone from a second story window. Boston won the series. The excitement of the series was scarcely equalled by the enthusiasm at the Carlyon park diamond when slugger Pete Flagstead, described by the *Olympian* as "a virtual Ty Cobb," led the Olympia Senators to victory in the Southwest Washington minor league.

The war in Europe still seemed far distant, although the increasingly aggressive German U-boat campaign was awakening American resentment which became steadily deeper following the torpedoing of the first American merchant vessel, the full-rigged ship *Wm. P. Frye* in March. Indignation reached a new high following the torpedoing of the Cunard liner *Lusitania* later in the year, and patriotism kept pace with indignation. On July 14 the legendary Liberty Bell, en route from Philadelphia to the San Francisco Panama-Pacific exposition, arrived at Olympia by special train and was placed on exhibition at the Northern Pacific yards. Superintendent Faulkner had the street lights turned on for the first time in four months and a crowd of 15,000 welcomed the symbol of American independence. Three bands joined in the national anthem while, according to the *Olympian*, *"hats were tossed in the air and patriotism reigned in every heart."* The crowd was described as the largest in Olympia history and the *Olympian* reporter seemed on the verge of sentimental tears as he recorded that *"pretty maidens stand in line to press their fair lips to the bell's metallic form."*

That lone-time mainstay of the town's industrial economy, the brewery, was closing down its production of famed Olympia beer while its officers cast about for other means of utilizing its plant. The Olympia Dairy Products company was organized, with Adolph Schmidt as president, for the cold storage of eggs and dairy products. Later in the year the Fruju Fruit Products company was formed to produce fruit beverages. After some experimentation with other flavors, the firm concentrated on "Appleju." Its label carried the traditional "It's the Water" trademark, and there were rumors that unless the contents were stored in a cool place, fermentation might take place, producing an illegally alcoholic beverage. Appleju should have caught on, but it didn't, and before long the big Tumwater brewery locked its doors to wait out the long drought which beset the state and nation.

Any tendency on the part of Olympians to grow complacent was taken care of by the *Douglas County Press*, a Waterville Democratic weekly, which reported rumors of a new effort to move the capital to "a more central location." Owners of a new land development at Three-Tree Point between Seattle and Tacoma were said to be drafting a referendum for the 1916 election which would move the seat of government to their as yet unborn community *"as part of a selling scheme on a monstrous scale."*

Citizens of the current capital city viewed the scheme as monstrous indeed, and kept a wary eye on the 1916 ballot. The referendum did not appear upon it.

The new year of 1916 arrived amidst scenes of mixed revelry and melancholy. The *Recorder* of January 1 noted that *"a white blanket of snow fell upon the streets last night emblematic of the new state of purity."* The 17 Olympia saloons had entertained capacity crowds at their own wakes. By midnight their remaining stocks had vanished. Thirsty citizens had been buying up cases of potables for months and storing them against the coming drought. At dawn on January 1, wreaths of black crepe were seen on the locked doors of most of the saloons, *"in tribute to the death of Bacchus, who passed away with the dying of the year 1915."*

The *Recorder's* obituary on the rosy-cheeked god of conviviality was, in the words of Mark Twain, "somewhat exaggerated," although there was considerable evidence at the time that the city and state had, indeed, gone dry.

The *Recorder* story pointed out that *"almost every keg and bottle were drained dry and there are not over two cases and a barrel left at the brewery and Seattle and Tacoma wholesalers are sold out."*

The saloons might be gone forever, at least in their traditional form, but the flow of alcoholic beverages had not been dammed. Out-of-state mail order liquor houses had begun advertising their postpaid wares in Washington newspapers even before the dry law took effect and the little orange liquor import permits from the county auditors' offices became extremely popular. Thurston county Auditor Annie Gaston reported by mid-March that permit requests were averaging seven a day and the demand increased steadily as hoarded stocks were depleted. Seattleites purchased 18,000 permits in August alone, while Spokane, with 44,000 registered voters, accounted for 34,000 permits during the year.

In an emergency situation, one's friendly neighborhood doctor was authorized to issue a prescription for a bottle of drug store whiskey, provided he added detailed directions for the self-administration of the medication. Before the year was over, Police Chief Caton, who kept a Bible on his desk at the police station and had run for congress on the Prohibition party ticket, was complaining about the number of such prescriptions being filled in Olympia drug stores. No less than 123 prescription bottles had been sold in the week ending October 7, he said, adding with some sarcasm that there must be an epidemic of some kind in town. He added that a couple of local practitioners were getting rich on booze prescriptions at from 50¢ to a dollar each. Dr. Partlow challenged the chief to name names, which he did. His survey was duly published in the *Olympian:* Dr. Riley, 35; Dr. Mustard, 26; Dr. H. W. Partlow, 16; Dr. K. L. Partlow, 11; Dr. Pettit, 8; Dr. Story, 5; Dr. Murphy, 4; Drs. Beach and Roberts, 2 each, and Drs. Bridgford, Longaker and Redpath, one each.

By December old Dr. Riley, a pioneer physician who believed, with "Old Bacchus," ship's surgeon of Captain Bligh's *Bounty,* that enough rum would cure anything, tried Chief Caton's patience too far when a very drunk logger was picked up with no less than two quarts of Doc Riley's prescription booze in his possession. The logger was fined $50 and costs in police court and Dr. Riley was arrested for being too free with his prescriptions. City Attorney George Bigelow, who brought the charges against the doctor, was lectured in the courtroom by the defendant, who told him, according to the *Olympian,* *"Whiskey is good for everything and the only real cure. Take a little whiskey and put some hot water in it and a little lemon and honey and it's mighty good for you. Try some some time . . . get a prescription."*

Bigelow, like Caton a teetotaller, was not amused by the old doctor's homely advice, but the justice court jury of six male admirers of old Doc Riley was. After hearing his explanation of why he led the prescription-issuing list . . . "I have a bigger trade than the other doctors do" . . . they found him not guilty.

Despite such liberality, the demand for liquor exceeded the supply. By the end of the year moonshine whiskey of doubtful quality was selling for as much as $5 00 a quart. Many of the saloons reopened as 'soft drink shops," most of them thinly disguised speakeasies. Enterprising hoodlums were quick to scent the potential profits and highjacking and violence began to take their places as integral parts of the dry years.

Out-of-town newspapers frequently pointed to the capital city as a center of the illegal booze industry, carrying lurid stories of "blind pigs" bootleg liquor and other evasions of the dry laws. Prosecutor George Yantis and Chief Caton protested that there was no truth to the reports . . . that "there is almost no drunkenness in Olympia." The chief, on March 2, claimed that his department had made only one drunk arrest since January 1, compared to 41 in the last month of 1915. He added over-optimistically that he expected no drunkenness at all when the hoarded stocks of liquor were used up.

Things started picking up soon after Chief Caton's hopeful forecast. Officer LeBarre, a former cowboy who had gained fame as the first Olympia policeman to lasso troublesome drunks, roped and brought in a logger who had been quaffing from a bottle of Jamaica ginger. The logger was soon followed by a local laborer who had consumed a half gallon of cider which turned out to be hard. "I never had cider effect me that way before," he told Justice Crosby as he was sent off to jail to sit out a $14 fine. He was soon joined by Raleigh George, who had absentmindedly consumed his whole bottle of prescription whiskey at a single sitting. Two more miscreants were picked up for ignoring their doctor's neatly-lettered prescription instructions . . . "take one teaspoonful in hot water before retiring."

BETTER SHOES THAN BOOZE

By the Fourth of July, when loggers from the outlying camps traditionally arrived in town to celebrate, the number of jailed drunks became a drain on the police budget and they were ordered to work eight hours a day on the Priest Point park woodpile. Those who complied continued to get three meals a day. Malingerers got only one.

Wet forces hoped that the many problems which beset the enforcement of the dry law would change public opinion and pave the way for initiative measures to open things up again, or at least permit civilized drinking on a limited basis.

The dries did not let their victory result in over-confidence. They continued a propaganda barrage, focused mainly on the alleged benefits of enforced abstinence. They claimed that drunk arrests were down 65 percent in Spokane and 80 percent in Walla Walla; that govern-

ment costs had been reduced markedly, tax delinquencies had been cut 50 percent, bills were being paid on time and bank deposits were up. George Cotterill, retired as mayor of Seattle by Hi Gill, who had come back as an advocate of civic purity, had been appointed to the highway commission. He reported that not a single new convict had entered the penitentiary since the dry law went into effect; that as a result of the convict shortage it had become necessary to hire outside labor to convert large rocks into small ones for surfacing the state highways.

Even the doughty Alden J. Blethen of the Seattle *Times* became convinced that prohibition was good for business. Conceding that *"my paper fought its damndest against prohibition,"* he had decided that *"it's better to buy shoes than booze."*

Members of the scientific community added their voices to the dry chorus. Much publicity was given to laboratory evidence that alcohol

County courthouse and Columbia Hall.

The (Captain Nathaniel) Crosby House, Tumwater.

was a poison, producing brain damage and defective children and contributing to crime, prostitution and poverty. Many scientists publicly gave up drinking and a considerable number of laymen followed suit, much as in the case of cigarettes following the surgeon-general's reports of the 1960s.

The wets managed to get two of their measures on the ballot; one to permit in-state breweries to manufacture beer for direct sale to customers and a new version of the "hotelmen's bill" permitting sale of liquor by larger hotels which had dining facilities. Another, which would have repealed the dry law entirely, failed to attract enough signatures to qualify.

Although most of the economic benefits claimed by the dries were more the result of the newly-opened Panama canal and the growing wartime economy, most people attributed them to prohibition and it became increasingly evident throughout the year that the spirit of temperance was stronger than it had ever been before. Even Seattle's Mayor Gill, the long-time advocate of a wide open town, had become as objectionably pious as a reformed prostitute. He personally led his cops in raids on premises suspected of harboring illicit booze and manfully swung an ax to demolish everything in sight whether evidence was unearthed or not. Ignoring constitutional niceties in regard to illegal search and seizure, Gill's dry squad even burst into the mansions of such establishment leaders as William Boeing and D. E. Skinner, confiscating hoarded stocks of excellent wine and liquors. Both Boeing, who was building airplanes in a small way, and Skinner, who was building ships in a large way, threatened to move their homes and businesses to a more civilized state.

In Olympia, Mayor Mottman resisted any impulse to similarly gain revenge on his old enemies of the business establishment, but Chief Caton and his men vied with Sheriff McCorkle and Prosecutor Yantis in ferreting out and raiding dens of alcoholic iniquity. McCorkle and Yantis scored first, on February 28, and gained the distinction of making the first prohibition raid in the town's history, although the *Olympian* reported that *"the leader of Yantis's raid was a gumshoe person who has been sleuthing here for several weeks"* and that Chief Caton *"was also along."*

The Taylor brothers' former Oxford saloon, now a bowling alley, pool room and dispensary of soft drinks was the first to be raided. It yielded a pint of whiskey and "part of a quart of ginger brandy." A room above the water company office at 3rd and Columbia was next on the agenda. The raiders emerged with two dozen empty whiskey bottles.

Prosecutor Yantis spoke in ringing tones to the crowd which had assembled to watch the forces of purity in action. "I am going to enforce the law," he said.

ARSENAL OF DEMOCRACY

Despite the sensational affairs at home, the local papers of 1916 increasingly headlined the warlike events in Europe and Mexico. General "Black Jack" Pershing had been dispatched south of the border to put an end to the depradations of bandit Pancho Villa and the 2nd Regiment of the Washington National Guard was with him. As in later wars, the headlines were often misleading. On April 1 the Olympia dailies proclaimed, "BEATEN BANDIT HIDES IN TERROR," but three days later their story had changed to "VILLA FOOLS PURSUERS . . . SEND MORE TROOPS TO PERSHING."

The terrors of a new technological warfare were splashed across the front pages during those spring days of 1916 . . . "ZEPPS RAID ENGLAND: KILL 28: WOUND 44" . . . "WAR IMMINENT! PRESIDENT TELLS CONGRESS SUB CAMPAIGN MUST STOP" . . . "11TH BRITISH BATTLESHIP SUNK!"

By September the new wartime economy was sweeping away the hard times as the United States girded to make itself "the Arsenal of Democracy." The Olympia Shipbuilding company was formed, with E. R. Ward of Seattle as president and local business leaders J. L. Peters, C. J. Lord and P. H. Carlyon as officers. A five block area on the new fill north of the Standard Oil plant was taken over and work was rushed on launching ways and plant buildings. By mid-November the keel of the 250-foot auxiliary schooner for Norwegian owners had been laid. A month later 400 men were working day and night shifts to frame the first ship and the keel of a second had been laid.

The change in the status of working men was dramatic. In January 31 jobless men were living at the city jail. Food and blankets were contributed by the more fortunate citizens and the men earned their keep by clearing snow from the streets or doing odd jobs. By fall the new shipyards and war-related industries were springing up throughout the Puget Sound basin and jobs could be had for the asking . . . and at premium pay.

Olympia labor unions, which hadn't been a very potent force in the town's limited industrial community, began to feel their oats. Six hundred members of the local labor organizations formed the Home Labor League, with master carpenter A. J. Phillips as president, "to see that home labor gets the local jobs."

Another long-delayed promise of increased prosperity was made good in January when the first train of the Union Pacific's Oregon, Washington Railway and Navigation company came clanging into the yards at 4th and Jefferson. The new brick station wasn't completed, but a large crowd was on hand and about a hundred passengers, including Chamber of Commerce officials and other civic dignitaries, jammed themselves aboard the day coach behind the baggage car and locomotive for the 7½-mile trip to Chambers prairie and the junction with the Tacoma-Portland main line. Doc Carlyon, whose industrial fill and belt line railway had provided the potential traffic to bring the new line to town, made a speech and broke a bottle over the locomotive pilot, christening it "Olympia Booster Train No. 1."

Two passenger trains were subsequently scheduled each way daily over the new short line, which reached the downtown depot from the south rather than from the north over the original Union Pacific grade of the 1890s. The dredgers had deposited some of their spoil along the edge of the old right of way, filling in a couple of tidal coves and making possible the completion of East Bay drive to Priest Point park.

Another civic celebration was staged, two weeks after the departure of the inaugural train, to dedicate the new depot. Mayor Mottman formally welcomed the railroad on behalf of the city and Governor Lister predicted that the Northern Pacific would soon replace its original wooden station with a more pretentious structure.*

*He was partly right, but his timing was off. It took the NP about fifty years to get the job done.

A month after the Union Pacific arrived the Northern Pacific abandoned the Port Townsend Southern branch line to Tenino. The prairie right of way, surveyed and cleared by the volunteer labor of Olympia citizens nearly a half century before, reverted to brush and pasture land and the brave little Olympia-Tenino railroad soon faded from memory.

It seemed for a while that even the tidal estuary along which the Olympia-Tenino line had meandered from Tumwater to Olympia might soon disappear. Doc Carlyon, the civic visionary, unveiled a plan to dam the Deschutes waterway at the site of the 4th street bridge and create a fresh water lake and park to reflect the future buildings of the hilltop capitol group at all stages of the tide. Carlyon's proposal included a tree-lined boulevard along the old railroad right of way on the west shore and an "auto hotel" on the forested slope across fromthe capitol grounds.

The city fathers embraced the Carlyon plan fervently. Not only would it provide the town with a lakeside park in the city center; it would solve the problem of that pesky draw-span on the 4th street bridge. The state land commissioner and capitol commission also viewed the Capitol Lake proposal favorably, but there were voices of dissent. The Olympia Light and Power company feared the damming of the waterway would reduce the power output of Tumwater falls and the brewery wanted to continue to ship Appleju by water. The argument was settled by the state attorney general, who ruled that Land Commissioner Savidge didn't have the authority to vacate a part of the Deschutes waterway to build a lake.

FRUSTRATIONS OF A FRUGAL MAYOR

Carlyon's Capitol Lake project was filed away for several more decades and the city council received notice from the army engineers that it was going to have to build a new draw-bridge across the waterway.

City government faced other frustrating problems, Mayor Mottman in particular facing the old political truth that the citizens favor government economy in principal but become annoyed when it inconveniences them. Even the steadfast mayor felt some doubts about the wisdom of having blacked out the street lights when he was grazed by an automobile while crossing 4th street from his store in the gloom of night.

More trouble beset him when he changed the current procedure for raising the 4th street draw span. The city hall janitor had been assigned the additional duty of bridge tender and was paid an additional $30 a month for rushing to the span when a tugboat whistled.The mayor, in the interests of municipal frugality, assigned the bridge-tending duties to the police department . . . without increase in pay. When the next boat whistled for the draw, Officer McReavey dashed to the bridge and set the rickety machinery in motion. The span rose ponderously, the tug started under . . . and something slipped. The span descended again, knocked the smokestack off the tug and ground to a lop-sided stop, the motor smoking and the whole mechanism hopelessly jammed.

This was the culmination of a frustrating year for Chief Caton. He had puttered about town tacking up "No Spitting" signs on telephone poles. He had issued orders to his force to blaze away with their revolvers when they encountered a stray dog which could run faster than they could. Since a well-conditioned turtle could outrun the average Olympia policeman,* there was a great deal of gunfire. The chief had even occupied himself in providing the town's first automotive traffic signals. He painted the manhole covers white on downtown street intersections and ordered the local motorists to go around them in the manner of racing yachts rounding marker buoys. He even inaugurated the taking of thumb prints of booked prisoners for the national crime clearing house at Leavenworth penitentiary. But all his busy work was forgotten in the public downfall of Officer McReavey and the 4th street draw-span.

---

*The *Recorder* of May 1 described a case in point when William Thompson, *"an old man with rheumatism,"* suspected of having stolen brass from local junk yards, escaped from Officer LaBarre, dashed up alleys, through the Bolster and Barnes feed store and down Water street to a dock, from which he jumped 16 feet into the Deschutes waterway. The tide happened to be out at the time and the force of his leap drove him into the mud up to his waist, giving Officer LaBarre time to come puffing up and haul him out with a rope. It was the opinion of the *Recorder* that *"LaBarre did well for a portly man."*

The fire department didn't escape the mayor's pruning knife either. The purchase of the new auto fire trucks had so depleted the firefighting budget that no new fire hose had been purchased since 1909. In mid-June the Capital City Iron Works caught fire and the mechanized fire department responded quickly. Hose was laid from the nearest hydrants . . . and immediately burst. The process was repeated several times until a single line was found that would hold. One of the engines was sent back to the station to bring a second line. It was coupled up and burst in three places as soon as pressure was applied. The firemen were drenched and furious and devoted themselves to denunciations of the mayor, the fire having been extinguished by company equipment.

The morale of the smoke-eaters was further depressed in August when they were summoned to a blaze at the home of Chester Chatfield, a salesman for the Olympia Knitting Mills. The hose broke five times, a few drops of water drizzling from the nozzles while hundreds of gallons sprayed the firemen and spectators and flowed down the gutters. The fire department spent five minutes in further caucus regarding the pernurious mayor while more hose was brought from the fire station and the fire at the Chatfield house raged out of control.

Mottman threw up his hands, pushed through an ordinance to equip the fire department with 1,500 feet of new hose and 86 new fire hydrants, recommended construction of a new concrete bridge across the Deschutes waterway and announced that he was retiring from public life. Jesse T. Mills filed on the Republican ticket and swept the Smokehouse gang back into power over Charles Talcott and the Citizens party. Like practically every other candidate for office in 1916, the former sheriff promised to stamp out the bootleggers.

HOW DRY WE ARE

Aspirants for policital office at all levels vied with one another to be the dryest. Former Governor McBridge tried hard to overcome his past saloon support by campaigning loudly against both wet initiatives, but the Democrats insisted on harping on his past record. His

279

major opponent for the Republican nomination, "Colonel" Roland Hartley, toured the state by atuomobile, ignoring the wet vs. dry issue and concentrating on the anti-union open shop issue. As a leader of the Everett industrial establishment, he was a veteran strike-buster and had helped organize the vigilante force which had specialized in beating members of the IWW half to death and running them out of town. The battle had culminated in a confrontation at the city dock when a steamboat load of Wobbly "free speech marchers" tried to land in defiance of the orders of Snohomish county Sheriff Donald McRae. Wobblies and vigilantes died in the ensuing hail of bullets as the "Everett Massacre" took its place in Northwest history, and Roland Hartley's attitude toward organized labor moved about as far to the right as it was possible to get.

McBride beat Hartley and seven other candidates for the Republican nomination. Lister won the Democratic nomination from his only opponent, W. E. Cass, by an overwhelming 28,620 votes to 3,794. The two nominees then stumped the state in campaigns largely devoted to their total opposition to alcohol in any form. When Lister proclaimed that he had never in his life taken a drink of intoxicating liquor, the *Olympian* observed that *"when Lister was paving 4th street he had his headquarters in the Oxford bar."*

*"He's English,"** the writer explained, *"and thus partial to highballs in a tall glass,"* although he conceded that *"he never reached a state of talkativeness or near inebriation."*

Woodrow Wilson was returned victoriously to office on the campaign slogan "He Kept Us Out of War," carrying Washington by more than 21,000 votes over Republican Charles Evans Hughes. Lister was returned for a second term* by a margin of nearly 14,000 over

---

*Lister, born in Halifax, England, in 1870, was the only governor of Washington state of foreign birth. Two territorial governors, Pickering and Salomon, were naturalized citizens. Lister had come to Tacoma with his family at the age of 14, was elected to the city council at the age of 23 and appointed chairman of the state board of control by Governor Rogers four years later.

---

*It is interesting to note that only two non-Republicans, Rogers and Lister, were elected governor in the 43 years from statehood in 1889 to 1932. The only governors elected to second terms during that period were Populist Rogers and Democrat Lister.

McBride and C. C. Dill was returned to congress, but all other offices, along with a majority of the legislature, went to the Republicans.

All initiatives were defeated, the brewers' bill by 146,000; the hotel men's bill by an overhwlming 215,000. The voters also elected the dryest contingent of legislators in the state's history.

The heat generated by the wet-dry campaign of 1916 was dramatized when Tom O'Leary, successful candidate for Thurston county prosecuting attorney, sued the publisher of the Tenino *Journal* for printing a photo of some of his political supporters sharing a bottle of whiskey.

The cause of enforced temperance was clearly victorious in Washington. Even the traditionally wet cities of Seattle and Spokane had voted dry on the 1916 amendments. The old-fashioned saloon had, in fact, outlived its function in society as the poor man's club. With the onset of wartime prosperity, workingmen were buying silk shirts and Fords and moving into the middle class. The automobile, the motion picture theater and, in a few years, the radio, provided spare-time entertainment and relaxation, and the former patrons of Olympia's 17 vanished saloons didn't miss them as much as they had expected to.

1917

The 15th legislature began to assemble, as usual, in early January of 1917 amid "slush" and snow, although its members had escaped the worst blizzard of the 20th century, which had dumped three feet of snow on the captial city in February of 1916. For the first time in many sessions no pre-legislative caucus was held, patronage committees having been appointed to fill staff positions, theoretically at least on the basis of ability and experience. All clerks, it was announced, would have to be qualified stenographers and typists would be required to prove that they could actually type. It sounded businesslike and logical, but the new job specifications simply couldn't be met by many of the legislators political and personal favorites. A bitter patronage fight broke out in the house within 24 hours and committee assignments were held up until some compromises were worked out.

Governor Lister was incommunicado, locked in his office working on his message to the legislature. His inaccessibility further widened the gulf between the executive and legislative branches of state government as leading Republican senators and representatives who called to offer support for executive request bills were turned away. Although it wasn't generally known yet, the governor's once robust health had broken down under the strain of office and of campaigning as a Democrat in a solidly Republican state. The responsibilities of the chief executive had increased tremendously during his years in office. The time was past when a Washington governor could lead a quiet life in the quiet capital city, riding the street car home from his office in time to milk the family cow. Edmond Meany described the change in his *Governors of Washington*, published by the University of Washington in 1913:

"The extra gubernatorial duties have reached a climax in Gov. Lister's term. Eastern conferences of all the governors, Western conferences of groups of them, two expositions in California, the open Columbia river celebrations and other occasions have called him out of state. Within the state events have frequently arranged themselves seemingly in chains so that the governor makes a tour with functions in the morning, afternoon and evening for a week at a time. His friends marvel that he is able to keep his health and his good nature throughout the never-ending strain. He is still in the prime of life. There is every probability that he will continue for years an energetic, robust and useful citizen of the state he loves after his release from the burdens of public office."

Professor Meany's usually reliable gift of prophecy was faulty in this case.

Since his little book was written, the gathering clouds of war had further complicated the governor's life as the state geared for the worldwide conflict which seemed increasingly inevitable. It seems probable that he was gathering his strength for the coming legislative ordeal rather than locking himself up simply to concentrate on his literary efforts.

Both houses met shortly after noon on January 8. Guy E. Kelley of Pierce was quickly and unanimously elected speaker of the house after the call to order by Chief Clerk Maybury. Senator Nichols of King was just as quickly elected president pro-tem after Lieutenant Governor Hart banged the opening gavel and

advised the new senators to vote no on any bills they didn't understand. "Many think we have enough laws now," he explained.

NO PLACE FOR A GENTLEMAN

The senators took note of the current direction of the wind of public opinion by passing a joint memorial to congress asking for a national prohibition amendment even before they approved the bill appropriating funds for their own expenses. Despite the businesslike beginning, the 15th legislature ended up spending just under $200,000, which was almost twice as much as any other in the state's history to date.

A truce was declared in the running battle with the press, a third floor room in the capitol being fitted up with telephones and typewriters for the convenience of the state's political correspondents. This created some muttering among the few remaining old-line politicians and the complaints increased when the second biggest committee room in the building was converted to a "ladies card room" for the wives of senators. With 51 senate and 57 house committees, according to the *Recorder*, "scurrying about the state capitol in wild desperation seeking some place to light," there was considerable feeling that the senatorial wives had gotten more than their share of the available space. The press became similarly outraged when it was discovered that the taxpayers had been hit for the costs of furnishing and decorating the room, including a French mirror, $5.00; three card tables, $9.00; six oak rockers, $24.70; two fine oak tables, $27; two Wilton rugs, $65: 12 folding chairs, $12; and four yards of cretonne (price unspecified).

What with all the hanging of cretonne, lack of bourbon and cigars and pampering of the press, prohibitionists and females, old-line Senator Linck Davis, defeated in the previous year's primaries, may have been right when he grumbled that "the legislature is no longer a place for a gentleman anyway."

It was not exactly a haven for women either. Only one lady legislator, Representative Ina P. Williams of North Yakima, appeared for the 1917 session. A 41-year-old Republican and mother of five children, Mrs. Williams had been left an orphan at the age of 10; had begun earning her own living as a school teacher at the age of 15. She held her own well in her male-dominated environment. When a male colleague asked her, "Where are your children?" she replied "Where are yours?"

"Home with my wife, of course," he huffed.

"Mine are home with my husband," Mrs. Williams told him, no doubt enjoying the feminine prerogative of getting in the last word.

ECONOMY, MORALITY AND PATRIOTISM

Governor Lister addressed the legislature on January 10, pointing out that the state treasury contained a million dollar surplus despite the fact that he had inherited a sizeable deficit when he took office. He urged the retirement of all outstanding bonds as quickly as possible, the holding of the line on highway taxes to one mill and the passage of an absolute prohibition measure similar to those recently approved by the legislatures of Oregon and Idaho.

The legislature went through motions of attempting to rid itself of the clinging embrace of lobbyists. Lieutenant Governor Hart observed with uncharacteristic naivete that they weren't really needed because copies of all bills would be mailed to any interested party upon request. Senator Phipps of the rules committee was quoted by the *Recorder* as making an even more outspoken speech on the subject:

"Corporations and other interests who pay agents $200 to $300 a session to keep informed on bills introduced and presumably to retard or expedite legislation at their will, are simply wasting their money, for these lobbyists have absolutely no influence with us whatever and they are generally discredited. They are grafters pure and simple."

No doubt the more sensitive of the lobbyists winced at the attacks on their professional ethics and effectiveness and the more effective must have resented Senator Phipps' charge that they were either pure or simple, which they certainly were not.

The number of lobbyists was not noticeably diminished by the efforts of the senate, either then or subsequently.

There were the usual number of personal encounters in the chambers, one of the more spectacular involving Senators Ed Brown of Whatcom and Howard Taylor of King. An altercation prompted by a Brown bill to require the muzzling of all dogs in areas where rabies existed, moved Taylor to strike his colleague "a stinging blow on the face which was plainly heard throughout the chamber." Brown, who was recovering from a broken leg, retaliated by whacking Senator Taylor about his head and shoulders with his cane until the combatants were separated by other senators.

There were the usual weekend junkets to the livelier and larger cities of the Sound. Joshua Green, president of the Puget Sound Navigation company, which had established a virtual monopoly on the steamboat business, dispatched his fine steel steamer *Sioux* to Percival's dock to transport 300 legislators, state officials and political hangers-on to the annual Lincoln day banquet in Seattle. Cannon fire was heard in Olympia for the first time in years when the *Sioux* fired thunderous salutes on entering and leaving the harbor.

There were the usual trivial bills, including a last-ditch effort by the Pierce county delegation to get the name of Mt. Rainier changed to Mt. Tacoma. The first venture into tourist promotion was made with a $45,000 appropriation for a joint advertising campaign with Oregon and British Columbia. Three hundred Centralia boosters descended on the lawmakers wearing large tags which proclaimed "We Want a State Normal School at Centralia." A bill by Victor Zednick requiring military training in all high schools was defeated, but a military reserve act was passed, permitting Pierce county to donate a large tract of land near American Lake to the federal government for the establishment of a new army post. A bank deposit guarantee bill was approved, along with a measure prescribing a single moral standard for both sexes. The increasing war hysteria prompted passage of a regressive criminal syndicalism law, which was described by its sponsors as "designed to end IWW riots."

Governor Lister enraged the legislators by vetoing an additional $10,000 appropriation for their last week in session. They quickly passed it over his veto and retaliated by ordering an investigation of his personal and political friend, State Printer Frank M. Lamborn. Lister had asked for an investigation of the state auditor's office. This was turned down by the lawmakers, but they appropriated $43,-000 to investigate practically every other department of state government. Lister vetoed that bill after the session had adjourned. He also redlined measures eliminating osteopaths from the state medical board and creating a state board of chiropractic, requiring regulation of jitneys in second and third class cities, and eliminated some of the more obvious pork barrel segments of the omnibus appropriations bill. Another one million dollar appropriation to complete the Temple of Justice and begin construction of the capitol group became law without his signature.

But prohibition and capital punishment were the overwhelming issue of the 1917 session.

House bill 4, introduced by Representative W. C. Elliott in the opening days of the session, was a bone dry prohibition measure advocated by the Grange and the WCTU. It would end the mail order permit system except for clergymen and druggists and eager members vied with one another in offering amendments to dry up even these meageer sources of supply.

Superintendent Conger of the Anti-Saloon League had opposed the introduction of the bone dry law. His time table still called for a more gradual attack on Demon Rum and he feared the Elliott bill was so radical that it might result in a public opinion backlash. Although he couldn't very well fight it openly, he made no secret of his lack of enthusiasm. When Speaker Kelley invited him to take the podium during debate on the bill, he declined politely and remained in the gallery.

House bill 3 passed overwhelmingly . . . 75 to 18 in the house; 46 to three in the senate. Most of the opposition, Such as it was, came from those who felt the people should be given the final say on the matter by referendum. Lister promptly signed the prohibition law, surrounded by WCTU ladies, Grangers, ASL officials who had decided to get in on the act at the last minute, and the dryest of the dry legislators.

The state would, presumably, go bone dry 90 days after the adjournment of the legislature.

The remaining devotees of Bacchus managed to stave off the evil day by procuring 23,000 valid signatures on a referendum petition submitting the prohibition issue to the people, but their victory was a hollow one. The federal government had already prohibited mail shipments of liquor into states with dry laws, regardless of whether or not a permit system was authorized and the ardently dry state supreme court, disregarding the referendum, upheld the conviction of a Tacoma Italian who had been caught making a few gallons of wine for his own use.

RETURN OF THE GALLOWS

The matter of repealing the Goss bill* of 1913, which had abolished section 12, page 78 of the laws of 1854 prescribing capital punishment for murder in the first degree, was brought to the attention of the legislators in a much more dramatic manner than the prohibition issue.

The quiet of the capital city and the equanimity of the statehouse were simultaneously shattered at 1:30 p.m. on the afternoon of February 1, 1917. A black-haired giant in workman's clothing strode into the office of the industrial insurance commission as the legislature was about to reconvene after lunch.

The office employees sighed and shook their heads as they recognized John Van Dell, a six-foot-three, 206-pound logger, who had been haunting the office and making a nuisance of himself for days. Six months earlier, while working in the woods at Bordeaux, he had been struck by a broken haul-back line and hurled 20 feet into the underbrush, landing on his back. He was taken to St. Peters hospital, from which he had only recently been discharged. He filed for industrial insurance compensation of $30 a month, claiming that he had been totally disabled. Dr. J. W. Mowell, the commission surgeon, reported the logger's injuries as "superficial" and he was offered a final payment of $50 as full settlement of his claim.

Van Dell had been waiting at the office when it opened that morning. He buttonholed Commissioner E. W. Olson when he arrived, but the commissioner brushed him off with the comment that the case had been closed and couldn't be reopened. Van Dell was then heard to utter a statement which was to be more widely quoted than any oratory of the legislators down the hall and would grimly affect the lives . . . and deaths . . . of 58 convicted murderers over the next 47 years:

"By God, the state of Washington will take care of me all the rest of my life!"

Following a later unsuccessful attempt to enter Olson's private office, the big logger left

---

*Representative Francis P. Goss, King county journalist, had first introduced his bill substituting life imprisonment for hanging at the 1911 session. Similar bills had failed to pass in 1897, 1899, 1901 and 1907. The reform-minded legislators of 1913 passed the Goss bill after one of the most heated legislative debates in history.

the capitol, cut across Sylvester park and strode down Main street to Mills and Cowles hardware store, where he bought a 38-caliber revolver and a box of ammunition. He then walked back up Main street to Harbst's soft drink and card rooms, where he unwrapped and loaded the weapon; then returned to the capitol. He arrived at ten minutes to one and was again denied admission to Olson's office. Again he left, but returned 20 minutes later, moving grimly toward the closed door of the commissioner's office.

"You can't get in there. Mr. Olson is in conference," commission secretary Percy Gilbert told him. Van Dell ignored the secretary and thrust aside a stenographer, Ruby Lenherr, who was blocking his path. He flung open the office door. Olson was talking on the telephone, his back to the door. With him was J. E. Leonard, a former state senator.

"Hello, old timer," Van Dell said pleasantly. Then he fired three shots at point blank range. Two of the bullets struck the commissioner in the head and he slumped over his desk, killed almost instantly. Leonard, too shocked to move, was not injured.

Van Dell then turned and walked quietly from the office, out of the building, and went directly to the sheriff's office in the Thurston county court house on east 4th street. "Better lock me up quick," he told a startled deputy sheriff. "I just killed Olson, the insurance commissioner. He tried to starve me, damn him, and I fixed him." Deputy McCorkle was unbelieving until the huge logger handed him the revolver, the price tag still affixed to the trigger guard and a thin wisp of smoke still curling from the muzzle.

During the ensuing excitement at the state capitol, the fateful words of Van Dell were given wide publicity and the obvious connotation . . . "By God, the State of Washington will care for me all the rest of my life" obviously meant "You can't hang me, so now the tax-payers are going to have to support me."

In vain Van Dell insisted that his statement to Commissioner Olson had not been meant as a cynical death threat. "I couldn't work and I wouldn't beg," he said. "I only meant if they wouldn't pay my claim I'd have to go to the poor house and be supported the rest of my life." The impulse to buy the gun and kill Olson had come suddenly, he said. "It was as if a rope had been tied around my neck. It dragged me to buy the gun. Nothing could have stopped me

that morning. I never thought about whether the state could hang me or not."

No one paid attention to the words of the self-confessed murderer. The *Morning Olympian* editorialized, *"If the law of the state provided capital punishment for murderers, the crimes would be fewer."* Other newspapers throughout the state made similar editorial pronouncements. Senator Cox of Walla Walla, the day after the crime, announced that he would introduce a bill reinstating the death penalty.

On March 13, while the Van Dell murder trial was still in progress, the ubiquitous ex-senator, Leonard, the eye-witness to the Olson shooting, was eating his lunch in a cafeteria across Sylvester Park from the statehouse. A young man entered the restaurant and ordered a roast beef sandwich and milk. Senator Leonard noted approvingly that the young man was extremely polite to the waitress who served him. Then a passerby stopped to look at the menu posted on the cafeteria window and the polite young man appeared to go berserk, leaping to his feet, cursing and waving his arms violently. Senator Leonard, his nerves still unsteady, suggested that somebody call the police and Sergeant Benjamin Peck responded. The agitated young man met him at the door, displayed a long-barreled 38 caliber revolver and gesturing toward the back of the restaurant, told the police sergeant, "The man you want is back there."

There ensued another Keystone Cops episode with elements of slap-stick comedy in contrast to the shocking tragedy of the Olson murder, but at the time it seemed not at all funny to numerous people, including Governor Ernest Lister of the state of Washington. It was another major factor in the public outcry which was to re-erect the gallows at the state penitentiary.

Sergeant Peck was joined at the restaurant by recently appointed Police Chief Harry Cusack and the two officers then engaged in what the *Morning Olympian* described as a "pursuit" of the armed man, who nimbly dodged a Tumwater-bound street car on Main street and crossed Sylvester park toward the statehouse. The pursuit was apparently a slow and stately one, for the strange young man paused at the capitol entrance to engage in conversation with State Treasurer W. W. Sherman, then proceeded to the office of Governor Lister. Leveling his long-barrelled revolver at

Irvin W. Zigaus, the governor's private secretary, he said, "I am a Mason and I want to have this out with the governor and the first one to try to stop me will get it."

He backed toward the open door of the governor's private office, where Lister was in conference with State Adjutant General Maurice Thompson. Understandably gun-shy, they took one look at the intruder's formidable weapon and vacated the office simultaneously and at a much higher rate of speed than was being displayed by the Olympia police, who were still presumably engaged in the "pursuit," but were nowhere in sight. The governor beat the general to the state auditor's office by several lengths and locked himself with the state archives in the auditor's vault.

Hearing the commotion, Chief Clerk Maybury of the house of representatives and his assistant, A. W. Calder, armed themselves with golf clubs and approached the governor's office. The gunman was leaning from a window of the office talking to an Olympia businessman, Charles Dufault. "I won't come down," he explained, "because I would be crucified or burned at the stake like Jesus Christ. They want to make a Roman holiday out of me." Eventually the three men convinced him that he should throw down his gun and surrender to the police officers, who had at last arrived on the scene. This he did, and he was later identified as Charles Lorenz Wagner, 33, who coincidentally had been employed at the same Bordeaux logging camp as Van Dell.

Wagner was committed to the hospital for the insane on March 17, the same day that John Van Dell was sentenced to life imprisonment at the penitentiary.

Three other apparently demented individuals, probably attracted by the recent publicity regarding the insurance commission scandals, invaded the statehouse and added to the nervousness of legislators, state officials and employees during the course of the 15th session.

Governor Lister, still smarting from the indignity of being *"closeted in a vault"* as the *Olympian* tactfully put it, and claiming that he had received threatening letters from the Wobblies, announced publicly that "state officials can expect but little if any protection from the police authorities of Olympia." He demanded a special capitol police force to protect state officials upon whom, according to the governor and the news media, open season appeared to have been declared.

The legislature, which was not then accustomed to going into overtime, adjourned in mid-March without having reinstated capital punishment, but its members did not, during the interim, forget the gunplay which had taken place so uncomfortably close to their chambers. It was a foregone conclusion that the gallows would be re-erected at Walla Walla as soon as a bill could be drafted and submitted to the next session.

Sine die adjournment was accomplished at 5:00 a.m. on the morning of March 9 after a last-minute deadlock over the removal of a $4,000 pension for Mrs. Olson from the supplemental appropriation bill. While the conference committee wrangled, the *Recorder* recorded, *"Legislators with nothing to do but sit and wait got noisy, indulged in horseplay, shouted and sang and paraded in lockstep to the tune of 'John Brown's Body', the house members through the senate and the senators through the house."*

House members of the conference committee refused to reinstate the pension. Senate members were just as determined that it should be. Just before 4:00 a.m. two of the three committee members from the house gave in, but the full membership refused to accept their capitulation. It was then the senate's turn to surrender. After indulging in a series of eulogies to the late insurance commissioner, its members voted to leave his widow pensionless.

Even without Mrs. Olson's $4,000, the legislature managed to set another record appropriation of $6,789,000 from the general fund and a total from all funds of $30,800,000.

PLUGGING THE LEAKS

The reorganized Olympia police department may not have done the greatest job in the world of protecting public officials, but it was doing its best to make good on the mayor's pledge to enforce the dry law. Chief Harry L. Cusack, who fired all but one of ex-Chief Caton's force, took a page from the book of Seattle Mayor Hi Gill and directed a series of surprise raids on hotel rooms, private abodes and places of entertainment. Legislators who voted dry and drank wet lived in constant fear that, even though they couldn't be arrested for liquor violations during the session, their names might appear in the public press, blasting their political careers forever. Chief Cusack's men even raided a meeting of the Washington Education Association lobby in the hotel room of the Franklin county school superintendent. They caught the educators drinking something, but they weren't sure whether it was booze or Appleju. The police decided to leave the matter to the discretion of the mayor and he decided to pretend that it had never happened.

Nobody was safe from the aroused forces of total abstinence, as Dr. Story was to discover when he was arrested for prescribing a bottle of drugstore whiskey for one Dan Dunbar without bothering to write the usual directions to take a spoonful in hot water before retiring. A six-man jury of the doctor's friends and patients, including Robert Blankenship, Bill Klambush, W. S. Wotton, and C. W. Maynard, quickly found him not guilty, but newly-elected Prosecutor O'Leary, apparently determined to correct the wet image created by the libelous photo in the Tenino *Journal,* brought new charges in Judge John R. Mitchell's superior court. The predominantly female jury brought in a guilty verdict and the judge assessed a $100 fine, which the good doctor paid with indignant reluctance. He suspected that the prosecutor had been set upon him by a professional colleague who was nearer the top of the list of prescription-issuers and relations between the two physicians remained strained thereafter.

WAR IS A GLORIOUS EXPERIENCE . . . FOR THE HOME GUARD

The rush toward full participation in the European war brought with it a full measure of bigotry and intolerance along with a spirit of dedication and self sacrifice. Booze became not only immoral but unpatriotic as it was pointed out that its production diverted grain, money and manpower from the national defense effort.

The resumption of unrestricted submarine warfare by Germany in January had prompted President Wilson to ask congress for authority to arm American merchant vessels, but his effort was blocked by the filibuster of a small group of "willful men," which included Washington Senator Wesley Jones. Super-patriotic Spokane civic organizations issued resolutions of censure and Jones recanted. Following the April 6 declaration of war he was the first to speak in favor of Wilson's proposed draft.

His colleague, Senator Poindexter, probably best typified the less endearing aspects of the new spirit of reactionary jingoism. Elected as a liberal reform candidate, he made a sudden right turn after the outbreak of hostilities, declaring that "war is a glorious experience and a great character builder." He also came to the conclusion that labor unions, particularly in Washington, were part of the "anarchist conspiracy" and introduced a bill to make all strikes illegal. He remained an ultra-conservative throughout his subsequent career, alienating all his old progressive backers, particuarly when it was discovered that he was the recipient of an $80,000 campaign fund raised by big business. William Boeing had contributed $1,000, making Poindexter the first Washington politician to be tainted with Boeing Airplane company money. After Warren G. Harding's election as president, Poindexter became a prominent member of his informal cabinet of hard-drinking cronies and was rewarded with an appointment as minister to Peru.

Washington's lone Democratic congressman, C. C. Dill, was the only one who remained true to his principles. He was a member of the tiny minority in congress which voted against the war resolution. He further enraged such over-age patriots as Senator Poindexter by suggesting that the names of all the pro-war members of congress should be turned over to the recruiting offices as volunteers. His constituents at home screamed for his recall and he was rewarded for his profile in courage by being temporarily retired from political life in the following year's election.

In Olympia, as in the nation as a whole, the World War I years became a glorious opportunity for busybodies, snoopers, frustrated fascists and the self-righteous to bask in the glow of patriotism and public approval.

The day after the declaration of war 40 men had signed up for Captain W. B. Marsh's home guard company and mustered at the "armory" in the Elks building (the old Woodruff block) on lower Main street. All were determined to defend the town to the death after listening to the captain's warning that "the capital of the state is always the center of attack in war." Within a month a half dozen other home guard companies, including the uniformed orders of the local lodges, were drilling on vacant lots all over town. W. J. Cook of Tumwater, a veteran of the Cuban, Puerto Rican and Philippine campaigns, was searching for 30 or 40 horses with the intent of forming a home guard cavalry troop.

By August the proliferating home guard units were getting in each other's way and there was a move toward consolidation. Even attorney Tom Vance, a leading voice of local patriotism, admitted that "the organization up to date has been more or less farcical." After much arguing and a public meeting sponsored by the Chamber of Commerce, a single "official" company was authorized, captained by E. A. McClarty. The local citizens were given the patriotic privilege of chipping in for uniforms and the fund was over-subscribed the first day.

Soon afterward a youth described by the *Olympian* as a *"pink-capped scoffer"* found the maneuvers of the guard company funnier than a Charlie Chaplin comedy as they marched down Main street in their new uniforms. He kept pace with the hometown warriors, mocking Captain McClarty's martial commands in a falsetto voice. The captain brought his company to a halt at 4th and Main and marched across the street to confront the heckler. "Do you consider this drill to be anything to laugh at?" he demanded.

The misguided youth stifled his guffaws and responded, "It's a joke."

The captain put an end to the conversation with a well-aimed left hook to the young man's jaw. Gazing sternly at the recumbent figure, he proclaimed, "The Olympia home guards are not a joke and do not intend to be so considered in any sense of the word."

The *Olympian* wrapped up its military communique with the opinion that the heckler *"had received his just deserts"* and that *"he was chastened so that he apologized for his conduct."*

Thus was the first blow for Democracy struck in Washington's capital city.

There was less martial spirit among those who received draft numbers after the local registration board was formed in May with Sheriff Gifford, Auditor Gaston and Dr. Partlow as its members. On June 6 the citizenry, with the exception of the prospective draftees, celebrated Registration Day. Six hundred registrants, looking apprehensive, marched to the capitol behind the brass band, the home guard and veterans of the civil and Spanish-American wars. They were addressed by lawyer Vance, who told them, "You are not making a sacrifice; you are enjoying the privilege of defending your country."

Some of the potential draftees looked unconvinced, but the home guard cheered loudly.

SHAME ON THE SLACKERS!

Those who failed to register for the draft were "slackers" and open season was declared on them. Some 25 members of the business community, all safely exempt from the draft, met at the Elks club and formed a vigilance committee to help Prosecutor O'Leary track down those cowardly youths who refused to "do their bit."

"Pro-German" soon became another popular hate phrase. Anyone who was un-American enough to voice a preference for peace over war was considered a pro-German, and that included Congressman Dill. Herman Meyer, a used furniture dealer and Socialist, refused to contribute to a Chamber of Commerce fund drive for the establishment of a servicemen's center designed to "make the Sammies happy."* Meyer said the "Sammies" were always welcome at the Socialist hall and anyway, he wasn't in sympathy with the war, which he belived to have been "started in the interests of a few parasites."

The community was aghast at this heresy. The Perkins press heralded the outrage with screamer headlines, the County Council on Defense urged similar public disgrace for all "agitators" and there was talk of a special committee on disloyalty. The Methodist

*An effort was being made at this stage of the war to popularize the nauseatingly cute pet name "Sammy" for the citizen soldiers of the new army. Presumably it was derived from Uncle Sam. Fortunately it failed to catch on and the more incomprehensible but somewhat less objectionable "doughboy" soon replaced it.

Episcopal brotherhood issued a long resolution supporting the war and denouncing "disloyalty."

Spy scares vied with pacifist-baiting for public popularity. A few days after America's entry into the war Mrs. W. A. January and the J. D. Kinseys reported an airplane "flying at high speed low over their Bush prairie homes." The mysterious aircraft had, they said, been sighted almost daily for a week, its occupants singing "My Old Kentucky Home." There was conjecture as to whether the rendition of this popular American folk ballad was a ruse to cover up the pro-German proclivities of the airmen or a pre-arranged signal to henchmen on the ground.

Further fears of an imminent attack by the Central powers upon Olympia were engendered by another mysterious and never-explained event described as follows by the *Recorder* of June 6:

"Sneaking around at night, some uniden-tified person has placed mysterious marks on nearly every house in Olympia. One woman says she rubbed the mark off three times yesterday and each time it returned. One man says he saw a woman dressed in a blue tailored suit marking his door. He caught up with her as she left and accused her, but she flatly denied having done so. Most of the marks are in the forms of circles with lines of crosses through them and B or C above or encircled."

This was followed, in August, by the *Washington Standard's* grim warning that *"sinister influences are at work in this county,"* it having been established that *"Von Alvensleben, the German spy arrested in Seat-tle was in Olympia earlier, busying himself on some mysterious mission."*

As the war fever increased, patriotic business men, observing the law of supply and demand, raised the price of American flags by 100 percent. Liberty bonds were hawked by increasingly high-pressure methods. Senator Piles added his voice to the cries of Washington's congressional hawks when he came to town and told the citizens at a mass meeting that "we will be cowards and poltroons if we do not over-subscribe the Liberty Loan." Olympians duly over-subscribed their quota by $102,000.

The public library was collecting books and magazines for soldiers and a box was placed in the Kneeland hotel lobby for the deposit of old kid gloves to be made into aviators' jackets. Olympia women were urged to knit their way to victory by producing sweaters and other warm garments for the troops. Meatless days were proclaimed, with the slogan, "Be asham-ed to eat what the soldier needs!" Two ounces of bread was ruled the maximum serving at restaurants and anybody who took more than a "pinch" of sugar in his coffee was likely to be publicly branded a pro-German by some self-appointed guardian of patriotism.

The police department had to give up its time-honored high helmets when home front heroes decided they resembled the headgear of the hellish Hun and took to throwing rocks at them, and somebody set fire to the bandstand in Sylvester park, presumably because its spik-ed pergola roof also bore a fancied resemblance to Kaiser Bill's helmet.

Women flocked to join Miss Florence Lister's Red Cross first aid classes and to sign the National League of Woman's Service volunteer forms. The women's commiteee of the National Council of Defense had charged that more than half of the women of the United States were "flappers," defined by the commitee as "women who do not work." No decent Olympia woman wanted to be classified as a flapper, which was the feminine equivalent of a slacker.

Employees of the Olympia National bank were engaged in growing potatoes on a vacant lot at 15th and Main, while Perkins press staff members planted a victory garden adjacent to the newspaper plant at 3rd and Main. Local business leaders freely offered their vacant properties for more such patriotic vegetable patches, but showed no more inclination to personally grub in the dirt of Olympia than to volunteer for service in the trenches of France.

SHARING THE PROFITS

The Carlyon fill hummed with increased shipbuilding activity as the Sloan Ship Yard company, armed with contracts for four ocean'going motorships for Australian owners, began construction of a plant adjacent to the established Olympia Shipbuilding company yards. On July 13, the first of the Olympia Shipbuilding vessels, the 292-foot auxiliary schooner *Wergeland* was launched at a civic celebration which featured a band concert and free Appleju.

Applju

The Famous New Process
APPLE JUICE
Pure and Unfermented
CONTAINS NO PRESERVATIVES

Northwest Fruit Products Co.
SALEM, OREGON, OLYMPIA, WASH, U.S.A.

Producers of *Loju* Loganberry

Prohibition substitute for Olympia beer failed to achieve the popularity of the real thing.

NOBLE EXPERIMENT: Unloading carloads of apples at the Olympia Brewing company's Tumwater plant for production of "Appleju" during early prohibition days.

The shipyard workers were willing to march in the numerous patriotic parades with the home guards and the Grand Army of the Republic, but they also wanted a share of the wartime cost-plus profits. By mid-summer the first of a series of periodic strikes for higher pay began to slow down production at the local yards.

Workers in other fields, eyeing the lucrative shipyard jobs, became increasingly annoying to the business community as they demanded wage increases. Car men led the chorus with an ultimatum to the street car company that they would either have to get a 5¢ an hour raise . . . to 28¢ an hour . . . or they would march from the carbarn to the Carlyon fill and go to work at the shipyards. The company capitulated, but began experimental operation of one-man "pay-as-you-enter" cars, which eliminated the conductor from the rear platform.

City employees quickly followed the lead of the motormen and conductors, demanding . . . and getting . . . a $10 a month raise. Word spread to the loggers in the surrounding woods and they, too, began demanding higher pay, an outrage attributed by many to the work of IWW agitators. Soon the workers in local sawmills were talking bravely of an eight-hour day and a minimum wage of $3.00. Those whose demands weren't met followed the shipyard workers' lead and went on strike. Telephone girls, aware that the Olympia Canning company was working around the clock and hiring hundreds of female employees, walked out in October when the company refused their demand for a daily pay scale of from $1.50 to $2.75, with union recognition. The company said it would break the strike and never, never recognize a labor union, but communications became chaotic in the capital city for some time.

Six local newsboys employed by the Tacoma *Tribune* became inspired by the new defiance of their elders and staged a strike of their own when the publisher ruled that they must sell *Tribunes* only, at 3¢ a copy, instead of with another newspaper for a total of 5¢.

The Olympia Brewing company, now doing business as the Northwest Fruit Products company announced that it had pressed a million gallons of Appleju during the first year of prohibition, but it didn't say how much it had sold. In the fall Leopold Schmidt the younger, viewing the failure of the last wet initiative, announced sadly that "prohibition is a sickness that will have to run its course" and authorized the sale of the brewery's beautiful horse'drawn beer wagon to E. L. Blaine of the state public service commission. There were nostalgic tears in Tumwater when it was learned that Mr. Blaine had shipped the symbol of grandeur to his ranch in Grandview . . . to haul prunes to market.

Old-timers also sighed sadly when the ancient New England Hotel, which had entertained Governor Stevens upon his arrival over the Cowlitz trail . . . and hundreds of territorial politicans in later years . . . was declared beyond repair and demolished.

FREE SPEECH MAY BE HAZARDOUS TO HEALTH

Militant patriotism reached new heights in 1918 as American troops began to take their places in the trenches of France. The county council of defense and the Minute Women, commanded by Mrs. Mowell, observed the coming of the new year with the announcement of "a campaign against pro-German liars. The *Recorder* headlined the news, warning grimly that *"the names of some of the kaiser's liars have been obtained"* and that they were to be either *"cleaned out of the county or interned socially."*

Early in February the council brought charges against South Bay school teacher Charles R. Carr before Josephine Corliss Preston, who had taken office the previous year as the state's first female superintendent of public instruction. Young Carr was charged with making "seditious statements" and the council wanted his teaching certificate revoked.

Carr introduced evidence that he "had always prayed for the president and the United States at prayer meetings," had worked for the Red Cross and YMCA and organized pig, poultry and garden clubs, although he admitted that he might have publicly described the current conflict as "an unholy and unrighteous war for commercial purposes." Tom O'Leary and Mrs. Fred Agatz testified that they had, in fact, personally heard the teacher make "anti-war statements" at a Liberty Loan meeting in the South Bay school.

The public inquisition was held in the senate chamber before an audience of several hundred, including 20 children brought by Carr as witnesses. According to the *Recorder* they

"capered about the gallery and occupied the president's chair and desk," which probably didn't strengthen their teacher's case. Although 95 percent of the South Bay school parents had signed a petition supporting Carr, the document was ignored as lawyer Vance delivered an eloquent and patriotic speech demolishing the teacher's defense as "a deathbed repentance."

Mrs. Preston forthwith revoked Carr's certificate for "unpatriotic and un-American remarks," following this up with an order to all public schools to stop teaching German.

Soon afterward a local resident with the unfortunate name of John Kaiser was accosted on the street by Chief Cusack, who asked him if he had been born in Germany. Kaiser said he was a naturalized American citizen and advised the chief to mind his own business. He was immediately thrown in jail. "Campfire Bill," a local character described by the *Recorder* as *"delighting in liquor and iconoclasm,"* wandered to Tacoma and was likewsie jailed *"for making injudicious utterances against the government."*

C. H. Goodpasture, a candidate for the Olympia school board in the spring election, was branded as a traitor by unnamed Red Cross workers, who complained that he had refused to contribute to any of their constant fund drives and that "he has no bonds or thrift stamps." His opponent, W. W. Manier, proved that he had contributed to and joined every patriotic organization in town. Manier garnered 800 votes to Goodpasture's 68.

Mr. Vance reached new heights of Americanism at a patriotic meeting in the house chamber sponsored by the local carpenters' union. He not only established once and for all the righteousness of the American revolution, War of 1812, Civil and Spanish-American wars, but was even able to defend the Mexican war as "a glorious struggle to free Texas and secure our southern border." He concluded with the pronouncement that "all pacifists are traitors." The audience responded with cheers and the county council of defense with the appointment of a committee to censor all pacifist motion pictures and literature.

By mid-October, with the fourth Liberty Loan drive under way, most Olympians had been drained of most of their ready cash by the continual round of fund drives for a myriad of worthy patriotic causes. Strong means were found necessary to stimulate the lagging enthusiasm of prospective bond buyers. Full page advertisements were run in the local papers advising citizens to *"either buy bonds or forever stand before the world as a pro-Hun."* The Perkins papers also began running a *"Slacker List"* front page center in every issue. At first the actual names of the non-buyers were deleted, although the culprits could usually be identified, as in the case of the local dentist who had *"traded his Buick for a new six-cylinder auto last spring,"* but had claimed he couldn't afford to buy the $500 worth of bonds the committee had decided upon as his quota.

The papers subsequently named names, including those of Thomas Ismay, a confectioner near the log cabin station of the Olympia-Tumwater car line and Goodpasture, the defeated candidate for the school board. Those scheduled for subsequent publicity surrendered at the last moment and found means to buy some bonds.

Housewives, in addition to coping with the increasingly high cost of living . . . beef was up to 15¢ a pound; bacon to 31¢ . . . were saving fruit pits and nut shells for gas mask filters, making surgical dressings, serving doughnuts and coffee to soldiers at the Camp Lewis Hostess House . . . and knitting. Especially knitting. During the first two months of the year Mrs. Robert Prickman completed 75 sweaters; far ahead of her nearest competitor, Mrs. Fred Guyot, who had turned out 22. Mrs. A. E. Bigelow, Mrs. D. J. Larison and Mrs. George Talcott were racing for the sock-knitting championship. A woman who wasn't knitting was considered as unpatriotic as a man who wasn't buying liberty bonds.

Land Commissioner Benson, in a burst of enthusiasm, presented the ladies of the Red Cross with four lambs, which were pastured on the statehouse lawn, hopefully to flourish and provide still more wool for the knitting needles of American womanhood. The idea seemed reasonable, but the lambs created unexpected problems. The Red Cross ladies made pets of them and complained bitterly that the state had failed to provide roofs for their pens during the rainy season. Acting Governor Hart responded with a promise to order Benson to issue umbrellas to the lambs. When the lambs gained 66 pounds during their first month and became full-fledged sheep, Commissioner Benson emerged from seclusion and demanded to know, "Who said it wouldn't work?"

He retreated again when he received a petition from a number of statehouse employees demanding, "for the sake of suffering humanity, the removal of those musical sheep." The constant blatting, they said, was driving them out of their minds and the banishment of the woolly beasts would "save the state the expense of a lot of new boarders at Steilacoom," the site of the Western Washington state hospital for the insane. Benson explained that local children had been feeding the sheep cookies and popcorn, causing them to "blat continually when not fed." He gave in to public pressure at this point and sold the flock, turning over the profits to the Red Cross.

The Red Cross chapter was also the recipient of the big Tumwater Clubhouse, which was presented to it by Peter G. Schmidt and Joseph R. Speckart of the Olympia Brewing company. This example of large-scale patriotism prompted the *Olympian* to quote from *"a letter of Leopold Schmidt prior to his death in September, 1914, which proves he was against the Kaiser even then."*

CONCRETE AND BRICKS

Although work was halted on the recently authorized completion of the Temple of Justice and the first office building of the capitol group, due to high costs and a shortage of skilled labor, the excavation was begun at the corner of 6th and Washington for the erection of the long-awaited new hotel, to be built of concrete and faced with brick. Upon its completion it was to be operated by H. M. Pierce, who had managed the Mitchell hotel since 1908, and his two sons, John, currently an ensign in the navy, and Thad, who was manager of the Hotel Puget at Port Gamble. A downtown landmark, beloved of generations of small boys, gave way to progress as hotel construction began. The huge old cherry tree on the corner, which had been the pride and joy of Captain Sam Willey when his home was located there, was chopped down at the ripe age of 50 years.

The same contractor who was doing the preliminary work at the hotel site was also putting the finishing touches on the impressive new brick and concrete William Winlock Miller high school on Main street just north of the stylish Capital apartments. The original high school building had been taken over by the state with the expansion of the new capitol grounds. It had been intended to refit it as a temporary office building, but on the evening of July 1 it caught fire and was completely gutted. Low water pressure and the lack of a pumper engine made it impossible to control the blaze and a high wind swept firebrands across the south end residential area, setting fire to numerous houses. High school classes were held in temporary quarters until late December, when the student body assembled at the new building across Main street.

Another progressive proposal aimed primarily at solving the ancient problem of the west 4th street bridge generated bitter controversy within the civic leadership. The city council proposed a $300,000 bond issue to construct a new concrete span and pave parts of the Tacoma and Tenino highways. Doc Carlyon, still thinking big, advocated a $600,000 bond issue to make additional road and street improvements, including the grading and paving of the west 4th street hill. Attorney Funk insisted that "for $12,000 you could put in a cheap wooden drawbridge that would answer the purpose." Secretary Kenney of the brewing company didn't want to spend any money at all. Any construction during wartime would, he insisted, be "unpatriotic." He further quoted William G. McAdoo, secretary of the treasury, to back his stand.

Walter McDowell, a west side resident, replied heatedly that "McAdoo is in no position to tell how bad a new side bridge and county paving is needed."

Funk sprang to the defense of Kenney and economy. "You knew the hill was there," he told the westsiders, "now you want the city to give you a nice easy grade." Ex-Police Chief Caton, also a west side resident, delivered a religious blow to Kenny and Funk with the pronouncement that 'you would criticize God the almighty for putting the hill there."

As usual, Doc Carlyon got his way and the $600,000 bond issue was duly passed by a majority of 70 votes.

The firm of Morrow and Blackman, anticipating the improved highways, inaugurated the first Olympia-Tacoma auto freight line, operating their single truck daily from the Rose-Nepple garage.

Despite the continuing signs of modernity, Olympia managed to retain a degree of its traditional bucolic charm. The *Olympian* took note of a couple of examples during the year. In mid-January "a middle aged gentleman of rural appearance" attempted to mail several letters in one of the city's fire alarm boxes at the corner of 4th and Main. Apprised of his error by amused bystanders, he rushed down the street toward the fire station a block away, waving his arms and shouting at the firemen, who had the Seagrave cranked and half way up the block before he could get them stopped. Soon afterward a newly-rich eastern Washington cattle farmer arrived in town with a large bankroll and set out to see the sights of the capital city. He expressed the opinion to a statehouse janitor that the octagon-towered stone structure was "a real beauty." The janitor jokingly offered to sell it to the cattleman, who immediately began peeling bills of large denomination from his roll to make the down payment. The janitor had considerable difficulty explaining that it was all a joke.

By early fall a deadly influenza epidemic was sweeping the Northwest. Dr. Kincaid urged the wearing of gauze "flu masks," public meetings were banned and the schools were closed but the disease continued to take its toll, especially of the very young and the very old.

Those who were not yet infected forgot the flu and threw away their masks on November 8 when a false report of an armistice ending the war raced across the nation. The town abandoned itself to the premature victory celebration. Automobile owners salvaged old radiators and other scrap iron from the ruins of the burned high school, attached them to their vehicles and raced up and down the streets madly honking their horns. Factory whistles shrilled, school bells clanged and there was a major run on drug store supplies of a popular brand of "stomach bitters" which had an alcoholic content of 25 percent.

The real armistice, three days later, came as something of an anti-climax. It came too late for some, including Mrs. C. C. Cater, who had received word on November 3 of the death of her son, Ira, who had left high school and his job as an usher at the Rex theater to enlist in the infantry. He had died at a field hospital in France on October 16 of wounds received in action on the western front.

Governor Lister, who had been forced to remain for some time in a Chicago hospital while returning from a trip to the national capital, was back in town, but not living in the mansion. Legislators, who were smarting under continuing charges of extravagance, had been firing periodic counter-barrages of criticism at the governor practically since he had moved into the big red brick house on the hill. He was accused of having a garage built at state expense and without legislative approval, of using Filipino convicts from the state penitentiary as house servants and of having charged five gallons of oysters to the taxpayers for a state dinner. In high dudgeon, the chief executive had packed up and moved across Main street to the Capital apartments, leaving the governor's mansion vacant. A number of local youths broke in and began systematically looting the rugs and furnishings, but the plot was fortunately discovered before they could arrange transportation for the final removal of the neatly stacked haul.

1919

The legislators returned to the capital city on January 12, amid rain, wind and flu masks and without a single bar to provide a drop to ward off the chill. Rumors were prevalent, however, that a number of the statesmen had brought their own bars with them in their suitcases. Three members checked into St. Peters hospital before session opened, joining Representative Charles W. Gorham, state printer under Governor Mead and a legislator since 1917, who suffered a stroke on the floor of the house.

The survivors convened on January 14, electing Don Carlyon president pro-tem of the senate and Fred A. Adams of Spokane speaker of the house. Joint resolutions were then dispatched to congress requesting adoption of the nationwide woman suffrage amendment and a change in the name of the Panama canal to Roosevelt canal. The national Volstead act was also ratified on the first day without opposition.* Two days later a total of 36 state legislatures had approved the nationwide prohibition measure and the Noble Experiment was scheduled to go into full effect one year hence. As a matter of fact, the country went officially dry in July of 1919 when the war prohibition act banned all manufacture of beer and wine until demobilization was completed.

POST-WAR PROBLEMS

In his message to the legislature on January 15, Lister urged a program of public works to provide jobs for returning veterans, with particular emphasis on the Columbia basin irrigation projects. He branded the acts of the IWW as disloyal and cautioned that there was still need to guard against anarchy and sedition. He asked for a $100,000 emergency appropriation to cope with the influenza epidemic and $50,000 to erect a monument to the war dead on the new capitol grounds. He continued to defy the highway lobby, objecting strongly to Carlyon's proposal for a $30 million highway bond issue, pointing out that it would cost $11 million in interest by the time the bonds were retired. He did, however, recommend a lesser speedup of road projects as another means of finding jobs for the 50,000 Washington men who had been in uniform and the thousands more who were being laid off from shipyards and war industries.

The lawmakers displayed their patriotism by passing a criminal anarchy law which banned "all seditious banners and emblems" and made

---

*This was the first legislative session of which I have a personal recollection. At the age of five, I was taken to the capitol by my father to witness the historic ratification ceremonies. In the corridor outside the chambers I was fascinated by the sight of several gentlemen wearing long overcoats which nearly reached the floor. Quite regularly, other gentlemen would emerge from the legislative halls and hand money to the overcoated ones. Although the transactions were quick and cautious, I was able to observe that cloth loops were sewed inside the overcoats and each loop contained a small bottle filled with an amber liquid. The bottles were exchanged for the currency. When I asked my father what was happening he explained, "Those are our senators and representatives getting drunk enough to vote in prohibition."

it a crime to "flaunt the red flag" or to carry the red membership card of the IWW, a tougher criminal syndicalism law and a sabotage statute. The senate, however, turned down Senator George B. Lamping's bill to provide a modest state bonus to returning war veterans. The American Legion, in its formative stages, had not yet become an effective lobbying force for veterans, but the Seattle Elks lodge issued a resolution to "condemn and denounce as slackers and as men to be classed with the bolshevik and IWW element the members of the senate who voted aginst the soldiers' bonus." The Olympia Elks quickly held an indignation meeting to which brethren of the legislature were invited, to likewise condemn the action.

A major bone of contention in the senate was a proposed new divorce law, recommended by a committee of superior court judges. It would remove "personal indignities rendering life burdensome" as a cause, this, according to the judges, being the bases for two-thirds of the state's divorce cases. Senator Rockwell of King delivered a passionate oration for an amendment to also strike "incurable chronic mania and dementia after 10 years," claiming that the clause was put in the present divorce law by "a man who was in this legislature and who wanted to divorce his poor, stricken wife and marry his hired girl."

Senator Hall of Whitman got in a blow against one of his pet peeves by offering an amendment to include among the grounds for divorce, "when a wife leaves her husband and children and becomes a lobbyist at the legislature."

He was relatively safe in making this male chauvinist statement, for no woman had yet penetrated the masculine stronghold of the state senate. The single lady representative that session was Mrs. Frances Haskell of Pierce, who proved herself a good fellow on opening day by moving to suspend the rule against smoking on the floor of the house, and then relapsed into the silence befitting a freshman legislator and a woman.

By February all the items vetoed from the 1917 appropriations bill were restored, including $43,700 for the state bureau of inspection, a $6,000 salary for the state law librarian, $9,000 for the maintenance of the governor's mansion and $1,500 for the department of labor.

The house debated a bill by Representative Bassett of Spokane to establish a state con-

stabulary of four companies, each with 45 privates, officers and specialists. The state Federation of Labor waged an all-out fight against the measure, using the Pennsylvania state constabulary as a horrible example of strike-breaking brutality, which had placed it in the same relationship to union labor as the cossacks to Russian peasants. The representatives decided to postpone action until a less objectionable plan for a state police force could be worked out.

A bill introduced by Senator W. Lon Johnson to restore the death penalty for capital crimes was passed, although not without some opposition and much discussion. Senator French wanted a remarkable amendment added to imprison the condemned at hard labor for one year, the governor to then fix the execution date and decide whether the gallows or the electric chair should be utilized. French felt this might prevent the execution of innocent persons, but it was agreed by the majority that it was somewhat cruel and unusual. Senator Johnson argued that the restoration of capital punishment "will be a big deterrent to murder, which is increasing rapidly in the state." The bill passed the senate 26 to 12 and sent to the house on the same day that an Olympia shipyard worker named Norman Burnette took his wife and two small boys on an automobile picnic excursion to Hawks Prairie. He was equipped with a gun and a shovel as well as a picnic basket and after lunch he brutally murdered his family, burying his wife and one son in shallow graves, the smallest child in a hollow under a tree root. The publicity didn't help the advocates of mercy, but Representative Shattuck of Kitsap put up a good fight. He said he had heard it argued that the death penalty was approved in the Book of Genesis, but that Christ had brought a different law. Thompson of Lewis, also a student of the Scriptures, rose to observe that "Christ on the cross did not condemn the capital punishment of the two thieves."

Shattuck disagreed and, according to the *Olympian, "Uproar followed, with Speaker Adams pounding his gavel and demanding order."* When peace was restored the capital punishment bill was passed by a 75 to 18 vote. Hart, who was acting governor at the time, announced immediately, "I will take great pleasure in signing it."

The sixteenth legislature passed other bills authorizing the manufacture of metal license plates at the penitentiary, establishing a licensing board to certify "drugless healers" and a Columbia basin survey commission, and a new motor code which required rear license plate lights and banned "glaring headlights." The $50,000 for a war memorial was approved, along with a $3.5 million capitol appropriations bill to begin construction of the new legislative building. Appropriations from all funds reached a new grand total of just under $50 million.

A LOAD THAT SHOULD
HAVE BEEN SHARED

On January 31 Governor Lister did not appear at his office in the statehouse. It was announced that he was resting at home under the care of Dr. Ingham, who issued a reassuring bulletin, attributing the governor's condition to overwork and "blood pressure." By February 4 he was still confined to his bed at the Capital Apartments and rumors were prevalent that he had "abdicated," but he let it be known that this was not the case. He had asked Attorney General W. V. Tanner and Dr. Henry Suzzallo, president of the University of Washington,* to take care of things for him at the executive office, but was signing bills and conducting business from his bed.

The Seattle general strike, which had failed to paralyze the city as had been predicted, *was* scaring the daylights out of people, who viewed

it as the first step in the take-over of the nation by the dreaded "Radicals." Although ambitious Ole Hanson, currently mayor of Seattle, was beginning to see visions of the presidency as he issued pronouncements that "the seat of government is still in city hall" and that "any man who attempts to take over the control of municipal government will be shot at sight," the problems of the strike placed added strain on the governor.

On February 13 Louis Hart took over as acting governor and Carlyon as president of the senate, while Lister was transferred by ambulance to the state hospital at Steilacoom, where he was placed under the care of his old family doctor and close friend, hospital Superintendent W. M. Kellar. Two days later he was brought home, apparently much improved, and consented to reoccupy the mansion. The legislature, which had done so much to raise the governor's blood pressure, immediately appropriated $5,000 to finance a sea voyage for his health. The sea voyage was never made. Instead, Lister was transferred in the late spring to Swedish hospital in Seattle, where he died at 8:35 a.m. on June 14 from what physicians diagnosed as "a cardiovascular-renal disease." The next day he would have been 49 years of age.

Like the state's only other two-term governor in the first three decades of its history, Lister died in office, but he had established the record for the longest term of service of any governor so far . . . nearly six and a half years, or 18 months longer than that of his old friend John Rogers.

Lister, the youngest man yet elected governor of the state, was noted for his physical strength and robust health, but he had broken under the strain of the sudden precipitation of his office into a complicated 20th century. The office still functioned much as it had in the halcyon days of 1889. With a staff of a couple of secretaries and a stenographer and faced with a politically hostile legislature and state elected officials, Lister had been forced to do the job himself.

Republican Louis F. Hart drove to the Temple of Justice at 10 o'clock on the morning of June 15 and received the oath of office from Chief Justice O. R. Holcomb of the state supreme court. Then he issued a proclamation in which he said of Lister, "He attempted to carry a load that should have been shared by others, and one which was too much for even his wonderful strength."

*Dr. Suzzallo, a native of San Jose, California, was appointed to the presidency of the university following years of political, religious and philosophical bickering which had embroiled the institution since the days of Governor Rogers and resulted in frequent turn-over of presidents. Even Professor Meany became embroiled in the political in-fighting and barely survived a strong effort by Rogers to have him fired. Dr. Franklin Kane, Suzzallo's immediate predecessor, was fired by the board of regents in 1913 against the wishes of Lister. In the resulting showdown, an entirely new board was appointed by the governor and Suzzallo was employed after a long search for a top-flight administrator, which Suzzallo was. He gained nationwide prominence during the war years as an arbiter of labor disputes and was much in demand as a public speaker, having the ability, it was said, "to make speeches all day long without repeating himself" and could "talk to experts in any field and inform them of things they had not known in their specialties."

On July 28 the last of a dozen wooden Ferris-type freighters built by the Sloan yard for the U. S. Emergency Fleet Corporation, the *Dacula,* was christened by Miss Ruth Peters and duly launched to take its place with hundreds of similar hulls which were never destined to sail the seas. Two unfinished hulls remained on the ways at the Sloan shipyard, but the wartime shipbuilding boom was ended. Workers, used to wartime wages, were unwilling to face the fact that the nation was facing a post-war economic slump. Strikes continued to plague the nation and the Northwest. The widely publicized Seattle general strike made the biggest headlines, but pickets were walking everywhere. National strikes tied up the railroad, steel, telegraph, electrical and coal mining industries. Even in Olympia, where labor militancy was less evident than in more industrialized cities of the area, 1919 was a year of strikes.

The local bakers walked off the job, demanding raises from $42 to $53 a week. Telephone operators tried again. Some of them were still getting $2.00 a day after seven years on the job and they demanded $4.00 a day after three years service. Building laborers delivered an ultimatum on a $5.50 per day miminum scale and the piledriver crew working on the east 4th street bridge walked out on strike for $8.00 a day. All paving work on the new Pacific highway was shut down by labor disputes and in November Governor Hart ordered Adjutant General H. J. Moss to place the 3rd regiment of Washington national guard on standby alert to prevent violence and property damage in a statewide coal strike. Even the pay of city employees was up 20 percent . . . $150 a month for the fire and police chiefs, $132 for firemen and $120 for policemen.

It was feared that the continuing rash of strikes would seriously delay a number of major construction jobs scheduled for the capital city following the relaxation of wartime restrictions on materials and labor. The contract had been let to complete the marble interior and sandstone exterior of the Temple of Justice at a cost of $283,267 . . . nearly 250 percent above the architect's pre-war estimate. The Elks lodge had successfully raised $75,000 to build an impressive three-story brick lodge building next door to the Mitchell Hotel on Main street. An all-out drive, similar to that which had raised the money to build the legendary Hotel Olympia nearly three decades earlier, lifted the new hotel project from the doldrums and work was resumed at the corner

LOUIS F. HART, 10th governor, kept tight rein on state spending.

of 6th and Washington. The Olympia Hotel Building company was capitalized by local stock subscriptions, with J. L. Peters as president, C. J. Lord, treasurer; C. H. Springer, vice president; L. B. Faulkner, secretary; and trustees P. M. Troy, Millard Lemon, Peter Schmidt, Harry Van Arsdale and Thad Pierce. Inflation had raised the original cost estimates by 300 percent . . . to $300,000.

A new organization, the American Legion, had established its local post, named for Alfred William Leach, who had served with Battery D, 6th Field Artillery and was killed in action on the Argonne five weeks before the armistice was signed. The ex-doughboys were occupying space in the old Elks building, but they too were busily raising funds for a new building of their own.

EXECUTIVE CLEMENCY

The year was not without its amusements. The public was titillated by the trial of Ruth Garrison, a sexy 18-year-old redhead who had allegedly poisoned Grace Storrs, the wife of her paramour, in the restaurant of a Seattle department store. Women, including a few from Olympia, were tramped in the rush to get seats in the courtroom. Leading society matrons pulled hair and cursed like fishwives in the battle for seats, but they later chose a delegation to call on Colonel Blethen of the *Times* with a request that he stop publication of the names of those who suffered minor injuries in the melee. They explained that they didn't want their husbands to know that they had been involved in such a sordid affair. Pretty Ruth was declared mentally irresponsible and placed in the insane ward at the state penitentiary, but this was not the last that would be heard of her.

Prison authorities subsequently discovered that male inmate workers in the laundry had tunneled through the wall to the laundry room of the women's section and were engaging in illicit sex with the female convicts. One young prisoner was caught in the act with Ruth and the outraged warden dispatched a telegram to the governor asking him to rescind the young man's probation, which was being processed at Olympia.

Hart asked his new secretary, Hollis B. Fultz, why the parole was being held up. Fultz explained what the prospective parolee had been doing in his spare time. The crusty chief executive, who was Washington's only tobacco-chewing governor, fixed his secretary with a disgusted look, ejected a large wad into the executive cuspidor and roared, "Hell, man, any young feller that's spent over two years in the pen and wouldn't tunnel through a wall to get at Ruth Garrison wouldn't *deserve* to get a parole."

He then took the papers from the bottom of the pile, signed them vigorously and handed them back to Fultz.

POST-WAR PROGRESS

There were, of course, more respectable forms of recreation and civic celebration to be enjoyed. On June 27 a 30-block parade, the longest in the city's history, made its way to Priest Point park, where three steers were barbecued to feed and honor the returning service men of Thurston county. The parade, which included scores of patriotically decorated floats, was led by the fire department's latest pride and joy, a 70-horsepower White combination, pumper, chemical and hose wagon, carrying, according to the *Olympian, "six of the city's prettiest girls."* The mining town of Tono declared a holiday and chartered a special OWR & N train to convey the entire population to the celebration. Major General William H. Johnson of the 91st Division addressed the crowd, after which dances were held in the Red Cross and Central halls and all men in uniform were admitted to the movies free.

The Ellison-White Chautauqua again set up its giant tent across from the new capitol grounds on Main street, bringing culture and such national figures as William Jennings Bryan to town. Local society was likewise delighted by the dance recital of Mrs. Edward Platt Gardner's class on the lawn of the A. A. Phillips home. Mrs. Gardner's "little fairies," dressed in fluffy white costumes, performed to the music of Miss Marjorie Holcomb on the mandolin and Mrs. Roy Huggett on the piano. The performers included such winsome tots as Arleta Satterlee, Charlotte Huggett, Elizabeth Kevin, Mary Lasher, Jean Mustard, Claire Nulton, Clara Louise Schmidt, Virginia Rowe, Mary Lindley, Edna McCaughan and the red-headed Clem twins, Frances and Florence.

The town's first public kindergarten was established at the Christian church, providing the rudiments of education to a class of 37 toddlers, including Richard Phillips, Stanley Lilian, David Dahlquest, Harry Lewis, Albert Hart, Julia Eaton, Elizabeth Standford and Virginia Isom. The first Boy Scout troop was organized at the home of Norman Funk, with Smith Troy elected its first scribe.

That heroic figure, the street car conductor, began to disappear from the city streets with the arrival of a fleet of seven of the ultra-modern Burney "one-man safety cars" as the Puget Sound Power and Light company took over the operations of the pioneer Olympia Light and Power company, tied in the capital city to its power grid and began phasing out the old power plant at Tumwater falls. The new street cars, designed as the traction companys' ultimate weapon against the automobile, were highly efficient and equipped with air brakes and folding steps which would emerge only when the car was at a full stop. They were entirely enclosed and people could no longer hang from the open platforms or entertain their fellow passengers and passers-by doing pratfalls from still moving cars. But another bit of romance was lost when the old open "wind-scoopers" stopped making their summer runs to the baseball grounds at Carlyon park, which were being crowded out, in any event, by the modern bungalows of the recently platted Carlyon addition.

The drinking driver had also established himself as one of the real hazards of the highways. At 3 o'clock on a July morning a carload of celebrants missed the turn at 5th and Adams, crashed through the fence of the OWR & N railyards and demolished itself against a steel freight car. One girl was seriously injured and police noted "the odor of liquor" in the wrecked car.

These sad events failed to curb the exuberance of local motorists and the *Recorder* noted late in the year that *"Speed cop Peterson continues to arrest 'scorchers' on the city streets."*

Prompted perhaps by the increasing harvest of the automobile, the Sisters of Charity announced plans to build a new concrete and brick hospital in the near future to replace the old wooden structure of the 1880's.

And the county replaced its old outside jail behind the courthouse with a new escape-proof dungeon in the building's basement.

The automobile also brought an end to the 66-year era of the passenger steamboat at Olympia. The *Nisqually* had operated profitably during the war when train service was curtailed and gasoline scarce, and even the old *Greyhound* had returned briefly to service. Early in March, Mark Reed, who owned the Shelton steamer *S. G. Simpson,* purchased all the other shareholders' stock in the Olympia-Tacoma Navigation company and tried to make the racy *Nisqually* show a profit, but it just wasn't possible. Reed finally gave the steamer free and clear to her old skipper, Captain Fred Willson, who took her to the Columbia river to try and make a living on the Portland-Astoria run. For a few months the little *Magnolia* struggled to maintain the down-Sound steamboat service, but by 1920 water passenger service to the upper Sound, inaugurated in 1853 by the little *Fairy,* had ended. Reed kept the *Simpson* on the Shelton run for awhile longer, but she soon gave up also and was relegated to a freight run between Shelton and Tacoma.

THE ROARING TWENTIES

The decade of the Roaring 20's was ushered into the capital city amid the falsetto

recriminations of Washington's militant women who charged that equal suffrage was being sabotaged, and Governor Hart was in the crossfire. Carrie Chapman Catt, president of the National American Woman Suffrage Association, was firing broadsides at him from national headquarters claiming that male chauvinist legislators had convinced him that he should drag his feet in calling a special session to ratify the suffrage amendment, which had passed congress the previous year. Emma Smith DeVoe was zeroing in on the embattled chief executive at closer range. Hart said he couldn't call a special session because he had to go to Washington, D.C., to promote irrigation projects for the state. This put the heat on Secretary of State Howell, who would be acting governor in Hart's absence. Auditor Clausen entered the fray with a declaration that if Howell called a special session he wouldn't pay the legislators.

Hart and Howell had a "mysterious consultation" in the first week of January and it was suspected that they had worked out a technique for passing the buck. Hart would go to Washington, D.C., and tell Mrs. Catt that a special session was up to Howell. Howell would stay in Olympia and tell Mrs. DeVoe that only Hart could call the session. A further complication was added when Mrs. G. Kilbeth of New York, president of the National Association *Opposed* to Woman Suffrage, began firing off telegrams to Hart urging him not to call the session.

On March 2 the governor gave up and called a special session for 20 days hence to consider the suffrage amendment and provide emergency funds for state institutions of higher education, which were filling up with returned service men. He did not, however, attempt to extract a pledge from the legislators that they would limit the session to these topics.*

If Hart had needed further proof of the problems that could be created by dedicated women, he received it from state School Superintendent Josephine Corliss Preston.

---

*The state constitution provides that only the governor can convene the legislature in extraordinary session, but it does not give him the power to limit the deliberations or the length of time to be spent on them, which explains why most governors have been markedly reluctant to thus assemble the lawmakers.

When she heard about the special session she issued a proclamation from New York, where she was attending a convention of the National Education Association. calling for an assemblage of all county and city superintendents and all high school principals at Olympia on March 22. The governor was horrified at the thought of a mass meeting of public school officials when the legislatuve convened. He fired off a plaintive telegram to Chicago for Mrs. Preston, who was on her way home by train:

"Nothing is anticipated which can in any way affect public schools. Can you defer state conference to March 29? In interests of general public I beg you to assist us in holding the work of the legislature within reasonable bounds."

Mrs. Preston was determined that the special session *should* do something affecting the public schools and she wired a defiant message to the governor:

"The crisis in education in our state makes a conference of teachers, superintendents and principals imperative if anything other than ratification is to be considered by the legislature. I am sure you will join me in presenting the needs of our schools to the honorable body in their true light."

When she arrived home on March 13 she dispatched a more conciliatory message to the executive office, congratulating Hart for calling the session to ratify woman suffrage and compromising on a March 20 to 22 meeting time for the forces of education. The governor was well aware that they would be buttonholing legislators when they convened and, according to the *Recorder,* he *"appeared slightly pained"* when he received Mrs. Preston's latest missive.

On March 16 Mrs. Preston and W. F. Geiger, chairman of the teachers' committee, met with Hart, the chairmen of the legislative appropriations committees, house and senate leaders and others, described by the *Recorder* only as *"several other brave men."* The governor tried to soothe the superintendent by informing her that the extraordinary session was only supposed to consider emergency matters and the public school situation just wasn't that emergent.

He didn't get very far. Mrs. Preston and Mr. Geiger informed him that the only difference between the college and public school crises was the fact that "Public school teachers haven't threatened to quit and close down the system as the University of Washington

professors have." They pointed out further that teachers were leaving the classrooms in droves, unable to subsist on the average public school teacher's pay of $900 a year . . . compared to the $3,000 to $5,000 sinecures of the university instructors.

By the time the legislature convened, Hart had apparently been somewhat brain-washed by the educators. After pointing out a million dollar treasury deficit and urging rigid economy rather than more taxes, he conceded that "public school conditions are almost as deplorable as those of the colleges, with teachers quitting by the hundreds," but he left the lawmakers with the succinct advice regarding the special session to "keep it short and don't pass any appropriations bills." He suggested committees to study the educational proglems of the state and report to the 1921 regular session, but his principle emphasis was on government reorganization.

He pointed out to the legislators the multiplicity of state departments, boards and commissions which had popped out, like bureaucratic mushrooms, since 1889, "adding numerous hitherto unknown governmental functions." He reminded them that, while they had been adding new bureaucracies for the past 30 years, they had made only one effort to organizing or consolidating them. The result had been an increase in the per capita cost of state government from $4.70 in 1890 to $21.81 in 1920, while the assessed valuation of property had increased only three percent in the past six years. He declared that the property tax had "reached the line between taxation and confiscation" and that the state "does not require greater appropriations as much as it needs the exercise of a sensible rigid economy in all departments." To achieve more efficient and less costly state government he proposed to have drafted a bill completely reorganizing the basic governmental structure for submission to the 1921 session.

The legislature quickly ratified the national woman suffrage amendment, becoming the 26th to do so, the 12th to vote ratification unanimously and the 28th to convene in special session for the purpose. It appropriated funds to keep the colleges operating for the balance of the biennium, appointed a committee to study the common school crisis and adjourned *sine die* at 4:45 a.m. on March 24 after another heated inter-house battle over the veterans' bonus bill. The senate had passed it with an emergency clause, which would make it effective immediately, but the house insisted on a referendum to the people. The senators finally receded from their position, earing the house would kill the bill entirely by indefinite postponement, and the referendum was approved for the fall ballot.

The legislature had been in special session just two days and had spent a modest $8,700.

Hart spent the interim between the special and regular sessions stumping the state on behalf of his governmental reorganizational proposal. He hammered away on the theme of escalating state taxes, telling audiences that the levy had more than doubled in eight years . . . from 5.3 mills in 1912 to 10.44 mills in 1920 . . . and that the legislature had contributed to the current $49 million per biennium cost of government* by, in its last four sessions, creating 20 new boards and commissions with 76 members, many with duplicating functions and all "without system or proper placing of responsibility."

Citizens of Willapa Harbor were given a first-hand lesson in the blessings of bureaucratic consumer protection when the state public service commission ordered the Willapa Electric company to raise its electrical rate from 40¢ a month minimum to $1.00 and to install meters, on the grounds that the private utility was facing financial ruin. The company protested that it was making plenty of money and both its stockholders and customers were happy, but the state bureau was adamant. The company would either raise its rates 150 percent or lose its certificate.

Another political bone of contention during 1920 was Referendum 1, sponsored by Senator Carlyon, which would authorize a multi-million dollar bond issue for a major program of paving the state's major highways. The measure was specific as to the kind of paving to be used. Anything except Portland cement was banned. Representatives of the asphaltic paving industry muttered darkly that this was the greatest rip-off in the state's history; that Carlyon and certain other legislative power brokers would share a 5¢ a sack payoff from the cement industry for every grain of their

*For those readers who like to make comparisons, it may be pointed out that the record budget of the 1919-1921 biennium was approximately eight percent of the current state budget.

product used in surfacing the state highways. The state Good Roads Association shrugged off the innuendos and voted 234 to 37 to support the Carlyon road bill, but the people turned it down at the polls in November. As might be expected, Doc Carlyon considered his pet measure to be only slightly wounded, not dead, and he was determined to nurse it back to full health and vigor.

CAMPAIGN 1920

No less than six candidates for governor filed against Hart on the Republican ticket in 1920 . . . George Lamping, author of the veterans' bonus bill, the determined Roland Hartley, John Stringer, E. T. Coman, John A. Gellatly and the state's first female gubernatorial candidate, Anna MacEachern of Seattle. Judge Black, still convinced that Ernest Lister had robbed him of his chance at the governorship, filed for the Democratic nomination, along with three relatively unknown candidates.

Lamping's campaign by automobile of southwest Washington ended in disaster when his car was hit by a falling tree a few miles west of Olympia. He was taken to St. Peter's hospital, where surgeons sewed one of his ears back on, rejoined the tendons in high right hand and otherwise patched him up. He was on his feet again by September, but Hartley, who was also embarked on a whirlwind automobile campaign, was a good many laps ahead by that time. He showed up at Sylvester park in Olympia with a male quartet of University of Washington students, who entertained the voters. Hartley then made a speech vociferously denying that he was an enemy of organized labor, although he made it plain that he denied the right of labor organizations "to interfere with or prevent any man from working for whomsoever he pleases at any wage satisfactory to him whether he belongs to a labor union or not." He promised economy in government and the reduction of state boards and commissions, but Hart had firmly established that issue as his own and, as incumbent, was getting much more publicity for his views.

The 1920 campaign also brought a personable young politician from New York to Olympia. Franklin Delano Roosevelt, assistant

300

secretary of the navy under Wilson and vice-presidential running mate of Democratic presidential nominee James M. Cox, spoke to a modest crowd of about a thousand people at Sylvester park on the morning of August 21. He emphasized the need for reclamation of arid lands in the west and voiced strong support for Wilson's League of Nations, before turning the platform over to all the Democratic candidates for governor, who were traveling with him on his special train. The *Recorder* noted that *"his good natured smile and pleasing personality made a favorable impression of Mr. Roosevelt as an individual regardless of his political policies,"* but seemed to share the general opinion of the state's press that he was a nice enough young fellow who lacked the aggressiveness and force of character to get very far in politics.

Roosevelt's impact on the voters of Washington supported the belief that he wasn't very effective. Republican Herbert Hoover swept the state by the biggest majority in its history. Hart, who had easily taken the nomination from Hartley and his other opponents, beat Democratic nominee Black by nearly 22,000 votes. Wee Coyle, former football star and legislative clerk, was elected lieutenant governor by a similarly healthy majority, while the five Republican congressmen were all returned to office. The soldiers' bonus bill was approved by a better than two to one majority, but aside from those who were war veterans, it was another bad year for the Democrats.

The December municipal election came as an anti-climax. Colorful and controversial George Mottman had renounced politics forever and was concentrating on the operation of his department store. His Citizens party had lapsed back into futility and the Republican ticket, backed by the powers of the Elks club and the Smokehouse, had no difficulty in electing its mayorality candidate, C. H. Bowen, over D. R. Hester by a vote of 611 to 107.

THE CHRISTENING OF
THE HOTEL OLYMPIAN

The local Elks lodge came close to losing its reputation for solid respectability in June. Both the splendid New Hotel Olympian and the adjacent Elks temple had been completed

OLYMPIA'S NEW $300,000 HOTEL

With excavation work started for the foundation of Olympia's new $300,000 six-story hotel, under a contract calling for the completion of the building by May 1, 1920, J. G. Day, superintendent of construction for the H. L. Stevens company, of Chicago, architects for the building, yesterday announced the details of the plans and arrangements for the structure.

Located at the corner of Sixth and Washington streets, the hotel will occupy the entire site, 120 by 120 feet, with entrance on both streets, the main entrance being on Sixth street. The structure will be of reinforced concrete with the enclosing walls of brick and eight-inch hollow tile. On the street sides the walls will be of selected light face brick. The lower floor will be trimmed with terra cot-

space 80 by 88 feet. Adjoining the main dining hall will be three private dining rooms, each 12 by 36 feet, with folding doors opening into the main dining room. The lobby and main dining room will be two stories in height, ceilings of decorative plaster, the sides with walnut wainscoting. In the lobby will be the hotel office, telephone booths, cigar and news stands, check rooms, vault and the usual conveniences of a modern hotel. A large fire place will add to the attractiveness of the lobby.

A marble stairway leads from the lobby to the second floor. The mezzanine floor is provided with a promenade 50 by 70 feet, overlooking the lobby and main dining room with a well opening to the lobby of 25 by 40 feet. On the mezzanine floor will

rooms will be equipped with telephone service and hot and cold water. The woodwork in the rooms will be finished in silver grey stain with papered walls to match the finishing. An enclosed fire escape with openings to the alley will make all rooms accessible to a safe exit in case of fire, while the main stairway will be enclosed in a fire tower. In all the hotel will contain 155 rooms, 75 of which will have private baths.

The basement will contain eight large sample rooms, general storage rooms and the help's locker rooms. The refrigeration and ice machinery will also be in the basement, while the heating plant will be installed in a separate unit.

The elevator service will be located at the northeast corner of the main

Architect's drawing of proposed Hotel Olympian, front paged in the *Morning Olympian* of May 24, 1919.

and the formal openings were scheduled for June 25 and 26 respectively. More than 5,000 of the benevolent and protective brethren flocked into town for the ceremonies. Seventeen Elk deputies were appointed to help the limited local police force maintain order, but, according to Hollis Fultz, who had been chairman of the building committee and was exalted ruler of the local lodge that year, *"by one o'clock in the afternoon, all the deputies themselves were a little unruly."*

In his book *Elkdom in Olympia,* Fultz provided details of the day's festivities which were tactfully ignored by the contemporary press:

"There was a bootlegging joint just a block and a half from the police station; at times the line extended beyond the front door of the jail. Rowdy crowds filled the streets; and only while the parade was being held, and it was more than 20 blocks long, was there much semblance of order. By dinner time, restaurants had to lock their doors to avoid destruction of property. The Olympian Hotel

was dedicated the same day; fire hoses were turned on until one of the floors was flooded. It was midnight before order was restored. Yet all this trouble was caused by less than 100 wild individuals out of 5,500. No one was hurt; few fights, or other trouble, and all the events were a great success. Nevertheless, this Exalted Ruler, gazing out of the upstairs window of the Chamber of Commerce, across at Crane's Restaurant, where chairs had been strung across the doors, shed a few tears, for his future reputation and that of B.P.O.E. 186."

The new Olympian hotel had formally opened for inspection the previous day, with visiting hours form four to ten p.m. It was described by the *Recorder* as "*a triumph of comfort and beauty, the constant stream of visitors finding continual delight in the elegancies of furnishing and arrangements.*" The main dining room, with its huge arch windows and two story high ceiling was pronounced "*superior to the Isabella Dining Room of the Hotel Davenport (in Spokane), which has been conceded to be the finest in the state.*"

When the first formal dinner was held in the new hotel dining room with state and local dignitaries toasting the capital city's latest civic achievement, Peter Schmidt chartered an airplane to transport him from Seattle in time for the speeches, which made him the first Olympian to make a commercial flight. (The following month a pilot named Pop Maroney moored his seaplane at the city float for several days, taking local citizens on sightseeing flights at $15 a head. Mrs. Mowell got her delayed airplane ride with this first of the postwar barnstormers to work Olympia.)

The Olympian quickly became the center of social and political life. It housed the local branch of the automobile association and the central stage terminal, as well, and increasing numbers of people started their journeys from there as the Thompson-Smith stage line, which had transferred its five deluxe motor coaches from California to the Olympia-Tacoma route, brought a new standard of elegance in highway transportation. Their "big red stages" . . . elongated sedans with separate doors for each seat . . . were a marked improvement over the cold and drafty touring car-type stages of the past with their flapping side curtains. The new ones had plate glass windows, gray plush upholstery and three compartments . . . one for the driver, one for "ladies and escorts" and a smoker for unattached males.

The motor vehicle, particularly the Model-T Ford, had become commonplace by 1920. The *Recorder* noted that local dealers had 1,000 automobiles on order for the year, which would require a 250-car freight train if they all arrived at once. The motor truck had virtually eliminated the horse-drawn delivery wagon and was moving onto the farm. In May a 40-truck caravan, representing every make sold on the Pacific coast . . . GMX, Maxwell, Clydesdale, Day-Elder, Garford, Commerce and many more . . . arrived in town to publicize the "Motorize the Farm" campaign of the dealers' association.

The popularity of the automobile exceeded the available supply of fuel during the summer of 1920 and motorists were horrified to find themselves grounded by a major gasoline shortage. The *Recorder* commented on "*the long, dismal lines at every gas supply station*" and noted that when a 6,000-gallon railroad tank car finally arrived in town, its contents was "*lapped up tremendously by famished tanks.*" The 6,000 gallons lasted only four hours and the price was raised from 25¢ to 38¢ a gallon.

The community's grip on the capital became somewhat firmer on April 30, when the cornerstone was laid for the new $890,000 office building which was the next step in the Wilder and White plan for the new capitol group. Listed as "Office Building A" on the architects' plans, it is now known as the Insurance building. A $257,000 contract was also let by the capital commission for a power house and heating plant at the foot of the bluff on the shore of the Deschutes waterway. It was to be built of Tenino sandstone to match that salvaged from the burned high school building, which the commission had thriftily ordered used "as far as it will go."

As usual, the advance of progress demolished old landmarks as it created new ones. The once grand and gaudy Olympia opera house, former pride of John Miller Murphy and the town, but last used three years earlier for a boxing exhibition, was condemned as a fire trap and torn down. The old Lobby Building, erected the same year as the opera house as Farquhar's general store and later used as a legislative building and social center, also fell to the wreckers' crowbars and sledgehammers.

Although the street and bridge bond issue had been approved by the voters, the deepening post-war financial slump was making it difficult to market the paper. In April the *Recorder* headlined the ominous news . . .

"BEWARE THE CITY BRIDGE." The city council had been forced to close the 4th street span to heavy traffic and to inform automobile owners that they could cross it only at their own risk. The omniverous Budd Inlet teredos were as hungry as ever and it was reported that one of the bridge bents was supported by only a single piling, while several others had only two or three remaining. The paper reported flatly that *it is about to collapse."*

The paving of East Bay drive to the park was also delayed by trouble in disposing of $12,000 in bonds to fund the city's share of the project. And there was already talk of a new bond proposal to replace the old brick Lincoln and Washington schools, which were being propped up with timbers to prevent their complete collapse.*

THE DEVIL AND MR. HAYCOX

The major community feud of 1920 was generated by a proposal to permit the students of William Winlock Miller high school to hold co-educational dances in the gymnasium "under proper adult supervision." The school board, scenting trouble, decided it wanted a public hearing on the matter. Apparently the first meeting was attended by only a few parents . . . and liberal ones at that. Those present voted 18 to one to permit the dances, but as soon as the result was announced the supporters of the puritan ethic began to make themselves heard. C. E. Beach resigned as school superintendent during the ensuing furor and high school Principal Elmer L. Breckner replaced him. Leland P. Brown, former vice principal and athletic director, took over the high school and the board decided it had better have another public hearing. That one was held on January 16, the same night that national prohibition became effective and a grand victory celebration was staged in the Methodist church by the ladies of the WCTU. The forces of godliness were feeling their oats and their spokesman, Councilman W. E.

*As a member of Miss Amelia Dittman's second grade class at the old Lincoln school that year, I can testify that the building was more than a little scary, especially when a strong wind made it shake and groan.

Haycox, delivered a long homily to the school board. A vote of the parents meant nothing, he said, because the issue was one of right or wrong, and "any dancing is altogether wrong . . . the devil's wedge designed to be driven into the heart of the church."

Haycox was followed by a number of Protestant ministers who declared that "such diversion is apt to be immoral and likely to drive children away to other schools," and by highly vocal mothers, one of whom announced fervently that "I would let my children grow up without education rather than permit them to attend Olympia high school if dances are held in the gymnasium." Another topped that with the announcement that she was keeping *her* daughter out of school because the proposal had been made in the first place. J. Grant Hinkle, assistant secretary of state, observed that dancing leads to drinking and fighting and he couldn't "comprehend why people don't prefer to go fishing."

An effort was made to compromise when somebody suggested that girls be required to dance with girls and boys with boys, but that interesting proposal was lost in the general uproar. A few of the more liberal finally made themselves heard. Mrs. George Naden suggested that perhaps the students should be consulted "somewhat," but such arrant permissiveness was not viewed favorably. C. J. Lord pointed out that no high school students would be *forced* to attend the dances and Mrs. Charles Lindley ventured the opinion that "if old maids would learn to fox trot they wouldn't be old maids much longer." Frank Owings provided a historical note with the reminder that "Martha Washington was an unrivaled dancer" and an unidentified old gentleman, apparently not quite sure what the meeting was about, rose to declare firmly that *he* wasn't afraid of the devil.

The school board passed the buck to Principal Brown, who wisely waited until the defenders of morality found something else to view with alarm; then quietly approved the high school hops, which proved far less conducive to schoolgirl pregnancies than the outlying commercial dance halls, where bootleg booze was readily available and automobiles found plentiful secluded parking places on the way home.

The new outrage which had distracted the attention of the righteous from the high school gymnasium was the increasing obscenity of motion pictures. The PTA committee on movie censorship complained that "many plays are suggestive in theme and worse in production; that many films are unfit for children to view and, in some cases, pass beyond the borderline of common decency."

Local theater operators argued that "we give people what they want," but agreed to provide one "family night" each week, at which all film fare would be guaranteed "free from objectionable features," but things kept getting more outrageous. One theater, the *Recorder* announced breathlessly, was *"advertising an alleged 'sex' play with a poster of a nude couple embracing,"* although it conceded somewhat ruefully that *"no scene in the play carried the suggestiveness of the poster."*

Councilman Haycox was moved to new heights of indignation when the Strand theater posted a big sign, "LIVE BABY GIVEN AWAY!" The councilman confronted manager C. P. Mervin and demanded an explanation. The manager explained that it was only a baby pig that was to be the door prize, but Haycox was not mollified. He demanded that the sign be taken down immediately as "immoral and misleading" and departed "to consult with the humane society."

1921

There was more than the usual atrocious January weather to depress the spirits of the legislators when they arrived early in January for the 17th biennial session. The post-war slump was rapidly assuming the proportions of a full-scale depression. The number of unemployed workers in the nation had reached 2,325,000 . . . the highest since the panic of 1897. Pay and prices were dropping and tax delinquencies were increasing. Labor union membership had dropped 40 percent as hard-pressed workers vied for any kind of jobs at any kind of pay.

The legislative clerks, more anxious than ever to hang onto their patronage jobs in the face of the increasingly bleak economic outlook, arrived several days before the legislators and bustled into the statehouse to set up their committee rooms. Regular employees of a half

dozen departments, boards and bureaus were sent packing from their comfortable offices and sought refuge in the new Insurance building, which wasn't quite finished yet. The plaster was damp and the building's interior tomblike. The civil servants muttered and sniffled and came down with head colds, cursing the legislature as bureaucrats are want to do even to the present day.

When state government had moved into the sandstone statehouse 15 years earlier there had been room to spare, but even though the supreme court, attorney general and library had been transferred to the Temple of Justice, things were getting crowded under the octagon clock tower by 1921.

After electing E. H. Guie of Seattle speaker and Howard Taylor president pro-tem, the legislators prepared to consider Governor Hart's governmental reorganization plan, which he now referred to as the civil administration code. Ex-legislator McArdle, who was currently working for the bureau of inspection and had drawn up the proposed code for Hart, presented its salient features to the house of representatives, convened as a committee of the whole, in mid-January. There were immediate shouts of indignation from a variety of sources. Many legislators, particularly senators, who tend to be somewhat more paranoid than representatives, saw it as a power grab by the governor. School Superintendent Preston said she didn't like "its effects on the public schools," but didn't explain just what she thought those effects might be. The various lobbies which had evolved friendly working relationships with the existing bureaucracies didn't want some big, impersonal . . . and perhaps efficient . . . state department taking over in their areas of special interest, and organized labor also lobbied against the administrative code.

Most of the state's press favored it on the grounds of promised efficiency and economy, a notable exception being the Seattle *Star,* which seldom agreed with the *Times* and *P.I.* on anything and didn't like Governor Hart anyway. Hart, a diabetic, had been in poor health throughout his term as lieutenant governor and hadn't been able to afford proper medical treatment. His illness made it difficult for him to remain alert during the interminable meetings he had to attend as chief executive. He would grow drowsy and sometimes take refuge in actual slumber. The *Star's* political cartoonist lampooned this weakness by always drawing Hart with his eyes closed. The governor didn't think that was very funny and sued the publishers for libel. Relations between Hart and the *Star* remained strained throughout his terms of office.

Most newspapers including Olympia's Perkins twins, featured pro-code editorials pointing, like the *Recorder,* to *"the appalling facts on taxation in this state"* and decrying *"the total tax load on Washington citizens of over $72 million . . . nearly $54 per capita."**

The governor's message to the legislature had concentrated on the administrative code. He had done an excellent selling job throughout the state in 1920 and had succeeded in having its adoption included in the state Republican party platform. The entire membership of the legislature, with the exception of two senators and three representatives was Republican and all were faced with the growing public demand for more efficiency and less taxes. The voters were sobering up painfully after the wartime binge, during which they cheered any expenditure which might be construed as patriotic or useful to the war effort. And, as Hart pointed out in no uncertain terms, the general fund had a deficit of over a million dollars and the various institutions were crying for deficiency appropriations of a million and a quarter dollars.

Regardless of what their private thoughts on the matter may have been, the legislators passed the governor's administrative code bill almost unanimously.

It is strange that Louis Hart, a poverty-stricken country lawyer and poorly paid fraternal lodge secretary, should set as his goal the achievement of the first "business administration" for the state, but he did and he subsequently achieved that goal so effectively that business leaders came to Olympia to take a few pages from his famous account book.

GOVERNOR HART RUNS
A TIGHT SHIP OF STATE

Although Hart was preoccupied with his administrative reorganization plans in 1921,

he made recommendations in other areas, some of them surprisingly enlightened considering his background and political philosophy. They included probation or suspended sentences for first offenders in felony cases, registration and control of firearms and vocational and agricultural training for the inmates of state institutions. He opposed the move by ardent prohibitionists to establish a state police for the primary purpose of enforcing the dry laws and by industrial and business interests for a strike-breaking constabulary. If a state police force was established, he told the legislators, it should be primarily a highway patrol, financed by a $1.00 license fee for every automobile driver. He wanted the general fund property tax levies abolished and, although the legislature failed to do so, he saw to it that none were levied thereafter during his term in office. As another means of achieving that objective, he asked for and got a one cent per gallon gasoline tax to finance future highway construction and maintenance.

A bill was passed making bootlegging and "jointism" felonies punishable by five years in prison and the state highway patrol was established, much as Hart had recommended. A new anti-alien land law was passed "to prevent the best agricultural lands in Washington from passing into the hands of Japanese farmers*, a measure also advocated by the governor, and his one cent a gallon gasoline tax was adopted. A measure was passed making the sale of narcotics to addicts a felony, but permitting liberal prescriptions through doctors, dentists and veterinarians. Enrollment at the university was limited by law to 5,000 and at the state college to 2,500. The national "Black Sox" professional baseball scandal prompted a measure making it a felony to "fix" any baseball game and Olympians were delighted when continued development of the capitol group was approved, along with a $30,000 appropriation as the state's share for the much discussed and long postponed new concrete bridge across the Deschutes waterway on east 4th street.

There were predictable howls of protest when the legislators finally got up the courage to pass a joint resolution raising their own salaries from five to ten dollars a day while in

---

*again, for those who like to make comparisons, state and local taxes in 1965 totaled $879 million. By 1970 the figure had reached 1.5 *billion,* with an average cost per family of $2,836 for the year 1972.

---

*The U. S. supreme court, two years later, ruled both the Washington and similar California "anti-Jap" land laws unconstitutional.

session, but the bill which generated the most heat, particularly upon Hart, was a $5.00 per head poll tax which the governor favored because it would pay off the $11 million bonded debt the voters had imposed on themselves to pay the veterans' bonus. His political enemies, almost all from his own party, found this a convenient issue to focus public criticism upon the governor, but the real issue, as far as they were concerned, was Hart's stubborn refusal to fire competent Lister appointees and replace them with deserving Republican hangers-on. There is no bitterness like that of a disappointed political job-seeker, and there were many of these during the years that Hart commanded a tight ship of state.

The chief executive gave clear evidence that he meant business when the legislature adjourned in mid-March and he reached for his red fountain pen. He outdid Lister in vetoes, setting a new record of 31, plus 11 line item vetoes in the appropriations bill. These included a fourth normal school at Centralia, a women's industrial home and clinic, a $50,000 gift to the Children's Orthopedic hospital in Seattle and $30,000 to ten other charitable institutions, and a $50,000 contribution to the Pacific Northwest Tourist association. Although he had favored the much discussed blue sky law aimed at controlling fly-by-night stock promoters, he turned down the version passed by the legislature, terming it "a nefarious act to aid wildcat sales." The measure, doubtless drawn up with the aid of interested lobbyists, carefully excluded oil, gas and mining stocks . . . the favorite wares of the quick-buck artists . . . from all regulations, and Hart "refused to become a party to foisting such a bill upon an innocent public."

Less understandably, he also vetoed a bill reaffirming the treaty right of Yakima Indians to fish at Prosser falls in Benton county, but he redlined this one before adjournment and it was passed over his veto. The *Recorder* noted that *"even the usually silent and sententious Mark Reed declaimed against the governor's view."*

The highway patrol became a reality on August 1 when Louis M. Lang, former supervisor of capitol buildings and grounds, was appointed commandant and began recruiting his two dozen motorcycle officers. Ten days later one Mike Furin was encountered on the highway east of Olympia driving at the

NEMESIS OF SPEED MANICAS was Olympia's first traffic cop, complete with helmet, gauntlets and Yale motorcycle, posed in front of the Masonic Temple on Main Street in pre-World War I days.

breakneck speed of over 45 miles an hour. Major Lang personally chased him all the way from Camp Lewis to the Boulevard road before he got him stopped and Mr. Furin gained the historic distinction of becoming the first citizen arrested by the state patrol.

Governor Hart wasted no time in establishing the ten administrative departments authorized under the new code law. By spring the baffling multitude of bureaucracies which had sprung up helter-skelter during the 33 years of statehood was reduced to the departments of efficiency, public works, business control, taxation and examination, health, conservation and development, labor and industries, fisheries and game, agriculture and licenses, plus a highway commission, finance committee, capitol committee, humane bureau and state historical society.

Unlike recent governmental consolidations which were sold to the legislature on promises to cut costs and increase efficiency, Hart's plan began to work almost immediately. He appointed the best people he could find to head the new departments . . . his first choice was his old highway adversary, L. D. McArdle, as director of efficiency . . . and he kept them on a tight financial rein. Each department was required to submit to him a weekly financial statement, showing its total appropriation, its expenditures to date, its expenditures as of the past week and its balance. These the governor preserved in a loose-leaf ledger which he kept always at hand on his desk.

"That damned black book," as it soon became known in state governmental circles, was the terror of legislators and bureaucrats alike. It must have been an unnerving experience to try to outmaneuver a chief executive who knew to the penny exactly how much money each department had available at the end of every week and how it was being spent. Certainly it is one which nobody had had to face in recent years.

Under the careful supervision of Hollis Fultz, the contents of the black book was utilized to prepare elaborate balance percentage charts for each month of the biennium, showing graphically in colored ink exactly where every state agency and the general fund stood financially at any given moment. Hart kept a stern eye on the wall charts and if a misguided official overspent his allowable percentage of funds by so much as a fraction of a point, he found himself almost immediately sweating profusely on the executive office carpet. Hart also held regular monthly "cabinet meetings" of elective and appointive officials to establish communications between the various state agencies.

By the end of the year the million dollar treasury deficit had been wiped out and there was a cash balance of more than $650,000. The general fund tax levy had been reduced 50 percent and 474 surplus state employees had been eliminated . . . about 20 percent of the total payroll.

Despite these evidences of efficient administration, recall movements against the governor gathered momentum during the year, particularly after a bank scandal rubbed off on him during the summer, despite his best efforts to avoid contamination.

The Scandinavian-American bank of Seattle had collapsed spectacularly, leaving a great many trusting depositors holding the bag. The bank's chief officer, who had been playing fast and loose with the funds, escaped to California and displayed his political clout by getting the governor to turn down the extradition request to return him to Washington. The bank's number-two man, Ole Larsen, was less nimble on his feet and was duly arrested and convicted for his part in the shenanigans. He, too, had powerful political allies and much pressure was put on Hart to grant him an executive pardon. Larsen was not popular with the common people of the state, who had suffered once too often from the activities of defaulting bankers. A popular saying of the time had it that "We got three kinds of larceny in this state . . . petty, grand and Ole."

Hart compromised by leaving the state after advising Coyle, the ex-football player lieutenant governor, that he thought it might be an act of Christian charity to issue a pardon to Banker Larsen. As acting governor Coyle signed the papers and Mr. Hansen became a free man. By the same act he committed political suicide and inflicted grievous wounds on Hart.

A comparatively minor scandal, but one which was the forerunner of perennial outbursts of public indignation over the years, resulted from the discovery that certain drivers of state automobiles were using their tax-supported vehicles for private purposes. Director McArdle of the department of efficiency announced that he had found a solution to the problem by devising a mileage form which was to be filled out under oath and turned in monthly, along with a check to the state treasurer to reimburse the general fund for any non-official mileage. It was, McArdle pointed out, the same "honor system" used in making out state expense vouchers. What he didn't realize was that many an individual who wouldn't embezzle cash from the public treasury would drive a public car to the grocery store or picnic grounds . . . which is still the case.

POMP AND CIRCUMSTANCE

On June 1 the *Recorder* announced the beginning of a major change in the personality of state government. Since territorial days the small town atmosphere of Olympia had pervaded the modest halls of state. Hifallutin' airs were frowned upon and public officials, including the governor, were easily buttonholed by their neighbors and constituents in hotel lobbies, front porches and street cars. Hart, the champion of common-sense government and the elimination of costly frills, ironically set the trend toward governmental grandeur when, as the *Recorder* noted, he *"occupied the spacious executive offices in the new Insurance building, second story front, more elegantly finished and lighted than ever before in the history of the state. With the change has gone the old fashioned simplicity and easy method of seeing the state's highest officer that marked the capitol building used by governors of the state since Rogers' time. That is doubtless a distinct gain in time saved for the governor, as no one can see him now unless it is somebody he wants to see, and the present settings are such as to discourage any notion of familiarity. Visitors must first make themselves known to Mrs. Pearl Kelly, assistant secretary in the reception room; then to the governor's private secretary in his private office."*

It took people a while to get used to the idea that high state officials were not ordinary mortals who welcomed impromptu visits, but the trend was established. Mrs. Hart was sometimes interrupted in her housekeeping activities by unknown sightseers who knocked on the mansion door and demanded to be admitted and shown around because they were taxpayers and co-owners. The day was coming when a detachment of state troopers almost as large as the whole highway patrol of 1921 would be assigned to guard the executive mansion from close inspection by the citizenry and the countdown probably started when Mrs. Hart's husband moved to that "spacious executive office" in the new stone and marble Insurance building.

State government in general was likewise emerging from an era of simplicity. With two buildings of the new capitol group completed, its functions were no longer confined to the old gray stone statehouse in downtown Olympia. It had begun the bureaucratic spread which would eventually expand its operations throughout the capital city and its environs.

ALCOHOLIC ALTERCATIONS

Local law enforcement agencies were much preoccupied with the continuing and not very effective effort to enforce the Volstead act. A number of the town's less respectable hotels, including the Carlton, which had slipped badly in recent years, were periodically raided and there were complaints that bootleggers had set up shop in Sylvester park, doing a brisk business with thirsty service men from Camp Lewis. The sheriff's men spent a lot of time bouncing over back country roads matching wits with the operators of stills. The sparsely settled areas of the Black and Bald hills were favorite hiding places for such illicit distilleries, but a large one was discovered going full blast on the beach near Fishtrap cove, economically fueled with driftwood.

Mayor Bowen and his chief of police found themselves in a liquor-inspired controversy from the time that the mayor, beginning his second term, announced the reappointment of Chief Endicott. Councilman Haycox immediately leaped to the fray, violently protesting the mayor's decision. "There is gambling and bootlegging going on here," Haycox warned the council. "Boys under age are buying cigarettes and 16-year-old boys buy booze in notorious dives." He concluded with the dramatic proclamation that he would "stand for a clean town 'til judgement day." The audience, packed with ardent dries, applauded and cheered.

Chief Endicott managed to survive until late in the year when it was discovered that 82 bottles of confiscated liquor had disappeared from an empty cell at the city jail which had been used as an improvised evidence locker. The local ministerial association learned of the depredation and its president, the Reverend T. H. Simpson, announced that it was "a fine state of affairs." He demanded a full public inquiry into police department activities. Outrage grew when a raid on the Olympia Junk company turned up 13 quarts of bonded whiskey, which proprietors Berkowitz and Schomber claimed they had purchased from Olympia cops.

The city council, meeting in emergency session, recommended the dismissal of the chief and two of his patrolmen. Mayor Bowen had apparently scented trouble and gone on a hunting trip to Copalis beach. Chief Endicott fervently informed the council that he was "innocent as a newborn baby" and, taking a page from ex-Insurance Commissioner Schiveley's book, wept copiously. Also paraphrasing ex-Mayor Mottman, he sobbed,

"This leaves a black spot where I have never had one before."

Mayor Bowen returned a few days later and let it be known that he wasn't going to resign, although he did fire the three policemen, one of whom charged that the mayor had made frequent trips to the junk company for "nips" during the recent Armistice day celebration at the American Legion hall.

The Reverend Simpson appeared at the council meeting which formalized the police department shakeup and became engaged in a bitter quarrel with the mayor, insisting that he "wouldn't be dictated to" by the city's chief executive. Mayor Bowen replied heatedly that, for his part, he wasn't going to be dictated to by "nosy preachers."

Warming to his theme, the minister charged that immorality had spread to the town's youth and that Olympia high school students were "a bunch of little animals."

A group of some 30 high school lads subsequently called upon the Reverend Simpson at his home and invited him to the front lawn for a "ride out of town." It required his best persuasive talents and liberal refreshments to appease the youthful indignation committee.

Burton Troxell was named as Chief Endicott's successor and peace was restored for time being at city hall.

THOSE INSANE MOTORISTS

The proliferation of the automobile was dramatized in 1921 when part of the floor in the statehouse basement collapsed under the weight of 40 tons of prison-produced license plates awaiting shipment to motorists. The street commissioner was complaining that the city streets were likewise sagging under the weight of heavily loaded logging trucks and the Schmidt family, convinced that Appleju was never going to replace the real thing, had expanded into the hotel and auto stage fields, taking over the Mitchell Hotel and operating a fleet of 11 modern motor coaches on the Olympia-Grays Harbor route. It was evident that the bus was taking over the intercity transit business and the talk now was of abandoning rather than building electric interurban lines.

Irascible George Mottman, who had never accepted the coming of the horseless carriage and continued to ignore its presence at intersections, was again grazed by one as he made his stately progress toward his mercantile establishment. This time he gave vent to his feelings in a two-column full-length advertisement in the *Recorder* which should warm the cockles of a pedestrian's heart even to the present day. Captioned "AN APPEAL TO SANITY AND REASON," the announcement pointed out that *"It is an ordeal valued by your life and limb to cross any street or alley or road, and people unfortunate enough to have anything tangible in the way of real or personal property are taxed to death to pave streets, roads and highways to enable somebody else who pays nothing for the upkeep of the government to kill and maim and cripple others and their children and aged folks, just to satisfy an instinct to do as others do."*

"Three generations from now," Mottman concluded with almost clairvoyant foresight, *"we will have to confine the sane people to asylums to protect them from the majority of insane motorists."*

WONDERS NEVER CEASE

On April 1 the first radio concert was held at St. Martins college by Father Sebastian Ruth. Army Sergeant Benoit helped the good father hook up what the *Recorder* described as *"a large horn to which is attached a special sensitive phone in connection with a set of new apparatus lately installed in the college wireless station."* Some 300 college students and faculty sat spellbound as music and voices from the army radio station at Camp Lewis *"could be plainly heard at a distance of 200 feet."*

Early in May the new concrete bridge across the Deschutes waterway was opened to traffic, ending the decades-long civic battle against the marine borer. Captain Sam Percival's son H. A. Percival was granted the privilege of being the first to cross the new span, driving "Old Betsy," his faithful Dodge touring car. Captain Sam had furnished the timber for the original Marshville bridge of 1868, hand-hewn from his west side claim. Ribbon-cutting had not yet become a political art and the highway engineer proclaimed the opening by simply moving the barriers. A few days later the street cars resumed service over the new bridge, providing through service to the west side for the first time in more than a year. The *Recorder* noted that the Perkins press staff *"has resumed the sport of watching autos and trams try to avoid each other on the sharp turn at the corner of 3rd and Main."*

Post-war preparedness was indicated when Captain Edward C. Dohm, late of the army corps of engineers, was appointed a provisional captain of coast artillery to recruit an Olympia national guard company. Captain Dohm wasted no time and within a month the 3rd Company, Coast Artillery corps, Washington National Guard was mustered into service at the recently completed American Legion armory at 6th and Columbia. W. W. Rogers was first lieutenant, Neil McKay second Lieutenant and K. L. Partlow medical officer. Mrs. R. G. O'Brien, widow of the first adjutant general, and her daughter Mrs. George Aetzel were present to see the 73 enlisted men and four officers of the capital city's first post-war militia company sworn into state and federal service. A little competition for recruits was generated by the arrival in port of the *U.S. Eagle Boat 57* (generally known in maritime circles as "the Pickle Boat") to promote the enlistment of local young men in the naval reserve.

Another direct reminder of the little governor's era vanished earlier that year when his old territorial executive office building at 11th and Main was destroyed by a midnight fire. The little structure had been used as the governor's office from 1854 to 1860 and as general headquarters for the militia during the Indian war. It was here that Leschi's brother Quiemuth was murdered after his surrender to the governor.

The historic *Washington Standard,* last edited and published by J. M. Tadlock, made an ill-fated effort to go daily and compete directly with the Perkins twins in 1921, its first daily edition appearing on January 31. Although it launched its ambitious project with a grand subscription contest with two Ford roadsters, two talking machines, two electric kitchen ranges and eight gold watches as prizes, it failed to prosper. In a little over a year, on March 18, 1922, the last issue of the *Standard* was delivered to subscribers and the old wooden printing office on 2nd street was closed forever. A 62-year chapter in the journalistic history of the territory and state was ended. John Miller Murphy had not lived to see its demise. He had died in 1915 . . . and the town would never be quite the same again.

Times remained hard and the surviving dailies, the *Olympian* and *Recorder,* despite the elimination of this competition, cut back from six page editions to a modest and economical four. James A. Sloan, one of the proprietors of the now abandoned wartime shipyard on the fill, became a victim of the depression in midsummer when he shot himself in the head in a cheap Japanese rooming house in Seattle. He had pawned his gold cufflinks to buy the suicide weapon. Sloan had borrowed to the limit of his credit and eventually bankrupted himself in an effort to fit up the two remaining uncompleted hulls at the Olympia yard to enter the steamship business.

1922

Things were so quiet in Olympia in 1922 that such events as the eighth birthday of Master Trane Burwell were published as front page news, but progress wasn't entirely at a standstill. A new financial institution, the Security Bank and Trust company, had hopefully opened its doors in the new Columbia building and C. J. Lord was having a new Capital National Bank building of concrete and stone erected on the southeast corner of 4th and Main. A new industry, the peeling of plywood sheets from Douglas fir logs, had come to town with the completion of the Olympia Veneer company on the east waterway and the East Bay drive paving had finally been completed at the reduced depression cost of only $57,989.11.

By September the first of the handsome new stucco and tile school buildings, the new Lincoln school adjacent to Stevens field, was ready for classes and the towered brick building of 1890 was abandoned. Civic leaders put pressure behind the long discussed plan to create a Thurston county port district and things began to move. Homer T. Bone, attorney for the port of Tacoma, came to town in May to tell the Chamber of Commerce that a port of Olympia would pay for itself many times over. In September the recently formed Rotary and Kiwanis clubs approved the idea and the county commissioners agreed to place the issue on the November ballot.

The Chamber of Commerce campaigned actively for the port proposal, pointing out that 10 million feet of logs were towed out of the harbor every month . . . enough to support two large export sawmills if cargo-handling facilities were made available. The port project was duly approved by the voters and a site for ocean piers selected at the old Sloan shipyards site.

Governor Hart was reelected with little difficulty, along with the five solidly Republican congressmen and another Republican state legislature. The ill-starred poll tax was overwhelmingly repealed by initiative and the constitutional amendment to raise legislators' pay was rejected by almost as large a majority. The only bright spot for the Democrats was the senatorial contest, which young C. C. Dill won over the ultra-conservative ex-liberal, Miles Poindexter, and Farmer-Laborite James Duncan. Dill, a former farm boy and a YMCA member who didn't drink or smoke, had the support of both farmers and labor, upon whom Poindexter had turned his back, and was listed as an honorary member of the state WCTU.

THE NOBLE EXPERIMENT FALTERS

The old reform coalition of labor, granges and church people and the emerging urban middle class was foundering on the shoals of prohibition controversy by 1922. The dour grangers were humorlessly opposed to any relaxation of prohibition or, seemingly, to anything except hard work and godliness. They were officially opposed to prohibition jokes, drinking, smoking, dancing and movies and anathematized organized labor, which appeared to be taking too soft a view of such venial sins. When the state Grange master, William Bouck was excommunicated by the national organization for being too friendly with labor, he took a third of the Grange membership with him and organized the rival Western Progressive Farmers.

The prohibition enforcement agencies did little to endear themselves to the general public. The enforcement officers, or prohis, were exempt from civil service and their jobs were frequently the result of political pull rather than law enforcement abilities. Cynicism was in the air. President Harding had his own bootlegger, who supplied the private brothel and speakeasy of the president and his cronies on K street in Washington, D.C.

Treasury Secretary Andrew Mellon, charged with over-all enforcement responsibility, was generally known to have millions of dollars invested in the liquor industry. The ill-paid and ill-trained prohis in the field took their cue from on high and took their profits where they could. Senator Wesley Jones was the chief dispenser of prohibition patronage and he appointed a bespectacled ex-librarian named Roy C. Lyle as chief enforcement officer for the state. His assistant was a former King County Republican party chairman and unsuccessful congressional candidate, William Whitney. A jovial and talkative politician, he was best known for an affair with a lady member of the state legislature which scandalized the righteous and made unlikely his election to a non-appointive political office.

These top prohibition officers never made over $500 a month and the top pay for field agents was $200. Many were incompetents, drunks and outright hoodlums, the most notorious being one "Kinky" Thompson, who was famous for entertaining prostitutes in drunken orgies while engaged in "undercover assignments." He enjoyed beating up helpless prisoners and once clubbed a handcuffed man through the streets of Port Townsend to the jail. Juries soon refused to accept his testimony and when he was shot to death by a Tacoma policeman there was talk of awarding the cop medals for both marksmanship and public service. Another prohi agent was rebuked by a judge for brutally beating an 82-year-old man.

There were increasing charges of bribery, corruption, brutality and immorality against the prohis, two of them pleading guilty to staging a drinking orgy with a couple of teenage school girls, but Senator Jones consistently protected Lyle, Whitney and their "boys."

By 1922 it was estimated that 10,000 stills were operating in the state and decent whiskey was flowing in from nearby British Columbia in a rising flood. An open convention of bootleggers was held at Seattle during the year, with prices set and a code of ethics established, all under strict Roberts' Rules of Order.

The Noble Experiment was fast becoming a cross between low comedy and a nightmare.

Certainly the brightest event for the capital city in 1922 was the awarding of the contract on March 13 to Pratt and Watson, Tacoma and Olympia contractors, for construction of the foundation and first floor of the splendid new Wilder and White designed Legislative building, the domed keystone of the proposed capitol group. The low bid from among 11 firms was $397,514. Actual construction was soon under way and, although not much was said about it, the ancient "Rogers foundation" of the 1890's was quietly demolished. The new building would be considerably larger than the one originally planned for the site and the old foundation wouldn't fit the new building.

The new state highway patrol, consisting of 30 officers, reported that it had made 266 arrests during its first year of operations and weighed 144 trucks. Fourteen drunks had their driving licenses revoked and 209 errant motorists paid fines. The commandant had been fired as an economy move and that governmental man-of-all-work, McArdle, had assumed the office of chief along with his numerous other duties.

George Draham was elected mayor of Olympia in a lightly contested December election. Police Chief Troxell immediately resigned to enter the automobile business and was replaced by J. E. Kuntz. G. E. Henderson, a veteran Seattle police sergeant, was appointed assistant chief. New uniforms with roll collars and vizored caps replaced the old Keystone cops regalia and it was noted that Olympia's finest, a full half-dozen strong, were all over six feet tall. The two Dodge police cars gained a new impressiveness too as hand-cranked sirens were mounted on their doors and they began shrieking like banshees as they sped, with side-curtains flapping, to the scenes of crimes and misdemeanors.

Olympia's police force, like the town itself, was becoming sophisticated as the roaring 20's Charlestoned toward their midpoint.

IN MORE TRANQUIL TIMES, Governor Mead takes time out from affairs of state for a family cruise to Hartstene Island aboard the state fisheries boat *Bessie.* Governor and companion on the bow; family group seated in stern.

BROKEN PROMISES: Descendants of Indians who signed treaties with Governor Stevens came to Olympia in 1921 to plead with legislature for fishing rights guaranteed by the treaties. Stevens' daughter, Kate Stevens Bates, is in the front row, center, with the venerable Meninock, head of all the tribes of the Yakima nation on her right, and Chief Tchumse Yakatowit on her left.

GOVERNOR HARTLEY and his Pierce-Arrow touring car pose in front of the governor's mansion.

CHAPTER NINE
The Eighth Decade
1923-1933

If Washington state government emerged from infancy in 1889 with the shedding of the swaddling cloths of territorial status, it might be said that its period of childhood ended in 1923. Like an adolescent youth, it henceforth grew rapidly and expensively.

During the first 34 years of statehood, from 1889 through 1923, the *total* expenditures from the general fund amounted to slightly less than $76½ million . . . an average of about $4½ million for each two-year biennial period.

The general fund appropriations for the 1971-1973 biennium were in excess of *$2.3 billion*, or 31 times the entire expenditure of general fund money during the first three-plus decades of statehood.

The grand total expended from all funds from 1889 through 1923 was about $271 million. The figure for the current biennium, as this is written, is over *$5 billion*.

The cumulative cost of all the legislative sessions during the first 34 years of statehood was slightly over $1.8 million. An average regular session today costs well over $5 million, with biennial funding in excess of $14 million.

It cost the taxpayers of the state $680,000 to keep the governor's office in operation during those first 34 years . . . about one fourth the costs of a single biennium today. The lieutenant governors from 1889 through 1923

managed to spend the grand total of $31,-618.86, while the state highway system represented a total investment of $48.5 million, compared to an average biennial expenditure of around $800 million in this age of freeways, floating bridges and super-ferries.

And the state taxes collected from 1889 through 1923 amounted to a grand total of well under a quarter of a billion dollars. The present-day take for a single biennium amounts to about 10 times the total for the first 34 years.

By 1923 state government had burst from the confines of the old sandstone statehouse which had, for many years, housed virtually all offices and departments, the governor and the legislature. The massive bulk of the new Legislative building was rising above the ancient foundations on the hill between the Temple of Justice and the Insurance building and things would never be the same again.

Governor Hart still kept a stern eye on his percentage charts and a firm hand on his weekly account book, but he and succeeding governors, no matter how tight-fisted, would be fighting a losing battle against a state bureaucracy that continues to multiply itself like an eager amoeba.

The governor indicated no spirit of defeat or compromise when he addressed the two houses of the 18th legislature on January 10, 1923. He urged "a budget law with teeth" for both state and local government and pointed out that no department head under his administration was going to be foolish enough to ask for a deficiency appropriation. That treasury deficit he had inherited in 1920 had been replaced by a comfortable balance of nearly $4 million, and he made it clear that his veto pen was well sharpened to eliminate any extravagant notions that might reach his desk from the legislature.

He asked for a two cent gasoline tax to keep the state highway system on a self-supporting basis, a moderate blue sky law to regulate stock sales and a more stringent narcotics law.

The senate, all Republican except for two Farm Laborites and a lone Democrat, had already elected Carlyon as president pro-tem for another term, with Victor Zednick as secretary. The house of representatives, with 85 Republicans, nine Democrats and three Farm Labor members, quickly placed Mark Reed on the speaker's dias, with Ed Sims wheeling and dealing on the floor as majority leader. Sims had dropped out of the legislature for a couple of sessions and done some extensive traveling. In Mexico he and his wife had been captured by bandits, but he apparently regained his liberty with little difficulty (there were rumors that the bandits had paid *him* a ransom) and upon his return to Port Townsend had re-entered the political arena.

OLYMPIAN STATESMEN

The house boasted the largest female representation in its history with four members, Belle Reeves, Jessie Kastner, Mrs. H. J. Miller and Maude Sweetman. Mrs. Sweetman, a King county Republican of rather conservative persuasion who served four terms in the legislature, became a knowledgeable politician. She was also observant and literate and in 1927 she published a small book entitled *What Price Politics . . . The inside story of Washington Politics.*" Many of her observations on the statehouse politics of the 1920's provide a forthright appraisal of the people and issues involved. Of those legislative power brokers, Reed and Sims, she wrote:

"The overshadowing personalities of the Washington House of Representatives during my days in the legislature were Mark Reed of Shelton and Ed Sims of Port Townsend. These men differ from each other as a lion differs from a tiger. The one heavy, poised, thunderous in his expression; the other alert, tense, shrewd and persistent. The one wins his following by the qualities of his personality, drawing men and women in their weakness to the protection of his strength. The other, a machine builder, whips his human factors into the structure of his politics by promise, cajolry, bluff, threat, and every effective means that the shrewd mind can devise."

Mrs. Sweetman learned early in her legislative career the frightening results of crossing Sims, even inadvertently. During her freshman term in 1923 she was prevailed upon by the Seattle port warden to introduce a bill "authorizing cities of the first class maintaining a harbor department to install, maintain and operate telegraph stations in connection therewith." The measure seemed innocuous enough and carried no appropriation, so it passed unanimously, but Sims "took a walk" from the chambers before the roll was called. Although the lady representative was aware that Sims could have ordered her bill bottled up in committee or defeated on the floor, she was a bit miffed that he had slighted it by his absence when the vote was taken.

A few minutes later a pet fisheries bill of Sims' came up for a vote. Mrs. Sweetman decided to teach the floor leader a lesson by voting against his bill, *"and therefrom,"* she wrote, *"I learned a lesson:"*

"Mr. Sims' seat was directly behind mine. When he heard my vote, he sprang toward me, white and angry. I thought for a moment he was going to strike me, which of course he would not have done. Between his white lips he said: 'What did you do that for? I went out of the room to avoid a statement and to be absent from the roll-call on your bill; if I had said one word, I could have prevented its passage.' I replied, 'You would not have prevented its passage, of course, because there was nothing objectionable in it and it carried no appropriation. Why would you have wanted to prevent its passage?' 'Well,' said Mr. Sims, 'I am opposed to municipalities going into that sort of business. The bill is in itself harmless but once passed its promoter will be down here at*

the next session of the legislature for an appropriation. From then on, there is no telling to what proportions it may grow, to burden us financially and create an endless piece of administrative machinery. I could have killed your bill in a minute on the floor, but I didn't, because it was your bill!' "

Sims, wiser to the ways of the bureaucratic empire builder than the then politically innocent Representative Sweetman, was right. The Seattle port warden was on hand at the next session to lobby for a sizeable appropriation to finance his telegraph station. Mrs. Sweetman had also learned about the unwritten legislative law of the vote swap, as she explained further in her book:

"He did not say more but I understood then one of the most common and significant tricks of legislative achievement, the log-rolling process. My vote of 'No' had endangered the passage of his bill. I had not been fair in the horse trade. I had not yet learned the game of horse-trading."

Following the legislative ball, held that year in the spacious new American Legion hall in downtown Olympia, the legislators settled down to wrestle with bills, run the gauntlet of lobbyists and cope with the abominable winter weather. By mid-February a Caterpillar tractor had given up the ghost as it struggled to clear the street car tracks of snow and a good old-fashioned four-horse team and scraper took over. The streets were covered with two feet of snow on the level and up to eight feet in drifts. Buses from the south and west stopped running and, since there were no more steamboats, the railroads remained virtually the only means of getting in and out of town.

Not all the bills introduced were essential to the welfare of the commonwealth, although their sponsors no doubt thought they were. Representative H. F. Kennedy of Columbia county introduced a measure which he proudly called the "the poor schoolgirls' bill." Designed to promote modesty and prevent poor schoolgirls from feeling inferior to rich schoolgirls, it would have charged the superintendent of public instruction with setting a maximum cost of materials for the dresses of girls enrolled in the common schools of the state. It would also require all high

school girls "to wear skirts which come within 14 inches of the floor and waists closed at the throat not lower than the clavicle."

To the anguish of Mr. Kennedy, whose pet bill this was, it never got out of committee.

H. P. Rude brought out another cobwebbed proposal of previous sessions which would divide the state in two down the crest of the Cascade mountain range, creating the separate states of Washington and Lincoln. According to the *Olympian,* Mr. Rude's proposal *"started a big ha ha during the final hours in the house."*

The major uproar of the session was created when a house bill sponsored by Adam Beeler to appropriate $150,000 for the defunct women's industrial home and clinic failed by three votes. Veteran Whatcom county legislator Charles I. Roth noisily threatened to resign in protest.

No sooner had he subsided than a Sims-sponsored bill appropriating $15,000 to permit the state to prospect for oil on public lands was passed by an overwhelming vote. Roth leaped to his feet again and roared, "This is the straw that breaks the camel's back! I give notice that I intend to withdraw from this house immediately and hand in my resignation to the governor tomorrow. I cannot stand for such corruption!"

After much debate a motion was passed excusing Mr. Roth for the balance of the day, with the assurance that "the best wishes of the House go with him." This wise and kindly move restored peace and permitted the choleric representative to cool off in private.

B. N. Hicks, appointed Anti-Saloon League superintendent upon the death of Conger, pushed for a law requiring state officials to enforce the Volstead act. Although legislators were flooded with letters, sermons and telegrams, the bill died in committee, while the state's bone dry law, which was even more stringent than the national prohibition law, barely survived a repeal move.

Governor Hart vetoed the oil prospecting bill, pointing out that the average cost of drilling a single well was over $100,000 and that the state's entry into such a chancey business would create a bonanza for stock swindlers who would claim state backing. He also vetoed a bill raising the speed limit on state highways from 30 to 35 miles an hour and let the two cent gas tax bill, which he had asked for in the first place, become law without his signature.

---

*The advice of those who knew Mr. Sims best might well have been, "Don't count on that, Mrs. Sweetman."

The governor got his blue sky law and narcotics bill and even had the satisfaction of seeing legislative frugality reduce the cost of the session by $10,000 under the last previous one.

PLANTING THE CONCRETE JUNGLE

Later in the year Governor Hart, in his shiny Pierce-Arrow touring car, passed through what the *Olympian* called *"the symbolic gates of the paved Pacific highway at 9th and Main."* The highway patrol, still without uniforms, but sporting bright red armbands with the initials "HP" in blue and the state seal in black and white, led the 500-car caravan to Salem, Oregon, for the final dedication of the splendid new highway which boasted of "no mud or heavy grades" from California to the Canadian border.

That winter the highway department bought 50 big snowplows to be mounted on its trucks to keep the mountain highways open "except in very heavy snow."

The endless circle of more money spent on highways generating more money spent on automobiles had become well established by 1923. It was reported that 12,000 motor vehicles passed 4th and Main streets on Labor Day, with the average traffic count for that intersection 5,000 a day.

E. J. Thompson, the founder of the new Olympia-Tacoma stage line, purchased the big two-story masonry building across from the statehouse at 6th and Washington and had it completely rebuilt as the town's first consolidated bus depot. Some 80 of the big vehicles, now being referred to by their operators as motor coaches, rolled to and from the terminal each day, serving Olympia, Seattle, Tacoma, Portland, Grays Harbor and Shelton.

The city council, appalled at the destruction of streets by the ever increasing fleet of ever more heavily loaded log trucks, passed an ordinance barring the monsters from the city limits, but the resulting howls of outrage from mill owners and logging operators forced reconsideration of the ban and the problem has not been solved very satisfactorily to this very day.

Times were getting better as a post-war demand for lumber brought increasing prosperity to the forest products industry, which still dominated the state's economic structure. The Sound Construction company was awarded a $781,000 contract to complete the Legislative building to the base of the dome which, when completed, would be the fourth largest in the world. C. J. Lord's new Capital National Bank building at 4th and Main was completed and thrown open to the public, "ablaze with lights and decorated with a wealth of floral offerings", and the Sisters of Charity were well along with their imposing new red brick St. Peters hospital on the west side hill. The old power poles with their hanging street lights disappeared from Main street as ornamental boulevard lighting was installed from 4th to 27th and the fire department reached a new peak of mechanized efficiency with the purchase of still another motor truck, a powerful Seagrave pumper with a speed of 45 miles an hour and a pumping capacity of 1,000 gallons a minute.

THE SHIPS RETURN . . . CAUTIOUSLY

Enthusiasm for the proposed development of the port of Olympia increased with the arrival early in the year of the Charles Nelson company steam schooner *Saginaw,* described by the *Olympian* as *"the first deep-water vessel in many years"* to load 700,000 feet of lumber from local mills. The *Saginaw* tied up to the old Sloan shipyard wharf and loaded overside from scows. Although her cargo was to be topped off at Port Angeles, she was drawing nearly 19 feet of water when she departed. Some parts of the entrance channel had only 20 feet of water at low tide and her skipper, Captain A. A. Carlson, was understandably nervous and, according to the *Olympian's* newly assigned maritime reporter, *"took constant soundings".*

The *Saginaw* was followed by the company's larger flagship, the *Port Angeles,* and the *Mukilteo.* For some time the three coastwise steam schooners made monthly calls to load partial lumber cargoes from the Olympia Fir Lumber company and Buchanan mill, but even this evidence of potential world trade wasn't quite enough to get Thurston county citizens to vote a port development bond issue on themselves. With 4,353 votes cast, the bond proposal was 72 short of passage.

SOUNDS OF
THE ROARING TWENTIES

More and more Olympians were spending their evenings huddled around family radios which ranged in sophistication and efficiency from monstrous, many-tubed commercial "superhertrodines" to scratchy home-made crystal sets. Father Sebastian's college broadcasting station at St. Martin's had been assigned the official call letters KGY and was transmitting regular programs, including such grand operas as "Carmen" and "The Masked Ball". Those with the more powerful sets were tuning in, amidst much static, the Rhodes station, KDZE and Northwest Radio's KJR, as well as the thunderous Sunday sermons of the Reverend Mark Matthews, broadcast by the First Presbyterian church of Seattle.

The coming of the electronic home entertainment media may have provided the final straw which, added to the summer mobility of the family motor car, broke the back of paid admission baseball in the capital city. The sport itself was popular enough. The local merchants organized a twilight league and the sawmills fielded amateur teams in the sawdust league. The Olympia Senators even began the season bravely under the leadership of ex-major leaguer Ham Hyatt, but by the end of July the lack of patronage caused the semi-pro players to give up in disgust and turn the new Stevens Field diamond over to the high school and amateur teams.

The Chautauqua came to town as usual and set up its giant tentfull of culture at Main and Union, but the turnout there was also disappointing and there was talk that this great national institution would soon be going the way of semi-pro baseball.

The good old days when the activities of the police department were limited mostly to rounding up stray cows and rousting drunks had ended. The department made 1,514 arrests in 1923 and generated $20,580 in fines, mostly for traffic and liquor law violations. The Carlton hotel was raided again and its proprietor thrown into jail for 30 days for dispensing bootleg whiskey. Police kicked in the door of what the *Olympian* called *"that notorious liquor drive, 'The Orchard' at 8th and Chestnut"* and took its operators to join the lady from the Carlton. The federal authorities didn't neglect the capital city. Deputy Sheriff Bush Baker, an expert on the tricks of the local bootleggers, led the prohis in frequent search and destroy missions against the stills, and narcotics agents continued to keep a wary eye on Olympia's Chinatown. A massive raid on four Oriental establishments at once, all on the 400 block of Water street, added 15 Chinese to the jail population, charged with selling both opium and liquor. A later raid in the same area broke up a thriving opium den, with a number of local citizens caught in the act of puffing on the forbidden pipe. The police were quick on the trigger in those days, as young Tom Giles discovered when he decided to race Traffic Sergeant Matt Bartholet through Priest Point Park on his motorcycle. The officer emptied his revolver at his quarry, Tom hit a roadside tree and bail was set at $115.

As was the case almost everywhere, Olympia law enforcement officials had great difficulty in retaining the illicit liquor siezed in their continuing raids. Following the fiasco of the Olympia Junk company, a sturdy liquor locker had been built at the city jail, but it proved to be not impenetrable. In December an enterprising prisoner named Joe Foley, working out a fine on the Priest Point Park woodpile, decided that he and his fellow inmates needed a drop of something to ward off the chill. He sawed open the police liquor locker and when Captain Ed Herndon and Sergeant George Burtch came to inspect the cells they found the entire jail population hilariously drunk and most of the hoarded evidence consumed.

Poor Foley, in on a misdemeanor, was given a one to 15 year prison term for violating the prohibition law, but the amiable liquor thief held almost no hard feelings and even seemed pleased by the publicity his escapade had generated in the local press. Before he was hauled off to Walla Walla he composed a letter to Chief Kuntz, in which he wrote, *"You gave me a good write-up in the paper. I thank you for what you've done and am not sorry because the smile cannot be taken off my face. Goodbye and good luck to all except Officer Braun".*

YEAR OF THE RAT

The sheeted order of the Ku Klux Klan had somehow come to Washington in 1923 and its organizers, promoting it as a one hundred percent all-American patriotic brotherhood, were signing up members by the hundreds. During the summer Major Luther D. Powell, King Kleagle of the state klans, asked Governor Hart to send national guard troops to protect a mass initiation meeting at Renton. The crusty Hart was not much impressed with the Kleagle's assurance that his klansmen "will defend the rights of American citizens to the last drop of their blood." He quoted a state law which forbade masked assemblies "except for masquerades or amusement" and pointed out that the militia was getting ready for its annual summer encampments anyway. The Olympia artillery battery, commanded by Captain Dohm, duly embarked for the Harbor Defenses of Puget Sound to man the giant 12-inch disappearing rifles of Battery Kinzie and the knights of the white sheet were left to burn their crosses and recite their incantations without military protection.

The waterfront rats, temporarily displaced by the creation of the industrial fill, had migrated uptown and were again thriving. The municipal water supply, now drawn entirely from artesian wells, was much improved in quality, but the milk wagons, which had replaced the famous Olympia family cows, were delivering a less pure product than had the individually owned bossies. Eighteen cases of typhoid were reported in a single month during the spring, and the disease remained a threat throughout the summer.

The epidemic died out during the mild winter and civic pride was restored when ancient Ezra Meeker returned to repeat his December flower-picking of 1870. H. R. Woodward, who had helped him in his botanical ramblings of half a century earlier, was gone, but his surviving son, A. E., took his place and helped the white-bearded Meeker collect 62 varieties of blossoms . . . nine more than he had found in 1870.

and built smudge fires to protect the undamaged material.

The second of the new grade school buildings, the Washington school on the east side, was completed and two new theaters were built downtown, the Liberty on Washington street across from the new Hotel Olympian, and Wilson and Zabel's Capitol a half block away on 5th. The latter was designed by a rising young architect named Joseph Wohleb, who had made a name for himself with the palatial tile and stucco mansion recently completed in the stylish south end residential district for banker C. J. Lord.* The new Capitol theater had its grand opening in October, with a concert on "the immense new organ" and a local talent performance which featured the Chamber of Commerce glee club and a dance act by Ed Kevin's daughter Elizabeth. This was followed by a film entitled "Never Say Die", starring Douglas MacLean. The new brick and concrete St. Peters hospital was completed and the capitol commission let the contract to demolish the ornate old wooden structure which was in the way of the expanding capitol campus.

The opening of the splendid new hospital was not the only event to focus public attention on the west side in 1924. A local chapter of the Ku Klux Klan had received its charter from national headquarters in Atlanta and on the seventh anniversary of the reorganized klan the Olympia sheet-wearers made their presence known by constructing a 100 by 50 foot cross of old auto tires on the hillside above the Deschutes waterway and setting it afire, while shooting off parachute bombs with American flags. The spectacle was enjoyed by most of the community's white Anglo-Saxon protestant population, but nobody bothered to ask the local black community of half a dozen or so what its reaction was.

1924

By January of 1924 the weather had changed for the worse. An intense cold spell set in, cracking many of the cut sandstone blocks for the new Legislative building and causing $5,-000 damage to expensive cornerstones and round column sections. The huge stone pile at the construction site was valued at $300,000 and the contractors quickly erected tarpaulins

*The Wohleb-designed California Spanish style mansion is presently the State Capital Historical Museum. Another oversized dwelling, of red brick, built a little later by logging magnate Henry McCleary and designed to eclipse the Lord home, has now been converted to a medical center. The two adjacent structures remain as the last of the expansive dwellings built by wealthy Olympians as monuments to their success in an age of cheap servants and relatively painless income tax.

THE OLD ORDER CHANGETH

A major change in the nomenclature of Olympia's streets occurred in 1924 with the passage of an ordinance declaring all east-west thoroughfares to be avenues; those running north and south to be streets. It was felt that Main street was too small townish a designation for the capital city's principal thoroughfare with its expensive paving and boulevard lights, which would soon lead to the magnificent new Legislative building towering 27 stories above Capitol hill. The street was renamed Capitol Way. There was also considerable agitation to rename 4th street Oregon Trail Avenue, but purists pointed out that the Oregon trail had officially ended at Cowlitz Landing and merchants along the street felt the proposed name was too cumbersome. It remained plain 4th avenue, but 3rd street subsequently became State avenue and 6th street Legion Way.

The advance of the air age was dramatized in late September when Olympia citizens craned their necks to watch the United States' around-the-world flyers pass over the uncompleted Legislative building on their way from Eugene to Seattle. The following month it was announced that the navy dirigible *Shenandoah* would likewise pass over the capital city on a flight from San Diego to the mooring mast at Camp Lewis. The giant aircraft was delayed by a series of storms and when she finally took off was driven 70 miles out to sea, but her engines were finally heard at 6:45 on the foggy morning of October 18. Citizens rushed into the streets in the hope of seeing this marvelous flying machine, but *Shenandoah* was cruising 2,000 feet above the fog and they were rewarded only by the buzz of her multiple gasoline engines. On her return flight in the evening she was clearly visible in all her majesty, however, and those who had waited so long for a glimpse of her felt amply rewarded.

The port of Olympia commissioners, undeterred by the failure of the special bond levy the previous year, sold the maximum of bonds possible under their statutory right to levy a two-mill county tax, and plans proceeded for the construction of a deep-water terminal at the old shipyard site on the fill.

Law officers, with the notable exception of the highway patrol, continued to dash about in search of illicit stills and bootleg liquor. Governor Hart, who was no teetotaler, frowned on the use of state police to enforce the Volstead

act. It had been passed by congress and congress could finance the futile efforts to enforce it. It would probably have made little difference anyway. The first flush of self-righteousness had worn off and the public was becoming less enchanted every day with the heavy-handed efforts to enforce an unenforceable law and the increasingly harsh penalties inflicted for violations. The old morality was laughingly rejected by the bell-bottomed "shieks" and short-skirted, bobhaired "flappers" of the post-war generation, and even solidly middle-aged business men took pride in the quality of their illegal cellars and the professional qualifications of their bootleggers. The popularity of the prohis was not increased when a carload of them, careening through the streets of Washington, D.C., in pursuit of suspected bootleggers and firing wildly, dropped a United States congressman on the sidewalk with a bullet through the head . . . three blocks from the national capitol.

Chief Kuntz, sharing the general disenchantment, resigned from the police department and joined the highway patrol, having modernized the department with a criminal identification division, fingerprint files, modern equipment and prowl cars. He was replaced by Carl Hansen, an experienced police officer and former special investigator for the Indian service.

THE COOL CAMPAIGN
OF CALVIN COOLIDGE

The election of 1924 was largely a triumph for the Republican party at both the state and national level. Warren G. Harding, his administration sinking around him in a sea of corruption, had died while returning from a trip to Alaska the previous year. His vice president, colorless and tight-lipped Calvin Coolidge, received the nomination for president by an overwhelming vote and "Keep Cool With Coolidge" became the Republican battle cry.

Democrats, in a rare display of their ability to defeat themselves, became embroiled in a bitter inter-party fight between the wets, who supported Alfred E. Smith, and the drys who backed William McAdoo. Both sides were willing to accept a Republican victory at the polls rather than the nomination of the candidate they opposed and the nomination went to John

W. Davis, a stuffy and relatively unknown New York corporation lawyer. His running mate was William Jennings Bryan's younger brother, Charles. Davis chased away the liberals and Bryan the conservatives. The Progressive party, in an effort to give voters an alternative to the equally conservative and unimaginative presidential candidates of the two major parties, nominated Robert LaFollette, with Senator Burton K. Wheeler of Montana as his running mate.

Coolidge had little difficulty in winning the election and carried Washington with a vote of 218,000. The Progressive ticket made an impressive showing, coming in second in the state with 150,000, while the ill-fated Democratic team of Davis and Bryan trailed dismally with 42,000 votes.

Republicans, with one exception, were elected to the state's five congressional seats. Democrat Sam B. Hill of the fifth district defeated his Republican opponent, J. E. Ferguson, by about a thousand votes.

Continued ill health, plus the political heat generated by the ill-fated poll tax and the pardon of banker Ole Larsen, prompted Governor Hart to retire from public life at the close of his first full term. He made an effort to choose a successor, but without success. Lieutenant Governor Wee Coyle had also been tarred with the Scandinavian-American bank scandal brush and was overwhelmed in the primary. Hart's other choices, Mark Reed and Clark Savidge, refused to run. The race was wide open and 14 candidates filed for the primaries, ten Republicans and four Democrats. Persistence paid off at last for perennial candidate Roland Hartley, who won the Republican nomination from E. L. French by less than 2,000 votes. The Democratic nomination went to Ben F. Hill, but he got only about 7,700 votes, which was well under the total of the seventh-place Republican contender.

Republicans took every state elective office. Hartley had achieved the executive office he had so long coveted. W. Lon Johnson was the new lieutenant governor and, of course, the legislature was as overwhelmingly Republican as ever.

The three initiative measures submitted to the voters that year all went down to defeat, although it is difficult to understand why this was so in the case of Number 50, which would have imposed a 40-mill property tax limit. Number 49, which would make public school attendance compulsory for all children between the ages of seven and 16, was opposed by numerous religious groups and many conservatives, who thought teen-agers should be working and contributing to the family support. The private power forces succeeded in beating a Seattle City Light-sponsored initiative to permit the sale of municipal power outside the corporate limits of cities.

The election results would seem to indicate that Washington citizens were entering the midpoint of the 1920's still basically conservative, although the remarkable showing of the Progressive party in the state made it apparent that there was a growing discontent with the old politics and an awakening awareness of the need for sweeping changes in the social and political structure of the state and nation.

The Olympia municipal election, which hadn't generated much heat since the retirement of George Mottman from city politics, took on new life also. Mottman gave full backing to James C. Johnson, an attorney, who filed on the Citizens' ticket against the establishment's hand-picked candidate for mayor, George Draham. The Perkins press threw its weight to Draham, charging that Johnson was *"the friend of the bootlegger and gambler"* and printing front page lists of those for whom he had posted bail, but the Mottman magic apparently rubbed off on Johnson, who won the election.

The ensuing uproar at city hall would have done credit to Mayor Mottman at his best.

1925

The local political warfare began to reach a crescendo early in 1925, although for the first weeks of the year it was overshadowed by the more thunderous salvos fired from the statehouse. Normally the first official meeting of a newly-elected Republican governor with a newly-elected Republican legislature took place amid a honeymoon atmosphere, but although a honeymoon took place at the state capitol in 1925 it was certainly the shortest one on record.

Governor Hartley and Lieutenant Governor Johnson were duly inaugurated on the stage of the splendid new Liberty Theater* and the inaugural ball followed, again held at the Legion hall. The arrangements committee, in a burst of originality, had erected a special box for the chief executive and his party, made of

GOVERNOR STEVENS' MANSION, shortly before it was demolished.

rough logs, decorated with evergreens and labelled "Our Logger Governor's Pole Shack." Hartley, who had gotten his start in the timber business by marrying the daughter of ex-Governor Clough of Wisconsin, a millionaire Everett mill owner, and who occupied an imposing mansion in that city, did his best to look at ease in the "pole shack."

IN LIKE A LION

On the third day of the session Hartley, who, at five feet six inches, was one of the shortest governors since Issac Stevens, mounted the speaker's dias in the house chambers to deliver his inaugural address to the assembeled solons. It turned out to be more like a declaration of war.

---

*There were fears that the floor joists under the old statehouse might give way under the weight of the expected crowd.

He gave full vent to his political philosophy, which was far to the right of Calvin Coolidge, and to his animosity for the professional politicians whom he was convinced had frustrated his ambitions for the past nine years while ensnarling the state in bureaucratic socialism. Mrs. Sweetman, serving her second term in the house and an outspoken admirer of the little governor, described his opening gambit this way:

"On the third day of the session Governor Hartley faced the new Legislature with all the pentup feelings of nine years of combat seething in his volcanic nature. In a brief half hour this extraordinary Governor transformed the fresh and placid Legislature into a boiling caldron of contradictions, confusions and dispute.

"With even voice and direct stroke he aimed bomb after bomb, violating every discretion and thoughtless of political consequences. If there was method in his madness, and his purpose was to bring all of the varitey of forces that in past years had worked through sub ways and in secret, into the open, he achieved it.

322

"The Legislature sat amazed and dumb-founded."

Hartley told the legislators that they had created "too much government" and too many taxes and that he proposed to straighten out the mess they had created by "applying the simple standards of plain business" to state government, although he strongly inferred that he knew the pork barrel politicians of the legislature would resist his efforts.

Declaring that "we are too much governed," he warned that the state and the nation were fast drifting upon the deadly shoals of socialistic paternalism, which was "submerging the self-reliance of the citizen and weakening the responsibility of the individual."

He urged elimination of the 1½ mill highway levy, a pay-as-you-go system of highway financing and much stricter budget requirements and demanded a stringent belt-tightening in the costs of public education. The only diversion from his tone of extreme conservatism was his recommendation for a reforestation program (which would assure an adequate supply of raw material for his Everett mill).

Having gotten all this off his chest, Hartley told the legislators, like a group of naughty school children, to go home and behave themselves after appropriating sufficient funds to keep state government operating and taking action *not* to ratify the federal child labor measure which, if ratified, would become the 20th amendment to the United States constitution. He would, he said, call them back into session in November, after both he and they had had more time to consider the error of their ways and the true needs of the state.

Hartley was vehement in his opposition to the child labor amendment, which he viewed as the ultimate in socialistic legislation. He continued to make his views known, ever more vehemently, throughout the year. Hollis Fultz, former secretary to Hart, had gone back to his original trade of newspaperman (he had come to town in 1911 as foreman of the *Recorder* printshop), and was editing a lively new weekly, the Olympia *News*. In April he noted that Hartley was still *"ranting and raving"* regarding *"pampered and petted children"* in his *"rabid denunciation of the child labor law."* His lead editorial compared Hartley very unfavorably with the old Populist, John Rogers and his deep concern for the children of the state.

Somewhat dazed, the senators passed a joint resolution agreeing to the short session and rejected the child labor amendment after much debate and oratory. The representatives accepted the short session resolution with only eight negative votes, but rejected the section which would have limited the measures to be considered to the child labor amendment and appropriations.

A bill to create a new tax commisssion, which Hartley favored, came up for action and was described variously in the legislative chambers as "a panacea for the state's tax troubles" to "one of the most vicious pieces of legislation ever proposed." Opponents in the house made unusual efforts to assassinate the bill by removing the enacting clause and "trimming the Christmas tree" with myriad amendments, but it was eventually passed.

Another bill, introduced by the legislative farm bloc, with strong Grange support, provided a $400,000 emergency fund to underwrite seed wheat for eastern Washington farmers. It quickly passed both houses and was just as quickly vetoed by Hartley, who blasted it as "class legislation" and "paternalism." He further enraged the farm bloc by emasculating a bill authorizing a Kittitas valley irrigation and reclamation project.

At that point the battle lines were drawn and war was declared. The senate failed, by one vote, to muster the two-thirds majority needed to override the veto, but the house declared it would refuse to adjourn until the seed bill was passed. The 27 farm-oriented senators stood with them solidly on this ultimatum. The *Olympian* observed on February 12 that *"From a docile and agreeable legislative body ready to do the governor's bidding, the condition was changed to almost open revolt among senators and representatives who opposed the governor's veto of the seed wheat bill."*

After two days of threats, thunderous speeches and general uncertainty, the legislators caved in and adjourned *sine die* on February 13, one day before the deadline they had agreed upon. During the abbreviated session they had suspended the Centralia Normal School levy and reverted $400,000 to the general fund, ruled that 50 percent of all registered voters must cast ballots to validate local bond issues, appropriated $1,220,000 for capital improvements at institutions of higher education, and authorized $4 million in bonds against the state timber lands to finance completion of the Legislative building.

The higher education appropriation, lobbied by Dr. Suzzallo and his cohorts, was sent to the secretary of state without the governor's signature . . . and Suzzallo's name took its place at the top of Hartley's list of bad guys. He did sign the capitol completion bill, an action he would later recant in a spectacular manner.

FUROR POLITICUS

The legislators returned home and Hartley went to the Hotel Olympian to defend his economy moves before the Olympia Chamber of Commerce in a speech broadcast by radio station KGY. Hartley was the first Washington governor to make wide use of the electronic media to communicate with the public.

Personal and political controversy raged during the interim between the January and November sessions. Former Governor Hart did not escape the sniping. A flood of criticism had resulted from his pardoning of a great many convicts . . . including some serving life terms . . . in the last week of his administration. A few months later he was actually arrested on a Pierce county prosecutor's warrant charging that he had solicited a bribe from the attorney and liquidator of the Scandinavian-American bank. The charges were subsequently dropped, but the incident probably deepened Hart's conviction that he had been wise in retiring to non-political life.

The opening sortie of Hartley against Suzzallo was led by Duncan Dunn, a Yakima legislator close to the governor, who in April issued a statement blasting the university president for "running around the state and the United States playing politics and seeming to advance his personal interests." Suzzallo, in an address to the Grange, had previously attacked Dunn for trying to cut down the university's appropriation. This was the beginning of one of the loudest and bitterest battles in the political career of the combative Hartley.

Hartley soon proved to have more in common with Isaac Stevens than short stature, short temper and large ego. During the period between the regular and special sessions of 1925 there was ample time to draw up the battle lines and, as in Stevens' day, the legislature ignored party loyalties. Members were either pro-Hartley or anti-Hartley and the majority caucuses in both houses were very anti indeed.

The moody Mark Reed had, for reasons apparently known only to himself, isolated himself from the political conflict and refused to issue orders to the representatives who came to him for leadership. Ed Sims took over by default, but found himself, as a defender of Hartley, in a position of minority leadership.

Hartley's second legislative message was more belligerent than his first. He wanted the boards of regents of the university and state college and the boards of trustees of the normal schools abolished, along with the office of superintendent of public instruction. He blasted Suzzallo by name and announced that the state had far too many libraries. A number of them, including the state traveling library, should be abolished. He wanted the indeterminate sentence law revoked and the parole board abolished, voicing the opinion that "the best way for an individual to get out of jail is to keep out by observing the law." He wanted the reclamation and land settlement acts repealed and the ½-mill reclamation levy abolished. He boasted that he had fired 130 more code department employees and was requiring the survivors to work an extra hour a day.

Open warfare was declared between the legislative and executive branches a few days later when Senator D. V. Northland of Yakima delivered a scathing denunciation of Hartley, branding him as "an executive without the capacity for leadership." He called upon the senate to take up the burden of leadership, which the governor had cast aside. Most of the senators applauded.

This was followed up with the delivery to the executive office of a bill taking reclamation functions away from Hartley's department of conservation and development and turning them over to the more friendly land commissioner.

Hartley vetoed the measure and stalked to the legislative chambers to deliver a second message, as conciliatory a one as he could utter without choking to death.

"I can't see why there is antagonism between the legislature and the governor," he told the lawmakers plaintively. "I have been a a Republican all my life. This is a Republican legislature almost to a man and woman, so why is it necessary for abusive things to be said on one side or the other?" Then, in a final burst of burst of what his enemies viewed as combined schizophrenia and paranoia, he announced dramatically, "I have been misrepresented, lied about and abused!"

The legislators, now more confused than ever, declared that they couldn't decide whether to give up and go home or stay and fight it out.

The next day the governor backed up his talk of peaceful intentions by signing a compromise Kittitas irrigation bill making it possible to obtain $9 million dollars in federal funds for the reclamation project in central Washington. The legislators decided to stay awhile, but the session did not develop into a love feast.

A further head-on conflict developed over that ancient controversy, the disposal of public lands. The governor inferred strongly that the practice of turning over state assets to favored customers without competitive bidding was being carried on by Land Commissioner Savidge, who was a major power in state Republican politics. The legislature appointed a committee to investigate the matter, but the governor refused to meet with it because he believed its membership was made up largely of Savidge henchmen. The committee was unable to unearth any skullduggery in the land office, but the affair further widened the rift within the Republican party.

Perhaps to goad the governor further, or to dramatize his antediluvian conservatism, the more liberal legislators introduced a number of "social welfare" bills, including one to resurrect the women's industrial home and clinic, another permitting counties to build and operate charity hospitals for "the medically dependent" and another, sponsored by the Fraternal Order of Eagles, which would grant a $25 a month old age pension provided very stringent citizenship and residence requirements were met. Still another "radical" measure, which was defeated in the senate, declared labor unions to be lawful organizations and granted the right of peaceful picketing. When it failed to pass, the statehouse was picketed by union members carrying signs proclaiming "Senate Unfair to Organized Labor." Senator Charles Myers and Representative O. F. McCall delivered outraged denunciations of this impudence, apparently feeling that the militia should be called out to break the heads of the pickets.

A move to produce a single appropriation bill for the coming biennium was sidetracked by Mark Reed, who was getting fed up with Governor Hartley. He forced a separation of the general and supplemental bills and had the $1,300,000 college capital improvement appropriation, which Hartley opposed, placed in the supplemental measure. His strategy was to submit the supplemental bill first and, if the governor line-vetoed the higher education clause, carve up the general appropriation bill.

The legislature then adjourned for the Christmas holidays amid screams of a Reed double-cross from Hartley and the house minority.

Hartley spent a pleasant Christmas eve vetoing bills, including the supplemental appropriations bill, increased millage for higher education, improved workmen's compensation, authorization for second and third class counties to establish law libraries, authorization for first class cities to build auditoriums and museums, provision for condemnation of land for park purposes . . . and even a bill changing the color of the fringe on the state flag from green to gold. A few days later he vetoed a highly controversial basic science law, strongly lobbied by the medical establishment and bitterly opposed by chiropractors, drugless physicians and a number of old-time dentists who had been practicing successfully for years with little knowledge of abstract science or human anatomy below the neck.

The legislators returned on January 30, refreshed and eager to do battle. The senate immediately passed four of the measures over the governor's veto, but the wily Sims was able to marshal his house minority so effectively that the necessary two-thirds majorities couldn't be mustered there.

The politically memorable year of 1925 passed into history with the legislature deadlocked and its members feeling a growing urge to go home. Two of the lady members of the house, Mrs. Reeves and Mrs. Miller, took a final swipe at Hartley on New Years eve, directing a remonstrance against the "persistent and repeated violation of the rule against lobbying on the floor by the governor's appointees" and urging that the offending state employees be thrown out by the sergeant at arms.

Peace on earth and good will toward men did not reign at the statehouse that holiday season.

IT'S NONE OF THE PEOPLES' BUSINESS!

City politics were also volatile in 1925. In January, as the governor and legislators grappled at the capitol, Mayor Johnson made a clean sweep of all city appointees and appointed new ones of his own. The council refused to approve his selections and he demanded that two of the councilmen either resign or be recalled. Annoyed by the attentions of the local press and its reporting of the city hall feud, the mayor proclaimed, "—t's none of the peoples' business what the mayor or council do until after action is taken" and demanded that the papers stop sending reporters to the council meetings.

When the February payday came around, the mayor refused to sign the checks of Police Chief Hansen, Police Sergeant Fred McNeill, Fire Chief Rogers, Assistant Chief Bolton, Water Superintendent McClarty, Health Officer Dr. J. J. O'Leary, and their assistants. The council got a writ of mandate from Judge Wilson forcing Johnson to sign the paychecks and extra chairs were ordered into the council chambers to accommodate the overflow crowds of fascinated citizens who came to watch the fireworks. Councilman J. C. Bricker, obviously a man of peace, resigned a few days later. He was soon followed by Councilman George L. Jones. A. J. Phillips, builder, and Joseph Wohleb, architect, were appointed by the remaining councilmen to fill the vacancies. The mayor protested that the action was illegal and soon appointed his own councilmen. Councilman Roy Hendrickson was recalled by his constituents and Ed C. Johnson was appointed over the violent protests of the mayor.

The controversy died down somewhat when, in November, the voters reelected Mayor Johnson, but likewise approved a commission form of government. After 52 years the old ward councilman system was abandoned and the number of city fathers reduced to three . . . Mayor Johnson as public safety commissioner, E. N. Steele, finance commissioner, and Frank Phillips, public works commissioner. The commission functioned more amicably than had the council and mayor. The former city department heads, with the exception of O'Leary and McClarty, were given their walking papers. A. J. Peterson was appointed chief of police, W. J. Kingsley, fire chief and Julia Waldrip Ker, police judge, replacing old Judge Crosby and becoming the state's only female magistrate.

The tempo of the twenties was well established by 1925. The radio was fast becoming a household entertainment center. A second local station in the community center was broadcasting regularly, with legislative reports three times a week during the session. It was reported that the station had been picked up as far away as Berkeley, California, and the *Olympian* reported that many farmers in a 50-mile radius of the station were enjoying the church services and Sunday school lessons on their home-made crystal sets, although some of the more sophisticated radio fans complained that the local signal was interfering with their compulsive efforts to bring in the most distant possible stations. The farmers' simple crystal sets were rapidly giving way to store-bought models housed in handsome wooden cabinets and equipped with ornate "loudspeakers" to replace the earphones of the earlier and more primitive sets. Sticklin Augo Supply was advertising a wide range of models, including the Kennedy, Greve and Atwater-Kent, and business was good, but the new station didn't last long. Local merchants weren't yet willing to entrust their advertising dollars to such a new-fangled medium.

Proprietors of the town's traditional grocery stores and meat markets were keeping wary eyes on another new development. A chain store with the peculiar name of Piggly Wiggly was operating on a cash and carry basis with its wares displayed in such a manner that shoppers could make their own selections. This pioneer "super-market" was soon followed by a similar establishment called Skaggs United Stores, which shortly changed its name to Skaggs-Safeway.

Another tradition . . . the "hired girl" or Chinese houseboy . . . was vanishing from the domestic scene as houswives discovered the electronic household appliance. The Martin Hardware company was prepared to deliver a Maytag electric washing machine, while the Olympia Light and Power company (now a wholly-owned subsidiary of Puget Sound Power and Light) had an excellent stock of Hot Point electric ranges.

Science also provided a new delight for the juvenile population, the Capital City Creamery advertising its "frozen chocolate malted sucker," later referred to by its youthful addicts as the "popsicle."

Bootleg liquor continued to flow freely, ranging in quality from that produced by Bald hill stills from stagnant swamp water and aged as long as eight hours, to excellent bonded whiskey imported from Canada by speedboats, log booms, railroad cabooses, fast automobiles and a variety of other ingenious devices.

A second large plywood mill, the Washington Veneer company, was under construction at the foot of Capitol Way on the fill and local boosters were proud of the towering brick smokestack, which upon its completion was viewed as a symbol of economic growth rather than a polluter of the atmosphere. The adjacent shipyard site was cleared by the port commission and additional fill created by the Tacoma Dredging company's *Washington,* which also covered the last of the original shoreline along west 4th avenue. While the new ocean dock was still under construction, the port of Olympia played host to its first trans-Pacific steamship, the *Milan Maru* of the Japanese K Line, which lifted a lumber cargo from the local mills late in September. She was soon followed by her sister ship, *Malta Maru* and the McCormick coastwise steam schooner *Wapama.* By the time the new port dock was completed it was handling cargo tonnages never equalled in the town's heyday as a seaport.

There was considerable unhappiness among movie fans when the Jensen-Von Herberg chain took control of all the local theaters and announced that it was going to close three of the four. The resulting outcry brought about a change of heart and the new owners agreed to keep operating the Ray, for movies only; the Liberty, for vaudeville and movies; and the Capital for road shows. Only the Rex theater was closed.

The site of the pioneer Acme movie house vanished from the scene when Dawley Brothers Construction company removed a row of ancient wooden buildings in the vicinity of 4th and Washington which had housed saloons and shooting galleries in earlier days. They were replaced with a modern business building which housed another new chain store, Woolworth's "five and dime," the Buster Brown shoe store, Wilmot Clothing company and Munson Drugs.

At about the time the new Dawley building was completed, the *News* announced that H. J. Maury and J. Frank Libby had purchased the old "Mann drugstore corner" across the street on the southeast corner of 4th and Washington. The frame building there, built in 1870, housed N. E. George's confectionery and newsstand and the C. B. Mann feed store. The price, $40,000, was said to be the highest ever paid for property in Olympia, and civic pride was increased further when it was announced that a modern five-story office building was to be constructed on the site for the Security Bank and Trust company.

The massive bulk of the new Legislative building was rising ever higher to dominate the city's modest skyline. On April 20 the huge construction project claimed its first life when Emmett Godat of Tumwater, working his first day on the job, fell down an 80-foot elevator shaft.

The capital city became headquarters for an enlarged national guard unit when Captain Dohm was promoted to major and placed in command of the first provisional battalion, 248th Coast Artillery (Harbor Defense).

There was a general feeling among Olympians that things were going well in 1925, but an omen of future poor peoples' militancy appeared in November when an inmate of the county poor farm set fire to the barn to protest alleged mistreatment. The county commissioners, shocked by the aged man's refusal to maintain the meekness expected of paupers, appointed a committee of three citizens to investigate the affair.

Like many such committees before and since, nothing was ever heard from the citizen investigators.

1926

The new year of 1926 found the extraordinary session of the legislature still locked in combat with itself and Governor Hartley. The Olympia *News* headlined its lead story of January 5, "VITUPERATION FLOODS LEGISLATURE!," quoting such bitter terms as *"liar . . . ruthless, ruinous tactics . . . deceit . . . despicable and contemptible conduct . . . coercion, etc."*

Roland Hill Hartley, nicknamed "Rollin' Hill" by the *News* because of his habit of frequently "rollin' down the hill" from the executive offices to scold the legislators in the statehouse, continued the practice, arriving on January 4 to deliver what the *News* termed *"a vitipurative address."* In this one he blasted the news media as well as the legislators, denouncing at some length the "partisan and biased press." He also complained that the majority leadership in the house, headed by Reed, "had tried to use the budget bill to browbeat and bulldoze the governor." The Reed forces, he fumed, had "used every possible method of coercion, intimidation, abuse, scheming and trading" to gain their ends.

The latest gubernatorial outburst did not advance Hartley's cause. Representative Brislawn, who had been wooed away from the majority by Sims, returned to the fold following the governor's speech and Representative Templeton, another of the Hartley supporters, was taken to the new hospital to have his appendix removed. That gave Reed's faction the clear two-thirds majority needed to override the governor's vetoes. A resolution was immediately passed by a 63 to 31 vote amending the rules to permit reconsideration of previous vetoes.

The *Olympian* so far overcame its Republican loyalties as to reprint a Seattle *Star* castigation of both governor and legislature in bold face type on the front page:

"Our honorable governor speaks up in meeting to the general effect that our equally honorable legislators are incompetents, crooks or what have you. The honorable legislators retort that our equally honorable governor is a liar, a dictator and what not.

"Well, what difference does it make? Peanuts in politics are peanuts, aren't they? And the public still pays the bill, doesn't it?"

The *Olympian* agreed editorially with this analysis, but pointed out that these were awfully expensive peanuts.

On Janury 6 Hartley returned his 16th vetoed bill . . . a measure allowing metropolitan park districts to raise their millage . . . and the legislature gave up and adjourned. Ed Sims summed things up pretty well with his comment that "It started wrong and it ended wrong. The best thing about this session was its adjournment."

Following adjournment, the governor continued to occupy himself for some time with his trusty veto pen. Among the measures which were redlined was the Eagles' old age pension bill, designed as an alternative to the county poor farm. The *News* observed with some sarcasm that *"Hartley's heart was racked with*

pity for the aged and infirm, but his judgment is that pensions are bad business."

The governor did, indeed, produce a veto message on this one which lacked only soft violin music to make it a genuine tear-jerker:

"Childhood and age! The innocence of the one, the helplessness of both! How they tug at our heartstrings and open wide the gates of our finer emotions!

"The time will never come when we shall fail, either through private or public charities, to administer to those deserving in their indigency . . . But how often do our emotions blind us in our fairer judgments and divert us from the pathway of plain, albiet sterner duty."

One might expect to find the paper stained with executive tear drops as Hartley penned the final paragraph . . . *"While I commend the effort, I cannot conscientiously approve the method proposed; therefore Senate Bill No. 57 is vetoed."*

That grand old institution, the county poor farm, had been preserved.

The governor, preoccupied with feuds, vendettas and vetoes, served further notice on the public that the old days of dropping in informally on the state's chief executive were definitely a thing of the past. He asked the citizens to write, not call . . . and if they felt they must appear in person he informed them that the governor's office would henceforth be open to the public only after three o'clock in the afternoon.

He also blasted the proposal of the capitol commission to have electronic pushbutton voting installed in the new legislative chambers. "With this system we'll get 500 fool laws each session, whereas now we get only 200," Hartley declared. "If I had my way I'd stop all legislation for 40 years and the state would be better off."

ROLAND HARTLEY GIVES 'EM HELL

The departure of the legislature permitted Hartley to concentrate his fire on President Suzzallo of the university, whom he had disliked heartily since the war years. Suzzallo, as chairman of the national defense council, had been instrumental in obtaining the eight-hour day and other reforms in the Northwest logging camps. Such pampering of timber beasts was contrary to everything Hartley stood for. Furthermore, Suzzallo's national prominence and fluent speaking ability probably caused the governor to suspect that he might be a potential political rival.

By October of 1926 Hartley appointees on the board of university regents outnumbered the holdovers five to two and the governor decided it was time to make his decisive move. He made a trip to Seattle, presumably to confer with the majority trustees, and a few days later the board met formally on the campus. By a five to two vote the members dismissed Suzzallo from the room and went into executive session, quickly adopting, by the same five to two vote, a demand that Suzzallo submit his resignation. The two non-Hartley appointees, J. T. Heffernan of Seattle and Mrs. Ruth Karr McKee of Longview, were shocked and angered by the tactics used. Both resigned from the board soon afterward, Mrs. McKee in a sizzling letter to Hartley which pointed out that no charges had been brought against Suzzallo, that he had not been given a hearing of any kind and that she "refused to participate in a rule of political expediency at the university." Hartley replied that he "did not feel that the state has lost by your resignation."

The indignation of the minority regents was widely shared by the press and public of the state. The *Times* political cartoonist, who was depicting Hartley with clothing much to big for him and a hat much too small, now portrayed him with five identical little regents on a leash. Other cartoonists pictures him as the leader of a trained seal act, the university regents being the seals.

William M. Short, president of the state federation of labor, denounced the action as attributable to "the governor's insatiable hatred of the University of Washington and education generally, and his determination to subordinate education and every other asset of the people to his own personal and political interests and his unbridled prejudices." The Reverend Matthews saw the hand of the devil in the sudden ouster of the University president and thundered that it was "a crime against the university."

The *Times,* although now a Republican paper, continued to fire editorial broadsides at Hartley,* predicting that he would leave office *"the most despised man in the state of Washington,"* and recommending that the leave-taking be hastened by recall or impeachment. The Tacoma *News-Tribune* called the firing *"the blind action of a dictator,"* and the Olympia *News* editorialized that *"Hartley has upset the state and made it the laughing stock of the nation . . . something for which the voters should not pardon him."*

A recall movement was under way by October, although Hartley blandly asserted that he had had nothing whatever to do with Suzzallo's dismissal. When the newspapers refused to take his denial seriously he declared a press boycott, telling reporters, "I won't give out any news as long as the papers you represent continue their present attitude toward me." A number of the governor's appointive code directors followed his lead and refused to talk to the capital press corps, but Hartley's business partner, Joe Irvine, issued a press release threatening to prosecute everyone who circulated or signed the recall petitions if the charges against Hartley couldn't be proved.

---

*The story of Blethen's break with Hartley was frequently told in the state's political circles. Here is Hartley's version as told to a statewide radio audience in August:

"Of course, you all know Clarence Blethen and the *Times.* Clarence wanted things fixed up so that he would outrank or rank ahead of the adjutant general of the National Guard. And despite his remarkable war record I could hardly see my way clear to grant such an unusual request. You know, I was just a little bit afraid that if I did that the General would become over-inflated and blow up. So when his request was denied General Blethen just resigned and left the National Guard flat on its back.

"Have you ever seen General Blethen in his uniform? It is an inspiring sight. One day last summer—the National Guard wasn't in camp at American Lake, either—one day a herald came into the office of the governor at Olympia and announced that Brig. Gen. Clarence Blethen was about to appear.

"He was shown into the governor's private office. With true military precision he marched in, executed a right flank, did a left face, clicked his heels together, saluted and announced 'Brigadier General Blethen reports to the commander in chief.'

"He was in full regalia with enough service stripes to cover a whole regiment. I was sitting at my desk in my shirt sleeves, working. I hardly knew what was happening. At first I wondered if we were at war or something, but it seems the General was doing only a little dress parade duty.

"It is hard for me to take the General or his newspaper very seriously."
(Seattle *Times,* August 20, 1926.)

Seattle *Times* delighted in portraying Governor Hartley as a very small man in clothes too big for him. This 1926 cartoon referred to the governor's bitter feud with University President Suzzallo.

Undeterred by this threat, Mrs. Clarence E. Maynard, Thurston county chairman of the recall movement, opened headquarters in the new Capitol theater building and the signature drive continued actively in the capital city and throughout the state for the rest of the year.

A less vocal but sizeable segment of the public supported Hartley and disapproved of Suzzallo for a variety of reasons, including the natural distrust of the uneducated for the intellectual, and the belief of many that the university was becoming a hotbed of radicalism and a sounding board for "anarchists." A motion brought before the university faculty criticising the action of the regents failed because nobody would second it. Timidity may have had something to do with it, but many of the teaching staff had little love for their former president. His salary of $18,000 a year was considered princely, whereas the faculty rank and file were dismally underpaid. When the legislature had appropriated funds for pay raises, Suzzallo had used it to hire more instructors . . . and he ran the University as unilaterally as Hartley was attempting to run the state.

In the end the Suzzallo affair proved to be something of a teapot tempest and it had no effect upon the Republican party's usual overwhelming victory in the off-year election. The pro-Hartley forces, masterminded by jowly, balding Jay Thomas, the state printer and Hartley's closest political crony, and former Governor McBride, concentrated on helping legislative candidates considered friendly to the governor, which was probably a waste of time and money. Once they got to Olympia the majority of lawmakers soon became disenchanted by the governor's remarkable ability to lose friends and alienate people.

The popular fifth district congressman, Sam B. Hill, easily defeated his Republican opponent. The other four seats went to Republicans, although Stephen F. Chadwick came within about a thousand votes of upsetting incumbent John F. Miller in the first district. The veteran Senator Wesley Jones, who didn't even bother to put on a campaign, beat his Democratic opponent, political new-comer A. Scott Bullitt, by a closer than usual 164,000 to 149,000 vote. Jones, a militant dry, favored Draconian enforcement of the Volstead act, while Bullitt was inclined toward it liberalization. Some political observers, the dry ones at any rate, considered Bullitt's defeat as proof that the majority still favored the Noble Experiment.

$47.50 SPIT-BOXES

Hartley, even as he found himself embroiled in the heat of the Suzzallo controversy, found other things to get good and mad about. On October 14, 1926, he placed the capstone on the graceful 47-foot stone lantern atop the Legislative building dome, which towered 287 feet above street level on Capitol hill. Taller than the domes of any other state capitols, it was exceeded in height only by the national capitol (307 feet), St. Paul's in London (319 feet) and St. Peter's in Rome (408 feet).

No sooner had the little governor descended from the airy scaffold than he discovered grounds for indignation in the marble halls below. Shiny brass cuspidors were set conveniently throughout the building, perhaps at the suggestion of tobacco-chewing Governor Hart, who had approved most of the final plans for the structure. Hartley looked up their cost and set up an immediate outcry against the "$47.50 spit-boxes." Savidge and Clausen of the capitol commission claimed he had taken his figures from the rejected bids; that the golden gaboons had only cost from $2.20 to $10.00 each, but by that time the irascible governor was discovering other evidence of profligate spending in the Legislative building and he continued in full cry for several months.

The majestic capitol had, in fact, cost a total of $7,385,768.21, including the imported marble paneling, the five-ton Tiffany chandelier in the rotunda and all the furnishings . . . including the controversial cuspidors. Even if it had been paid for by the taxpayers rather than by capitol timber grants, it would have represented a great bargain. It probably could not be duplicated today . . . the skilled stone-carvers and other craftsmen aren't around any more . . . but if it could the cost would be astronomical.

New architectural marvels weren't limited to Capitol hill in 1926. In January the *Olympian* announced that construction would soon start on *"the city's monumental new financial building at the southeast corner of 4th and Washington, designed in keeping with the elegance of the state capitol group."* The Security Bank building, Olympia's first multi-story office building since the 19th century McKenny building, was completed by the end of the year and the ground floor retail spaces were occupied by such firms as Merle Junk's picture shop, Kerr-Sjolund jewelers, Phillips cigar store, Grace beauty parlor and Stenger and Quass, the live wire druggists.

SECURITY BANK BUILDING was first modern office building.

Milan Maru, first deep sea vessel to dock at the new port of Olympia piers.

Talcott brothers were having a modern brick and concrete retail building constructed on the northwest corner of Legion Way and Columbia and the recently formed general contracting firm of Phillips and Newell (A. J. Phillips and Roy E. Newell) had completed a second unit of the luxurious Capital Apartments, an exact duplicate of the original half connected to it by covered cement walkways on all floors. The same firm was at work on the Wohleb-designed Eagles' temple at the corner of 4th and East Bay. The cornerstone was placed with much ceremony on October 28, with a parade headed by the chief of police and the Seattle Eagles' band and with the Tenino Eagles' band bringing up the rear.

The voters had approved a school bond issue for a major addition to the high school and construction was underway at the site just north of the enlarged Capital Apartments, while the firm of McLelland and Avery announced the opening of the city's first "super service station" for the convenience of motorists at 5th and Franklin.

The new deepwater port of Olympia continued to prosper, the *News* announcing in April that *"the port of Olympia will rise to a maritime height never before attained when two big Japanese lumber carriers the* Oridono

Maru *and* Malta Maru, *come in Sunday and take berths at the port commission docks to load for the Orient."* With the continuing demand for lumber sparked by the post-war building boom, the new pier would soon be lined with as many as five vessels busily loading lumber from the Olympia and Shelton mills. During the summer the six four-funneled destroyers of Destroyer Division 32, led by the flagship *Paul Hamilton,* were met off Dofflemeyer's point by pilot Delta V. Smyth, operator of the tugs *Sandman, Alice* and *Lumberman,* and guided to a berth at the port dock. Local citizens flocked to the ensuing open house aboard the destroyers, many getting their first close look at the port facilities. The resulting enthusiasm gave the port special levy bond proposal a better than four to one majority at the polls and the commissioners began plans for an extension of the pier and the construction of warehouse and cold storage buildings.

Another progressive step in 1926 was the first concentrated and scientific effort to control the rats, which had swarmed under and through the town since early territorial days. The joint effort of the city and biological survey bureau of the state health department revealed that the rodent population had extended its sphere of operations to Priest Point Park, where new generations of rats multiplied and grew fat on the stock of feed for the birds and animals of the small zoo, and also consumed the young birds, including the offspring of the park's famous flock of peacocks. The old city dump on the Swantown fill, recently converted to a fill operation, was also found to be swarming with the unpleasant animals and

315 were reported killed there in one day by a single dose of cyanide.*

BOOZE AND BEDLAM
AT THE OLYMPIAN

From its opening in 1920, the Hotel Olympian was, for four decades, the second capitol of the state of Washington. More laws were passed or rejected and more political careers decided there than in either the old sandstone statehouse across the street or the splendid new Legislative building on the hill. The Olympian was *the* hotel and all the important legislators and lobbyists made it their headquarters. Among its other amenities, it provided an oasis of excellent whiskey in the Volsteadian era of Bald hills white lightning and bathtub gin. The observant Mrs. Sweetman, serving her third term as a representative in 1927 (she was the only woman member that session), recorded an interesting sidelight on life at the Olympian during the dry years:

"One who spends the entire session or a large part of it in Olympia, usually draws the correct conclusion that the hotel's the place to get liquor. On one occasion at the last session (1927) as members and visitors thronged the lobby of the hotel, some wag started the rumor that federal officers were about to raid the hotel. A remarkable phenomenon resulted. The lobby was quickly vacated by reason of the fact that each man went straight to his own room and the fun of the following day came as a result of the broken glass from bottles dropped from innumerable windows in disposal of the evidence."

---

*The Olympia rats didn't confine their activities to such traditional breeding grounds as docks and garbage dumps in the 1920's and 30's. A favorite occupation of a local highway patrolman in those days was the sharpening of his marksmanship by taking his coffee breaks at the drug store fountain in the IOOF building at 5th and Capitol Way and taking pot shots at the rats which appeared from time to time at the door of the adjacent store room. Uninitiated customers sometimes spilled their coffee when the gunfire started, but the highway patrolman became one of the crack shots of the force.

Mrs. Sweetman was no friend of Demon Rum and her dry sentiments had been strengthened during the previous session when Representative Zent of Spokane committed what she described as *"a gurgling defection from the ranks"* of the pro-Hartley minority and, *"continuing in his unhappy condition 'stubbed his toe' smashing his face against the wall (or something) and passed out of the picture."* This, combined with the illnesses, the death of Thomas Kemp and the subsequent desertion of H. G. Goldsworthy of Whitman, who announced on the floor of the house, "It's hell if you do; it's hell if you don't, but now I'm going to do as I damn please," had given the anti-Hartley majority the votes needed to override his vetoes.

Mrs. Sweetman, still an ardent Hartley supporter, wrote further of boozey doings at the Hotel Olympian:

"A ridiculous object indeed, is the legislator who repeatedly, and especially in critical times when responsibility ought to weight heavily upon him, permits liquor to steal away his brain and confuse his tongue. When I have seen such a one, I have wished that his entire constituency might be brought to Olympia to witness his folly and thereafter to bury him forever in political oblivion. We have had within recent weeks state-wide publicity given to a senator of long legislative experience, whose soft footfall down the corridors of the Olympian Hotel at Olympia is known to many members and many lobbyists. His oft-repeated midnight mission from door to door was no more important than to add to the sum total of his cumulative night-cap."

The 1927 session led Maude to the firm conviction that what the Olympian needed was a real prohibition raid instead of just the rumor of one. Her writing indicated that, among other problems, it was impossible to get a decent night's sleep:

"Anyone who lives at the Olympian Hotel throughout a legislative session must more than once be filled with anger and disgust at the night revelry, the noises from which vibrate the hotel court. At the last session of the legislature there was no mistaking the frequently heard, the penetrating bass voice of one well-known lobbyist of tax fame, and the sweet tenor of another voice, of more or less legislative ill-fame, as their drunken voices gave to the early morning air the confusion of their tongues, night after night through a whole session."

"It will be well for Washington and for the men, women and children of our state, when this minority of imbibers shall be restrained from their contacts with lobbyist hospitality.

"Olympia of all places in our state should have the highest measure of law enforcement during a legislative session."

The Olympian did eventually get raided by the prohis, providing great excitement, numerous red faces and a rich store of political anecdote, but the big bust didn't take place until after Mrs. Sweetman's retirement from the legislature and she was thus deprived of the satisfaction of witnessing this dramatic example of "the highest measure of law enforcement during a legislative session."

LAST LEGISLATURE IN THE OLD STATEHOUSE

Although she was disenchanted by the hard-drinking habitues of the Olympian, Mrs. Sweetman was favorably impressed by the general quality of the 1927 legislature:

"In many respects the house membership of 1927 differed from all other sessions. They were an independent-thinking body of men, refusing to recognize any faction, organization, or self-appointed leadership. After going through so many sessions where Mark Reed cracked the whip or Ed Sims bullied, it was an interesting and amusing thing, and to one democratically minded, satisfying, to see the opinions of these former masters treated on a par with the opinions of any other man in the house. In the previous sessions, one who understood the situation, could mark in advance the roll-call of every measure to be voted upon in either the house or the senate. This was not true in the house of 1927. The members wore no man's collar. They were men who could not be handled, browbeaten, bluffed or told what to do."

Mrs. Sweetman listed among the strong-minded representatives of 1927 Chester Biesen of Thurston, Knute Hill of Benton, Rex Roudebush of Pierce and Theodore Haller of King. With the new independent spirit in the house, Mrs. Sweetman, who was in 1927 the 12th in seniority, had hoped for a place on the prestigious and all-powerful 15-member rules committee, but Ed Sims quickly made it clear to her that this legislative inner sanctum was still a club for men only. She recorded her conversation with the tough ex-crimp in her book:

"As my legislative experience grew, and particularly at the last session, when only eleven other members were of older service than myself, I wanted very much to be placed on the 'Rules' Committee. This favor would, of course, depend upon Mr. Sims, and I asked him for it. His reply was: 'You wouldn't want to be on the 'Rules' Committee and I wouldn't want you to be.'

"I reminded him of the extraordinary session when the minority needed my vote to become a majority and he had to include me in the star chamber sessions, and he made his meaning clearer by adding: 'You know that 'Rules' Committee is a rough place. We swear and smoke, put our feet on the table and call a spade a spade.'

"What he really meant was that the 'Rules' Committee is the real battleground. It is here where every ounce of energy is concentrated ... where every weapon that can be used in mental combat ... bluff, threat, and oath ... is brought into play. That it is in the 'Rules' Committee that the decision is really made, and the legislative decision comes to its final conclusion. His quizzical smile and statement that the 'Rules' Committee was not a place for a woman really meant that I was not yet a member of the house organization. It would be difficult, indeed, and under present conditions, absolutely impossible, for any women to become a member of the 'Rules' Committee."

The number of available positions on the house rules committee was drastically reduced in 1927. Traditionally it had been composed of 15 members with eight, including the speaker, representing the "organization" forces; the other seven from the independents, minority and other scattered forces. The independent and unpredictable nature of the new representatives caused the old-line organization leaders to doubt that 15 controllable members could be selected, so the number was reduced to nine ... four anti-Hartley men, four pro-Hartley men and the speaker, Ralph Knapp of King county.

Mark Reed had made it known at the opening of the session that he would be absent much of the time due to "the press of personal business" and proceeded to abdicate his position of leadership completely. Mark Moulton of

Benton, leader of the pro-reclamation, anti-Hartley majority and known as "the little giant of the majority," had been one of the legislators defeated by the Hartley-McBride campaign strategy, and Sims was thus enabled to expand his pro-Hartley minority of 1925 into a majority in 1927.

The senate majority, led by Lieutenant Governor Johnson and the gentleman from Thurston, described by Mrs. Sweetman as *"the ever-present, intriguing, manipulating and horse-trading Dr. Carlyon,"* was strongly anti-Hartley. Johnson appointed Carlyon and four other solidly opposition senators to virtually all the important committees and they managed to control them firmly. According to Mrs. Sweetman, *"Johnson took care to see that where a Hartley man was on a committee, he was there alone."*

But the governor retained that ultimate weapon, his veto pen. Before he was through he had redlined 59 bills in whole or in part, cutting a total of nearly $2½ million from the general fund budget of $34,600,000.

Hartley did, however, open his negotiations with the legislature on the most conciliatory note he had ever struck. Sam Crawford, who had taken over the editorship of the Olympia *News*, noted that *"Hartley faltered over his conciliatory message as if he was not familiar with its contents"* and believed that *"a tight rein is being held upon Governor Hartley by those now guiding the destinies of his administration. He is saying the things they want him to say and doing the things they want him to do. The man on the hill is not now master of his own tongue."*

While the moderate tone of his legislative message would indicate that the governor was listening to and accepting some advice, there wasn't a political rein strong enough to hold him in check once his dander was up.

His 1927 message was largely devoted to a detailed summary of the needs of the state institutions, which had degenerated through years of neglect. He predicted that inmate populations would expand spectacularly in the immediate future, basing his opinion on a typical bit of the Hartley social philosophy:

"We are living in an age of cold hearthstones and relaxed parental restraint; of bright lights and late nights; of jazz and joyriding; of haste and waste. We are reaping the harvest in the criminal, the insane and the defective. In everyday affairs we have opened wide the door to improvidence and extravagance, and wider spreads the way to the prison cell, the insane ward and the almshouse. As public officials, we cannot stay nor halt the procession. We must receive it. Our duty is plain. We must incarcerate, shelter, care for and protect, whatever the cost."

He was unable to forego another blast at the administration of the state lands, quoting Pliny Allen's investigative committee of 1910:

"The looseness and laxity of the land laws, the dishonesty, incompetency and inefficiency of cruisers, together with other conditions, convince the committee that the state has been for years systematically defrauded, and the people of the state have lost millions of dollars by the sale of state and timber lands for grossly and ridiculously inadequate consideration. Reliable cruises that have been made under our direction disclose that careless, inaccurate, and perhaps dishonest cruises, heretofore made by state cruisers, have resulted in the loss to the state of great amounts of money, running into incredible figures."

He then expressed the personal opinion that *"the same looseness and laxity of laws, the same inaccuracy of cruises, the same obscurity of sale, and the same lack of competition, exists today."*

He urged that Governor Hay's measure of 1911, requiring that private logging roads and railroads be operated as common carriers to haul the logs of other than their owners be rewritten *"and made to mean what it was intended to mean."*

It had been widely predicted by Hartley's political opponents that, as a timber and logging magnate, he would turn the state's forest resources over to the robber barons of the industry. It somewhat took the wind out of their sails when he told the legislators that *"if our constitution renders us powerless properly to protect and safeguard the great heritage of our school children and leaves us to sit idly by to watch certain great powerful timber interests gobble up sections 16 and 36 of each township in our forest areas, and whittle away piecemeal the state's great stand of Douglas fir on the Olympic Peninsula, then most certainly it is time to amend the constitution."*

His biggest concession was a budget recommendation for total highway expenditures of $24,701,000, whereas he had, at the opening of the previous session, insisted that the highway budget should be limited to $10 million a biennium. This, as the *News* pointed out, *"removes the lid from the state highway appropriation and opens the lid to the pork barrel . . . and does much to restore rapport with the members of the legislature."*

The governor closed his message with the wish that *"harmony may characterize our relations and success attend our common efforts."*

And, for good measure, he sent invitations to all the legislators, even his bitterest political enemies, to attend a lavish reception at the mansion.

On March 9, 1927, the members of the 20th legislature of the state of Washington deserted their modest chambers in the old downtown statehouse and marched in a body up the hill to the monumental new Legislative building. Mounting the broad stone steps at the north entrance, they passed through the 30-ton ornamental bronze doors and into the rotunda of gray Alaska marble, with the great seal of the state in bronze set in the mosaic marble floor and the huge Tiffany chandelier 50 feet overhead, hanging from the inner masonry dome by a 101-foot bronze chain. Then they separated, the senators taking over their new desks and comfortable swivel-chairs in the heavily carpeted chambers of Formosan marble; the representatives moving into their south chambers, finished in French Escalette marble of cream and yellow with delicate veining of warm pink and red.

NEW CAPITOL: OLD CUSTOMS

Maude Sweetman, who missed little that went on in legislative circles, noted that one of the first facilities to be furnished and equipped was an oasis of relaxation and hospitality which became known over the succeeding years as committee room X or committee room 13. Mrs. Sweetman wrote: *"This fountain of refreshment was established in the few days of the occupancy of the new quarters by the Legislature in the last session."*

The legislature had come a long way from the drafty wooden territorial capitol, which had stood just to the east, between the current sites of the Legislative and Insurance buildings, but the custom of "taking the oath of allegiance" had survived . . . in a somewhat more sophisticated milieu.

Three days later, at midnight on March 11, the constitutional 60-day term was supposed to end, but the legislature was locked in an inter-house battle over the highway and general fund budgets. The joint conference committee appointed to reach a compromise on the distribution of the concrete pork barrel was made up of anti-Hartley senators and pro-Hartley representatives and there was little rapport between them. While the conference committee haggled in the privacy of the new rules committee room on the floor above the chambers legislators, lobbyists, employees and townspeople danced in the rotunda to the beat of a jazz band. The temporary clocks had been removed from both chambers and, officially, time was standing still at the capitol.

As is usual in such cases, fatigue and an overwhelming desire to pack up and go home forced one side to capitulate. In this case it was the senate segment of the conference committee. They wearily approved the $34,600,000 general fund budget, including $319,000 which the senate and Hartley had wanted to trim. It included $18,000 to investigate the governor's office.

The legislature adjourned *sine die* at 5:34 p.m. on March 12, having run 17 hours and 34 minutes overtime.

The lawmakers had responded to Hartley's request for an institutional building program, making the largest appropriation yet to begin mending the results of the neglect of 20 years. In the final confusion the federated industries lobby had succeeded in pushing through a senate bill making it more difficult than ever for injured workmen to collect industrial insurance. The new measure prohibited workers from suing employers and made any appeal from the rulings of the governor's insurance commission virtually impossible. The state's industrialists, who were required to co-finance the insurance program, had traditionally opposed the concept that an employer had any responsibility for an injured employee. The majority, including Hartley, held firmly to that opinion and his commissioners had turned down every possible application for benefits. The courts, however, had frequently overruled them and supported the injured worker. Senate bill 230 plugged that legal loophole . . . and was typical of the last-minute special interest rip-off legislation which persists to this very day.

Folowing adjournment the governor pared that $319,000 and then some from the budget. His vetoes cut a total of $2,473,172.69 from the legislative budget, including the funds to investigate his office, $10,000 for a formal dedication of the new Legislative building and more than a million dollars from the highway budget.

Having rested from his labors for a month, the governor then embarked upon what the *News* called "a firing rampage." Among those whose heads rolled under the executive ax were J. Webster Hoover, the popular highway engineer, O. O. Calderhead, supervisor of transportation, H. O. Berger and Thomas D. Jennings, traffic experts, and L. D. Conrad, supervisor of the motor vehicle division, all employees of the department of public works. The *News* reported much indignation in the capital city, where the men involved had many friends and were considered to be among the more capable public servants.

The governor's communications with the ousted employees were characteristically brusque and to the point. His letter to Hoover was typical:

"Dear Sir: In accordance with my message to you, through our Mr. Lane . . . you are hereby notified that your appointment and services as State Highway Engineer will terminate and cease on Saturday, April 30, 1927."

Lieutenant Governor Johnson expressed the feelings of Hoover's supporters in his letter to the ousted highway engineer . . . *"—t is difficult to write a temperate letter in this matter. * * * You were compelled to resign when there was no justification, in fact, for such an action."*

The governor's pride and joy, the state highway patrol, now nattily attired in field green whipcord uniforms with leather leggings and Sam Brown belts and commanded by Hartley-appointed Chief William Cole, met in a body at the old statehouse in the first of a series of seminars aimed at improved traffic safety on the state highways. There were complaints from some of the state's motorists, however, that it was as much as your life was worth to get in the way of Governor Hartley when he went tearing down the highways in his powerful touring car with red light flashing and siren screaming.

LUCKY LINDY AND THE MODEL-A

All the school children of Olympia marched to the new capitol grounds in mid-September to crane their necks and cheer when the current national hero, Charles Lindberg, circled the capitol dome three times in his ocean-spanning monoplane *Spirit of St. Louis* and dropped a message from his plane to the people of Washington.

Early in December residents of the capital city flocked to the Hotel Olympian to see another historic sight . . . the unveiling of the wonderful Model-A Ford. For months the nation had waited with baited breath to see what mechanical marvel was to supersede the legendary Model-T. The first of the "new Fords," a turquoise blue coupe, was enshrined in shiny splendor in the center of the lobby as the public admired the stylish lines, the "70 percent wool tapestry upholstery," the four-wheel brakes and the "vibrationless 40-horsepower engine," said to be capable of developing the breathtaking speed of 60 miles an hour. Prospective buyers rushed to L. E. Titus's Olympia Motors to place advance orders for the automotive wonder of the 1920's.

The various independent stage lines serving the Puget Sound region were consolidated as the North Coast Lines, with big new motor coaches revolutionizing public highway transport as much as the Model-A affected private motoring.

The contracting firm of Phillips and Newell completed a new multi-level department store building for J. C. Penney on the northwest corner of Capitol and Legion ways, and the big brewery at Tumwater, vacant since the demise of Appleju, was rented by a new local stock company, the Tumwater Paper Mills. The evening *Recorder* became the evening edition of the *Olympian* and a few months later the weekly *Chronicle,* published since 1899 by M. D. Abbott, suspended, leaving only the morning and evening *Olympian* and the weekly Olympia *News.*

With the capital seemingly anchored safely for all time by the multi-million-dollar group of pseudo-Grecian buildings rising on the hill and the city's industrial base strengthened by the coming of plywood and paper mills, Olympia was developing a new civic self-confidence. The lumber market was booming as it had never boomed, the new port piers were lined with ocean steamships hauling forest products to the ports of the world and even a few of the old windjammers were being hauled from waterfront boneyards to help carry the timber cargoes. One of these, the graceful barkentine *Conqueror,* was towed to the pier by Captain Volney Young's wood-burning steam tug *Prospector* to lift a lumber cargo for South Africa. She was the last of the fleet of commercial sailing ships that had put in to Budd Inlet since the days of Mike Simmons' little brig *Orbit.* The *Robert Dollar,* largest freighter under the American flag, was one of 90 ships of nine nations which loaded 130,000,000 board feet of lumber, doors and plywood at the Port of Olympia in 1927.

Times appeared to be changing for the better and even women were proving that they could compete in the new society of the twenties. Margaret McKenny, daughter of the territorial Indian agent and capitalist, received a commission to landscape a 1,500-acre estate in New York and departed for the east, admitting that she would "miss the wild blackberry and mushroom hunting seasons."

1928

Governor Hartley increased the volume of his outcries against the extravagance of the capitol commission in furnishing the new Legislative building as the election year of 1928 rolled around. Land Commissioner Savidge, in January, felt constrained to buy air time on radio stations KOMO in Seattle and KHQ in Spokane to defend the actions of the board, but it was impossible to drown out the governor, once he was aroused.

On February 27, the eve of the formal move of the governor and state elective officials to their posh new offices on the second floor of the capitol, Hartley delivered himself of a blast at the building itself, as well as its amenities. It constituted, he proclaimed, "a monument to extravagance in architectural design and waste and profligacy in furnishings" . . . although he had originally taken great pride in it and even suggested that the legislature appropriate an extra $500,000 to line the dome with marble.

The governor became apoplectic when the commission hired the nationally noted landscape firm of Olmstead brothers to lay out

the grounds around the capitol, insisting that a state highway engineer could do the job just as well.* He objected with equal violence when sculptor Victor Alonzo Lewis was engaged to create the soldiers' and sailors' monument authorized by the legislature of 1919. The price had gone up from $50,000 to $65,000 and Hartley felt a contest should be held to choose the best . . . and presumably cheapest . . . statue. When the other commissioners pointed out that a nation-wide contest would require cash prizes and other costs and that they could hardly call on other artists to bid on the model already created by Lewis, the governor decided that he "liked the design," which was non-abstract and heroic, and added his blessings to the contract. (The mind boggles at the thought of what the little governor's reaction would have been to the kind of sculpture currently in vogue for public grounds and buildings, which have the appearance of bronzed stools left behind by some prehistoric race of gargantuan metalic monster.)

Although he may have capitulated in that minor skirmish, Hartley continued to do battle against the "spenders at Olympia." As his campaign for a second term warmed up he appropriated several items of hand-carved furniture and jammed them in his car. Then he affixed one of the biggest of the "golden spitboxes" to its top and toured the state, letting the peasantry see at first hand the hifallutin' and costly nicknacks they were presumably financing. Hartley's "Cuspidor Caravan" has become legendary in the annals of Washington politics.

The governor, despite his preoccupation with the Legislative building, had plenty of energy left over for forays in other directions. He feuded consistently with the attorney general, John H. Dunbar, who was not one of his admirers. Hartley and his right-hand man, Jay Thomas, charged that Dunbar's hostility was prompted by the refusal of the governor to appoint Judge Wilson to the supreme court and then appoint Dunbar to Wilson's post on the Thurston county superior bench.

Whatever its origins, the hostility was dramatized in Judge Wright's court where

---

*Judging from the concern displayed over the years by state highway department engineers for the landscape, Hartley's proposal could have led to disastrous results.

Hartley had brought suit against the majority members of the highway commission to prevent their appointment of Thomas Beeman as secretary of the commission. Convinced that Dunbar had neither the legal skill nor willingness to handle the case properly, Hartley kept butting into the proceedings. The attorney general finally lost his patience and told the chief executive, "Tend to your own affairs. I'll run this case the way I please!"

Hartley vented the excess steam pressure created by this courtroom confrontation by going on the air via station KJR to blast the Seattle *Times* and *Post-Intelligencer* for their biased and unfriendly reporting of his accomplishments and their failure to print a long news release he had issued to them summarizing the tax savings he had accomplished and lauding the unprecedented efficiency of Jay Thomas's state printing plant.

THE CANDIDATES TAKE TO THE AIRWAVES

The 1928 political campaign in the state of Washington was marked by the first wide use of radio broadcasts by candidates and the usual overall sweep by Republicans of offices from the White House to city hall.

Calvin Coolidge, having issued his famous "I do not choose to run" statement, the Republican presidential nomination easily went to his secretary of commerce, Herbert Hoover, who was still regarded as a hero of the world war food drive. Senator Charles Curtis of Kansas was his running mate. Both were conservative and dry.

The Democrats, still smarting from the wounds of their 1924 convention, gave almost unanimous support to colorful Al Smith, wet, Catholic, and Tammany-supported big city mayor. To offset this image among the more conservative voters, they selected Joseph T. Robinson, dry, Protestant small town politician from Arkansas as their vice presidential candidate.

Washington Republicans aimed their big guns at Democratic Senator Dill. Miles Poindexter resigned as minister to Peru to return and do combat with his old adversary. Perennial candidate Austin Griffiths also threw his hat in the ring, but Republican organization leaders doubted that either could defeat the popular and charming Dill. They selected Judge Kenneth Mackintosh as the man to receive the blessing of the party bosses.

All the incumbent congressmen, with the exception of the previously invincible Albert Johnson, received easy renomination. Johnson barely edged out a political unknown named Homer T. Bone, who was thereafter viewed as a man who would be heard from in the future.

Controversial Roland Hartley had apparently struck a responsive chord in the bosoms of the taxpayers. He easily won nomination for a second term, garnering more votes than his two opponents combined. John A. Gellatly was nominated for lieutenant governor over Paul Houser, Victor Zednick and W. L. LaFollette, Jr. The more cynical political observers attributed the large field of prominent names in this contest to the historic fact that no Washington governor had yet lived to complete a second term.

A. Scott Bullitt edged out four other candidates for the Democratic gubernatorial nomination, while Harry M. Westfall beat Representative Belle Reeves by a few hundred votes for nomination as lieutenant governor.

In November 518,713 of the state's 596,888 registered voters went to the polls, but very few of them marked Democratic ballots. Smith and Robinson carried only sparsely populated Ferry county. Hartley's victory was less overwhelming. Although Bullitt carried only five counties, the largest of these being Grays Harbor and Lewis, he garnered 214, 334 votes to Hartley's 281,991 . . . an unprecedented number for a Democrat in the 1920's.

The only Democratic victory was that of Dill, who defeated Mackintosh in a close race. All the incumbent congressmen also won new terms. All the state elective offices and the usual one-sided majority in the new legislature went to Republicans.

Josephine Corliss Preston had managed to make her office as superintendent of public instruction almost as controversial as the governor's. She had quarreled constantly with her upper level staff, particularly the female members, and had run through a half dozen assistant superintendents during her first term in office. In 1928 she found herself under vigorous attack for having permitted the distribution to schools of "industrial and vocational material" provided by the private power companies. The public power advocates called the school publications "thinly veiled propaganda for private ownership of public utilities." They joined the pro-Hartley forces in opposition to the lady school chief and she lost the Republican nomination for reelection to Dr. Noah Showalter. No Democratic candidate filed and Showalter thus took over the post by default.

George G. Mills, denying his campaign was, as rumor had it, backed by Governor Hartley, was elected mayor and commissioner, carrying the Republican victory to city hall.

The airplane had thoroughly captured the popular imagination of people everywhere, and Washington's capital city was no exception. The daring aviatrix Amelia Earhart, following the course set the previous year by "Lucky Lindy" spanned the Atlantic by air and the University of Washington was establishing aeronautical research facilities with grants from William Boeing, pioneer Seattle airplane manufacturer, and the Guggenheim foundation.

AIRPORT

Infant airlines were springing up to compete bravely with the railroads for express and passenger business and H. L. Whiting, president of the Olympia Knitting Mills, back from a trip to the east, announced that Olympia should immediately start building an airport. He reported tremendous development of air travel from Chicago east and ventured the daring prediction that "airlines may become as important as railways."

Olympia civic leaders, no longer preoccupied and impoverished by the long battle to keep the capital, were more receptive to new ideas in 1928. By mid-April a plot of prairie land south of Tumwater had been cleared, a runway graded and the Olympia airport dedicated. The dedication ceremonies, bravely held on Friday, April 13, featured the dramatic arrival of J. B. Story, youthful manager of the Olympic Aeronautical corporation who, according to the *Olympian, "glided smoothly down from the sky and landed his trim Alexander Eagle Rock plane, just 59 minutes from Portland."* The Eagle Rock, on the last leg of it flight from the factory in Denver, was to be stationed at the new airport to train students for the company's Olympic School of Aviation. Another Eagle Rock, piloted by C. L. Langdon, also arrived carrying two passengers, John Sparling, an Olympic shareholder, and his guest, Walter Lytle. After becoming the first air passengers to arrive at the Olympia airport, they drove to the Olympian Hotel to address the Rotary club on the wonders of aviation.

A number of prominent local citizens made flights the same day, Mrs. W. W. Rogers becoming the first woman to fly from the airport. Others included John Pierce, Joe Kershner, *Olympian* writer, and B. F. Hume, secretary of the Chamber of Commerce. L. E. Titus, the local Ford dealer, was the first to make a business flight, winging his way to Tacoma and Centralia. Within two weeks Titus had become president of the reorganized Olympic Aeronautical corporation, with Story as vice president and Langdon as chief pilot. Titus announced that it was the company's purpose "to put Olympia on the map from the aeronautic standpoint and work for the development of the new airfield." Mr. and Mrs. Titus and Story then flew from Dearborn, Michigan, in a new six-passenger Bushel air sedan to be stationed at Olympia in the company's commercial service. Competition soon arrived in the form of a Waco monoplane, flown in from Troy, Ohio, by local pilot Ross Dye for Charter Service.

In December Santa Claus arrived by airplane and was driven from the airport to the capitol to meet the town's tots. The traditional Christmas lights were augmented by a 75-foot aviation beacon tower in suburban Lacey.

COSMOPOLITAN TOUCHES

Signs of progress continued in other areas as the optimism of the late 1920's approached its zenith. Phillips and Newell, who had just finished moving a whole block of houses from the expanding capitol campus to a new location east of Capitol Way, were at work on two new buildings on opposite sides of east 4th avenue, a three story brick department store for Montgomery-Ward and the Wohleb-designed Avalon theater of Spanish stucco, with a half block of retail store space in addition to the central theater section. In mid-summer it was announced that the Pacific Coast Investment company and Schmidt estate would soon begin construction of a "seven-story addition to the Mitchell Hotel" on Capitol Way across from Sylvester park. The same group had taken over management of the Olympian and the new structure, which absorbed the old Mitchell and became the Governor Hotel, was an alternative to an earlier plan to add two floors and a grand ballroom to the Olympian. Occupants of the stone courthouse at 4th and Washington were complaining that it was unsafe to venture inside, and so were lawyers who had to go there when court was in session. It was generally agreed that Thurston county needed a new courthouse, and that it should be built adjacent to the splendid new capitol campus.

The long dormant capital city was definitely growing and expanding. There was no doubt that, by 1928, it had at last exceeded the 10,000 population it had been bravely claiming since 1890. The Chamber of Commerce, anxious to retain Capitol Way as a fitting approach to the capitol group and to provide some control over the community's expansion, accepted the new-fangled concept of civic planning and urged the creation of a nine-member city planning commission. E. N. Steele, E. M. Chandler and Millard Lemon became the "nucleus committee" to set up the new advisory group.

Metal stop signs sprouted on all the arterial streets, replacing the painted warnings on the street surfaces which had been the earlier form of traffic control. The controlling stock in the Capital National bank was purchased by the Marine Bank corporation of Seattle and the Harris Drygoods company, a leading locally-owned department store since 1896, was sold to the Miller Mercantile company of Oregon, proprietors of eight stores in the neighboring state. A new firm, Olympic Homes, organized by Carlton Sears, proprietor of Rexall drugstores, and Ford dealer Titus, took over the 1,600 lots and five miles of salt waterfront of the old Boston Harbor townsite and announced that the land would be made available on easy terms to 800 new settlers.

The Weyerhaeuser Timber company began logging operations from its new company town of Vale in southeast Thurston county, delivering 350,000 feet of logs daily over its private railroad to its huge log dump on South Bay, from whence they were towed to Everett for milling.

The expanding port of Olympia continued to add new lustre to civic pride. In June a pretty Olympia schoolgirl, Hollys Brazeal, rechristened the Tacoma-Oriental line's trans-Pacific freighter City of Spokane, S.S. Olympia. The ceremony was followed by an inter-city love feast at the Winthrop Hotel which banished any lingering hostility which might have remained from Tacoma's last effort to steal the state capital from Olympia.

Early in September the sleek new Mitsubishi line motorship Olympia Maru arrived in port to load a cargo of lumber. Ship's officers, company officials and the Japanese consul were guests of civic officials and dignitaries at a banquet in the Hotel Olympian. Local Japanese school children performed traditional dances to Japanese music and Mayor Johnson concluded his speech of the evening by pressing a button which turned on the newly extended boulevard lights on Capitol Way all the way to 27th avenue.

The affair provided a new cosmopolitan touch, dramatizing the fact that the long-isolated town had emerged from its mudflats and placed itself on the world's trade routes. The name of Olympia was being carried to the seaports of the Pacific rim on the counters of two big merchant ships and auto supply stores began doing a big business in license plate frames which proclaimed "Olympia . . . the Capital Port."

The waterfront was further enlivened on June 21 when the first Capital to Capital Yacht Race began amid pageantry and half-day holiday. Ten cruisers, convoyed by the coast guard rescue cutter Snohomish, set out on the long voyage to Alaska's territorial capital, Juneau. The Olympian's paripatetic reporter, Kershner, went along on E. J. Thompson's yacht Dell, skippered by John Pierce, and was subsequently able to report that the Dell had won the first prize, $100 worth of Alaskan gold nuggets. Adolph Schmidt's Winnifred took second place and the handsome Sidney Laurence painting, "Race to the Potlatch."

After witnessing the race start, Governor Hartley celebrated his 54th birthday by swinging a scythe to harvest the hay on a vacant lot near the capitol grounds at the invitation of the owner. The governor thus dramatized his firm belief in the work ethic and, as he put it, proved that "I've still got a lot of pep and I wanted that fellow to know I wouldn't be stumped by his dare."

Steadily increasing prosperity prompted a revival of semi-professional baseball, the reorganized Olympia Senators fielding a team in the Timber league. The Chautauqua, soon to fall victim to increasingly sophisticated radio broadcasting and other leisure time activities, made its last stand on the vacant lot across from the capitol grounds, already selected as the most likely site for the county's proposed new courthouse. The local Elks lodge had made earlier use of the area for a less cultural and much noisier tent show. School Superintendent Breckner protested to the city commissioners that the Elks' carnival, adjacent to the high school, had served as a distribution center for postcards and other pictorial material which he considered "obscene and semi-obscene." He enclosed samples of the erotic material, which he said had been purchased at the carnival by pupils and was being passed around in classrooms and during study periods. The commissioners, blushing, declared that carnivals were forbidden under existing ordinances and that the event had been held illegally, but the carnival had already folded its tents and disappeared, so there wasn't much they could do about it.

A further sign of moral decay, according to those who viewed with alarm the activities of the post-war "lost generation," was the wide publicity given to the taking of the Old Gold cigarette "blindfold test" by J. P. Morgan's daughter Anne. Miss Morgan declared via radio commercials and newspaper advertisements that "Old Gold's smoothness was so obvious," thus placing the stamp of social respectability upon the use of tobacco by American womanhood. Although not proclaimed in the advertising of the day, it was also generally evident that females of respectable middle class background, who wouldn't have been caught dead in an old-fashioned saloon, had no such compunctions about appearing in public in the fashionable speakeasies and downing the illicit liquor, which was somehow much more glamorous than the tax-stamped and government bonded product of the pre-Volstead days.

A new pre-war generation of college students had departed from tradition and elected a radical young law school senior named Marion Zioncheck president of the associated student body at the University of Washington. Zioncheck had graduated from Olympia high school in 1919 under the name of Marion Potter

(his step-father's), and a more prominent local high school graduate, Wilbur "Mickey" McGuire, was a leading member of the coalition of fraternity men and athletes who opposed the slum-born Polish-American "barbarian" as student body president. They gave vent to their feelings by donning hoods, cornering Zioncheck, shaving his head and tossing him, fully clothed, into Frosh pond. McGuire was among those expelled for their participation in this bit of campus activism. Zioncheck, soon afterward, was dropped from law school for low grades, but he got himself reinstated, graduated, passed the bar examination and set forth on an even more colorful political career.

THE CLOCKS ARE STOPPED

The most spectacular event of 1928 in the capital city was the near destruction by fire of the old statehouse on the afternoon of September 9. The eight illuminated clocks on the octagonal stone tower came to a stop forever as seething flames roared through it as through a chimney, and the west wing (the original courthouse) was reduced to blackened and gutted masonry.

Origin of the blaze, one of the worst in Olympia's history, has never been determined. The building was practically deserted when janitors smelled smoke and turned in the alarm at 3:35 on that quiet Saturday afternoon. When it became evident that all the apparatus of the local fire department was insufficient to cope with the erupting blaze, a combination wagon from the Tacoma fire department made the run to Olympia in the then remarkable time of 35 minutes.

Hampered by a crowd of 6,500 people and with the clock tower seemingly about to crash into the street, the Tacoma firemen managed to get to the roof of the building, where they thrilled the crowd by scampering across the slippery metal roof like squirrels. One nimble Tacoma smoke-eater, according to the *Olympian,* carried a length of hose directly into the tower, which was belching smoke and flame, and sat nonchalantly in one of the arched windows directing the stream at the heart of the blaze, while other firemen below

OLD STATEHOUSE IN FLAMES, September 8, 1928.

protected him with spray from another hose. As the fire progressed, one clock after another stopped, the eighth one ticking its last at 13 minutes to five when a stream of water struck it full force.

The combined efforts of the Olympia and Tacoma firemen and citizen volunteers succeeded in controlling the conflagration before it did serious damage to the newer east wing, but the ornate Victorian tower, which had dominated the downtown Olympia skyline for nearly three decades and given the old building much of its character, was doomed. Part of it had crumbled and dropped on the roof below and the remainder was too far gone to save. When the wing was rebuilt the famous eight-sided clock tower was demolished.

Soon afterward another landmark of more halcyon days, the 19th century wooden bandstand in Sylvester park, succumbed to the ravages of time, termites and incendiary efforts and was torn down. Old-timers mourned its demise, along with that of the statehouse clock tower, but young Marvin Glavin, a sharp-eyed *News-Tribune* carrier boy, found a 1913 five-dollar gold piece in the ashes, proving the truth of the old adage that it's an ill wind that blows no good.

1929

The 21st legislature of 1929 was the first to convene amid the marble, bronze and tapestry splendor of the new Legislative building, but the January weather which greeted it was just as disagreeable as that which had been cursed by the sturdy pioneers of the territorial legislature. The lawmakers also faced a similar problem. The legislative chambers were back at the site of the territorial capitol, 13 long uphill blocks from the downtown hotels. By the end of the month 13 inches of snow had accumulated, making the streets and sidewalks nearly impassable and causing the street cars to hum like hornets, spin their wheels and run only spasmodically. Representative Maude Sweetman skidded on the ice and continued her legislative duties with a cast on one arm. Chairs were placed in the marble corridor between the senate and house chambers to provide frigid lobbyists with a place to thaw out while waiting the opportunity to buttonhole legislators. Somewhere along the way that crowded marble hall became known as "ulcer gulch", a designation which has achieved virtually official status.

By January 13 the legislators had gathered amid rumors of an unprecedented contest for the office of president pro-tem of the senate. That august body had received its first feminine member in the person of Miss Reba Hurn, a politically ambitious Spokane attorney who had run for congress in the primary election of 1924. Senator Hurn was no shrinking violet and she was not intimidated by her masculine colleagues. She was an announced candidate for the top leadership position, claiming upon her arrival, that she was in a 17 to 17 vote tie with Senator Fred W. Hastings of King county. Hastings' supporters said their candidate had 25 votes safely sewed up, with only 22 needed for election.

Their predictions proved accurate, Hastings was named president pro-tem and Miss Hurn was relegated to the position deemed proper for an overly ambitious freshman senator . . . and a female at that. Senator Heifner was the unanimous choice as minority leader. He was the only Democrat in the upper house.

Ed Davis of Columbia county was duly elected speaker of the house, while Sims and Reed continued to run the show in their usual self-effacing but highly effective manner. Mrs. Sweetman may have been tempted to use her plaster cast as a bludgeon when she was not only passed over for the rules committee, but denied membership on the roads and bridges committee; furthermore, several of the more chauvinistic male members told an *Olympian* reporter that *"she should be satisfied with her seat in the house and not hanker after the deeper cushions of the committee rooms,* thus adding insult to injury.

The senate gallantly set aside one of the new committee rooms for the use of the lady lobbyists of the WCTU, PTA, Federated Women's Clubs and others dedicated to "seeing that no bill passed to lower the moral standards of the state." The male lobbyists, relegated to the crowded confines of ulcer gulch, complained bitterly of discrimination. The usual ineffective steps were being taken to keep them out of the chambers during deliberations and operators had even been placed in the automatic elevators to prevent their sneaking in by that means. The ladies of the purity group protested that they weren't really lobbyists at all, but self-sacrificing guardians of public morality.

The senate solved the thorny problem by ejecting the WCTU ladies and their colleagues from committee room 13 and installing a bar.

Governor Hartley, the first Republican governor in the state's history to win a second term in office, addressed the assembled legislators on January 16, following the inauguration ceremonies for himself, Lieutenant Governor Gellatly, Secretary of State J. Grant Hinkle, Treasurer Charles W. Hinton, Attorney General Dunbar, Auditor Clausen, Land Commissioner Savidge, Superintendent of Public Instruction Showalter and Insurance Commissioner H. O. Fishback. The ceremonies were held in the evening to permit a statewide radio broadcast on prime time and were preceded by a band concert in the rotunda by the regimental band of the 148th Field Artillery. A formal reception in the Italian violet marble state reception room, lighted by the Tiffany chandeliers of Czechoslovakian crystal, ended the night's events.

NO EASY TASK

Tacitly conceding that his first four years in office had been stormy ones, Hartley declared that *"so far as I am concerned, what has been done was done in the interests of courageous, efficient, good government."* He further conceded that *"I realize that some of my recommendations for greater economy were so unexpected and so contrary to the long uncontrolled trend of public business as to appear drastic,"* but he insisted that *"grievous conditions demand drastic action."*

He then delivered an opinion of such accuracy that it might well have been engraved in the marble of the capitol rotunda:

"It is no easy task to close the sluices of public expenditure when the long-opened gates have become so fixed in their grooves as to yield downward only to sledge-hammer blows."

Although the booming economy had resulted in a $16 million surplus in the state treasury, he considered this to be an indication that taxes should be cut rather than expenditures increased. *"The truth is,"* he observed dryly, *"the state's affairs are today in better condition than are the private affairs of those from whose pockets has been taken that $16,000,000 now in the state treasury."* He further warned the lawmakers that *"I shall regard it as the performance of plain duty to disapprove any legislation calling for new appropriations, unless such legislation provides the means of its own financing in some manner that does not add to the already too great tax burden borne by the people as a whole."*

While a number of legislators fumed under the chastening words of the governor, thousands of simple taxpayers tuned in to the state capitol and, amid the static, blessed the name of Hartley.

The methods proposed by Hartley to reduce the costs of government would, coincidentally, add vastly to his personal power. He urged abolishment of the highway commission and formation of a department of highways under a director appointed by the governor. Having quarrelled continuously with Auditor Clausen over Legislative building expenditures, he proposed that that official be replaced on the capitol commission by one of his closest political allies, Olaf L. Olsen, director of the department of business control.

THOSE OUTRAGEOUS OUTHOUSES

All three members of the state fisheries board having resigned two years earlier and never been replaced, he called for an appointive supervisor of fisheries. Convinced that public education was running amuck with the taxpayers' money and viewing with alarm the recent development of the junior high school and junior college, he wanted a nine-member board of education for the university and colleges and a constitutional amendment abolishing the elective office of superintendent of public instruction, which he considered, with some justification, to be a sounding board of the spendthrift education lobby. The superintendent would, of course, be replaced with a Hartley appointee. He also wanted the state tax commission (appointed by him) to give final approval to all appraisals of his arch enemy Savidge before any state lands or timber could be disposed of. The state parks committee had enraged the governor by a tendency to spend money on public picnic and camping facilities, including *"community halls, kitchens, shower baths, playgrounds, rowboats and other knickknacks."* His voice squeaked with outrage when he pointed out that the park committee had spent $116,000 for *outhouses!* He wanted the committee, made up of the land commissioner, secretary of state and treasurer, abolished and the parks turned over to the director of conservation and development. He likewise made the sensible suggestion that the multiplicity of annual and biennial reports be consolidated in a single report to be published by the department of efficiency.

Hartley reported that he had slashed nearly $5½ million from the requested general fund budget of $66,850,970, making it only slightly higher than that of the previous biennium. The total budget, including federal and non-appropriated funds, was $75,435,584.

The legislators did not feel constrained to limit themselves to the consideration of executive request measures. A total of 762 bills was introduced, of which 453 died in committee or on the floor, 227 became law, and a new record of 82 vetoed bills was set by the fiesty governor.

TWADDLE, ALTRUISTIC AND OTHERWISE

Hartley's highway department bill passed easily, with Mark Reed speaking in its favor and voting for it in the house, but his other reorganization proposals were rejected. A complete investigation of the current tax system, recommended by the governor in a supplementary message, was approved, however. The tax equalization council subsequently issued its report, recommending a graduated state income tax, a gross revenue tax on railroads, classification of property for tax purposes and an amendment to the federal statutes permitting states to tax national banks. The further suggestion that the governor call a special legislative session in the fall to act on the tax proposals, was rejected by Hartley in the interests of economy.

The Pierce county delegation was pushing for a suspension bridge across the Tacoma narrows to the Kitsap peninsula, a proposal which alarmed Olympia port boosters. The ocean terminal was jammed with ships and a 420-foot pier extension was being rushed to completion to handle the overflow. There were fears that a bridge across the narrows might constitutute a hazard to navigation and relief when the bill took its place among those that passed, but didn't receive an appropriation.

Reba Hurn, who had been stripped of her chairmanship of the senate public morals committee by the lieutenant governor, presumably for insubordination, introduced a bill to bar cigarette advertising from billboards. "It won't be long," she predicted with a shudder, "before girls will be pictured smoking!"

Eastern Washington apple growers lobbied for a memorial to congress for a high tariff on bananas and the Daughters of the American Revolution, horrified to discover that people were walking on the bronze face of George Washington in the capitol rotunda, demanded that a railing be placed around the great seal. A bill was passed authorizing the patriotic barrier, but no appropriation was provided. A bill was introduced to levy one mill per kilowatt hour on electric power companies and was efficiently lobbied into a quiet death in committee. The same thing happened to a measure sponsored by a few bleeding-heart liberals which would have raised the mothers' pension from $15 to $30 a month. It would doubtless have been vetoed by Hartley had it passed, for he had already made it clear that he considered child welfare efforts to be "altruistic twaddle."

Representative W. P. Totten of King introduced an income tax bill to authorize a tax of two percent (on the first $1,000) to six percent (on all income over $4,000) for individuals and a modest two percent on all businesses except public utilities. It was felt that action on such a delicate matter should await the findings of the tax equalization council.

Senator Heifner, perhaps to prove that although he was the only Democrat *he* wasn't one of those bleeding-heart liberals, sponsored a measure to return the whipping post as a means of rehabilitating criminals. With evident relish, Senator Heifner went into great detail. In addition to authorizing from one to 100 strokes, "well laid on the bare back," at the discretion of a judge in felony cases, he specified that the lash was to be "a single piece of leather, 36 to 38 inches long and from one to 2½ inches wide, not less than one-eighth inch thick," and that the culprit was to be "tied to a post, triangle or other contrivances so he may not escape and the lashing will be effective." It was made clear that the corporal punishment was just an added fillip and should in no way effect the prison sentence to be meted out by the judge.

The attorney general offered the opinion that the proposed rehabilitative method constituted cruel and unusual punishment and it was shelved, along with another Heifner-sponsored bill to establish a state sales tax. Representative Sam W. Webb proposed a revolutionary measure to establish a form of state-administered no-fault insurance which would pay up to $4,000 to automobile accident victims from a fund financed by a $10 increase in license fees. It didn't get very far either.

Neither of the session's two most controversial bills survived. One, sponsored by the Grange in the form of an initiative to the legislature, would permit governmental units "to own, operate and maintain electric power plants and sell electrical energy." This precipitated first all-out public vs. private power fight and the private power lobby was successful in this onen The Grange public utilities district bill passed the house, but was killed in the senate. The senators were not burdened with scruples about "open government" in those days. The vote was taken behind closed doors and public power was rejected, without debate on either side, by a 20 to 17 vote, five senators having taken a walk.

The other headliner, the Eagles old age pension bill, would have provided $25 a month to indigent citizens over 65 years of age, provided they had been residents of the state for 15 years and of the county for five years. It passed the senate, but the house apparently decided it was too liberal and killed it.

The gasoline tax was raised another penny . . . to three cents . . . to finance a Grange-backed farm to market road program; enforcement of the blue sky law was transferred from the secretary of state to the governor's department of licenses; fire and police pensions were increased and the first state airway was established between Spokane and Puget Sound.

A number of bills which survived the legislative battles succumbed to the sharpened veto pen of Governor Hartley. Among these were the propoed constitutional amendment to raise legislators' pay, mandatory jail sentences for drunken drivers and three bills sponsored and ardently lobbied by the WCTU . . . one making the manufacture and transportation of liquor a felony, another making its sale to minors a felony and a third requiring the state to seize vehicles used to transport liquor. Hartley, who as mayor of Everett, had let horse manure pile up in the city streets to dramatize the loss of saloon revenue, was even more determined than his predecessor, Hart, that the state wasn't going to waste its time and money trying to enforce a damnfool law like the Volstead act. Although he had seen to it that Chief Cole's highway patrol, which was self-sustaining through drivers' license revenues, was increased from 40 to 60 men, they continued to concentrate on traffic violations and didn't concern themselves with booze . . . unless it was being carried in undue quantity inside the driver.

The governor also vetoed a measure permitting larger school districts to establish junior colleges, commenting that 77¢ of every dollar was already going to education and that "the way to reduce taxes is to quit spending the peoples' money." For good measure, he redlined a bill authorizing construction of a toll bridge across Deception pass, which had been the personal pet of a determined freshman legislator named Pearl Wanamaker, who was one of the four female state representatives that session. Mrs. Wanamaker, who was also one of the four Democrats in the lower house, led an inspired fight to override the veto, but failed by a vote of 48 to 47.

Mrs. Wanamaker was destined for a long and distinguished political career, and Hartley was one of the few men to come out victorious in a pitched battle with her.

The 1929 session, like those which had preceded it and those which would follow, had its lighter moments. Lobbyists were populating ulcer gulch in great profusion, led by the rival cohorts of the cement and blacktop industries, the free-spending advocates of green trading stamps and the dour contingent from the Anti-Saloon league. All but the latter provided abundant and convivial hospitality to the legislators who were so minded.

Senators were lulled by the mellifulous tones of their new reading clerk, the Reverend R. Franklin Hart, rector of St. Johns Episcopal church, and enjoyed an impromptu style show when Grant Barnes, 12-year-old son of Senator Frank Barnes of Longview, was called to the rostrum to model the snappy new blue, green and gold uniforms which had been prescribed as a means of matching the splendour of the pages with that of the marble halls they inhabited.

The house of representatives, not to be outdone in status symbols, had an electric voting machine installed and used it the first time on March 12, no doubt to the disgust of Governor Hartley, who had no control over the expenditures of the legislature on itself, but it soon short-circuited and the representatives returned, for several years, to the traditional voice vote.

THE GOVERNOR IS FOR THE BIRDS

The governor, to the delight of newspaper photographers and bird lovers, was proving that, although he didn't approve of handouts to hungry humans, he was willing to bend a little in the case of a seagull named "Tee", who had taken to alighting on the ledge outside the executive office window and mooching snacks. The papers were full of pictures of Hartley feeding Tee and the partnership worked well for both of them. The publicity tended to humanize the governor and the executive gull became the best fed bird on the Olympia waterfront.

When President Herbert Hoover was inaugurated the Bunce Music company installed its latest model radios in the house and senate chambers and the members paused in their deliberations to hear the president promise the nation "an administration of constructive prosperity."

The 21st legislature stopped the clocks and set a new record for overtime, finally adjourning *sine die* at 9:30 p.m. on March 15 after a long and bitter deadlock over the $24 million highway budget. The major bone of contention was the proposed purchase by the state of the Pasco-Kennewick toll bridge across the Columbia river in eastern Washington. The conference committee finally alloted $400,000 for the purchase and the sleepy solons departed from the capitol after 21½ hours of unremunerated overtime. There had been the usual third house frivolity while bored members awaited a conference committee compromise, with Pliny Allen presenting Ed Sims with a large oil can and lauding his ability to "keep the peace," but eventually most of the legislators found comfortable leather davenports in committee rooms and lounges and went to sleep. Some hyperactive practical joker mixed up their shoes while they slept, causing a great deal of confusion and ill-feeling when they awoke.

All in all, it had been a prolific session. A total of 227 bills became law, 453 failed to pass . . . and 82 were vetoed by Hartley.

As is always the case, a large segment of the state's editorial writers expressed disenchantment with the legislative process. The *Olympian* editorialized that *"the governor's action on the legislative grist indicates to a considerable extent the uselessness of the legislature and the wasteful manner in which it operates,"* and ventured the opinion that *"the state needs a small body of trained men acting as business managers of the state."*

"Abolish the legislature," the *Olympian* urged its readers, *"and replace it with the initiative and referendum."*

This remarkable suggestion would, if it had been adopted, have accomplished Hartley's goal of reduced law-passing. Of the 53 iniative measures filed since 1914, only 14 had qualified for the ballot and just three had passed . . . state prohibition, abolishment of fee-charging employment agencies, and the repeal of the poll tax.

INTERIM WARFARE

With Roland Hartley occupying the executive offices in the new capitol building, Olympia no longer relpased into a state of calm tranquility when the legislature adjourned. The peppery little governor kept the fireworks popping during the interim.

Early in May he fired off a letter to Attorney General Dunbar demanding that charges be brought against the state officials responsible for paying $4,449.29 to an Olympia firm, the Bookstore, for office supplies which he claimed had never been delivered. The letter was a classic bit of Hartleyana, bristling with denunciations of "appalling conduct" and "great mismanagement in the state treasurer's office." Dunbar pointed out that if, indeed, a crime had been committed, Thurston county Prosecutor W. J. Milroy would have to bring the charges, but Milroy showed little inclination to become embroiled in this latest capitol feud.

He did take action a few weeks later, however, when Hartley's supervisor of banking, H. C. Johnson, was charged with two counts of accepting bribes totaling $3,260 from the North Pacific Bank of South Tacoma to turn down applications of rival banks which wanted to set up business in that community. When Johnson was arrested in his office and taken to jail until he could post bail, Hartley quivered with indignation and denounced Milroy for filing charges against Johnson and not against Treasurer Hinton and ex-Treasurer William Potts in the Bookstore case. "It shows Mr. Milroy can act against state officials when he *wants* to!" the governor declared.

Milroy defended himself as best he could, but Hartley was in full voice and could not be drowned out. "That man's untruthful statements cut no more figure with me than the chirping of a chipmunk in a brush pile," he roared.

When Johnson came to trial the governor took the stand in his defense, testifying that the plot had been engineered by J. E. Hansell, the young editor of the South Tacoma *Star,* who was supposed to have been the go-between in the solicitation and payment of the alleged bribes. Hartley said the journalist had first approached him with an offer to "frame" Dunbar if the governor would appoint him as his private secretary. He then offered to do the job in return for appointment as the governor's

press agent,* but, Hartley explained, ingeniously, "He wasn't the right type."

This blew the case. The two bankers involved were found not guilty by the jury and Milroy then threw up his hands and asked Judge Wright to dismiss the charges against the state bank examiner. The judge did so.

Dunbar had, in the meantime, filed a civil suit against the past and present state treasurers and the Bookstore to recover the money for the supposedly undelivered office supplies. In the course of the dispute Prosecutor Milroy declared that Hartley "is a bigoted ass" and "greedy for power and publicity." Judge Wilson eventually dismissed the suit on the grounds that other goods of like value had been substituted for those appearing on the state vouchers and that no fraud had occurred. He did, however, condemn "the irregularities of the transactions." But even that didn't end the battle. Well over a year after the original charges were made by the governor, Dunbar complained that Director of Efficiency E. D. Brabrook had seized $840 worth of purchase coupons from Treasurer Hinton during the investigation. The coupons were issued by the Bookstore, which went bankrupt before they could be redeemed, and the state was thus out $840 through the inefficiency of Hartley's director of efficiency.

FEUD OUT THE OLD YEAR: FEUD IN THE NEW

The governor continued to quarrel with his fellow capitol commissioners, Clausen and Savidge. He objected violently to the Olmstead plan for landscaping the capitol grounds, declaring that "this affair is a tragedy," as well as "disgrace to the state and the present-day civilization." In the midst of this he discovered cracks on the lower floors and walls of the Legislative building and insisted on taking the capitol commission on a personal tour and lecturing them on the faults. Soon afterward he found that the roof leaked and the floor tiles

---

*The forthright term "press agent" has not been used in governmental circles for many years. The position sought by the enterprising editor of the *Star* is currently referred to as "press secretary."

were coming loose and he would frequently emerge from his office to guide amazed capitol visitors to see these examples of wasted tax dollars.

The contractors eventually made good these minor failings, but by that time the governor was in full cry on another trail. By November he was more convinced than ever that Land Commissioner Savidge was engaged in a massive give-away of state timber and shore lands. He fired off one of his explosive letters to the commissioner, demanding that he turn over all applications for purchase of state lands to Director Ernest Brabrook of the department of efficiency for investigation before any sales were made. The letter was followed by H. H. Hook, license department auditor, who had been ordered to make a full investigation of the alleged multi-million dollar bungling in the land office.

The embattled Savidge said that Hartley's claim was "too ridiculous to answer" and made poor Mr. Hook sit outside the land office railing while employees reluctantly brought him the records.

Apparently feeling that things were moving too slowly this way, Hartley demanded the complete record of all land sales and a description of all lands held by the state . . . immediately if not sooner. Savidge blandly asked for an appropriation from the governor's emergency fund, pointing out that "it would take one man at least one and a half years with nine months aid from a stenographer" to comply with the demand.

He did not explain why the stenographer would be useful for only nine months.

The feud continued into the following year, although the governor took time-out on Christmas eve to issue greetings to his constituents:

"As your governor I extend to you the season's greetings this Christmas of 1929. May your holiday be a happy one and may the coming year bring to each and every home health, happiness and a reasonable amount of prosperity, and may it bring payrolls to our state that each of us may have honest work to do, for work is the salvation of the human race."

Nor did he forget to convey greetings to President Hoover. Shingle manufacturer Hartley added a bit of advice there, too, pointing out that, in his opinion, a high protective tarriff is the best aid to prosperity . . . par-

ticularly a high protective tariff on shingles.

He closed the year with another of his sudden and unexplained firings. John C. Denny, director of the department of public works and a former superior court judge, had made the mistake of firing Fred K. Baker, an Everett friend of Hartley's, as supervisor of transportation. Denny was the recipient of one of the governor's abrupt letters demanding his immediate resignation.

"One never knows what's going to happen next here, you know," the ousted director philosophically told the United Press correspondent at the capitol.

Hartley immediately appointed his old buddy Baker to replace Denny as director and issued orders to his secretary, "No newspapermen today."

Thus, incommunicado but still making headlines, Roland Hill Hartley saw the old year out.

THINGS WERE BOOMING IN '29

The capital city, the stage upon which these interesting and noisy events transpired, continued to stride into the air age under its own momentum. Postmaster Frank S. Clem disclosed that increasing numbers of Olympians were willing to entrust their letters to airplanes and that the average number of airmail communications had increased within six weeks from 60 to 125 a day. The planes, he pointed out, cut from one to three days from the train time to the east coast. The Graf Zeppelin was making regular crossings of the Atlantic and endurance flights were much in the news. Amelia Earhart was the winner of the national women's air derby, but a former Olympia boy, Harold Bromley, was unable to get his monoplane *City of Tacoma* off the ground for its projected flight across the Pacific to Tokyo. The city purchased the Olympia airport site for $29,000 and the Alaska-Washington Airways seaplane *Ketchikan*, a four passenger Lockheed, was carrying passengers from the city float to Tacoma at speeds of from 125 to 140 miles an hour.

The local banks were issuing a new style paper currency, considerably smaller than the old banknotes and the telephone company was offering a newfangled instrument with the receiver and transmitter in one piece. Local citizens, headed by Roy (Red) West, "the singing highway patrolmen," were becoming radio stars as the Elks club inaugurated its annual Jingle Club appeal for Christmas funds for needy children over station KGY. At the professional level, the Warner Brothers— Vitaphone extravaganza "On With the Show," starring Marian and Madeline Fairbanks, was playing at the Liberty, billed as "the first 100% natural color talking, singing, dancing production."

The *Olympian,* reporting that *"the short skirts of the girl workers at the capitol are causing comment,"* interviewed several state officials as to their reactions. Attorney General Dunbar averred that *"if the knees are shapely, dimpled and pink I think short skirts are fine."* Secretary of State Hinkle felt that the skirts *"should be short enough to be interesting and long enough to cover the subject,"* while Chief Cole responded enthusiastically that *"they keep men wide awake and alert at all times and are good for traffic safety."*

The *Olympian* also front-paged the prediction of the style advisory board of the National Association of Cotton Manufacturers that women would soon be wearing trousers! (The exclamation point was the *Olympian's*).

The police department had doubled in size and boasted eight nattily uniformed officers, including Chief Frank Cushman, Assistant Chief Cleo Beckwith and Sergeant Jack Brazeal, and was even dignified by the presence of a detective, H. A. Gregg. Tacoma had recently installed fancy red and green lights which changed colors automatically to direct traffic on some of the busier downtown streets and the Olympia police department purchased one of Tacoma's surplus hand-operated stop-and-go signals. During the evening rush hour a patrolman was assigned to carry the contraption up to 4th and Capitol Way and risk life and limb at this principal intersection in the city's first efforts at mechanized traffic control.

The department's two rakish Model-A Ford prowl cars worked around the clock to maintain order and decency, but it was difficult to cope with the new morality. School Superintendent Breckner and neighborhood residents petitioned for lights around the new Lincoln school and Stevens field to discourage an activity which was becoming popularly known as "necking".

Another portent of things to come occurred when black militants, who had long been demanding jobs in state government, won a victory of sorts. Three white janitors in the Temple of Justice were fired and replaced by blacks. Department of business control Director Olaf Olsen explained that the changes were made "to be fair and give some Negroes jobs in the statehouse," although he hastened to add that one white custodian had been left on the payroll to see that the new janitors did their work properly. It is interesting to note that even this minor victory in the battle for equal employment rights occurred during the administration of the state's most reactionary 20th century governor.

PROGRESS, POLLUTION AND POLITICS

The lumber market and the port of Olympia continued to boom. The 420-foot pier extension was completed, but in March it was announced that six ocean steamships were in the harbor, a couple of them loading in the stream for lack of dock space. One of the docked ships was the recently rechristened S.S. *Olympia,* on her first voyage to her namesake city. A civic banquet was held for her officers and company officials at the Olympian and Captain C. W. Jacobs was presented with a brass plaque to go under the picture of the capitol which had been presented to the ship at the rechristening ceremonies. By the end of the year 224 deep-sea ships had loaded 228 million feet of lumber and 9,000 tons of general cargo and had unloaded 4,000 tons of inbound cargo.

S. S. *Olympia* on Puget Sound — Oriental route.

The Tumwater Paper Mills in the old Tumwater brewery building, which had been closed for some time as a result of financial troubles, was sold to a Portland group said to have long experinece in the business, and confidence was expressed that the mill would soon be back in full production. Growing evidence of the town's increasing industrial activity was recorded by the *Olympian* when it announced proudly that *"Olympia residents may expect to see smoke pouring out of the Washington Veneer company's gigantic smokestack about the middle of July."* Big smokestacks were considered monuments to prosperity in 1929, and the thicker the smoke the better the economy. Civic leader Peter Schmidt was quoted as predicting that the belching 225-foot stack *"will help to advertise Olympia industries more than any other one thing."*

The completion of the smokestack was greeted by a full-scale civic celebration on June 8. All the other mills closed down and an estimated 4,000 people followed the Fort Lewis band to the industrial fill to watch E. F. Ross, inventor of a portable fire pump powered by a Johnson outboard motor, shoot a jet of water over the towering structure. Then Grace Carr and William Jackstead were hoisted to a temporary platform at the summit of the seck and joined in holy matrimony by the Reverend Chester C. Blair of the Tumwater Methodist church as newsreel cameras ground and the crowd cheered. Mrs. A. N. Anderson won the $20 prize for guessing most accurately the number of bricks in the smokestack. She guessed 94,241. There were actually 94,390.

The citizens of the county finally conceded that the old courthouse at 4th and Washington was in danger of collapsing and authorized a

Capital Way, circa 1929.

bond issue of $274,000 to build a new one on the old Chautauqua grounds across from the capitol. Although the county commissioners had convinced the electorate that the old building was about to go the way of the wonderful one-horse shay, it proved to be about as flimsy as the great pyramids of Egypt when the new one was completed and Phillips and Newell were given the contract to demolish the abandoned courthouse. By the time the monolithic basement jail was finally chipped away the contractors were convinced that they, if not the county's voters, were the victims of political propaganda.

A more historic structure succumbed more quickly to the wreckers' hammers, although not until it had precipitated another controversy about the heads of the capitol commission. The old mansion of Governor Stevens on the north edge of the new capitol campus, was ordered demolished to make way for the landscaping. There were howls of outrage from the remaining pioneers, but the Daughters of the American Revolution and Stevens' surviving daughter, Kate Stevens Bates, finally agreed to its removal if the commission promised to erect a life-size statue of Stevens and a plaque on the site. The promise was made and the old house knocked down, but the life-sized image of the little governor was never erected.

A more localized controversy in 1929 involved the return of gambling paraphernalia to the capital city. The *Olympian* complained that, within a week of the inauguration of Mayor Mills, who had campaigned on a promise to "wipe out gambling," both slot machines and punch boards had reappeared on the scene. The one-armed bandits . . . nickle machines in town; twenty-five-centers in the county, dispensed a roll of violently violet-flavored mints with each play and Chief Cushman said this made them merchandizing rather than gambling appliances. After more editorial heat, the mayor announced that he had banned the trade stimulants, but later in the year the lady cashier of Frye's Capital market admitted that she had stolen $2,888.16 and spent it all on Olympia punch boards. Chief Cushman said this was impossible.

Convinced that Olympia, with its gambling devices, short-skirted stenographers and necking couples in rumble-seats, was destined to go the way of Sodom and Gomorah, a bearded and eccentric gentleman named William Greenfield erected a replica of Noah's ark on the West Bay mudflats. He christened it *Noah's No. 2,* plastered it with signs urging repentance and seldom left its shelter. Sightseers who drove past observed that Mr. Greenfield frequently glanced aloft, as if checking the weather.

BLACK FRIDAY

Disaster did, of course, strike in 1929, but it came from the direction of Wall street rather than heaven. The great stock market crash of October set prices tumbling in a panic-stricken avalanche of selling. Investors lost $10 billion dollars the first week and ordinary people who had convinced themselves that permanent prosperity had come at last and they would never suffer another depression shared the panic of the Wall street high-flyers.

The great depression which followed the market collapse was slow in reaching the Pacific Northwest, but when it did everybody knew that it had arrived.

1930

The decade of the thirties dawned with President Hoover predicting confidently that "prosperity is just around the corner," Rudy Valee crooning "Vagabond Lover" in the talkies at the Capitol theater and Amos n' Andy keeping radio fans in stitches. A "cute little fast-spinning toy on a string" called a yoyo had taken Olympia by storm and Raymond Grim became the hero of the younger set when he won the all-city yoyo championship. A 16-year-old Washington girl named Helene Madison was making headlines in the nation's sports pages for her swimming feats and was considered a celebrity when she stopped off at the Hotel Olympian for an oyster luncheon on her way from Portland to Seattle.

But the best entertainment in town in 1930 was the three-ring circus which continued its performances up on Capitol hill.

Auditor Clausen, who was nearing his 79th birthday, had taken a three-month vacation in California for his health. His nephew, C. L. Clausen, an assistant accountant in his office,

had gone along as his driver, apparently on full pay.

When the short-fused Hartley learned of these goings-on he exploded spectacularly, demanding that Clausen's office be declared vacant on the grounds that he was neglecting state business. Attorney General Dunbar informed the governor that an elected official can stay away from his office as long as he wants to as long as he maintains his legal residence in Olympia.

The governor bitterly denounced Dunbar, demanding that Clausen return the three months salary of his nephew and that Prosecutor Milroy bring charges against both Clausens for misuse of the state payroll. The venerable auditor announced wearily that he was leaving San Diego for Olympia to do battle with Hartley. Upon his return he found that his nephew had been overpaid in the amount of $262.50 and repaid that amount to the state treasurer. He then called upon the long-suffering Dunbar to force the return of salaries and expenses paid to Amy Albright, the governor's confidential secretary, Highways Director Sam Humes and Lacey V. Murrow, the Spokane district highway engineer, while they were in Seattle testifying in a damage suit brought by Miss Albright against the North Coast stage lines, one of whose buses had collided with her car. Clausen alleged that the two had collected witness fees as well as their state pay, and that Humes had bought lunch for another of Amy's witnesses on his state expense account.

Prosecutor Milroy, unable to avoid the crossfire, winced when Clausen let it be known that he might demand criminal prosecution of all three Hartley appointees.

The governor was, in the meantime, embarked upon a diversionary maneuver against Land Commissioner Savidge. Brabrook of the department of efficiency began an investigation of the land office, calling 10 of Savidge's employees to a sort of pseudo grand jury hearing. The Seattle *Star* sent a reporter to the capitol and published a highly senational story claiming that thousands of dollars in shortages had been revealed in the first day's hearings.

Dunbar fired a broadside, declaring Brabrook's "star chamber sessions" to be illegal and pointing out that Savidge and his employees had been denied right of counsel.

The *Olympian* noted that this was *"the bitterest fight yet in the Hartley administration"* and that *"the other elective officials have taken the offensive against the governor."* Reverting to wartime terminology, the dispatch continued, *"the war correspondent at the Olympia front line trenches interviewed the generals and their lieutenants with the following results:*

"Hartley . . . I have nothing to say at this time.

"Amy Albright . . . I have not seen Clausen's charges yet.

"Humes . . . I have no statement to make.*

"Savidge . . . I'll have something to say tomorrow.

"Clausen . . . That fellow Hartley has tried to crucify me on his political cross. These charges I have filed are just a starter."

By the next day the combatants had become more vocal. Hartley still insisted that shortages in the land office accounts had been deliberately covered up. Savidge denied there were any current shortages, while conceding that there had been some covering up. *"The trouble,"* he told the *Olympian's* Capitol hill war correspondent, *"was with W. W. Hopkins, the assistant land commissioner under Lister in 1913. We didn't prosecute because of his father, a fine old pioneer, an earnest preacher . . . a man with a splendid civil war record."*

Having thus deftly secured the sympathies of the pioneer association, the Grand Army of the Republic and the ministerial association, Savidge explained that Hopkins, a former Thurston county Republican central committee chairman and deputy county auditor, had been fired and *"died blind in the insane ward at Steilacoom."*

Highway Director Humes informed the correspondent that *"All this talk is just dust to divert public attention from their own pilferings."*

Hartley gave vent to his feelings with another blast at the attorney general, demanding that Dunbar *"quit passing the buck and do your duty for once in your life,"* presumably by seeing to it that the venerable state auditor and the insurance commissioner spent the rest of their lives in the penitentiary.

---

*A typical highway department response if there ever was one.

Since the law requires that all suits involving state government be filed in Thurston county superior court, the unfortunate Milroy, as county prosecutor, found himself still in the role of innocent bystander at a full-scale guerilla war. After giving due consideration to the charges and counter-charges of the embattled officials, he announced that he was dropping all charges against Amy Albright, Humes and Murrow on the grounds that a conviction was impossible. After another day's cogitation he decided to also drop charges against Clausen . . . on the grounds that a conviction was impossible.

While all this was going on, Judge Wright further complicated the governor's affairs by ruling that his department of public works was no longer a duly constituted state agency and was barred from performing any governmental functions. Both the supervisor of transportation and supervisor of public utilities positions were vacant as the result of the internicine warfare at the capitol, leaving Director Baker as the only commissioner. Judge Wright ruled there had to be a quorum of at least two.

Fortuitously, the University of Washington football coach, Enoch W. Bagshaw, was ousted at about that time. A star back on the legendary teams of Coach Gloomy Gil Doby, Bagshaw had later been the coach at Everett high school, where his no-nonsense approach to athletics had won the admiration of Mayor Hartley.

The governor appointed him supervisor of transportation, putting the department back in business and making Bagshaw the first, if not the last, former Washington gridiron coach to hold high state office.

COUNTER-ATTACK

Following a week or two of relative calm, the anti-Hartley forces regrouped and began a series of counter-attacks. Savidge asked Dunbar to ask Hartley why the state highway department had paid $30,398.75 more for the Metaline Falls bridge than the highway commission had declared it to be worth in 1926.

Hartley responded, "Let Savidge and all the rest of that moonshine cabinet make as many charges against me as they want to." Then departed for Seattle to address the citizens of the state by radio on his favorite subject . . . "The Misconduct of State Officials."

In his fireworks chat, Hartley gave special attention to an inference by Dunbar that a number of legislators were, contrary to law and ethics, employed in state departments under the governor's control. Hartley averred that Dunbar had "slipped a cog," because the only legislator holding a state job was John C. Hurspool who, as a representative from Walla Walla, had voted in favor of a pay increase for assistant attorneys general . . . then gone to work for Dunbar as an assistant attorney general.

The remainder of the program was devoted to a further raking over the coals of Savidge, with detailed attention to the much publicized office fund shortages of 1913-1917, and a generalized attack on the attorney general, whom he referred to as "Johnny the Fixer."

Called upon by the *Olympian* reporter for their reactions to the governor's electronic blitz, only one of the embattled officials was willing to make a comment. The exception was Clausen, who said *"Blah!"*.

The attorney general quickly regrouped and returned to the fray, charging that Hartley's director of labor and industries, Claire Bowman, was using workers' contributions to the compensation fund to fight against their claims in court. He announced that he was filing suit against the director to recover $10,-492 in such illegally used funds. He added that Bowman had refused to provide department records for his inspection and quoted Hartley's latest radio address, in which he had said that "no honest public official should be afraid to have his office inspected."

Dunbar followed this up with threats to prosecute Mrs. Florence Phelan, another of Hartley's former Everett neighbors, whom he had appointed superintendent of the girls' training school at Grand Mound. Parents were complaining of brutality at the juvenile institution, but Hartley brushed aside the charges with the statement that "the school is being operated better than ever before;" after he had time to think things over he made a more typically Hartleyish proclamation:

Attorney General Dunbar was, according to the governor "an insidious menace to the state," who was miffed because the governor had appointed somebody else (Judge Adam Beeler) to a vacancy on the supreme court. "The perfidy of your official acts," he informed

Dunbar, "will live long after you have gone from the high post you hold."

Between skirmishes, Olympia Boy Scouts Donald Dobrin, Tilford Gribble, Oliver Beatty and William Mitchell ventured into the executive office to ask Hartley if it would be all right for the scouts to carry on a fund raising drive in the state buildings. The governor took a long lunch and kept them waiting for two hours, but when he got back it was obvious that he had been filled with geniality as well as food. He placed Scout Dobrin in his chair and announced to his staff and visitors that "this young man is chief executive until I resume the chair."*

THE LEGISLATURE REDISTRICTS . . . RELUCTANTLY

The major accomplishment of the off-year election of 1930 was the passage of Initiative 57, which accomplished what the legislature had been unable to do since 1901 . . . legislative redistricting as required by the state constitution. In 1901 a reapportionment bill had been passed which provided that each of the then 36 counties should have at least one representative and establishing a 94-member house and 42-member senate. The creation of Benton county in 1905, Grant in 1909 and Pend Oreille in 1911 increased house membership to 97, but no other changes had been made. The population west of the Cascades had increased four times as rapidly as that of eastern Washington, with the result that the ultra-conservative "cow counties" carried far more legislative weight than they were entitled to.

Skamania county enjoyed 593 percent representation, Wahkiakum 403 percent and Jefferson 427 percent, with 100 percent being the constitutional requirement. On the other side of the coin, the most populace counties were badly under-represented . . . King 61

---

*Donald didn't get to sit in the thronelike brown leather chair with the state seal embossed on the back in gold which came with the new capitol and has been use by all later governors. Hartley apparently felt that the massive piece of office furniture emphasized his diminutive stature and used a smaller chair during his occupancy of the executive office.

Merely A Modest Request

NOW ALL I ASK IS MUNICIPAL HOME RULE FOR MYSELF AND A REAPPORTIONMENT ENABLING ME TO GOVERN THE REST OF THE STATE AS WELL

COW COUNTIES

KING COUNTY

LEGISLATIVE REDISTRICTING was an unpopular subject with rural legislators, who viewed it as a power-grab by populous King County, as illustrated in this *Recorder* cartoon of 1913.

percent, Pierce 97 percent, Kitsap 42 percent. Spokane county came closest to equitable legislative representation with 99 percent.

The initiative aimed at correcting this legislative imbalance was filed by King county representatives Dan Landon and E. B. Palmer, but Secretary of State Hinkle refused to accept it on the grounds that only the legislature could redistrict itself. The supreme court ruled that a redrafted version of the initiative was legal and it went on the ballot. Legislative redistricting is a complicated and confusing subject. Few citizens understand it or care very much about it. Of the 360,000 voters who cast ballots in 1930, only about 232,000 bothered to register an opinion on the redistricting measure and it passed by less than a thousand votes. Of the state's 39 counties, it carried only King, Kitsap, Kittitas, Yakima, Whatcom and Chelan counties.

As a result of the close and apathetic vote, the house of representatives was increased to 99 members; the senate to 46. Eastern Washington counties lost five representatives, while the western counties gained seven. It was a step in the right direction, although a number of counties were still over-represented and eastern Washington generally continued to enjoy more legislative voting power than it was entitled to.

THE NOBLE EXPERIMENT FALTERS

Disenchantment with prohibition was growing in 1930. With the deepening depression people were no longer convinced that enforced

355

temperance was the sure road to prosperity. Hard-pressed Olympians recalled with nostalgia the humming activity and steady payroll of the brewery, and their feelings were echoed throughout the land. Moves were afoot in congress to repeal the Volstead act and thoughtful citizens were increasingly aware that the law simply couldn't be enforced. The liquor business was flourishing, but enriched neither honest men nor the coffers of government. In Thurston county alone, 455 stills were seized between 1926 and 1930 . . . one for every 70 men, women and children . . . and only a small percentage of those in operation were seized.

Militant prohibitionists viewed the change in popular opinion with much alarm and reacted by urging more punitive measures against violators of the prohibition laws. Although Governor Hartley had scornfully vetoed such measures pressured through the 1929 legislature by the WCTU-ASL forces, old Senator Wesley Jones had responded the same year by getting the Jones law passed by congress. This raised the penalty for prohibition violations to a maximum of five years in prison and a $10,000 fine. All but the most rockbound advocates of enforced morality viewed the Jones law as harsh and savage and the senator from Washington was generally pictured as a cold, rigid and humorless old man. The senior senator, still firmly anchored to the philosophies of Herbert Hoover and the Anti-Saloon League amid a storm of changing times, was facing political shipwreck.

The strident cries of the moralists did nothing to change public opinion in their favor. The Reverend Percival Clinton, on the Pacific coast for the Methodists' celebration of the 10th anniversary of nationwide prohibition, provided an interesting Christian view of the matter:

"I cannot see that there would be any crime in shooting at sight the man who violates any law and especially the prohibition law. He should be tortured and then executed."

In Olympia the celebration was staged by the ladies of the WCTU, with the cooperation of the town's less liberal Protestant churches. The Washington State School Directors association, meeting in the capital city at the same time, added its voice to the forces of decency, unanimously passing a resolution opposing the hiring of any public school teachers "who smoke or drink."

ONE-HORSE TOWN

The capital city, according to the 1930 census, could legitimately claim a population of "over 11,000", the official figures showing 11,733. And during the year the number of Olympians was further increased through the first annexations since the town was incorporated in 1859. Forty blocks east of the old city limits were annexed in April and the new Wildwood-Carlyon residential district between Olympia and Tumwater in November. The latter action eliminated the gap between the pioneer communities of Smithville and New Market and made Olympia and Tumwater effectively a single community in all but legal incorporation.

Olympia was no longer a one hotel town. The seven-story brick Governor was in operation diagonally across Sylvester park from the Olympian, the newer section of the old Mitchell forming an annex to it. The Kneeland had slipped to a second-rate status and the once stylish Carlton had become an increasingly frequent target of prohibition raiders. A new company had been formed to jointly operate the two leading hotels, headed by Peter G. Schmidt and with Thad Pierce as vice president and manager.

The capital city was in danger of becoming a one-horse town, however. The annual inventory of personal property by the county auditor showed that only 20 horses were left within the city limits. The *Olympian,* noting this dramatic decline in the equine population, predicted that *"Olympia will be a one horse town by 1935."* And according to the record, the once teeming throng of milch cows had entirely vanished from the urban scene.

The splendid new courthouse on upper Capitol Way was completed and the county offices moved from the old downtown location. Among the first occupants were Harold and Smith Troy, prosecuting attorney and deputy prosecutor respectively. Smith, the youngest son of the late P. M. Troy, had joined his brother's law firm after graduation from the University of Washington law school. When Harold, a 1927 graduate of the University of Washington, was elected prosecutor in the fall election he chose Smith as his chief deputy.

The Daily *Olympian* was occupying new and modern quarters in a Wohleb-designed stucco and tile plant at its old location. The original plant, which had originally been the 19th century Burmeister building, was not

BURMEISTER BUILDING at 3rd and Main, later
the plant of the *Olympian* and *Recorder.*

demolished prior to construction. Owner Sam Perkins had insisted that business continue as usual during construction and Phillips and Newell had been faced with the rather formidable task of building the new structure around the old one; then removing it piecemeal after the job was done.

Pollution continued as an adjunct of 20th century progress in the thirties. The Olympia Harbor Lumber company, Tumwater Lumber company and Tumwater Lumber Mills, all of which maintained huge trash burners along West Bay drive for the purpose of incinerating unused lumber, were sued by west side householders who claimed that the resulting soot and ashes damaged their property, blackened family washings, choked gutters and killed shrubbery.

The growing blight of abandoned junk automobiles prompted City Commissioner Charles Dufault to organize a civic drive to get rid of the hulks. Local garages provided trucks with which to haul the old cars from vacant lots and back yards to the port dock, where they were loaded on barges and dumped in 20

fathoms of water on the lower bay. The antique car buff had not yet appeared on the scene to cherish and restore vintage motor vehicles and the *Olympian* reported that *"scores of Olympia's earliest 'benzine buggies' go to their final rest."*

It may be that Ashley's Reo, Dr. Strickland's high-wheeled auto-buggy, banker Lord's Pope-Toledo and many more of those wonderful jallopies of the town's pioneer motoring era still repose beneath the placid waters of Puget Sound, a haven for barnacles and octopi.

A unique form of pollution afflicted the waters of upper Puget Sound in the spring when a number of the old wooden shipping board hulks of world war days, beached in Carr Inlet, drifted off on a high tide and converted themselves into a menace to navigation between Olympia and Tacoma. The coast guard cutter *Chelan* succeeded in rounding them up and rebeaching them before any damage was done to passing shipping.

The increasing hazards of the automobile age prompted the organization of the first school boy patrols to guard children at school crossings and such public-spirited youngsters as Abe Bean, Fred Chesnut and William Conser donned cross-belts and badges and took over responsibility for the safety of their younger colleagues in the public schools.

1931

The convening of the 22nd legislature on January 12, 1931, provided a more resonant sounding board for the internecine strife between Hartley and the other state elective officials. In his message to the assembled solons the governor demanded a $25,000 appropriation to investigate Commissioner Savidge and the land office "to straighten out intolerable conditions."

He also hammered away at "the chaotic situation in Washington's taxation, with local government costs increasing alarmingly and taxpaying sources diminishing."

"Taxation," he said, "is still the most vital problem facing our state. Since my incumbency we have wrestled with the subject from every angle and chaos still reigns."*

He asked for the abolition of the three-member paid tax commission, which had been created at his request in 1925, its duties to be taken over by a supervisor of taxation under the director of efficiency. This recommendation caught everyone by surprise, including the tax commissioners.

The general fund budget of $10,488,682 proposed by the governor was below the $11,737,737 of two years before, but the total recommended budget from all sources added up to $82,499,112 . . . $11,792,394 more than the previous biennium.

Hartley was finding himself in the frustrating situation of economy-minded executives in which they find themselves to the present day. Parkinson's law had not been passed by any legislative body, but it was in effect. Bureaucracy seemed to proliferate and feed upon itself like runaway cells in the body politic. No matter how he tried . . . and he certainly did try . . . the governor was forced to watch the costs of government go up each

biennium. He probably felt like a deep-sea diver grappling with a maritime monster which grew new tentacles faster than he could lop off the old ones.

The governor continued to view education as the rathole down which the taxpayers' dollars flowed endlessly and he reiterated his belief that "retrenchment in educational expenditures is absolutely essential." He also continued his battle to abolish the fixed tax millages for institutions of higher education and to replace the boards of regents and trustees with a nine-member unpaid board of education. He stated emphatically that "administrative functions carried on by ex-officio committees and boards have proved diabolical, extravagant, incompetent and unbusinesslike," and asked for the abolishment of the state capitol commission, state parks committee and judicial council. He also referred obliquely to a state sales tax as a possible "medium through which values can be restored to property," but stopped short of its outright endorsement.

The legislature was, as usual, overwhelmingly Republican, with only eight Democrats in the house and one in the senate, but the party was hopelessly split between the pro-Hartley forces and the anti-Hartleyites, led by Lieutenant Governor Gellatly and the other elective officials. The governor's life was complicated by the fact that he was afraid to leave the state lest Gellatly, as acting governor, should marshal the forces of the opposition and do him in in his absence. Furthermore, neither his legislative champion, Ed Sims, nor Mark Reed returned to the capitol in 1931 to keep a tight rein on things.

The number of women legislators was reduced from five to three . . . Representatives Belle Reeves, who had made a political comeback after six years absence, Ida McQueston and Mary Hutchinson. Pearl Wanamaker and Maude Sweetman had made unsuccessful bids for congress and the state senate, and Reba Hurn had been defeated in the primaries, leaving the senate again a masculine stronghold.

When the house convened on January 12 a freshman representative from Clark county named Clement Scott arose to second the nomination of Edwin J. Templeton as speaker. "If this is the last thing I ever do," he told his colleagues, "I want the people of Clark county to know that I made a speech in the house."

---

*The same statement could well have been made by Governor Evans in his message of 1975.

He then sat down, had a heart attack and fell to the floor dead.

Templeton was, after a decent pause, elected speaker of the house.

As the session progressed into one of the mildest winters in the history of the Puget Sound country, desperate efforts were made to bring forth a legislative redistricting bill to replace Initiative 57. Legislators from the lesser counties joined forces to reduce the heavy representation given King county, but their efforts were fruitless. When a bill was finally rammed through, the attorney general's office pointed out that the legislature must wait two years to change or repeal an initiative.

By 1931 it had become fashionable to haul school busloads of public school students to Olympia to see the processes of democratic government (or at any rate its public facade) at close hand and crowds of gawking adolescents and harrassed teachers got in the way of preoccupied legislators and lobbyists.

Senator E. B. Benn of Grays Harbor infuriated Superintendent Hicks of the ASL and his embattled cohorts by introducing a bill prohibiting wire-tapping, which passed the senate by a 35 to four vote. It was prompted by the wire-tap conviction of Roy Olmstead, former Seattle police lieutenant and a popular and highly ethical bootlegger, and by the belief of Senator Benn that the prohibitionists had been responsible for ousting him from his job as United States marshal for western Washington. According to Benn, his opposition to wire-tapping "had incurred the wrath of the great temperance organizations with their king fish* who dispenses Washington federal patronage" (through hide-bound old Senator Jones).

The antiwire-tap bill died in the house, as did the $30 a month old age pension bill, which had again passed the usually more conservative senate.

Both houses passed a bill providing for an individual and corporate income tax, although not without some confusion in the house of representatives. M. B. Mitchell pointed out in some outrage that the record showed 60 members had voted for the bill and 22 against, although a nose-count showed that only 65

representatives were present on the floor at the time the vote was taken. The speaker, as speakers are wont to do, simply ignored the protests of Mr. Mitchell.

This too proved to be a moot point, since Hartley vetoed the measure on the grounds that the two to five percent individual tax and five percent corporate tax would cost more to administer than they would earn and wouldn't reduce the property tax. He added the gratuitous opinion that the legislature should have reduced rather than increased taxes, but that this had been thwarted "by a little band of willful men in the senate."

The governor started vetoing on February 23, when he redlined a bill to grant military leave with pay to members of the national guard and reserve, and he kept it up until well after the legislature had departed from the scene. He trimmed $210,000 from the omnibus appropriations bill and $1,390,000 from the supplemental appropriations bill, including $400,000 to help Seattle build a sea wall along its waterfront. The King county legislators had succeeded in getting the sea wall substituted for the Deception Pass highway bridge which had been recommended by the governor.

The legislators had already anticipated the governor's action and reciprocated by cutting the requested $56,200 for the operation of his office to $53,000, reducing his requested investigative fund from $25,000 to $18,000 and extradition fund from $25,000 to $16,000.

The session ended in the usual deadlock over the general and highway appropriations bills. The infighting was particularly vicious over the $25 million highway pork barrel, with the senate cow county faction demanding more money for eastern Washington roads and the house urban faction holding out for increased appropriations for the ocean beach and Olympic loop highways. There was little floor action as the conference committees wrangled in private and by four o'clock on the morning of March 12 only four Democrats and one Republican remained on the floor of the House. This gave the Democrats the opportunity to get the feel of power and Harry C. Huse of Spokane was ushered to the presiding officer's chair. Later he has replaced by Democrat George E. Brown, the youngest representative that session. There was, of course, no quorum, so the Democratic occupancy of the rostrum was, at best, a hint of things to come.

---

*The influence of Amos n' Andy was having its effect upon the oratorical terminology of the legislature as well as the speech of the general public.

The session finally ended at 12:11 a.m. on the morning of March 16, having set a new overtime record of 76 hours. The vote on the last bills was taken in the house in the late night hours and many of the members had given up and wandered off somewhere. Newsmen counted 34 absentees, with the clerk voting for 20 of them as he called the roll. A number of measures were shown on the record to have passed with 83 aye votes, no nayes and 14 absent or not voting.

Thus did the 22nd legislature of the state of Washington come to an end, if not with a whimper certainly not with a bang. It had, in fact, accomplished little that was noteworthy and had almost completely ignored the plight of the thousands of its constituents who faced poverty and hunger as a result of the ever-deepening worldwide depression. This was thoroughly in accord with the philosophy of the governor. When the Exchange club of Toledo, Ohio, telegraphed the governors of the states for their opinions on "the proposed movement to develop a happier outlook on business and conditions in general," the crusty Hartley fired off a reply advising one and all to "quit blathering one another. Print only the truth. Let the people do the business while the government keeps order. All will be better off."

If, at the national level, Herbert Hoover was seemingly incapable of dealing with the human tragedy of the great depression, Hartley, at the state level, seemed incapable of realizing that it was occurring.

RAID ON THE GRAND HOTEL

Probably the brightest event to enliven the 1931 legislative session was the great liquor raid on the Hotel Olympian.

The raid on the capital city's previously sacrosanct hostelry was led by federal prohibition agent D. E. Dunning, along with Sheriff Claud Havens and Chief Frank Cushman. According to the *Olympian* of March 3, the crime fighters *"swooped down on the Hotel Olympian with dramatic suddenness to the surprise of state officials, legislators and others who were congregated in the lobby."*

The part about the surprise was the understatement of the year.

Much mystery surrounded the raid. The law officers would reveal only that six people had been arrested and a keg of moonshine confiscated. They refused to name names, but Jay Thomas, Colonel Thomas Aston, a Spokane attorney and lobbyist and Roscoe Balch, a University of Washington regent, were observed in conference with Havens and Dunning the next morning. Those arrested subsequently journeyed to Tenino, pled guilty under assumed names, paid their fines and returned to their various pursuits.

Anti-Saloon League Superintendent Hicks was the occupant of a lobby chair, a happy smile wreathing his stern countenance, as the raiding party burst into the hotel. The legislative session and the intransigent wetness of the governor had tried his patience. He had charged that "one of the smoothest wet organizations in the country is working at Olympia to put through repeal of the state dry law," and that it was useless to push through dry legislation "with a vetoing governor sitting in the capitol."

Informed legend has it that Hicks had received an advance tip that Governor Hartley would be among those tippling at the Olympian that night and, as surrogate for Senator Jones, he had applied pressure upon the prohis to stage the raid in the hope of catching the little governor in *flagrante dilecto*. Only Hartley's knowledge of the back corridors and fire escapes of the Olympian saved him from falling into the net, which so embarrassingly ensnared the lesser political fish.

When the state PTA urged Hartley to remove University Regent Balch from office for having been arrested for possession of liquor, the crusty governor quoted Lincoln, informing the ladies of the delegation that if he knew the brand of booze favored by Balch he would send a case to each of the other regents.

DEEPENING DEPRESSION

In the capital city, as in the state as a whole, the depression had moved westward like a black and dreary cloud. Ships no longer jostled for space at the port docks and the local mills began to cut production. Construction, which had been active until 1930, ground to a halt. President Hoover had signed the emergency unemployment bill, which allotted $1,734,000 in federal funds to Washington for new construction, highways and harbor improvements, but it was too little and too late. At Thanksgiving and Christmas of the previous year the Olympia labor unions had served meals to 300 hungry people at the labor temple.

Even as the legislature and the governor ignored the disaster, the unemployed and desperate people were rioting from Connecticut to California. A drought was making a dust bowl of the state of Arkansas and the *Olympian,* on January 20, published a front-page photograph of a nine-year-old Arkansas boy named Isaac Busby receiving a loaf of bread from a Red Cross worker . . . the first food he had eaten in three days. Hoover and Al Smith were making a joint nationwide radio appeal for a $10 million Red Cross emergency fund drive.

And in Washington's capital city, the county established a charity woodyard at which the poor were permitted to "chop and take" on a 50-50 basis; the Red Cross distributed "relief garden seeds," presumably on the theory that if the jobless and destitute could avoid starving to death until harvest time they could dine lavishly on home-grown vegetables.

Although a growing segment of the population was concerned about where the next meal was coming from, bootleg liquor continued to command an excellent price and was available all the way from such disreputable hostelries as the Carlton and Bayview to those stylish centers of social and political activity, the Olympian and Governor. City authorities made sporadic efforts to enforce the traditional morality of the capital city, concentrating on the more sordid and less affluent establishments. Mayor Mills and the city commission instructed City Attorney W. W. Manier to take action to remove floathouses moored at street and alley ends along the waterfront. *"Many occupants, particularly along East Bay and State street are undesirable citizens,"* the mayor told the *Olympian,* adding that, in his opinion, *"moral conditons in that district are very bad."* Chief Cushman objected to the proposed abatement proceedings on the grounds that, as happened in 1910 when the lower Main street restricted district was closed, *"they'll just move their activities uptown."*

The final result was a sort of latter day restricted district. Most of the dilapidated shanties on cedar logs congregated on the mudflats west and south of the Northern Pacific depot and yards. As the depression deepened, more improvised shelters were erected there, both ashore and afloat and the district was given the unofficial designation of "Little Hollywood". It remained, a picturesque if squalid and unfragrant segment of the capital city for many years.

The citizens of Thurston county gave further evidence of their stern morality when a gangling 16-year-old named Walter Dubuc was convicted, along with adults Harold Carpenter and Ethel Willis, of killing an elderly farmer named Jacobson in the course of an attempted robbery. Young Dubuc and the 41-year-old bespectacled Carpenter were sentenced to death; Mrs. Willis to life imprisonment. No clemency was granted the boy and he was carried, blubbering and retching, to the scaffold, where he was duly hanged.

The citizens continued to find themselves confronted not only with increasing crime and immorality, but with increasing pollution as well. The department of licenses had cheerfully granted an unrestricted permit for the operation of a huge paper mill at Shelton. The mill proceeded to pour its noxious liquors into the restricted waters of the upper Sound and by 1931 it was noted with alarm that those legendary and succulent gourmets' delight, the tiny Olympia oysters had been virtually wiped out.

The city, having outgrown its garbage dumps, purchased a ravine near Gull Harbor and began hauling its trash to that site, to the intense disgust of citizens of the rural community, who began circulating abatement petitions against the city.

The citizens of Lacey, headed by L. C. Huntamer, soon joined the chorus of outrage, claiming that Olympians were dumping their garbage along the Lacey road rather than making the long haul to Gull Harbor. When the county commissioners asked the Laceyites if they had posted their road they replied that they had, but that the signs were now covered up with tin cans.

1932

Despite such continuing problems, Washington's capital city strode bravely into the year 1932 and the depths of the great depression trying, as best it could, to pretend it wasn't there. A new golf club, Glangarry, bravely opened west of town at the head of Eld Inlet, and radio station KGY moved from St. Martin's college to full commercial operation in the Dawley brothers' handsome new Capitol Park building just north of the capitol campus.

In July five destroyers arrived in town for fleet week and to escort the cruisers of the Capital to Capital yacht race on their way to Juneau. A parade was staged from downtown to the capitol grounds, led by highway patrolmen and the high school band and including uniformed postal employees and a naval contingent. The second-hand traffic device from Tacoma had been junked and the paraders marched under brand new electric traffic lights at the downtown intersections.

Amid these festivities and signs of affluence and progress, the surplus food warehouse in the basement of the courthouse, which had been issuing staple commodities to a thousand families a month, was abruptly closed. The county commissioners explained that relief funds were short and there was plenty of summer work in berry fields and on farms and all able-bodied poor "must now shift for themselves."

In September the local merchants went all out, turning on all their store lights and subsidizing the street car company to provide free rides downtown for their annual fall opening.

The following month the Olympia National bank, which had closed its doors earlier in the year, attracted much bigger crowds. The receivers had announced an 18 percent payment on accounts and most of its 2,740 depositors lined the street to claim their share of the salvaged $240,000.

LANDSLIDE

It was apparent to most political observers by this time that the biggest political upset in the state's history was due to take place at the fall elections. The inability of the Hoover administration made it evident that almost anyone chosen by the Democratic convention as its presidential candidate was going to win. At the state level, the Neanderthal reaction . . . or lack of reaction . . . by Hartley to widespread unemployment, hunger and despair, plus the continuing and widely publicized political bickering at the capitol, made it equally apparent that a qualified Democratic guber-

natorial candidate would have an excellent chance to send Hartley into well deserved political retirement.

One of the few who was unable to read the political handwriting on the wall was Hartley himself, who insisted upon filing for an unprecedented third term. He went down to humiliating defeat in the primaries at the hands of his arch-enemy Gellatly, who beat him 119,015 to 68,718, with three other candidates trailing far behind.

The Democratic nomination went to Clarence D. Martin, a slight, mustached and bespectacled flour mill owner from the eastern Washington town of Cheney. A moderately conservative Democrat, Martin was considered to have the perfect solid business man image . . . "neither too rich nor too poor."

In his campaign the Democratic candidate promised to give priority to unemployment relief, reform of the banking system and property tax relief, all popular issues with the voting public, which responded at the polls. Martin received 67,168 votes, Judge William Pemberton 57,124 and Lewis B. Schwellenbach 55,094.

The Olympia *News* added insult to Hartley's injuries by commenting that *"as a result of the primary election last week the next executive of this state is sure to be a man of dignity and integrity."*

In the general election Franklin D. Roosevelt swept the state with nearly double the vote given Hoover. Nationally he garnered 472 electoral votes to Hoover's 59. Martin did almost as well as the Democratic presidential candidate, beating Gellatly by 240,515 to 144,659.

Two politicians who had seen the writing on the wall were elected as Democrats despite cries of turncoat and opportunist. Homer T. Bone, who was accused of being a socialist as well as a "political hitch-hiker," and had run for congress on both the Republican and Socialist-Labor tickets, overwhelmingly defeated Wesley Jones, rolling up a considerably larger vote than either Roosevelt or Martin. The other, Otto A. Case, a flambouyant militiary officer who had campaigned previously as a Republican and Bull Mooser, was elected state treasurer.

All the embattled elective officials were ousted along with the governor. Dr. E. N. Hutchison became secretary of state, Cliff Yelle auditor, Hamilton, attorney general, and Martin, Land commissioner. Of the elective officials, only Showalter survived, probably because no Democrat bothered to file for superintendent of public instruction.

The lieutenant governor's office went to a colorful character named Victor Aloysius Meyers, who had gained some local fame as a band leader at the old Butler Hotel in Seattle during prohibition days. The debonair and neatly mustached Meyers had been prevailed upon by Seattle *Times* reporter Douglass Welch, the last of the great newspaper humorists of the Pacific Northwest, to engage in a comic opera campaign for mayor. While Meyers clowned about in a Mahatma Ghandi costume leading a goat, delivered campaign oratorq from a beer truck and promised to place hostesses on the city's street cars, Welch gleefully recorded his campaign in the *Times,* and a surprisingly large number of voters cast their ballots for the clowning candidate.

EDITORIAL

GOODBYE, ROLAND!

On September 14, 1932, the Seattle *Times* frontpaged its unkind farewell to the defeated Governor Hartley.

Meyers became bitten with the political bug and, when the 1932 election rolled around, journeyed to Olympia to file for statewide office. According to legend, he had intended to run for governor, but found he couldn't afford the filing fee. The cheapest job available was lieutenant governor, so he filed for that and beat Republican Judson Falknor 191,000 to 166,000.

Vic Meyers remained a major political figure in the state for a generation, the horror of the stuffy *Times* increasing steadily as it came to realize that it had created a seemingly indestructible Frankenstein monster.

All the Democratic candidates for congress were also elected, including the erstwhile radical university student body president, Zioncheck and an Everett jeweler named Mon C. Wallgren.

The state house of representatives ended up with an overwhelming 70 to 29 Democratic majority, which would have been greater except that Democrats had gotten out of the habit of filing for the legislature. It was the first time since early territorial days that the Democrats had controlled the house. The senate, whose members only had to stand for election every four years, experienced a less dramatic turnover, with a 25 to 21 Democratic majority, but that was quite a change from the 45 to one Republican majority of the previous year. And most of the 21 holdover Republican senators had a feeling that their days were numbered.

That was the great Democratic landslide of 1932. Those who rode it to power and glory had waited a long time and so they relished it the more. It ushered in a weird and wonderful and zany political era, but it also brought about greater progress toward meeting human needs and enhancing human dignity than any other phenomenon in the political history of the state and territoy.

And Washington's capital city would never be quite the same again.

CHAPTER TEN
The Ninth Decade
1933-1943

In all its 90 years as Washington's seat of government, the staid and tranquil capital city of Olympia had never seen a year like 1933.

Defaulting public officials, noisy revelry in downtown hotels and occasional bouts of fisticuffs during legislative sessions had long been taken in stride, but nothing had prepared the citizens for the events which transpired in 1933. Nothing quite like them had been witnessed by the oldest inhabitants.

In addition to the traditional fist-fights and noisy feuds, Olympians were treated to a continuing extravaganza of pageantry which included a portly senator mounting the Legislative building steps aboard a donkey and preceded by a brass band, the unseating of a representative who was a convicted rapist, a commune of unemployed legislators cooking beans in the home of the town's founding father, an influx of hunger marchers with stomach aches, parades of militant, sign-toting communists and the antics of a lieutenant governor who was possessed of an earthy sense of humor.

Even before the 23rd legislature convened the unemployed victims of the ever-deepening depression were shattering the traditional image of the meek pauper who gratefully accepted the county's thin and grudging charity.

On January 5, weeks of bitter wrangling between the unemployed and county welfare workers culminated in a semi-riot at the courthouse. A throng of angry people jammed the corridors outside the welfare office and when Director H. L. Thornton tried to elbow his way through he was firmly grasped and held in place to hear shouted demands for food requisitions. Sheriff Havens and his men eventually rescued the welfare director and jailed nine of the more aggressive demonstrators, but the remainder threatened to storm the jail and release their friends, giving the sheriff's department an apprehensive and sleepless night.

The courthouse confrontation was an omen of things to come.

Associated Press correspondent E. Q. Anderson was under the impression that things were going to be more sedate at the capitol with the departure of Hartley and the embattled Republican elective officials. A week before the new state officials were inaugurated he wrote:

"On Wednesday that notable company of stars who provided many an hour of thunderous melodrama in the statehouse at Olympia during the past eight years will make their last appearance and then give way to a newer, but surely not more entertaining troupe."

Mr. Anderson couldn't have been less accurate in his prediction.

A SEX FIEND IN THE HOUSE

One of the 70 newcomers of the Democratic house majority was one N. G. Robinson, who had been elected from a King county district while in jail awaiting transport to the state reformatory for the rape of a pre-teen age girl. Things like that happened in the Democratic landslide of 1932, but the Robinson case was something of an embarrassment to his colleagues of the majority caucus. They comforted themselves, however, with the happy thought that, as a convicted felon, Representative Robinson wouldn't be coming to Olympia. The King county commissioners would select a replacement who would be quietly seated and the over-sexed gentleman from

GOVERNOR CLARENCE D. MARTIN

SMITH TROY as State Attorney General.

King would quickly sink into the anonymity of a numbered inmate at Monroe.

They hadn't counted on the terrible-tempered governor who, as a lame duck, was smarting uncontrollably under the humiliation of his dismal failure in the primaries. Two days before the legislature convened, Hartley announced with a straight face that statements of the girl's mother and doctor had convinced him that Robinson was innocent after all. Although not noted as a pardoning governor, one of his last official acts was the granting of a full and unconditional pardon to Representative Robinson, who was released from King county jail in time to get to Olympia to assume his high elective office.

Quietly cursing the name of Hartley, the Democratic caucus was forced to meet and vote their erring colleague out of office, a proceeding which made front page stories across the state.

The two Democratic King county commissioners, Dr. Brinton and "Radio Speaker" John C. Stevenson, appointed one Edmund Miller to replace Robinson, but the Democratic leadership viewed him as a doubtful improvement. He was a maverick who insisted on marching to his own drum. Finally a number of the top Democrats cornered him and attempted moral 'suasion to get him into line.

"Don't you have any regard for your constituents?" they asked him reproachfully.

"I only got two constituents . . . Doc Brinton and John Stevenson," he replied.

THE FIRST DEMOCRAT
TO SHOW HIS ASS IN OLYMPIA

When the legislature convened on Jaunary 9, Senator Corydon (Nifty) Garrett, publisher of the Sumner *Standard,* Democrat, uninhibited practical joker and bosom buddy of Lieutenant Governor Vic Meyers, felt that something special should be done to make memorable the Democratic take-over of the capitol.

Dressed formally and wearing the rakish derby which, it was rumored, he slept with, he mounted a symbolic donkey and preceded by a brass band, which he had hired for the occasion, rode the full length of Capitol Way to the Legislative building, bowing and smiling at bemused bystanders. Upon his arrival he urged the nimble donkey up the broad granite steps to the great bronze doors, dismounted gracefully and proceeded to take his seat in the senate chamber.

The affair, colorful enough in itself, had a fascinating aftermath.

That evening Senator Garrett, no doubt exhilerated by his morning's triumph, was being even noisier than usual in the lobby of the Hotel Olympian. A pair of impressively bosomed and hatted WCTU ladies, probably suspecting that the senator's high spirits were engendered by alcoholic stimulation, huffed their way to an innocent looking gentleman seated in one of the lobby chairs.

"Who", they asked with great disdain, "is that uncouth person in the derby hat?"

The gentleman in the chair was a veteran newsman named Jim Brown, who operated an insurance agency in the hotel building and served as capitol correspondent for the Seattle *Argus*.

Brown fixed the indignant ladies with a twinkling eye and informed them, "That's Nifty Garrett . . . *the first Democrat to show his ass in Olympia*."

The reaction of the two virtuous guardians of the public morality can be better imagined than described.

THE IMPOSSIBLE TAKES
A LITTLE LONGER

Amid such minor distractions, the legislators met to face unprecedented problems. The most terrible economic depression in the nation's history was approaching its darkest depths. Nearly 350,000 of the state's 1,500,000 citizens . . . one out of every four . . . were keeping body and soul together through some form of relief. Banks and other financial institutions were toppling like dominoes and the property tax rug had been rudely jerked from under the feet of the legislators by citizen action.

Five initiative measures had been approved at the 1932 election . . . one more than the total number passed in all the years since 1914. The measures included provision for permanent registration of voters, creation of separate departments of game and fisheries and repeal of the state bone dry law. The fourth, Initiative 64, imposed a constitutional limit of 40 mills on property taxes, eliminating $13 million in state revenue. It was believed at the time that the passage of the fifth initiative, Grange-sponsored Number 69*, which authorized a state income tax, would reduce the shortage to $8 million, but in subsequent court litigation Judge Wright ruled that the law was unconstitutional on the grounds that "a graduated income tax is not a uniform tax on the same

---

*Rather inexplicably, the 40-mill tax limitation was approved by a bare 54 percent majority, while the income tax proposal passed by an overwhelming majority of well over two to one. Perhaps present-day advocates of "tax reform", the modern euphemism for a state income tax, should study the selling techniques employed by their counterparts of 40 years ago.

class of property" as required by the state constitution. The supreme court, by a five to four decision, subsequently upheld Judge Wright's opinion.

The *Olympian* observed as the legislature convened that its major responsibilities would be *"unemployment relief, reduction of the budget and taxes and finding new sources of revenue to replace that lost by passage of the 40-mill limit initiative"*.

Just how a vast program of relief was to be established while the budget was cut and new revenues were to be raised while reducing taxes, the *Olympian's* editorial writer left to the ingenuity of the lawmakers.

The legislators were also beset by the spokesmen of local taxing districts, particularly the school districts, who wailed that the 40-mill limitation would wipe them out unless some new means of raising revenue was quickly devised. Major Dohm, who was president of the Olympia school board as well as the town's ranking militia officer, announced that the capital city schools could be operated for only five months unless state support was markedly increased.

To further increase the tension, there were reports that Seattle and Tacoma "communists" were organizing a gigantic hunger march to descend upon the capitol. County Prosecuter Harold Troy warned a joint committee of the house and senate that "rioting will follow in the wake of the threatened hunger march" and that he was convinced the marchers were bent on storming the county jail, where eight of the "alleged communists" from the courthouse fracas were still being held on charges of inciting a riot.

Members of the local business community, determined that the "so-called hunger marchers," as the *Olympian* consistently referred to them, were not going to endanger their precarious security, checked their shotguns and filled lengths of garden hose with lead to serve as bludgeons in case the "communists" tried to help themselves to the remaining material resources of the capital city.

In the meantime, the legislature, made up predominantly of freshman, did its best to get organized and gird itself for the troubled times ahead. Even the speaker of the house, George Yantis of Thurston county, was a mere second-termer in the halls of state. With a total of six ladies, one in the senate and five in the house, the 1933 legislature also enjoyed the largest feminine membership in its history. The fair lawmakers were treated somewhat better by their male counterparts than had been the custom in the past. Senator Kathryn Malstrom of Pierce County was delegated to fly to the national capital with a joint memorial asking congress to depreciate the currency by placing a duty on imports equal to the difference in par value of U.S. currency and that of the nation where the goods were manufactured.

Upon Senator Malstrom's return, Mollie Grace Chamberlin, the 10-year-old daughter of Senator George C. Chamberlin of King, was appointed honorary page for a day to help escort the emissary of the senate to the rostrum. Little Miss Chamberlin acquitted herself so well that Senator Henry Foss, Tacoma tugboat man and Democrat, moved that she be hired as a regular page for a week. The *Olympian,* overlooking the girl page of the late 19th century, viewed this as a brand new precedent and observed that *"another male stronghold has been crashed by the weaker sex."*

The representatives, unable to provide cross-country flights for its feminine members, presented potted plants to Representatives Pearl Wanamaker, Belle Reeves, Lulu Haddon, Florence Myers and Esther Lanz.

The Democrats further broke with tradition when they did away with the coterie of gold-braided militia staff officers which had added comic opera pomp and circumstance to previous inaugural ceremonies.

LONG LIVE THE GOVERNOR

On January 10 Roland Hartley made his last pilgrimage to the legislative chambers to deliver his farewell address to a joint session of the two houses. He spoke of the "most insidious and bitter opposition" which had hindered his eight-year effort to reduce the costs of state government, and urged the legislators to continue on the course of economy which he had plotted. He expressed bitter opposition to proposals to transfer welfare responsibilities from the counties to the state, warning that it would "open the door to unlimited opportunities for waste, inefficiency and graft."

He was particularly proud of an executive request bill which would transfer the public printing plant and its accumulated profits to the state as an outright gift. The appraised value of the plant was $78,261 which, with accrued profits amounted to a total of $113,556.

The legislature cheerfully accepted this windfall, the plant was placed under state operation and, henceforth, salaried public printers were appointed by the governors.

At 12:20 p.m. on January 11 Clarence D. Martin received the oath of office from Chief Justice Walter B. Beals, becoming the first Democratic governor since the death of Ernest Lister 14 years earlier, and the second in the state's history.

Hartley, the 19th century arch-conservative, made way for Martin, the enlightened 20th century man, with surprisingly good grace. The two met in the governor's office the morning after the inauguration. Hartley shook hands with Martin and told him, "Here are the keys to the mansion. The help is all ready to serve you." The new governor thanked him, smiled and said, "Come down here to see me once in a while." Then he extracted a key from his own pocket and handed it to Hartley. "I would like you to use my room at the Governor Hotel tonight." Hartley did and they exchanged beds. After the amenities were observed, the two posed for photographs, Martin in the big executive chair with the seal of the state on the back; Hartley in his favorite small chair. Martin's 13-year-old son Frank asked Hartley about the seagull, Tee, and the ex-governor asked him to be sure that food was put on the window sill for his old friend.

The new governor then strolled across to the mansion for lunch, but found that the thrifty Hartley had left nothing in the larder but bread and coffee. The chief executive's first meal in the mansion consisted of black coffee and unbuttered toast.

Martin had prefaced his inaugural address with a warning to the legislature that it must "revise old philosophies of government if it carries out the demands of the electorate which created it."

Failure of the preceding administration to take cognizance of changing conditions, the governor said, caused a revolt at the polls, but the incoming administration was given a direct and unmistakable mandate to produce "a fresh economic deal, a different social order and a new political spirit."

The old philosophy followed "by those who have been in control . . . the rejected leadership," he declared, "embraced the idea of rule by the strong and cunning." This must be replaced, he said, by the philosophy of "thy brother's keeper," and "the gospel of the helping hand must be proclaimed."

The governor then appealed "to those who are pleading for tax relief to submit patiently to some new imposts that may at first glance look like extra taxes," explaining that any tax changes would be "the beginning of the shift of a reasonable portion of the load from those who are burdened to those who are escaping their share of taxes."

Like his predecessor, he urged strict economy in the routine operations of state government, suggesting that it might "be well to adopt a policy of forced economy by cutting all appropriations in the budget (prepared by Hartley) by 25 to 40 per cent. For his part, he promised to effect a savings of more than $3 million dollars in the code departments "through salary revisions and elimination of deadwood."

He proposed creation of an unemployment commission to "seek out public work that might be done by otherwise unemployed men" and warned that "we might be required to consider a bond issue of from $5 million to $10 million to be made available for immediate unemployment relief," adding that "it is possible, as an emergency measure, some form of a selective or a general sales tax will be the easiest and surest way to secure the needed $8 million (lost by passage of the 40-mill initiative), and I request the legislature to give this plan its thoughtful consideration."

He further insisted that he did not favor "a reactionary policy for our public schools" (another mild slap at Hartley), and urged that entrance requirements at the university and state college be lowered to "open the door, with reasonable fees, to every girl and boy who graduates from an accredited high school."

He recommended a sweeping rewriting of the state banking laws, including the authorization for large banks to establish branches, and a strong effort to obtain construction of the proposed Grand Coulee dam on the upper Columbia river. The highway patrol, he believed, should be transformed into a state police force as a means of relieving small counties and communities of law enforcement costs. Foreclosures on homes and farms should be made more difficult, a "conservative system of child welfare" should be adopted and a contributary system of old age insurance should be established to "banish the poor farm from Washington."

THE WHEELS SPIN FASTER

The legislature wasted little time in responding to the governor's message. On the afternoon it was delivered, Senator E. B. Palmer of King county introduced a sales tax bill which, he declared, "collects a tax from everyone, but does not pyramid taxes." His bill was 22 pages long and contained over 7,000 words. The complicated measure was a sort of graduated sales tax, with a wide and confusing range of assessments . . . 42/100 of one per cent on minerals and timber, 21/100 on manufactured goods, 2/20 on property sales, 3/10 of one per cent on retail goods, etc., etc., etc.

The next day Representative Myron Titus of King introduced a house bill permitting county commissioners to grant monthly pensions of $30 to persons 65 years of age or older, provided they had lived in the state 15 years, the county five years, and had incomes of $360 a year or less. A bill introduced by Representative E. F. Banker of Okanogan would establish a Columbia Basin commission to work for the "immediate development of the project by means of the Grand Coulee dam and adjacent power plants and development of power, water and soil resources vital to the development of the state, Pacific Northwest and United States."

Governor Martin demonstrated similar alacrity in keeping his part of the bargain. On January 13 he ordered pay cuts of from 10 to 25 per cent in all code departments and institutions. State employees accepted the cuts without a murmur, happy to have steady jobs at any pay, but there was apprehension as the governor explained that the pay cut was "preliminary to a survey to see how many state employees can be eliminated." Department directors, who were paid $500 a month, didn't escape the pruning knife. They received cuts of from 10 to 35 per cent.

The new state auditor, Cliff Yelle, struck a blow for economy the same day, asking Treasurer Case not to issue warrants to ousted Republican state workers for accumulated vacation pay.

TO HELL WITH OLYMPIA BEANS!

On January 16 the advance guard of the hunger marchers . . . about 200 people . . . arrived in town, some on foot and others riding in broken-down flivvers and trucks. They were not the ravening communist horde the locals were expecting. Most of them appeared to be ordinary people, just a little more ragged and undernourished than the average. They limited their activities to the distribution of handbills setting forth the objectives of the march, which was sponsored by the Washington State Hunger March committee, acting for the Unemployed Citizens' League of King county, United Producers of Washington, Unemployed Council and United Farmers' League.

By the next day the ranks of the hungry had increased to about a thousand. An *Olympian* reporter interviewed and described a "typical" marcher . . . a 32-year-old man *"in a torn 'tin' coat, overalls and boots,"* who had *"been out of a steady job for about three years."* He said he had a wife and two babies, most of his savings had been lost in a savings and loan closure and his house had been foreclosed. *"We can't sit back and starve,"* he told the reporter.

Although the man in the tattered working clothes wasn't carrying a bomb or a red flag, the *Olympian* writer was able to record his subversive avowal that he would be *"tickled to death if he could go to Russia tomorrow."*

The sound of armed, alert and well-fed business men and legionnaires gritting their teeth was widespread as they read the evening paper.

On the afternoon of January 17 the ragged army gathered to march up Capitol Way to the Legislative building. Merchants grimly guarded their premises, prepared to defend their inventories and plate glass with their lives, but there was no violence. The marchers carried some inflammatory signs . . . "THE COMMUNIST PARTY LEADS THE STRUGGLE OF THE WORKERS," "DOWN WITH THE COMMISSARIES" and "WE DEMAND FOOD AND CLOTHING . . . and they did a lot of shouting once they had marshalled outside the capitol.

Inside the marble halls the apprehension was even greater than that which prevailed in downtown Olympia. All the doors were locked, including those of the legislative chambers and the governor's office. Elevators which gave access to these critical areas were made inoperable and highway patrolmen stalked the corridors.

Until then the weather had been mild and rainy, but the marchers stood outside in a snow storm which deposited four inches on the capital city by evening. They amused themselves and further outraged the local patriots by voting honorary membership in their committee to the imprisoned Wobblies of the Centralia shoot-out and to two Anacortes men who had been thrown in jail for boldly removing groceries from a chain store to feed their families.

Finally a delegation of 25 was admitted to the capitol to present the demands of the marchers, the principle one being passage of a "social insurance bill" to provide $10 a week to jobless family heads, plus $3 per dependent.

Olympia citizens, pleased that their city did not lie in smoking ruins, opened up a number of vacant store buildings as dormitories for the male marchers and provided rooms "in one of the cheaper hotels" for the smaller number of women and children. The Volunteers of America set up a kitchen and served beans and coffee, after which a number of the hungry ones became violently ill. Whether the volunteers' beans were bad, or the marchers simply weren't used to having food of any kind in their stomachs is unknown, but henceforth signs were added to the line of march proclaiming "TO HELL WITH OLYMPIA BEANS!"

Such excitement prevailed in the capital city that it didn't even make front page headlines in the *Olympian* when Wallace Nicely, former supervisor of savings and loan, was convicted of misappropriating $14,000 in the closure of the Puget Sound Savings and Loan at Seattle, and sentenced to a four to 15 year term in the penitentiary.

Although the hunger marchers soon dispersed after making their damands known and the widely expected violence failed to develop, there was a grim determination about them that couldn't be ignored. It was apparent to less sensitive and intelligent politicians than Martin that people weren't going to keep marching peacefully while their families went hungry . . . not unless clear evidence was given them that government was concerned for their plight. At his urging, a relief bill was rushed through both houses of the legislature and signed on January 20. A five-member relief commission was appointed to administer relief funds from the Reconstruction Finance corporation. Frank S. Baker of Tacoma was named chairman and Charles F. Ernst, manager of the King county relief department, became the director of emergency unemployment relief.

There was, in fact, more contention and outright violence among the legislators than among the hunger marchers in 1933.

UNHAND ME, YOU RUFFIAN!

One of the most prickly of the lawmakers was a distinguished old gentleman with a white goatee and tender emotions named Charles Roth, a retired Whatcom county lawyer and former Bull Mooser who had served in the legislature off and on since 1893 and in 1928 had been elected to the house from Whatcom county as a Republican. During a floor debate in which remarks of individual members were limited to 10 minutes, Representative Roth refused to relinquish the floor when this time was up. *His* remarks, he insisted, were too important to be subject to a time limitation.

After banging his gavel futilely, Speaker Yantis summoned Sergeant at Arms P. F. McElroy, a brawny ex-bouncer for the Pantages theatrical circuit, and ordered him to stifle the gentleman from Whatcom.

The sergeant at arms gingerly approached the orating Roth and placed a hamlike hand upon his arm.

"Unhand me, you ruffian!" the old gentleman shouted with great emotion. Then, with goatee trembling, he broke down and wept at the indignity which had been inflicted upon him.

The members, including Yantis, forthwith turned upon the unfortunate McElroy, drove him from the floor and gave old Mr. Roth their time allotments so that he could speak as long as he wanted to.

Although well paid, a legislative sergeant at arms does not always occupy a bed of roses.

Representative Roth proved, before the session was over, that he didn't have to rely solely on his histrionic ability to survive in the legislature. He could practice that time-honored legislative art of horse-trading when he had to.

George Adams, the first full-blooded Indian to be elected to the legislature, introduced a pet bill permitting Indians to acquire state oyster lands on favorable terms. Roth, declaring that this constituted "special interest legislation," announced dramatically that he was "sworn to fight it tooth and nail as long as I am in this legislature."

The wily Adams did a little checking and learned that Roth's son was the operator of a profitable fish-trap on Puget Sound. He promptly introduced a bill banning all fish-traps. Roth shortly approached him in great agitation, offering to go along with the oyster bill if Adams would keep the fish-trap bill in his fisheries committee. Adams, doing his best to hide a triumphant grin, agreed and they shook hands on it.

But to the horror of both parties to the deal, the fish-trap bill caught on. Sports fishermen and offshore commercial fishermen wrote letters to their representatives and there was great pressure to get it on the floor. The unfortunate Adams had to stay on the floor of the house constantly to defend his keeping the bill bottled up in his committee and avoid breaking the unwritten but sacrosanct law of the log-roller.

Another running feud was carried on by Democratic Representatives Fred Schade and Frank (Scotty) Anderson of Spokane county.* Each consistently worked and voted against

*The ill feeling began when Mr. Schade, full of good spirits, announced on the floor of the house that his fellow Democrats were just Republicans with their brains knocked out. Anderson apologized for him and the feud was on.

the other's bills until the closing days of the session. Then, with a Schade bill up for a final vote, Anderson rose to speak. Schade gritted his teeth and braced himself for the expected verbal blast. Instead, to the amazement of everyone, and Schade in particular, Anderson gave the measure his unstinted support, urging all his colleagues to vote favorably upon it. It passed with only one negative vote.

Representative Schade, apparently convinced that if the hated Anderson was for it there must be something wrong with it, cast the only nay vote against his own bill.

The decorum of the senate was somewhat marred when a young senator in his 20's, Charles Todd, who worked on the Seattle *Times* copy desk, lost patience with the aggressive lobbying of the King county commissioners. John C. Stevenson, a verbose politician who had gotten his start as street barker for an advertising dentist, later became a radio commentator and, for political identity, had his name legally changed to *Radio Speaker* John C. Stevenson, was the leader of the courthouse delegation. Todd, normally a restrained and courteous young man, spotted Stevenson in the gallery, rose to a point of personal privilege and pointed an accusing finger at the radio speaker. He then delivered himself of an unflattering opinion of tax-paid lobbyists in general and of "that overstuffed county commissioner cruising about the legislative halls like a blimp looking for a mooring" in particular.

Stevenson was not easily abashed, but this public reference to the fleshy padding that had come with political prosperity, and the ensuing hilarity in chambers and gallery drove him from the house in humiliation and confusion.

Todd subsequently progressed further in the newspaper business than Stevenson did in politics. The radio speaker, in spite of determined efforts, never rose above the courthouse level, but Todd later became attorney for and publisher of the *Times*.

VIC SOOTHES THE SAVAGE BREAST

The senate was also the scene of an incipient display of pugilism as it debated a bill to place a modest tax on chain stores ($5.00 for one establishment to $125 for 20 or more). Senator Kebel Murphy, Spokane county Democrat, was a staunch advocate of the bill. Senator Paul Houser, Republican of King, was just as stoutly opposed to it. As the debate grew heated, Murphy accused Houser of "shady actions."

The gentleman from King arose in flushed indignation to demand, "When did I ever do anything shady?"

"When did you ever do anything else?" his opponent snapped.

Lieutenant Governor Meyers pounded the gavel and asked Senator Murphy to "tone down his remarks," but to no avail. Senator Houser dashed across the floor toward Senator Murphy shouting, "If you will come closer I'll give you an answer right on the end of your nose!"

Senator Howard, King county Republican, ventured the opinion that "I think Senator Murphy should retract his remark."

This conciliatory advice wasn't needed. Murphy was already retreating before the frontal attack of Houser, fingering his nose nervously and loudly asserting, "I'll take it back! I was just joking!"

Mollified, Houser ceased his advance and politely requested, "Permit *me* to apologize."

Taking advantage of the lull in hostilities, the lieutenant governor announced heartily, "Well, we need some harmony now." He then summoned the Pacific college quartette to the floor to render a number of soothing melodies, the savage breasts were calmed and harmony did, indeed, prevail in the chambers presided over by the state's best known musician.

Despite the calming influence of the musical Meyers, the legislators of 1933 faced most of the frustrations of previous sessions and a number of new ones.

OLD FRUSTRATIONS AND NEW

The continuing and wholly ineffective efforts to exert some sort of control over the lobbyists resulted in a house resolution requiring members of the third house to register with the chief clerk and disclose their clients for the public record upon pain of being barred from the chambers.

A particular target of legislative wrath was the Washington Education Association, which was becoming an increasingly strident voice for the traditionally meek and down-trodden school teachers of the state. The teachers certainly needed a voice . . . in addition to being fired if caught smoking, drinking, cussing or getting married, a number of those in Thurston county were subsisting on salaries of $315 a year . . . but many of the lawmakers felt they were being unduly pressured by the forces of education.

The house approved a resolution castigating the WEA as "an invisible government" and "a private racket preying upon the teaching profession of the state," and setting up a five-member committee to investigate its activities.

While a number of present-day legislators might agree in principle with the opinions expressed in the resolution, such a document would have the survival potential of the proverbial snowball in hell at a contemporary legislative session. The education lobby has replaced the railroad, liquor, timber, concrete and fisheries lobbies as one of the state's most powerful, and it can marshal countless thousands of votes to provide its muscle.

Apparently alarmed by the ill-feeling between legislators and educators, Governor Martin quickly dispatched a special message, described by the *Olympian* as *"a heart-wringing plea in behalf of the common schools and a specific request for a $10 million bond issue to relieve unemployment."* The governor warned that *"the cherished barefoot schoolboy principle is threatened"* and that more than 100,000 Washington workers were unemployed.

The electronic marvels of the new Legislative building provided further frustrations. The new-fangled electric roll-call machine in the house had short-circuited itself into oblivion and members were again forced to undergo the droning boredom of verbal roll-call votes on even the most trivial issues. The chamber elevators were bitterly denounced in the senate, the presiding officer and several members having been trapped in the bronze confines of one of them for a quarter of an hour that morning.*

---

*The original elevators have since been replaced, but they are apparently lineal descendants of the original balky cages. A legislator is not considered properly seasoned until he has been imprisoned in one.

IT'S NOT POLITE TO SAY YOU'RE HUNGRY

Late in February the capital city was alarmed to learn that another and larger hunger march was being planned for the first week of March. Efforts by liberals at the capitol to repeal the state's punitive criminal syndicalism law were thwarted when Representative Miller, who had replaced King county's pardoned rapist, warned that, without its protection 50,000 wild-eyed hunger marchers would descend upon the seat of government and give it a terrible kicking. Instead of repealing the repressive syndicalism law, a measure was introduced to investigate whether "there is a conspiracy under way in King county and elsewhere to tear down our government."

The Olympia city commissioners warned that participants in a second hunger march would approach the capital city "at their own risk" and made it clear that no food, shelter or transportation would be provided. They then passed an emergency ordinance prohibiting "seditious or anarchistic demonstrations within the city." For good measure, Dr. Bridgford, the city health officer, announced that such an influx of the unwashed would constitute a menace to public health.

The unemployed and hungry insisted on coming anyway. On March 1 the Central Federation of Unemployed Citizens Leagues of Seattle issued a demand that the city of Olympia "make every possible preparation for caring for and protecting the marchers," while denouncing the previous efforts to discourage the event:

Olympia responded by beefing up its deputized vigilante force to 800 men.

On the morning of March 2 most of the downtown business establishments were closed and securely locked, while a large segment of the citizenry lined the streets to watch the arrival of the marchers, who were herded out to Priest Point Park by the law officers. They arrived in a downpour of rain, wet, cold and many of them sick. Most of the unwelcome visitors were too exhausted and miserable to stage the parade which had been scheduled for 10 a.m. After one night under the dripping trees at Priest Point, the less hardy and determined began to straggle toward home. Five who ventured back into town were quickly jailed for vagrancy.

The park department complained that the tires of the marchers' jallopies had ruined the turf, picnic tables had been converted into improvised shelters, garbage had been strewn about and most of a three-years supply of fire wood had been burned in futile efforts to keep warm. For good measure, Dr. Bridgford condemned the campsite as "unsanitary and a hazard to the health of the general public." Sheriff Havens forthwith ordered the park evacuated.

Defeated and dispirited, the 1,200 marchers gave up and left town without having marched. Many of them, possessed of some wistful hope that help was to be obtained at the capitol, had set out with barely enough gasoline in the tanks of their fender-flapping flivvers and broken-down trucks to get to Olympia. The highway patrol reported the highway to Seattle lined with out-of-gas vehicles throughout that cold and rainy day and night.

Sympathy and violence were equally absent from the reactions of Olympia citizens to the arrival of the hunger marchers. Nobody clubbed them. Nobody gave them so much as a crust of bread. The marchers didn't come back.

Not that there wasn't compassion for the plight of the depression's victims. It was just that when they appeared in large numbers, grim, angry and pathetic, they were an affront to the consciences of those who could still buy food, but feared to share it because the ranks of the hungry reminded them that, next day or next week, they might join those ranks.

LEGISLATIVE COMMUNE

A fair percentage of the legislators were, themselves unemployed, and were required to subsist upon their five dollars a day per diem. Eleven of them rented the ancient mansion of the town's founder, Edmund Sylvester, for $150 a month. They pooled their resources, hired a cook and a waitress and slept on army cots. Although the old house had many rooms, only one was a bath and the hot water supply was limited. Two of the legislators were permitted a bath each night, but aside from that minor inconvenience they lived quite well for about a dollar a day. One of the communal lawmakers was a young attorney and first-term representative named Warren G. Magnuson, who had a job as a deputy King county prosecutor, but was living with the group "to learn the needs of the jobless."

James J. Bond, King county Democrat, as spokesman for the unemployed legislators, insisted that "the only way to fight capitalism in these times is to issue scrip, rather than Governor Martin's proposed $10 million bond issue proposal, which will place a burden on our children." The inhabitants of the Sylvester mansion "dormitory" favored the issuance of $50 million in scrip, underwritten by the state, which would lose its value after a short period of time. They pointed out that such short-term scrip couldn't be hoarded and would so go directly into circulation as a badly-needed transfusion to the state's economic arteries.

The governor's more conventional proposal was accepted by the legislators, who passed the bond measure with little delay and sending it to Martin for his signature on March 7.

NEW DEAL

Despite the bickering, confusion and uncertainty at the capitol, the Democratic legislature of 1933 did a far more effective job of meeting and solving the economic and social needs of its constituents than had the single other non-Republican session in the state's history, the even more motley and philosophically divided Fusionist assembly of 1897.

The local efforts to combat the great depression were given tremendous impetus with the inauguration on March 4 of President Roosevelt. Unlike Hoover, who had seemed more concerned with the possibility that any unorthodox action by him might be declared unconstitutional than with the plight of the nation, FDR took vigorous and decisive action almost immediately. His first step was the declaration of a national bank holiday or moratorium. All banks were required to close and were not permitted to reopen until they had demonstrated their financial stability. A statewide bank closure had been ordered by Governor Martin two days earlier, when a run on a major mutual savings bank in Seattle spread to commercial banks. The legislature followed this up with a bank stabilization act and a change in the banking laws permitting larger financial institutions to establish branch banks.

Within two weeks the majority of banks were reopened, along with the stock exchange, which had also been closed by presidential order. In Olympia the Capital National, which had not closed during the two-day holiday, and the Washington National, which had taken over the premises of the defunct Olympia National with the backing of the Seattle First National, reopened as soon as the banking ban was lifted. The latter, managed by Reno Odlin, became a branch of Seafirst as soon as the branch banking law became effective.

Before the month of March was ended, Roosevelt had pushed through congress a $500 million relief grant to the states and a measure creating the Civilian Conservation Corps to employ young men in forestry and construction projects. And, difficult as it may be for those who have watched Richard Nixon and Gerald , Ford struggle futilely to control runaway inflation, Roosevelt worked just as hard to *create* inflation. All gold in excess of $100 was ordered returned to the treasury on pain of $10,000 fine and 10 years in prison. This was his first step toward abandonment of the gold standard and an increased flow of devaluated currency.

In addition to the $10 million emergency employment bond issue, the legislature passed a graduated business and occupation tax to provide $6 million in increased state support to the hard-pressed public schools. Both the bond measure and the business tax were challenged in the courts, but both were upheld by the supreme court justices, who could read a voter mandate as well as any other politicians and decided that "it is better to cure insurrection or incipient insurrection by promoting prosperity than by the use of bullets."

Horse racing with parimutuel on-track betting and 10-round boxing were approved, with the proceeds earmarked for funding the Eagles' old age pension bill, which was finally passed. The conservative Martin signed the measure with the warning that such possibly sinful activities would be "on trial" and if there were any signs of gangsterism they would be quickly abolished. Boxing and horse racing commissions were appointed to regulate and control the newly legalized sports.

A major victory for the public power advocates was achieved when the Homer T. Bone power bill, previously turned down as an

initiative to the people, was passed by the liberal new legislature, permitting publicly-owned utilities to sell surplus power anywhere in the state. Commissions were authorized to survey the feasibility of both the Grand Coulee dam and Puget Sound-Grays Harbor canal projects and a moratorium on mortgage and tax foreclosures was approved. Martin vetoed the latter measure upon the solemn promise of lending agencies to be lenient, but within a few months he was engaged in considerable controversy with them as to just what constituted "leniency."

The chain store license fee bill was passed, but also vetoed by Martin, the quarterly tuition fee at the university was reduced from $10 to five dollars, and the state highway patrol was accorded full police powers and the new designation, Washington State Patrol.

The reorganized highway department, as requested by Martin, was approved and Lacey Murrow, Spokane district highway engineer, was appointed director. The change was aimed at eventually eliminating the traditional pork barrel method of road financing through legislative log-rolling, and at promoting efficiency and economy.

Murrow found himself at the head of a poverty-stricken organization, three cents of the five cent gas tax having been diverted to the counties to eliminate local road and bridge levies. Furthermore, the depression was making serious inroads on pleasure driving, resulting in a big drop in gas tax revenues. Murrow cut the highway department staff drastically, but a few days later Auditor Yelle made an examination of the department and issued a report critical of its excessive number of state-owned "pleasure cars," many of them luxury models, excessive telephone and telegraph costs, imprudent spending, a lack of uniform accounting and wages between districts and "a tendency to accumulate junk." Later in the year Yelle's accountants audited the department in greater depth and revealed that things had been worse under the old system, particularly in the matter of highway right of way purchases. Numerous incidents were recorded of property having been acquired at twice its appraised value as a favor to financially or politically potent owners.

With the distribution of the highway pork barrel no longer a major basis for last-minute wrangling, a joint conference committee, which included Representative Magnuson and Thurston county Senator E. N. Steele, spent many hours arguing over the business and occupation tax.

As they deliberated, the press corps served "near beer" and pretzels to the senate as punishment for having killed a house bill which would have permitted the manufacture and sale of real beer.*

The clocks were, as usual, stopped when time ran out, the session finally adjourning *sine die* late on the night of March 11, having been in session 62 days by real time.

The failure of the state beer bill became moot soon afterward when, on March 22, President Roosevelt signed a congressional bill authorizing the legal sale of 3.2 percent beer after midnight on April 6.

The Schmidt family immediately announced that a new $300,000 brewery was being planned for Tumwater and brewery stocks shot up as much as $14 in a single day on the stock exchange.

By November the necessary 37 states had ratified the complete repeal of prohibition and Governor Martin had called a special legislative session for December 4 to consider state liqour control laws.

THE HONEYMOON ENDS

The legislators reconvened amid torrential rains, the enthusiasm of many of the Democratic members for their conservative governor considerably chilled. Martin was different from most chief executives in a variety of ways. While earlier governors, including Hartley, had shudderingly resisted all efforts to lure them aboard airplanes, Martin routinely used aircraft to get around the state. Unlike most politicians, he enjoyed brisk give-and-take with the press and held regular press conferences. Hartley hadn't called a single one during his eight years in office.

But the Martin peculiarity which annoyed the Democrats the most was his unwillingness to apply the old political axiom that "to the victors belong the spoils." He stubbornly insisted upon retaining on the state payroll the Hartley appointees who performed their jobs capably. At least 60 of the more impecunious Democratic legislators had their applications in for state jobs and they arrived in Olympia with the avowed intention of "prying Martin loose" from his policy of protecting the "black-hearted Republicans" who were holding down state jobs.

The hostility erupted within an hour of convening when senate Democrats proposed a $100,000 legislative appropriation, plus $12,000 for "incidentals," to finance a 60-day session. That five dollars a day was looking good to a number of the members. The Republicans, who were generally more affluent, demanded a short session. Senator E. B. Palmer offered an amendment to reduce the appropriation to $50,000 as a means of forcing an abbreviated session. The senators compromised on $75,000, and the house finally went along after making an abortive effort to raise it to $199,999.99.

Governor Martin backed the Republican stand in his address to the special session, stating emphatically that "enactment of a sane, strict plan of state control over all liquor is the only issue facing this legislature." He outlined a recommended five-point program to accomplish this:

A state monopoly or control of hard liquor to eliminate private profit.

Exclusive state licensing of wine and beer sales.

Prices to be kept as low as possible to discourage bootlegging.*

Revenue to be distributed to the state, cities and counties.

Liquor control to be kept as far out of politics as possible, with management and responsibility "separate, visible and absolute" so the people will know who is accountable.

Although an advisory commission, headed by Senator Steele, had been laboring on a measure designed to meet the governor's criteria, there were as many different ideas as

*Near beer, a puny substitute for the real thing, was purchased by old-time saloon patrons when gripped by nostalgia and by those who were in the habit of "needling" it with alcohol to give it a decent whallop. Lest the largess of the press should puzzle experienced capitol observers, it should be pointed out that the near beer was furnished the newsmen without cost by Cammarano brothers, an Olympia beverage distribution firm.

*Subsequent governors and legislators have certainly ignored *that* one. Washington state monopoly liquor prices are currently the highest in the United States.

to how liquor should be dispensed as there were members in the legislature. Nearly a dozen bills were actually introduced and most of them had lobbyists on the sidelines. Officials of local government, headed this time by Seattle Councilman David Levine, were opposed to the Steele recommendations because liquor revenues were to be shared by the state. Druggists, remembering the profitable days of their liquor monopoly, plugged for sales "by package only through drug stores." Hotel and restaurant owners wanted to serve liquor by the drink, which the Steele proposal didn't contemplate.

The vanquished forces of total prohibition, headed by ASL Superintendent Hicks, formed ranks for a counter-attack to salvage what they could. Hicks demanded a long list of restrictions . . . no liquor sales near schools, no Sunday sales, no liquor at such public gatherings as picnics, dances and marathon dance contests and heavy restrictions on newspaper and billboard advertising. Public officials found intoxicated were to be removed from office, all bottles were to bear the warning "Alcohol is a narcotic drug and poison," alcohol education was to be a required subject in the public schools and a fund was to be established from liquor profits to pay for any damages resulting from the return of Demon Rum.

National prohibition ended in the midst of the squabbling . . . December 5, 1933 . . . but the effects were scarcely noticeable in the capital city. The flow of beer had been turned on back in April, although the newfangled "beer parlors" were considered by the unregenerate as pale shadows of the lusty pre-Volstead saloons, lacking such traditional amenities as brass rails, swinging doors and free lunches, but the existing city ordinance still forbade hard liquor. The city fathers decided to keep it in force until the state lawmakers had made up their minds.

As the noble experiment faded from the American scene, 90-mile-an-hour winds struck the coast and almost nine inches of rain descended on the sodden capital city in five days. Then things improved a little, with only 20 inches falling in the succeeding 20 days. Power and telephone lines collapsed and bridges floated away. The Christmas recess was brief, for most legislators couldn't get home. On December 22 all mountain passes were reported closed, 100,000 acres of land were flooded, the Pacific highway was closed north

of Kelso and 975 homes in that community were flooded and wrecked. The flooding Nisqually river flowed over the highway to Tacoma and four inches of muddy water covered the Olympic highway just west of Olympia.

Charles Norrie, Olympia's weather observer and temperance advocate, told the *Olympian* that he attributed the situation to the state going wet.

The one legislator who was completely unconcerned about the widespread flooding was Senator Henry Foss, who was living comfortably in his 58-foot yacht *Thea Foss,* moored at the Delta Smyth tugboat moorings on the waterfront.

The Steele liquor control bill passed the senate by a 33 to four vote (with nine members absent) on December 16, with Governor Martin keeping an alert eye on the proceedings from behind a velvet drape. The equally sharp eye of Vic Meyers spotted the chief executive and he was invited to a seat on the president's rostrum, which he accepted with some trace of embarrassment.

The legislature did not, however, confine itself to this "single issue." Bills had already been introduced to reinstate the anti-mortgage foreclosure and chain store bills vetoed by the governor, to prescribe the death penalty for kidnapping (the state's "little Lindberg law"), to require one to 10 year sentences for hit-and-run drivers and to authorize a constitutional amendment permitting joint county-city government.

No less than three measures were introduced to put the state in the wholesale and retail gasoline business, the price-rigging practices of the major oil companies having caused great public indignation. The *Olympian,* aghast at these socialistic proposals, published a front-page editorial with the punch line, *"Every service station operated by a political appointee! What an amazing political machine that would create!"*

The legislators accepted a $150,000 federal grant to build another office building on the capitol campus without debate, but they made up for this in deliberating charges that numerous lawmakers had been working for the state and federal governments during the interim and that this was contrary to law. Eleven members, including Speaker Yantis, Warren Magnuson, Donald McDonald, the majority floor leader and E. Morris Starrett, Port Townsend postmaster, were mentioned specifically.

A special house committee was appointed to scrutinize the charges. In due time they delivered a report exonerating all the accused legislators except Starrett. It would take them a little longer to make up their minds about him, they said.

Having settled that, the house members set to bickering over the senate-passed Steele bill, with a strong push for amendments to permit liquor by the drink in hotels and restaurants. Three days after Christmas the senate voted to "go on strike" against the representatives' "dilly-dallying." A vote to cancel all afternoon sessions resulted in a 20 to 20 tie. Debonair Vic Meyers tossed a coin, ruling, "Tails we adjourn to 10 o'clock tomorrow morning." It came up tails and the senate adjourned, with President Pro-tem W. G. Ronald, 76-year-old "dean of the senate," tarrying to inform newsmen that "The house is dilly-dallying. We are drifting into general legislation."

That evening the eloquent Representative Schade took up the cudgel in defense of the house. Waving a copy of the *Olympian* which headlined the charges of the venerable Senator Ronald and with vocal chords well lubricated, he thundered, "The senate has impugned the honor to the house! * * * It is committing sabotage * * * driving spikes in the logs of legislation and throwing emery dust into the wheels of state!"

It was upon this note that the embattled lawmakers adjourned for the new year, the issues of the special session, specific and general alike, unresolved.

THINGS LOOK A LITTLE BRIGHTER

Aside from the melodramatics of the two legislative sessions, there wasn't much excitement in Washington's capital city during that depression-ridden year of 1933.

The return of beer created a flurry of revelry which drained the kegs of many of the newly opened beer parlors by noon and caused numerous tipplers whose stomachs were unaccustomed to honest brew at five cents a glass to throw up, but the novelty soon wore off and beer-drinkers came to take the ready availability of their favorite beverage for granted.

In June the grand old frigate *Constitution*, rescued from decrepitude and restored to her original glory by the nickels and dimes of American school children, arrived at the port dock on a nationwide voyage in tow of the minesweeper *Grebe*. "Old Ironsides" was escorted into the harbor by a flotilla from the Olympia yacht club and 9,443 visitors filed aboard during her nine-day stay. One of them was 15-year-old Pauline Newman of Tumwater, who was proclaimed to be the four millionth guest since the ship began her voyage Pauline was greeted by the *Constitution's* commanding officer and taken on a personally-conducted tour.

The Chamber of Commerce attempted to capitalize on the world-famous Tenino wooden currency by issuing plywood "oyster money" to commemorate the visit of the famous fighting ship. Shaped like an Olympia oyster shell and bearing a picture of the *Constitution,* the 25¢ tokens were accepted by all local merchants, but failed to gain the kind of publicity that had been enjoyed by Tenino's one and only original wooden money.

Considerable interest was displayed when the new Ford V-8 arrived on the scene to replace the marvelous Model-A, particularly since things were beginning to pick up a bit and people had hope that they might sooner or later be able to afford to buy one. The Olympia Brewing company was moving ahead on its new plant and by early summer many of the closed mills were reopening. . . the Olympia Harbor Lumber company after 15 months of idleness, Buchanan Lumber company after 14 months and the Washington Veneer company after eight months. Many of the fleet of idle vessels on Lake Union got up steam and returned to the sea lanes. Port tonnage began to move upward, along with the stock market, and the cheerful sound of mill whistles signalled the good news each morning that there might be light at the end of the tunnel after all.

In November excavation began for the huge Grand Coulee dam and for a new four-lane "super-highway" between Olympia and Tacoma which was eventually dedicated as Martin Way.

But there was also tragedy.

Birney one-man safety car waiting for passengers in front of the Mottman Mercantile company at 4th and Capitol Way, 1929.

REQUIEM FOR THE TROLLEY CAR

Early in September the Puget Sound Power and Light company informed the city commission that it wanted to be released from its street railway franchise. The sun of the trolley car had been setting everywhere since the high point of the first world war. The traction industry had survived the pre-war onslaught of the motorized jitneys, but the post-war love affair between the American people and the motor car was too much for it.

The trolley was no longer considered a thrilling and glamorous means of transportation. Rather it was viewed as a proletarian and somewhat frowzy hindrance to unrestricted automobile traffic. The coming of the Birney "one-man safety cars," a last-ditch effort by Charles Birney, engineer for the Stone and Webster power and traction empire, had banished such glamorous adjuncts to trolley travel as the summer rides on the open cars and the ministrations of the lordly but accommodating conductors.

A single "operator" handled the standardized single-truck Birnies and he wasn't supposed to carry on conversations with passengers, even if he had the time. The little cars, designed for economical operation, developed only 50 horsepower and were not noted for their speed or acceleration. They were rather easily derailed by youthful delinquents who placed grease or railroad signal torpedos on the tracks and, if more than and inch or two of snow covered the tracks, they had an unfortunate tendency to hum loudly and remain firmly in place when the operator swung the controller handle to full speed ahead.

The power company reminded the city fathers that a federal grant was available for paving streets if the tracks were removed, but city hall announced scornfully that the street cars weren't going to be "sacrificed for a few thousand dollars." There was no sentiment involved. The commissioners just wanted bargaining power to insure that the buses, which would replace the trolleys, would provide extended service beyond the limits of track and overhead wire.

Agreement was reached in a couple of weeks and the *Olympian* announced matter-of-factly that the buses of the new Olympia Transit company, headed by former chief clerk of the house and license director Charles R. Maybury, would replace the street cars within about 45 days. The fare, which had remained at a nickel since the horse car days of 1889, would be raised to four rides for a quarter.

Henceforth the Dodge buses of the Olympia Transit company held fourth, adding their noxious fumes to the growing carbon monoxide level of the streets. The fleet of little Birnie trolleys was hauled off to a Tacoma junkyard.

The proud and ponderous big brother of the trolleys, the interurban, had been even harder hit by the inroads of the gasoline engine, for the inter-city bus and truck lines had joined with the private automobile to skim the cream of the passenger and freight traffic. The dream of an express electric line from Oregon to Canada was never realized and, despite the dozen or more announcements that the interurbans were coming, Olympians were never treated to the stirring sight of the great cars rumbling majestically through the city streets. The Seattle - Tacoma interurban line had folded back in 1927 and the last of the passenger steamers on the route were withdrawn three years later. The local passenger trains still operated, but with an ever declining clientel. By 1933 the big motor coaches of the North Coast lines had emerged triumphant in the inter-city transportation business of the Puget Sound country. The evolution had been a colorful one. The little sloops and plungers had displaced the Indian canoe, the steamboat had displaced the mosquito fleet sailing craft and managed to hold its own against the inroads of the steam train and, later, the electric interurban, but in the end it was ordained that all must give way before the concrete-mixer and the internal combustion engine. The only surviving relics of journies past are the ferryboats, which have lost the jaunty independence of the steamboats and are tolerated only as slaves of the conquering motor vehicle.

1934

By the second day of the new year of 1934 the house of representatives was again locked in debate over the provisions of the Steele act, which had passed the senate back in mid-December. Speaker Yantis expostulated mildly as the bill's opponents resorted to delaying tactics in the hope of getting it indefinitely postponed. Many of the representatives believed the measure wasn't liberal enough, was unenforceable and would encourage bootlegging. Others insisted that the electorate had voted prohibition *out*. Period! To wrap the simple process of buying a drink in legislative red tape was contrary to the will of the majority. And some, of course, were acting as spokesmen for such special interests as the druggists, the hotel owners and the restaurateurs.

The Steele act became one of the gaudiest Christmas trees in legislative history. Amendments were hung upon it by the dozens. Amendments to permit drugstore sales and to substitute city and county liquor stores for state dispensaries were beaten down, as were dry efforts to include local option clauses. By January 9 the bill was festooned with no less than 106 amendments and the representatives seemed to lose interest in the whole thing. Yantis, overcome by frustration, pounded his gavel futilely and announced, "We might as well recess if the members don't stay in their seats and keep order."

Equally frustrated, the members voted to refer the liquor control bill to a committee of senate-house conferees, which came up with a reasonable compromise by January 12. The house then receded from four of its 106 amendments and the measure was passed . . . 29 to 13 in the senate; 62 to 23 in the house.

Senator Houser, acting as spokesman for the minority, expressed eloquently their discontent with the legislation which put the sovereign state of Washington in the booze business:

"The passage of this act is the most flagrant violation of the will of the people ever carried into effect by any legislature in the history of the commonwealth," he thundered.

The special session adjourned *sine die* the next morning. Only 29 of the 99 representatives and 19 of the 46 senators were in the chambers as it faltered to its close. Vic Meyers was among the absentees and Senator Ronald signed the liquor bill, along with Speaker Yantis. Henceforth the sale of beer and wine by the glass and the sale of packaged liquor in state-operated stores would be legal, provided the purchaser was equipped with a liquor purchase permit, which cost 50 cents a year.

THE RETURN OF JOHN BARLEYCORN

Before the end of the month the governor had appointed the first state liquor control board. Luther E. Gregory, a retired admiral and a Democrat, got the nine-year term, William J. Lindberg, Spokane attorney, secretary of the senate in 1933 and likewise a Democrat, was appointed to the six-year term, and Henry Gregerson, Battle Ground merchant and a Republican, had to settle for a three-year tenure. Miss Gay Grigsby, who had been assistant secretary of the senate during Lindberg's term as secretary, and had earlier been a secretary to C. C. Dill for ten years, became the first secretary to the board. It was announced that liquor stores would be open in major cities by March 26, and eight inspectors were hired to check on the flood of applications for tavern licenses.

Olympia's first liquor store, in the Talcott building on west Legion Way, opened on April 5, the Olympia *News* reporting that 20 men and two women were lined up outside the doors and Mrs. Hazel White had the honor of being issued liquor permit number one. She immediately utilized it to purchase a 60-cent bottle of sauterne from Manager Jess Leverich.

Prices were unbelievably low compared to the greedily padded costs of today's state monopoly. A reasonably good straight bourbon could be had for a dollar a fifth or 65 cents a pint and an adequate California port or sherry for 65 cents a full quart. The original guiding philosophy of the state liquor board was to hold down prices to the bare minimum to make the illicit liquor trade unprofitable. Over the intervening years that philosophy has been scrapped for one of getting the last possible dollar of revenue from the clients of this governmental monopoly and the result has been a new form of rum-running. Respectable citizens touring neighboring states usually take advantage of the opportunity to purchase as much booze as they can afford and/or stuff into the trunks of their automobiles, and smuggle it across the Washington state line. The pastime is growing in favor so rapidly that Washington's liquor profits are declining, despite the outrageously inflated mark-up and taxes, and citizens may yet witness the unique phenomenon of a state tax actually being reduced as legislators seek to circumvent the law of diminishing returns.

During the first full year of operation the state liquor stores *sold* a total of $10 million worth of potables. In 1971 they contributed $66.3 million to the general fund in *taxes and profits.*

The special session of 1933-34 passed a number of trivial and a few significant bills in addition to the Steele act. Representative Magnuson's "little Lindberg law," prompted by the brutal kidnap-murder of Charles A. Lindberg's little son Charles, was approved, but others didn't fare so well. The senate passed a dog racing bill, but the house of representatives, whether believing that horse gambling was moral and dog gambling immoral . . . or convinced by other cogent arguments of the new horse racing lobby . . . killed it. Nor did any of the proposed sales tax measures survive legislative scrutiny.

RIGHT OF WAY REBATES AND RIOTS

After thanking the lawmakers politely for their efforts, Governor Martin announced that "I have told Dick Hamilton (his executive secretary) to dig out my red ink pen." He then proceeded to veto a number of the bills that *had* passed, including one which stipulated that university and college regents and trustees and liquor board members could only be removed from office by court action, and another which would have put the state in the insurance business to underwrite loss or damage of public buildings.

State Auditor Cliff Yelle continued to flail away at that political dead horse, the Hartley highway department, pointing out that it had paid the Bryant Mill company $149,733 for Seattle land valued at $30,000. A few square

feet of the expensive property was used for piers supporting the Aurora bridge,* completed in 1932, the remainder being then turned back to the mill company for perpetual use, rent free. The firm thus realized a fat profit on the property, while retaining its use without having to pay taxes on it. The aggressive auditor also criticized the engineering costs of the span, which accounted for 12.35 percent of the total construction cost. Yelle felt that 4½ percent would have been a more realistic figure, and pointed out that nearly half of the engineering funds went to outside bridge engineers, although state-employed bridge engineers were sitting around with nothing much to occupy their time.

Governor Martin could ignore this unsavory revelation from the past, but he couldn't ignore the sudden costly riot that broke out at the state penitentiary on February 12. His recently-appointed warden, J. M. McCauley, a Dayton business man and farmer, had instituted "prison reforms," substituting moral 'suasion for solitary confinement and insisting that the hard-bitten $50-a-month guards treat their charges kindly.

As is often the case when amateurs become involved in penology, the inmates took advantage of the relaxed discipline to air their grievances, many of which were real enough. The 19th century dungeons were jammed to more than twice their capacity and the vast majority of the convicts spent almost all their time in tiny iron cells without plumbing or proper ventilation. When they cut loose they killed a guard and stabbed several staff members, including the assistant chief turnkey. The chief turnkey and his bleeding assistant were used as hostages when a group of prisoners unsuccessfully rushed the main gate. When the break-out failed they vented their frustrations by setting fire to a number of the prison buildings.

The continuing struggle of the Indian tribes to regain the fishing rights which had been granted them by the Stevens treaties had not yet resulted in the violence and bitterness which it generates today. A group of Lummi tribesmen in colorful costumes descended on the old statehouse to perform war dances, but

---

*It was officially designated the George Washington Memorial bridge, but nobody has called it that since the dedicatory ceremonies.

they weren't really very hostile. They invited Governor Martin to join them, made him an honorary chief and bestowed upon him the name *Pal-Awk-Ten,* which means Tall Male Cedar Tree. The governor responded by taking his fellow tribesmen to the Hotel Olympian for lunch. After the festivities, the Lummis joined with members of other tribes to discuss fishing rights and the coming loss of traditional fishing places on the Columbia river as a result of the construction of Bonneville and Grand Coulee dams.

In the fall an interesting proposal was made by a constitutional revision commission which had been appointed by Martin and which met in Olympia to present its recommendations. Among them was a plan for a "continuing legislature" to meet annually for 30 days; then adjourn to go home and take the political pulse of the various districts and reconvene to work as long as there was work to be done. The concept didn't get a fair test, because it also suggested that the legislature reduce itself to a unicameral body of 46 . . . one from each of the state's legislative districts.

Since politicians have seldom been known to vote themselves out of their jobs, nothing much came of the commission's efforts to streamline the legislative process.

By late February it was reported that 1,239 Thurston county workers were employed on various jobs sponsored by the federal Civil Works Administration, forerunner of the Works Progress Administration or WPA. Some were building a new runway at the Olympia airport and making repairs to the public school buildings, but the largest force was employed in the construction of the new office building on the capitol campus. Designed to house the highway department (which quickly outgrew it and two subsequent structures), it was faced with yellow brick, which clashed with the esthetics of the classic stone buildings of the Wilder and White-planned main capitol group. It was explained that the architectural plans for the highway building contemplated an eventual stone facing to make it less of a sore thumb on the campus, but nobody has gotten around to it and, as the present Institutions building, it still resembles a shabby bungalow in a neighborhood of stately mansions.

The taxpayers did get a bargain, however, no contracts were let, the state handling the federal funds and hiring day labor to do the job. Three hundred men worked two shifts and the building was completed in a little over six weeks at a cost of 158,000.

Today a great deal more than that is spent in *planning* a new state office building.

1935

At the midpoint of the thirties the world was becoming increasingly tumultuous and considerably smaller. The Pan American clippers, huge multi-engined flying boats, inaugurated flights from California to the Orient via Hawaii. The trip, which had taken days or weeks by ship, was made in 17 hours and 45 minutes. Americans were being stripped of the comfortable feeling of isolation from the distant doings of European and Oriental war lords. The depression had become worldwide, but the dictators, Hitler in Germany and Mussolini in Italy, were finding the wherewithal to create mechanized war machines and the confidence to shout increasingly menacing threats against their neighbors. There were some who wondered whether the professional army of 150,000 men was sufficient to adequately protect the United States in the face of the world's growing hostilities.

Others feared that the republic was endangered more by domestic radicals than by foreign dictators. People were searching for means of escape from poverty and hopelessness and they were willing to clutch at idealogical straws. The Townsend plan, the 30-hour week, the greenback bonus plan and unemployment insurance all had their advocates, while out-and-out Communists found increasing numbers of the depression's victims who were willing to listen to their doctrines.

After notable lack of success at the polls under its real name, the Communist party in the United States . . . and in Washington . . . had begun to make use of front organizations with high-sounding titles, the Washington Commonwealth federation becoming the most effective advocate of Marxist evangelism within the state.

WHO'S A COMMUNIST?

With a Democratic majority of 91 to eight in the house of representatives and 37 to nine in the senate, the 1935 legislature took on the organizational overtones of earlier sessions. With the long dominant Republicans reduced to a sad state of impotence, the rival caucuses were organized on doctrinal rather than party lines, the more conservative Democrats, along with Governor Martin, seeking to hold the line against the ultra-liberal Democratic faction, which referred to itself as "progressive." (The use of the term Communist was frowned upon as apt to upset the decorum of the chambers and, except in the heat of battle, the conservatives usually referred to their liberal colleagues as, at worst, "left-wingers.")

The selection of house and senate leadership, usually well cut and dried before the session convened, was still very much in doubt when the lawmakers arrived. With factionalism rife in both houses, it was apparent that the large number of first-term legislators (freshman were in the majority in the house), would have the final say on whether the conservatives or the left-wingers gained control. On January 14 the house was deadlocked on the selection of a speaker. Ralph Van Dyk, a Whatcom county left-winger, garnered 40 votes, while the conservatives were divided between John T. Ledgerwood of Garfield, with 29 votes, and Robert Waldron of Spokane, with 28. After several days of frustration, with the governor urging a united front against the left-wingers, the 30-year-old Waldron was elected as the second youngest speaker in the history of the house. (Meigs of Yakima was 29 when he was elected in 1909.) Waldron, a baby-faced 200-pound lawyer with a disarmingly boyish smile, proved to be an excellent choice for presiding officer of the house during that tumultuous session. Although he might look as innocent. and guileless as a cherub, the *Olympian's* political reporter, a young journalist named Don Magnuson, pointed out that *"he rules like a Mussolini and makes them like it."* His tactics were described as *"stern but fair,"* permitting no "dilly-dallying." By January 31 the *Olympian* reported the *"that Democratic majority, with a few Republicans helping, get the left-wingers under control in the house and get the legislature moving."* Bitter wrangling over committee chairmanships ended with only one left-winger getting an appointment,

Jurie B. Smith of King being named to head the unemployment relief committee.*

The plight of the unemployed was dramatized during that winter of discontent as a mid-January cold wave of record-breaking intensity swept over the state, dropping temperatures to nine degrees above zero at the capital and causing four deaths in the state. Later in the month a heavy snowfall arrived with the warming Chinook wind, followed by a steady downpour of rain. There was little to cheer the one in nine Washington citizens on relief, or the legislators who sought means of financing the resulting drain on the state's archaic revenue structure.

Matters of legislative controversy were almost unlimited in both number and scope. Courthouse politicians gathered with the convening legislators to denounce a proposed new highway code drafted by Director Murrow, which would remove $6,750,000 in gas tax revenues from the counties and place all road building and maintenance under a state highway commission. Many legislators were equally outraged when they discovered that Murrow's proposal would eliminate the last of their prerogatives to make pork barrel appropriations for roads, bridges and ferries in their home districts.

A brief return to the religious feuding of earlier sessions was precipitated when liberal senators introduced a birth control bill aimed at reducing the population explosion. The venerable Senator Ronald made an impassioned speech against it, quoting the scriptures at great length to prove that any legislative interference with the human reproductive processes would be sinful.

---

*This was a major committee in the depression days, an effort by the conservatives in the previous session to toss a meaningless committee bone to the left-wingers having backfired. One of the more voluble of the ultraliberals, who frankly admitted to Marxist leanings, was appointed chairman of the committee on ditches, dikes and drainage, which hadn't had a bill referred to it in the memory of man. To the amazement of the majority, the committee's new chairman arose almost daily to announce meeting of the committee on ditches, dikes and drainage although, as usual no legislation had been referred to it. It took them some time to discover that this was a code phrase to summon a caucus of avowed and under-cover Communists of the house.

The irrepressible Nifty Garrett then rose to move that the section of the Bible quoted by Senator Ronald be repealed.

Fierce resentment in the senate against the state relief administration (WERA), which had been gathering throughout the interim, came to a head with the appointment of a committee to investigate the conduct of the department. The chamber echoed to bitter charges of extravagant administration costs, money spent for political purposes and the families, friends and followers of various politicians awarded the better jobs at the expense of the deserving needy. "There is nothing to show for these millions spent except a lot of tubercular children!" Senator James Daly of King county shouted. The house appointed an investigative committee of its own the next day and federal relief authorities agreed to assist in the probe of state welfare practices following an executive request by the governor.

When Martin addressed the joint session of the house and senate before packed galleries and a battery of radio microphones, the chambers remained noisy, Lieutenant Governor Myers shattering Speaker Waldron's gavel in his efforts to restore decorum. (The Vancouver Chamber of Commerce thoughtfully replaced the speaker's broken badge of office with a one-pound replacement made from the wood of an apple tree planted by Dr. McLaughlin at Fort Vancouver in 1826.)

The governor's message, according to the *Olympian, "teemed with optimism over the economic picture."* He pointed out that the farmer's purchasing power, which had dropped to an index of 61 toward the close of 1932, had risen to an index of 79, that the state's business and industrial payroll was up from a late 1932 low of $129 million to $168 million, and bank deposits were up $100 million since the Roosevelt bank holiday of 1933. He congratulated "those who are without the independence of work who might be expected to yield to the temptation of false prophets" for having "remained patient and shown no disposition to follow the malcontents and agitators who would lead them into communism and insurrection."

He conceded, however, that grave social problems still faced the state and he proposed that $39 million in new revenues be raised to meet them. The additional money, he said, should come from "a luxury tax" on cigarettes and tobacco, an increase in gift and inheritance taxes and corporation fees, and a boost in the "business tax" from $5,775,000 to $18,500,000.

The current business tax was limited to the business and occupation levy on gross proceeds and there was some confusion, not to say apprehension, as to how the governor proposed to nearly quadruple the take from that source. Martin was, in fact, indulging in a bit of evasive rhetoric. He was talking about a retail sales tax, to be paid directly by consumers, but he was extremely careful not to say so.

He also urged resubmission of two proposed constitutional tax amendments which had been turned down by the people at the last election, one permitting a graduated new income tax and the other giving the state wider supervision over taxation.

He recommended a $5 million welfare appropriation to be used under a flexible program to be coordinated with future federal relief measures. Like most governors, he advocated more centralized control of state agencies, suggesting that the function of the controversial relief commission and the department of efficiency and of business control might well be turned over to two new departments, public welfare and finance, budget and business.

The proposal to create a state department of welfare and abolish the WERA aroused the immediate and vociferous opposition of the left-wing legislators, who charged that it would "only perpetuate the present unsound system of the dole." Representative Yantis replied that such a coordinated department was necessary in order to become eligible for the maximum in federal grants . . . an argument which has subsequently been used effectively to justify the most outrageous bureaucratic monstrosities.

Apparently feeling that enough ammunition for legislative strife had been provided, the governor stepped gracefully out from behind his highway director's highly controversial highway code proposal, at the same time managing a vote of confidence for Mr. Murrow. While he endorsed the centralization of highway building and maintenance in the state, he said, he doubted that allocation of funds by a three-member highway commission, as proposed by Murrow, would be practical. He tactfully suggested that the legislature retain control of road funds, with the department designating individual projects according to the needs of the state road system.

PAPER BLIZZARD

With the departure of the chief executive, the legislators returned to their respective chambers and set about the introduction of a flood of bills. The left-wingers competed among themselves for the sponsorship of the most enlightened measures. There were bills to exempt all homes with a value of less than $3,000 from property tax assessments, to pay $40 a month to every citizen of the state over the age of 50 and to prohibit welfare workers from asking questions or making investigations "of a vexatious nature or character." A resolution was proposed to establish a legislature of 24 members, four from each congressional district, the members to receive $400 a month and act as heads of the various state departments, and a bill was submitted to give cows the right of way over automobiles at highway crossings. The drys, who never seemed to give up, sponsored a bill limiting the maximum alcoholic content of beer and wine to 2.75 percent.

The conservative majorities saw to it that these proposals were laid quiety to rest in committee or defeated on the floor, as in the case of a proposed senate memorial asking congress to adopt the Townsend plan, which would provide $200 a month to every citizen over 60 years of age, with the proviso that it must be spent before the next monthly check arrived. They then proceeded to pass a number of "law and order" bills, apparently prompted by the heroic battles of G-men like Elliot Ness and J. Edgar Hoover against the forces of organized crime.

The proposals to "disarm the gangster" included measures to regulate the sale and possession of firearms, a uniform narcotics act, abolition of the indeterminate sentence and creation of a state parole board to replace the independent boards at each of the correctional institutions, the latter presented by Warren Magnuson, the King county prosecuting attorney and U.S. Marshal A. J. Chitty. The house enthusiastically adopted a bill barring communists and others who advocated violent overthrow of the government from the primary ballot. The vote was 94 to two, one of the dissident duo being Thurston county's Ben

Sawyer, who said the measure was "vicious, silly and unconstitutional." For good measure, the conservative representatives killed the latest efforts to repeal the criminal syndicalism law. The senate majority showed similar alacrity in squelching a resolution asking Martin to remove state officials and educators from the legislative chambers, where they continued to lobby for pay raises in the best tradition of John Miller Murphy's "bread and butter brigade," and rebuking him for failure to reduce the general expenses of state government.

The advocates of law and order pointed to the case of 15-year-old Herbert Nicolls to prove that long prison sentences were good for people. Herbert had, at the age of 12, been caught by the 72-year-old sheriff of Asotin county stealing a plug of tobacco from a general store. Herbert shot and killed him and was sentenced to life imprisonment in the state penitentiary. It was pointed out that he had arrived at the walls "tattered, barefoot and nearly illiterate, a mouth organ and a battered bugle his only possessions," but that after three years of tutoring by the prison librarian he was at the high school level and displayed an IQ of 110.

THE LEGISLATORS
LOSE THEIR COOL

Legislative tempers continued to flare over the alleged transgressions of the WERA and the investigative efforts of the committees. Senator Kebel Murphy announced that his committee had satisfied itself that the relief agency had "squandered or misspent at least $3 million," although he admitted that he hadn't accepted any of the numerous invitations of the governor to meet with him and T. J. Edmonds, who was representing the federal relief administration. When chided for this unilateral attitude, Senator Murphy shouted, "Edmonds isn't worth wasting our time on!"

His colleagues directed him to attend all future meetings anyway.

The Grange-sponsored blanket primary initiative, which had quickly passed the house by an 86 to 11 vote, ran into rough sledding in the senate. The vote there was tied, 22 to 22, with 24 needed for passage. When it became obvious that its proponents couldn't muster the necessary majority, Fred Norman of Pacific county had changed his vote to no in order to be in a position to request reconsideration. It might even have been 24 to 20, had not the secretary of a small local Grange in Clark county taken it upon himself to write a hell-and-damnation letter to Senator H. L. Nelson of Vancouver, warning him to vote for the measure on pain of bringing down the wrath of God and the Grange upon himself.

Nelson, who had intended all along to vote for the blanket primary, dug in his heels and asserted that he'd be damned if he would in the face of the Grange threats. A number of legislators shared Nelson's dislike for the heavy-handed pressure tactics of the Grange, which included the editorial opinion expressed by the *Grange News* that *"any public man who is opposed to the blanket primary is a political buzzard,"* but the bill finally passed by a 27 to 19 vote on reconsideration.

A few days later, after quarrelling with Murphy and his investigative committee, the senate changed its mind again, called for another reconsideration and began debating the merits of placing the blanket primary question before the people in a form of a referendum. Then, frustrated and with the legislative wheels spinning badly, it voted not to observe the traditional Lincoln's birthday adjournment. Tempers wore thinner than ever. There were charges that the more impecunious members were dragging their feet deliberately in order to insure a special session and con-tinuation of their daily pay. Early in March the senate rules committee aroused a storm of indignation when it asked for another $35,000 in legislative appropriations, bringing the total to an outrageous $175,000 for the session. It was explained that the huge number of bills which had been filed had caused printing costs to skyrocket, and there were a lot more legislative employees than in the past. The latter point was fairly obvious. The state was full of hungry and deserving Democrats and the patronage committees had gone to some lengths to take care of as many of them as possible. Each chamber door, for example, was guarded by two doorkeepers, one on the inside and one on the outside, with three shifts working around the clock.

The request for additional funds prompted Senator E. J. Miller of King to inform his colleagues in angry tones that "Our work has been the rottenest ever seen and we have done less in a longer period of time than any other body that ever sat in the senate."

The senators responded by engaging in a day-long filibuster on the proposed new highway code.

The mood of self-recrimination appeared to be catching. Three days after Senator Miller's unkind critique, Senator George Gannon of Whitman was moved to even harsher words.

"Crookedness and sabotage are rampant!" he thundered, bringing his fellow senators to sudden attention. After what the *Olympian* described as *"a fiery denunciation of lobbyists and their methods,"* he struck even closer to home:

"We're crooked in the senate. One lobbyist is saying he bought 22 votes in this body. I want to say he was gypped, because I know the man that sold them to him and he couldn't deliver more than three or four."

"If this senate doesn't get down to work and quit worrying about this or that pet bill," he thundered, "I'll show you some sabotage that *is* sabotage!"

While a number of senators sat stunned by the frank remarks of the gentleman from Whitman, others were prompted to make public their own tales of woe. Senator John Ferryman of Chelan, chairman of the appropriations committee, rose to complain that "I'd save the state two or three million dollars if they'd leave me alone, but they're shooting at me from every hand."

Senator James A. Dailey of King expressed full agreement. "I've been through more hell in the past eight weeks than all my 44 years," he announced bitterly.

"—'ve been through more hell in the past *two* weeks than ever before in my life," Ferryman responded.

The house of representatives was less con-cerned with decorum and good order and didn't confine itself to mere verbal mayhem. On March 4 a small and usually mild-mannered representative from King county, Myron H. Titus, entered the chambers after spending some time examining the problems of the state through the bottom of a whiskey glass in committee room X. Liquor had a tendency to transform the legislative lamb into a tiger and he proceeded to take over the floor, ignoring the thunderous banging of the speaker's one-pound applewood gavel and embarking upon a long and inarticulate oration.

Speaker Waldron, who had sweated off 20 pounds during the session and spent a week in the hospital recovering from nervous prostration and the flu, was in no mood to play games with Mr. Titus. He summoned Sergeant at Arms C. Pat Hooper and his assistant, Al Meyers, to remove him firmly but gently from the floor.

Hooper was still nursing a couple of mutilated fingers which had been very nearly amputated a couple of weeks earlier when a member of the house, seeking to escape from the chambers after a call of the house had been ordered, slammed a massive door on them. His assistant led the effort to remove Representative Titus from the floor. Mr. Titus, bracing himself on his desk, delivered a kangaroo-like kick at Meyers' head with both feet. When the assistant fell to the floor, the solon delivered a drumlike tattoo on the ribs and injured hand of Hooper. Both officers of the house were taken to the hospital. Hooper's wounds eventually healed, but Meyers' entire right side was paralyzed. He never fully recovered. One of the last acts of the turbulent 24th legislature was the appropriation of funds to pay the hospital bills of the sergeant at arms and his assistant.

A resolution was introduced to expel Mr. Titus from the house for being drunk and disorderly, but the majority of the members seemed to feel that this would be setting a dangerous precedent and the resolution failed to pass.

At the end of the prescribed 60-day session on March 14 the senate was still deadlocked over the proposed two percent sales tax and the clocks were stopped. The next day some unknown culprit restarted the clocks in both chambers and, before anybody noticed, they had run past the legal adjournment hour. This precipitated another debate, numerous legislators insisting that the session was over and everybody should go home. In the midst of the discussion further sabotage occurred. The power of the Legislative building was cut off. Nobody could prove that is was Senator Gannon making good on his threat, but there was much outrage. Senator Reardon of Snohomish demanded that the culprits should be found "and brought before the bar of the senate and punished."

During the noon hour somebody set the clocks back to 11:30 and the proceedings continued for a total of six days overtime.

On March 20 the *Olympian* announced that *"probably the wildest legislature in history* *was drawing to a close today and everybody concerned was glad that it was over."* The more fascinating highlights were recapitulated, including the mayhem performed on the sergeant at arms and his assistant, the hospitalization of the speaker and the fact that *"Chief Clerk Si Holcomb hasn't been able to go to bed for the last three days and nights trying to keep the legislation in order, and the newspapermen didn't ever get any sleep."* "Yep," capitol correspondent Magnuson concluded. *"It was a humdinger."*

Frank G. Gorrie of the Associated Press also pointed out that it was *"the longest-winded Washington legislature in history,"* that it had appropriated more money to operate the state and itself than any other, and had come close to breaking the all-time record for bills introduced . . . 1,064 compared with the 1,121 of the 1913 session. The house had set a new record for itself . . . 697 . . . but only 189 measures were actually passed by the two houses. A total of $128 million was appropriated, which was about $16 million more than was spent in the previous biennium. This included $10 million for old age pensions and $10 million for unemployment relief.

WHEN THE DUST SETTLED . . .

The two percent sales tax was passed, as was the Grange blanket primary initiative. Public power enthusiasts had pushed through a constitutional amendment which, if approved by the voters, would permit the state to enter the power business and build transmission lines. Another constitutional amendment would authorize a graduated net income tax and, as an anchor to windward, a bill establishing a flat income tax of three percent, with a surtax of four percent on all incomes over $4,000. The state support of public schools was increased from 16¢ per day per pupil to 25¢. The governor's requested welfare and finance, budget and business departments were authorized, as was his full-time central parole board.

"Eugenical sterilization" of inmates in institutions was legalized, the uniform firearms regulation act was approved, a radio libel act was passed, placing broadcasters under the same restrictions as newspapers, a $400 annual pension for the blind was funded and the salaries of state department heads were reduced to a maximum of $4,000 a year.

Much major legislation fell by the wayside including the birth control bill, Sunday beer and wine, liquor by the drink, the measure to put the state in the gasoline business, Lacey Murrow's highway code, prohibition of compulsory military training in schools, permitting use of the Bible in the public schools and a three-day waiting period for marriage license applicants. A bill requiring that state-licensed pilots navigate deepsea vessels into Puget Sound, defeated regularly by the large mill owners and shipping companies since territorial days, was finally passed, and a state pilotage commission established. Boosters of the port of Olympia viewed the passage of this measure with some alarm, fearing that pilot fees might discourage shipping companies from patronizing the Sound's furthest inland port.

Governor Martin vetoed a $25,000 appropriation for an interim investigation of the WERA, apparently on the theory that it would constitute the beating of a dead horse, since the agency had already been abolished by legislative action. He also redlined sections of the revenue bill imposing the special chain store tax and levies on stock purchases and sales, a gift tax and a somewhat discriminatory 10 percent sales tax on cosmetics and toilet preparations.

The income tax was subsequently declared to be "wholly unconstitutional" by Judge Wright in Thurston county superior court hearings.

Another grandiose plan for the development of Boston Harbor was submitted to the federal rural rehabilitation authorities by Martin, who proposed to create the state's first New Deal rural industrial community on the site of Hillman's dream city. Under his plan, homes for 300 families would be built on about 2,000 acres, the National Plywood company having evinced interest in building a plywood mill on Zangle cove adjacent to the community. The mill failed to develop, the federals declared the project "economically unsound" and Boston Harbor retained its bucolic tranquility.

GOVERNOR MARTIN LIVES DANGEROUSLY

As the worst gloom of the depression was lightened somewhat by the massive transfusions of state and federal money into the economy, strikes proliferated as workers sought to force wages back up to pre-depression levels. No sooner had the port of Olympia recovered from a protracted dock strike than its pier and the local mills were again tied up by a Puget Sound tugboat strike. The statewide lumber and timber industries were soon embroiled in a major strike and Martin's response goaded the more liberal members of his party to new heights of indignation.

He issued strict orders against aggressive action by pickets, many of whom were, according to the governor and most of the state's press, "outside agitators" and the national guard and state patrol were alerted to insure compliance. Although the guardsmen spent most of their time in armories, out of sight of the public, and the patrolmen showed considerable restraint, Martin was branded by a number of labor leaders as a strike-breaker and there was some effort to recall him and to cut off the pay of the militia. Nothing came of it and Martin brushed off the controversy as having been fomented by "the Seattle left-wingers."

On the first of May the governor's popularity was more seriously threatened with the imposition of the retail sales tax. It had first been proposed to issue paper scrip books, with certificates in denominations as low as one-tenth of a cent, but aluminum tax tokens of one-fifth cent value were substituted. An initial order for two million of the metal tokens was placed at a cost of $6,000. There was some bureaucratic delay in getting them into distribution, only 8,000 being doled out to Olympia businesses by opening day. The tax commission ruled that, in view of the token shortage, the tax could be ignored for a while on sales of less than 15¢. This, according to the *Olympia News, "eased the situation somewhat and buyers and sellers became more reconciled."*

It took the average citizen a long time to become fully reconciled to "Martin's Chinese money," and some never did. Handsful of the tax tokens were frequently flung in the governor's face as he journeyed about the state and many political wishful thinkers convinced themselves that he had less chance of passing through the next election to a second term than of passing through the hole in the middle of a tax token.

And even as the first of the tax commission's funny money appeared to enrage the citizenry, Martin threw his Democratic enemies into paroxysms of indignation by appointing Charles Ernst, the first WERA director, to head the new department of public welfare. Ernst was a prominent Republican and much of the legislative antagonism to the WERA had been focused upon the director himself.

AN HONEST DAY'S WORK
FOR AN HONEST DAY'S PAY

May was also the month that the legendary WPA began its operations, immortalizing in American folklore the stereotype of the shiftless WPA worker leaning endlessly on his shovel. Pay scale for technical and professional workers was set at $61 to $95 a month, semi-skilled personnel at $45 to $65, and common labor at $40 to $55. By the end of the year 1,143 people in Thurston county had transferred from the dole to WPA jobs.

Those fortunate enough to be on the payrolls of private enterprise learned that they would soon find a small sum being deducted from their checks for something President Roosevelt called social security. It was explained that, within a generation, practically everyone too old to work would be receiving a comfortable social security check each month and poverty and welfare would be things of the past.

1936

By the spring of 1936 more than $326 million in federal recovery funds had been pumped into Washington's economy and the capital city had received its share. The projects ranged from the famous WPA sanitary outhouses ($13.80 for a single-holer; $20 for a two-seater) to another major building for the state capitol group. In its first issue of the new year, the *Olympia News* reported that *"patriarchal pines are being cut down"** as ground was

---

*The *News* had sacrificed accuracy to alliteration. The trees were actually fatherly firs.

cleared south and east of the Legislative building for the new Social Security building, designed to house the new department of public welfare, which was the fastest-growing agency of state government, and the state land commissioner's office.

The new building, designed by Joe Wohleb to Wilder and White specifications, cost $717,-405.15, of which nearly $320,000 was provided by a federal PWA grant. Some $200,000 from liquor profits made up most of the state's share. The cornerstone was laid early in August with Governor Martin and Secratary of State Hutchinson presiding. The stone contained enough artifacts to start a small museum, including small American and state flags, a Bible, a copy of the *Olympian*, copies of the state and national constitutions, a statement regarding social security in the state of Washington, a brief (and probably expurgated) history of the department of public lands, a photostatic copy of the first old age pension check issued by the state, a list of all current state officials and a hand-written letter from Governor Stevens begging Dr. Tolmie of the hated Hudson's Bay company to provide supplies for the treaty Indians on credit.

The depression was far from over, but the basic problems of survival had been met. The poor farm was no longer the last, fearful alternative to outright starvation for the old and poor and even the pay of a WPA worker could provide at least a subsistence living for an average family. The new state banking laws and the inauguration of the federal deposit insurance program had gone a long way toward restoring public faith in financial institutions and the fireside radio chats of Franklin Roosevelt were convincing Americans that, indeed, they had nothing to fear but fear itself. Affluence was not yet achieved, but hope was rapidly displacing despair.

ELECTION '36

One way to get a fairly well-paying job . . . with a rent-free house thrown in . . . was to get elected governor, and no less than 14 hopeful candidates filed for that office in the primary election of 1936. Martin, the solidly conservative Democrat, was opposed for the Democratic nomination by two major candidates, King county Commissioner John C. Stevenson, who was backed by the left-wing Washington Commonwealth Federation, and State Treasurer Otto Case, who was the champion of the Townsendites. Presumably as an effort to confuse the electorate even more than was normal, a political unknown named H. G. Stevenson was persuaded to file, prompting the "real" Stevenson to insist that his name on the ballot should include the designation "Radio Speaker."

The Radio Speaker, who appeared to be a man of some wealth, was an enigmatic figure in Washington politics. He was widely believed to be a Canadian citizen and ineligible to run for political office in the United States, but the issue does not appear to have been brought to a showdown. Not long before the primaries the governor of New York issued an extradition request on him, claiming that he was actually one John Stockman, wanted for fraud by the Buffalo police. Martin characterically refused to comply and thus rid himself of a powerful opponent, and the charge was later withdrawn.

Roland Hartley, a man who did not easily say die, charged back into the fray and it was generally believed that he could not lose in the primary or win in the general. The recently-passed blanket primary gave voters the opportunity for the first time to engage in cross-voting in the primary and there is strong evidence that thousands of Republicans did so. Terrified at the thought of the Radio Speaker winning the governorship and hoisting the red flag over the capitol, they opted for the lesser evil among the Democratic candidates and gave their votes to Martin. That this was the case is indicated by the fact that, while Republican nominees for other state elective offices, who usually receive considerably fewer votes than the gubernatorial candidates, averaged more than 150,000, while less than 100,000 Republican votes were cast for governor.

In commenting on this phomonemon, Claudius C. Johnson wrote that *thousands of Washington voters are exceedingly mobile, even politically ambidextrous."**

Martin's campaign for a second term was simple and low key. During his first bid for office he had been criticized for having spent more than $18,000 to win the governorship,

some of his critics charging that in spending such a tremendous sum of money he had actually bought his way into office. In 1936 he ran simply on his record as "the governor of all the people." His tactics were far from flamboyant. Even his "Martin for Governor" buttons, not much bigger than a dime, were probably the least gaudy in political history.

Stevenson, who had launched his campaign in February with the sponsorship of a 135-page initiative to provide a minimum income of $100 a month for disabled persons and all those over 60 years of age, made good use of his mellifluous voice, both on the air waves and in stump speeches, but the state's silent majority, including thousands of cross-over "Martin Republicans," gave the incumbent governor 166,000 votes to the Radio Speaker's 129,000. Case trailed with about 86,000, mostly cast by the geriatric set of the state's Townsend clubs.

Hartley easily won the Republican nomination, although he trailed well behind both Martin and Stevenson. The Everett mill magnate, who had been unable to adjust to the relatively mild social changes of the 1920's, was as out of date as Elisha P. Ferry amid the tidal wave of social and political change in the mid-thirties. Roosevelt blitzed Alf Landon in Washington with a vote of 459,579 to the Kansan's 206,892, but Martin led the ticket, swamping Hartley by 466,550 votes to 189,141.

Death had thinned the ranks of the state's Democratic congressional delegation and there was a primary scramble for the vacant seats. Warren Magnuson, assistant U.S. district attorney for western Washington, replaced the erratic Zioncheck who, after a series of wild escapades in the national capital, had leaped to his death from an upper floor of the Arctic club in Seattle. Charles H. Leavey beat out a covey of candidates, including C. C. Dill's wife Rosalie, to claim the 5th district seat, while in the sixth a gaggle of hopefuls, including that derbied donkey-driver Nifty Garrett, placed their hats in the ring. John M. Coffee won the nomination and the position. Incumbent Mon C. Wallgren defeated Pearl Wanamaker in the primary and retained his seat.

Lieutenant Governor Meyers took the nomination from Charles R. Maybury and he, along with a full slate of Democratic elective officials, was swept into office. The last of the Republicans, Noah Showalter, lost his job this time, Stanley F. Atwood having won the nomination against him as a Democrat.

*"The Washington Blanket Primary," *Pacific Northwest Quarterly,* XXXIII, Pp. 27-39.

By 1937 the state capital, from the governor's mansion to the courthouse, was solidly in the hands of the Democrats. Only city hall, with Dr. Longaker at the helm, remained as an enclave of good, solid downtown establishment conservatism.

1937

It was apparent by 1937 that the world was in violent ferment and was likely to stay that way. Even the most hopeful were becoming aware that there would be no going home to the simple, placid way of life that ended with the outbreak of the first world war.

In America, labor was growing increasingly militant as the AFL and CIO jousted for power and prestige. Pent up frustrations of years of depression-spawned wage cuts, shutdowns and a "take-it-or-leave-it-you're-lucky-to-have-a-job" management attitude resulted in a year-long series of national, regional and local strikes.

A bitter west coast maritime strike, which had shut down all ports the previous fall, had dragged into its 67th day by January 1, and would continue for another month. In Michigan, the national guard was holding back pickets as carloads of strike-breakers were hauled to the General Motors plant, and badge-wearing goons of the company security force beat and clubbed union leaders at the Ford plant.

On Puget Sound the 25 ferries of Captain Alex Peabody's Black Ball line were tied up as 400 unionized crewmen demanded an eight-hour day and a minimum wage of $64 a month. Governor Martin tried his hand with no great success as an arbitrator. The ferryboat crews turned down his suggestions and the state eventually had to grant Captain Peabody a rate increase to meet their demands. This was the first in a long round of free-for-all battles between governors, ferry patrons and Captain Peabody which would make periodic headlines for 15 years and result in the eventual take-over of the ferry fleet by the state.

Soon after the maritime strike ended, putting longshoremen back to work at Olympia and the other Puget Sound ports, the plywood workers walked out. Local auto repairmen joined them the same day, demanding a wage scale of 90¢ an hour for mechanics and a dollar an hour for body and fender men.

A NEW AND TROUBLED WORLD

On the international scene, Hitler and Mussolini continued to scream threats against the rest of the world, while giving their fighter and bomber pilots a little advance training by helping General Franco blast the socialist forces and take over as dictator of Spain. In the far east the first rumblings of the Sino-Japanese war were heard and before the year was over, patriotic Americans were enraged by the bombing and sinking of the U.S. navy gunboat *Panay* by the Japanese on the Yangtze river.

Newspaper readers and newsreel viewers were titillated when the Duke of Windsor, having renounced the British throne for the American divorcee he loved, *"swept Wallace Warfield Simpson into his arms at the moss-covered Castle de Cande in France,"* proving that fairy tales sometimes do come true. They were horrified at the newsreel film portraying the awesome, fiery death of the great trans-Atlantic passenger dirigible *Hindenberg* at Lakehurst, and proud when young millionaire oil man and film producer Howard Hughes set a new transcontinental air speed record, flying from Los Angeles to Newark in seven hours, 29 minutes and 27 seconds. There was mild interest when Justice Hugo Black of the United States supereme court admitted, under congressional questioning, that he had been a member of the Ku Klux Klan.

The year began with G-men and local law enforcement agencies combing the Puget Sound country in a feverish effort to solve the state's most publicized crime of the decade, the kidnapping of 10-year-old Charles Mattson from his parents' fashionable Tacoma home. Eleven days later the boy's nude body was found, stabbed, bludgeoned and sexually assaulted, in brush alongside a highway near Everett. His perverted killer was never found.

GENTLEMEN, COME OUT FIGHTING

The legislature of 1937 assembled amid snow and sleet, more overwhelmingly Democratic than ever . . . 91 to eight in the house of representatives; 41 to five in the senate. The majority could hardly be called a solid one, however. The left-wingers, though somewhat reduced in numbers, still constituted an aggressive and highly vocal minority within the majority and they believed they saw an early opportunity to make their weight felt when the Democratic caucus found itself embroiled in a four or five way fight over the speakership.

Jurie B. Smith was the candidate of the progressives, Representative Waldron was backed by the more conservative element. George Adams and Edward J. "Fresh Water" Reilly* were strong contenders, and there was a move by some to draft former Speaker Yantis, who wasn't a candidate.

When it became evident on the first ballot that the Smith backers couldn't muster a majority, they made a quick deal and threw their support to the 235-pound Irishman, Reilly. Waldron had withdrawn in favor of Adams and, had it not been for the liberals, the Indian legislator from Mason county would have won the gavel. As it was, Reilly won by a vote of 60 to 23, with only 17 of his supporters from the ranks of the regular Democrats.*

A terrible howl of outrage went up from the ranks of the progressives when the speaker they had elected awarded only five of the 14 major committee chairmanships to their members. They asserted their determination to "upset Reilly's apple cart" and held secret meetings to sound out Yantis, Belle Reeves and J. T. Ledgerwood as candidates who might prove acceptable to the moderates and conservatives in a plot to unseat Reilly.

Reilly moved with equal rapidity to arrange a treaty meeting with Adams at which the peace pipe was smoked, potlatch gifts presumably offered, and a working coalition was arranged. Reilly remained on the rostrum throughout the session.

The debonair Vic Meyers was having troubles of his own across ulcer gulch in the senate as members of that august body who did not approve of his committee assignments threatened to drag out that hoary bill to

*"Fresh Water" Reilly was so designated to distinguish him from Representative Edward Riley of King, who was predictably known as "Salt Water"Riley, being a Puget Sounder.

*There were 37 left-wingers in the Democratic caucus, 36 conservatives and 17 "wish-boners" or middle-of-the roaders, who might potently throw their weight in either direction.

abolish the office of lieutenant governor. Vic, too, cheerfully survived the crisis as he would a host of subsequent ones, soothing his critics with beaming smiles and the rhetorical question, "Why pick on Vic?"

Senator John H. Ferryman, a veteran oldster of Chelan county, suffered the most disjointed nose of any victim of organizational strife. After being defeated in his bid for the office of president pro-tem, he was further humiliated by an effort to replace him as chairman of the powerful appropriations committee with a younger man. When he was subsequently appointed to represent the state at the second inauguration of President Roosevelt he seemed pleased, but upon reflection decided that it was all a plot to get rid of him. He returned to Wenatchee in high dudgeon and announced, "I quit 'em . . . I walked out. They tried to shelve me."

GOVERNOR MARTIN
SETS THE PACE

Governor Martin delivered his second inaugural address to the legislature shortly after noon on January 13 after being sworn in by Judge William J. Steinert, who had just assumed the chief justiceship of the state supreme court. He told the lawmakers that the people had "set the pace" when they rejected "proposals for new forms of taxes and a number of radical and experimental propositions." The pace, he made it clear, should be one of moderate and cautious progress. He cautioned against any liberalization of the liquor laws, urging the members to "remember the common promise not to return to the saloon and open drinking." Tippling, he felt, was a vice which should be pursued in secrecy, or at least in places shielded from the innocent gaze of the temperate, and the procuring of potables should, for the sake of men's souls, be made as inconvenient as possible.

As to the Sunday closing law, which was notably ignored, he expressed the opinion that it should either be "revised, repealed or enforced."

Other suggestions included: Retention of the 1935 revenue act without substantial changes; an expanded social security program, including a new unemployment security act and an increased budget to support the plan; a state tribunal with broad power to settle labor disputes; another public building program, to include a second "custodial" institution for retarded children in western Washington; and "practical machinery for state prosecution through the attorney general's office, in the event of failure of county prosecutors to act."

As an example of the need for such authority, the governor cited the "slot machine racket," which he said was making illicit profits of from $4 million to $7 million a year.

Following the inaugural ball in the American Legion hall, described as usual by the *Olympian* as *"the finest in the history of the state of Washington,"* the oddly assorted legislators set about producing an equally oddly assorted group of nostrums designed to cure the ills of the state. The result was a flood of bills which ultimately numbered 1,154, finally breaking the previous all-time record of 1,121 set by the 1913 session.

GETTING DOWN TO SERIOUS SQUABBLING

Little time was wasted in getting down to serious squabbling, primarily over the confirmation of Martin appointees to code department directorships. The first to rock the senate chambers was a pitched battle between liberals and conservatives in regard to the durable Olaf Olsen, who had been named to head that prototype "superagency," the department of finance, budget and business. It was charged that he had little concern and no compassion for the inmates of the state institutions, which were numbered among his diverse responsibilities. It was said that he had helped defeat a bill to raise the pay of prison guards and attendants at institutions for the insane and mentally retarded, who were working a virtual seven-day week at an average pay of about $50 a month. Senator Reardon, pointing to the unrest in the state's correctional institutions, pointedly questioned Mr. Olsen's "capability as responsible head of the penal institutions."

After nearly a month of simmering hostility, all but Senator Reardon gave in to the tradition that the governor should be permitted to choose his political bedfellows and then lie with them as comfortably as possible, and Olsen's appointment was confirmed by a 41 to one vote.

But by that time a fight over the governor's request measure for increased social security services had spilled over from the house, where the controversy had, as usual, raged about the head of Director Ernst, who remained the favorite whipping boy of the ultra-liberals. They charged that Ernst, like Olsen, was possessed of a heart of stone; that he had removed rehabilitative programs for the blind and eliminated their minimum pension level, had failed to help needy veterans of the world war and otherwise failed to meet the human needs of the state. The liberals were supported from the wings by Radio Speaker Stevens, King county Commissioner Tom Smith and Tacoma attorney John T. McCutcheon, who lobbied for an entirely different and more generous program than that recommended by the governor, claiming that his proposals were "too restrictive."

The senate took up the heated debate regarding Mr. Ernst and its own social security committee, which had failed to deliver a requested investigative report on Ernst and his department to the members.

Visitors to the galleries enjoyed an excellent choice of entertainment in either house, but guests of the house of representatives on January 28 had enjoyed a particularly rare treat when they witnessed the first punch on the nose delivered to a member of the press by a member of the legislature in the new capitol building.

The punchee was Ashley Holden, political writer of the *Spokesman-Review,* a man who felt that Elisha P. Ferry had been rather too liberal; the puncher was Representative Bert H. Collins of King, a member of the left-wing caucus. Strong feelings had been generated in the course of a debate over a resolution to bar all newsmen from the chambers. When it failed to pass, Mr. Collins strode to the press table, thoughtfully plucked Mr. Holden's spectacles from his nose, and swung a wicked right cross which connected with a fine thud. Fellow members rushed forward and removed their enraged colleague from the vicinity of the dazed Holden, but decorum was not entirely restored. The left-wingers introduced another resolution specifically banning Mr. Holden from the chambers. After much heated debate, the measure was defeated and Representative David Cowen moved to tidy things up by striking all reference to the press squabble from the record.

The ill feeling between Holden and Collins had originated the previous day when the political pundit from Spokane interjected himself into an argument over a left-wing resolution which would have authorized a legislative investigation of the trial of Ray Becker, one of the convicted Centralia wobblies of 1919. According to the legislators involved in the discussion, Holden had bustled up and told them, "He ought to have been hanged or lynched when he was caught."

Holden insisted that his comment had been of a more moderate and kindly nature . . . "It would have solved the whole problem if he had been hanged."

In any event, Holden became the recipient of an historic if somewhat painful distinction and Collins had the deep personal satisfaction of actually doing something that countless legislators have said they were going to do.

A lot of noses were out of joint that session, but Holden's the most literally and painfully.

Further threats to the decorum of the house emanated from the speaker himself when Vic Meyers began commuting through the marble corridors to organize house liberals in an effort to defeat Martin's labor arbitration bill, which was violently opposed by the state federation of labor, and to pass social security legislation more liberal than that proposed by the governor.

Fresh Water Reilly announced that he would "pull out Vic's mustache, one hair at a time, unless he keeps the nose above that mustache out of the house." It was noted that the lieutenant governor had closely trimmed his mustache, but he claimed it wasn't a precautionary measure . . . "They cut so much from my budget I can't afford wax any more," he explained plaintively. He then offered to let Reilly go ahead and pull out his prized hirstute adornment if the speaker would go along with his bills.

Both the governor's industrial relations bill and a counter-proposal by organized labor which would create a state commissioner of industrial relations, bogged down in controversy. Martin's measure was buried in the rules committee and it appeared for a while that the labor bill would have easy sailing on the floor of the house. It had 67 sponsors . . . far more than enough to pass it . . . but when it came up for action many of them claimed that it had been misrepresented to them; that they had been told the governor approved of it. They demanded that their names be removed and, in the end, no arbitration bill of any kind passed.

The failure of a bill with 67 sponsors to muster a bare majority in the house aroused the deep disgust of the lieutenant governor, who issued a statement to the press advocating a one-man legislature. "Most of them are just stooges of the governor anyway," he proclaimed. "He cracks the whip and they jump through the hoop. They don't think for themselves; they wait until the governor sends them an idea through a mental pneumatic tube and presto! They're happy as a child with a new toy. We might as well let Martin do it all. It would save the taxpayers $170,000."

When asked by the capitol correspondents if his suggestions weren't a bit on the facetious side, he replied, "The folks of the state are paying for this show. We might as well give 'em some laughs for their money. They're not going to get anything else apparently."

Incensed, the Democratic senators called a caucus to discuss an additional cut of $1,200 from the lieutenant governor's modest budget request of $6,000 for the coming biennium. Aghast, Meyers went to the caucus to apologize and plead for a restoration of funds, leaving the tiny Republican minority in charge of the floor. Senator Chapin Mills of Clark, a horticulturist, observed the occasion by throwing prunes to the galleryites. A little old lady who had been dozing and was thus unaware of what was going on, was struck on the forehead by one of the senator's prunes and awoke with a piercing shriek.

Republicans and Democrats appear to have shared an equal concern for the decorum of the chambers during those sensational sessions of the thirties.

The next major debate in the senate was sparked by a bill to establish a maximum 60-hour week for domestic servants, sponsored by one of the three current female members of the upper house, Senator Mary U. Farquharson of King.* The measure was strongly opposed by Spokane and eastern Washington small town legislators, who viewed it as the kind of socialistic pampering that, if not stopped, might someday extend even to itinerant farm workers. Senator Mills offered a facetious amendment to include husbands, "who are often domestic employees as soon as they get home."Senator Henderson felt that it was "too regulatory." "Why the first thing you know," he warned darkly, "we'll be having a law that you can't kiss your wife except on Sundays after church."

The house was currently arguing over two proposals offering differing methods of public school equalization. Charles W. Hodde, a freshman representative with a good head for figures, had lobbied the previous session on behalf of a Grange-sponsored bill to decrease state support to wealthy school districts and increase payments to the poor ones. Hodde, still somwehat naive in the ways of legislatures, proudly pointed out that his proposal would do the job without increasing taxes a single penny.

Representative Yantis had worked out a different equalization bill with Pearl Wanamaker, who had transferred to the senate and was already making herself a viable candidate for superintendent of public instruction by serving as a powerful legislative voice for the Washington Education Association. Her bill, backed by the WEA, would add $3 million in subsidies to poor school districts, while maintaining the current 25¢ per day— per pupil support to all districts.

Hodde, speaking with the confidence of a man who has logic and mathematics on his side, pointed out that the Wanamaker-Yantis bill, while costing the taxpayers an additional $3 million, would merely preserve the advantage of the wealthy districts. It did not provide for equalization, he said, but subsidization.

Senator Wanamaker responded with the opinion that there should be a few very rich school districts in the state to serve as examples for the others, a belief similar to that held by members of the upper classes that there should be a few multimillionaires with sea-going yachts to provide motivation to the rest of the population.

---

*The other two were Pearl Wanamaker of Snohomish and Island and Lulu D. Morgan of Kitsap, the house had four . . . Belle Reeves, Gene Bradford, Violet Boede and 24-year-old Margaret Coughlin, who was the "brain" behind the liberal faction.

The conservative Democrats and Republicans in the house joined forces with enough wish-boners (of which Hodde was one) to kill his bill by indefinite postponement. The Wanamaker-Yantis bill was later passed.

This defeat, according to Hodde, taught him an important lesson . . . "Your bill will never get passed if it's the cheapest one."

By March 1, the 50th day cut-off date for introduction of bills, the house had produced 736; the senate 417, of which 101 had been passed and 27 signed by the governor. Among them was the usual weird and wonderful assortment of expensive left-wing measures, ranging from statewide adoption of the Townsend plan to the Commonwealth Federation's pet bill to put the state in the gasoline business, the latter pushed with evangelical fervor by E. L. Pettus, a Pierce county minister and ardent federation member. Conservatives, liberals and wish-boners alike sought to return the state highway system to the pork barrel by introducing a flood of bills to enlarge the primary highway system by construction of new roads and assumption of maintenance responsibility in all the various legislative districts of the state. Having thus labored mightily for the good of the state, the Democratic legislators embarked that evening for a dinner dance cruise aboard the Black Ball line's streamlined flagship *Kalakala,* arranged by State Committeeman George Sheridan to commemorate the fourth anniversary of the Roosevelt landslide.

Governor Martin was moved to address a warning to the prolific lawmakers in mid-session, pointing out that if they approved even a fraction of the special appropriation bills being introduced with such abandon "it will wreck the financial condition of the state."

Representative David D. Cowen, Spokane dentist and chairman of the house appropriations committee, agreed with the governor. He estimated that the hundred or so extra money bills would exceed the state's income by $20 million during the next biennium. Both Cowen and senate appropriations chairman Judson W. Shorett of King pledged themselves to stand solidly with the governor in his recommendations for a balanced budget.

A LITTLE SCANDAL NOW AND THEN

On March 8, with the 25th session rapidly drawing to a confused close, the voice of scandal was added to the verbal strife at the capitol. The day started with the news that bribery charges had been filed against ex-Representative Rex Strickland, an unsuccessful candidate for land commissioner in the last election and that $500 bail had been set by Thurston county Justice of the Peace Van R. Hinkle. The former member had been lobbying on behalf of the state's small loan companies, which were in a state of hysteria over a bill to limit their interest rates to 12 percent a year. Their melancholy plight had seemingly touched the hearts of a number of legislators, who girded their loins to fight to the death for the basic American right to squeeze as much as possible out of a debtor.

That afternoon Representative Edward E. Henry of King demanded immediate action on the 12 percent small loan bill, making the direct accusation that "certain members have received bribes" and pointing to the fact that Representative James T. Sullivan, also of King county, had testified that Strickland had offered him $50 to vote against the bill.*

"I have absolute evidence that certain members of this legislature have received money in bribes for votes on the small loan bill," Henry thundered, "and I demand that the bill be put on the calendar to smoke out the dishonest members of this legislature."

Visibly shaken, the membership hurriedly voted, 73 to 16, to give the bill immediate consideration, then passed it by a 76 to four vote, 19 having left the chambers for brisk walks in the fresh air.

The next day Representative Joseph D. Roberts of King became the second legislator to pack up and go home in a huff that session. He departed after losing a battle with that strong and invincible female senator Pearl Wanamaker. Both had introduced bills to establish a state publicity bureau "to counteract adverse publicity such as the over-emphasis of minor social disturbances." His bill had been pigeonholed and Pearl's passed.

Attention was not long diverted from the charges of bribery, which by March 10 were resounding from both the house and senate. Henry, a former King county deputy prosecutor, was loudly demanding a grand jury

probe of bribes paid to legislators by lobbyists during the session. "The activities of various lobby interests in Olympia this session would shock the honesty of every decent citizen of Washington," he thundered.

King county left-wing Representative Michael B. Smith was equally outspoken during debate on a bill to regulate funeral directors.

"I happen to know that lobbyists spent thousands of dollars buying senators right and left to get their bill passed," he said, speaking darkly of "a big organization in Seattle" which was backing the undertakers' bill.

Not to be outdone in citing specifics, Henry charged that lobbyists spent $25,000 in their efforts to throttle the small loan bill. He said he expected more arrests, including "higher-ups."

There was no grand jury investigation, no further arrests and lobbyist Strickland was assessed a fine, which was immediately suspended. Governor Martin line-vetoed some of the more restrictive clauses from the small loan bill and in October the state supreme court voided the rest of it, ruling that it was discriminatory and unconstitutional.

THE GOVERNOR BATS .714

The governor got 20 of his 28 executive request measures, giving him a respectable batting average of .714. The failure to set up any kind of industrial labor dispute arbitration system was his major failure.

The state publicity measure was passed and a seven-member progress commission established to administer the funds. A new school for retarded children was funded, the 60-hour week for domestic employees was established, and the names of the three normal schools were changed to colleges of education.

State support was authorized for junior colleges, the requirement was set that members of the liquor board must have their appointments confirmed by the senate, and all city policemen were placed under civil service.

Other bills provided special education facilities for retarded and handicapped children, established an institute of child

---

*According to current and authoritative statehouse rumor, the price of a vote to raise interest rates has increased by approximately 2000 percent over the intervening years.

development research at the university, provided state aid for public libraries, made marathon dances and walkathons illegal, prohibited the possession or use of slot machines except in private clubs, raised the gasoline tax a half cent, and imposed a 1.5 percent excise tax on the value of all automobiles, payable at the time of annual licensing. Representative Adams of the Skokomish tribe, a winery representative in his spare time, succeeded in getting the ancient law prohibiting liquor sales to Indians repealed. The *Olympian,* taking note of Adams' profession, commented, *"Indians are now selling fire water to whites."*

Martin's requested department of social security was established (with Ernst still clinging grimly to its directorship) and its functions were liberalized. A division for the blind was made a part of it, charged with providing for the welfare of the sightless. Public assistance was extended to cover "the blind, aged and dependent," and state aid for tubercular patients was increased from five to seven dollars a week, with the requirement that at least one dollar of the weekly grant must be expended on rehabilitation services.

In the closing hours, with the clocks stopped and the more impatient legislators drifting homeward, the two percent sales tax was extended to bread, butter, milk and fresh fruits and vegetables, which had been excluded in the original sales tax bill. An amendment by Representative Hodde calling for a sales tax on service businesses such as barber shops and laundries died in conference committee, as did another graduated net income tax proposal.

The 25th legislature adjourned *sine die* at four o'clock on the morning of March 10, having appropriated $53 million for highways, $43.3 million for social security programs and $33.5 million for schools, all somewhat higher amounts than those proposed by the governor. By and large, however, it had hewed reasonably close to the moderate line he had set, rejecting the more far-out bills from both the left and the right.

Governor Martin tidied things up a bit after the departure of the legislature by vetoing the half-cent gas tax increase and cutting the highway budget back to his recommended $33 million. He also redlined the $400,000 appropriation to help public libraries, the $100,-000 for support of junior colleges, the $20,000

for the child development center at the university, $100,000 for state aid to noxious week control and the $15,000 appropriation for the Oregon-Washington boundary commission. All told, his veto pen trimmed some $20.7 million from the legislative budget.

Among those who had, from time to time, observed the legislative process was the president of the University of Washington student body who, like two of his recent predecessors, Marion Zioncheck and Smith Troy, was a law school student. Young Nat Washington was advocating more student self-government at the university. When asked by a capitol newsman if he had any ambition to go into politics he replied cautiously, "Well, I've thought about it a little, but you can't tell what will happen."*

THE CONCRETE JUNGLE GROWS APACE

The automobile continued to exert its ever-increasing impact upon the state and its citizens. Although the added half-cent gasoline tax had been vetoed, the service stations had already raised their prices to more than compensate for the increased tax and none of them bothered to revise them downward. With more than 600,000 sets of license plates turned out by the penitentiary that year, there were a lot of cars on the road and the oil companies made a tidy profit on the gasoline tax raise that had been red-lined by the governor.

The narrow, winding highways of the previous decade were no longer adequate for the increasing burden of faster and more powerful automobiles, especially on the heavily traveled sections between the cities along the eastern shore of Puget Sound. The Seattle-Tacoma "skyline highway" had introduced Washington motorists to the lethal delights of the high-speed multi-lane highway and they were clamoring for more.

*As this is written, Nat Washington is serving his sixth four-year term as a Democratic state senator from the 13th district (Kittitas and part of Grant and Yakima counties), having first spent one term as a representative.

In September another four-lane highway, from Olympia to Fort Lewis, was dedicated with great pomp and circumstance as Martin Way. Following a luncheon at the Hotel Olympian for 50 dignitaries including Martin, his director of Highways, Murrow, Mayor Longaker, Charles Maybury, president of the Chamber of Commerce, the commandant of Fort Lewis and Doc Carlyon, the ceremonies were held on the "O. R. Elwell Memorial Bridge"* across the Nisqually river, with the Alfred William Leach American Legion post band playing and aerial bombs bearing aloft the American flag.

Shortly afterward, observant motorists noticed what looked like lengths of garden hose lying across the new thoroughfare. They were part of a marvelous new gadget called an "electric eye", which faithfully counted the number of cars which passed that way.

The recent legislature had, among its multifarious activities, passed a new highway code requiring that all Washington motorists must take physical and mental tests to qualify for driver's licenses and the state patrol recruited 27 new officers to help carry the added load. All but three of the recruits were over six feet tall, among them rooky patrolmen Oliver Furseth, George Amans and John Agee. Sergeant J. E. Kuntz, the former Olympia police chief, was chief instructor for the 60-day recruit training program.

The lot of a state policeman was a somewhat happier one in 1937 than in earlier days. Most of the man-killing motorcycles had been replaced by black and white "paddy wagons," which provided considerably more protection from accidents and the weather, although the more conservative members of the force felt somewhat self-conscious in the new and gaudy uniforms which were issued to them that year. The regalia, which would do credit to President Nixon's palace guard, included maroon breeches, light blue shirts, dark blue blouses with Sam Brown belt and brass buttons,

maroon bow ties, red and blue caps and shiny boots.

It was not considered good policy for motorists to laugh when stopped by one of the dazzlingly colorful troopers.

By 1937 Governor Hartley's free-loading seagull, Tee had apparently winged his way to that great garbage dump in the sky, replaced by a Democratic successor named Bilbo, who visited the Insurance building every day except Sunday to share the lunches of state workers.

The electronic computer had not yet arrived upon the governmental scene, but the statistician had, and people with $50 adding machines were able to produce just as impressive statistics as the multi-million-dollar monsters which IBM had succeeded in establishing as the bureaucratic status symbol of the 1970s.*

Among the fascinating facts and figures was the information that 35 million sales tax tokens had been manufactured which, if stacked one on top of the other would reach 34 miles into the stratosphere, and that the state industrial insurance department had, during the 25 years of its existence, paid $96,706,281 in injury and death benefits to workers and the surviving heirs of the 8,104 who had been killed in extrahazardous industries . . . mostly logging camps.

ALARMS, FALSE AND OTHERWISE

In addition to politics, the local news of the capital city was dominated by fire alarms. Early in January a late night fire gutted a major downtown landmark, the tall-windowed Odd Fellows building with its ornate clock tower at 5th and Capitol Way. The old brick structure, the first three-story building in town, housed the lodge rooms and library on the third floor, a 26-room hotel on the second, and three stores, including Carlton Sears' Rexall drugstore and fountain lunch.

---

*This span was named for a former highway department bridge engineer. Like the George Washington Memorial Bridge in Seattle, its official designation has been long since forgotten although it is still in use, carrying north-bound traffic lanes of Interstate 5 across the river at the Thurston-Pierce county line.

---

*There are numerous observers of state government, of whom I am one, who are convinced that the clerk with the five-key calculator also produced the information more quickly and accurately.

The fire was reminiscent of the one that had destroyed the old HotelOlympia and decimated the ranks of the fire department. Fire Chief Holcomb and firemen Ab Huntley, Larry Rogers and Stewart Tatro were hauled off to St. Peters hospital, overcome by smoke and gas. Like most Olympia conflagrations of earlier years, it was more spectacular than deadly. There were no deaths or serious injuries.

A few weeks later a heavy windstorm came up during the night and toppled the brick walls of the fire-gutted building. One of them crashed through the roof of the one-story building which housed the Pantorium Dye works and the Capitol Way Inn. After-theater diners at the inn leaped over the counter and through the shattered plate glass window. Again there were no serious injuries.

And, as the saying goes, it's an ill wind that blows no good.

A committee of Odd Fellows had met earlier that evening and accepted a bid to raze the remains of their building. Noting that much of the demolition had been accomplished by the forces of nature, they voted to call upon the contractor and demand a lower bid.

The second fire alarm to achieve public notice was a false one. Late in January a teacher at the new Washington school sent two third grade boys to mail a letter. Older students directed them to a fire alarm box and their efforts to insert the teacher's letter resulted in emergency runs by the fire department, police cars and off-duty employees of the city's public safety department through knee-deep snow to the school. They found the third-graders seemingly fascinated by the cacophony of sound they had precipitated and debating whether or not letters were conveyed from the red box to the post office by means of a pneumatic tube or electricity.

It seemed that major conflagrations always prompted the city fathers to buy a new fire engine. A couple of months after the Odd Fellows blaze Mayor Longaker and Honorary Fire Chief Grant Talcott formally accepted a new Seagrave combination pumper, and none too soon either.

A month later a fire of undetermined origin swept the Capitol theater, resulting in a $70,-000 loss. This time the entire fire department, with the exception of Captain Everett Holmes, ended up confined to their beds from injuries and smoke inhalation. The friendly Tacoma fire department sent a full company down to take over the capital city's fire station during the period of convalescence.

In mid-June a fire and explosion ended the days of the chubby little Sound freighter *Capital*, which had replaced the ill-fated *Chaco* on the daily voyages from Seattle and Tacoma to Percival's dock. The early morning fire broke out as the *Capital* was trundling up Dana passage near Johnson's point. The crew escaped to Briscoe point* at the southern tip of Hartstene island in the lifeboat. The little freighter, a homely favorite with shoreside shipwatchers, sank in deep water off Itsami shoal and 1,500 cases of empty Olympia beer bottles went floating off on the tide.

Returning, as it always did eventually to things political, the attention of the capital city was focused upon the town's fourth presidential visitation; the second by a Roosevelt.

HERE HE COMES! THERE HE GOES!

Jaunty and grinning, complete to uptilted cigarette-holder and gray fedora, FDR arrived in town in a Lincoln phaeton after an inspection tour of Grand Coulee and a 250-mile trip around the Olympic loop. Governor Martin had met him at Quinault lodge and they had transferred from a closed sedan to the open car outside the city. Crowds lined the streets and cheered themselves hoarse as the man who had licked the depression was driven toward the capitol. There more thousands waited under the threatening early October skies, among them Kate Stevens Bates, the spry, apple-heeled old lady who had come to the muddy hamlet of Olympia in 1854 with her father, Isaac Stevens. All the state elective officials and most of the supreme court justices along with Mayor Longaker and his fellow city commissioners. George Yantis, chairman of the welcoming committee, had arranged for a loudspeaker system and microphone and had alternated with the American Legion band under Phil Vincent in entertaining the restless crowd during the hour and a half waiting period between the announced and actual arrival times of the president.

---

*This landmark has, from time immemorial, been known to upper Puget Sound tugboatmen and the saltier yachtsmen as Raggedass point.

Behind schedule and tired, FDR was taken to the governor's mansion, where gubernatorial secretary Dick Hamilton presented him with a mess of Quinault river trout which he had just caught. Fifteen minutes later the Lincoln emerged from the wooded mansion grounds and passed in front of the Legislative building, the president grinning and waving. After a brief pause at the recently completed Social Security building, the first major monument to the Roosevelt era in Washington's capital city, the party moved back down Capitol Way and up the 4th street hill toward Tacoma. Halfway up the hill, with darkness beginning to fall, along with a preliminary splattering of Puget Sound rain, the Lincoln halted briefly, the top was raised, and it roared off toward the Tacoma union station and a presidential special train. From the rear platform he addressed another massed crowd, describing the dogged determination with which Senator Bone and Congressman Coffee had been "literally haunting the White House" trying to get his O.K. on the construction of a Tacoma Narrows bridge by the PWA. At 8 p.m. the presidential special pulled out of the Tacoma yards and headed for Hyde Park.

Franklin had come a long way since, as a young sub-cabinet officer and vice-presidential candidate, he had addressed a moderate crowd in Sylvester park and prompted the *Olympian* to observe that he seemed a nice enough young fellow . . . for a Democrat . . . but he would probably never go very far in politics.

When the taillights of the presidential Lincoln disappeared over the 4th street hill, Olympians returned to the normal pursuits of a drizzly evening in October. Some went home and tuned in Paul Whiteman's orchestra on KJR or the Promenade Cafe orchestra on KOMO or the Hollywood Barn Dance on KVI. Others went to see Tyrone Power and Sonja Henie in "Thin Ice" at the Liberty, or Ramon Navarro and Lola Lane in "The Sheik Steps Out" at the Avalon, or Shirley Temple in "Stowaway," Laurel and Hardy in "Our Relations" and "The March of Time" at the rebuilt and refurbished Capitol. At the downtown taverns sporting types quaffed nickel glasses of Oly and replayed the Stevens field game of the previous day in which Captain Billy Brenner had led his blue and white clad Olympia high school Bears to a 19 to 0 victory over the Kelso high school gridders. Some drove to the Evergreen ballroom on the old

Tacoma highway to dance and some to Hawks prairie to make love.

And some, it can be presumed, warded off the autumnal chill by throwing a couple of five-dollar-a-cord logs on the fire and addressing themselves to $1.65 fifth of straight bourbon from the state liquor store.

The town's serious drinkers made every effort to make their weekend purchases early, before the legal liquor dispensary closed. Until mid-summer it had only been necessary to telephone for a cab and an obliging driver would deliver liquid refreshments at a reasonable mark-up. Then the bothersome inspectors of the state liquor board descended upon the hacking industry of the capital city on an otherwise tranquil Saturday night in June. Practically all the cabbies in town ended up in jail. Al's Taxi, Airline Taxi and Eight-Five Taxi were temporarily out of business, as were several independents and, according to the *Olympian, "the city was practically without taxi service for a short time Sunday morning until bail was posted."*

After that the cab drivers performed their after-hours public service more circumspectly, catering only to those they knew to be trustworthy, appreciative and badgeless.

It was also a bad year for the town's rats. Nobody will ever know how many perished in the holocaust at the Odd Fellows hall, where they had been nesting in the foundations since 1888, but the U.S. Biological survey estimated that 75,000 had flourished at the old city dump on the waterfront until they were poisoned by a mighty dose of red squill and their malodorous breeding place graded and covered with a heavy layer of hogged fuel from the Washington Veneer company.

1938

By 1938 it was becoming apparent that the world was going to hell in a handcart. The *Daily Olympian* ushered in the year with the screamer headlines, "GERMANY THREATENS WORLD PEACE! HITLER TAKES OVER ALL MILITARY FORCES AND DEMANDS RETURN OF PRE-WAR TERRITORY. As it drew to a close the headlines proclaimed, "WORLD FACES

YULETIDE WITH FEARS . . . RUMORS OF WARS DOMINATE SPIRIT OF CHRISTMAS!" From time to time the rumble of massed flights of B-17 bombers on long-range reconnaissance flights from Gray Field at Fort Lewis added ominous overtones to the shrill cries of newsboys hawking war extras on the streets.

Despite the drift toward world cataclysm, the United States had not yet assumed its role as "the arsenal of democracy." It appeared to many that Roosevelt had not, in fact, whipped the depression. The nation seemed to be slipping backward in its struggle to regain full prosperity. The number of Washington citizens existing on relief had increased from 16 percent of the population in February of 1937 to 22 percent in February of 1938. Grays Harbor county was hardest hit, with more than one out of three on the dole. By March Director Ernst of the social security department had ordered the state's 188,000 able-bodied recipients off the welfare rolls because funds were running out. Welfare groups and liberal legislators besieged Governor Martin demanding an emergency legislative session.

VICTOR, WHERE ARE YOU?

The special session issue reached dramatic proportions when, in mid-April, Martin made a flying trip to the national capital to do battle against Senator Wallgren's bill to create a very large Olympic National Park. Martin, the practical businessman, strongly favored a very small national park, which would permit the lumber industry to profitably cut down a very large number of trees.

Martin must have had strong feelings on the matter, for he had heretofore been careful not to get very far from the state line. In his absence Victor Aloysius Meyers was governor, and Vic was the darling of the Commonwealth Federation and most of the state's other relief, pension and assorted ultra-liberal groups. There was no telling what Vic's fertile imagination might contrive once he had assumed the reins of government.

The governor may have been encouraged to believe that he could slip off safely to Washington, D.C., and back again, because

Meyers was also away somewhere. He hadn't bothered to tell anybody where he was going and had apparently broken all lines of communication.

No sooner had the chief executive boarded his plane for the east than Meyers' liberal friends began a frantic search for the lieutenant governor. Commercial radio messages were aired begging him to call home, wherever he might be. His secretary, Claire Jackson, was under the vague impression that he was fishing somewhere in the vicinity of San Diego and two days after Martin's departure Representative Kenneth Simmons, Pierce county ultra-liberal who was one of the most ardent backers of the special session, managed to run him down and contact him by telephone. He had, indeed, been fishing in southern California and, for the past two days, Washington had, without knowing it, been governed by the first and so far only woman chief executive in its history.

Dr. Ernest N. Hutchinson, the veterinarian who had entered politics at the age of 68 "to do something for the dairy industry and promote Washington," had died late in January at the age of 73. Belle Reeves, the veteran state representative from Chelan county, was appointed secretary of state in his place. With both Martin and Meyers out of the state, Mrs. Reeves was acting governor. As far as is known, her only official act while filling that office was the traditional pitching of the first ball of the season when the Olympia Senators met a Seattle semipro team at Stevens field.

THE GREAT AIRPLANE RACE

Meyers, having been informed by Representative Simmons that his great opportunity was at hand, made haste to board a fast Southern Pacific train for Portland, where he was met by a state patrolman and whisked toward the capital city with siren screaming and red lights flashing.

Martin had, in the meantime, been informed of these developments at home. He hadn't completed his mission, but he wasted no time in turning his attention to the more immediate crisis. No form of land transportation could possibly get him back to Olympia in time to avert Meyers, as acting governor, from calling the special session; neither did the limited commercial airline schedules of that era provide a sufficient margin of safety. Arrangements were made with Northwest Airlines, the governor boarded the limited express train for Chicago and was whisked to the airport in that city, where a 10-passenger airliner awaited him. He had chartered it at the special rate of $60 an hour and it wasted no time in taking off for an all-night flight to Spokane.

Meyers won the race, but lost the battle. He arrived at Olympia a few minutes after the secretary of state's office had closed on April 19. It was too late to file his special session proclamation, so he gave up, proceeded on to Seattle and enjoyed three hours of peaceful sleep. As the lieutenant governor slumbered, Martin's chartered plane was bucketing through the stormy night carrying its grim, sleepless and presumably white-knuckled passenger toward Spokane.

Vic arose early on the morning of April 20 and likewise took to the air. As his plane landed at the Olympia airport, Martin's expensive transport having rolled up $600 worth of flight time, was skimming over the Idaho panhandle. It touched down at the Spokane airport at 7:58 a.m. as, 300 miles away, the debonair Meyers sprinted toward the granite steps of the Legislative building. He puffed into the secretary of state's office at 8:01 a.m.

But he was wasting his time. The mantle of leadership had dropped from his shoulders a few minutes earlier as Martin's plane roared across the Idaho-Washington line 18 miles east of Spokane.

Governor Martin had triumphed, but he showed no elation. He had spent an uncomfortable night in the air watching ten $60 hours tick off. He had missed a lot of sleep, his neat business suit was rumpled and he needed a shave. His neatly clipped mustache bristling and indignation flashing from his horn-rimmed spectacles, he observed less than his usual restraint in discussing the drama with the newsmen who had been awaiting his arrival. *"Maybe he was just playing up to those red devils,"* he conjectured when the motive for the lieutenant governor's action was questioned.*

The insouciant Meyers responded glibly that, if Martin was willing to call a special session in 1933 to give the people beer and whiskey, another special session was now justified to give them bread and butter.

It speaks well for the character and will power of Clarence D. Martin that, having been a heavy smoker for years, he successfully kicked the cigarette habit during that year of crisis. He remained firm even when congress went ahead and authorized the 860,000-acre Olympic National Park, which he had flown to Washington to argue against.

1939

The last slim hope for world peace vanished with the last year of the thirties. In the early months of 1939 Olympians sometimes heard the distant drone of monstrous new warplanes which were being produced by William Boeing's airplane factory in Seattle. The B-27 "flying fortresses" were tested in the stratosphere thousands of feet above the winter overcast, but there was an awareness that they were there and their presence was both reassuring and ominous.

In mid-March the German *blitzkreig* erupted in Czechoslovakia and the Nazi legions turned toward Poland. England announced that an attack on Poland would result in an immediate declaration of war. Hitler shrugged off the threat of England's "contemptible little army" and the grim developments in Europe crowded the glamorous marriage of Carole Lombard and Clark Gable from the front pages.

In mid-April President Roosevelt asked Hitler and Mussolini to pledge a decade of peace. Hitler refused and Mussolini remained silent, letting his actions speak for him as he increased Italy's military budget by $25 million a year. Pope Pius XII asked for a world prayer crusade for peace, but neither Divine

---

*After a period of reflection, Martin came to the conclusion that Vic had deliberately lost the race. The lieutenant governor was taking his duties more seriously, had surprised everybody by becoming an excellent parliamentarian and was in the process of gracefully and almost imperceptibly moving from the far left limits of his party. The governor was probably accurate in his opinion that Vic's dash from California was pure show biz, designed to make "those red devils" think he was going all out for them, while he carefully avoided being too closely identified with them in the public mind.

nor presidential involvement slowed down the war machinery of the Axis powers.

In mid-summer the U.S. navy submarines *Stingray* and *Perch* docked at the port of Olympia, but unlike visiting warships of the past, they did not welcome townspeople aboard. Their conning towers remained grimly closed and sentries politely but firmly turned back strollers on the pier.

On September 1 the German *luftwaffe* bombed Warsaw, France mobilized its armed forces and British troops prepared to cross the channel to join their allies. On Wall street, the stock market boomed, with the leaders up from 19 to 25 points. Peter G. Schmidt, president of the Olympia Brewing company returned a few days later from the first all-air tour of Europe made by an Olympia resident. In a remarkable burst of wishful thinking he told an *Olympian* reporter that the Germans he had talked to were all sure that Hitler would keep them out of war.

Down at the port dock the steamship *Florida Maru* was busily loading scrap iron for Japan, but the longshoremen were annoyed by a picket line of local Chinese . . . mostly children . . . who suspected that the rusty cargo was destined for a fiery rebirth as munitions of war. A committee of city officials met with the Chinese community and patiently explained that the scrap iron would be used to manufacture cheap toys, inferior cigarette lighters and other harmless gadgets; certainly not weapons of war. They then asked that the pickets disperse "for the good of the port of Olympia."

The Chinese children, bowing to the superior wisdom of the round-eyed mandarins, complied with the request.

In mid-October the Olympia units of the 248th Coast Artillery (Harbor Defense) were mustered into the new 205th Coast Artillery (Antiaircraft). The new unit was a full regiment, complete with military band, and Major Dohm was promoted to colonel.

In December there was general indignation at Russia's sudden attack on little Finland and amazed delight at the manner in which the Finnish army knocked the stuffing out of Joseph Stalin's vaunted Soviet war machine until it was finally overwhelmed by sheer weight of numbers.

HOLD THAT LINE

Of course neither wars nor rumors of wars could prevent the biennial gathering of Washington's legislators at the capital city. The group which assembled in January of 1939 was still dominated by Democrats, although the Republicans had embarked upon a period of gradual ground-gaining which would within the next eight years restore their political potency.

The house of representatives had lost 20 of its Democrats since the previous session and the balance was now 73 to 26. The Republicans had made a net gain of one in the senate and the line-up was now 40 Democrats to six Republicans. Most of the house Democrats who had fallen by the wayside had been of the left-wing persuasion and the more conservative wing of the party was firmly in control. Taxpayers were comforted with the predictions of political pundits that this would be a no-nonsense session in which expensive ultra-liberal proposals would be given short shrift, the governor's sharp-penciled budget of $176 million (down from the $196 million of the last biennium) would be closely adhered to, and taxes would not be increased.

John N. Sylvester, a solidly conservative Seattle attorney, was elected speaker of the house by a vote of 75 to 24, with only the surviving left-wingers opposing him. George Adams, who hadn't made it back that session as a representative,* was quickly elected sergeant at arms and Si Holcomb was returned as chief clerk without opposition.

Keiron Reardon of Monroe was elected president pro-tem of the senate, Joe Mehan of Seattle, sergeant at arms, and Earl McCroskey of Tacoma, secretary. Lieutenant Governor Meyers meekly attended the conservative caucus and gave his blessing to its selection of officers.

Governor Martin, who had not grown more liberal during his years in office, was being referred to by many Democrats as "the best Republican we ever elected." His message to

---

*Adams, the legislature's only full-blooded Indian, was defeated by Charles R. Savage in the 1938 election. In 1940 Adams plastered his district with signs reading "Vote for an Indian — Not a Savage" . . and won his seat back.

the legislature urged cooperation, prudence and economy. He wanted the relief programs administered strictly on the basis of "need," old age pensions granted only to the demonstrably destitute and the 40-mill tax limit made permanent. He also asked for the removal of sales tax exemptions (which he had vetoed last session), and reaffirmed his stand against the growing pressure to raise liquor prices as a means of increasing state revenues.

Opposition quickly developed to the governor's hold-the-line budget proposal, particularly in the area of social security where fund requests had been reduced from the previous $43 to $30 million. Senator Reardon complained that the relief budget was woefully inadequate, particularly in view of the fact that the social security fund was already $6 million overdrawn. He predicted more marches on the capitol and his prophecy was borne out in a small way the very next day.

Two Olympia area dirt farmers picketed the capitol carrying signs which read, *"Ernst Gets $7,500. We Get Nothing"* and *"For a New Deal in Washington. Work or Relief."*

The conservative majority responded by tightening its grip on the house of representatives, revising the rules to require a two-third vote rather than a simply majority to move stalled bills out of the conservative-dominated rules committee.

Thurston county's superior court judges in mid-January granted Smith Troy's request for a grand jury investigation and Chief Cole, head of the state patrol since 1926, immediately resigned, giving rise to the suspicion in the minds of the legislators that more scandal might soon be emanating from the capitol.

A few days later 3,500 unemployment compensation checks . . . the first in the nation . . . were mailed out from the Social Security building. Two Olympia men were the first to receive them; one for $7.00 and the other for $15. The legislature had already passed a bill to establish a department of unemployment compensation apart from the department of social security and the new agency became operative early in February under the direction of Jack E. Bates of Bellingham. It immediately became the largest agency of state government with nearly 500 employees.*

---

*By current bureaucratic standards a payroll of 500 is considered pretty small potatoes. The department of social and health services has somewhere between 15,500 and 16,000 employees. Nobody seems to know the exact figures.

A minor league version of the great Martin-Meyers race to the capitol occurred at about the same time. Several conservative representatives had taken long weekends away from the seat of government and left-wing Michael B. Smith of Seattle thought he saw an opportunity to break the two-thirds rule for getting legislation out of committee. The remaining conservatives pressed the panic button and Majority Leader "Fresh Water" Reilly and David Cowen made an aerial dash back from Spokane in time to defeat the threatened insurrection.

By February 19, with the session two-thirds over, the leadership had maintained such a deliberative pace that only 18 of the 822 bills in the legislative hopper had been passed. The Democratic take-over had not changed the traditional and highly inefficient way of doing things. From territorial days to the present, the legislative time table has changed little if at all. Following pious promises of a businesslike, no-nonsense session, legislators become political tortoises, pursuing a leisurely and rambling course. Then in the final days, with the adjournment deadline staring them inexorably in the face, they metamorphize into hares, leaping wildly toward *sine die,* passing bills in a dazed state and with few having the vaguest idea what they are voting upon.

On March 5, with five days left to go, the 26th legislature entered the usual better-late-than-never flurry of activity. The controversial omnibus social security bill, the result of six weeks of special hearings by legislative committee, was passed, but not without recriminations and parliamentary fencing. In the senate a rule was adopted limiting speakers on the measure to one two-minute hearing after Senator Herbert Sieler, Lewis county Republican, went on a one-man campaign to love it to death with amendments including motions to remove all penalties against false statements by relief-seekers and the requirement that immediate relatives contribute to the support of their indigent kinfolk.

The capitol clocks were stopped during the night session on March 10 and time stood still within the marble halls for the next four days and nights. Near midnight, with tempers growing short, Representative Van Dyk led a group of eight ultra-liberal members off the floor in protest of a ruling made by Speaker Sylvester. They holed up in the men's lounge during a call of the house and dared Sergeant at Arms

Adams to come in after them. M. T. Neal announced that he was going home and Van Dyk expressed the opinion that "the speaker has broken all the rules of the house and we can break 'em too."

With the rest of the membership unable to proceed on the bill at hand (broadening vocational education programs for the state) until the eight dissidents returned, soothing moral 'suasion was applied and Van Dyk was mollified. He led his squad back on the floor and the bill was duly passed.

On March 12, with the session in its second night of overtime and a number of the members approaching a somnambulistic state, the conference committee on appropriations slipped in a $5.00 per month tax on every pinball and slot machine in the state. Although they were strictly illegal according to the state constitution, the number in operation is indicated by the fact that the $5.00 license fee would, it was estimated, raise $10 million to help balance the budget. Only two legislators objected to this somewhat cynical proposal to share in the proceeds of illicit gambling devices.

YOUNG AL ROSELLINI SPEAKS OUT

In the senate an assistant King county prosecuting attorney, Albert D. Rosellini, who was serving his first term and was, at the age of 29, the youngest member of either house, made his first major speech. "It legalized gambling by taxing pinball, slot and other machines. Since when has the state lost its moral fibre to permit slot machine gambling?" He also objected strongly to another section of the appropriation measure which removed the sales tax exemption from food.*

In the house, crusty Representative Van Dyk wanted a graduated net income tax instead of a gambling tax. "The state hasn't made an attempt to sell the graduated income tax to the people," he complained.

At 11 p.m. on March 13 the speaker of the house turned the rostrum over to wise-cracking

---

*Another freshman legislator that session was young Charles R. Savage of Mason county. As this is written, he is a member of the 44th legislature, the only survivor of the class of 1939.

"Salt Walter" Ed Riley of Seattle, who uttered one of the frankest statements of that or any legislative session . . . "I had no ideas when I came here and have very few to take home, but it was a great education." Before relinquishing the rostrum, Speaker Sylvester had finally designed to recognize one of the more obstreperous left-wingers, whose efforts to be heard he had thwarted throughout the session. "For what purpose do you rise?" he asked the frustrated one. "To make a motion," the left-winger replied. "State your motion," Sylvester intoned. The long-slighted legislator thereupon rose to his full height, placed his thumb against his nose, waggled his fingers vigorously in the direction of the speaker and seated himself without a word.

Later, in the wee hours of the morning, the 26th legislature adjourned *sine die*. Having been heralded 64 days earlier as an "economy session," it ended up by passing an all-time high budget of $215 million, which was $39 million more than the governor had requested and $50 million higher than that of the 1937 session. About $11 million in new taxes were authorized to provide some semblance of precarious balance to the fiscal package.

Governor Martin did about as well as in the previous session on executive request bills. He got his requested revision of the social security system, the sales tax on food, the requirement to show need in order to qualify for old age pensions, the separate social security and unemployment compensation departments and broadened vocational education programs removed from the control of the superintendent of public instruction.

But he lost the one he probably wanted most of all . . . a strict limitation on the lieutenant governor's power to call a special legislative session.

Other bills passed included an increase in the cigarette tax from one to two cents a pack, extension of the sales tax to liquor, the requirement that state, county and municipal governments pay sales tax on their purchases, authorization for prison honor camps for forestry work, the inmates to receive 25¢ a day for their labors, and a remarkable piece of special interest legislation permitting the lieutenant governor and state senators of over six years seniority to take the state bar examination regardless of whether they had attended law school, or for that matter, completed grammar school. The Pierce county delegation finally got its Tacoma Narrows bridge and King county a floating concrete bridge across Lake Washington, which the Seattle *Times* predicted would surely sink.

Among the hundreds of bills which failed to pass were measures to permit the serving of liquor by the drink, to reorganize the public school system and merge districts, to abolish straight ticket voting at primary elections, to regulate the shell fish industry, to revise forestry policies to foster sustained yield cutting, to encourage local independent gasoline refining, and to return fish traps to the Washington side of the Columbia river until such time as Oregon banned them from its waters. Among the more controversial casualties was a small loan bill granting highly usurious interest rates. Described by Van Dyk as "the stinkingest measure to come before the legislature," it was defeated amid specific charges that one legislator had been promised a $25,000 gratuity if he succeeded in pushing it through.

Governor Martin further winnowed the legislative chaff, vetoing $238,610 from the general and $56,470 from the supplementary appropriation bills. He likewise line-vetoed parts of the new social security bill which would have permitted court appeals from department rulings and require relief records to be kept confidential. He redlined the bill which would have made lawyers out of Vic Meyers and the senate and deleted the two million dollar appropriation from a measure authorizing Seattle to hold an international exposition in 1942. He did give his full blessing to authorization for the state to take over the C. J. Lord mansion as a state capital museum. It came as a gift from the late banker's wife and daughter.

After resting briefly from his veto session the governor issued orders for a 15 percent cut in all code department spending. Relief funds in Thurston county were cut in half . . . from $300,000 in 1938 to $145,000 . . . and 59 WPA workers supporting 212 dependents were laid off in a federal slash of funds for that agency. A lien clause in the latest public assistance act effected further economies, prompting 10 old age pensioners in the county to return their $30 a month subsistence checks rather than have state liens placed on their homes in the amount of their total grants.

GRAND JURY

The governor's life remained full of complications even after the legislators gave up and went home. The Thurston county grand jury had been continuing its deliberations throughout the legislative session.

On May 7 the capital city was rocked by the news that indictments had been handed down against Chief Cole and E. Pat Kelly, director of the department of labor and industries. Both were arrested by Sheriff Huntamer. Cole was subsequently released on $1,000 bail and Kelly on $5,000.

Kelly was charged with misconduct, grand larceny and misappropriation of accounts by a public official, more than $300,000 in accident and medical aid funds, it was said, having been diverted "for use of numerous persons not entitled thereto." Additional charges were added later, alleging that as an added exercise in petty larceny, he had arranged with a local garage to credit $4.00 a month to his account as his share of the storage fee for an imaginary state automobile, that he had failed to keep proper accounts, and that he had padded his expense account, the latter indiscretion adding perjury to the specific charges against him.

J. Webster Hoover, highway department construction engineer, was appointed acting director while the charges against Kelly were processed, Harry Huse having taken over Cole's chieftainship of the state patrol.*

Cole was charged with a single indictment . . . grand larceny involving fraudulent misappropriation of state property and the illegal use of state equipment and employees . . . but the jury's written report to the superior court judges was a detailed and damning document. It asserted that conditions in the Washington State Patrol under Cole were "shocking and almost beyond belief" and that the organization "had no business management at all." It cited the case of 23 slot machines stored at the Olympia headquarters, which had been rifled of their cash contents, as an example of rather lax stewardship. (Huse had the slots destroyed the day after he took over and turned over the few remaining coins to the state treasurer.)

---

*Times have changed and the current governor, taking the liberal view that everyone is innocent until proven guilty, has felt no compulsion to suspend his appointive officials who may happen to be under grand jury indictment.

The report stated further that "a virtual parade of paddy wagons and state trucks had for the past several years wended its way over highways from Olympia to eastern Washington and back to Cole's ranch carrying sacks of wheat, livestock, loads of potatoes and other produce." Continuing in an embarrassingly specific manner, it reported that the state vehicles had also transported pipe, cement, shingles, veneer and lumber, as well as a big bulldozer from the Coulee dam construction site . . . under the guise of "an experiment in overloading on state highways" . . . and the ponderous shipment was convoyed across the state by "numerous state patrolmen."

The jury further charged that Cole "would enter into strike troubles at the slightest provocation in order to later personally benefit thereby"; that phony license plates had been attached to the misused state vehicles, and that the patrolmen operating them had been ordered to disguise themselves as working men. Frequently the working clothes were authentic, it was said, because Cole was accustomed to order crews of state cops off the highways (where the traffic death rate was skyrocketing) to serve as farmhands on his ranch.

The jurors expressed the opinion that "several patrolmen, aping their chief, purchased small tracts and commenced to build and stock the premises in the manner they had observed practiced by the chief." Many other misdeeds among the rank and file were noted, including "misuse of requisition books and state credit cards for their own cars."

Martin's critics pointed to the state patrol fiasco as an example of what happens to Democratic governors who keep Republicans on in upper level state jobs when plenty of destitute and deserving Democrats are available to take over.

One of the long-time loyal Democrats of the capital city, Harry L. Parr, serving on the staff of Attorney General G. W. Hamilton, while criticizing Martin's subsidization of the grand jury with $3,000 from his emergency fund as "an attempt to run the state by grand jury," voiced that feeling when he conceded, "I don't mind Cole being indicted because he's a Republican."

The grand jury used its windfall from the governor to hire an ex-G-man, C. C. Spears, who had set himself up in business as a private eye after gaining wide fame in his solution of the Weyerhaeuser kidnapping case, and it continued to keep officialdom at Olympia in a state of nerves. The jurors even visited the city jail and found it in such a deplorable state that they ordered abatement proceedings against it if it wasn't cleaned up in a hurry.

When a 65-year-old former deputy county treasurer named Oscar Pritchard received a subpoena to appear before the jury he declined firmly by shooting himself to death with a 45-caliber automatic. The next day the jurors issued a statement that a $3,000 shortage had been found in the county treasurer's funds, embezzled by "one person" with the aid of a "poor bookkeeping system." Later secret indictments were handed down against two state tax commission agents, one at Seattle and one at Longview, charged with having pocketed taxpayers' money in the amounts of $300 and $3,500 respectively.

By the time they had finished, early the following year, the grand jurors had investigated 14 state departments as well as county and city agencies and had handed down seven indictments. Their final report was more critical than ever of the city jail and urged "greater enforcement against local vice and gambling, particularly bookmaking on horse races." It also criticized the lack of harmony between the Olympia police department, the sheriff and the state patrol and "the lack of harmony between the sheriff and the prosecuting attorney."

At the height of the grand jury furor, state Auditor Cliff Yelle was charged by the Clallam county prosecutor with nonfeasance in office for having failed to audit the books of the treasurer of that county for a two-year period from 1936 to 1938. The incoming county treasurer had discovered a $100,000 shortage, which he attributed to the delayed state audit. Yelle went to Port Angeles to post bond, explaining that the death of two of his top staff men had slowed the state's auditing processes.

To add to the general confusion, the Black Ball ferry crews went on strike again at the height of the summer tourist season. Martin, still nursing the wounds of his last involvement with Captain Peabody, his employees and indignant ferry patrons, was reluctant to get into the same mess again. Several hundred commuters from Vashon and Bainbridge islands invaded his office early in August to demand that he do something immediately to restore ferry service. When his secretary, Dick

Hamilton, explained that the chief executive was out of town, the islanders grew hostile. When the harassed secretary tried to soothe them by pointing out that federal mediation was under way and that Martin "wasn't trying to dodge the issue," they drove him away with a prolonged chorus of boos and Bronx cheers. When they learned that the governor was inspecting the state hospital for the insane at Steilacoom they expressed the opinion that he should be kept there indefinitely.

Violent crime was much reduced that year, the most sensational case being the kidnapping of a 22-year-old Olympia housewife from the steps of the post office by two knife-wielding men. She was driven to Grand Mound prairie, held four hours, raped several times and eventually released. Two suspects were quickly arrested, holed up in a shack in Little Hollywood, the Deschutes waterway slum. One of the abductor-rapists, a 16-year-old lad named Robert Kimmich, quickly confessed, attributing his actions to a three-day "bay rum drunk" and the smoking of three marijuana cigarettes, which he had purchased on the street shortly before the crime was committed. His 40-year-old companion, an ex-con named Jack Marable, was less talkative, but young Kimmich had done enough talking for both of them. The jury quickly recommended hanging for Marable and life imprisonment for Kimmich.

Although the police department had thus distinguished itself by quickly solving the only major crime of violence that year, the fire department suffered humiliation reminiscent of the days when the fire horses had to pull the mud-scraper and the hoses always burst at the first application of pressure. When the home of supreme court Chief Justice Bruce Blake on east 25th street caught fire on an early October afternoon, the firemen discovered that the 1910-model hook and ladder truck had succumbed to the infirmities of age. They couldn't get it started. In desperation, they summoned police aid and the decrepit fire engine was finally towed to the blaze by Officer Couch, with state patrolman Roy Carlson at the wheel of the disgraced apparatus. The *Olympian* reported that *"it was funny to onlookers, but not to the fire department."*

Judge Blake was presumably not overcome by mirth either. His three-story house was gutted by the fire before the hook and ladder made its ignominious trip up the hill to 25th street.

There were a few developments at which the community could point with pride. Another new office building, a duplicate of the Social Security building, was being constructed south of the Legislative building to the west and its completion would see the original Wilder and White design for the capitol group almost realized. All that remained was a sixth structure matching the Insurance building to replace the tottery brick veneer governor's mansion, which Martin complained was leaky, drafty and termite-ridden. The sixth building was essential to give proper balance to the dome-dominated capitol complex and there was general agreement that the sooner the mansion, which was three years older than the town hook and ladder truck, was demolished the better for all concerned.

A handsome new state armory was completed at the east side site of the old Washington school and the local national guard units moved out of their rented quarters in the American Legion hall. The move was made in the form of a full-dress parade, led by the Legion band, which would soon give added lustre to Olympia's image by winning the grand trophy at the American Legion national convention in Chicago.

Bud Ward won new laurels as national amateur golf champion and the recently organized Olympia little theater group presented three one-act plays under the direction of Mrs. B. F. Hume. Avid readers of movie magazines went into ecstacies of delight when 11 genuine Hollywood stars arrived in town to plug Warner Brothers' current motion picture epic, "The Old Maid." The stars were guests at a civic banquet in the Hotel Olympian, leading lady Rosella Towne being escorted by chubby Mayor Gammell, and leading man Ronald Reagan by Miss Helen Engel, who later disclosed to the *Olympian's* society editor that she had found Mr. Reagan to be *"a clean-cut type of young man surprisingly well versed on almost any subject."*

Early advocates of women's rights may have sneered at the public adulation of Hollywood sex symbols, but they were cheered when Olympia attorney June Fowles was appointed the state's first female assistant attorney general.

The increasing signs of wartime prosperity had, by early September, convinced the state finance committee that the state wouldn't have to go on a warrant basis to finance the latest legislative spending spree, but this proved to be an over-optimistic prediction. By the end of the year the committee ruefully admitted that the state treasury was in hock by more than five and a half million dollars, and the new year would start with all checks marked "unpaid for lack of funds." Major banks had agreed to accept them at par at one percent interest.

The great depression had maintained its icy grip on the nation for a decade and even after the economic sun began to shine, the thawing process was a slow one. The Tumwater Paper Mills became a victim of the depression's death throes when its mortgage was foreclosed by Portland and San Francisco banks.

The word "ecology" still wasn't in general use, but county Sanitarian William Fultz struck a blow for it anyway, urging people to stop just dumping garbage in the bay or on the surrounding beaches. His interesting solution to the problem of environmental pollution, according to the *Olympian,* was to *"flatten cans, break bottles and wrap garbage. Take well out in the bay, where cans and bottles sink to the bottom and the garbage floats out of Budd inlet."*

And, as if the capital city hadn't been shaken up enough recently, a sharp earthquake near midnight on November 12 came as an unexpected climax to the earlier celebration of the golden jubilee of statehood. Downtown buildings swayed and shed fragments of their cornices, windows rattled, dishes were broken and the Legislative building skylights crashed onto the desks in the house and senate chambers. Some felt it was providential that the legislators hadn't been occupying their seats at the time. Others expressed differing opinions. Governor Martin, riding it out in the tottering mansion admitted afterward, "—'ve never been so scared in my life."

1940

In the spring of 1940, 34-year-old Smith Troy, having achieved a remarkable 1,000 percent batting average in convictions for capital crimes during his terms as Thurston county prosecutor, was appointed state attorney general to succeed 81-year-old G. W. Hamilton, who died in office. His deputy, John S. Lynch, Jr., formerly the town's most beautiful baby, replaced Troy as prosecuting attorney.

Although the nation's wartime economy was reaching boom proportions, the last vestiges of the depression had not yet disappeared. A system of food stamps for the needy was instituted in Olympia early in the year and grocers and recipients joined in demand for countywide distribution. By early fall the food stamp program had, indeed, been extended to 11 southwest Washington counties as a means of providing surplus foods and alleviating hunger.

By that time the inevitability of full American involvement in the second world war was becoming apparent and it was dramatized by the alerting for federal service of all Washington national guard troops as part of a general mobilization of reserve forces. By mid-October 4,317 Thurston county men between the ages of 21 and 35 had registered for the draft. The citizen army was assembling and the streets of the capital city became crowded with uniformed service men from nearby Fort Lewis. Crowds jammed the Liberty theater to boo and hiss as Charlie Chaplin portrayed Adolf Hitler in "The Great Dictator."

The highway department was deeply embarrassed when, on November 7, the long-awaited and much heralded new Narrows bridge collapsed awesomely into the waters of Puget Sound. The span, which had earned the name of "Galloping Gertie" as result of its tendency to gyrate wildly when the wind blew, was the victim of an autumn storm which brought gusts a bit higher than usual. Its death agonies were caught by a motion picture cameraman and the film is still shown from time to time on national television.

Even more embarrassed than the highway engineers was the Tacoma insurance agent who had written the policy on the bridge. Reasoning that it was about as indestructible as the great pyramids of Egypt, he had pocketed the premiums. The bridge, most of which reposed on the bottom of the Narrows, was not insured.

The elections of that year also proved embarrassing to some, including Clarence D. Martin. Despite general predictions that he would be beaten if he ran for a third term and the harassments of his years in office, he decided to give it a try. Party Democrats favored former Speaker of the House George Yantis or Congressman Warren Magnuson, but Yantis' health was failing and Magnuson was convinced that he might enjoy a reasonably successful career in congress.

Others were urging Congressman Knute Hill to make the race and C. C. Dill was actively testing the political waters. Democrats conceded that they would need a strong candidate because it was generally believed that Stephen F. Chadwick, popular and personable former national commander of the American Legion, would be the Republican gubernatorial candidate in the general election.

Students of politics are still puzzled by Martin's determination to try for an unprecedented third term. He was only the second governor in the state's history to have survived two full terms and Republicans were making the third term issue a major basis of dispute as they termed Roosevelt's candidacy a threat to American democracy which verged on tyranny. Martin could easily have won the nomination for the senate seat which had recently been vacated by Schwellenbach, who had been appointed to the federal bench, and would almost certainly have won the position.

The best conjecture is that he probably fell victim to the messiah complex which has afflicted several Washington governors. For eight years he had seen himself as the defender of the state against "those red devils," the Seattle left-wingers, and their plots to plunder the treasury and bankrupt the working taxpayers. He was probably convinced that he was the one man who could continue to keep the ship of state on an even keel; that he was, in short, the indispensable man.

More practically, he may have also convinced himself that many Republicans, who shared his conservative philosophy, would come to his aid in the primaries as they had in past elections. If so, he had failed to take into account the strong and sometimes violent opposition to the third term principal engendered among Republicans by the Roosevelt campaign.

In the primary election he lost to Dill by a vote of about 186,000 to 114,000, with Tom Smith, later to become a much publicized warden of the state penitentiary, coming in a poor third.

THE VIRGIN POLITICAL BIRTH OF ARTHUR LANGLIE

Chadwick having decided to go after the senate seat vacated by Schwellenbach, the Republicans came forth with a rising young political prodigy as their standard-bearer in the race for the governorship.

Arthur B. Langlie had begun his career as a struggling lawyer in Seattle and might have continued in that role had it not been for a Seattle political phenomenon known as the New Order of Cincinnatus. It was organized by idealistic young men who were fed up with the civic corruption which had, ever since the days of John Pennell, festered in the heart of the Queen City of the Pacific Northwest. They established an almost superhumanly moralistic code of ethics and embarked upon a search for city council candidates who would subscribe to it.

By 1935 the Cincinnatians had one unsuccessful campaign behind them, had learned a good deal about politicking on a shoestring, and were loaded for bear. They had assembled what they believed to be an impressive slate of councilmanic candidates, but an unfortunate turn of events eliminated one of them at the last minute. He was endorsed by a local Republican club. This violated the order's code of strict non-partisanship and he was considered to be disqualified.

At this critical juncture the pious young attorney, Langlie, was produced as a possible alternative. Although not a member of the order, he let it be known that their high principles were exactly in accord with his own and that he would be only too happy to sign their pledge of nonpartisanship, refusal to accept more than $25 in campaign contributions from anyone, etc. He would also be proud and pleased as punch to be one of their candidates for the Seattle city council.

Two of the Cincinnatus candidates won and Arthur B. Langlie was one of them. Having thus gotten his foot in the political door, he soon forgot all about the vows of poverty he had taken with the Order of Cincinnatus, launched a well-financed campaign for mayor, was elected and served two terms. He had discovered a formula for successful civic leadership in Seattle. If one assumed a role of sanctimonious righteousness and, from time to time, issued statements reminiscent of the Sermon on the Mount, while ostentatiously attending church and participating in Boy Scout, Sunday school, evangelical and other good works, the illicit gambling, prostitution and police payoffs could continue relatively undisturbed while the local pastorate and press proclaimed that all was well.*

The Seattle mayor's office has traditionally been a political cemetery. No one before or since Langlie ever got very far in the practice of statesmanship, although Ole Hanson was at one time convinced that he, rather than Herbert Hoover was going to be the Republican candidate for president.**

Langlie was the exception. The Order of Cincinnatus had broken up in his wake, but he didn't need them any more. The fat-cat Republicans of the state were solidly behind him in his bid for higher office.

As expected, Langlie swept the Republican primary, rolling up over 160,000 votes to a combined total of less than 20,000 for his two opponents.

Chadwick easily won the Republican nomination for U.S. senator, while Mon Wallgren defeated Frank T. Bell of Ephrata, former secretary to Senator Dill and considered by many to be the man who got the Grand Coulee project for Washington, and Martin's political trouble-shooter, Harry Huse.

A young ex-newsboy who appeared to have his head screwed on right, Henry M. (Scoop) Jackson of Everett, got the Democratic nomination for Wallgren's former house seat and was faced in the general election by the Republicans' perennial second district congressional candidate, Payson Peterson.

With one notable exception, the 1940 general election was another Democratic landslide. Roosevelt won his third term and, for the first time in Washington, led the ticket with more

Governor Arthur B. Langlie.

than 462,000 votes. All six Democratic congressional candidates were successful, all state elective offices went to Democrats, and the legislature received a 68 to 31 Democratic majority in the house; 37 to nine in the senate. Two of the new state elective officers were women, Belle Reeves, who won the office of secretary of state in her own right, defeating Albert Johnson, and Pearl Wanamaker, who ousted Stanley Atwood from the state school superintendency.

The exception was the race for the governorship. Arthur Langlie nosed Dill out by such a narrow margin that the results weren't known for sure for several months. As is usual in such close elections, there were cries of voting irregularities and demands for recounts, but when the political dust settled, Langlie was declared the official winner by a margin of less than 4,000 votes. It was aparent that the "Martin Republicans" of past years had eased their consciences and returned to the party fold.

Clarence D. Martin, having turned the executive offices and mansion over to his successor, returned to Cheney and private life with a record of accomplishment which would place him on the level of such landmark

---

*Three subsequent Seattle mayors successfully adopted this technique and its efficacy is demonstrated by the fact that their images have remained untarnished through bombings, police scandals, gambling exposes and grand jury investigations.

**Holy Ole may not have been elected president, but after the city purchased the rickety street railway from Stone & Webster during his administration, he migrated to California and staked out a new city which he named San Clemente. It might be said that Ole never got to the White House, but the White House eventually came to him.

governors as John Rogers and Marion Hay. Rogers' administration had seen the reform of the public school system, Hay's administration the reform of governmental processes, and Martin's the emergence of public concern for human needs and human dignity. The specter of the poorhouse had been removed from the lives of thousands through the old age pension. Workers, out of a job through no fault of their own, could rely upon unemployment compensation to feed their families.

On the other hand, the state had been kept solvent as Martin led the way along a path of moderation, unshaken by the slings and arrows of the radical left-wingers who howled for panaceas that would have bankrupted the treasury in a matter of months.

During Martin's tenure in office the Grand Coulee-Columbia basin projects had become a reality, the Lake Washington and Tacoma Narrows bridges had been built (although in the latter case the job had to be done over again), the state had begun the operation of ferries on a limited basis and the highway system had begun to emerge from the Model-T era.

The state had weathered the worst of the great depression. Although there was still unemployment and economic distress, industry was gearing up for all-out war effort and the unemployment rolls were dropping monthly. It was obvious, as Arthur Langlie took the helm of the ship of state, that the corner around which Hoover had insisted a decade earlier property lay, was about to be rounded at last.

1941

The year which was to end in infamy at Pearl Harbor began in Washington's capital city amid an atmosphere of business as usual. The 27th legislature would soon be assembling to give a boost to Olympia's already strengthening economy. The sawmills, the plywood plants, the brewery, the cannery and the knitting mills were back in full production and the relief rolls were declining, although 856 Thurston county residents were making use of the federal government's surplus food stamps. By mid-year 107 men, women and children in the county were collecting a total of $1,952 a month in social security payments, and it was predicted by many that the marvelous new plan would eliminate poverty from the nation with the coming generation.

The state liquor store was still dispensing good Kentucky straight bourbon whiskey at $2.00 a quart and Safeway was advertising prime beefyeaks at 29¢ a pound, bacon at 23¢, salmon at 17¢ and bread at 9¢ for a full pound loaf.

The citizen who might be moved to trade in a jalopy he had been nursing through the depression years could buy a new Nash "Big Six" sedan from Ray's Texaco for $961, or a six-passenger Packard from Frank Thorp for $990. The home-seeker could look at Capital Realty company's brand-new five-room house on the east side, listed at $3,200, Gerald Sophy's 40-acre farm with house, barn and spring water, on the highway just west of town at $2,200, or rent a three-bedroom south end home near the capitol for $40 a month. Penneys was featuring men's suits . . . single or double breasted . . . for $15, and Keeton-Smith Furniture company would install a new Kelvinator refrigerator for $149.95.

There remained some doubt at the beginning of the new year as to just who would be running the state for the next four years. Democrats, who had achieved an otherwise clean sweep of the last election, were unwilling to concede that Arthur Langlie had, in fact, defeated Dill. Olympia Postmaster Ben Sawyer, a loyal Democrat if there ever was one, filed a petition with the secretary of state challenging Langlie's election on the grounds of voting fraud. The point at issue involved the large number of voters who had voted an otherwise straight Democratic ticket, but had crossed over to mark an individual vote for Langlie. Democrats claimed that many of the cross-overs were marked "by other than the voter" and that since a change of one vote per precinct would have elected Dill, he should, in fact, be the state's chief executive.

The legislature convened the day after Sawyer's petition was presented to Belle Reeves and there was considerable confusion as to whether the inaugural ball could be held until after it was decided who the governor was. Realtor Sophy, president of the chamber of commerce, announced that it *would* be held . . . at the new armory . . . that Langlie *would* lead the grand march, and that music would be provided by Joe E. Bowen's Washington Athletic club orchestra.

Election uncertainty spread to the state senate soon after it was called to order by Vic Meyers and George Lovejoy of King county had been elected president pro-tem. The senators refused to seat Agnes Gehrman, Grays Harbor Republican, whose election was being challenged by her opponent, who had lost by 10 votes, and Lenus Westman, Snohomish Democrat, who was charged with being a former member of the Communist party. Senator Gehrman was soon permitted to take her place in the august assemblage with the other lady senator, Mrs. Farquharson, King county Democrat, but Westman, a 31-year-old farmer, was less fortunate. Although a senate investigating committee headed by Senator Shirley Marsh of Cowlitz submitted a majority recommendation supporting Westman, the vote was 27 to 17 against him on the floor. Super-patriotism was again becoming popular in the brinksmanship atmosphere of 1941 and the majority of the senators felt it prudent to placate the American Legion, DAR and the far from silent majority which knew that communism was bad.

The house of representatives, having been called to order by Chief Clerk Holcomb at noon on Janury 13, proceeded to elect "Fresh Water" Reilly to a second term as speaker,* and confirm Holcomb as chief clerk for another session. Charles Maybury, having devoted himself to repeated unsuccessful efforts to unseat Vic Meyers as lieutenant governor, Holcomb had by this time achieved the all-time record for longevity among chief clerks.

On January 14 Clarence Martin made his farewell address to the legislature, pointing to the progress of social security programs as the major accomplishment of his administration. He recommended a welfare budget of $59 million for the coming biennium, which was almost the exact cost of all state government in the Hartley year of 1925.

Amid the nostalgic atmosphere of farewell Martin apparently even forgave Meyers for the expensive cross-country airplane flight he had been forced to undertake. When the lieutenant governor queried, "Well, Governor, aren't you going to kiss me goodbye?" the usually somewhat prim Martin scarcely turned a hair.

"Sure," he replied, embracing the debonair Meyers and kissing him on the cheek, while the galleries roared with delighted laughter.

There was little doubt by this time that Langlie would be inaugurated as governor, although the Democratic die-hards, led by Sawyer, continued to petition the legislature to declare the office vacant pending some sort of investigation. George Kinnear of King, floor leader of the 31-member house minority, issued a strongly-worded statement in defense of Langlie, charging that efforts to block his inauguration were "initiated by henchmen of the Seattle machine," and that the move was "not only left-wing in its origin, but also an effort to place a particular state political power similar to those machines which have wrecked several eastern states."

Speaker Reilly, a political realist even though a Democrat, responded with the assurance that unless direct evidence of election fraud were presented the issue would not be brought before the legislature. The Democrats, in caucus, followed this up with an overwhelming vote to ignore all contests of Langlie's election. Vic Meyers, who had argued heatedly for a legislative investigation of the election fraud charges, ended up meekly signing the certificate along with speaker Reilly.

The former Cincinnatian was duly sworn in at 11:01 a.m. on January 15, 1941, by Chief Justice John S. Robinson, along with the solidly Democratic corps of lesser elected officials . . . Lieutenant Governor Meyers, Secretary of State Reeves, Attorney General Troy, Auditor Yelle, Insurance Commissioner William A. Sullivan, Treasurer Otto Case and Land Commissioner Jack Taylor. Case, a dedicated politician at all levels of government, had served one term as treasurer in 1932, when incumbents in that office were limited to a single term. Taylor had served the two terms as King county commissioner then permitted by statute before moving up to state elective office.

At 40, Langlie was the youngest governor in the state's history, and he had other reasons to congratulate himself as he took the oath of office. On election eve the odds had been five to three against him and he had survived one of the closest . . . and certainly the most loudly contested . . . gubernatorial elections since 1889.

*A tradition had existed in the house of representatives since statehood that a member should serve only one term as speaker, then step politely aside and give somebody else his 90 days in the limelight. The tradition was dying out by 1941.

John L. O'Brien, 35-year legislative veteran.

Among the young legislators who watched the inauguration ceremonies were 31-year-old Senator Albert Rosellini, 29-year-old sophomore Representative Perry B. Woodall and a 30-year-old freshman representative named John L. O'Brien.

The senior political figure present that day was patriarchal Senator Charles M. Baldwin of Pomeroy, who had been a member of the house of representatives in the first state legislature of 1889 and subsequently from 1921 to 1925. He had thus served in all three capitol buildings . . . the territorial capitol of 1856, the old sandstone statehouse and the new Legislative building.

PAINLESS TAXES?

Langlie's inaugural message to the legislature recommended balancing the budget through economy and "comparatively minor new taxes", including a license fee on pinball

machines. He wanted a merit system for the state's 7,500 employees "to attract capable workers, freed from political control," a further consolidation of state agency functions, and immediate reconstruction of the ill-fated Narrows bridge.

Martin's proposed budget had totaled $211,201,517 for the coming biennium, an increase of about $4½ million. Receipts were estimated at $200,169,850, with the balance sheet showing a deficit of more than $11 million without new taxes. The social security budget was up $17,603,000 to nearly $59 million, of which federal grants accounted for slightly less than $22 million.

Auditor Yelle was less optimistic. In his opinion, the passage of Initiative 141 at the 1940 general election, which raised maximum old age pensions to $40 a month, would result in social security costs of $81 million.

Langlie's version of the budget proposed $6 million in "painless taxes," which included a gift tax, increased inheritance tax, higher fuel oil tax and the licensing of such constitutionally illegal gambling devices as pinballs, slots and punchboards. He proposed to effect $3½ million in governmental economies, transfer $2.2 million in available cash to the general fund from other sources, and predicted confidently that the improving economy would increase revenue from current sources by $8,251,500.

The Domocratic majorities in house and senate immediately began a strategic campaign to "put Langlie on the spot" for heavier taxes to meet the needs of the state. They also threatened that if he didn't keep his campaign promises to curtail overlapping state bureaus and commissions they would solve the problem for him by amputating most of his code departments and transplanting them into the bodies politic of the Democratic elective officials.

Speaker Reilly bravely pointed the way toward governmental economies by cutting the pay of all house employees to save $2,000 weekly. So pleased were the legislators by this display of fiscal responsibility that they forthwith voted themselves an additional $5.00 a day for expenses. This cost the taxpayers an extra $5,180 a week, for a net loss of $3,180. It was also quite unconstitutional.

The governor, blandly ignoring the gathering storm clouds on Capitol hill, attended a prayer breakfast at the Olympian as guest of the Washington State Breakfast Groups. It was reported that *"a religious atmosphere pervaded the room, for the organization is founded upon Christian precepts."* The 300 guests were doubtless comforted when Langlie rose to announce that he was going to *"count on Divine guidance in the solution of the state's problems."*

Such an aura of righteousness surrounded the young and balding governor that one could, indeed, visualize the Supreme Being dropping in from time to time at the mansion to advise him on affairs of state, although as his years in office multiplied, it was believed by many that Langlie was giving the advice to the Almighty.

PROFITEERING AND PUGILISM

The authorization of increased daily expense money for the legislators focused their attention on the ancient charges that Olympians, like resort hotel operators, raised their charges to astronomical heights during sessions and lived high off the hog on the proceeds of their profiteering throughout the interim.

Senator Joe Drumheller of Spokane sponsored a bill giving the department of public service control over the price of food and lodging in all cities with populations of between 12,500 and 13,500. When it occurred to Thurston county's dapper Senator Carl Mohler that Olympia was the only city in the state falling within that population bracket, he girded for battle, leading off with an amendment that the rate regulations also apply to cities with populations of from 121,000 to 122,000, which would have taken care of Drumheller's home town. Mohler's amendment was tabled amid a storm of indignation and the most impassioned oratory of the session. Drumheller roared that his bill was designed to "stop Olympia profiteering on legislators," charging that "the capital has the champion robbers of the state" and "takes us for a swell ride every session."

"I never saw such a place with such a disregard for justice and fairness," chimed in Senator Charles F. Stinson of Benton county. He was followed by most of the out-of-town senators, all of them expressing similar opinions. After tabling Mohler's amendment,

the bill was sent to committee for revisions. The debate had given the senators an opportunity to let off steam and it did not reappear on the floor, but the bad blood between Drumheller and Mohler continued to simmer. It reached the boiling point when Drumheller got Mohler's per diem payments cut off on the grounds that he already lived in Olympia and so suffered no out-of-pocket loss in performing his legislative duties.

The *Olympian* subsequently reported in great detail an encounter between the two embattled senators *"in the wee small hours of Saturday morning, March 2 in an Olympia cafe."* Mohler, it seems, was already in the cafe with a party of friends and relatives when Drumheller and Earl Maxwell, a one-legged senator from Seattle entered. Drumheller and Mohler, according to the *Olympian, "became engaged in an altercation,"* with Mohler ending up under a cutting table in the kitchen.

When the three principal figures in the pre-dawn drama failed to show up for the Saturday session of the senate, *"rumors flew thick and fast".* It was said that Mother had been dragged bodily to Percival's dock and thrown into the chilly waters of Budd Inlet and that Maxwell, who claimed he hadn't even been there, had *"suffered an irreparable fracture of his artificial leg".*

All three eventually put in an appearance, Drumheller explaining that he had been "cooling off in his room", Mohler denying that he had been dunked in Puget Sound, and Maxwell displaying his wooden leg to newsmen to prove that it was still sound. Drumheller attributed the melee to Mohler having called him a double-crosser because he and Maxwell had refused to approve Mohler's expense account. Mohler, explaining that he had "stayed home today to get a little rest", said he thought Drumheller was mad because he and other newer senators had been meeting prior to sessions to "go over the day's calendar."

"A bunch of the old wheel-horses are sore about those meetings", he added, inferring that Drumheller was a leader of the old guard senators who favored secrecy, smoke-filled rooms and a reasonable degree of corruption.

The *Olympian* concluded its commentary on the affair with the information that a large sack of Yakima onions was *"scattered willy nilly about the cafe premises",* causing those who sought to intercede to suffer humiliating pratfalls and adding to the old-fashioned two-reel comedy atmosphere which seemed to prevail.

It concluded with the jocose suggestion that *"if a rematch is arranged, Senator Maxwell, the little man who wasn't there, would be a knockout as the invisible referee".*

WHO EVER HEARD
OF A GOOD WAR?

Although this constituted the only recorded case of physical violence during the 1941 session, there was no lack of verbal jousting. A particularly noisy encounter took place early in the session when resolutions were introduced by conservative Democrats commending President Roosevelt for his "aid to the democracies", and by left-wing Democrats voicing criticism of the undue power of the president in granting war aid to Great Britain. As the house chambers echoed to the voices of those arguing for unlimited aid to the warring democracies of Europe and those arguing for no aid, a delegation of "Women for Peace" entered the galleries carrying placards expressing anti-war sentiments. The ladies let their signs speak for them until Representative H. C. (Army) Armstrong of King responded with a chandelier-shaking "Aye!" on the pro-aid resolution. Then they began chanting, "We want peace!" After banging his gavel futilely for some time, Speaker Reilly summoned Sergeant at Arms W. Newton Fry and assigned him the unenviable task of throwing the demonstrative ladies out of the galleries.

Emotions ran high on the floor as well as in the galleries. When the house voted down the anti-aid resolution of Pierce county liberal Edward Pettus, the white-haired pacifist leaped to his feet and thundered, "This is a war for economic empire!"

His seat-mate 28th district Pierce county Representative J. H. Ryan, who believed like most red-blooded Americans that anyone who preferred peace to war was unpatriotic, ventured the opinion that if Pettus had dared to make such a speech while campaigning in the 27th district, "he wouldn't be here today".

After the worst of the tumult and chanting had subsided, the house voted 76 to 20 to support President Roosevelt in his efforts to make the United States the arsenal of democracy. The action was doubtless a great comfort to FDR.

While the representatives thus exacerbated one another's feelings in hot debate on matters of worldwide import, the senators were engaging in somewhat naughty jollity. President Pro-Tem Lovejoy presented brightly colored nighties to the two lady senators, Farquharson and Gehrman, on behalf of Mrs. Anna Romanovsky, who operated the Legislative building cafeteria. The lady senators giggled and blushed in a fitting manner and the risibilities of members and galleryites alike were tickled mightily when some wag suggested that Senators Farquharson and Gehrman should save their gift nighties to wear at the inevitable night sessions which would be coming up in March.

THE RULES COMMITTEE
IS UNRULY

A couple of days later Senator N. P. Atkinson of King, who didn't approve of Vic Meyers' committee appointments, arose on a point of personal privilege to denounce the lieutenant governor's choices. "These committees do not represent their purpose," he thundered. "The personnel of the social security committee makes it look unsocial; the judiciary committee unjudicious and the rules committee unruly!"

Soon afterward the *Olympian,* echoing the journalistic complaints which have echoed down the corridors of time since 1854, announced that the legislature had been in session 15 days and that *"their one accomplishment, aside from oratorical outbursts brought on by numerous investigations of one kind and another, was passage of a bill providing their membership with personal expense money for the session."* The *Olympian's* political analyst then hazarded the wishful opinion that *"Monday may see the legislature get down to actual business."* Two weeks later the writer conceded defeat. *"Little has been accomplished thus far because the leaders are too busy figuring ways to embarrass the Republican governor and still appear friendly toward him."*

Ostensibly in the interests of cooperation between the legislative and executive branches, a unique house-senate "contact committee" of 15 members was appointed to provide liaison between the third-floor chambers and the governor's office on the second floor, but the Democratic wheeler-dealers were concentrating their real efforts on the move to take most of Langlie's powers away from him.

It was originally planned to give the tax commission to Treasurer Case, the state patrol to Attorney General Troy, the license and agriculture departments to Secretary of State Reeves and all auditing functions to Auditor Yelle. The scheme soon ran into problems brought about by the traditional proclivity of Democrats to quarrel among themselves. Otto Case insisted he wanted the license department, not the tax commission. Smith Troy said he wouldn't touch the state patrol with a ten-foot pole, and Belle Reeves and Vic Meyers both demanded the state progress commission as their spoils of the political wars.

In an effort to reach some sort of agreement, closed-door Democratic caucuses were held for the purpose of twisting enough arms to insure a two-thirds majority, which would surely be needed to override the governor's veto. This generated much anger among independent-minded Democrats, of which there are always plenty, and it was reported by insiders that the house lacked 10 to 15 votes and the senate four of the number needed to quash a veto.

As alternatives, bills were quickly prepared to create a state safety commission, to remove the state patrol from Langlie's control, and a highway commission to replace his appointive director, Burwell Bantz.

Langlie, apparently secure in the knowledge that God was with him, ignored the political machinations and delivered a supplementary message suggesting that the sales tax be raised from two to three cents to meet increased old age pension costs. The number of pensioners had risen, since the passage of Initiative 141, from 40,000 to 60,000.

The senate turned down another proposal to raise old age pension money by a constitutional amendment to permit a state lottery and Senator Mohler demanded, "'Let's have a graduated net income tax. Let's get legitimate revenue. Let's not let the state be put into illegitimate business."

He did not attempt to explain why he thought it was alright to gamble on horse races or state-licensed slot machines, but not on a state lottery.

In any event, the income tax proposal didn't even get as far as the lottery bill, and in the midst of the confusion some black-hearted Republican dropped a measure in the hopper to abolish the elective office of state auditor and turn Yelle's duties over to Langlie's department of finance, budget and business. Representative Hugh J. Rosellini countered with a marvelously simplistic proposal to put the governor down in grand style. His bill would create a state executive board consisting of Republican Langlie and Democrats Reeves, Case, Troy, Yelle, Taylor and Wanamaker. By majority vote, this body could appoint or remove all code department directors and members of administrative committees.

The session had started amid torrential January rains caused by the bank behind the under-construction Transportation building to give way, burying a tractor and its operator in mud (both were rescued and put back to work), but by early March the sun was out and temperatures rose to an unprecedented 75 degrees. The pace of legislative action accelerated with the thermometer. On March 8, the agreed-upon cut-off date for the two houses to act upon their own bills, the clocks were stopped for seven hours while legislators shouted at each other over the highway appropriations bill. The *Olympian,* which seemed to hold the wooden-legged senator from King county in rather low regard, reported that *"Maxwell, the Seattle pundit who seems to feel his oats on Saturdays, very nearly precipitated fisticuffs".*

On March 9, with five days left, the senate was plowing at full steam through 200 house bills, while the house was engaged in winnowing 155 senate bills. Many fell by the wayside, including Langlie's executive request bills to institute an employees' merit system, reorganize the department of labor and industries, place the state patrol under the highway department and set up a forestry conservation program.

So did all the Democratic bills to remove authority and state departments from the governor, to tax chain stores, submit an income tax referendum to the voters, legalize a wide range of gambling and liberalize the liquor laws.

To the credit of the senate, it must be recorded that it refused, after eight years of reform, to return to the pork barrel highway appropriation system in which individual legislators earmarked funds for pet projects within their districts. Although the house had marched angrily on the senate to demand reconsideration, the highway planning process remained more or less in the department of highways.

The 27th legislature staggered to an end at 11:38 a.m. on March 15, the clocks having been stopped for two days. The galleries were deserted and only 17 senators and 54 representatives remained on the floor. When a committee was appointed to inform the governor that the legislature was about to adjourn *sine die*, he said, "I can't say I'm sorry" (which was certainly a masterpiece of understatement); I've been warming up the red ink until you leave here."

He was as good as his word, vetoing, among other measures, bills permitting beer taverns to operate an extra hour on Saturday nights, liberalizing libel laws relating to radio stations, apportioning a bigger share of the gasoline tax to county road funds, and giving wives equal control with husbands over community property.

Among the bills which survived were the three cent sales tax (with provision that the tax would revert back to two cents "if and when a graduated net income tax is put into operation") the unconstitutional licensing (and taxing) of pinballs, slots and punchboards, the gift tax and a measure plugging loopholes in the inheritance tax. In all, 274 bills were passed, most of them, as is always the case, of interest only to their sponsors, lawyers and the special interest groups or individuals they were designed to serve.

Among the less widely publicized bills was one which designated the former C. J. Lord mansion as a state capitol historical museum. In anticipation of the event, a State Capitol Historical association had been incorporated earlier and had helped Thurston county representatives Ralph Armstrong and Earl R. Warnica draft the bill.

The biennial budget for 1942-1943 totaled $259,075,652, of which $190,199,429 was "state money." It set another "all-time record," an accomplishment which the legislature had been achieving with monotonous regularity for most of its 27 sessions.

Vic Meyers, who had long since metamorphized from buffoon to astute politician and polished parliamentarian, proved his political clout by getting his budget raised from the $4,800 recommended by Langlie to $12,000,

including a new and rather vague line item headed "maintenance . . . $7,200."

The *Olympian's* valedictory to the late session included the information that *"phrase coiners agree the 1941 legislature should be dubbed the Raucous Caucus or the Anti-Pork Barrel Session."*

THE BANDS BEGIN TO PLAY AGAIN

In the capital city, as in the state as a whole, there was much preoccupation with the war in Europe. The democracies had their backs to the wall and the totalitarian powers were winning. The inevitability of eventual direct involvement was becoming more widely accepted every day.

On February 2 the 194 Olympia national guardsmen of the 205th Coast Artillery were mustered into the Army of the United States at the armory on Legion Way. The streets were given a martial touch three times a day as they marched back and forth from the armory to the Elks club on Capitol Way for meals. Ten days later the citizen soldiers moved on to the 41st Division cantonment area at Fort Lewis.

A local unit of the Washington State Guard was already in the process of organization to take over the armory and perform home guard duties during the absence of the federalized national guard. Captain Clarence B. Shain, county engineer and a former master sergeant in the 205th, carried on an active recruiting campaign and was well on the way toward mustering in an effective force when Governor Langlie, in a remarkable display of prescience, suddenly ordered the state guard units dissolved . . . five days before the national guard was ordered into federal service. It was a second frustration for Shain, who still hasn't forgiven Colonel Dohm for not taking him along on active duty with the 205th, and he was not placated by Langlie's bland explanation that he deemed it "inadvisable to attempt to finance and maintain armed forces other than the state police." By mid-summer, however, the governor had changed his mind and Captain Shain had the satisfaction of mustering into service the Olympia company of the 4th Washington Volunteer Infantry regiment, along with units of 14 other Washington cities.

417

SHOWN IN PHOTOGRAPH

First Row: T. A. Randall, A. K. Bowlin, I. W. Dorland, R. E. Dye, R. D. Phillips, W. C. Engdahl, W. S. Fultz.

Second Row: C. A. Sulenes, L. K. Pennington, D. W. Simon, M. E. Schoppe, F. J. Irish, R. F. Clem, R. R. Hawkins.

Third Row: R. B. MacConnell, A. C. Peringer, W. H. Wagner, J. D. Walters, V. L. Hull, E. M. Petty, C. E. MacConnell, G. F. Andresen, T. A. Randall.

Two hundred local women were being recruited as volunteer observers in the aircraft warning service, Red Cross ladies went back into uniform and a women's motor corps was organized and uniformed. Its members learned to change tires and make mechanical repairs; skills which almost all of them have forgotten over the intervening years.

The Junior Chamber of Commerce opened the Olympia Army-Navy club on the ground floor of the old statehouse to provide hospitality of sorts for the increasing numbers of lonesome soldiers from Fort Lewis who were haunting the city streets in a vain search for something to do on a 12-hour pass.

EDWARD C. DOHM
Major, Commanding 248th Coast Artillery

IT'S THE WATER: Modern plant of the Olympia Brewing company, upper Tumwater Falls and park in the foreground.

The shipbuilding boom of the first world war did not repeat itself as far as Olympia was concerned, although Al Lewis of the Reliable Welding works, who had been building occasional small steel craft in association with H. C. Hanson since 1929, * was turning out welded steel oil barges of 100,000-gallon capacity for use in inland waters, and it was announced in August that three Tacoma residents had incorporated the Olympia Shipbuilding company. A lease was signed for 40 acres at the north end of the port fill (the original name of Carlyon fill had fallen into disuse by 1941), where it was planned to build a shipyard for the construction of concrete barges and other specialized craft. A payroll of

3,000 was predicted, but the company's operations never approached such a grand scale. Its major accomplishment was the production of a half dozen big wooden coal-burning steam tugs for the British admiralty.

CIVIC PROGRESS . . . AT ANY COST

The preoccupation with martial affairs was not so great as to bring civic progress to a complete halt. A one-way traffic pattern was established on 4th and State streets (over the outraged protests of merchants along those thoroughfares, who yelled to a man that they would all be out of business within six months) in an effort to solve the colossal traffic snarls caused by the routing of all cross-state highway traffic through the city streets. Traf-

*Hanson, a well-known Seattle naval architect, was superintendent of the old Sloan shipyard during first world war days. Currently semi-retired, he is the owner of the Hotel Olympian.

fic lights were installed at intersections along the new one-way thoroughfares, allegedly synchronized for continuous traffic flow at 20 miles an hour.

Parking meters suddenly blossomed like metal toadstools along miles of streets. Preoccupied pedestrians, unused to such obstacles, frequently collided with the meters and seemed to hate them even more than the motorists who were forced to feed them pennies.

The citizens of Tumwater held a town meeting and announced that they were no longer opposed to the construction of a dam to transform the southernmost tip of Puget Sound into a lake. The brewery had long since rebuilt its plant away from tidewater and no longer felt the need for sternwheel steamboats to transport its product. It was felt that, unless the outbreak of war interfered, the long-discussed Capitol Lake would soon become a reality, and the city fathers decided, as a preliminary step, to eliminate Little Hollywood from the shores of the Deschutes waterway along the Northern Pacific railyard.

The capture of the two kidnapper-rapists of the town's last sensational crime in one of Little Hollywood's shacks had given the place a bad name and it was undeniably a civic eyesore. The residents were, in fact, mostly decent poor and elderly people trying to hold onto the last of their independence. Most had bought their shoreside shacks and floathouses from previous owners for anywhere from $10 to $50. There were about 50 WPA families, 30 old age pensioners and a few direct welfare recipients. Some of the more able-bodied supported themselves by odd jobs and scavenging. One resident was said to be a formerly prosperous farmer who had lost everything except $50 in the depression. He had spent his remaining fortune on the floathouse he occupied.

The city had been offered federal funds to provide low-cost housing, but Mayor Trullinger didn't believe in federal handouts. Besides, low rent housing might bring an undesirable class of people to town ... the kind who had the bad taste and judgment to be aged, handicapped, poor or some color other than pure white.

The people of Little Hollywood were served eviction notices and the civic authorities turned deaf ears on their pleas for someplace to go. One after another, the shacktown occupants surrendered and went away . . . some to rundown rooming houses and fleabag hotels, some to other towns. A few of the old age pensioners moved to a modernized version of the old fashioned poor farm which was appearing on the Northwest scene. First euphemistically called "havens for old folks," they later became "nursing homes." The proprietors of some of them, then as now, adopted the adage of the poor farm supervisors ... "The less you feed 'em the better the profit."

One after another the shacks and floathouses were burned or demolished and a civic eyesore vanished and was forgotten . . . just like the people who had been driven from it.

It was listed as one of the proudest accomplishments of Mayor Trullinger's administration.

DAY OF INFAMY

No one who was alive and aware of events in Olympia or anywhere else in America on the morning of December 7, 1941, will forget where he was or what he was doing when the word flashed over the airwaves that Japanese bombers had raided the great Pearl Harbor naval base on a quiet Sunday morning and virtually wiped out the Pacific fleet along with what American air power had existed in the Hawaiian islands.

As the last days of that fateful year ticked off, the citizens of the Pacific coast and its pitifully ill-equipped and largely untrained military garrisons braced themselves for the assault of Japanese battle fleets and bombers and the Banzai charge of assault troops across the sand dunes of Moclips or Copalis or Pacific Beach. Experienced military men conceded privately that when they came there would be no stopping them west of the Rocky mountains.

The new war time year was ushered in with a more ominous sound than that of the traditional Chinese firecrackers and mill whistles. Early in January the Olympia *News* reported that *"Olympia's immense air raid warning siren blasted out its shrill notes Tuesday in a try-out effort. As anticipated, it proved the noisiest thing in Olympia and well suited to the purpose for which it was intended.*

"While its wail produced an eerie sensation in the ear drums its grave warning, in the

420

future, may save the lives of many Olympians should Axis bombers suddenly appear over the area."

The siren, the gift of O. R. Rockway and C. H. Leland, was mounted atop the new Rockway-Leland building at State and Washington. It was a good central location and had the added advantage that radio station KGY had moved its studios to that location, so the city's air warning center was in direct electronic communication with the rest of the nation.

Such defense preparations were taken seriously in 1942. Little in the way of air or naval defenses stood between the Pacific theater of war and the hospitably broad and flat sand beaches of the Washington coast and people would have been much less surprised than was the garrison at Pearl Harbor to have sighted Japanese warplanes making their bombing runs on the capitol dome. Nerves had not been comforted when, late in December, a Japanese submarine nonchalantly surfaced to shell a Vancouver Island lighthouse, the ancient Spanish war coastal fortifications at Fort Stevens on the mouth of the Columbia river, and a California oil refinery.

On an otherwise quiet Saturday in mid-June Olympians did get a sample of aerial carnage. A light army plane from McChord Field near Fort Lewis came smoking out of the sky to sideswipe St. Peters hospital on the west side hill and crash to the street in flames. The pilot died in the hospital four hours later of a fractured skull and burns. A military policeman helping in the rescue operations was knocked unconscious when he touched a downed power line and Deputy Sheriff Ed Stearns was, according to the *News, "thrown to the ground by an exploding bullet."*

Later the same day another air corps plane crashed in a pillar of fire and smoke on the prairie between Olympia and Tacoma, killing another young pilot.

HOME FRONT HEROES

The civilian war effort was reminiscent of the patriotic activities of a quarter century earlier. Citizens who had bought Liberty Loan bonds until it hurt in 1918 were buying war bonds in 1942. All Thurston county farmers were asked to participate in the voluntary registration of horses and mules between the ages of three and 10 for possible military use, as requested by headquarters, Western Remount Area. A number of highranking military men were still convinced that the deciding battle of the second world war would be decided by a cavalry charge.

The Army and Navy club in the old statehouse gave way to a new USO center on east 4th street, which provided hospitality to an average of 2,100 young men in uniform each week. Not completely satisfied that Captain Shain's militiamen would be able to protect the outlying areas of the county, Don Major, publisher of the Tenino Independent, formed the Tenino Minute Men. Armed with hunting rifles and fowling pieces, Major's Minute Men were prepared, upon an instant's notice, to take to the hills and prairies to protect the county's second largest incorporated municipality from Japanese paratroopers.

General J. L. DeWitt, the understandably nervous commander of what defenses the Pacific coast had, ordered a "dim-out" from the beaches to a point 150 miles inland. This was followed by reassuring counsel from Governor Langlie, who advised his constituents to keep calm, stay home and do their best to ignore any Japanese planes which might drop bombs upon them.

Patriotic citizens gathered scrap iron, tin cans and grease for the war effort and E. A. Zabel staged a "grease matinee" at his Capitol Theater. Any kiddies who came bearing a pound or more of grease, preferably in containers, were admitted free.

Rationing was reintroduced, partly to make the home front folks aware that they were in a war and partly because of actual or potential shortages. Coffee, sugar, liquor, gasoline and tires were soon available only by coupon. Chairman Evro Becket, Langlie's liquor board chairman, complained that some unpatriotic individuals were bootlegging liquor ration books and warned that the board was going to crack down hard on both buyers and sellers.

The fear and suspicion of "enemy aliens," which had provided such an unsavory chapter in the history of the first world war, was just as rampant in the second. In March the *News* reported that city police and sheriff's deputies had raided 22 homes of "Thurston county's enemy aliens" and arrested three middle-aged men of German ancestry who had been found in possession of a couple of shotguns, three cameras and a radio capable of receiving short-wave broadcasts. The culprits were, according to the *News, "jailed to await FBI instructions."*

It was also reported, with a tinge of disappointment, that *"the only thing found in the homes of Japanese living at Mud and Oyster bays were large stores of supplies, mainly sugar and rice."*

Since a goodly proportion of the town's white Anglo-Saxon population was feverishly engaged in hoarding coffee, sugar, tires, booze and anything else scheduled to be rationed, it was difficult to make out a case against the Japanese for their sacks of rice.

It wasn't necessary to find bombs and machine guns, however. The color of their skins and the shape of their eyes provided all the guilt that was required. In June, upon the demand of the nervous General DeWitt and practically everyone else in a position of military or civilian authority, all persons of Japanese ancestry were rounded up for removal from the "West Coast Military Area" to inland concentration camps. A total of 13,391 . . . a majority United States citizens who couldn't even read , write or understand the Japanese language . . . were "relocated" from the state of Washington. Those from the Olympia area went to Tule Lake, California, near the Oregon border.

Aside from the fact that the basic constitutional rights of thousands of loyal American citizens were trampled in the march of "national defense," it is interesting to note that nobody of German or Italian descent was "relocated." Fortunately for those who need somebody easily identifiable to hate, thousands of blacks soon began a migration to the state for employment in the burgeoning war industries and provided a new focus for frustrated bigotry.

The manpower shortage of the first world war was also repeated. The Boeing Airplane company plant, turning out armadas of flying fortresses, and the great steel shipyards of Seattle, Tacoma and Vancouver, absorbed thousands of workers at high rates of pay and the basic forestry, agricultural, mining and fishing industries were going full blast to meet the demand for raw materials and food.

The Olympia post office was, by the end of the year, operating with only 75 percent of its normal staff and deliveries were cut to one a day. The state automobile testing stations were closed for the duration to conserve manpower and fuel. In the heat of late August the city's garbage men walked off the job in a body when their demands for salaries of $35 a week was denied by the city fathers. Noisome effluvia from overflowing trash cans was reminiscent of the summer odors of earlier days and Sheriff Huntamer was enraged by the monumental heaps of garbage which citizens deposited along rural roads. One garbage truck, manned by an inexperienced crew, threatened to further pollute the capital city when the driver forgot to set the brakes on a steep hill and the vehicle ran away backward. Fortunately an alert bystander leaped aboard and got it stopped before it demolished itself and festooned the surroundings with garbage.

City hall finally gave in and decided that it could afford to pay its garbage men $140 a month after all, even though it seemed outrageous.

Another reminder of old Olympia resulted from gas and tire rationing when an unnamed farmer rode his plow horse to town to do his weekly shopping and, finding no hitching-posts left, tied it deftly to a parking meter.

POLITICS AS USUAL

The saintly atmosphere of the Langlie administration was disturbed somewhat in 1942 when the press noted that some 40 state patrolmen had resigned from the force within four months, including a number from the Seattle detachment who had quit in a body, bitterly denouncing "political manipulation" of the patrol. The *News Tribune* reported the discontent had spread to the Tacoma detachment as a result of the "to the victor belongs the spoils theory of the Langlie administration".

It was rumored that "similar disrupting influences are at work in the highway department" and that the liquor board was likewise badly affected. Most editorial opinion tended to the conviction that the pious governor simply couldn't be aware that his "over-officious subordinates" were engaged in widespread political finagling within the various agencies of state government.

Langlie turned the other cheek and ignored the restrained criticism of the press, letting his obvious virtue speak for itself.

The procedure appeared to be successful. It looked as if the Republican party in Washington had stemmed the decade-long tide of Democratic dominance and was starting its comeback in earnest when the results of the 1942 elections were toted up.

Republicans recaptured three of the state's six congressional seats. Fred Norman defeated Martin Smith in the third, Walt Horan torpedoed the hoped-for political comeback of C. C. Dill in the fifth, and the seemingly unbeatable Knute Hill of the fourth district was ousted by the glib and dapper dean of men at Central Washington college, Hal Holmes.

The more urban districts remained loyal to the Democratic incumbents. Magnuson and Coffee won by healthy majorities, as did Jackson over his perennial Republican opponent, Payson Peterson. The state legislature remained in the hands of the Democrats, but by a slimmer majority than at any time since 1932. The house of representatives had 57 Democrats and 42 Republicans; the senate 27 Democrats and 19 Republicans, which was an impressive gain in view of the fact that there hadn't been more than nine Replublican senators at Olympia since the 1933 session.

SMOKE-FILLED ROOM: The fate of much legislation is determined behind the closed doors of party caucus rooms off the legislative chambers. This 1971 photo shows the Democratic caucus of the 42nd Legislature hard at it.

CHAPTER ELEVEN
The Tenth Decade
1943-1953

For Olympia landlords, the second world war years were just like having the legislature in session all year-round. The most dilapidated shanties and converted chicken coops were snapped up by Fort Lewis and McChord Field service men desperate for some kind of housing for their families and the rent schedule was based on whatever the traffic would bear. Owners of rental properties drank New Year's toasts to 1943 and the city fathers, who had had the statesmanlike foresight to turn down federal low rent housing funds.

So critical was the housing situation in the capital city that Harold Van Eaton, chairman of the legislative housing committee appointed by Governor Langlie, suggested delicately to members of the 28th legislature that it might be a good idea to leave their wives and families at home. Decent housing was almost impossible to get and the usual dances and social events would not be held during this first wartime session. The *Olympian* reassured the legislators that they *"won't have to sleep in tents, but will pay higher rents".*

A number of rooming house proprietors did their bit for the legislature by serving eviction notices on soldiers' wives and renting the vacated premises to lawmakers at twice the previous rent. Lobbyists, it was noted, had reserved almost all the first class hotel rooms and citizens were urged to rent spare bedrooms to legislators. Many of them did.

A number of wife-dominated legislators were enabled to enjoy a bachelor session after convincing their spouses that it would be unpatriotic to further complicate the war housing situation in Olympia.

Most of the state solons arrived in town on January 11 for pre-session caucuses. "Fresh Water" Reilly, the first speaker of the house to serve two consecutive terms and aggressively campaigning for a third, predicted that this one would be "a very businesslike session", but that it would run the full constitutional 60 days despite some agitation to limit it to 43 days.

Thurston county's Representative Armstrong was a leading contender for the speakership, along with Julie Butler Hansen, a second-term legislator from Wahkiakum county, who had wasted no time in embarking on the path toward becoming the most astute and powerful female politician in the state's legislative history. Mrs. Hansen had already written to Reilly that she was withdrawing in his favor, but at the Sunday pre-session caucus the vote was tied between Reilly and Armstrong.

By the next morning, Armstrong had decided to also withdraw and conservative Democrat Reilly became the first three-term speaker of the house. The senate quickly elected Al Rosellini president pro-tem and returned Joe Mehan as sergeant at arms. Newt Fry was elected his counterpart in the house and Si Holcomb, who was becoming something of a legislative institution, continued to preside as chief clerk. The senate's first order of business was the appropriation of $240,000 for expenses of the session.

In keeping with the wartime spirit of austerity, the opening night festivities were limited to a legislative reception in the Jade Room of the Hotel Olympian, at which a completely non-alcoholic punch was served and the Olympia high school double string quartette played soothing melodies. The *Olympian* reported that this restrained gathering *"was held in lieu of the extravagant social activity of past sessions"*, since such festivities were deemed unfitting in times of such grave national peril.

On January 13 Governor Langlie addressed the still strongly Democratic legislature and presented another "all-time record" budget of $267,700,000, including a $5 million emergency fund in case the state was bombed by the Axis powers.

He reiterated his support of a civil service system for the state's 7,000 employees and a cost of living raise for them, as well as the 8,000 public school teachers. In these proposals he was vigorously supported by the WEA and the newly-formed state employees' union, headed by Langlie's close associate and admirer, Norm Schut.

His major executive request bill, aimed at giving him control of the state timber resources, proposed a state forestry board to be appointed by him to replace the existing forestry board and capitol committee. Land Commissioner Jack Taylor was, understandably, vigorously opposed to the governor's suggestion, and before long he had the satisfaction of seeing it routed off to the house logged-off lands committee to quietly expire.

Pointing out that he had converted a $5 million treasury deficit into a $20,600,000 surplus, Langlie urged that a savings account be set up for post-war building programs, to include $120 million in new highways and $22 million in public buildings. He also submitted a package of 10 "war power bills", which would grant him dictatorial powers over almost every type of public activity if he deemed it necessary in the interests of the defense of the state and nation.

The Republicans in both houses were feeling their oats, convinced that the days of Democratic dominance were ending, and their augmented numbers provided them with considerable weight to throw around. They succeeded in doubling their chairmanships of house committees and organized a putsch against Vic Meyers' senate committee appointments. Nine dissident Democrats, David Cowen, W. R. Orndorff and Thomas Bienz of Spokane, Don Miller of Okanogan, E. A. Edward of Whatcom, Ted Schroeder of Pierce,

and Henehan and Reardon of King, formed a coalition with the 19 Republican senators to reject Meyers' committee list and, after a great deal of fighting and name-calling, the lieutenant governor and senate leadership were required to make a number of painful concessions.

96

Including the strong-minded Julia Butler Hansen, there were nine lady representatives that session . . . Violet Boede, Emma Taylor Harman, Jeanette Testu, Mrs. Thomas Kehoe, Mrs. Jurie B. Smith, Ella Wintler, Gertrude Johnson and Georgianna Behm. The senate chambers were graced by the presence of three feminine lawmakers . . . Lady Willie Forbus of King, Kathryn Malstrom of Pierce and Agnes Gehrman of Grays Harbor and Pacific. Of the 12 feminine legislators, only Mesdames Wintler and Gehrman were Republicans.

The house did away with its legendary committee on dykes, drains and ditches and, since nobody wanted to be continually reminded of that constitutional requirement for legislative redistricting after every census, the legislative apportionment committee. The void was filled by new committees on naval affairs and civilian defense.

Charles Savage, who was well embarked upon his in again-out again legislative career, was appointed chairman of the labor committee, a position which he currently holds as this is written, exactly 32 years later.

IT'S NEVER TOO LATE
TO INVESTIGATE

On Friday, January 15, the legislators convened just long enough for the house to pass a resolution demanding an investigation of the liquor board. Stocks in the state's monopoly boozeries were already depleted and the war seemed to be just getting well started. Why, the aroused representatives wanted to know, was rationing necessary? Why hadn't the board purchased a reserve supply while it was available? Why had teetotaler Langlie appointed only drys to the board? There were those who suspected a conspiracy to again force abstinence upon the citizens of the state under the guise of wartime shortages.

Having thus let off steam, they adjourned for the week-end, returning on January 18 to hear the details of Langlie's latest record-breaking budget, which represented an increase of $9,-200,000 over that of the previous biennium.

Lieutenant Governor Meyers was heard to voice his lament, "Why pick on Vic?" when he discovered that Langlie had deleted his hard-won "maintenance" appropriation of $7,200. Land Commissioner Taylor had stronger words for the chief executive when it was revealed that his departmental request for $225,000 had been pared to $60,000, apparently on the highly optimistic belief by Langlie that his requested forestry board would be created to relieve Taylor of most of his responsibilities.

The atmosphere was even colder outside the capitol. One of the worst cold spells in years had descended upon the Puget Sound country, with the morning temperature at seven degrees. Local business men quickly raised $2,000 to buy bedding and blankets and the old Totem Market building on west Legion Way was donated by Safeway Stores for conversion to an emergency dormitory to house up to 300 shivering servicemen. A couple of days later the inevitable Chinook wind arrived from the Pacific, mixed itself with the Arctic front and deposited 14 inches of snow upon the capital city.

Legislators warmed themselves with whatever potables were available and braved the weather to demand further investigation of the executive branch. There were loud outcries in the senate over the fact that the governor had paroled, pardoned or granted commutations of sentences to 67 inmates of the state prison and reformatory, including 20 lifers in for murder.

Public and legislative feelings were further lacerated when a parolee, out less than a month on parole after serving 18 months of a 15 year burglary sentence, was arrested for a new burglary in Renton. Furthermore, one Maurice Larius, convicted of kidnapping, beating and robbing a semi-invalid Olympia taxi driver in 1936, was turned loose on "work release" to help harvest the eastern Washington apple crop and failed to return from the orchard after the picking was completed.

Thurston county Prosecutor John S. Lynch asked for a supreme court ruling on the legality of the prison exodus and the senate penal committee requested an attorney general's opinion. When the opinion was offered that the procedures used to release the lifers were il-

legal, Senator Mohler demanded a legislative investigation of the state's probation and parole operations.

Langlie, who was nobody's fool when it came to politics, deftly fielded the barrage of criticism, leaving his board of prison terms and paroles alone in the field of fire. Before the senate could appoint an investigating committee, the governor announced blandly that *he* had appointed a three-man committee consisiting of two superior court judges and Richard A. McGee, the state supervisor of institutions, "to investigate the actions of the state board of prison terms and paroles in releasing a number of long-term prisoners".

Although a number of senators complained that McGee had joined with the parole board in recommending the releases, the governor's maneuver had taken the wind out of the sails of Mohler and his cohorts and the senate investigation proposal lost by one vote. As is customary in such cases, Langlie's three-man committee continued to investigate until public indignation had abated and then quietly dissolved itself.

The major bones of contention in the 28th legislature were Langlie's request for virtually dictatorial emergency authority for the duration of the war and an initiative to the legislature authorizing public utility districts to join together to condemn and buy privately owned utilty companies.

Second term Representative John L. O'Brien led the move to amend the governor's requested "war power" bills to remove individual power from Langlie and place it in the hands of a defense council consisting of the governor, secretary of state, insurance commissioner, auditor and attorney general. Republicans complained that the proposed board was too unwieldy and a compromise amendment was worked out reducing it to three . . . the governor, attorney general and auditor.

Charles Hodde, back in the house representing Pend Orielle county, and chairman of the powerful revenue and taxation committee, piloted the public power initiative through the legislative shoals with such skill that by late February it had passed the legislature with an emergency clause to place it in affect immediately.

When the senate had second thoughts and sent a resolution to the house to refer the measure to the people at the next general election, Hodde displayed a finely coordinated agility of mind and body. When the reading clerk announced the arrival of the senate resolution, the gentleman from Pend Orielle jumped to his feet and moved for indefinite postponement while Speaker Reilly still had his mouth open to assign it to a committee.

Such a motion isn't debatable. It quickly passed and the senate's buck-passing effort died when Representative Perry Woodall's motion to reconsider was ruled out of order by the speaker, who was a fairly quick thinker himself.

This public power ploy was followed early in March by what the *Olympian* described as *"the worst knock-down, dragout fight of the entire Washington state legislative session to date"*. The ruckus in the house of representatives was precipitated by debate of Langlie's requested war powers bills. On three votes, all point-blank tests of the governor's strength and prestige, his supporters were defeated in their efforts to force two of the Langlie bills out of the civilian defense committee, where O'Brien and the rest of the Democratic leadership had them decently buried. The anti-Langlie vote wasn't strictly along party lines, five Republicans voting with the majority and eight Democrats with the Republican minority. Insult was then added to injury when a Democratic civilian defense bill, just submitted, was placed on the calender ahead of the languishing Langlie measures.

Three days later the governor got the word that his far-reaching forestry board bill had been relegated to the logged-off lands committee as an exercise in legislative euthanasia.

Two days after that, Langlie got a little of his own back by vetoing a bill designed to get around the unrealistic constitutional limits on elected officials' salaries, which ranged downward from the $4,000 a year of the treasurer and superintendent of public instruction to the $1,200 of the lieutenant governor. Vic Meyer's maintenance appropriation had worked so well that a bill was passed to provide additional maintenance payments to all the deserving Democratic officials. Langlie had previously been allotted a separate maintenance allowance which had the effect of doubling his constitutional $6,000 a year, so he felt no pain when he red-inked Senate Bill 154 "because of irregularities in the bill". From that point on the governor and legislature were bogged down in partisan and personal bickering.

Two days after *that* the legislature passed the three principle Langlie war power bills,

first amending them beyond all recognition. The war council consisted of Republican Langlie and Democrats Vic Meyers and Insurance Commissioner Sullivan.

The 28th session adjourned *sine die* at a little after 5:00 a.m. on March 12, having run only about five hours overtime. Despite the running feud between the legislative and executive branches, it *had* been a reasonably businesslike session. A resolution was passed to submit the 40-mill property tax limit to a vote of the people for inclusion in the state constitution, it directed that employers must pay women the same wages as men for performing the same work, and the state's 15,000 employees (including public school teachers) were granted a $30 a month cost of living raise for the remaining three months of the biennium, plus a 13 to 15 percent raise for the coming biennium, and old age pensions were raised to an average of $40. The budget was balanced well within the limits of anticipated revenues. Langlie got a central purchasing agency and a state motor pool, but not his top priority requests. At adjournment, left-wing Representative H. C. (Army) Armstrong shouted, "Notify the governor what we did to him this session!"

The public power initiative, which had supposedly become law before the session ended, was challenged in the courts by private power interests and the supreme court knocked out the emergency clause, giving its opponents 90 days to collect the 30,000 signatures needed to submit the measure to the people at the next election.

WAR WORKERS AND TEEN-AGE WEREWOLVES

Except for the legislature and the increasing activities of the local civilian defense forces, 1943 was a quiet year in Olympia. Wartime restrictions had brought construction to a virtual standstill. The $150,000 project for shipways and buildings of the Puget Sound Shipbuilding company on the port fill was the only large one, accounting for well over half the construction money spent that year. The first of its products, the 157-foot wooden steam tug *Compeller,* was launched with considerable ceremony on Columbus Day and duly transferred to the British Admiralty. By the following month the ReliableWelding plant on the west side had completed 16 steel tugboats for the government and received a contract for a half dozen 85-footers with 600-horsepower diesel engines. At Portland the liberty ship *Nathaniel Crosby* was launched at ceremonies attended by Olympians Charles Burr, grandson, and George Harrigan, brother of Mrs. Harry L. Crosby, who was the daughter-in-law of Captain Nat and mother of the by now famous Bing Crosby.

Although there was growing evidence that Olympia wasn't going to be bombed from the air or invaded from the sea, the civil defense authorities didn't let down their guard. County Engineer Shain had been promoted to lieutenant colonel and, as operations and training officer of the state guard, was converting the states motley militia of aging first world war veterans and 4-F's into a well organized and disciplined force. Air raid wardens and other civilian defense workers were issued white enameled steel helmets with brightly colored decals indicating their branch of service and there was some disappointment among them when General DeWitt, having decided that the Japanese high seas fleet was no longer lurking outside the three-mile limit, suspended the coastal dimout in November.

The nearest Olympia came to being a combat center had been back in August when a small replica of the town was laid out on Stevens field as a set upon which a cast of 900 participated in what the *News* called *"a pageant depicting in realistic fashion the bombing of the state capital."* The spectacular event was, the *News* continued, *"the nearest thing to war that is possible without actually killing people."*

Under the direction of county CD Director Joseph Wohleb, all hell broke loose on Stevens field. As bayonet-wielding state guardsmen chased saboteurs, medical workers rushed to the rescue of dramatically dying victims of explosion and gunfire. Three waves of planes from McChord field then swooped down to drop simulated bombs upon the simulated town. It was a noisy and satisfying spectacle, particularly enjoyed by the small boys of the community.

The war of 1944 was a more sophisticated one than the war of 1918, but the similarities remained. The Olympia papers, like newspapers across the country, published the sad news of hometown boys killed or maimed or missing in action. The stories grew more frequent after June 8 when the allied invasion

forces crossed the channel to the beaches of Normandy. There were bond drives, paper drives, scrap metal drives and Red Cross drives. The home guardsmen drilled and the streets were filled with lonesome G.I.s from Fort Lewis, just as they had once been filled with lonesome doughboys from Camp Lewis.

And just as the motormen and conductors of the Olympia Light and Power company's trolley line had threatened to quit and move to the shipyards if they didn't get a pay raise, the drivers of the Olympia Transit company's buses threatened to go to work for Boeing unless their salaries were raised from 90 cents to a dollar an hour. After due deliberation, the regional war labor board granted them 95 cents an hour.

More distinguished visitors came to town . . . Wendell Wilkie, the Republican candidate for the presidency in 1940 to be introduced by Governor Langlie at the Lincoln Day dinner in Tacoma . . . and a little man from Missiouri named Harry Truman, who came in October, following his selection as Franklin Roosevelt's vice presidential running mate. Senator Truman spoke from the steps of the capitol after being introduced by his close senatorial friend, Mon Wallgren. "This war," he told the citizens of the capital city, "has been the most efficiently conducted war in the world's history . . . no one can deny that."

Langlie called a special session of the legislature for February 28 for the purpose of setting up absentee voting provisions for servicemen. The governor intimated that he thought it would be nice if the lawmakers limited themselves to that task and immediately adjourned. The house refused to thus limit itself, but did agree to a rule barring any consideration of bills after March 2. Not yet having heard the Truman phrase about "the buck stops here," the representatives neatly passed it to the senate, with the comment, "It will be up to them to decide the length of the session."

Langlie urged the legislators to avoid new pensions which might erode the treasury surplus, but Senator Rosellini called the address "a typical say-nothing message from a do-nothing governor" and legislators vied with one another to introduce bills designed to show the appreciation of the state's taxpayers to the returning veterans, once the war was over. A bonus was proposed at the rate of $50 a month for every month of service in the armed forces, with a maximum payment of $800. As an alternative, veterans could choose free tuition and books at any state institution of higher education. Another proposed bill would provide free college tuition in addition to any bonus granted by the state. Still another called for a 10 percent preference on civil service examination scores.

Having gone on record in support of such hero bills, the lawmakers adjourned at the end of six days, having passed only the servicemen's voting bill and a memorial to congress requesting the granting of citizenship to Filipinos in the United States.

RETURN OF THE RED MENACE

With the Democratic legislature out of the way for the time being, Governor Langlie had time to observe the international scene and come to the conclusion that, with the Axis powers on the run, communism remained the great threat to liberty and freedom. In a statewide radio address in August he cautioned that voters must be alert to "the subtle infiltration of subversive elements into the bloodstream of our government."

Communists, he said, would "yell that I am dragging red herrings across the trail," but he was, in fact, "trying to put up a red light on the great American road warning us against the dangers we head for if we turn * * * into totalitarian by-ways."

Suspicious Democrats had a feeling that the governor's warning might, in fact, be the opening chorus of the Republican theme song for the 1944 general election. A number of the state's more successful Democratic politicians had embraced the ultra-liberal cause during the depression years, and Republican strategists felt the time was fast coming when such "left-wing" tendencies could be effectively used against them, as had been the case in the defeat of C. C. Dill.

The theory had merit, but its application was premature. Stalin's Red army hordes were still viewed as our gallant allies, the cold war was still in the future and the hot war hadn't been won yet. It was bad business to change horses in the middle of the stream.

The Republicans, reviewing the strong gains they had made in the 1942 off-year election, were convinced that the tide would continue to flow in their direction. A good many Democrats seemed to agree with them. United

States Senator Wallgren filed against Langlie for the governorship, but he was so pessimistic about his chances of being elected that he clung to his senate seat. The betting odds against him remained overwhelming throughout the campaign.

The optimism of the state's Republican politicians was exemplified by the field of 11 candidates which filed for the senatorial seat of Homer T. Bone, who had resigned to take a federal judgeship. Harry P. Cain of Tacoma won the Republican nomination for the vacant seat, while Congressman Warren Magnuson garnered three times the vote of his primary opponents, Martin F. Smith and John A. Hogg.

Hugh DeLacy won the Democratic nomination for the vacated Magnuson first district congressional seat over Tom Smith, Howard Costigan and several others. He faced former Seattle mayor Robert Harlin in the general election.

State Representative Charles Savage was nominated to run against incumbent Fred Norman, who had unseated Democrat Martin Smith in the third district.

Victor Zednick, who had begun his legislative career in 1911, won the right to face Vic Meyers in the lieutenant governor's race, winning the nomination over Charles Maybury and several lesser candidates. The genial Meyers easily won the Democratic nomination from the puritanical former state senator and Seattle mayor, George Cotterill. The Democratic voters had a clear choice in that one. Vic Meyers and George Cotterill were about as different as two human beings could be.

To the dismay of the hopeful Republicans, the state of Washington returned to its habit of voting Democratic. Magnuson, who had served in the navy with Admiral Bull Halsey and campaigned on both his congressional and war records, rolled up a majority of nearly 100,000 over Cain. Savage, who pledged to work with FDR "in his efforts to win the war, prevent future wars, provide full employment, security and prosperity after the war," and urged voters not to "handicap President Roosevelt with a congressman obligated to a political party hostile to the president," defeated Republican Norman.

Roosevelt and Truman outpolled Dewey and Bricker by 486,750 to 361,700 and Wallgren, to the amazement of everyone, especially Langlie and himself, took the governorship by a vote of

428,834 to 400,604. Meyers downed Zednick by more than 100,000 votes.

The Democratic campaign song of 1944, "Happy Days Are Here Again," proved both timely and prophetic. They came out of the election with a net gain of one in congress, retained their senatorial monopoly and regained the governorship. The Democratic majority in the state legislature was also increased ... to 63-36 in the house and 32-14 in the senate.

Lame duck Langlie, who had spent too much time working for Dewey instead of himself, wound up his last months in office with a commendable display of bi-partisan statesmanship. Although Magnuson had won Bone's seat in the senate, it was technically vacant until the winner was sworn in early the following year. Republican politicians descended upon the governor beseeching him to appoint some deserving party workhorse to the short-term vacancy, thus giving him the lifetime title of senator and brief membership in the world's most exclusive club. Langlie refused to go along with the proposal. Instead he appointed Magnuson to fill out the last months of Bone's term, thus giving the new junior senator from Washington seniority over all the rest of the crop of new senators.

As for genial Monrad C. Wallgren, former Everett jeweler and amateur billiards champion, he prudently clung to his senate seat until he was sworn in as governor in January of 1945.

Although Langlie had behaved magnanimously in regard to the Magnuson appointment, Wallgren no doubt felt that the opportunity to appoint a Republican to a full four years in the U.S. senate might be an unfair strain on the outgoing governor's principles.

1945

The wartime baby boom was typified on a small scale in Olympia when the maternity section of St. Peters hospital reported three babies born between midnight and dawn of New Year's day, two of the three to wives of servicemen. In past years it had often been necessary to wait a day or two to welcome the town's first New Year baby.

The infant influx would cause expensive problems for future legislatures, but the session

Governor Mon C. Wallgren.

of 1945 had too many current problems to deal with to waste time wondering what was going to happen when all those bundles of bliss metamorphized into swarms of school children.

Governor-elect Wallgren was already in town on January 1, sharing temporary office space with Vic Meyers. Langlie and Wallgren had studiously avoided any personal contact after the incumbent's first political defeat. Even before he formally took office, Wallgren learned something of the arm-twisting to which governors are so frequently subjected. The party faithful flocked to the lieutenant governor's office suite off the senate chamber to urge Wallgren to appoint Congressman Coffee to his soon to be vacated senate seat. After listening patiently to a long series of eulogies to the congressman, he announced casually, "I've chosen the man to succeed me as United States senator and it isn't John Coffee." A few days later he finalized matters by the announcement that he was going to appoint his bright young executive assistant of several years' standing, Hugh B. Mitchell. At the same time he let it be known that his new right hand man would be Jack O. Gorrie, chief deputy for the federal internal revenue service in the Washington and Alaska district.

The rejection of Coffee, probably prompted by the fear that a Republican would capture the congressman's vacated seat in a special election, aroused considerable party strife within the Democratic organization. State Chairman Harry Huse called the central committee into session at Olympia to consider the situation. Since there wasn't much they could do about it, the party leaders opted for a show of unity and officially approved the Mitchell appointment.

Nobody complained when it was learned that crusty 72-year-old Admiral Gregory, who had headed the state liquor board during its first eight years of operation, was coming back as board chairman after four years of involuntary retirement. It was also general knowledge that Wallgren was contemplating a modest liberalization of the state's almost stupefyingly complex, illogical and restrictive liquor laws. Gregory, although straight-laced and quite incorruptible, was no blue-nose, as were the Langlie appointees to the board.

When the legislature convened at noon on January 8, George Yantis, who had been elected to another term as speaker, let it be known that he opposed any liberalization of the Steele act except by initiative or referendum. It was apparent early in the game that liquor by the drink was going to be a major issue.

The senate chose Carl Mohler as president pro-tem, making this the last session in which Thurston county legislators had occupied the top elective offices in both houses.

RETURNING TO NORMAL

By 1945 it was apparent that an allied victory was inevitable and some of the wartime facade of patriotic sobriety was abandoned. The *Olympian* noted that *"long frocks are back in the shop windows in place of the short and severe substitutes,"* and that the streets were thronged with women shopping for the inaugural ball. The wartime housing shortage was as bad or worse than during the last session, however, the *Olympian* reporting that *"the chamber of commerce has been sleuthing for weeks for housing for the legislators."* The town echoed with the outraged screams of statesmen learning what their monthly rentals were going to be.

Outgoing Governor Langlie delivered his farewell address to the legislature on opening day, pointing with pride to a $63 million state treasury surplus and the relative harmony which he felt had existed between the Democratic legislature and the Republican governor. He defended his liquor board as "a model among state monopolies throughout the nation" and urged that it not be "hurled into the maelstrom of political manipulation."

He said he had "carried the ball in public office a long time and would like to see others take it," that he was "retiring from public office without further political ambitions," and that he was "leaving without bitterness toward the new administration."

Despite these protestations of good will, it was pointed out by the *Olympian* that *"there has been no meeting between Langlie and Wallgren since the latter's arrival at the capital and the atmosphere is so chilly there is little prospect of them meeting at all in the exchange of office. Neither of the two men or their assistants have met to discuss the turning over of office."*

Eventually the transfer was made without personal contact. Just before noon on January 11, Langlie, accompanied by a few of his appointees, ducked out the back door of the executive offices. At noon Jack Gorrie arrived and Langlie's secretary, Inez Lewis, handed the keys to him "and departed." Langlie claimed he had invited Wallgren to meet with him; Wallgren insisted he hadn't received any messages from the outgoing governor.

Few men had less in common than the dour, cold and puritanical Langlie and the genial, gregarious, whiskey-drinking and pool-playing Wallgren. Langlie, never a good loser, doubtless believed that the forces of Anti-Christ, as personified by Wallgren, had triumphed over him with the help of Satan;* Wallgren considered Langlie to be ineffective as a governor . . . he had been known to wisecrack that the state would be better off if Langlie had a few friends in Washington, D.C., instead of in Heaven . . . and considered him a crashing bore as an individual. It was a twain that was probably better off not meeting.

---

*This feeling was expressed by Seattle *Times* editor Elmer Todd in a post-election letter to Langlie: *"I did not think it was possible . . . the powers of evil seem to be in full control and the public's enemies are lurking in the shadows."*

Reaction to the outgoing governor's remarks varied widely. Conservative Democratic Speaker Yantis considered them to be "well presented" and said he accepted them as "sincere remarks." Senate Majority Leader Al Rosellini classified them as "an humble attempt to justify the mistakes of his administration" and left-wing Representative Pettus asked, "why doesn't the old governor shut up and get out? We've got a new governor who knows what to do!" As for the new governor, he commented succinctly, "it was an *if* speech . . . *if* I'd been elected."

13th GOVERNOR: 29th LEGISLATURE

Two days after Langlie's valedictory, Wallgren became the 13th governor of the state of Washington. The ceremonies were held on the broad steps of the Legislative building, whence Wallgren was escorted by a committee from the house and senate. Rare January sunshine illuminated the scene as Chief Justice Walter B. Beals "intoned the oath" and a crowd estimated at 7,500 looked on. Among the onlookers was the governor's 84-year-old mother. His 93-year-old father, Swan Wallgren, was feeling poorly and his doctor had made him stay at home in Everett.

The armory, manned by the Olympia company of the state guard, was swathed with red, white and blue bunting to provide a patriotic motif for the inaugural ball, but wartime austerity was abandoned and, as usual, the local press described it as the most gala affair in the long history of inaugural balls.

With the essential ceremonies out of the way, the 29th legislature got down to serious business. The first order of business was the quick passage of the bill introduced by Representative Henry of King raising legislators' expense money from $10.00 to $15.00 a day.

Langlie, much more liberal now that he was leaving, suggested that old age pensions should be raised to $50.00 a month, that $5 million should be appropriated to "eradicate tuberculosis within 20 years" and that teachers' retirement should be increased. He urged the creation of a state aeronautics department, an agency to control pollution in streams and lakes, a veterans' welfare commission, and passage of forestry protective, cutting practices and reforestation measures. To finance this enlightened program he proposed a biennial budget of $357,513,149.38 . . . up nearly $90 million from the last one.

Governor Wallgren, having perused the inch-thick budget document of his predecessor, observed that it looked way too high to him. "We may have to write the whole thing over again," he predicted.

In *his* message to the legislature, Wallgren had proposed higher old age and teachers' pensions, an all-out recreation and tourism program, and the encouragement of a new post-war industrial development "from the ore to the finished goods." He pointed out that the state's new hydroelectric resources could bring major aluminum and magnesium plants . . . "the magic metals of the future." He also observed, with equal accuracy, that "the state has a patchwork government" and needed a constitutional convention for the purpose of streamlining it.

After recovering somewhat from the shock of learning that the supposedly defeated German army had turned around and unleashed its panzer divisions on the allied forces in the Ardennes, the lawmakers turned their attention to outrages closer to home. Finding that the tripling of their expense money had barely kept pace with inflated living costs at the capital, they passed a resolution demanding that the OPA place controls on rents in Olympia. Representative George Hurley of King denounced Olympia landlords, charging that they had been known to "have increased rentals of housing units as much as 100 percent and 200 percent." His colleagues agreed that "legislative rents have increased in many instances to fantastic proportions."

Mayor Trullinger took quick and decisive action. "I believe it is every landlord's patriotic duty to keep rents at 1942 levels," he proclaimed.

It was certainly not his fault that few of the local landlords appeared to hear him.

The house of representatives passed a rule prohibiting wives of representatives from working on the legislative staff. This ruling was contrary to everything the legislature had stood for in the way of nepotism and it raised such a furor, particularly among those members whose spouses were feeding from the public trough, that it was quietly abandoned.

NEVER DO TODAY WHAT YOU CAN PUT OFF UNTIL TOMORROW

Other than that, the early weeks of the session passed with a minimum of histrionics and even less action. Republicans asserted that the slow pace was attributable to the fact that Wallgren had wasted no time in making a clean sweep of Langlie department heads. The result, they said, was chaos and confusion in the various agencies of state government.

Others were convinced that the normally savage legislative breasts had been soothed by the melodious strains of organ music which daily floated from the marbled state reception room across from ulcer gulch. The gregarious Vic Meyers had, prior to the session, met a former theater organist from Klickitat county, Phil Raboin, who had just been released from army service. Vic, always a lover of music, genially invited the young organist to come to Olympia and play a concert for the legislature. He did, was subsequently put on the payroll as a clerk, and has been playing the organ in the capitol ever since.

Vic doubtless needed the calming strains of organ music, for 10 conservative Democrats in the senate were again threatening to form a coalition with the Republicans unless his committee assignments met with their approval.

It is an interesting aspect of legislative history that Democrats frequently bolt their caucuses and climb in bed with Republican minorities to make their own party ineffective. Republicans never have been known to commit such political adultery.

By late January a few legislative investigations had been proposed, including a probe of the liquor board's purchase of two Kentucky distilleries, and of the state's juvenile correctional institutions, which were scenes of repeated riots and runaways. The latter proposal was backed by senate majority leader Rosellini, who was developing a strong interest in the state's snakepit institutions. He urged a $25,000 appropriation to provide the investigation with muscle and teeth.

Robert Harlin, former Seattle mayor and director of labor and industries under Langlie, requested an audit of that department, having been informed by Cliff Yelle's financial sleuths that $10,000 in state funds appeared to have been embezzled by a former employee. Little time was lost in complying with this request and the capital city was soon shocked to learn that another of its promising young men, a former high school athletic star who was currently serving in the navy, had lifted the $10,000 in public funds.

J. M. Dawley, Olympia builder and Langlie's hand-picked and notably inept Republican state chariman, interjected charges of his own at this point, claiming that "about 300 cases of the finest and most expensive liquor available" had been dispensed to "influential lobbyists and politicians via the back door of the Olympia state liquor store." He said the shipments were released upon "written orders from trusted employees of the Democrat-controlled legislature."

Governor Wallgren, scarcely bothering to register his full confidence in his liquor board, observed offhandedly that "if any liquor is being issued in the amounts he describes, I'll be willing to bet the Republicans are lapping up just as much of it as the Democrats."

At the end of January, Wallgren introduced his liquor by the drink bill under local option control, telling the legislature, "We should offer our guests the same hospitality we rceive in other states." The state restaurant association, displeased with the local option provision of the executive request measure, immediately began lobbying against it, letting it be known that it would be presenting its own bill.

Despite the general lethargy which had marked the legislative deliberations, the senate, at the end of February, brought forth a budget totaling $304,557,922. Although it was about $33 million below the Langlie request, the state taxpayers' association immediately announced that it was "out of line."

A time honored tactic of legislative leaderships is to guide each session along a path of bumbling lethargy, droning endlessly over trivialities, until the closing days. Then a terrible crunch occurs. The two houses convene early and keep at it until the wee hours of the morning. The majority of the members become completely befuddled and have only the vaguest of notions as to what is going on about them. Some try to sustain their flagging energies with ardent spirits and others take refuge in sleep. It is then that the wheeler-dealers take over and push through the more outrageous legislation aimed at enriching themselves and the various special interests which are their true constituency.

The 1945 session provided a good example of this technique. In mid-February the press was commenting with obvious boredom that there was little action at Olympia and few bills introduced, but things changed in March, after the senate brought forth its proposed budget.

By early March the sessions were extending well into the early morning hours. The Senate passed 40 bills in one sitting, bringing its total to 166. A three-minute limit was placed on legislator's oratory, but this rule was honored largely in the breach as emotional issues reached the floor.

THE HOWLING HENRYS

On March 6, with adjournment looming closely, the senate became engaged in a bitter fight over a proposal that the state take over the Bellingham-San Juan Island and Tacoma-Fox Island ferries, both of which were navigating on mounting seas of red ink.

The *Olympian* reported the ferryboat fight led by what it termed "the howling Henrys" . . . Senators Al Henry of Klickitat and Ed Henry of King. Senator Al, a man of positive opinions and forthright speech, thundered that the whole affair was a monstrous boondoggle engineered by the Pierce and Spokane county delegations. The Fox Island ferry was costing Pierce county $25,000 a year and the Spokanites had agreed to back a state bail-out of the ferry line in return for a bigger share of the gas tax money for Inland Empire highways.

Seattle's Ed Henry demanded that the state also take over the Black Ball Line's Seattle-Bremerton route. "If you're going to vote against operating a ferry that makes money," he argued, "I don't see how you can logically vote to absorb a money loser such as this Fox Island thing!"

The senate, upon the motion of Hugh Rosellini, placed the ferry controversy in the hands of a free conference committee on the grounds that the members didn't really understand the amendment relating the the Fox Island purchase.

"They did too understand," Al Henry commented vociferously afterward. "They understood it was a fraud!"

In the last-minute confusion the conference committee approved both controversial ferry

purchases and, for good measure, added the Astoria-Megler system across the Columbia river and another small privately-owned ferry operating between The Dalles, Oregon, and Dallesport, Washington.

Governor Wallgren, who was in the throes of bargaining with Captain Peabody for full state ownership of all the Puget Sound ferries, frowned upon this piecemeal approach and settled the controversy by vetoing all the ferry legislation, along with a large number of other bills.

By March 12 the legislature was still in overtime, the clocks stopped and time standing still in the marbled halls of state. A considerable number of the members had wandered away and gone home, but there were enough left to keep things lively to the last, the *Olympian* reporting what it headlined as a "NEAR RIOT!":

"Actions in both chambers were on the rugged side yesterday, with members scurrying hither and yon with last minute business.

"A near riot broke out in the house when labor members were beaten down in an attempt to amend the rules to permit forcing of bills from the rules committee upon presentation of a petition by 33 members, later increased to 50 members.

"Rep. George Hurley, Seattle, beat his desk with his hands, kicked his knees shoulder high and screeched. Rep. Chart Pitt, Mukilteo, not to be outdone, thumped boxes and desks with a bat. All in all, the setting greatly resembled that of a movie jungle war scene."

MARBLE ZOO

The legislature has always prided itself upon its "decorum," but such traditional scenes as these were earning the Legislative building the descriptive if uncomplimentary title of "the Marble Zoo."

On March 13 the *Olympian* announced that the legislature had adjourned *sine die* "*after going on the greatest spending spree in history.*" The weary lawmakers called it quits at noon that day, having been in unrenumerated overtime for five days. The budget for the coming biennium totaled $561,-

734,291.69. Governor Wallgren did fairly well on his request measures, although the house turned down his proposal to permit liquor by the drink and the senate killed his request that counties be required to levy property tax on realistic assessed values in order to qualify for state school equalization funds.

The state progress commission and planning council were combined to form a division of progress and industrial development under the department of conservation and development, a state timber resources board was created to control reforestation and sale of state timber lands, $70 million was appropriated for post-war public works, the public service department was divided into separate departments of public utilities and transportation, the bi-partisan requirement for liquor board appointments was repealed and the governor was given the right to hire and fire members of the state game commission.

With healthy Democratic majorities in both houses of the legislature and Mon Wallgren in the governor's mansion, the 1945 session was fairly generous in its dispensation of public funds. Old age pensions were raised to $50 a month, unemployment compensation to $25 a week for 26 weeks and teachers were given a $75 a month pension at age 60, provided they had accrued 30 years of service. An appropriation of $1.5 million was authorized to establish a firemen's pension fund, and even the state's elective officials were not forgotten.

Their constitutional salary limitations were conceded to be riduicuously low in an era of post-war inflation, but taxpayers have traditionally been easily upset by legislatures which raise their own or other elective officials' pay. Such pay raises were, then as now, political dynamite, and means were constantly being sought to accomplish financial readjustments with a minimum of public outcry.

The legislature of 1945 came up with the ingenious idea of creating a state commission on interstate cooperation, to be made up of all the Democratic elective officials. Their pay as members of the commission would be such as to raise their total legitimate income to $6,000 per annum. The originators of this strategem felt that, having doubled their own pay, it might be wise to cloak the legislative largess to the elective officials in a different guise.

Although the final budget was well over $200 million more than the Langlie proposal, which Wallgren had felt to be a bit high, Represen-

tative Richard Murphy, chairman of the house appropriations committee, blandly explained to the press that it wasn't really as bad as it might seem. Much of the budgetary increase, he said, was attributable to the transfer from a war to a peace economy and the financing of needed public works which couldn't be accomplished during the war years.

"Thus, he concluded, "the total appropriation is far in excess of any normal past or future budget,* and does not represent an actual substantial increase in the operating costs of state government."

Not all the legislative gifts cost the taxpayers money. One bill, for example, provided for the admission of Lieutenant Governor Vic Meyers to the Washington state bar without examination "by virtue of his long service as presiding officer of the senate."

Governor Wallgren cheerfully signed the measure, perhaps reassuring himself with its provision that the transmorgification of bandleader Meyers into a barrister must first receive the approval of the state supreme court. It may be that minor technicality which prevented Vic from becoming the Clarence Darrow of the west. It cannot be denied that he was possessed of the quick wit and fine sense of timing required of a good lawyer. A typical example occurred at *sine die.* Most of the legislators had departed the marble halls before the final ceremonies were completed. Only 23 of the 99 representatives were at their desks and the senate chamber was empty except for Meyers on the podium and Senator E. A. Edwards of Deming at his desk. Unphased, the lieutenant governor scanned the almost empty chamber, fixed his gaze grimly upon the sleepy Edwards and intoned, "Will the senator please come to order!"

Among the additional accomplishments of that session were the creation of a pollution control commission, authorization of a survey for a possible highway tunnel through the Cascade mountains, the appropriation of $100,-000 to pay bounties for killing sea lions, and another million dollars to begin work on the long-discussed damming of the southernmost

---

*Representative Murphy was not a very good fiscal prophet in regard to future budgets. The state's biennial budget has now reached a figure more than ten times that of the one proposed by Governor Langlie in 1945.

Olympia from the west side of Capitol Lake, 1974.

arm of Puget Sound to create a fresh water lake beneath the capitol group, as envisioned in the original plans of Wilder and White.

Another million dollars was authorized for construction of the final building of the Wilder and White capitol group. This structure, marked on the original plan as the Education building, was to be identical to the insurance building, giving symmetry and balance to the group and the massive capitol dome. An additional $100,000 was earmarked for "removal or replacement" of the governor's mansion, but sentimentalists objected (and still object) to any tampering with the tottery brick-veneer structure. The appropriation was never spent and the almost perfect capitol group remains lopsided and incomplete to make room for the carpenter-Georgian structure of early Grand Rapids vintage.*

Although Governor Wallgren was generally castigated by the almost wholly Republican daily press of the state as a wild-eyed spendthrift, he applied his veto pen to more than 30 bills, lopping off about $15 million from the legislature's budget. In addition to the various ferry purchases, the scuttled measures included authorization for the state to purchase the Manette bridge at Bremerton, the $75 a month school teachers' pension fund, the state supervised firemen's relief and pension fund and a $1.4 million appropriation for the purchase of new school buses. He also vetoed a revolutionary bill which would have established a joint house-senate legislative council of seven senators and eight representatives to function throughout the interim . . . the first serious effort to make the legislative branch a continuing agency of government on a year around basis.

The governor sought to soften the blow of his pension vetoes by promising a better pension bill next session.

As a result of Wallgren's trimming, the actual general fund budget ended up only about one million dollars over that proposed by Langlie. The over-all budget was much higher because of appropriations from other funds and surpluses. (The new office building and Capitol Lake development, for example, were to be funded by capitol timber grant money.)

The people subsequently asserted *their* veto power by passing a PTA-sponsored referendum killing Wallgren's state timber resources board.

One of the highlights of the session, as far as Wallgren was concerned, was the discovery that the capitol dome, which had previously echoed only to the oratory of legislators and the outraged shouts of demonstrators, provided perfect acoustics for more melodious sounds.

---

*This historical sentimentality, which did not surface during the demolition of such truly historic buildings as the Stevens mansion and the territorial capitol, is proving expensive to the taxpayers. The 1973 legislature appropriated more than $600,000 for the latest repairs to the mansion, which was built originally as a temporary structure for less than one-twentieth that amount.

THUNDER UNDER THE DOME

Shortly after the legislature departed, the governor's discovery was announced in the Olympia *News:*

"What we have discovered and scientifically proven is that the capitol of the state of Washington possesses a musical sounding board the equal of the most famous in the

436

world and possibly the greatest in the world . . . at least the equal of those in the Vatican at Rome and the great Morman Tabernacle in Salt Lake."

Time magazine gave national publicity to the audio-phenomenon in an article headed "Thunder Under the Dome" and legislative clerk Raboin was officially appointed state organist, beginning the daily noontime concerts which have continued ever since. Raboin had learned of the dome's peculiar qualities when he moved his organ from the state reception room into the rotunda and began idly playing the "Lost Chord." After a few moments he stopped, awed at the amplified perfection of the notes, and the great discovery had been made.

The thunder under the capitol dome was in contrast to the thunder of arms as the war reached its crescendo in Europe and the Pacific. As the legislature met in the early months of 1945 American battle casualties had reached a tragic level. The state of Washington listed nearly a quarter of a million of its young people in the armed services; nearly 5,000 had been killed and 10,000 wounded. The *Olympian,* like other daily papers across the state, published casualty lists with somber regularity.

Infantry Lieutenant Dan McCaughan, who had worked for Mills and Mills mortuary in the days when death usually came less violently, was wounded in action for the second time somewhere in Germany. Lieutenant Robert Jackson, one of the three national guardsmen who had unveiled the first world war veterans' monument on the capitol grounds, died of wounds suffered on the western front. The 25-year-old graduate of Olympia High school had worked for the local branch of the National Bank of Commerce in happier days. Mr. and Mrs. A. J. Phillips were notified of the combat death of their 21-year-old son, Staff Sergeant James A. Phillips, who had been an architecture student at the University of Washington. Young Phillips was one of the four Olympia boys who had reported together for army service 18 months earlier. Two of the others, Ralph Wickstrom and Bud Lewis had been critically wounded. Only one, Curtis Johnston, was reported still in action.

A touch of wartime action came to Olympia late in January when Patrolman John Morgan, on routine patrol, noted an army sedan moving through town at a crawl. Officer Morgan became suspicious. "It struck me as odd," he explained later, "that an army vehicle should be moving slowly." He stopped the car and discovered that its four occupants, equipped with packsacks full of food, couldn't speak English. They turned out to be four enterprising German prisoners of war who had escaped from the Fort Lewis stockade and had lost themselves on the streets of the capital city. Officer Morgan escorted them to jail and 20 heavily armed soldiers soon arrived to take them back to the fort.

ATOMIC AGE

Soon afterward citizens jammed the Olympia airport to view one of the new Boeing B-29 "superfort" bombers and there was general agreement that Germany and Japan would soon be pulverized into submission. Those who took their science fiction seriously hoped so, for the president of the United States rocket society was insisting that "a rocket could be sent to the moon tomorrow if somebody would put up the money." His fears that the Nazis might get there first and bomb the allied nations from the lunar surface received considerable publicity.

Fortunately the Thousand Year Reich of Adolph Hitler collapsed before German rocket experts were able to reach the moon and on May 8 mill and factory whistles signaled V-E Day to the citizens of the capital city. Jubilation was restrained by the death of Franklin D. Roosevelt less than a month earlier. People turned on their radios to listen to Truman, Churchill and other allied leaders and then went to churches and to the capitol rotunda to attends solemn memorial services.

It was a different story in August when the nuclear holocaust at Hiroshima ushered in the atomic age and sparked the swift disintegration of the Japanese armed forces in the Pacific. All the whistles, sirens and automobile horns in town cut loose as the news spread and the streets were jammed with jubilant crowds of service men and civilians. Stores and offices closed and joy was unrestrained.

In late June the new president of the United States, Harry S. Truman, was back in Olympia visiting his old friend, Mon Wallgren. After meeting informally with the press in the governor's office, wearing a Cowichan Indian sweater borrowed from Wallgren, he and his host vanished on a fishing trip for a couple of days before Truman's departure for San Francisco to make the closing address at the United Nations world security conference.

In September the Japanese surrender party boarded the mighty battleship *Missouri* in Tokyo bay and the war was officially ended. Among the honored quests on the *Missouri's* surrender deck was General Jonathan Wainwright, who had inherited McArthur's hopeless ccommand in the Philippines and had suffered with his surviving troops through years of Japanese imprisonment.

In mid-November Wainwright was welcomed to Washington's capitol by Governor Wallgren as he toured the Northwest to promote the national victory loan drive. With four local heroes of Corregidor, Sgt. Seth Bish, Captain Harold Proff, Corporal Ronald Robbins and Corporal Leslie Gilbert, he had lunch at the mansion before proceeding on this mission.

1946

The transition to the post-war era was made gracefully in Washington's capital city, primarily because it had been even less involved in defense industry than it had been during the first world war. Nothing more impressive than tugboats had been produced at local yards for the war effort, and the unprofitable Olympia Shipbuilding company plant on the port fill was taken over by a new industry, the Olympia Wood Preserving company, which manufactured teredo-proof creosoted piling. The Reliable Welding yard was at work on a welded steel motor vessel, which was launched in April as the *F. H. Lovejoy,* flagship of the nine-vessel Puget Sound Freight Lines fleet.

Early in the year the War Shipping Administration announced plans to establish a major reserve fleet moorage in Budd Inlet. It was expected that as many as 300 war surplus vessels would eventually be moored from Priest Point to Boston Harbor and that 450 men would be employed in their care and maintenance. Waterfront residents were vocally displeased by the prospect of having scores of battered freighters, tankers and troop

transports moored in their front yards, but the Chamber of Commerce pointed happily to the estimated million dollar a year payroll to be generated by the reserve fleet installation and Jack Taylor, director of the state pollution control commission, declared himself satisfied that the moored ships would not add appreciable amounts of impurities to the already sewage-polluted waters of the inlet.

By mid-April, two tiers of ships were already firmly anchored in the outer harbor and maintenance crews were busily spraying them with unlovely rust-colored protective paint. By August 80 ghostly vessels were enrolled in the Olympia reaserve fleet and more kept coming throughout the year. For the next quarter of a century there would be more ships in Olympia than in all the other ports of Puget Sound combined, but few of them were going anywhere.

PEACE: IT'S WONDERFUL!

War surplus stores sprang up to dispense unneeded military items at a fraction of their original cost to the government, and, by January, veterans' organizations were busily initiating large classes of second world war veterans. Military traditionalists of Alfred William Leach post were somewhat taken aback when Muriel Hopp, ex-WAC, presented herself for membership with the January 10 class of 65 second world war veterans, but she was duly initiated as the first feminine member of the Olympia American Legion post.

There were also signs of the new American affluence. The days when a handful of doctors sat in their offices hoping for patients had ended. A modern medical clinic was opened on east 4th below St. Peters hospital, complete with spacious parking lot. The old McCleary mansion on upper Capitol Way, which had operated throughout the war years as the Majestic Apartments, was remodeled as a medical center when ex-military doctors Ralph Highmiller, J. A. Rose, Frank Hartung and F. J. Cornelius returned from the service and, finding no suitable office space, formed the Olympia Medical and Dental Building corporation.

Out on the east edge of town along Martin way, the transition from the modest tourist cabin to the luxury motel was epitomized when

H. B. Bailey opened the new Bailey Motel. The new motor hotel boasted "showers and bath with each room, venetian blinds and draperies, wall to wall carpeting, radios and hotel service, with the lobby open 24 hours a day."

Post-war automobiles were rolling off the assembly lines and buyers were waiting to snap them up as fast as they arrived at the local dealerships. A. G. Schaefer diverted a new Plymouth sedan to become Olympia high school's first driver training car and crusty advocates of the three R's pointed to this latest example of fads and frills in the public education system.

And if survivors of the crusade against "mixed dancing" in the high school gym remained to view the post-war scene, they must have been further horrified when the high school band blossomed out with high-stepping drum majorettes in skirts daringly above the knee.

West Coast airlines announced that it was inaugurating four trips daily to the Olympia airport by 24-passenger DC-3's and the post office department prepared a special envelope cachet to commemorate the first regular air mail flight. Federal red tape resulted in a series of postponements of service from early fall to mid-December, and even then the *News* reported that *"flights are intermittent because of the bad weather."*

Passenger service from the Olympia airport has remained at best "intermittent" to the present day, ranking approximately on a par with railway service to East Olympia.

In city politics the establishment candidate for mayor, Ernest Mallory, narrowly defeated colorful Olympia old-timer Ed Henderson, a realtor who billed himself as "the One-Man Chamber of Commerce" and devoted much time and energy to devising newspaper advertisements urging such civic improvements as a sewage treatment plant, arterial streets and the Puget Sound-Grays Harbor canal.*

The 1946 general election in November also proved to be triumph for the forces of conservatism as voters evinced their tendency to turn out of office the party in power after the war.

---

*Although viewed by many as a wild-eyed dreamer, most of Henderson's projects have achieved reality ... with the notable exception of the canal ... and he was posthumously honored by having one of the city's more noteworthy arterials named Henderson Boulevard.

RETURN OF THE REPUBLICANS

Flamboyant Harry P. Cain, campaigning as a major of paratroopers still on active duty, decisively beat slight, bespectacled Hugh Mitchell for the United States senate, while five of the state's six congressional seats went to Republicans. Homer R. Jones of Bremerton ousted DeLacy, Fred Norman regained his seat from Charles Savage and Thor Tollefson unseated Coffee, with the contests clearly between the political philosophies of the left and the right. DeLacy was suspected of outright Communist party membership and every effort was made to discredit Savage and Coffee by innuendo and guilt through association. The end of the war had transformed our erstwhile Soviet allies into the Red Menace, events were leading up to the national paranoia of the McCarthy era, and communist scare tactics could be used with great effectiveness by conservative politicians.

Hal Holmes, the loquacious ex-college dean, beat off efforts of Earl Coe to defeat him and Walt Horan had little difficulty with the less well-known Democrat, John T. Little.

Even worse, from the standpoint of Democratic Governor Wallgren, was the fact that the Republicans gained an overwhelming majority of 71 members in the statehouse of representatives. Hold-over Democratic senators gave that body a theoretical Democratic majority, but eight of the dissidents quickly joined forces with the 23 Republican senators to turn over leadership of sorts to Zednick and Harry Wall. The house was managed with considerably more skill by Herbert Hamblen of Spokane, who kept the 31 eager Republican freshmen on a tight leash. All three Republican leaders had higher political ambitions, Wall having dreams of the governorship and Zednick and Hamblen both eyeing a possible race for lieutenant governor. They hoped to appear as statesmanlike as possible, but only Speaker Hamblen enjoyed much success.

Senator Rosellini, leader of the loyal Democrats, was likewise casting hopeful glances at the governor's mansion and he did his best to harass the coalition leaders. Rosellini's best was impressive. Pandemonium reigned frequently in the senate as Rosellini charged into the fray, enthusiastically abetted by the more liberal senators and by Vic Meyers, who seldom used his gavel against the Rosellini forces. The strong desire of Zednick and Wall to maintain decorum and avoid controversy made them appear inept in the fact of Rosellini's slashing attacks, which were backed up with a thorough knowledge of parliamentary procedures and legislative psychology.

In the house, where control rested on a solid majority rather than a shaky coalition, Hamblen and Majority Leader Perry Woodall announced that no Democrats would be given committee chairmanships. The Republicans had more than the two-thirds majority needed to override vetoes by the governor.

Wallgren was thus faced with the situation which had plagued Langlie . . . firm legislative control by unfriendly forces.

No sooner had the legislature convened than Pearl Wanamaker, by now one of the most astute and powerful politicians in the state, announced that she wanted $161,550,962 to implement her 19-point educational program, which included new buildings, salary increases and higher pensions for teachers, education for handicapped children, nursery school and junior college support and fleets of new school buses.

Although the coterie of back bench Republican freshmen in the house were loudly celebrating frugality with calls for a pared budget and no new taxes, the legislative leaders had no difficulty in achieving quick passage of a bill providing $602,000 for legislative expenses . . . a considerable increase from the $322,000 of the 1945 session. Having accomplished this, the Republican leaders issued a blast against "willful negligence in social security expenditures" by the Wallgren administration, thus joining the fledgling representatives in the formalized celebration of thrift so dear to the legislators' heart.

Governor Wallgren put the best face possible on the situation, informing the hostile legislature that the state was "in the best financial condition in its history" and that he was opposed to Washington becoming a "pinch-penny narrow-minded state" . . . an obvious slap at his predecessor, Langlie. He recommended approval of a state veterans' bonus, pay raises for state workers and increased industrial insurance benefits, along with "a thorough survey of the state tax structure on the principle of ability to pay," to include consideration of a graduated net income tax. He urged construction of the much-discussed Cascade highway tunnel, a pet project of his highway director, Shain, and com-

pletion of a four-lane "super-highway" from Vancouver to the Canadian border, which he considered "the most urgent job of highway completion facing the state today."

He placed the treasury surplus at $129 million and presented a somewhat unrealistic budget of $516,725,000. Republican legislators were soon thundering that the document was "tricky, deceptive and alarming" . . . a feeble attempt to make the budget look lower than the last biennium's by leaving out all mention of capital expenditures, teachers' retirement, increased industrial insurance payments and other costly programs.

Wallgren had been prepared for the worst and, after presenting his budget to the legislature he quickly divested himself of all responsibility for its ultimate fate. "I'm past the point of recommending," he announced plaintively. "I'm sitting here ready to execute. I'll take care of the executive end. The Republicans are going to have to write the laws."

Senator Clinton S. Harley, chairman of the appropriations committee, put the Wallgren budget on a back shelf and hired former budget supervisor Brabrook as a financial consultant to write a new one. Curmudgeon Brabrook, who acted as if he would have preferred to work standing up at a counting house desk with a quill pen, harrumphed that Wallgren's real budget was probably closer to $720 million, with a probable deficit of $170 million. Brabrook cut capital spending by $20 million and included it in a total budget of $557,324,581, with an estimated deficit of over $25 million.

The back row chorus of frugal freshmen complained bitterly, but the Republican advocates of austerity were caught by Wallgren's threat to call a special session in the fall of 1948 if the legislators didn't face up to the responsibility of financing state government for the full biennium. The prospect of dealing with emergency appropriations on election eve was a chilling one.

A PINK TEA PARTY

As the majority party in the legislature contemplated its dilemma, Wallgren took the offensive, charging into the fray with the war cry that the Republican leaders had "spent four weeks . . . running for governor and building up the Republican party."

"What?" he asked the capitol newsmen gathered in the executive office, "are they doing for the state?" The 30th legislature, he averred, was "a pink tea party."

Senate majority leader Wall blandly responded that "no legislator I know of is running for office in 1948."

Eventually the Republican leaders simply shoved the issue of deficit spending under the rug, rationalizing that possible reversions from the various departments and a possible $10 million increase in revenues through the activities of newly authorized tax commission auditors would balance the budget. They had been cast in the role of fiscal responsibility and preferred a certain deficit to the political embarrassment of inflicting new taxes upon the electorate.

The Republican daily press of the state helped to paint the Republican legislators into a corner in its effort to damn Wallgren as a spendthrift. A typical editorial appeared on the front page of the *Olympian* on February 11:

"The legislature is one of the best that ever met in Olympia. Its members may be counted on to do their utmost to relieve Washingtonians of the highest per capita tax burden in the nation, and try to clean up an ineffable mess resulting from mismanagement, incompetence, waste, lack of judgment and from adherence to New Deal policies that are accountable for deplorable conditions everywhere."

But, the *Olympian* cautioned in a tender defense of the Republican-dominated legislature, citizens must be patient with it. *"The state has become a very sick patient . . . too ill to be restored to health by ordinary legislative remedies."*

While showing little inclination to face up to the financial problems of the state, the leaders of the 30th legislature evinced a strong urge to investigate the governor. There was much talk of "willful negligence" in handling old age pensions, of hanky-panky in the expenditure of a million dollars in scarce park department funds to develop Sun Lakes (Dry Falls) state park in eastern Washington, near which Vic Meyers was co-owner of a dude ranch, and demands to find out what had caused the most recent of a long series of riots at the training school in Chehalis.

CONTINUING LEGISLATURE

By late January the house had voted to appoint a committee to investigate the department of unemployment compensation and placement regarding charges of one of Yelle's auditors that improper safeguards had resulted in overpayments, as well as liquor club licensing, misuse of state cars, operations of the liquor board and social security department and what the *Olympian* termed *"various rackets countenanced by the administration and sundry off-color matters of concern to the public."*

A few days later, Associated Press correspondent Leroy Hittle revealed that *"a reliable source who declined to be quoted by name"* had told him that *"a move is under way to establish an interim committee with broad powers to investigate any and all administrative departments, boards and commissions."*

This modest news release heralded the first major step toward what is currently termed a "continuing legislature," with its functions not limited to the constitutional provision for a 60-day session every other year. Although Republican legislators had bitterly assailed the legislative interim council concept when it was proposed by the Democrats during the Langlie first term in 1945, and it was vetoed by Langlie, they enthusiastically adopted it now that the shoe was on the other foot.

While financial problems remained in the background, the legislative chambers continued to resound with cries of outrage over alleged improprieties of the Wallgren administration. Representative Loomis Shadbolt of Yakima introduced a resolution for the marking of all state cars, complaining that he had seen such vehicles at the racetrack on Sundays, at supermarkets with wives at the wheel, and had once interrogated "three drunks" in Portland, Oregon, who insisted they were "on state business."

There were complaints of mismanagement and financial losses in the state-owned ferry operation which had replaced the ill-fated Narrows bridge and charges that 23 Democratic legislators had been given state jobs by Wallgren, in violation of the constitution.

In a burst of political probity, the majority pushed through a bill to enforce the ban against publicly-employed lawmakers, but when it was found that a *Republican* legislator

441

was in line for a *county* job, they hastily amended the measure to exclude county jobs, providing Wallgren with an excuse to veto the whole thing on the grounds that it was inequitable.

Given top billing during this session of investigations was the "Capitol Club," an unincorporated and unaudited organization of state employees, some of whom were complaining, according to the *Olympian,* that *"it is purely for the purpose of collecting large sums for political campaigns."*

Representative Woodall introduced a resolution in the house for an investigation of the club, waving a membership card signed by Jack Ballew, director of finance, budget and business, and the campaign files of Arthur B. Langlie, biding his time and thirsting for revenge against the pool-playing, whiskey-drinking Wallgren, fattened daily.

As a means of coordinating and continuing its muckraking, the legislature approved various interim subcommittees of the legislative council with subpoena power, to make a two-year investigation of almost everything.

Meanwhile, in mid-February, 800 veterans converged on the capitol in a noisy mass demonstration for a state veterans' bonus. The male heroes were indignant when a distaff warrior, ex-WAVE Cappi Stevens of Olympia, took an opposition view.

"I'm not in favor of a bonus," she proclaimed. "I have two feet and two arms and I can care for myself. Why don't you go out and see what you can do for yourself?"

The self-reliant Miss Stephens was booed and shouted down with angry reference to "women holding down men's jobs" and challenges for her to "find jobs for us."

Legislators, preoccupied with finding new matters to investigate, passed the bonus buck to Wallgren with the comment that he would have to find some way of financing it.

Two weeks later a thousand demonstrators marshaled by Old Age Pension Union president Pennock appeared at the capitol to demand increased pension benefits. The small army of discontent included labor unionists, veterans and minority groups as well as oldsters and it tended to be unruly. One group of 25, including a number of veterans, was ejected from the senate gallery after one of its members began shouting about a "runaround" in regard to the bonus. A second group tried to force the door to the senate chambers, while a third banged and kicked away at the house door, chanting the words of a popular song of the day, "Open the Door Richard."

Legislative reverence for orthodoxy was outraged by the antiestablishment sentiments of the demonstrators, one of whom carried a sign reading, "the Communist party supports the March." Some of the veterans pitched puptents on the capitol lawn and vowed to stay, but, as usual, the weather was terrible and they abandoned their cold and wet encampment the same evening.

Between demonstrations the senate engaged itself in a noisy dispute over confirmation of Wallgren's appointments to the University of Washington board of regents, rotund Teamsters boss Dave Beck, maritime unionist John Fox and John King, all of Seattle. The committee on higher education had been sitting on the confirmation action throughout much of the session and finally the coalition Democrats bolted to support their party caucus on the vote to relieve the committee of the matter. At the last minute, however, Senator Grieve bolted back from the Democratic caucus to the Republicans and the 24 to 22 vote to relieve was insufficient.

The issue finally came to the floor in March with a recommendation from the committee that Fox and King, a Grange representative, be rejected . . . on the grounds that they had denied knowledge of subversive teaching at the university. Senator Bienz of Spokane evinced the greatest outrage at this, quiveringly asserting that "We have heard of this for years!" He said he had been told by "one person" that there were five Communist professors and, by "another person," that there were 30.

Fox was finally rejected, amid charges and denials of subversive teachings at the university. King was reluctantly confirmed. But not a soul, either in the committee or on the floor, had uttered the slightest criticism of Beck, who was at the height of his power and several years away from a term at the McNeil island federal penitentiary.

Despite the many problems and distractions, the legislature found time to assert its traditional preoccupation with trivia. Indian Representative George Adams was angered by the shabby condition of the capitol grounds totem pole and wanted it transferred to the jurisdiction of the superintendent of public instruction. Representative Arthur Cory of Lewis county introduced a bill to remove the comma from the official title of the state board of prison, terms, and paroles. The institutions committee wrangled long and bitterly over the matter. Should the comma come out? Would such an action set a dangerous precedent? Might it involve the state in legal problems? Eventually the committee moved courageously to delete the surplus punctuation and Cory was prankishly nominated as chairman of the committee on commas. Salt Water Riley sponsored a bill to change the name of Hood Canal to Hood Inlet, and Representative Army Armstrong submitted his periodic measure to place a tax on pay toilets. The jaunty Armstrong, an extreme left-wing Democrat, was engagingly frank in his explanation of his motive for stubbornly submitting the pay toilet tax bill each session.

"Every session I sponsor it and every session I get $200 to see that it stays in committee. That pays my room and board while I'm in Olympia."

The ingenious Armstrong had come up with the perfect "fetcher" bill; one which could be used session after session to mitigate the financial sacrifices of serving in a citizen legislature.

Two bills which were to have a major impact on the political resurrection of Arthur B. Langlie were passed by the 1947 session. One, which progressed unobtrusively into law, abolished the straight party ballot, which had permitted voters to mark an X at the top of the party slate, thus casting a full party ballot. A potential boon to Langlie, it has had the ultimate result of weakening the state's political parties to a state of chronic ineffectiveness. The other was the approval and funding of the legislative council and its various investigative subcommittees, which would provide the Republican leadership and its friends with year-around publicity and per diem payments and the Wallgren administration with embarrassing headlines in the state's hostile press.

Among the interim investigating groups was a joint fact finding committee on un-American activities, presided over by a slight, gimlet-eyed and paranoid representative from eastern Washington named Albert Canwell. This well-funded agency had just one moderately liberal member, George Yantis, who died before it

began its deliberations, and it soon provided Washingtonians with a prologue to the frightening McCarthy era which was to grip the nation as a whole. This, too, would ultimately provide targets of opportunity for the political wars as fought by ex-Cincinnatian Langlie.

By February 21, the cut-off date for introduction of bills and with the session two-thirds over, 994 measures were in the hopper and the matter of the budget could no longer be kept under the rug. Brabrook addressed the representatives in committee of the whole and told them the original $14,578,000 deficit of the Wallgren budget had been increased "by urgent requests" to $186 million. Republican floor leader Woodall observed that "the governor's budget was conceived in confusion and dedicated to the proposition of attempting to embarrass the Republican party," but when the tumult and shouting died the legislators proceeded to approve a budget based on wishful thinking and the wistful hope that the $84 million wartime treasury surplus might somehow tide them over.

Toward the close of the session the attention of lawmakers and governor was further diverted by a flareup of the endemic "ferry crisis" which had afflicted Puget Sound for years. In the face of a strike threat which would tie up the entire Black Ball ferry fleet, Director of Transportation Paul Revelle granted Captain Peabody a 30 percent temporary rate increase pending a thorough study of the rate structure. The house had already made an inconclusive study of the same matter and, for good measure, the senate voted to investigate both Black Ball *and* the transportation commission. Company president Peabody offered his employees a 10 percent pay raise, but by mid-March the marine engineers had gone on strike and tied up all 22 ferries on all cross-Sound routes. The navy provided two landing ships to transport shipyard workers to Bremerton and the state's Narrows ferries speeded up schedules on the only crossing to the west side of the Sound, but the area was in the grip of a full scale transportation crisis.

By March 13 the supplemental appropriations bill was up to $55 million as, according to the *Olympian*, "the 30th legislature, its minority and majority members in acrimonious debate to the very last, adjourned sine die at 4:45 Thursday afternoon ...

the first time in 22 years a legislative session has been concluded in the statutory 60 days."

In a feeble effort to increase revenues, the lawmakers had raised the pinball, slot machine and punchboard taxes . . . an exercise in hypocrisy as well as futility, since all these devices had been declared illegal under the constitution . . . and, as a conservative tweak of the public power advocates' noses, had boosted public utility district taxes. They had provided raises of up to $750 a year for teachers, with a $100 a month pension, without making a serious effort to fund their largess. The state department of veterans' affairs was abolished and replaced with a veterans' rehabilitation council with representation from the various veterans' organizations. The division of budget within the department of finance, budget and business was replaced by a director of budget under the governor and nine interim investigating committees were funded to investigate liquor and bottle clubs, Puget Sound ferry rates, taxes, inter-state fisheries, highway administration and policies, the Capitol Club, state institutions and Un-American activities.

Bills to build the Cascade tunnel, raise the gasoline tax one cent, restrict labor unions and provide a veterans' bonus were among the major casualties of the session.

A majority of the legislators departed the capital with the comforting thought that, while they might not have solved many of the state's problems during the 60 days just past, they would have the whole interim to collect per diem while seeking solutions as members of one interim committee or another.

And the 30th legislature made another bit of political history. It was the last one to date at which a member of the working press was punched by a lawmaker.

Robert Cummings, now the benign dean of the capitol press corps, but then the fire-breathing capitol correspondent for the *Post-Intelligencer,* had annoyed Senator Albert D. Rosellini by pointing out that the Democratic leader had, under the eyes of a large delegation of PTA ladies, seconded a motion to remove one of their pet education bills from committee. Rosellini, according to Cummings, had been instrumental in keeping the measure bottled up in committee in the first place.

Robert C. Cummings, dean of capitol newsmen.

The injured senator repaired to committee room "X", that traditional fourth floor oasis above the legislative chambers, to quench his outrage. As he departed, Cummings arrived to enjoy that time-honored prerogative of capitol newsmen . . . freeloading. They met in the doorway and big Al swung a mighty left, knocking the wiry but unprepared Cummings backward to land upon his fundament. The senator then stepped over the recumbent form of the scribe and departed, no doubt feeling considerably better.*

---

*While history does not record the violent downfall of any newspaper men in the capitol since the Rosellini-Cummings bout, a young UPI correspondent named Robert McDaniel suffered what he considered an even worse indignity during the 1967 session. The editor of the Yakima *Eagle,* an extreme right wing publication, had been denied press credentials and barred from the floor of the house that session. Although the *Eagle* man had a mustache and McDaniel was smooth shaven, they were otherwise somewhat similar in appearance. When McDaniel approached the press table on his first day at Olympia, he was mistakenly identified as the *Eagle* editor and two security men were dispatched to eject him. "You can't fool us by shaving off your mustache," they told him. When the nonplussed McDaniel sought to expostulate with them, they seized him, one on each arm, and frog-walked him, before a delighted gallery full of spectators, to the chamber doors. They then ejected him bodily. This public indignity so chagrined the young newsman that he planned to resign as a political reporter, but his colleagues calmed him down and he has been covering legislative sessions ever since without suffering bodily harm or humiliation.

MORE ELECTRONIC MARVELS

With the legislature embarked on a course of year-around activity, the modern age of politics was well on its way, and the bureaucracy was in the process of inflicting that space age Frankenstein monster, the computer, upon the public. The *Olympian* devoted considerable space to the development of the electronic marvel:

"Occupying 7,200 square feet of floor space in the newly constructed building at 215 south Washington street is the Tablulating and Machine Unit of the Acunting Division of the State Department of Unemployment Compensation and Placement.

"To the stranger it is a bewildering jungle of noisy electrically operating auditing machines through which stream hundreds of thousands of variously punched cards and figure-covered papers, all used in processing wage and contribution statements, claims and benefits for roughly 650,000 wage earners."

The operation had just been moved from the third floor of the old statehouse when engineers, with apparent seismic sixth sense, expressed fear that an earthquake might cause the floor to collapse under the weight of primitive computers and card files. The program already employed 106 workers on a three-shift, six-day-a-week basis, their tending of the machines lighted by 1,200 feet of fluorescent tubing.

By 1947 the KING broadcasting company was installing equipment for the transmission of television programs to the Puget Sound country, a few gadget-loving Olympians were amazing their friends with Edward H. Land's new Polaroid camera, which miraculously produced a finished picture in 60 seconds, and the telephone company was experimentally installing telephones in automobiles. The Olympia post office was issuing stern warnings against the chain letter fad, which had been declared illegal and the new Studebaker was being hailed as the car of the future.

Contractor A. G. Homan was retained to build a new fire department substation on the west side near the Garfield school, to cost $29,000 and house a captain, lieutenant and three firemen. Power doors were also installed on the central fire station at city hall. The new substation was officially designated as the Grant Talcott substation, in honor of that pioneer smoke-eater of the old Columbia engine company. Later in the year a surplus 40-foot government fireboat was purchased by means of a 90-day loan from various waterfront industries and a fund-raising drive planned to make it a permanent part of the city's firefighting equipment.

Mayor Mottman's long fight for an adequate and potable water system was vindicated when a two million gallon reservoir and pumping plant was built at McAllister Springs near Nisqually and eight miles of reinforced pipe installed to link the new municipal waterworks with the city mains. City fathers were also negotiating for purchase of an east waterway site for a new sewage treatment plant designed to stop the century-long dumping of raw sewage in Budd Inlet. Modern mercury vapor lights replaced the old ornamental light standards on 4th avenue and on the west side bridge, and the former USO on east 4th, obtained with a down payment of $5,300 donated by the Elks lodge, was opened as a community center. Local motorists, fuming in the traffic jams of cross-state and ocean beach traffic which funneled through city streets, were cheered when Highway Director Shain announced that the new super-highway between Portland and Seattle would by-pass downtown Olympia.

The post-war army national guard was well established at the armory, with a brigade headquarters commanded by General Neil McKay and a self-propelled automatic weapons battery of the 700th antiaircraft artillery battalion being recruited by Captain Gordon Newell, recently returned from command of a similar unit in Europe.

The landmark Kneeland hotel, originally the McKenny building and ex-officio state capitol, appeared to have received a new lease on life in June when William Shively, formerly of the Savoy hotel in Seattle, and R. L. Eagan purchased the business. A month later, however, Fire Marshal H. L. Lynch and Building Inspector W. R. Turner condemned the old structure, finding flammable doors, open light wells, defective fire escapes and other violations of 20th century fire and building codes. The upper floors of the historic building were sealed off to gather dust for the next couple of years. For good measure, the inspectors closed down the Hutson hotel, ordering its 20 residents to leave at once and the crumbling hostelry razed. This was the once splendid Carlton House, which had survived two major fires and the revelry of countless territorial politicians and lobbyists.

DEPARTMENT OF DIRTY TRICKS

An interesting exercise in politics occurred in May when Congressman Fred Norman, who had defeated Charles Savage for the office in the last election, died and a special election was called to replace him. Savage and Attorney General Troy filed for the Democratic nomination; Russel V. Mack, Hoquiam publisher, Tom Hall, Herb Seiler and Olympia real estate man Monroe Burnett for the Republican choice. In the May primary, Savage defeated Troy 16,800 to 12,000; while Mack outpolled his nearest Republican rival, Hall, 9,000 to 3,700. The total Democratic vote was 29,000 to 17,000 for the Republicans. Savage garnered more votes than all four of his Republican opponents. He appeared to be a shoo-in to regain his congressional seat.

But between the primary and the June general election, somebody within the state Republican organization established an early version of Richard Nixon's "department of dirty tricks." The third congressional district was suddenly flooded with pink pamphlets urging voters to *"support your next congressman and ours . . . Charles Savage."*

In bold-face type it was attributed to the *Progressive Communists of America!*

There was no such organization. It was the product of the fertile imaginations of those engaged in character assassination on the easy-going, totally honest Mason county logger, but it did the job. In the finals Mack edged out Savage 33,400 to 31,800.

One of the mysterious perpetrators of the smear, identified in the newspapers only as "Mr. X," later recanted, expressing "regret that the man with one of the best records in Congress had to go," but Savage's congressional career was over.

Harry Truman was back in town in 1948 to spend two days with his old congressional buddy Wallgren, bringing Mrs. Truman and his daughter Margaret with him in the course of a campaign tour of 18 western states. The presidential party was conveyed from Bremerton to Olympia on the *Olympus,* a luxurious motor yacht which the state fisheries department had purchased as government surplus. Wallgren solemnly asserted that the teak-paneled beauty was just a workaday fisheries patrol boat, but Langlie was loudly proclaim-ing the extravagance of "the governor's yacht." In any event, the Trumans enjoyed the Puget Sound cruise and Harry made one of his fighting speeches in Sylvester park before departing for McChord Field to take the presidential plane *Independence* for a flight over Grand Coulee.

The seven-car red, white and blue "Freedom Train" also arrived at the Jefferson street yards that year, carrying 127 of the nation's most priceless documents, including the Bill of Rights and Declaration of Independence. The patriotic streamliner, sponsored by the American Heritage foundation, had covered 33,000 miles from its starting point in Philadelphia. It was officially greeted by Governor Wallgren, the mayors of all southwest Washington cities, military brass from Fort Lewis and one honor student from each school in Thurston, Mason, Lewis, Pacific and Grays Harbor counties, after which it was opened to the thousands of ordinary citizens lined up to view the venerable documents of democracy.

The community drive to finance the ex-Coast Guard fireboat went over the top with $8,315 collected. This paid the government its $7,500 price for the $60,000 vessel and left a balance for needed renovations. The Chamber of Commerce asked a reluctant city government to take over future care and maintenance of the fireboat and a long-range Alfonse and Gaston act ensued between city hall and the Port of Olympia as to which agency should have the honor (and expense) of ownership. Meanwhile, out in the sleepy rural community of Lacey, a local booster club called the Elephants donated funds for the purchase of a second-hand Ford fire truck and the Lacey and Lakes District fire department was organized.

Bids were let late in the year for the Capitol Lake project, including the dam, spillway and fish ladder to be constructed just south of the west side bridge at a cost of $915,950.

Secretary of State Belle Reeves died in January at the age of 77 and a few days later Wallgren appointed Senator Earl Coe, chairman of the state Democratic committee, to serve out her unexpired term. Coe found himself in the role of acting governor on the day of his appointment, both Wallgren and Meyers having departed on out-of-state journeys.

ACTING LIKE A REPUBLICAN

On the political scene, Arthur Langlie, the erstwhile Cincinnatian and exponent of nonpartisan politics, continued his very partisan efforts to gain control of the state Republican party apparatus and woo local politicians, while working hard for the nomination of New York Governor Tom Dewey as the G.O.P. presidential nominee.

In a public recantation of his previous nonpartisan leanings, Langlie told a group of eastern Washington party faithful, "In Olympia I found myself surrounded by Democrats. Then we found the Democrats were knifing us in the back." The indication was that he had become a convert to the political axiom that "to the victors belong the spoils," and his audience responded enthusiastically. The very Republican *Spokesman-Review* commented approvingly, *"He has lost his Cincinnatus accent . . . he is acting like a Republican stalwart."*

Langlie had the party organization well sewed up by filing time and had only feeble primary opposition from Senator John T. McCutcheon, a progressive Republican who had some Grange and P.U.D. support and took credit for defeating Langlie's 1943 timber board bill, which he called "a design for industry mastery," and James M. Greene, a Chelan county insurance man who enjoyed some veterans' organization support. Firm party rule by Langlie prevented their campaigns from ever really getting off the ground.

This was not the case with Wallgren's primary rival, Clarence D. Martin, who leaped into the fray on the last day of filing, expressing dismay at Wallgren's "loose methods" and a feeling that "all is not well at Olympia." The primary contest thus evolved into a contest between three governors . . . one "in" and two "outs."

As Democratic primary challengers are prone to do, Martin relieved Langlie of much of the task of tearing up the Democratic incumbent. Martin zeroed in on the close association between Wallgren and University regent and teamster boss Dave Beck, calling them "political bedfellows" and "a morally bad combination loaded with power politics and all the evils that go hand in hand with machine politics." This provided Langlie with heavy ammunition with which to blast a virtually nonexistent "Wallgren political machine" in the general election campaign.

Martin's traditional plea for Republican support went unheeded in 1948 and he received only 89,851 votes in the primary. Wallgren garnered 165,775 and Langlie 206,851 in what the United Press called "a sensational political comeback," although the total Democratic vote was well ahead of the Republican total.

In the finals, Langlie ran on a "team basis" with former Speaker Herb Hamblen, who had political strength in the Spokane area and was the only Republican candidate who enjoyed labor approval.*

Langlie's campaign issues covered a wide spectrum . . . the Sun Lakes state parks "scandal," the "resignation" of Parks Director Tom Martin, the "yacht" Olympus and Wallgren's "two Cadillacs." He promised to remove the two bars which he said Wallgren had installed in the mansion and he harped on what he called Wallgren's "cellar gang" . . . left wingers in the administration headed by ex-Montana Congressman Jerry O'Connell. All had long since been kicked out or departed voluntarily to the ranks of the Progressive party, but Langlie delivered his strictures in the present tense, frequently referring to "an army of subversive termites swarming about the capitol."

Nor did he hesitate to quote the little McCarthy committee of Representative Canwell, which had been meeting amid a glare of publicity to declare the state threatened by hosts of "iron-disciplined Communists." He lumped former Wallgren confidant O'Connell with leftist Commonwealth Federation and Pension Union bosses Tom Rabbitt and William Pennock and Communists in general, thus pioneering the guilt by association technique used so effectively by Senator McCarthy.

And, for good measure, he climaxed his campaign oratory with the question, "Do you want a Dave Beck dominated governor?"

Wallgren probably did as much as Langlie to insure a change in administration in 1949. His uninspired and largely defensive campaign gave the impression that he had found the administrative tasks of the governorship boring and he didn't much care whether he was reelected or not. When Langlie charged him

---

*Although Hamblen lost the election, his effort was not unrewarded. Langlie subsequently appointed him to the first supreme court vacancy, which occurred in 1949.

with "machine politics," the debonair Wallgren replied "My machine is better than Langlie's any day." To his opponent's outraged cries of extravagance in regard to the *Olympus* and the two gubernatorial Cadillacs, Wallgren offhandedly announced, "If the voters don't want to go first class they better get another governor."

When Langlie began using the legislative investigating committee's findings on the Capitol Club . . . "The only regular activities in which all of the members are permitted to participate is the monthly payment of dues" . . . as a major offensive weapon, Wallgren appeared to lose his sense of humor. After the Langlie attacks prompted heckling in regard to the fund-raising organization, the governor would respond grumpily, "There isn't such a thing. I told the boys to cut it out two years ago."

The club had been the brain child of Wallgren's highly political chief of the state patrol, a former railroad brakeman and union official named Herb Algeo. Jack Gorrie, Wallgren's executive assistant, was president and Art Garton, director of conservation, vice president and secretary. The Capitol Club had gained additional adverse publicity when Algeo, who acted as treasurer, let it be known that "a shoe box" containing an undisclosed but presumably sizeable portion of the funds had been "stolen" from his desk at patrol headquarters in the Legislative building.

The Langlie forces also made much of a slick paper publication on the patrol produced by a pair of professional advertising solicitors and heavy on full page whiskey ads, and a "penthouse" constructed atop the Seattle patrol headquarters at a cost of $600,000.

Wallgren didn't improve his Langlie-inspired image as a machine politician when he took to the highways and byways of the state in a sound truck said to be the "gift" of the employees of the department of labor and industries. On his amplified tour of the hustings the governor occasionally went on the offensive, attacking Langlie as "do-nothing governor" who was "trying to serve the private power companies, ruthless timber barons and giant monopolies," but he was more often on the defensive . . . or attacking the state's press for its overwhelming support of Langlie.

FERRYBOAT SERENADE

Wallgren also made a serious mistake in making the Puget Sound ferry controversy a major campaign issue, putting himself in the position of having to find a solution to the long-standing and thorny problem before the election. In July of 1947 his administration had refused Black Ball ferries a permanent 30 percent rate increase over the 1937 schedule. The company had suspended operations early in 1948 and subsequently acquired county charters to resume service, raising its fares 169 percent. Wallgren, seeking a quick solution, ignored previous tax commission figures on the navigation company's worth and made an offer of $5,425,000 to Peabody and the stockholders, threatening a duplicate state ferry service if his offer wasn't accepted. The cost of the ferry purchase and Agate Pass bridge, essential to an integrated Sound transportation system, would be financed by toll bridge authority bonds and users were promised a one-third reduction of fares under state operation.

In August, with the primary election looming on the horizon, Wallgren announced that the toll bridge authority had agreed to meet Peabody's asking price of $5,925,000, but that fares would have to be increased 50 percent until completion of the Agate Pass bridge. This made Peabody's previous fare increase requests seem reasonable and cast doubts on the basis of Wallgren's plans for state operation of the ferries.

Langlie promised to find "a sound solution" to the ferry problem, pointing to his success, as mayor, in modernizing the decrepit street railway system of Seattle. He poked fun at the highway department's purchase of the ferry *Crossline* for the Narrows route . . . a former Peabody boat which had been sold to Canadian owners and which, the administration found to its embarrassment, couldn't be brought back into the United States without a special act of congress . . . and he was vociferously critical of the failure to begin construction of the Agate Pass and new Narrows bridges.

Wallgren got himself into more hot water when, in the course of his dickering with Peabody, he threatened to have the Kaiser shipyards in California build a whole new state ferry fleet to replace Peabody's aging vessels, most of which had been purchased second-hand in San Francisco after completion of the Golden Gate and Bay bridges. Puget Sound shipyards and industrial boosters were outraged.

On August 30 the ferry company stockholders gave the state a 90-day option to purchase and the hostile legislative council subpoenaed Wallgren to appear before that body and reveal his financing plans. The governor charged politics and refused to appear. He was further frustrated by a tax-payers' suit, which delayed the purchase; then by Auditor Yelle, who filed a demurrer against signing the bonds. Wallgren, in desperation, announced that bids would be called on the bonds anyway . . . on October 26; one week before the primary election.

During the final phase of the campaign Wallgren seemed totally preoccupied with the ferry issue, orating at length on the subject even in the drylands of eastern Washington where the voters couldn't have cared less.

The governor had embarked upon the sea of politics in a cranky craft, and when no bids were offered on the controversial ferry and bridge bonds he was sunk.

On November 2, 1948, Arthur B. Langlie outpolled Wallgren 316,151 votes to 294,437, becoming the first Washington governor to regain that office after having been defeated . . . and the only Republican elective official in Olympia for the next four years. The absence of the straight party ballot and of Franklin Roosevelt from the national ticket, coupled with Wallgren's lackluster campaign and an overwhelmingly biased press, had given Langlie his second chance.

Wallgren could take scant comfort only from the fact that the liquor by the drink initiative, which he had long advocated, was approved by the voters who, at the same time, rejected a Langlie-blessed initiative to remove beer and wine from taverns and make it available only at state liquor stores . . . thus closing "the glamorous dives that are seducing our youth." The veterans' bonus was also approved by initiative.

Langlie's triumph was doubtless dampened somewhat by the loss to his friend Tom Dewey to Harry Truman, who had been written off by practically all of the nation's political pundits.

The Democrats regained control of the state house of representatives and the lesser elective offices returned to full Democratic control. Otto Case, the venerable King county politician and militia officer, who had nimbly leaped back and forth between the Republican, Democratic and Bull Moose parties during his long career, ran as a Republican for land commissioner and was defeated by Jack Taylor, who thus joined Langlie as the only elective official to survive a past defeat. It was a tactical blunder by Case, who had believed the polls which predicted an overwhelming Republican victory and turned his coat accordingly. Charles Savage, in his last effort to regain his congressional seat from Russell Mack, also made a strategic error. He shied away from fully embracing Harry Truman and was supported largely by the old-fashioned liberals who no longer constituted the potent political force they once had.

Earl Coe, the Wallgren-appointed secretary of state, won the position in his own right, leading the ticket and running ahead of Truman.

When it was all over the governor-elect turned himself in at a California hospital for treatment of "overexertion and ulcers."

1949

Governor Langlie was back in Olympia by January of 1949 for his triumphant reinauguration and the *Olympian* announced that the capital city, *"ordinarily a quiet and peaceful community"* would soon *"take on its biennial circus atmosphere when the 1949 session of the state legislature gets under way on 'the hill' ."*

Immediately after the inauguration ceremonies, Wallgren departed for Washington D.C., where it was reported he would *"take an important post in the administration of his personal friend, President Harry Truman."* Langlie forthwith ordered the bar removed from the mansion.

The house of representatives, with a lopsided 67 to 32 Democratic majority, reelected Charles Hodde as speaker. Hodde, although small of stature, had developed into one of the toughest and most knowledgeable speakers in legislative history. Republicans sometimes referred to him bitterly as "Little Caesar" and claimed that he was blind in his right eye . . . the one which should have observed members of the minority demanding the floor . . . but he was generally respected for his thorough knowledge of state government as well as his parliamentary abilities. The senate, which was 27 to 19 Republican, chose Lester Parker of Aberdeen as president pro-tempore, but Democrat Meyers continued to preside as lieutenant governor, having evolved into a polished parliamentarian in his own right.

On the surface the state's financial goose was hanging high. Fat wartime revenues and delayed capital improvements had resulted in a $223 million treasury surplus, with only $3 million in ourstanding bonded debt, but in fact the governor and legislature were facing an economic crisis. Post-war tax collections were falling off. School costs were climbing astronomically. The highway system was obsolete and broken down, and Initiative 172, approved at the last election, was expected to result in increased welfare costs of $150 million.

Langlie expressed the opinion that "new taxes are inescapable" and met with Hodde to ask that Democratic legislators "shoulder a share of the tax burden." The "Capital News Letter" of C. E. Johns and Carl Downing, published in the Olympia *News,* predicted that *"Arthur B. Langlie will get along passably well with the house leadership, in particular Representative Charles Hodde of Colville, who is a sound thinker and not stampeded by the hysteria which certain groups are exhibiting with regard to a larger biennial state budget."*

The problems of both were eased somewhat by the fact that the "cold war" and the purgative effects of the Canwell committee's communist hunt had practically eliminated the left-wingers from the legislature, but the speaker and the governor were not in full accord as to what the sources of new revenue should be nor, indeed, upon the actual amount needed. Langlie estimated the coming deficit at $100 million; Hodde at $135 million. Although he had vigorously opposed any kind of income tax during the campaign four months earlier; Langlie was determined to impose a two percent flat rate income tax as a "temporary" two-year measure to meet school building needs. Hodde favored increased business taxes and an extension of the sales tax to personal services. And most legislators had their ideas

for raising new income which didn't agree with either the governor's or the speaker's.

Wallgren, as debonair and smiling as ever, made his farewell address to the lawmakers, urging purchase of the Sound ferry system, construction of the Cascade highway tunnel and increased appropriations for tourist advertising.

Langlie, looking as if his ulcers were still bothering him, attacked Wallgren's proposed budget as "unrealistic", claiming that the outgoing governor had overestimated revenues by $30 million.

A RAISE IN PAY AND A RAISE IN TAXES

Before tackling the fiscal problem, the legislators joyfully voted themselves the first real pay raise to come their way in the 40 years since statehood. The per diem of the lawmakers had previously been frozen into the constitution at $5.00 a day, while other elective officials' salaries had been constitutionally limited on a scale ranging downward from $6,000 for the governor to $3,000 for the lieutenant governor, auditor and superintendent of public instruction. The 1947 session had placed a constitutional amendment on the ballot permitting the legislature to set their own and the elective officials' salaries. The liberal electorate of 1948 had approved the measure and no time was wasted in implementing it. Legislative pay was raised from an unconstitutional $15.00 per day while in session to a legal $100 a month on a year-around basis. The governor's salary was tripled, from $6,000 to $18,000, the lieutenant governor got $7,500 and other elected officials $10,000. The senate, after indulging in the time-honored legislative celebration of abstract thrift by proclaiming the raises too high, gave in with seeming reluctance to the house proposal and turned to the financial welfare of the state as a whole.

Long and bitter debate ensued as to the kind of new taxes to be imposed. The house favored an $80 million bond issue for capital improvements in lieu of the governor's cherished flat income tax. The senate rejected Hodde's tax bill and substituted an increase in the sales tax to four percent. The house rejected the senate bill and forced a conference on alter-

450

natives. Langlie announced plaintively that the legislators' proposals were "merely an escape mechanism" which was "playing directly into the hands of the Communists".

Things had reached a total impasse as the first month ended, and on February 2 the governor delivered a special message to the legislature, condemning the bonding plan and calling for strict economy "to save the country from National Socialism". He then set about applying pressure on the shaky coalition leadership of the senate to get his income tax measure out of the rules committee. He succeeded and the bill appeared suddenly on the calendar, to the dismay of Al Rosellini and his loyal Democrats. They staged a five-hour filibuster, but the income tax eventually passed in that chamber, only to be rejected in the house by a 41 to 58 vote, with only four Republicans voting for it.

The senate then brought forth a $72 million package of nuisance taxes, including increases in the parimutuel, liquor by the drink, lubricating oil, utilities and business and occupation taxes and a raise in the gasoline tax from five to 6½ cents a gallon.

Speaker Hodde at this point made a deal with Langlie to get the income tax through the house if the governor would push the capital construction bond issue through the senate. After long and involved caucuses with the Republican senate leaders, Langlie came up with an unworkable compromise which would defer the issue of bonds until two years after the next legislative session. There was no provision for retiring them, so it would have been impossible in any event to put them on the market without action by the 1951 legislature. This "iffy" proposal did not impress Hodde or his Democratic cohorts in the house, so things were again stalemated, with both the bond and income tax measures in limbo.

On March 8 the senate released a biennial budget bill which was nearly $74 million out of balance and a conference committee met in overtime with the capitol clocks stopped. Langlie sadly predicted a special session "within 14 months". Johns and Downing reported that *"veteran observers agree the 31st legislature is the worst ever for its apparent inability to get down and face obvious facts".*

After 10 days of frustrating overtime the lawmakers threw up their hands, passed a hopelessly out of balance budget of $592,584,-234, and went home.

Langlie had little luck in getting passage of his pet measures. The income tax, the major government reorganization recommended by the Shefelman "Little Hoover" committee and his cherished timber board proposal all died. The only two major executive request measures to pass were a merger of the transportation and utilities and public utilities departments into a single public service commission, and the creation of the nation's first board against discrimination.

The latter looked like a major accomplishment on paper, but the board took the position that it could fight bigotry only by moral 'suasion and not through the police powers of the state. During the Langlie years, and for a decade thereafter, it limited itself to "exposing" cases of prejudice and was protective in theory only.

The Agate Pass and new Narrows bridges were funded, a quarter of a million dollars was alloted to tourist promotion and a measure was passed prohibiting motorists from installing television sets in automobiles unless they were screened from the view of the driver.

The final report of the Canwell Un-American Activities Committee was submitted, stating that 40,000 copies of material relating to Communism in the state had been accumulated. Armed state patrolmen conveyed the documents in three locked safes to a sealed room in the Legislative building, but efforts of right-wing legislators to reconstitute the committee were beaten down.

Langlie vetoed a bill making the state highway advisory commission an administrative agency, a measure which was more than a little embarrassing to him. Wallgren had retained Langlie's highway commission intact and they had become impressed with the performance of Wallgren's highway director, Clarence Shain, who was high on the list of political enemies the ex-Cincinnatian proposed to eliminate. After vetoing the bill, he dumped his entire commission, fired Shain and, after several months appointed William Bugge in his place.

THROW THE RASCALS OUT

Having purged himself of any lingering tendencies toward non-partisanship. Langlie set out to purge state government of actual and suspected Democrats. At least 3,500 state workers were fired, ranging from department heads to elevator operators, with genial E. A. (Eddie) Alexander wielding the ax as "director of personnel".

Soon after his inauguration the governor reappointed his political crony, Seattle Fire Chief William Fitzgerald, to head the state racing commission. H. P. (Dick) Everest took a leave of absence as head of the University of Washington school of journalism to become his executive assistant, and Kay Willis of Seattle was appointed as the first gubernatorial press agent, despite the fact that Langlie had bewailed the tendency of Mon Wallgren to hire "tax-paid propagandists". Ernest Brabrook returned as "the crusty czar of the budget office" and Evro Becket, another of Langlie's closest political henchmen, replaced Admiral Gregory as head of the liquor board.

Few of Langlie's appointees to top office were outstanding. Some were bland, colorless and reasonably efficient, while others were notable liabilities. Outstanding in the latter category was the Reverend "Doctor" Henry Ness, a fundamentalist preacher whom Langlie appointed chairman of the parole board. Willful, contentious and erratic, he soon had the board in turmoil and the inmates of the state's penal system in a state of sullen resentment which was no doubt a major factor in subsequent uprisings at the penitentiary and reformatory.

John R. Cranor, who had been in charge of Japanese prisons under General McArthur during the post-war occupation, replaced Democrat Tom Smith as warden of the penitentiary. Cranor had excellent credentials, but he had reached retirement age at the time of his appointment and seemed determined to close out his career as a leader in that vague field known as prison reform. One episode which caused amusement to many, although not to Langlie, took place when the warden hosted a number of inmates on a picnic outside the walls. Determined to make the occasion a memorable one for his charges, Cranor provided horses for them to ride. A couple of them galloped off into the sunset in true western style and never returned. As the ensuing years took their toll, Cranor let control of the prison slip more and more into the hands of convict bosses, further setting the stage for the violent riots which were to mark the Langlie administration.

The state park department, faltering under the widespread criticism of its Sun Lakes adventure, showed no improvement under Langlie appointee Sam Clarke, who was removed from office late in 1949 and replaced by John R. Vanderzicht, a former park commissioner, with Charles deTurk, former Indiana parks director, as chief planner.

One of the more interesting of the Langlie appointees was Roderic Olzendam, described by George W. Scott in his University of Washington doctoral thesis, "Arthur Langlie: Republican Governor in a Democratic Age", as *"a hard-headed Tacoma business man"* and *"a parsimonious hatchet-man"*.

Langlie, angered by the "ultra-liberal" Initiative 172, which he blamed for throwing his welfare budget out of kilter, was determined to mount a full-scale offensive against "welfare chiselers" and he found welfare career man Verne Graham unfitted for the task of squeezing the "fat" out of the social security budget. Olzendam replaced Graham as director.

Olzendam may have been "hard-headed", but he was also flamboyant and controversial. While setting out grimly to pare welfare costs, he instituted weird and wonderful expenditures of the taxpayers' money which set the pattern for present-day bureaucrats.

He ordered all stocks of stationery, forms and other printed materials in his department thrown out, to be replaced with new supplies printed in green ink. Green typewriter ribbons replaced the standard black ones. When asked for his rationale, he explained that, after all, Washington *is* the Evergreen State.

OVERPAID OLDSTERS

Wasting no time in his frontal attack on the welfare initiative, Olzendam began releasing a series of dramatized reports which all began with the oracular assertion, "I find . . . ." He hired an assistant director "for program development" . . . a forerunner of the present fantastic array of deputies, assistants, coordinators and consultants within the bulging state bureaucracy . . . and an internal auditor, who headed up an undercover investigative staff which put welfare recipients through the wringer, even to the extent of examining their credit ratings. As a result of the internal auditing activities Olzendam "found" that the welfare rolls contained three percent "unqualified" recipients and 16.3 percent who were "overpaid."

While Olzendam's "I Find" releases harped on the undue liberality of Initiative 172 and the manifold abuses which took place as a result of it . . . *"The benefits are about the highest, not only in the United States but in the world"*. . . Langlie provided a background refrain offering ratable reductions in welfare payments as necessary to "prevent a difficult situation in the state's business."

Olzendam fired 200 employees, mostly caseworkers whom he suspected of sympathizing with the lame, halt, blind and aged, although the workload under 172 had increased by 35 percent. He employed a teacher of elocution to instruct his upper level staff people in effective public speaking against Initiative 172, and an Irish tenor to render lullabies in the Olympia headquarters of the welfare department. His more portly staff members grumbled at his inauguration of a Swedish gymnastics program during the lunch hour.

The year was marked by a running fight between Langlie, Olzendam and the Old Age Pension Union. The union's president, William Pennock, had been widely publicized as a Communist by the Canwell committee and he was in a combative mood. In August he led 250 pensioners to the capitol, where they were joined by local sympathizers for a mass meeting on the steps to demand a special session to provide additional welfare money. Langlie ventured from his office to denounce Pennock and found himself hooted down by the crowd and outshouted by Pennock who told the governor, "We have been baited by experts." (the Canwell committee) "We didn't come here to be baited by a rank amateur."

The pension union followed up with a writ of mandamus barring ratable reductions. The writ was quashed in November with the provision that Olzendam must provide 30 days notice of pending reductions as required by law. The pensioners then flooded Olzendam's office with hundreds of protest letters. Olzendam "found" that this was an example of how Pennock and the other leaders of the union "use their elderly followers for burnt offerings at the slightest excuse."

In December Pennock and his colleague Tom Rabbitt, former state senator who had also been painted a vivid red by the Canwell committee, obtained a ballot title for an initiative to recall Langlie on the grounds of malfeasance (aiding monopolies in return for campaign funds), and violations of the Hatch act (permitting Olzendam and his newly trained orators to stump the state on speaking tours against Initiative 172).

Rising welfare costs and sniping at his efforts to reduce them were to haunt Langlie's entire second term, and it was quickly apparent that his battle was in vain. The legislature had appropriated $206,208,000 for welfare and Langlie's figures indicated tthat if the provisions of 172 were strictly adhered to, the cost would be $240 milllion. Although ratable reductions cut the average welfare grant from $66.50 to $63.35 per month, a severe winter and rising unemployment kept the total costs going up. The state was soon spending $3.5 million more each month than it was taking in and Wallgren's treasury surplus was dwindling rapidly.

THE GOVERNOR AND CAPTAIN PEABODY

Nor was the welfare conflict the only irritant to Langlie's ulcers in 1949. The much publicized ferry crisis remained unsolved, although the funding of the two major bridges made the state purchase more feasible by consolidating routes and releasing the highway department's Narrows ferries for other service. The legislation had also given Langlie, as chairman of the toll bridge authority, the authority to sell its own bonds instead of paying the normal four percent interest plus five percent discount. Still the unbending figure of Captain Alex Peabody, president of the Black Ball ferry line, blocked the path toward fulfillment of Langlie's campaign promise to get the company at "a reasonable price."

Early in 1949 the governor undertook his first strategic move against the embattled Peabody. The governor's agents set out to purchase equipment and landing sites at several key Puget Sound crossings. The theory was that a threat against Peabody's monopoly would force him to meet Langlie's offering price of $3 million. At a heated and stormy meeting in the executive offices in August, Peabody demanded the Wallgren price of $5,-975,000. Then, to compete with the upcoming state toll bridge traffic, Peadoby set about buying property for a new Lofall ferry crossing. Langlie countered by withholding lease of essential state tidelands. Peabody bought private tidelands 150 feet south. Langlie pressured the county commissioners into refusing to build access roads to the site. Peabody built privately owned "Black Ball boulevards."

There were unofficial reports that the governor's ulcer was kicking up.

Toll bridge authority attorney George Boldt advised Langlie that the navigation company wasn't worth $4.25 million and that the state purchase should be abandoned "unless at fire sale prices." The governor was in too deep to back off now, however, and he took to the air with an impassioned appeal to public opinion . . . "When a private monopoly defiantly and arrogantly resists regulation and * * * declares it is law unto itself, a responsible government has no honest choice but to break the unbridled grip." This he followed up with an offer of $3.9 million, mailed directly to the company's stockholders with a reminder, by way of a second radio speech, that his offer was well above the market value of their stock. He also threatened a suit by the public service commission to place the company back under state regulation, with "corrective legislation" as an ace-in-the-hole. Furthermore, he pointed out, navigation company stock would be completely worthless "in six or seven years when the Sound is bridged."

The company's board of directors responded with a unanimous vote of confidence in Captain Peabody. Attorney General Troy charged publicly that Langlie had intentionally made an unacceptable offer to save face and extricate himself as gracefully as possible from the ferry purchase, which he had branded as "socialistic" when Wallgren first proposed it. The governor, Troy insisted, should produce or admit that his campaign promises were "the mouthings of a political opportunist."

Troy's remarks added salt to Langlie's wounds. Captain Peabody had outmaneuvered and outfoxed the governor throughout the entire first year of his second term, and he was in a monumental snit.

The governor's efforts to set up a personnel committee aimed at establishing a statewide merit system also foundered on legal shoals in 1949, the courts ruling that it was beyond the powers granted by the administrative act of 1921. Langlie retained Alexander as head of what was euphemistically called "the central personnel office," but it was without legislative or legal sanction and state government continued under four different "merit systems," with the majority of employees covered by none of them.

A series of devastating floods which had put units of the national guard and the state patrol on emergency duty, the Russian mastery of the atomic bomb and the subsequent outbreak of

troubles in Korea prompted the governor to create a department of civil defense from his limited emergency funds. One of its first efforts was a drive to recruit 10,000 civilian aircraft spotters to alert the state against communist bombing planes, which was somewhat of an exercise in absurdity in an age of high-flying jet aircraft.

THE BATTLE OF CAMP MURRAY

Military matters further embarrassed the governor when he sought to remove Adjutant General Ensley Llewellyn from command of the national guard. The military code of 1943, pushed by Langlie during his first term as a means of taking the guard out of politics, made the office of adjutant general permanent unless specific grounds for dismissal were established by a court martial. Llewellyn stood on the law and Langlie hand-picked a review board of militia officers, most of whom were private power company executives in private life. Although they displayed little enthusiasm for their task, they dutifully sustained 11 of the 12 charges of "misconduct" against Llewellyn. Among them was the allegation, straightfacedly attested to by the loyal Chief Fitzgerald, that the general had permitted public gatherings in the monolithic Seattle armory, which Fitzgerald said was a fire trap.*

Llewellyn charged that the review board was made up of "Langlie stooges" and demanded a properly constituted court martial. The court agreed with him and issued an injunction prohibiting the governor from interfering with the adjutant general in the performance of his duties. Langlie ignored the court order, had the locks changed at the military headquarters at Camp Murray and appointed the proprietor of a Lewis county sewing machine shop, to replace Llewellyn, who eventually gave up and returned to his Tacoma advertising agency. Scott, in his thesis on the Langlie years, concluded that *"the unseemly incidents spanning a year were complimentary to neither man,"* although it must be pointed out that Llewellyn clearly had the law on his side and

---

*The building is still in use daily as one of the public facilities of the Seattle Center on the former "worlds fair" grounds.

that Langlie was in the position of being hoist on his own petard . . . the military code which he had sanctimoniously espoused as a means of "taking the national guard out of politics."

Finally the beleagured Langlie became more deeply enmeshed in partisan acrimony as a result of the pension union recall movement. The Communist *Daily Peoples' World* of San Francisco claimed that the Democratic party was behind the Pennock-Rabbitt recall effort. A meeting of Democratic leaders was hastily convened in the Seattle office of Warren Magnuson and Art Garton, the state chairman, disclaimed responsibility, stating that the recall was "sponsored by the same people who in large measure were responsible for the election of Governor Langlie." Langlie retorted somewhat shrilly that the Democrats were "desperately attempting to wash their hands of those extremist associations which they so zealously espoused a year ago."

The Olympia *News,* one of the state's few Democratic papers, ountercharged that Langlie had promised during his campaign to reduce the state payroll by 4,000 but that during the first five months of his term it was up nearly 25 percent over the first five months of Wallgren's last year in office.

At year's end the ferry problem remained unresolved, the national guard in considerable turmoil, the bureaucracy reluctant to reduce itself appreciably, welfare recipients screaming that they were being slowly starved to death, welfare costs rising and the treasury surplus melting away like the proverbial snowball in hell.

But Langlie had managed to sell the yacht *Olympus,* although at a sacrifice price that must have amused Captain Peabody.

EARTHQUAKE!

The capital city, the stage upon which the state's political drama was being played, received its greatest shock on April 13, 1949 . . . and so did the actors upon that stage. Just before noon of that day the worst earthquake

---

*It is now published by Eddie Alexander, Langlie's erstwhile "personnel director," and has changed its politics.

in the recorded history of the area struck the Puget Sound country. Two Olympians were killed, one by falling bricks, the other by a heart attack, several were injured and the town would never look quite the same again.

Up on the hill the massive dome of the Legislative building shifted on its base as the stone observation lantern at the top rolled and wallowed like a ship in a storm, trapping a pack of sightseeing cub scouts 270 feet above the unstable earth. Across the street the stone sides of the Insurance building collapsed like a dry waterfall in a haze of billowing dust.

Down town the ornate stone cornices and balconies of the old statehouse thundered to the street and the remaining 19th century business blocks showered the sidewalks with bricks and ornamental masonry. The condemned Kneeland hotel, built on the site of the town's first circus . . . the one with the collapsing seats . . . likewise collapsed and was subsequently demolished. Across Capitol Way the top two floors of the three-story Pacific building next door to the National Bank of Commerce were twisted and torn loose, sustaining such damage that they also had to be torn down. The pioneer Chambers block at 4th and Capitol Way lost its tall ornamental cornices and the Mottman building shed bricks and masonry into the intersection and through the roof of Ben Moore's restaurant. Automobiles were crushed by debris and the loss of life was actually extremely low in view of the havoc wrought by the quake. Had the quake occurred a few minutes later, with lunchtime crowds leaving the buildings and filling the sidewalks, it would doubtless have increased the death and injury toll many times.

The Legislative building and other state government structures were declared unsafe and bureaucrats sought temporary quarters in less damaged quarters. Within a few days emergency cost-plus contracts had been signed for repair of the state buildings and workmen were erecting a giant inclined timber tramway to the top of the capitol dome. The 100-ton cupola, designated by the architects as a "lantern of liberty," had not been anchored to the dome and was beyond repair, although the frightened scouts who had occupied it during the quake were all brought safely down the twisted circular staircase. The stone structure was demolished, to be replaced with the steel replica which still crowns the structure, having survived another severe earthquake in 1965.

455

REPLACING THE LANTERN atop the capitol dome was a major project following the earthquake of 1949.

1950

On January 9, 1950, Treasurer Tom Martin and Auditor Cliff Yelle called a joint news conference to announce that the treasury balance had reached zero. Attorney General Troy followed this up with an opinion that the warrants being issued against the non-existent state general fund were an illegal violation of the constitutional debt limitation statutes.

The Olympia *News* periodically annoyed Governor Langlie by its publication of specific examples of the difficulty the chief executive was having in keeping his campaign promises to control bureaucratic spending and reduce the state payroll. It pointed out that ex-Senator Ernest Huntley, Langlie's tax commission chairman, had employed five secretaries, whereas his predecessor had gotten by with one. It was suggested that the corps of secretaries was needed because Huntley, who was believed to have political ambitions, had taken to writing personal thank you letters to all citizens gracious enough to pay their taxes.

The state's financial crisis was alleviated somewhat in April when the supreme court ruled that deficit warrant financing was constitutional, applying the rather ingenious reasoning that the debt limitation applied only to money borrowed outright; not to the warrants, which were actually state IOU's, held by the banks to draw interest. In addition, the outbreak of the Korean war that spring had increased the flow of revenue dollars and there was hope that the treasury wouldn't be deeply in the red until mid-summer. The *News* was reporting *"much talk of a special legislative session,"* however, observing that *"many people wonder how long the banks can carry state government."*

RED INK SESSION

In mid-March Republican legislators met in the governor's office and expressed strong opposition to the calling of a special session. Democrats renewed their call for an emergency session the next day, promising to support the governor on supplementary revenue legislation.

At this point Langlie was clutching at financial straws and was pushing a proposal to shift the costs of welfare to the counties when state funds were exhausted. He scheduled a meeting with county commissioners on July 1 to submit his plan. Hodde and Garton conceded that Initiative 172 was "too broad in the standards set for unemployment under general asistance," but attacked Langlie's plan to shift the welfare burden to the local level. For good measure, Smith Troy ruled the plan illegal the day before the scheduled meeting and the commissioners sat tight agreeing only to await a court ruling on the matter.

At this point the governor decided that a special session was "inevitable."

By June 11, the ship of state was fully embarked on a sea of red ink, with deficit spending to be continuous during the final year of the biennium. After a meeting with the legislative council, Langlie called the special session for July 17. The upcoming election put the legislators on thier best behavior and the announcement of the Korean war by President Truman monopolized the front pages and discouraged grandstanding. The session was brief and relatively businesslike, although it made only a feeble effort to plug the state's financial leaks. Langlie, relying on the legislative council's reluctant promise to consider priority needs, submitted no specific requests for new revenue measures while asking for an emergency appropriation of $22 million to keep welfare going. The legislators performed their ritualistic celebration of frugality by reducing this to $16 million. They appropriated an additional $450,000 for the pensions of injured workers and their widows, extended the veterans' bonus to surviving next of kin and passed a bill allowing Korean servicemen to register by mail. With a wary eye on the 1950 elections, members of both parties pussyfooted delicately around the graduated net income tax amendment and departed from the capitol without taking any meaningful steps to make income meet expenditures.

The special session did, however, pass a bill which gave Langlie the clout he needed to come to terms with the redoubtable Captain Peabody of the Black Ball ferry line. The executive request measure, which the governor should have submitted in 1949, gave the public service commission jurisdiction over county-chartered ferries, thus negating Peabody's ploy to evade state regulation. This put Peabody in a corner from which he could not gracefully extricate himself and in December he accepted $4.9 million for the company's facilities and most of its fleet. On the face of it, Langlie had made a somewhat better deal than Wallgren had proposed, but under the final agreement Peabody retained two large and two small ferries. These he moved to Canada to form the nucleus of a British Columbia Black Ball line, which operated profitably until the provincial government subsequently bought that company at another plump profit for Peabody's stockholders. It also left the Puget Sound fleet short of boats to meet the Korean war traffic boom.

Langlie quickly assured the Seattle Chamber of Commerce that there was nothing in the state take-over that "even remotely strikes at the free enterprise system", and the following year the ferries' red and black stacks were repainted green and white, the Black Ball houseflag was lowered and an evergreen tree flag ceremoniously hoisted, and the state of Washington was in the ferry business. The state and local government coffers immediately lost some $200,000 a year in taxes and the following year the public service commission negated the state's original excuse for the takeover by ruling that Peabody's rate boost of 1947 had been justified all along. For good measure, Manager W. C. McDowell of the state ferries conceded that there had been "nothing basically wrong with the company's conduct".*

No sooner had the ineffective 1950 special session adjourned than the pension union filed Initiative 176, which it called "the Freedom from Want Act of 1950". It placed a mandatory $65 a month floor under grants and provided for free telephone, laundry and dry cleaning services for recipients, while specifically banning ratable reductions.

Langlie denounced the measure as "a disguised maneuver to hasten the insolvency of Washington" and, with the trusty Olzendam, set up a "non-partisan citizens' committee" to get the necessary 72,000 signatures for Initiative 178, "the Common Sense Welfare Initiative," which made a $60 pension floor subject to yearly revision based on the consumer price index and left it up to Olzendam to decide whether a recipient needed the full $60. It forbade automobile ownership by recipients, along with property of any kind "beyond a reasonable value" . . . and specifically *authorized* ratable reductions.

Pennock promptly labeled it "Langlie's Freedom to Starve Act", but the Seattle Chamber of Commerce just as quickly threw its full support behind it. Chamber President Tom

---

*The state ferry deal remained a politically sensitive area throughout the Langlie administration. Rate increases were avoided from 1951, when the state took over the operation until 1956, although basic operating costs increased by about one-third. In fact, rates were lowered by $300,000 a year just prior to the 1952 election when Langlie was running for an unprecedented third term. All this was accomplished by floating an additional $2,549,000 in second lien toll bridge authority bonds. When the house highway committee in 1955 questioned Langlie about his politically timely rate reduction he blandly replied that he was "not adverse to doing things the people like prior to an election".

Pelly, lugubrious spokesman for the Seattle establishment, stumped the state in its support and it eventually gained the endorsement of the American Legion, Grange, Farm Bureau and various other voices of the silent majority. The state medical association, too preoccupied with battling "socialized medicine" to take an active part in support of the Langlie-Olzendam initiative, confined itself to a denunciation of Pennock's 176. Attorney General Troy expressed the pre-election opinion that 176 was "a monstrosity", and that 178 "falls short of meeting the need". He advised the electorate to reject them both.

Enraged, the governor charged that the attorney general was "indulging in his habit of issuing opinions for political purposes", in this case, he was convinced, at the instigation of Speaker Hodde, who was of the opinion that the legislature should find the internal fortitude to provide enough revenues to maintain a decent welfare standard. As was often the case when frustrated, Langlie resorted to shrill invective and genteel demagoguery. He did not hesitate to capitalize on the anti-Communist hysteria generated by the Canwell committee, which reached its climax during the 1950 elections, frequently quoting Lenin's opinion that "the democracies can be drowned in red ink" in his battle for 178 and against 176. He told a meeting of the American College of Physicians and Surgeons, meeting in Boston, that "political blue sky has come about because political life is too often a dumping ground for broken down haberdashers and unsuccessful lawyers . . . and other incompetents who had failed at their vocations".

The *News,* in referring to the obvious slur upon the President of the United States, wondered about the "unsuccessful lawyers, pointing out that Langlie hadn't exactly set the legal world on fire before entering politics."

OFF-YEAR ELECTION

Despite his manifold problems, Langlie firmly maintained his position as active head of the state Republican party, leading the legislative and congressional fight, as well as campaigning indefatigably for Initiative 178. He held himself aloof from Senator Cain, who had proven himself a bombastic incompetent in the halls of congress. Cain had verged on paranoia as he filibustered to block Truman's appointment of Wallgren to the national security resources board on the grounds that he had surrounded himself with Communists, and television had brought the unedifying spectacle into thousands of Washington homes. The national Republican committee worked out a campaign schedule which kept Cain out of his home state except for one appearance in support of Payson Peterson against Henry Jackson, which was a lost cause in any event. Cain suspected that Langlie had arranged the scheduling and also quarreled with the governor over his plodding and ineffective state chairman, Dawley . . . particularly in regard to his lack of imagination and fund-raising abilities. In a notable reversal of traditional roles, the state Republicans were holding $1.00 basket socials and the Democrats $100-a-plate full course dinners.

Dissension was rife in other areas as well. Conservative Republicans were still good and mad at Langlie for twisting their arms on the corporate income tax at the 1949 session and for keeping a flat-rate income tax out of the party platform. The governor's hand-picked King county chairman, Ray Moore, added fuel to the flames when he moved to screen all Republican candidates for office and ruled that they "must agree to cooperate without reservations with the county organization". Although it was explained that these steps were taken to "prevent subversive or irresponsible persons from filing under the Republican label", the pre-primary endorsement policy precipitated a major hassle within the Republican ranks of the state's most populous county. Moore's arbitrary ruling was not made any more acceptable by the fact that he was proving to be as poor a fund-raiser as Dawley, having been able to produce only $4,000 of his $38,000 quota for the state organization.

While ignoring incumbent Cain, Langlie personally picked Seattle mortgage banker W. Walter Williams, like Tom Pelly a prototype of the Seattle establishment, to run against Democratic Senator Warren G. Magnuson. Like Langlie, Williams expressed himself frequently as favoring "morality in government".

When it was all over and Williams had been thoroughly clobbered by the mighty Magnuson, the loser wrote to Langlie thanking him for his help, "both openly and under cover".

The Republicans gained in total seats in the legislature, while losing the senate, although the eight dissident Democrats would continue their coalition with the Republicans to provide a nominal majority of conservatives.

The voters of 1950 took a far more conservative line than those of 1948. Initiative 178 passed with a majority of more than 80,000, while 176 was rejected just as decisively. A $20 million bond issue for the upgrading of state institutions was approved, but a similar measure to provide capital improvements for institutions of higher education was rejected.

Vic Meyers, discovered vacationing in Arizona with his dented and dusty state Cadillac, explained that he was soaking up the southeastern sun on doctor's orders as an "arthritic cure." Langlie, who was being driven about in a modest Oldsmobile, posed for a picture while C. Montgomery ("Gummy") Johnson affixed a "Keep Washington Green" tag to the executive vehicle as a means of publicizing the recently coined forest fire fighting motto of the Keep Washington Green association, of which Johnson was assistant director. There was considerable grumbling when the state public service commission granted in-state telephone rate increases which made it twice as expensive to call Vancouver, Washington, as Portland, Oregon, and made a toll call to Pullman as costly as one to San Francisco.

CITY CENTENNIAL

Male citizens of the capital city were growing beards for the town's centennial celebration, which took place in May, with 94-year-old Riley Ticknor, born in the Skookumchuck valley, and 89-year old Mrs. Mary Campbell Garson, born on Hawk's Prairie as king and queen of the pioneers, by virtue of being the oldest living natives of Thurston county. Betty Mayrent of Burbank, "queen for a day" on Jack Bailey's radio show, was rewarded by being flown with her husband to Olympia to participate in the festivities, and one of Puget Sound's two surviving passenger steamboats, the *Virginia V,* brought the "mosquito fleet" era briefly back to Percival's dock (now owned by the Puget Sound Freight Lines) as she carried excursionists down the bay.

In the arena of local politics, Mayor Mallory came out a poor third in the mayorality primary, real estate men Ralph A. Swanson and Ed Henderson (the one-man chamber of commerce) getting the nomination. In the finals, Swanson beat Henderson amid overtones of the traditional open town politics. Swanson made it clear he believed Olympia needed a bit more night life to attract and entertain the Fort Lewis soldiers . . . including at least one "good bottle club."

In the realm of civic improvements, bids were called for the new municipal sewage treatment plant on the east side of the port fill, citizens of the McKinley school district got a new building to replace the ancient wooden fire trap, and the Capital Apartments lost its traditional role of top prestige rental property with the completion of the modern six-story concrete and glass Maple Vista apartments a block south on Capitol Way where the ornate Victorian "mansion" of Governor Ferry had stood. County government had outgrown the Tenino sandstone courthouse and bids were opened for a new four-story annex behind it. The commissioners were somewhat nonplussed when the low bid was $275,000 . . . $75,000 above the estimate . . . but they went ahead and built it anyway and it was occupied in the spring of the following year.

Port and city authorities were still arguing over who should assume responsibility for that unwanted baby, the fireboat. The Lacey volunteer fire department, growing fast and feeling its oats, offered to take it over, but the suggestion was ignored and the once proud craft remained on the waterfront, forlorn and neglected.

At the mature age of 100, Olympia had achieved a population of about 15,000. Its modest skyline, with only the capitol dome rising above the taller fir trees, was even less impressive than it had been, a number of the older buildings having lost their upper floors and lofty cornices, or been demolished completely and replaced with modern structures of lesser height. During its century as a town it had slipped from first to twelfth in population, but the capital was secure at last . . . or so its civic leaders thought . . . and there was time now to promote new smokestacks, new payrolls and an expanded population.

Almost nobody except General McKenny's daughter Margaret, who wrote books about birds and mushrooms and kept a wary eye out for tree-choppers and parking lot builders, had given thought to pollution, either industrial or human. Everett was still proudly calling itself "the city of smokestacks" and Tacoma was filling in its tidal estuaries to provide space for stench-producing industries. Olympians hoped to emulate their neighboring cities and some day, perhaps, achieve a status symbol as impressive as Tacoma's monumental smelter smokestack, which daily belched out tons of arsenic and other deadly poisons to help hide the mighty mountain which the city had for so long insisted should be named after it.

1951

The 32nd legislature convened on January 8, 1951, amid an atmosphere of uncertainty regarding the state treasury's $147 million debt, the possibility that federal Korean war taxes might cut the ground out from under state revenue-producing plans, and the usual partisan problems to be expected with a Republican governor and Democratic legislature.

The 54 Democratic representatives were unanimous in their choice of Hodde as speaker for a second term, while the 21 Republican senators and eight conservative Democrats chose Ted Schroeder, a conservative Democrat from Puyallup, as president pro-tem. Arch-conservative Democrats Lindsay and Cowen were appointed chairmen of the revenue and appropriations committees. That was the only concession to non-partisanship in the senate, however. Rosellini and his loyal Democrats were denied membership on any important committees. The state Democratic central committee strongly condemned the eight dissidents, causing some nervousness among them.

The senate, with 46 members, employed a staff of 121, with salaries ranging upward from $7.50 a day (for pages) to $50 a day (for Secretary Herb Sieler, with a total bi-weekly payroll of $22,108.50. The Republican caucus dded the first political "flak," Bob Cummings of committee room "X" and Rosellini fame, although his position was disguised as "committee clerk" at $15 a day. Nepotism was as widely practiced then as now in the patronage hiring, with Daisy Sieler, daughter of the senate secretary, on the payroll as workroom clerk at $16, Mary Louise Meyers, Vic's daughter, as a secretary at $12.50 and Vic, Jr., as a law clerk at $15.

The house, with 99 members, had only 119 employees, Chief Clerk Holcomb having slashed the payroll to 20 below that of the 1949 session.

FISCAL TRINITY

Governor Langlie, in his address to the assembled legislators, took considerable pride in having converted Wallgren's $32 million surplus into a deficit of only $47 million. This had been accomplished, he said, by postponements of expenditures, pre-auditing and other economies which had made possible a reversion of $13 million. In view of the voter rejection of the higher education bond issue, he recommended delay in capital improvements and a delay in salary increments. He hopefully resubmitted his merit system proposal for state employees, a grand jury law ad inclusive pre-auditing authority. He proposed a bond issue to pay off the state debt, a $37 million reduction in total appropriations and a corporate franchise tax to raise $30 million to $40 million. He said he planned to "cut out governmental frills," but the *Olympian* expressed *"consternation"* at his unorthodox budgetary proposals. For the first time in history, a governor submitted not one, but *three* different budgets to the legislature.

The first, which he termed a "spenders' budget" totaled $473 million with a built-in deficit of $83 million. His "moderate" proposal included a $50 million underappropriation for welfare needs, even by the austere standards of Initiative 178, a $37 million cut in other spending and a $34 million deficit . . . assuming the four percent corporate income tax were approved. It further proposed that new public school requests of $31 million be passed on to local government through authorization of a one percent franchise tax and imposition of the sales tax by cities and counties and incorporated his unique suggestion that the $47 million existing deficit be wiped out by having the various state funds buy state bonds.

His "austerity" budget involved no new taxes, removed $36 million in liquor profits from counties and cities and reduced state services to a bare minimum.

Legislators viewed the three volumes with disgust, convinced that Langlie was dexterously shuffling off his responsibilities on them. The governor, on the other hand, awaited the praise of press and public for his statesmanship and was deeply pained when the opposite reaction took place. Even his former right-hand man, Ross Cunningham, editorialized in the Seattle *Times* that Langlie's fiscal trinity constituted *"arithmetical gymnastics."* Democrats circulated copies of the editorial and the governor took to lecturing reporters regarding their responsibility for "facts," claiming plaintively that the press was portraying him as "a confounded waster who makes Wallgren look like a piker."

Indeed, the governor seemed able to make nobody happy that session. City and county officials denounced him bitterly for his proposals to cut off their liquor profits and burden them with the state's share of school support. The PTA, WEA and the rest of the school forces, led by the redoubtable Pearl Wanamaker, called Langlie's school support proposals "disastrous," and the governor again lost his cool. When the PTA flooded his office with protest letters he wrote brusquely to the state president of that organization demanding to know where she proposed to raise the money and "whom would you tax and how?"

The state bankers' association screamed to high heaven that Langlie's proposed corporation franchise tax was "just an income tax in disguise," and other corporations and small businessmen joined in the outraged chorus.

In the meantime, legislators retaliated against Langlie's budgetary buck-passing by celebrating a veritable high mass of frugality. Senator Lindsay trumpeted against the regular salary increases of social security employees in the face of a certain deficit. Olzendam, under pressure from all sides for added administrative and payroll costs under initiative 178, proclaimed his intention to reduce all grants radically, remove 2,600 people from the old age assistance rolls and 8,000 employables from general assistance.

Legislators retaliated by pointing their fingers at a slick, full color publication of 10,000 copies, edited for Olzendam by Seattle publicist Leo Lippman for a fee of $1,000 to portray the "human interest" side of Olzendam's department. They went on from that to generally berate "the thousands of publications turned out by the state printing presses." One lawmaker, pointing to stacks of departmental biennial reports on his desk, grumphed to an *Olympian* reporter, *"A lot of that junk isn't even good for firewood . . . the booklets are too thick to burn. You have to tear them apart page by page to get a good fire."*

The state printer had billed the various departments for over a million dollars the past biennium . . . and that didn't count work turned out in small printing plants maintained by the secretary of state and departments of highways, labor and industries and social security. In addition to Olzendam's venture into photo-journalism, the legislative celebrants of economy took particular umbrage at Auditor Yelle's leather-bound report alleged to have cost more than $7.00 a copy, and a state institute of forest products survey of deadwood in logged off areas, which cost the taxpayers $90,000 and was duly reported in a small library of publications. A separate booklet was produced for each of the twelve districts involved in the survey, although the text was identical except for a few pages of tabulated matter.

The press agent and the lucrative "survey" of state functions by outside "consultants" had become an integral part of the Olympia scene and, despite the lamentations of legislators and taxpayers, the intervening years have been marked by a continuous proliferation.

As the celebration of thrift continued in the legislative halls, the chairmen of the house and senate appropriations committees demanded that department heads "submit written justification for every additional person they wish to hire," Lindsay proclaiming that his perusal of Langlie's budget proposals indicated a desire to hire 2,200 more employees during the coming biennium. Leroy Hittle of the Associated Press ventured the rather naive opinion that *"the leaders of the legislature have taken their first step to stem the ever-growing state payroll."* He was making the mistake common to legislative observers . . . that of confusing the time-honored and purely ritualistic celebration of thrift with a real intent to cut costs. How well that and succeeding legislatures have made good on their threats to invoke "spending reform" and to "control the bureaucracy" is evidenced by

the simple fact that the number of state employees increased from somewhat over 10,-000 in 1953 to about 54,000 in 1973, while the biennial budget has gone up from less than $700 million in 1951 to an astronomical figure of nearly seven billion dollars.

Also proliferating in 1951 were the number of computers, which were viewed by bureaucrats as the very latest in status symbols. They . . . and the representatives of IBM . . . were appalled when Representatives Charlie Johnson of Olympia and curmudgeonish Perry Woodall of Toppenish introduced a bill prohibiting the state agencies from paying rentals of over $100 a month to IBM, unless the contract included an option to purchase the equipment. The use of "punch-card accounting machines" had begun with the department of unemployment compensation in 1938 and, by 1951, had spread to the departments of budget, highways, labor and industries, the University of Washington and Washington State College. IBM was collecting $200,000 a biennium for rentals of equipment, a figure which Johnson and Woodall considered exhorbitant.

Computer services now cost the taxpayers many millions of dollars a biennium, with IBM still collecting the rental fees.

In late January the attention of the legislators was distracted by a horrifying blaze in a ramshackle Hoquiam "nursing home." Bitter cold, which had frozen Tumwater falls into solid ice, made it difficult for firemen to fight the blaze and only 16 of the elderly occupants were saved, while 21 were burned to death. Representative A. B. Comfort, named to head an investigating committee, urged that the state take over operation of all nursing homes, claiming with probably only minor exaggeration that "no poor farm conditions are worse than these nursing homes."

BOILING OUT THE FAT AND TRIMMING TO THE BONE

The lawmakers soon reverted to the celebration of thrift, however, with eastern Washington Neanderthal Cowen thundering that "not only will there be no new taxes, but there will be no need for any!", and Langlie calling such a parsimonious attitude "unrealistic and shortsighted."

It was becoming increasingly apparent that it was the strategy of the house majority to pass Langlie's $473 million "spenders budget," with some $65 million added, leaving the Republican-dominated senate to confirm it and pass the corporation tax to fund it . . . or bear the outrage of the educational, welfare and other special interest forces if they cut it.

Langlie took a look at the house budget and announced that "I have never seen a worse bill." He was especially exasperated by an $18 million welfare contingency fund appropriated to him, well knowing that it wasn't enough to fully fund the program and would put him on the hot seat throughout the coming biennium as welfare recipients and organizations demanded its expenditure. It was like having a handful of money to pour down an unlimited number of rat holes.

Langlie, seeking a course of fiscal moderation, was caught between the efforts of house Democrats to increase his "spenders' budget" and of Senators Cowen and Lindsay to carve the house budget to the bare bones. As Lindsay hacked away at the budget, Pearl Wannamaker and Hodde kept constant pressure on the governor to renounce the senate "economy bloc" on the grounds that it was patently unrealistic to trim an already inadequate budget to the point where no new taxes would be needed. Three Republican members of the senate appropriations committee felt the same way, Carlton Sears, Tom Hall and Asa Clark bolting the Lindsay-dominated committee and holding a rump caucus with house leaders to work out a more realistic budget bill.

With the committee itself split on the issue, that astute politician Al Rosellini kept pressure on to force the measure out and onto the floor, or turn it over to the senate as a committee of the whole. The coalition stuck together and the move was defeated after much bitter debate, the United Press quoting Speaker Hodde's appraisal that *"it looks to me like the good old French system of 15 parties with a new cabinet on every bill."* That night Lindsay threw up his hands and quit as committee chairman. *"I felt the committee should have a new chairman who can explain this budget,"* he told the press. *"God knows I can't."*

Tom Hall, a sandy-haired wiry Skamokawa farmer, was appointed foster father of the orphaned budget. The next day the legislators had reached an apparent agreement on a budget approximately $45 million out of balance, Hall announcing hopefully that the governor's four percent corporate tax would balance it.

At this hectic period the legislature authorized an interim budget committee to carry on a continuing study of fiscal affairs and administrative expenditures with the help of a full-time legislative auditor. An *Olympian* editorial set forth the optimistic opinion that this *"should mark the last time a session of the Washington legislature runs overtime because of prolonged arguments over appropriations and methods of raising revenue."*

Already well into overtime, the house passed the governor's corporate tax on a straight party line vote, all Republicans opposing it. The senate refused to concur and wrangled endlessly over three alternative proposals . . . a three percent flat income tax, a broadened sales tax as recommended by Hodde, and a 50 percent increase in the business and occupation tax. The marble halls swarmed with lobbyists, determined to insure that *their* particular special interest employers were protected from any tax increase, prompting outspoken Representative Rasmussen to observe that "the only people not represented by lobbyists in the legislature are the people." The 600 lobbyists, who now preferred to be called "legislative representatives," were not amused.

On March 16 the senate dumped Langlie's tax bill once and for all, with Republicans pushing for a typical last resort nuisance tax package . . . a five percent increase in liquor taxes, a one percent franchise tax, sales tax extension to personal services and a compromise two percent corporation tax. This was rejected three days later by the house, creating a final impasse with the plaintive requests of the governor for "legislative partnership" going unheeded. The next day Hodde announced a house-senate agreement to adjourn *sine die,* still deadlocked on the tax proposals.

Langlie announced with disgusted resignation that he would call a special session within ten days.

THERE'S ALWAYS TIME FOR TRIVIA

The air of crisis which pervaded the capitol had not discouraged the usual sideshow aspects of all legislatures . . . the solemn introduction of silly bills, the preoccupation with trivia and the ceremonial pomp an circumstance so dear to the legislative heart.

On March 2, with six days to go, the senate took time out to deliberate a bill introduced by Thurston county's Carlton Sears to declare the willow goldfinch the official state bird. A presumably facetious amendment to substitute the crow was beaten down and when some urban lawmaker wanted to know what the hell a willow goldfinch was, Senator Tisdale rose to deliver the ornithological information that "it's the little yaller wild canary you see flyin' around." The measure, sponsored by the ladies of the state garden clubs, was passed by a vote of 38 to 0.

Another bill by Senator Jess Sapp of Sedro Woolley, would have imposed a special tax of $5.00 a year on all television sets. His fellow senators, envisioning an uprising of red-eyed telly fans, voted it down decisively.

On March 11, with the capitol clocks stopped for the past three days, Representative John R. (Jackrabbit) Jones of Waterville proposed that a committee be appointed to "get the clocks back in working order," suggesting Tacoma watchmaker George Kupka as chairman. Speaker Hodde delivered the straight-faced ruling that "such an investigative group is beyond the legislative jurisdiction." While the overtime wrangling went on, laced with graveyard humor, a group of solicitous lobbyists hired Irv Sholund and his Evergreen Ten, a local dance band, to play in the rotunda outside the chambers, but Eldon Barrett of the United Press observed that *"most of the legislators didn't appreciate the music. They apparently had the blues because their expense checks had stopped with the clocks."*

In the final days, when it became apparent to the lobbyists that no tax bills were going to pass, they departed to rest and gird themselves for Langlie's threatened special session. Barrett reported that *"Senator Tisdale of Raymond is preparing to revive his 'Soup for Solons' movement. He pointed out that a majority of the lobbyists who had been supplying most of the lawmakers' meals had departed. Two years ago Tisdale's campaign brought 25 gallons of clam chowder, 200 cakes from Spokane, many gallons of rhubarb sauce from Sumner, and many other victuals for hungry legislators."*

POMP AND CIRCUMSTANCE are dear to the legislative heart. The state's business can always be postponed to escort a queen to the rostrum.

MID-WINTER MADNESS

In early March a 58-year former state liquor store operator named John Uleman was dragged off to the county jail charged with having offered bribes to Representatives Reuben Knoblauch and Kenneth Simmons, Sumner Democrats, to vote against a controversial bill requiring a vote of the people before Spokane PUD districts could buy the Washington Water Power company. Uleman, who had been out of a job since the Langlie purge of state employees, admitted having made the offer, but said he hadn't realized it was a crime. Representative August Mardesich was appointed chairman of a committee to investigate the matter and the unfortunate Uleman was subsequently found guilty and given a suspended sentence.

A number of legislators expressed themselves as outraged, not so much because the bribe had been offered, but because of its size . . . $25 per vote. With the Korean war inflation pushing pork chops to 65¢ a pound and a decent blend of whiskey to $3.50 a fifth, that kind of money wouldn't go very far in 1951.

Young Senator Nat Washington suffered an embarrassing moment or two early in the session when he took his wife and four-year-old son Nat, Jr., for a stroll in downtown Olympia. During an unguarded moment, little Nat dashed to a pretty red box on the corner and turned in a fire alarm. The elder Washingtons stood stricken on the street corner as traffic lights turned red, bells rang and, according to the *Olympian, "the air broke into a series of ear-splitting whirrs."* Representative Washington told the *Olympian* reporter, *"Olympia has a helluva lot of fire trucks."*

The 1951 session was enough to drive anybody crazy, but the only member to be so certified was Senator Miller of Spokane, who was shipped off to Eastern State mental hospital early in the session. Thurston county Prosecutor Hewitt Henry had ordered a sanity hearing after conferring with Democratic leaders including State Chairman Harry Henson and Floor Leader Rosellini. Sergeant at Arms Mehan testified that the senator's actions had been "far from rational," in that he had kept four or five pages busy on silly errands and a like number of stenographers "to turn out silly letters."*

It was further said that his behavior had been "erratic" during his attendance at a bar association gathering in the Hotel Olympian . . . that he had interrupted the speeches with loud applause and shouts and had greeted a chilly Governor Langlie with a hearty shout of "Call out the militia . . . it's revolution!" Miller explained that he had just been trying to "be sociable and warm up Langlie," but since he had presumably not been drunk, which would have made his behavior commonplace and reasonably acceptable. this was taken as further evidence of mental unbalance. Furthermore, Sergeant Wayne Thorp and Officer Chester Breuer of the Olympia police testified that the senator had been taken into "protective custody" during an early morning altercation in the bus station with a group of Canadian soldiers. Miller testified that he had become enraged when the Canadians found it impossible to believe that he was a senator.

*If such behavior were accepted as evidence of insanity in today's legislature a considerable number of lawmakers would be occupying "rubber rooms."

STOP THE CLOCKS AND PASS THE LEGISLATION

Strangely enough, the 32nd legislature did succeed in passing a number of bills, some of them of some importance. The most significant was the passage of the state youth protection act and creation of a division of children and youth within the department of institutions, to be assisted by a 21-member citizen council for children and youth. Although Langlie seemed peculiarly insensitive to the plight of those in the state's deteriorating institutions . . . lack of interest or planning had resulted in proposed expenditures of only one million of the $20 million institutions bond issue . . . this was the first step toward a general dramatic upgrading of all state institutions during the subsequent administration of Albert Rosellini. Julia Butler Hansen, who had gained the chairmanship of the powerful house highways committee, succeeded in pushing through a bill creating an appointive highway commission with administrative rather than mere advisory responsibility, along with a $62 million highway construction bond bill.

The pesky tax tokens, which had been flung in the face of Governor Martin and annoyed consumers ever since, were abolished and the state bought back all those in the hands of retailers. Regulation of nursing homes and bottle clubs was placed in the hands of the state and a $5 million revenue bond issue was approved for a University of Washington research hospital, to be retired by rental income from the downtown metropolitan tract, the site of the original territorial university. Funds were appropriated to build a fishway at the Capitol lake dam and begin construction of a parkway along the west shore route of the pioneer Olympia-Tenino railroad. Another appropriation of $2,450,000 was made for a non-classic and functional state office building to be built on the edge of the capitol campus. After numerous delays and appropriation of a lot more money, this became the present General Administration building, which marked the first structural and bureaucratic overflow from the original campus to its periphery.

The lawmakers also created a seventh congressional district, which Republicans branded as an exercise in gerrymandering, and passed a single tax bill . . . placing a license fee on pinball machines . . . including the automatic payoff kind the supreme court had just declared illegal. Langlie vetoed them both.

These accomplishments, such as they were, had necessitated the longest overtime session in the state's history to date . . . 11 days of stopped clocks compared to the former record of 10 days achieved in 1949. Although it was obvious that the legislature could no longer handle its business in a single 60-day session every two years, its membership displayed the usual legislative inability to face reality and refused to consider an annual sessions bill sponsored by Representative Ed Henry, which would have authorized off-year sessions limited to 30 days.

Soon after adjournment, the *Olympian* reported *"one of the most startling actions in executive-legislative history."* Langlie vetoed the entire omnibus appropriations bill because it was "unrealistic" and he considered it "unfair to deceive the people" by approving new services while "refusing to provide the revenue."

The bedraggled legislators were much opposed to having their noses returned to the grindstone without a reasonable period of recuperation, but the angry governor ignored their joint resolution to that effect and called them back into special session on March 27, appealing to them to "put aside petty political bickering and unite to provide the state with a balanced budget." Speaker Hodde probably summed up the feelings of the legislators when he told the *Olympian* that *"if the gentleman downstairs* (Langlie) *would read that book on how to win friends and influence people he and the legislature would be a lot better off."* The senate responded to the governor's plea by spending the first day in petty bickering over subsistence pay, the coalition finally beating down an effort to raise the per diem from $10 back up to $15.

Fortunately for the chief executive's peace of mind, none of the solons could draw *any* expense money until the matter was settled, which eliminated the possibility of a really long-drawn-out argument.

This was the ninth extraordinary session in the state's history, one third of which had been called by Langlie. The longest had been those of 1909 and 1925, which had both run 59 days; the shortest was that of 1920, which adjourned in one day after authorizing the bonus for veterans of the first world war.

On March 29 the governor's corporation tax bill was reintroduced in the house and failed to pass by two votes. After much lobbying by the governor's office it was reconsidered the next day and lost by two votes. The leaders of the senate coalition meanwhile drifted aimlessly in a sea of frenzied finance. A six-member ad hoc committee trimmed $7 million from the vetoed omnibus budget bill, but frowned upon a proposed 100 percent increase in the business and occupation tax. Langlie admitted ruefully to the press that the lawmakers were *"getting absolutely nowhere to date."*

Finally the house, in dithering desperation, gave birth to a two-headed monster, joining the appropriations bill to a varigated package of taxes and tax increases, although the constitution clearly states that a bill shall cover only one subject. Less than a dozen legislators so much as saw the 86-page bill before it passed on April 7 with only nine Republicans in each house voting for it.

The governor reluctantly signed the bill on the last possible day, expressing the opinion that it would probably be declared unconstitutional.

It was.

In August the supreme court ruled that it was unconstitutional on two counts . . . it covered more than one subject, and a net income tax on corporations, which was a part of the package violated the past court rulings that all classes of "property" (and the justices considered income to be property) must be taxed equally. All the state warrants issued since April were valueless and the commonwealth was financially paralyzed.

IF AT FIRST
YOU DON'T SUCCEED . . .

Langlie, breathing heavily, called the legislature back into another special session on August 24.

By this time the crisis in state government was such that even the most ostrich-minded of legislators could no longer bury his head in the sands of empty rhetoric and evasive tactics. With the fall elections looming on the horizon, a 16-member bi-partisan committee was formed to work with the governor in a serious effort to find new sources of revenue on a "share the blame" basis. It drafted a package including a 20 percent raise in the business and occupation tax, a ten percent increase in liquor taxes and new assessments against transient room rentals. It also included fractional increases in grain brokerage taxes, a half cent tax on soft drinks, a 40¢ per gallon tax on soft drink syrups, a 10 percent utility tax and increase in the charge for state liquor permits from 50¢ to one dollar. The philosophy seemed to be one of spreading the load around so widely that no one group . . . except the common folk who would ultimately pick up the whole tab . . . would be heavily affected.

The legislature accepted the hydra-headed tax package and a new $680 million budget. Langlie, the advocate of economy in government, vetoed from it an amendment by Rosellini that state agencies should cut expenses 2½ percent "if possible." The unfriendly Olympia *News* commented sourly that not only had the governor's bi-partisan committee confused the issue of who was responsible for another record budget and a whole gaggle of new taxes, but *"also lost in the shuffle was the governor's intent or ability to carry out any program of ecomony in the cost of state government."*

The second extraordinary session only lasted nine days and cost the taxpayers a mere $100,000. It had raised an additional $18 million and Langlie, with more optimism than accuracy, proclaimed the budget to be "approximately in balance." After a little time for reflection he conceded that a possible $18 million deficit constituted "an optimistic viewpoint."

The legislature, after three tries had, at any rate, met half its responsibility.

Higher education remained a major victim of the budget-making process, with a cut of over three million dollars. President Compton of Washington State University resigned after a protracted feud with the Langlie-appointed regents. The loss of 300 of the younger faculty members at the university prompted Dave Beck to resign in a huff, giving Langlie a majority on that institution's board of regents. President Raymond Allen likewise departed in the year, citing intolerable financial problems as the reason.

Even with the legislators back home, controversy continued to beset the Langlie administration. One of his more inept department heads, Fisheries Director Robert J. Schoettler, fired E. M. Benn, chief of enforcement, and 20 technicians and other key staff people resigned in mass protest. The department remained in a shambles throughout Schoettler's tenure.

Initiative 178 had been upheld by the courts and Olzendam, while expanding his bureaucratic trappings at Olympia, wielded the knife vigorously on welfare recipients. Ratable reductions reduced welfare costs from 49 percent to 42 percent of the total budget, relatives were pressured to provide support and by 1953 the rolls had been reduced from 107,000 to 93,000. Langlie and Olzendam were also embarked on a campaign to convince the state's oldsters that they weren't "pensioners" but "welfare recipients." The state's conservative press, with the Seattle *Times* in the vanguard, enthusiastically lent its help. A *Times* editorial of September 24, 1951, decried *"the mistaken notion fostered among the elderly that grants are something they are entitled to,"* and declared that they were rather, *"a kindly policy adopted by their fellow citizens."* It was made clear to the aged and destitute citizens of the state that they were damned well living on charity and they shouldn't forget it.

Olzendam eventually went too far, however. By September of 1951, with a serious question as to whether welfare funds would stretch, even with grants cut to the bone by ratable reductions, the Bremerton *Sun* broke the news that Olzendam had ordered each of his 500 field workers to arbitrarily terminate six old age pensioners to balance the budget. On a wave of resulting public indignation, Initiative 184 . . . another liberal welfare measure . . . was filed. Langlie viewed it as "a cleverly disguised time bomb to plunge the state into bankruptcy."

Over the next few months Olzendam's efforts cut the total welfare tolls so efficiently that ratable reductions were dropped and welfare ceased to be a major issue. The current federal Communist-hunt was finishing the job started by the Canwell committee and the red-tinged professional leaders of the state pension union were in the process of being completely discredited. There was enough bitter after-taste, however, that Langlie was prompted to ease Olzendam back into private industry the next year as he began campaigning for a third term and to make a further gesture of good will toward the senior citizens by appointing a state council on aging, which proved as ineffective as his board against discrimination.

The governor was apparently contemplating his third-term bid as early as 1951. Despite the legislative clamor over expensive state-financed publicity efforts he diverted $200,000 from his emergency fund to finance 25,000 copies of a 100-page slick brochure entitled

"Your Dollar's Worth of State Government . . . A Stockholders' Report." Roger Freeman, financial consultant to the governor, and publicist Lorin Peterson were the co-authors, the latter on a retainer basis with pay equivalent to that of the directors of major code departments.

There was further dissension on the hill . . . and the first of a long series of delays in construction of the new state office building . . . when Langlie complained bitterly that the 7½ percent architecture fee contemplated by Democratic capitol committee members Yelle and Taylor was too much; that *he* knew an architect that would do it for six percent. By late December, however, a new scandal had erupted in the capital city, diverting public attention from the continuing drama of the Langlie administration.

The *Times,* which disliked Land Commissioner Jack Taylor almost as much as it did its own political creation, Vic Meyers, had assigned its ace investigative reporter, Ed Guthman, to check out the land office. Guthman, who soon afterward won a Pulitzer prize for clearing the name of one of the Canwell-smeared university professors, was never able to find any "black spots" on Taylor personally, but his labors deeply implicated Sam Emmanuel, secretary of the state land board and Taylor's clerk, in highly questionable actions. Emmanuel was eventually indicted in Thurston, Pacific, Lewis and Pierce counties for allegedly soliciting bribes to "expedite" sales of state timber, a charge which he termed "preposterous." He was subsequently convicted on some of the charges, although like most indicted state officials, he never served a day in jail. There was no evidence that Taylor or anyone else had shared in his profitable sideline, but the much-publicized affair would have a profound effect on Taylor's fortunes in the next election.

KOREAN WAR DAYS

In the capital city itself, volunteer air observers, ignoring the availability of radar, worked around the clock scanning the skies for Communist bombers which would have been totally invisible even had they arrived. All citizens over 15 were urged by the civil defense authorities to join up. Wartime shortages and profiteering had prompted Harry Truman to clamp on tough price controls without loopholes for favored industries and Olympia housewives felt it was high time, what with choice sirloin steak up to an astronomical 90¢ a pound. There were increasing reports of strange unidentified flying objects . . . the first ever noted had been seen over Mt. Rainer . . . and alarmists feared that the Russians had beaten us into space. Some comfort was taken in the news that new U.S. air force jet fighters had broken the sound barrier without breaking themselves into fragments as pessimists had predicted.

The Olympia-Tumwater foundation, funded by the Olympia Brewing company, donated a replica of the famed Tivoli fountain in Copenhagen for the capitol grounds and it was duly accepted. On Easter, which happened to fall between special legislative sessions, hundreds of Olympia youngsters scurried about the landscaped grounds searching for eggs planted by the local American Legion members. It was observed by cynics that the children were the only people at the capitol that year who seemed to know exactly what they were doing.

The efforts of Mayor Ralph A. Swanson to provide a bit more "night life" for the capital city were frustrated by county Prosecutor Ralph G. Swanson, who annoyed local law enforcement authorities by going over their heads and personally closing certain walk-up hotels for offering too wide a range of after hours entertainment. Efforts of the city fathers to unsnarl the traffic bottlenecks on major streets were also frustrated as ever increasing volumes of traffic on state highways 99 and 101 overwhelmed the one-way streets. Local motorists fumed amid the fumes and wondered when the new "super-highway" from Portland would come to town. Another civic uproar was created by Dr. Bernard Bucove, the county health officer, when he suggested that it might be a good idea to fluoridate municipal water supplies . . . and concerned officials were still trying to find some way to finance the city's languishing fireboat.

The capitol commission bowed to history buffs and agreed to put a jog in the new Capitol Lake boulevard to avoid destruction of the pioneer Crosby house at Tumwater and the

Olympia *News* predicted dourly that the new scenic lake was going to silt up and become "Capitol Swamp."

Although the Crosby house was spared by the forces of progress, the last of the former governors' mansions was torn down at the site of the proposed new state office building just north of the capitol grounds at Union and Columbia. The 10-room house, built in the 1880s by banker Frank Gowey (who went broke in the panic of 1893), boasted a grand staircase brought around the Horn by sailing ship and four ornate fireplaces. Populist Governor John Rogers had lived there during his terms.

PUTTING THE CAPITAL BACK ON WHEELS

Some Olympians were alarmed by growing evidence that their city might lose the capital after all, not by legislative action this time, but by state agencies folding their tents like the Arab and silently stealing away to the more sophisticated and stimulating metropolitan atmosphere of Seattle. The park department, claiming that it was being crowded out of the old statehouse by the expanding comic opera bureaucracy of the civil defense department, signed a lease with the Seattle park board for office space in its Seattle headquarters. Director Vanderzicht insisted that no space was available in the capital city, although the chamber of commerce said it had located a suitable building at $1.00 a square foot compared to the $2.00 being charged in Seattle. The fisheries and game departments quickly joined the exodus and the division of programs and methods of the employment security department began looking for office space in Seattle on the grounds that it was "closer to the defense plants." The state board of pharmacy celebrated Independence day by making its move north.

The Chamber of Commerce showed no inclination to do battle as Langlie backed the wanderlust of his department heads. It was concentrating on "industrial development," trying to raise $50,000 to lure a garment factory to town and urging port Manager Ernest Gribble to start developing Puget Sound's last unspoiled and unpolluted estuarian area, the Nisqually delta, into an industrial site . . . presumably the smokier the better.

1952

In a sort of last hurrah for himself and the old age pension union he had for so long dominated, Pennock led a little band of a hundred or so protestors to the capitol early in 1952 to denounce the Langlie-Olzendam welfare cuts and demand a special session to fund the welfare program. The old people asserted they were going to "stay until we see Langlie" but his staff said he was "out of the state." At the five o'clock closing time state patrolmen arrived to eject them from the executive office. About half the delegation gave up and went home and the remaining 60 were invited by Secretary of State Cœ to spend the night in his office. Sympathetic Olympians contributed food and the next day the rear guard of Pennock's dispirited army straggled away from the capitol, pinning their hopes on still another liberalized welfare initiative, 184, to appear on the ballot that fall.

The state's welfare recipients weren't the only ones with an eye on the 1952 elections. Albert Rosellini, now a 14-year veteran of the state senate, had gotten himself the chairmanship of one of the proliferating crop of interim committees, the interim crime investigation committee, and he got more mileage out of it than anyone before or since. Like the good showman he was, Rosellini put his show on the road in the sticks, convening the committee's first session in the notoriously tolerant Grays Harbor timber and shipping town of Aberdeen. The drama was excellent from the start, leading off with spirited verbal exchanges between the chairman and Seattle attorney Joseph Diamond, who questioned the committee's legal authority to investigate crime on the local level. When Diamond interrupted the questioning of a witness who refused to answer questions about prostitution and bootlegging with an offer to "give the committee some advice," Rosellini drowned him out with his gavel and told him, "We don't want any advice from you! We know our authority and don't care to hear from you!"

469

AL ROSELLINI, CRIME-BUSTER

Among the more loquacious witnesses was a former Aberdeen madam who testified that she had paid over $5,000 in forfeited bail in recent years, but had never been brought to trial, and Grays Harbor Sheriff R. F. Simmons who conceded that "it is generally known that liquor is being sold by prostitutes and others on Grays Harbor, but there is no strong community feeling against the practice."

The big show was moved to Seattle next. Local television, which had been in its infancy during the last interim investigative drama, that of the Canwell committee, was prepared to take its cameras afield by 1952 and it brought the crime-fighting drama of the Rosellini hearings to thousands of viewers, with the big Italian-American ex-prosecutor as the hero. The committee inquiries were wide-ranging. It heard accusations against logging operators said to have stolen state highway gravel, but backed off when it was learned that the accused had previously testified against Sam Emmanuel, the indicted land board secretary. It heard testimony of state patrolmen and toll collectors that an estimated 25 percent of motorists crossing the Columbia river toll bridge at Longview escaped the $1.00 fee because they were friends, relatives or business associates of bureaucrats of toll collectors. State Patrol Captain Harold D. Austin took the stand to urge funding of a proper criminal identification bureau within the patrol.

Things really warmed up when witnesses were called to testify on the Seattle city government's "tolerance policy" in regard to gambling. An elderly man said he had lost $15,000 in the past 24 months in Seattle's "low-stakes" cardrooms and a stenographer claimed her husband had dropped $20,000 in a similar period, thus breaking up her home and marriage.

Mayor William F. Devin, who practiced the brand of pious respectability introduced so successfully to Seattle city government by Langlie, was at this time smarting under his recent defeat by non-establishment Democrat Allan Pomeroy. The lame duck mayor charged into the televised fray, challenging the committee to investigate "tie-ups with liquor and gambling interests among its members and other state legislators" and charging that the hearings were "purely political." He added that his administration had developed a program "which has effectively curbed commercialized gambling, prostitution and other vices."

State Senator William Goodloe, who could usually be counted upon to add verbal fuel to any controversy, got himself tossed out of the hearing room as the result of a heated debate with Chairman Rosellini following testimony of his client, the wife of a Walla Walla convict, that she had spent hundreds of dollars on unkept promises of lawyers and state officials to get her husband out.

Shaking his finger at the chairman, Goodloe demanded to know, "from the viewpoint of a Republican, whether you are running for governor." Gaveled down by Rosellini, he again rose to question the chairman regarding committee costs. Rosellini summoned Sergeant George Block of the state patrol and shouted, "Sergeant, you escort the senator out!"

The Associated Press reported that *still rumbling questions and protesting loudly, he was led from the room."* The mulcted wife of the convict *"had disappeared in the shuffle."* The Hi-Y "youth legislature" had declared "the dope problem" to be reaching crisis proportions and the TV drama reached new heights when a 20-year-old heroin addict wearing a white mask testified that he had taken up pimping to support a $30-a-day habit that had started at age 16 from smoking pot.

When the supreme court dismissed the suit of an Aberdeen police captain with the opinion that the committee could indeed investigate crime and vice at all levels, Rosellini took his show back on the road, holding hearings in virtually every major town and city of the state with the battle cry, "Help SWEEP and KEEP Washington CLEAN!"

The battle for the governorship was shaping up.

LOW ROAD TO VICTORY

After a protracted public display of coy indecision, Langlie announced for a third term at the state Republican convention in May, asserting bravely that he felt he must "finish the job of straightening out the state financially." The Olympia *News,* less friendly than ever following the filing of a $100,000 libel suit against it by the Langlie administration, snorted editorially, *"We can only assume that he uses the word 'straighten out the state' in the same manner as an undertaker speaks of 'straightening out' a corpse preparatory to a decent burial."*

Speaker Charles Hodde, perhaps the most competent, knowledgeable and statesmanlike individual to hold that office in the state's history, announced early that he was going to run against Langlie's "broken promise government." His campaign was based on a scholarly and somewhat verbose analysis of the Langlie administration, pointing out that Langlie's first term treasury surplus of $72 million was the result of the 50 percent sales tax increase which he had demanded, that the "largest highway building program in history," for which the governor claimed credit, was pushed through by Hodde's committee appointee, Julie Butler Hansen, "the only woman chairman of the roads and bridges committee in the United States," that the capital improvement program for schools and institutions had been pushed through by Hodde over the governor's objections, and that Langlie's foot-dragging had resulted in higher interest rate on bonds "and a loss of about one school house in five which could have been built for the same money had the governor given support when the program was proposed."

The Colville farmer had little base of statewide political power and his low-key and methodical attack on the Langlie administration was largely ignored amidst the strident charges and counter-charges of better known and less constrained candidates.

The Democrat's strongest candidate appeared to be Congressman Hugh B. Mitchell who, if nominated, would certainly provide the voters with a clear choice of political philosophies. A 1929 graduate of Dartmouth and former member of the Everett *News* staff, he had been Mon Wallgren's chief aid in congress and had been defeated by Harry Cain following his appointment to the senate by his former boss. An avowed liberal who poked fun at the Republican-Dixiecrat coalition in congress, he was an advocate of the Columbia Valley authority, a member of the Americans for Democratic Action and, in general, the direct antithesis of the conservative Langlie. For his part, Mitchell viewed Langlie as "a bumbler" and a "win-at-any-cost politician."

Rosellini, aware that Mitchell was the established darling of the state's liberals, departed from his former liberal leadership of the senate Democrats and bid against Hodde

for the more conservative vote, attacking Mitchell for his ADC membership, his tolerance for left wing causes and for "carpetbagging" from the national capital, where he had spent 16 of the last 20 years. Further capitalizing on his recent television role as the crusading crime-buster, he attacked "left-wingers, the political machine and crime racketeers."

Although Rosellini came in second in the Democratic primary, he had laid the groundwork for Langlie's final attacks on Mitchell and thus eliminated the liberal congressman as a viable Democratic nominee.

Langlie, using much of the ammunition provided him by Rosellini, was quick to take the offensive, demanding to know if the voters wanted "the state to revert to Wallgrenism" and claiming that he had "shrunk a $93 million Wallgren debt in four years to $76 million, while the state was "operating within its income for the first time since 1946." He did not mention the recent pronouncement of his budget chief, Brabrook, that the state was currently spending an average of $361,965 a month more than it was taking in for a 14-month deficit of over five million dollars.

Sensing the change in public opinion regarding welfare, he actively derided the latest pension union initiative, forcing Mitchell to also come out against it as financially unsound. Langlie then pointed to Mitchell's past support of Initiative 178, while claiming that under his administration, approvals of welfare requests had declined from 80 percent in 1950 to 66 percent in 1952, with the total rolls down from 192,000 to 111,000.

When the scholarly, bespectacled and mild-mannered Mitchell attributed the reduction in welfare costs quite accuratly to increased federal aid and the Korean war economy and attacked Langlie's appointees as "hacks," the governor invited comparison of his department heads with "the half-baked members of the ADA who surround Mitchell."

With his attacks on Mitchell amplified by the state's daily press, the *Times* and *Post-Intelligencer* in the lead, Langlie's charges became shriller as the campaign progressed, nor did he hesitate to capitalize on the paranoia of the Canwell and McCarthy eras.

Utilizing Mitchell's protest against the manner in which the University of Washington regents and president had supinely accepted the Canwell committee's demands for the firing of suspected professors, he scolded, "Mitchell and his ADA crowd defend the Communists' right to infiltrate our free institutions."

He blasted the proposed CVA as "a federal dictatorship on the state's resources" and castigated its proponent, Mitchell, as "a leg man for the big federal bureaucracy."

"The essence of a Marxian society," he warned grimly, "is its concentration of power in the hands of a central government, or to be blunt, the totalitarian state." He made it clear that a Mitchell victory would quickly turn the state of Washington into a "Marxian society." Making extensive use of radio and television, Langlie further warned that "his election would make Communist infiltration into our state not only possible but altogether likely." Mitchell, he said derisively, was "typical of the confused intellectual liberals whom the Communists use so effectively." He further damned him with the fact that he had voted against appropriations for the McCarthy committee and had been friendly with Pennock, Pettus and Delacy, who had recently been arrested by the FBI for alleged Communist activities.

Mitchell went on the air to blast Langlie's "blackout on decency," pointing out that while he might have voted to withhold funds from Joseph McCarthy's reign of terror, he had voted *for* a strengthened air force, the port security act, defense mobilization, Alaskan defense funds and military aid to Korea and "free" China.

Referring to one of Langlie's more demagogic television ploys . . . the display of a photo showing Mitchell sitting next to ex-Congressman Delacy at a Democratic luncheon . . . Mitchell pointed out that Senator Robert Taft had been similarly photographed with Earl Browder, chairman of the Communist party in America, and wondered if Langlie, applying his logic of guilt by association, considered arch-conservative Taft to be a Communist.

Unfortunately, however, Mitchell *looked* like a "confused intellectual liberal" . . . mild, scholarly and with a hesitant speaking style which gave the general impression of a college professor who had accidently gotten mixed up in politics. Anybody who had followed the deliberations of the Canwell committee or was watching the fulminations of McCarthy on television knew that college professors were soft on commies.

With the all-out support of his friend and golfing partner, *P.I.* Editor Charles Lindeman, who saw to it that Langlie's Communist innuendos against Mitchell got full and sympathetic treatment, the governor went all out in a speech responding to the charges of low-level campaigning.

"I plead guilty," he told partisan supporters at a Seattle rally. "It is low. I think corruption in government is bad! I think sloppy and wasteful administration is bad! But I think playing footsie with subversive elements who are boring to destroy the American system is just as low as you can get!"

Mitchell denounced Langlie bitterly as "a hypocrite, presenting a genial face to the world . . . but behind that smiling face is a cold, self-preserving politician."

But it was to no avail. Character assassination, innuendo and guilt by association were accepted means of fighting the Red Menace and Washingtonians, along with Americans in general, were on a conservative kick. When General Eisenhower decided he was a Republican and wrested the presidential nomination from Taft, it put the frosting on the political cake. In Washington, Republicans left the arena carrying most of the prizes.

Ike led the state ticket with a majority of 75,000 over Adlai Stevenson. Langlie became the first governor to win a third term, defeating Mitchell 567,822 to 510,657. He had carried with him his hand-picked candidate for lieutenant governor, Emmett Anderson, and the octogenarian ex-auditor, Case, who had decided to capitalize on the Sam Emmanual scandal and changed political parties for the fourth time to unseat Land Commissioner Taylor. An ill-starred post-election disclosure by Smith Troy that his Republican opponent, Don Eastvold, had apparently fraudulently collected a state veteran's bonus had the appearance of last-minute smear and backfired against the popular and capable attorney general, who lost by a narrow margin. Perennial Republican candidate Charles Maybury unseated Tom Martin as treasurer and Republican majorities were elected to both houses of the legislature. The only Democratic survivors among the elected officials were Secretary of State Coe, Auditor Yelle and Insurance Commissioner William Sullivan.

One of the few bright spots in the pervading gloom of the Democrats was in the congressional races, where an emerging young newspaper reporter with the magic name of Magnuson had upset 15 primary opponents, including Nat Washington, former senator and gubernatorial candidate John McCutcheon, Grand Coulee dam pioneer Frank Bell and novelist-lecturer Alice Franklin Bryant. Don Magnuson emerged the winner of the first "at large" congressional seat since 1912. His Republican opponent was none other than former Representative Canwell, who billed himself as "Communist-Fighter Al Canwell." It was a humiliating awakening from the grandiose political dreams of the dedicated witch-hunter who had expected to parlay his defense of Americanism to major elective office.*

SCOOP JACKSON AND THE TARPOT POLITICIAN

Henry M. Jackson, the stocky Norwegian congressman from Everett, rated by the mass

---

*The final chapter of the bizarre Canwell story was not written for another three years. In 1955 the legislature voted to exhume the anti-American activities committee records from the sealed capitol room in which they had been stored. In the presence of then Speaker John L. O'Brien, Lieutenant Governor Anderson and two FBI men, to whom the legislators planned to turn over the files, the room was unlocked. It was found that the combinations to two of the three safes had been lost and a locksmith was summoned. When the repositories were finally opened they were found to contain little but dust and a few old books and scraps of paper. The house voted to investigate and Canwell was subpoenaed. He testified that "much of the reports went through the fireplace of my home . . . nobody said how long we should keep them . . . they were for our own use." When O'Brien sternly asked him if he thought "the legislature set you up in business to the tune of $140,000 (it was actually $158,000) for your own personal use," it set off a sharp exchange, with Canwell remaining defiant. He declined to answer when queried as to the whereabouts of microfilm copies supposedly made of the more important documents. When O'Brien asked him if he was taking the fifth amendment Canwell replied scornfully, "No. Only Communists do that." He was duly threatened with charges of contempt and destruction of public records, but was never cited. The fiasco did, however, finally frustrate the repeated efforts of right-wing legislators to reconstitute the investigative committee.

circulation *Liberty* magazine as one of the 10 best members of either house of congress, took on incumbent Harry Cain, the former president of the Pierce county Young Democrats and liberal mayor of Tacoma who now considered his colleague McCarthy to be, if anything, a bit too easy on suspected Communists.

Cain was described by the *News* as *"a lean man of saturnine countenance who usually manages to look like a dying duck in his pictures but has a tongue as sharp and deadly as an adder's touch, and has been described in various leading national publications as one of the worst five senators in Washington, but who is looked upon by his adherents in this state as an outstanding patriot."*

In the closing days of the campaign Cain's good friend McCarthy came to Seattle to help reelect his fellow Commie-hater, and to get in a few licks at Scoop Jackson, who had referred to him as a "tarpot politician" a couple of years earlier.

The burly, blue-jawed McCarthy was less loveable than usual during his flying trip to Washington. He had recently undergone stomach surgery and was still sore and surly. His plane was diverted from Boeing field in Seattle to Portland by weather conditions and he missed his advertised appearance at a Republican rally in Jackson's home town of Everett. The next day he attended a press club banquet in Seattle, which turned out to be a politician-baiting gridiron affair with a surplus of ardent spirits and political partisanship. When efforts were made to gently roast McCarthy on the club's gridiron, he scowlingly announced that he hadn't "come 2,400 miles to be a funnyman." The gathering degenerated into food-throwing, shouting and general chaos and the great man departed in high dudgeon just before the police were summoned to restore order.

At his next stop, the television studios of KING broadcasting, he fell into the more convivial company of Canwell and other anti-Communist activists, but when he was told that part of his speech had been deleted as potentially libelous he flew into an even more towering rage and refused to go on the air. A soothing pre-recorded musical program replaced the expected fiery speech of Senator Joseph McCarthy.

And Scoop Jackson soundly defeated Cain, joining Warren Magnuson to give the state a solid Democratic membership in the United States senate.

DICK AND PAT AND HARRY AND IKE

McCarthy wasn't the only nationally prominent politician to inject himself into Washington's 1952 campaign. On September 22 Senator Richard Nixon, complete with five o'clock shadow and smiling wife Pat, arrived in Olympia to deliver a speech from the steps of the Legislative building before departing for Bremerton and eastern Washington. As Ike's vice-presidential candidate, he warned that continuation of a Democratic administration in the national capital might some day lead to recognition of Soviet Russia and Red China.

Early the next month Harry Truman spoke in Tacoma on behalf of the state's Democratic candidates, while Eisenhower attacked the Truman administration at the Seattle ice arena after arriving aboard an 18-car special train from Spokane. He called the fiesty little man from Independence "an expert in political demagoguery" and made the rather startling announcement that Grand Coulee dam and the other Northwest hydroelectric developments had been inaugurated by Herbert Hoover and the Republicans, not FDR and the Democrats.

Two much-publicized initiatives shared public attention on the 1952 ballot. Initiative 184, providing for a $75 old age and blind pension floor, eliminating the lien clause, which gave the state a financial claim on the homes of welfare recipients, and returning health care from the health department to the social security department, was the target of every conservative and taxpayers' group in the state. A well-financed advertising campaign portrayed it as the ultimate in socialism and a sure way to financial disaster. It was overwhelmingly rejected.

Initiative 180 provided that yellow oleomargarine could legally be sold in the state of Washington. It also provided an interesting insight into 'the composition of the true constituency of the legislature. For years the dairy and agricultural segments of the legislature's host-constituency had frustrated all efforts to permit such sales, on the high-minded stand that it might constitute fraud against the housewives of the state, who couldn't be expected to have sense enough to tell yellow margarine from the "high-priced spread." The protected housewives, straining to meet the inflated food costs of the Korean war period, were required to purchase margarine of an unpleasant off-white color which made it resemble congealed lard. A small color capsule was enclosed and the housewives, no doubt blessing their legislators all the while, had to laboriously stir the yellow coloring into the non-dairy product.

Despite an all-out campaign by the farm industries to educate the public on the horrors of yellow margarine, Initiative 180 was passed as enthusiastically as 184 was rejected.

1953

In the century that Olympia had been the capital city of Washington its population had increased more than one hundred times, but it was no longer the metropolis of the commonwealth. In 1853 it had boasted 150 citizens; by 1953 the state census board had placed its population at 16,800, putting it twelfth behind Seattle, Spokane, Tacoma, Vancouver, Yakima, Everett, Bellingham, Bremerton, Walla Walla, Longview and Aberdeen. It retained the traditional image of the quiet backwater town, satisfied to protectively clasp its seat of government and unable to compete for the belching smokestacks which were the coveted symbols of industrial progress. Despite the efforts of Mayor Swanson, its night life did not qualify it as Fun City and urban legislators still complained that the sidewalks were regularly rolled up each evening.

The most entertaining floor show in Olympia was still the state legislature.

HOLD ONTO YOU POCKETBOOKS, NEIGHBORS

On January 11, 1953, *Olympian* reporter Dick Lawrence warned the local citizenry, *"Hold onto your pocketbooks, neighbors, here we go again"* as he announced that the lawmakers were back in town *"to wrestle with an oversize budget."*

Displaying the usual complete lack of understanding of how legislatures actually function, the *Olympian* went on to hail the glad tidings of a Republican majority in both houses for the first time since 1931 . . . 25 to 21 in the senate and 58 to 41 in the house . . . and predicted naively that this fortuitous state of affairs would no doubt "help Governor Langlie balance the budget without new taxes."

The Seattle *Times* viewed the situation with greater caution, pointing out that *"the state is at the end of a dead-end street financially"* and wondering editorially *"Can the upward cost spiral be halted?"*

Solidly conservative Seattle publisher and 1952 Republican state chairman R. Mort Frayn replaced Hodde as speaker of the house, while that old political pro, Victor Zednick was named president pro-tem of the senate. Rosellini, defeated in his primary bid for the governorship, returned as senate minority leader, determined to claim the big prize in 1956. A hyperactive young Seattle attorney, R. R. (Bob) Grieve served as his caucus chairman.

The gravel-voiced but mild-mannered Frayn found his Republican caucus difficult to handle. Factionalism . . . frequently the curse of legislative majorities . . . set in quickly and the leaders had to "bind" the caucus to achieve even such routine objectives as the replacement of veteran Democratic Chief Clerk Holcomb with loyal Republican William S. Howard. Dawley, having been declared surplus as state party chairman, was elected sergeant at arms. The Democratic minority, under the leadership of the tough and canny Julia Butler Hansen, remained surprisingly united . . . for Democrats.

Tranquility did not reign in the senate either. The Republican majority was composed of six "liberals" who believed that some new taxes were needed, ten moderates, and an equal number of ultra-conservatives who were firmly convinced that it was preferable to have old age pensioners starving in the streets than to increase the budget. Although the leadership

The *Daily Olympian* of April 2, 1973, emphasized the current cost of legislative sessions.

was able, through patience, moral 'suasion and threats of excommunication, to reach general agreement in caucus, they appeared tongue-tied and somewhat inept on the floor. The Democrats' campaign of aggressive harassment, led by the astute Rosellini, was successful in making the majority look doltish at times, particularly when they were maneuvered into defending what Rosellini called the "profligate and spendthrift administration" of Republican Langlie. Six of the eight dissident Democrats, having been threatened with expulsion from the party, returned to the fold and embarked upon a waiting game to determine which would be the most profitable way to jump.

As the traditional pomp and circumstance of the session's opening, as stylized but not as purposeful as the mating dance of trumpeter swans, progressed, the *Olympian* further displayed its political nonpartisanship by running front-page pictures of the newly elected Republican state officials, introducing them as paragons of virtue who, *"by virtue of the purifying processes which were a distinguishing feature of the November 4 election,"* had fortunately replaced *"less desirable public servants."*

Land Commissioner Case, who was in his dotage, displayed a disconcerting tendency to

475

appear without his shoes or with his pants unbuttoned, and Attorney General Eastvold was busy ordering deep-pile carpeting, all new furniture and $40 ash trays for his office in the Temple of Justice, but Lieutenant Governor Anderson celebrated the Republican tenet of frugality by declining an increase in his subsistence allowance from $1,200 to $1,800 for the 60-day session.

While committee clerks struggled with a flood of pre-written bills introduced by the proliferating interim committees, legislators solemnly grasped each other by the arm and, preceded by the sergeants at arms, marched to the ceremonial joint session to hear the governor's inaugural address.

Langlie requested that the "temporary" taxes due to expire in March be extended indefinitely and repeated his conviction that the legislature should relieve the state of primary responsibility for public education. He believed, with a good deal of justification, that county assessors were maintaining valuations and tax collections at ridiculously low levels, safe in the knowledge that the state would pick up the deficit; that the state was, in effect, underwriting local governments and thus encouraging them not to collect their fair share of taxes.

Pearl Wanamaker sat with the tight-lipped smile of someone waiting for a dental appointment as Langlie announced that her $40 million request for the public schools had been pared to $10 million and her $30 million construction request deleted entirely. While conceding the urgent need for the funds, he felt the counties, most of which were "shirking their tax responsibilities," should pick up the tab. But he did not set forth any specifics for implementing a higher local tax rate except to suggest that the apportionment of liquor taxes to local government might be used as a club.

He said he wanted a lien clause in the welfare law, permitting the state to foreclose on the homes of deceased recipients, supported "government streamlining" as recommended by the interim study committee headed by Harold Shefelman, and observed that it might be nice to open confidential welfare case records to examination "on a limited basis."

He promised euphemistically to deliver a budget which, "without raising taxes, would hold present gains and make modest advances." It did neither, but the governor had evolved another ingenious method of evading full budgetary responsibility and passing the buck to the legislature. His $423 million budget was $40 million below that of the last biennium, which had proven wholly inadequate. He subsequently backed down from his original fulsome praise of the document, terming it "the minimum necessary to keep the state functioning," admitting that it provided ever poorer support for the state's snakepit institutions, and concluding with the confident hope that the legislature would "redesign" it . . . a political euphemism which meant raise it.

Having thus taken care of the state's financial crisis and dismissed Pearl Wanamaker's angry attack on his cheese-paring of the school budget with the prim observation that "Mrs. Wanamaker has never liked any speech I have made to the legislature," he departed smilingly for the inauguration of his good friend Dwight Eisenhower.

AND NOW TO THE AFFAIRS OF STATE . . .

With the departure of the governor the legislature set about resolutely ignoring all the real problems facing it by engaging in the compulsive attention to trivia so dear to the hearts of all such bodies. The house of representatives spent many hours haggling over a bill regulating barbers, which had been introduced by bald-headed Representative Vernon Smith, who certainly couldn't be accused of conflict of interest in the matter. Portly lobbyist James McDermott, operator of a 14-chair barber shop on Seattle's skid road, favored a stiff measure, including a 60-month apprenticeship for graduates of barber colleges. He complained bitterly that house amendments were rendering it "a butchered bill, trimmed right down to the cowlick." Representative Brigham Young, likewise a tonsorial artist who provided free haircuts for his colleagues in committee room X, agreed. "The only type of hair cutters left mentioned in the bill are female barbers," he mourned.

Representative Purvis of Bremerton thought the apprenticeship provision was "un-American." At this point, the *Olympian* reported that lobbyist McDermott sat in the front row of the gallery scowling and *"looking as if he were preparing to hurl his 296 pounds*

Step-By-Step Basic Training In Strategy & Tactics Of Lobbying

1. Circling the Prey   2. The Lapel Bend   3. Hand and Elbow Lock

DAILY OLYMPIAN PHOTOGRAPHER preserved lobbying techniques of James McDermott for posterity.

down on top of Mr. Purvis." When Young responded that *"this measure is for the protection of those people who are being flimflammed by inexperienced barbers,"* McDermott *"positively beamed,"* but his *"smile was erased"* when young Representative August Mardesich observed that fledgling barbers should have the same right as fledgling lawyers . . . to hang out their shingles as soon as they graduated. When Representative Slim Rasmussen likewise threw his support to the emasculated bill, the Olympian reported breathlessly that *"McDermott charged down and pounded loudly on the huge door of the house chamber."* A startled doorkeeper admitted him, *"but soon called for reinforcements and transported him back up to the gallery."*

Republican Floor Leader Elmer Johnston then came to the conclusion that too much time had been wasted and called for a roll call vote. The amended bill was passed by a vote of 96 to one and Johnston moved that *"the bill be enrolled and transmitted to the senate, and with it be transmitted Mr. McDermott."*

That the capital city daily devoted many columns of front page space to this exercise in statesmanship is indicative of the vital tasks to which the lawmakers were addressing themselves.

A freshman legislator named Stokes arose to assure one and all that he knew his place in the pecking order by announcing: "I stand up to be seen. I speak up to be heard. I shut up to be appreciated." Democratic representatives sought to embarrass their Republican colleagues by introducing a resolution of censure against Attorney General Eastvold for claiming a Washington veterans' bonus when he hadn't been living in the state. The diminutive but fiesty Representative Purvis, caught up emotionally in the political charade, charged the full length of the floor with the avowed intention of punching portly Fresh Water Reilly when he joined with the Republicans against the measure. He was stopped in the nick of time, Reilly, outweighing him by at least 50 pounds,* and was taken

---

*A few days later Pierce county Judge Bertil Johnson ruled that it was all right for Eastvold to keep his $245 bonus, although he hadn't been a resident of the state when he entered the service. Judge Johnson based his opinion on the ingenious argument that Eastvold had *intended* to become a resident of Washington at the earliest possible opportunity. Representative Rasmussen suggested that the same criterion might be used in regard to residency requirements for welfare. His remarks were subsequently expunged from the record.

away bodily while the gentleman from Spokane departed the chambers until things cooled off.

While the public interest was thus being served in the house, the senate was engaged in a battle of words over whether or not it was legal to stop the clocks and pretend time was standing still at the expiration of the constitutional 60 day session, a form of what John Miller Murphy had called *"boys' play"* which the solons had been engaging in since territorial days. Rosellini had determined that such action was illegal and threatened to challenge any actions taken after the legal cutoff time. "We are thwarting the constitution," he declared, "by hiding behind a stopped clock." The metaphor so affected the senators that they passed a resolution to end the session in 60 actual days, but the house refused to concur. The senate got its rule back and spent another full day of precious and fleeting time haggling over possible amendments.

When not otherwise engaged, the lawmakers considered a flood of proposals for new state commissions to, as the *Olympian* put it, *"regulate everything from the massage table to the grave,"* and to be provided with budgets of up to $15,000 a year. Although legislators have always loudly proclaimed their dedication to "the American system of free enterprise," they also proclaimed the virtues of a score of bills providing for the examination of matters ranging, according to the *Olympian*, from *"false teeth, fingerprints and architecture to dairy cows, dirt and alcoholism . . . and a multitude of other subjects."* By early February, 17 bills were under consideration, all establishing new regulatory and licensing agencies, or strengthening existing ones. They included examining boards for "the art of massage," beauticians, architects, real estate salesmen and sanipractic physicians. One real humdinger aimed at the preservation of public health, safety and morals would "prohibit the practice of naturopathy on the open highway."

Having failed to reach a meeting of the minds on the clock-stopping issue, the senate embarked upon a rural-urban conflict over daylight savings time and then outdid itself by voting to authorize red lights and sirens on the personal motor vehicles of all its members. The proposal was made by that chronic sufferer from foot in mouth disease, Senator Goodloe, who told the pathetic story of his six children who, upon observing the mayor of Seattle, and

King county commissioners speeding to lunch with screaming sirens and flashing lights, asked "Daddy, how come you are a state senator and they are only county officials and we can't have a red light and siren on *our* car?"

"So", the humiliated statesman-father concluded, "to save my face in my own family I thought I ought to do something about it."

Nat Washington proposed an amendment to make the bill applicable only to state senators with six children, but the august body ignored his levity and passed the measure unaltered. Fortunately, after having slept on it, the senators returned the next day and rescinded their action. It boggles the mind to reflect on the toll of death and injury that would have ensued had that bill remained on the books to the present day.

FANTASTIC CONGLOMERATION

Langlie returned from the national capital late in January to find the legislators completely stalemated as to any meaningful way of financing state government for the coming biennium. He summoned the leaders to his office to devise a packet of laws aimed at passing the problem to local government by forcing up property taxes to the current state average of 19 percent of true and fair value with the ultimate goal of 30 percent. (The state constitution mandated 50 percent.) The proposal included a state board of equalization to back the tax commission in a mandatory property tax formula based on sales tax receipts, with clout to be provided by the threat of withholding liquor tax receipts. It transferred two mills of property tax from higher education to the public schools, limited school equalization funds to counties in which a 14 mill property tax levy provided less than $1.00 a day per pupil, and permitted a majority of school districts in a county to petition the county commissioners for an excise tax.

The Democrats, charging that this constituted an evasion of the legislative responsibility to raise adequate revenues, proposed a graduated net income tax as an alternative. This Langlie shrugged off as "futility at its worst", prompting Julia Butler Hansen and the rest of the minority leadership to issue a reprimand which included the opinion that the governor had proposed "a fantastic conglomeration of legislation which will create many problems and solve none."

When Langlie responded with the opinion that local governments were better able to function under deficit financing than the state, Pearl Wanamaker joined the fray actively, scaring the daylights out of the state's property owners with the prediction that Langlie's plan would increase school levies by 67 percent. This generated such heat that Langlie took refuge in dignified silence while former Director of Agriculture Sverre Omdahl, the governor's current executive assistant, soothingly announced that it had never really been Langlie's intent to raise more money at the local level. He had simply wanted to "put the decision to the people."

By mid-February all Langlie's executive request bills were bottled up in committee and he was being besieged by county auditors demanding a softening of his stand on local taxes and insisting that his bills would upset the reassessment cycle begun in 1951, which they claimed had brought in an additional $16 million in revenue. To make matters more frustrating for the governor, Rosellini was loudly proclaiming that "the whole Republican revenue and taxation picture is going to collapse and the final budget will be $20 million above the governor's."

On February 26, after much nose-counting and arm-twisting in Republican caucus, the Langlie local tax package was rammed through the house over strenuous objections from the minority. As the last two were similarly railroaded through the senate, the Rosellini Democrats demanded a public school appropriation of over $162 million, plus $9.6 million for new construction. An unhappy Langlie visited the senate Republican caucus to mourn over a $479 million general fund appropriation bill which was $12 million over his figure and $4.5 million out of balance, even without any funds for critically needed school construction. Determined to make good on his no new taxes (at the state level) commitment, the governor insisted that the legislature either cut the budget or take the responsibility for raising new taxes. Several Republican senators balked, refusing to vote on the budget unless school construction funds were included. An embarrassed leadership, unable to muster enough votes to pass it, had to remove the measure from the calendar.

RETREAT FROM REALITY

The legislators continued to retreat from fiscal reality to the bitter end. The day before the Langlie local tax package was bulldozed through the house, the senate was involved in what newsman Hittle daringly referred to as *"one of the gosh darndest parliamentary hassles you ever saw."*

Such oratorical heights are often a signal that the legislature is embarked upon one of its most cherished ceremonies . . . the public celebration of orthodoxy, morality and the traditional American virtues . . . and such was the case this time. It began when Yakima freshman Representative Eugene Ivy sought to change that revered monument to legislative backwardness, the 1909 blue laws, to legalize the sale of "cooked and processed meats on the Sabbath." Although this, along with practically all the other provisions of the blue laws, had been disregarded since the day they went on the books, there was a strong conviction among lawmakers that such a monument to the Puritan ethic should be allowed to stand. And just as the solons most noted for groping under the mini-skirts of girl employees were the first to defend the statutes making seduction and adultery felonies, so those who spent every Sabbath at the race track were champions of the blue law prohibiting "any noisy or boisterous amusement distrubing the peace of the day," and those who got soused every weekend fought hardest to maintain the prohibition against Sunday serving of liquor.

When Senator Neal Hoff sought to amend the bill to include the sale of "books, toys, clothing, furniture, eye glasses, hearing aids, false teeth, kitchen appliances, dog and cat food, tooth paste, razor blades, bath salts, soap, baby powder, shoes, hair oil, veterinary supplies, Toni waves and Kodak film," Ivy angrily accused him of trying to ridicule his measure. Senator Lindsay moved that Hoff and his amendments be laid on the table. This was greeted by an indefinite chorus of ayes and nays, whereupon Senator Jack Rogers moved an amendment to repeal the entire set of blue laws as "archaic and obsolete" and "winked at and violated every Sunday," which was certainly true.

Lieutenant Governor Anderson ruled the amendment out of order on the grounds that it changed the scope of the bill. Senator Francis Pearson then asked for a suspension of rules to permit a vote on Rogers' appeal motion. Anderson ruled this also out of order, claiming that it violated the constitution (a document which legislatures have blithely violated almost every session since 1889). After a nervous huddle with the majority leadership, Anderson accepted a motion to adjourn and the blue laws remained intact. (They were eventually repealed quite recently, not by legislative action, but by an initiative to the people.)

And all this took place while state institutions were crumbling, state prisons smouldering toward bloody revolt, the public schools faced a crisis in space and funds, bright young teachers were leaving the state institutions of higher education in droves, the aged, blind and disabled had been relegated to new depths of deprivation and state government in general remained unfunded.

The state legislature is, indeed, a remarkable if thoroughly predictable agency of our democratic system.

On March 2, with less than a week to go and the senate still deadlocked on the Langlie tax package, the legislators reverted to pomp and circumstance, solemnly escorting each other and various state dignitaries to the house chambers for a formal celebration of the 100th anniversary of Washington's emergence as a territory.

Governor Langlie read a telegram from the president in which Ike assured the assembled statesmen, "I know your state. I admire her people. I share with you the pride you must feel as this centennial year begins." With Director Chapin Foster of the state historical society presiding, Langlie made a speech involving much quoting of Governor Stevens. His dry and humorless remarks were followed by those of R. J. Cordiner, president of General Electric, a hearty type and scion of a pioneer Washington family. Almost anything was a relief after a Langlie speech and Cordiner brought down the house with his folksy admission that "— remain at heart a rain worshipper, a salmon eater, a sagebrusher, an apple knocker, and possibly even a whistle punk from the big woods."

In a single sentence he had paid tribute to the regional lore of legislators from Pysht to Pomeroy, from Hoquiam to Humptulips, from Wenatchee to Walla Walla. No wonder he had become the president of a great corporation.

And, as a grand finale, the Chewelah high school band presented a concert in the rotunda.

Three days later the representatives were quarrelling over another effort to steal the capital . . . or at least a segment of it. Senator Sears had introduced a bill to expand the already authorized but long-delayed General Administration building by 70,000 square feet at an added cost of a half million dollars or so. Soon after Director Van Eaton of the public institutions department revealed plans for construction of a $2.5 million state office building in Seattle to be financed by state employee retirement funds. When the legislation to authorize the Seattle building reached the house floor, Representative Kermit McKay tried to amend it to place the structure in Tacoma. "If we're going to move the capital away from here by bits and pieces, I'm going to back Tacoma's bid," he proclaimed. His suggestion was shouted down, but that didn't prevent a hero speech from Representative H. J. Petrie of Yakima on behalf of his home town. Senators McCutcheon and Purvis insisted that it should be built in Olympia, while Representatives Richard Ruoff and Floyd Miller led the battle to retain the Seattle location. Fresh Water Reilly insisted that it should be built in *his* home town of Spokane which, he pointed out, "is the capital of the great Inland Empire. Representative Margaret Hurley, a petite Spokane school teacher who was already beginning to view the automobile as a not unmixed blessing, insisted that the municipal government of any city chosen for the building should be permitted to construct parking lots to keep employees' cars off the streets. Olympians living in the south end residential area adjacent to the capitol were already complaining bitterly that they couldn't find parking places in front of their homes or get into their driveways. The issue of city-operated parking lots was a hot potato that session . . . as it has remained ever since . . . and no action was taken on Mrs. Hurley's proposal. The day was consumed in haggling over the proposed office building, Slim Rasmussen getting in the final lick with his suggestion that the money should be spent "to build a bomb shelter for the Republican party in 1954." The bill was finally placed on third reading and held over for future action.

The next day, however, legislators' attention was diverted by a caravan of 200 teachers (far below the thousand or more predicted by C. Montgomery Johnson, who had deserted the Keep Washington Green association to flak for the WEA, but enough to stimulate the best histrionic abilities of the lawmakers). Half the teachers, who were seeking a pay raise, went to the senate gallery to hear Senator Grieve denounce the appropriations committee for failure to provide one, while the rest listened to house Democrats vainly attempt to relieve its appropriations committee of the budget bills. The WEA had vaguely threatened a teacher "hold-out" for higher pay and there was a belief among the more conservative legislators that the state's pedagogues were getting pretty "uppity." They blamed Pearl Wanamaker for inflaming their greed, but she coolly informed them that she had nothing to do with the teacher unrest . . . "the Washington Education Association is an independent organization."

When the teachers departed, the legislature passed bills authorizing both the Seattle and expanded Olympia office buildings and, for good measure, directed the purchase of more property on the edge of the capitol campus for additional parking.

The previous day the senate had finally taken action to balance the budget without resorting to Langlie's shift of school taxes to local government. They courageously lopped $10 million from old age pension appropriations.

The deed was done with the indispensable aid of the four Democratic Horsemen (the term was an appropriate one under the circumstances) . . . Reilly, Cowen, Lindsay and Rogers. It was then railroaded through the house.

Langlie subsequently denied that he had known the balancing process had been achieved at the expense of the aged poor, but his seems doubtful at best.

On March 12 the governor announced that vital legislative business had not been completed and that he was going to have to call a special session. He did so the next day, just 11 hours after the regular session had ended and amid the groans of angry lawmakers who felt they had done an excellent job of sweeping the state's problems under the rug for another biennium.

AT THE POINT OF DESPERATION

The opening prayer of the Reverend Richard Bingea indicated that he had sensed the mood of the solons. "Give us patience when we are at the point of desperation," he intoned, "kindness when we are at the point of hostility."

Divine intervention was not sufficient to remove the hostility of the legislature. When Langlie was escorted to address the joint session there was not a single handclap from floor or galleries. The profound and stony silence was unprecedented in the history of the legislature. Outrage had, for once, conquered the ingrained veneration of tradition, custom and orthodoxy. It was, by chance, Friday the 13th, 1953.

With a straight face and in measured tones, the governor explained that he had called the lawmakers into extraordinary session because he couldn't bear to see the state's needy senior citizens further deprived. He wanted $7.5 million of the $10 million cut restored. He also insisted that his half-dozen executive request bills still in committee be acted upon.

Open revolt flared in his own party, led by some of the most stalwart conservatives. Lindsay, pointing out that the governor had ineptly failed to produce his request measures until the session was more than half over, backed a motion requiring that all such bills be submitted during the first 20 days. Frayn stated publicly that Langlie's actions amounted to "political suicide." There was a strong move to adjourn immediately and go home . . . or recess for three months. The reaction among Democrats was even stronger. Mrs. Hansen charged that "the governor lacks understanding of any concept of the separation of powers of the legislature and executive." Rosellini was less restrained. He challenged the constitutionality of the special session and moved to ask the house to begin impeachment proceedings against the governor on grounds of malfeasance . . . spending $100,000 on the special session when their was no emergency as required by the constitution. The "four horsemen" of the senate bolted back to the Democratic caucus.

Even the press corps, writing for daily papers which shared an almost mystic veneration for Langlie, expressed disenchantment. Ashley Holden of the *Spokesman-Review* felt that the affair *"may have cost Langlie the party leadership,"* while Stub Nelson of the *P.I.* conceded the outbreak of *"one of the most serious interparty political wars in the history of legislative sessions."*

The legislators gave practical vent to their petulance by increasing their per diem allowance from $10 to $15 a day on the grounds that they had been called into overtime by the governor and were damned well going to collect overtime pay.

In the end the legislators provided the additional funds for the aged, approved Langlie's requested economies in the health plan for indigents and the consolidation of tuberculosis hospitals, and a minor request measure correcting the title of the unemployment compensation act to bring it into conformity with federal regulations. A proposal by Tom Hall, which had been opposed by Langlie, was also approved, authorizing a $20 million revolving fund bond issue for school construction.

Langlie's most cherished requests . . . civil service for state employees, his timber bill and reorganization of government under the Shefelman recommendations were all shunted off to the legislative council "for further study." This was accomplished partly by the inspired filibustering of Rosellini and his loyal forces in the senate, and partly by the disenchantment of Republican conservatives, who wanted to protect the elected officials and feared the Shefelman proposals placed too much power in the hands of the governor. Many of Langlie's appointees likewise lobbied suruptitiously against the government reorganization proposals, fearing loss of their own jobs. Even the aged Otto Case was a sad disappointment to Langlie, opposing his forestry board bill as stoutly as had his Democratic predecessor, Jack Taylor.

Only budgeteer Brabrook seemed to mourn the demise of the request measures with Langlie. In commenting on the need for the Shefelman proposals, he admitted sadly, "No single agency in state government knows how much money the state collects in a given year. If anybody should know it I should and I'm confused."

The days of innocence when Governor Hart kept the day-to-day accounts of every agency of government in the black book were long-gone, surely never to return.

On March 21 the *Olympian* reported that "*the capitol is quiet.*" The special session had adjourned and its participants departed, along with "*several hundred employees including doormen, postmasters, garage attendants, stenographers and clerks, hostesses and nurses and a clutch of attorneys and lobbyists.*" It was also pointed out that the combined sessions had cost just under a million dollars compared to the $140,000 of the long session of 1889.

PRISON RIOTS

Although quiet may have reigned on the upper floor of the Legislative building, tranquility did not return for long to the executive office downstairs. On August 21, with Langlie off on a European trip, the state reformatory at Monroe was swept by a riot involving some 300 inmates. The machine shop, garage and power house were burned and other areas of the institution gutted, with damages estimated at $1.5 million dollars. The violence not only revealed the desperation of the inmates but the total inadequacy of the prison administration.

Senator Rosellini, long a critic of the decaying institutions, demanded that Langlie return from Europe and launch a full-scale investigation.

Since prison riots have a way of spreading from one institution to another, the Spokane *Chronicle* sent an investigative reporter to the penitentiary at Walla Walla to size up the situation there. On September 7 his opinion that he found little chance of an outbreak there was published. The next day 800 rioters braved volleys of tear gas from the walls and set a half-million-dollar fire which destroyed the sheet metal shop and a million brand new 1954 license plates. Rosellini repeated his cries for a complete study.

Upon his return, Langlie removed the state institutions from Van Eaton's control and appointed Dr. Fred Dickson as superintendent of penal and custodial institutions. The Shefelman committee had recommended that the state institutions be removed from Van Eaton's "super-agency", which handled other functions ranging from purchasing to care of the capitol buildings and grounds. Langlie thus accomplished by fiat what the legislature had rejected. He also obtained the early retirement from the federal prison system of Lawrence Delmore, deputy warden at Alcatraz who had worked his way up from a rooky guard at McNeil Island. Within the year the permissive Cranor had been replaced by Delmore as warden at Walla Walla and the control of the institution by "con-bosses" was being dissolved.

The prison riots had not occurred without ample advance warning. Inmates at both Walla Walla and Monroe existed in general idleness and futility, many of those at the older institution in primitive iron "bucket cells" of the ancient territorial cellhouse. The reformatory had long since lost its original purpose as a rehabilitative center for young first offenders. It was just another barred warehouse and, like the penitentiary, it was jammed beyond its capacity with idle, bitter men. During the 1953 legislative session Judge Richmond of the Pierce county superior court had made headlines when, after a personal visit to Walla Walla, he refused to commit a convicted felon to the penitentiary because of "intolerable and impossible conditions" there. He mentioned terrible food, rampant sex perversion and lack of either a psychologist or doctor on the prison staff as specifics. He blamed legislative parsimony for the sorry state of affairs, which was justified, although Langlie had shown little enthusiasm for expending the several million dollars in available bond funds which had been approved by the voters for institutional improvements.

Reaction to the prison uproar was predictably varied. Van Eaton, in true bureaucratic style, bristled at Judge Richmond's statements, issuing the press statement, *"We need a full-time doctor and psychiatrist, and they are under consideration at the present time . . . but I doubt that those highly-dramatized off-the-cuff statements make for the best support as far as the legislature is concerned."*

Rosellini continued his demands for "a complete study and public hearing on all state institutions," while Senator Neal Hoff began his own probe of the penitentiary, an action which Frayn, as chairman of the legislative council, termed "silly at this time."

The undeniably sad state of the public institutions remained much in the public eye throughout 1953 and Rosellini's campaign promises to correct the situation would be a major factor in his successful bid to succeed Langlie the following year.

BUILDINGS, BUSES AND THE BOOB TUBE

In the capital city, municipal officials breathed a sigh of relief when bids were opened for Thurston county sections of the new freeway which would skirt the downtown area. Traffic engineers, police and maintenance crews were hard-pressed to cope with the ever-mounting volume of cross-state and local traffic funneled through city streets, a problem which was dramatized when a street department dump truck, dispatched to spread gravel on Decatur street, sank above its axles in mud and had to be ignominiously towed out of the quagmire. The municipality was further humiliated when its once proud fireboat, neglected and rusting throught several years of haggling over its financing, sank disgustedly at its moorings and was so permeated with salt water and mud that it was given up as a lost cause. The evil smelling transit buses, hailed 20 years earlier as the modern answer to the electric trolleys, were proving that they did not enjoy the mechanical longevity of the street cars. Repairs were frequent and costly, drivers' pay had gone up along with the price of gasoline, while the number of patrons consistently declined. Service was suspended after 7:00 p.m. and on Sundays and holidays. Public transit had declined sadly from the days of the jaunty and ubiquitous Birneys of the street railway and their 5¢ fare.

On the brighter side, construction of the enlarged General Administration building was finally getting underway in earnest, the beautiful Tivoli fountain was spouting picturesquely on the capitol grounds and the scenic drive along the west shore of Capitol lake was nearing completion. The last vestiges of the Olympia - Tenino railroad had disappeared, and so had the saltwater mudflats of the Deschutes waterway. Out at the bucolic suburb of Lacey, the theatrical Zabel family, which had been in the business in Olympia since 1909, was building a 500-car drive-in theater at a cost of $100,000.

KING-TV was providing such viewing fare as Hopalong Cassidy, Perry Como, Merceedes, Racket Squad, Hit Parade and My Little Margie. Before the year was out KTNT began broadcasting on channel 11 and video enthusiasm increased along with the size of the screens. People's store would install a brand new 21-inch Arvin for $209. The price of a 1953 Buick Special was up to $2,609 and gasoline cost 30.7¢ a gallon. There was hope that Eisenhower's Korean truce would reduce the runaway inflation that had beset the nation. The days when one could purchase a cheap and drinkable fifth of whiskey at the state liquor store had been ended by the legislative penchant for handy nuisance taxes. A bottle of Calvert Reserve was up to an outrageous $4.44 a fifth.

The McCarthy hearings in the national capital dominated the television screens of Olympia and the nation provided a major basis of conversation and disputation. The *Nautilus,* the world's first atomic-powered submarine was under construction for the United States navy and the British commercial jetliner *Comet* was making regular flights to South Africa at breathtaking speeds. A new craze was sweeping the maritime areas of the nation . . . water skiing . . . and memories of the happy Olympia couple who had been married atop the plywood company smokestack were awakened when a Florida couple were reported to have been wed on water skis, *"skimming along behind the minister in the motorboat."* As a matter of fact, *"the bathing suit of the bridesmaid split up the back"* and soon afterward both bride and groom were *"pitched into the ocean."* They ended up wading ashore where the waterborne minister *"had them repeat the vows while standing knee-deep in water."*

MADAM MAYOR

City politics became another major topic of conversation unprecedented since the days of George Mottman when a well-groomed, middle-aged credit agency manager, Amanda Benek Smith, was nominated to oppose Ernest Mallory for the mayorality. Swanson, no doubt frustrated in his efforts to convert the staid capital city into a center of night time gaiety, wasn't running for reelection. Campaigning on promises to investigate the police department and, hopefully get rid of Chief Roy Kelly, to lower water rates, raise city employees' pay, institute a youth program and work for new industries, she soundly defeated Mallory to become the city's first and . . . at least to the present time, last . . . feminine chief executive. Her term of office was marked by continuing hostilities with the two male commissioners, who frequently failed to appear for meetings, refused to vote, or took refuge in sulky silence like bad boys evidencing hostility toward a firm mother figure. The chief of police, who shrugged off the lady mayor's promises of a police department clean-up with the statement, "I like it here; I'm going to stay," did manage to survive the Smith years.

Much controversy was also aroused when proposals were made that the pioneer community of Tumwater should be annexed to Olympia. Loyal Tumwaterites fought the movement vigorously, backed by the brewery, and were successful in retaining their independence. Olympia high school, which served Tumwater, Lacey and seven other surrounding districts, was bulging at its seams with 1,300 students in a building designed for a maximum of 900. When steps were taken which would lead to the construction of a new building near the Olympia-Tumwater city limits, the citizens of Lacey and Tumwater decided to withdraw and form their own high school district.

There was further community dissent when 87-year-old attorney George Funk told the Chamber of Commerce, "Olympia is being robbed blind on the installment plan," reminding the membership of past efforts to steal the capital and blasting the proposed Seattle office building as proof of intent to achieve *de facto* transfer of the seat of government to that city. The chamberites, engaged in raising funds for the garment factory which never developed, and timidly fearful that opposition might lose the General Administration building for Olympia, were reluctant to take any sort of direct action, but Funk drew up a petition anyway, and 600 loyal Olympians signed it. It urged the city government to take legal action requiring the return to the state capital of the 18 governmental agencies which had slipped away to Seattle with Governor Langlie's blessings.

When city hall proved as timid as the Chamber of Commerce, which had dispatched an obsequious letter to Langlie assuring him that the chamber was not involved in the proposed court action and that it considered Funk's action "hasty," a group of four Olympia businessmen brought the suit. Judge Charles T. Wright (who had succeeded his father on the Thurston county bench) duly issued a ruling on behalf of Gerry Lemon, Fritz Mottman (a son of the redoubtable George), George Eklund and George Draham, requiring the agencies to show cause why they shouldn't come back home. State officials Maybury, Yelle, Anderson, Case, Sullivan and Wanamaker all supported the return movement, although the governor did not.

Wright subsequently ordered the agencies back with the strongly-worded opinion that "it was not the intention of the framers of the constitution that the state capital should be composed of empty buildings to collect cobwebs and stand in disuse."

In a bit of legal drama, Eastvold personally argued before the supreme court for a reversal, acting on behalf of Langlie. He was opposed by the man he had succeeded as state attorney general, Smith Troy. The face-to-face legal duel of the two political opponents resulted in a decision that the agencies must return to the capital city.

A century after the long war had started, Olympia appeared to have won it once and for all. There have been no subsequent efforts to, as John Miller Murphy used to say, "put the capital on wheels," and it seems probable that the long parade of rogues, buffoons and statesmen will continue to entertain, enrich and sometimes scandalize the citizens of the town that the Indians called *Chetwoot* and Levi Lathrop Smith called Smithfield.

THE MAPLES ARE CUT DOWN: A horse-drawn wagon was toiling up Main Street between the shade trees when the photograph above was taken about 1885. The square dormered building was Providence Academy; Priest Point in the right background. The photo below was taken from near the same spot in 1973. The street is Capitol Way now, the maple trees have vanished, and automobiles have replaced the horse.

MR. TAXPAYER WELCOMES THE LAWMAKERS BACK TO TOWN

Lacey *Leader* cartoonist views convening of
1973 Washington Legislature.

CHAPTER TWELVE
The Later Years
Part One: The Stage

Washington's capital city, the stage upon which the state's 120-year political drama has been played, changed more radically than the pattern of politics itself over the two decades since 1953.

Despite the best efforts of its civic leaders to lure the smokestacks of industry, Olympia is, in 1973, a less industrialized town than it was in 1953. The big plywood mills have closed down and relocated in areas of cheaper logs and labor. The site of the pioneer Springer mill and Olympia Veneer company on the easy waterway is in the process of being leveled and filled as the site of a giant pleasure boat marina, planned by the port commission to serve the remarkable number of affluent yachtsmen who fight for mooring space on Budd Inlet and its surrounding waters. The towering brick smokestack of the Washington Veneer company on the port fill, once the town's proudest industrial status symbol, has been demolished along with the sprawling plant it served. Symbolically, a part of the site is utilized now for the manufacture of aluminum mobile homes. The row of smoking waste burners and noisy sawmills along the West Bay shore is gone, and across the waterway at the port piers big foreign flag carriers load raw logs for processing in Japanese mills.

In the late 1960's and early 70's Olympia surprised itself by entering its greatest period of growth without the presumably essential ingredients of smoke, smog and pollution. The Nisqually delta, site of Stevens' confrontation with Leschi in 1854, remains much as it was then . . . a refuge for waterfowl and marine life . . . and the ancient treaty tree still stands, slowly dying beside the multiple concrete lanes of the Canada to Oregon freeway, I-5, which has replaced old highway 99. Where the freeway bridges cross the Nisqually river, the descendants of Leschi fight losing battles with armed state officers in defense of the treaty rights for which the farmer-warrior died.

General McKenny's daughter Margaret led the fight to save the delta from industrialization and to combat a plan to dig up the green and shaded downtown oasis of Sylvester park to build an underground concrete parking garage. She is gone now, but before she died she taught many people to share her almost mystic love of the green and gentle land in which she had lived out her life. Thanks in large part to this remarkable woman, a lot of Olympians have learned the true meaning of the word *ecology* while it still exists. Within the limitations of an age of commercialized vulgarity, Washington's capital city retains much of what Isaac Ebey was seeing when he called it "so fair a dwelling place."

Still, the 1970 census revealed that Thurston county had grown faster than any other county in the state, and old-fashioned civic boosters could take a measure of pride in the fact that Olympia had grown larger while the metropolis of Seattle had grown smaller. While there is little indication that it will ever rival that smogbound, traffic-choked urban center in commerce, trade and population, the capital city has seemingly found its place and lost its civic inferiority complex. Few of its citizens, if they had the opportunity, would be willing to roll back time, resurrect Ira Bradley and the Northern Pacific, lure John Pinnell and his Barbary Coast whores, and start over again to make their town "the commercial capital of our Northwest possessions." The majority seem more concerned with slowing and controlling "progress" than with courting it at any cost.

The pioneer settlement the Indians had called *Chetwoot* has grown larger than the

highway department signs at its city limits indicate. In the years since 1953 the rural crossroads of Lacey has burgeoned into a somewhat unlovely suburban community of 10,000. The once secluded Benedictine college on the hill is surrounded by sauna parlors, shopping centers, ribbon business developments, used car lots and traffic jams. To the south the one-time milling village of Tumwater, while managing to retain much of its traditional charm, has achieved a population of over 5,000.

Physically the three communities have merged into a modest urban center of some 50,000 people, although a fierce sort of neighborhood chauvinism has prevented technical consolidation. While their limits merge and intertwine, the three remain independent municipal corporations. Local independence has been achieved at considerable cost and little apparent logic. Although the taxpayers hold forth as firmly as ever for tax reform, reduction of bureaucracy and more efficient government, they happily support three city halls, three fire departments, three police departments, three mayors, three city councils or commissions, three water departments, three street departments and three school districts.

In recent years the three communities have been bound even closer together by the conversion of the faltering privately owned Olympia Transit company, successor to the old street railway line, to a publicly owned system. Laceyites, always suspicious of their neighbors in Olympia, held aloof for some time, but they eventually joined and the colorful new buses of the Intercity Transit system are providing the most efficient public transportation in the area's history . . . and unlike most municipal transit systems these days, its patronage is steadily increasing.

As in cities all across the nation during those years, much of the retail business has migrated from downtown Olympia to proliferating shopping centers on the outskirts, but there has been more progress than decay in the core area. The deserted Mottman Mercantile building moulders scabrously at 4th and Capitol Way, but new office buildings and apartments are going up to join the capitol dome which, for 45 years was the only structure to rise higher than the surrounding fir trees. St. Peters hospital has moved into its third home, an 11-story tower, and the old brick structure above the west side bridge has been converted to a low cost housing complex for the elderly. The once proud Masonic Temple has given way to a new office and parking complex of the Bank of Olympia, the Smokehouse, one-time core of local establishment politics, was demolished to make way for a savings and loan parking lot and the old Hotel Governor has been replaced by a new Governor House.

Contemporary Olympia street scenes.

488

The greatest expansion has been up on the hill, where the original capitol campus has bulged across Capitol Way to gobble up blocks of once quiet residential neighborhood. The highway department, protected and nourished by the 18th amendment to the state constitution and the clout of the highway lobby, and the recipient of a seemingly unlimited flow of federal dollars, has led the governmental proliferation. The WPA-built brick highway building of the 1930's, which still stands like a poor relative among the stone and marble edifices of the main campus, was outgrown in the 1940's and the roadbuilders moved to the new transportation building behind the capitol. By the next decade that was bulging at the seams and a seven-story highway-licenses building was constructed on the east campus. That has now been rejected for a concrete monolith twice as expensive and infinitely uglier than the majestic capitol itself. A similar architectural gem is now under construction to house that even hungrier and increasingly obese bureaucracy, the department of social and health services. And in this more sophisticated age those "golden spit-boxes" in the capitol which called down anathema from Roland Hartley have gone . . . auctioned off at a tidy profit to collectors of nostalgia.

The legislature, determined to become a full-time partner in state government as a means of controlling bureaucratic spread, is in the process of developing its own bureaucracy and has taken over much of the space on the original capitol campus and offices are still at a premium. Despite the huge construction program of the last decade, toilers on the state payroll are to be found tucked away in modern commercial office buildings, converted garages and prefabricated structures from the outskirts of Lacey on the east to the far reaches of Tumwater on the south.

County and city government have likewise outgrown their quarters of 1953. Municipal authorities hold forth in a handsome circular city hall, complete with moat, and the old building on the site of Rice Tilley's pioneer livery stable has become the fire department's central station. Despite the annex built behind the sandstone courthouse, that once proud structure is doomed to demolition . . . to make way for further expansion of the capitol grounds. The commissioners have made preparations to buy a nine-story office building downtown on the shores of Capitol Lake as the

Present (and third) St. Peters Hospital is 12-story tower.

nucleus of a county government complex to include a $3.5 million law and justice building. Many of the more conservative electorate, led by Managing Editor Dean Shacklett of the *Olympian*, owned now by the huge Gannett chain of newspapers and occupying an impressive new building on east 4th, feel that the commissioners of 1973, like those of 1890 who built the massive stone-towered courthouse which became the statehouse, are suffering delusions of grandeur. But judging from experience, the outraged cries of editors and taxpayers will not stay the swift expansion of state and local government.

The last of the pioneer maple trees which had once given Olympia its unique appearance of a quiet New England village, were sacrificed to the more recent developments on the east

489

STATE CAPITOL, Capitol Lake and a portion of the capital city in 1970. The route of the old Olympia-Tenino Railroad, at the left, is now a lakeshore parkway. The southernmost tiers of the now vanished Olympia Reserve Fleet are visible beyond the Port of Olympia piers in the right background.

. . . Photo by Bill Wojtech, courtesy of Eldon Marshall

LATE SESSION CRUNCH: Even Rice Toasties and hot coffee couldn't keep Governor Dan Evans, foreground, alert during the all night final frenzy of the 1972 legislative session. Republican House leaders Stuart Bledsoe and Tom Swayze seem to have also succumbed to the general lethargy.

GEN. R. L. O'BRIEN, fought Battle of the Budget with Gov. Ferry.

Just too late to call a special legislative session, Lt. Gov. Vic Meyers arrives in Olympia, proclamation in hand, on the morning of April 19, 1938. With him is Rep. Kenneth Simmons, who was instrumental in getting Vic back from his California fishing trip.

GEN. ENSLEY LLEWELLYN, fought Battle of Camp Murray with Gov. Langlie.

capitol campus. The strip of green grass and shade which had been deeded to the town as Maple Park by Governor Stevens' son Hazzard in 1877 was engulfed. The mighty maples, planted by Stevens that same year, were hacked down to make way for a few additional parking places, although the multi-million-dollar concrete catacombs of a 2,500-car underground parking garage are half occupied less than a block away.

The players in the game of politics have likewise become decentralized in recent years. In the early 1960's a glittering motor hotel, the Tyee, was opened at Tumwater. Although built of highly flammable tickytack, it had private swimming pools, padded vinyl bars and deafening music. Legislators and lobbyists took to it as their pioneer forerunners had taken to the ornate Victorian splendors of the gingerbread Hotel Olympia. The Olympian, once the state's second capitol, was deserted by all but the traditionalists. The Tyee was followed by other glittering hostelries . . . the Greenwood Inn on the old Mottman tract across Capitol Lake from the capitol, the Governor House which recently replaced the old Governor Hotel, the Brown Derby Inn further south on Capitol Way, and a score of generally garish and noisy watering places.

The Olympian, which traditionally echoed to the revelry of the buffoons, the plots and counterplots of the rogues and the oratory of the statesmen, has become an oasis of calm in a sea of politics for old-time Olympians. They go to its stately, high-ceilinged dining room to enjoy a meal in peace and quiet, far from the noisy hoopla of the ever more frequent legislative performances.

Out on the peninsula between Budd and Eld Inlets, where Athens University was supposed to have risen 80 years ago, a new state institution of higher education, The Evergreen State College, has replaced the third-growth timber. The legislators who authorized it had envisioned just another public four-year college, but Evergreen State has proven to be anything but that. Its unstructured curriculum, lack of grades and off-beat programs have attracted an *avante garde* student body, while the absence of an intercollegiate athletic program has discouraged the traditional Jack Armstrong types. Its administration has held aloof from politics, even annoying Governor Evans so badly by refusing to appoint his former state party chairman, "Gummy" Johnson, to the faculty that the trustees had to name the new college library after him to divert his wrath.

The once prestigious Capital Apartments undergoing demolition to provide more space for the ever expanding state government complex.

Many of the lawmakers who created it view TESC with a sort of horror, convinced that it is an educational Frankenstein's monster dedicated to upsetting the old-fashioned orthodoxy they so love to celebrate, but it is turning away applicants while other state colleges huckster for enrollees via television commercials.

Times are changing, and even that monastic citadel of masculinity, St. Martin's College, has gone co-educational.

Girls in bikinis undulate along downtown streets in summertime to the swimming beach at Capitol Lake Park, where the malodorous shantyboats of Little Hollywood were once moored on the mudflats. And if that isn't enough to make John Miller Murphy turn over in his quiet grave in the old Masonic cemetery, the movie theaters that have replaced his legendary Olympia Opera House frequently emblazon their marquees with plugs for X-rated films which wouldn't have been permitted even in Big Bill McGowan's waterfront boxhouse in the long-vanished Tenderloin.

On the other hand, the community which had twice as many saloons as churches at the turn of the century, now supports almost as many churches as cocktail lounges. A massive new metropolitan sewer system is under construction and may yet rid the harbor of its century-old pollution. New parks and playgrounds have been built, including the Olympia Brewing company's lovely oasis of green at the site of the old streetcar company park on Tumwater Falls, and Capitol Lake Park in downtown Olympia. A sweeping boulevard skirts East Bay to the old Oblat mission site at Priest Point and that long neglected civic asset, Priest Point Park, seems on the threshold of becoming a cultural and historical center.

Six public and private high schools serve the community which, in 1953, had only St. Martins and old William Winlock Miller. A modern vocational and technical institute shares space in the rapidly developing Mottman tract above Capitol Lake with new shopping centers, motels, townhouses and a high-rise condominium. The state library has moved from its grubby quarters in the basement of the Temple of Justice to a splendid structure on the south edge of the main capitol campus, and there is even hope that the venerable and crumbling Carnegie library downtown may soon be replaced with an adequate regional library complex. Capitol Pavilion, on the St. Martins campus provides space for public events ranging from roller derby and major league basketball exhibitions to political conventions and inaugural balls. The Governor's Festival of the Arts brings culture to town, and Lakefair, the annual civic Mardi Gras, brings tourists, carnival and a bit of extra income to local merchants.

And quite a few residents of the Olympia area still don't bother to lock their doors when they leave for the supermarket, the unemployment office, the yacht club or the golf course . . . even when the legislature is in session.

Regardless of what politicians may think of it as a place to visit, Washington's capital city isn't a bad place to live.

* * *

Capitol Lake and Budd Inlet from Temple of Justice.

Japanese log ship at Port of Olympia.

Part Two: The Players

Washington state government had, by the centennial year of 1953, assumed its present form. Over the intervening years that form has simply grown fatter.

The legislature had long since ceased to be an unpaid body which met biennially to subsist on $5.00 a day and the bounty of lobbyists. By 1953 it had contrived to unlock the constitutional bar on salary increases and had begun the cautious process of adding increased financial rewards to the personal satisfaction of dedicated statesmanship. It had been tacitly conceded that it was impossible to get the job done in two months every other year and "extraordinary" sessions were well on their way to becoming ordinary. The interim committee system was well-established and expanding rapidly, placing the legislative process on a year-round basis.

In 1965 the lawmakers tripled their modest salary of $100 a month and raised their per diem from $25 (authorized in 1957) to $40. In 1967 private secretaries and private offices were provided for all legislators, most of whom had been required to work from their desks in the house and senate chambers. It was explained that the efficiency of the legislature would be increased tremendously, permitting it to accomplish its tasks more expeditiously and at less cost. In 1969 the computer was brought to the legislative halls, likewise to increase efficiency and reduce costs.

Inexplicably, sessions have grown progressively longer and costs have risen to an estimated $45,000 a day.

Beginning with Arthur B. Langlie, Washington governors have displayed an increasing interest in national politics. Vice-presidential boomlets developed on behalf of Langlie and his successor, Albert D. Rosellini, and Rosellini even garnered one-half vote for President of the United States at the Democratic national convention of 1960. Currently there are increasing evidences that the third and current chief executive of the later years, Daniel J. Evans, may be suffering from the political malady known as Potomac fever.

As the prestige of Washington governors has increased on the national scene, so have their executive staffs. Langlie added such specialized underlings as a budget director, financial consultant and press agent and today's executive offices are graced by experts in fields ranging from women's rights to "Hispano-American affairs," the latter position currently held by an affable young man of Scottish descent who once made a trip to Tijuana.

Fattest of all has grown the government bureaucracy over the later years, but that pattern, too, had been set by 1953. That year each 100 citizens was served by .74 state employees . . . the fifth highest ratio in the nation. By 1963 the ratio was one state employee per 104 citizens; in 1967 one per 70 citizens and, by 1970, one per 68.

And the biennial state budget, still well on the shady side of a billion dollars in 1953, has grown, during the later years, to over five billion dollars; this despite 120 years of legislative dedication to the thrifty axioms of Benjamin Franklin and promises by several thousand legislative candidated over the years to "control the bureaucracy" and insure "spending reform." In the past 10 years, while the total state budget has nearly tripled . . . from less than $1,800,000,000 to more than five billion, the costs of the *legislature* have gone up almost *seven-fold* . . . from $2.7 million for the 1963-65 biennium to $14.4 million for 1971-73.

Some of the characters who held the political limelight of the capital city stage in 1953 are still performing; others have answered their last cue.

Langlie, whose efforts to shift school tax burdens to local government and to "streamline" • state government through the Shefelman bills went down to final defeat in the 1965 legislature, took on a last political crusade, seeking to unseat the state's senior senator, Warren G. Magnuson, in the 1956 election. Maggie was a carefree bachelor in those days, as was his junior colleague, Henry Jackson, but they were different kinds of bachelors. Jackson, who had a tendency to blush when approached by young women, was sometimes referred to as "Soda Pop" Jackson because of his peculiar custom of sipping straight ginger ale at capital cocktail parties. Magnuson, on the other hand, was something of a swinger. Sensational magazines delighted in articles with titles like "The Romeo of the Senate" and "The Senator and the Starlet," the latter referring to Maggie's dating of a minor Hollywood celebrity named Tony Seven.

Langlie's almost stupefying self-righteous-ness got the better of him in his ill-fated campaign against Magnuson. He seemed to view the contest as one between the forces of old fashioned Christian virtue and those of the devil. As Langlie fulminated publicly against the Magnuson life style, the Bremerton *Sun* summed up the reactions of many when it editorialized that Langlie's efforts were *"completely unbefitting a man who pretends to represent dignity and the responsibility of high office,"* and that he had *"cheapened himself and his party by using the weapons of the desperate, ruthless, politician."*

Julia Butler Hansen called the Langlie attack "a blood lusting below-the-belt campaign," but it was the unflappable Magnuson himself who had the last word. Just before the election Langlie challenged him to a debate on KTNT-TV. Magnuson responded with the message: *"Since your campaign has received national attention for its low level, I feel the only debate you have is with your conscience."* A *non sequiter* it may have been, but it was a dandy.

As in past campaigns, Langlie sought to shift the blame for his tactics upon his opponent, taking refuge in the sophistry that "I didn't set the level of this campaign. My opponent set it with his action over the past 12 years."

After the September primary, when he outpolled Magnuson only in tiny San Juan county, the least populated and most solidly Republican of the state's 39, Langlie revealed the depth of his frustration that the voters refused to share his almost fanatical disapproval of the incumbent senator's playboy social activities. In a letter to a friend, Dr. Wendell Fifield, soon after the debacle of the September primaries, he wrote, *"He (Magnuson) is morally bankrupt. He is a divorced man . . . his personal life is one of debauchery yet these things I cannot carry to the people, though this issue seems to me to be very important from the standpoint of a statesman making decisions on the basis of principle."* He added that he was *"fighting a righteous cause,"* but, as always, was *"willing to accept God's will in the knowledge it is best."*

Despite inspired efforts to build up the Langlie image . . . puffery as a vice-presidential potential, a cover portrait on *Time*

magazine and doubtful claims that he was "a key member of the Eisenhower team" and "a man of international stature" . . . his campaign didn't catch on. Even when Ike himself joined the candidate on television in mid-October and mildly praised him as "a man of honesty and sincerity," no wave of public enthusiasm was noted.

When the votes were counted in November Magnuson had snowed Langlie under by 61.09 percent of the vote to 38.91 percent. This time Langlie didn't carry a single county.

The former governor was offered the presidency of the McCall Publishing company by Los Angeles financier Norton Simon, who had recently secured a controlling interest in the firm and Langlie left the state which had rejected him for a Park Avenue office and a salary triple his $15,000 gubernatorial stipend. After a period of sagging profits and internecine strife during which the editor and a dozen top writers quit with angry blasts at Langlie, the publishing empire regained its feet, *McCalls* became the world's second largest magazine, and Langlie was promoted to chairman of the board. Early in 1961 he suffered a heart attack. Three years later he retired and returned to Seattle. He died on July 24, 1966, one day before his 66th birthday.

The 1956 election which ended Langlie's political career brought veteran state senate Democratic leader Albert D. Rosellini to the peak of his. The son of a poor Italian immigrant family was elected the 14th governor of the state of Washington by a healthy majority of 54.83 percent of the vote over one-term Republican Lieutenant Governor Emmett Anderson. To the horror of his original political sponsor, the Seattle *Times,* the amiable Victor Aloyicious Meyers was returned to office, this time as secretary of state, Earl Coe having deserted the office for an unsuccessful primary contest against Rosellini. Among the Meyers legends is the story that he was urged by some of his friends to run for state treasurer, but that he replied, "Putting me in charge of the state treasury would be like putting the rabbit in charge of the carrot patch." Vic remained in his new office until 1966, when the unfortunate and still unexplained theft of all copies of an anti-gambling initiative cast public doubt upon his efficiency and dedication and he was replaced by a young

Seattle city councilman, A. Ludlow Kramer. Kramer, having found the office a political dead-end, resigned early in 1975, replaced by an equally ambitious and hopeful ex-Seattle city councilman, Bruce Chapman.

Democrat Tom Martin returned as state treasurer, serving until 1964 when he was replaced by incumbent Democrat Robert S. O'Brien. Yelle continued his long tenure as auditor until 1964, when Democrat Robert V. Graham took over and has retained the office to the present day. Handsome Tacoma attorney John J. O'Connell ousted Republican Eastvold as attorney general, retaining the office until 1968 when he deserted it to make an unsuccessful bid for the governorship and was replaced by bespectacled Republican legislative leader and scion of a New England codfish ball manufacturing family, Slade Gorton. Democrat Bert Cole ousted the venerable Otto Case from the land commissioner's office. Popular Democratic Insurance Commissioner Sullivan retained his office until 1960, when he retired and was succeeded by his former chief deputy, Lee Kueckelhan. Former state legislator Karl Herrmann took over the office in 1968 and has since taken a uniquely populist stance for the holder of such an office, to the disgust of the insurance companies and the delight of the people who elected him. It is interesting to note that when he ran for reelection in 1972 he became the first candidate for any office to poll over one million votes in a general election.

The lieutenant governorship was assumed by a courtly and amiable ex-football coach at the University of Washington, John A. ("Cowboy Johnny") Cherberg, who had recently lost his job as the result of a noisy and much publicized player revolt. He, too, has retained his office to the present day.

The only hint of a Republican victory in 1956 was the ousting of veteran Superintendent of Public Instruction Pearl Wanamaker by Republican Lloyd Andrews, althouth the contest was technically a nonpartisan one. Andrews deserted the office after one term to run for governor and was replaced by Louis Bruno, who retired in 1972. The current incumbent is former Democratic Representative Frank (Buster) Brouillet.

Of the 146 members of the 43rd legislature of 1973, sixteen participated in the 1953 or earlier sessions. Senators Grieve, James E. Keefe, Reuben Knoblauch and Nat Washington were

Governor Albert D. Rosellini.

members of that body 20 years ago. Another nine who were representatives then have moved on to the "upper house" during the intervening years . . . Robert C. Bailey, Damon Canfield, Frank Conner, Fred Dore, Al Henry, August Mardesich, Slim Rasmussen, Gordon Sandison, and Perry Woodall. Only three of the house members of 1953 have remained there, John O'Brien, Charles Savage and Margaret Hurley.

Tough Julia Butler Hansen succeeded Republican Mack in the third district congressional seat and attained the same kind of clout she enjoyed in the legislature, exceeded only by that of veteran senators Magnuson and Jackson . . . the latter having become the first Washingtonian to receive serious consideration as a presidential candidate. Mrs. Hansen retired in 1974 and was succeeded by Clark County Auditor Don Bonker who defeated Repulican Kramer.

When incoming Governor Rosellini (who hadn't been allowed near the executive mansion until the Langlies had moved out) addressed the 1957 legislature it contained two freshman representatives who would assume a major place in the state's political history. Daniel J. Evans, a rather prim young civil engineer, scion of a pioneer Washington family and former Eagle scout, had campaigned decorously for his seat in a silkstocking Seattle district which always voted solidly Republican (until a personable young psychiatrist named James McDermott surprised everybody by winning Evans' old seat in 1970). Martin J. Durkan, descendant of Irish immigrants, ex-combat marine and a Seattle lawyer, campaigned in an equally partisan Democratic district in Seattle's south end against a candidate who had the blessings of a powerful and somehwat heavy-handed labor union. In the course of his electioneering, Durkan was waylayed one night and beaten so badly that he spent some time in the hospital. He emerged to campaign even more aggressively and to win the election.

In the previous session, with the return of a Democratic majority to the house of representatives, former minority leader Julia Butler Hansen and John L. O'Brien had fought it out for the speakership. Washington lost a chance to claim the first woman speaker of a state house of representatives when an ill member was brought to Olympia by ambulance to break a stubborn tie vote in the Democratic caucus. O'Brien, a parliamentary expert, continued to rule the house with an iron hand and gavel for five sessions, an all-time record to date, and currently serves as speaker pro-tem.

Rosellini, in 1957, faced a budget deficit of nearly $30 million as a result of the stubborn refusal of recent legislatures to match income with expenditures. Even worse, many of the basic needs of the state had been neglected during the Langlie years. The institutional crisis, a major base of Rosellini's campaign, had reached such proportions as to constitute a disgrace to the state and an affront to human dignity. The mental hospitals were jammed beyond capacity and had lost their accreditation. Competent staff was almost impossible to recruit and geriatric patients were vegetating in "back wards" which would have provided ideal locations for the screening of the motion picture "Snake Pit." Retarded children, locked up in equally overcrowded custodial "schools" were similarly neglected and the "correctional" institutions were barred warehouses of human misery, hopelessness and hate.

General fund appropriations of $681.8 million were made by the 1957 legislature, up from the $542.9 million of the previous biennium, a major share going to the new department of institutions, which had at last been legally removed from its secondary position in a larger agency of the state bureaucracy and had become, for a time at least, an autonomous department.

SENATOR MARTIN DURKAN as a member of the 1961 Legislature.

No new taxes were provided by the 1957 legislature and Rosellini's first biennium closed with the deficit up to $44.2 million, but much had been accomplished in the way of correcting years of neglect.

Governor Rosellini prevailed upon 66-year-old Dr. Garrett Heyns, who had already completed a long and distinguished career as prison warden, parole board member and director of corrections in Michigan, to undertake a new career in Washington as director of institutions. This was surely one of the wisest appointments ever made by a governor of the state.

Stocky, bespectacled and soft-spoken "Doc" Heyns was a rare combination of idealist, humanitarian and pragmatist. A man who liked to work in his shirtsleeves and think with his feet on the desk, he had avoided the Parkinsonian failings of most bureaucrats. He appointed the best division heads and professional staff he could find and delegated authority to them. He frowned on the buck-passing platoons of deputies, assistants and sub-chiefs so dear to the bureaucratic heart. Lines of communication became simple and direct, and from ward attendant and prison guard to superintendent, he had the rare ability to inspire pride and self-respect.

Aided by Rosellini's pledge to keep politics strictly out of the department of institutions, and by the subsequent achievement, through referendum by employee organizations, of a statewide civil service system, Heyns, during his nine years in office, brought Washington institutions from a national disgrace to

Dr. Garrett Heyns.

probably the best in the nation. Mental hospitals regained their accredited status and advanced treatment methods reduced populations dramatically. Schools for retarded children became schools in fact as well in name and juvenile institutions became treatment centers rather than penitentiaries in miniature. The success of Maple Lane school in rehabilitating seemingly hopelessly delinquent girls gained worldwide attention through a *Reader's Digest* feature published in many international editions and the United States state department began sending visiting corrections officials from around the world to Washington to see the programs of Maple Lane and other enlightened state institutions.

Dr. Heyns, a veteran of the political wars and legislative foibles of Michigan, had little difficulty in adapting to the processes at the Washington state capital. After all, legislatures function on exactly the same basic principles . . . or lack of them . . . in every state of the union. His ability to twist legislative arms and wring legislative hearts soon became legendary. Veteran reporter Bob Cummings once likened him to "an old sheep dog" in an article lauding his ability to "cut a

legislator out of the flock" and get him in a corner to be persuaded on the merits of some institutional improvement. Doc Heyns chuckled as heartily as any reader of Cumming's column.

This rare ability to pry funds from a legislature with a long track record of stinginess toward "human resources" programs resulted in such splendid new facilities as the Washington Corrections Center, until recent years a model for the nation in the rehabilitation of young adult felons, the Women's Institution at Purdy, which replaced the abominable female section at the Walla Walla penitentiary, the Echo Glen Children's Center for the state's youngest juvenile delinquents, adult and juvenile forestry camps and the Birch Cottage intensive treatment unit at Maple Lane which has done such remarkable work in rehabilitating profoundly disturbed girls.

Highway, educational, recreational and human needs, which had generally languished during the postwar years were brought to life, the state civil service system was instituted smoothly, a successful if somewhat euphemistically titled "world's fair" was staged and a department of commerce and economic development established during the Rosellini years.

A close associate of Rosellini once stated, with a degree of awe, "Al's as tight as the skin on a dill pickle." That was only a slight overstatement, but unlike most politicians and bureaucrats, he kept almost as close a grip on the public purse-strings as on his own.* While the state moved back into the mainstream of progress, budget increases were not dramatic. During his final biennium, 1963 to 1965, the general fund appropriations for the first time in the state's history exceeded one billion dollars, with a total from all sources of $1,795,-600,000.

Still, this was double the highest budget of the lean Langlie years and Republicans took to

*During the 1959 legislative session, Rosellini made use of the unique line veto power of Washington governors, seldom used until the later Evans administration, to delete his own salary raise from $15,000 to $22,500, thus setting an example of thrift. It must be recorded, however, that inflation had apparently caught up with him by 1961 and he made political history by actively lobbying the legislature to override his own veto.

referring to the Democratic governor as "Tax-ellini." Few Democratic governors have been as successful as their Republican counterparts in establishing images of personal piety and Rosellini's Italian ancestry made him a natural target for whispering campaigns of Mafialike goings-on. Despite the best efforts of politcial opponents and the ever vigilant investigative reporters of the Seattle dailies, only one scandal of any consequence broke during his eight years in office. It involved state purchasing, and the governor assigned his ace trouble-shooter, Hodde, to take over the department of general administration and straighten things out.

In the 1960 general election former eastern Washington farmer and state senator Lloyd Andrews, who had left his position as superintendent of public instruction to win the Republican gubernatorial nomination, came surprisingly close to winning. Although he was not a particularly appealing candidate and made numerous campaign mistakes, Rosellini gained a second term by only a fraction over 50 percent of the vote.

That was the year that Washington's governor became a candidate for president at the Democratic national convention. A delegate from Seattle refused to budge from his position and when the Washington delegation's vote was announced to millions of television and radio listeners, they heard this humiliating comment from the rostrum . . . *"Washington. Twenty-four votes for Stevenson; one half vote for . . . Rosenelli? Who the hell is that?"*

Fortunately for the self-esteem of the Democrats, the Republican national delegation selected none other than Senator William Goodloe to deliver *its* message to the rostrum. A customary bit of parochial puffery had been decided upon in advance and Goodloe was supposed to announce, *"Washington, the only state named for a president of these gerr-ate United States, votes . . ."*

He made it as far as *"Washington"* and then he blew it spectacularly with, *"the only state named after President George Washington!"*

By the election year of 1964 Daniel J. Evans had established himself as the leader of the Republican forces in the house of representatives and, in the previous year's session had succeeded in forming a coalition with the seemingly always available dissident Democrats to unseat O'Brien and place William S. (Big Daddy) Day, a Spokane

Governor Daniel J. Evans.

Democrat of conservative philosophy, on the speaker's podium.

During his legislative career, Evans maintained a properly conservative stance. He was strongly opposed to a state income tax and, when Governor Rosellini suggested at one point that the general fund borrow a modest sum from the employees' retirement system to solve a temporary financial crisis, he was horrified, castigating the proposal as "funny money financing." He frequently castigated the governor as a wild-eyed spender, and was as adept as any legislator in the ritualistic celebration of thrift, particularly after he decided to enter the 1964 gubernatorial race.

No Washington governor had yet succeeded in winning a third consecutive term in office, but Rosellini was determined to try, although the wise and politically acute Hodde, then director of general administration, told him, "Governor, it's time for us to go."

Evans, who started his campaign for governor with all the warmth and charisma of an iced halibut, developed an increasingly appealing television and platform presence, while managing to maintain the eagle scout image which gave him his most enduring nickname . . . "Straight Arrow."

Rosellini, who was at his best on old-fashioned political stumping tours, projected warmth and charm on a person-to-person basis, but when his personality was filtered through a television tube it emerged at its worst. The Evans forces, conceding privately that Rosellini's administration had been a good one, concentrated on a campaign of innuendo aimed at identifying the Italian-American governor as "Big Al," the godfather figure who just had to be guilty of unnamed high crimes and misdemeanors, and upon inviegling him into appearing at his worst in television confrontations with their young, clean-cut, all-American candidate. It is ironic that the man who first made use of television to gain political dominance was ultimately done in by it.

Having agreed to a series of television debates, Rosellini walked into a well-planned trap. New ground rules were constantly sprung upon him at the last minute. Evans demanded that he divest himself of notes and reference material which he brought to the studio to back up his arguments. Instead of cancelling the debates, the governor lost his cool and ended up showing thousands of television viewers an image of a flustered, angry politician unable to cope with a cool, precise young challenger, who set forth the wonders which would accrue to the state through his "Blueprint for Progress."

Evans also performed the usual celebration of thrift, casting the incumbent in the role of "Taxellini," the big spender of the taxpayers' hard-earned dollars.

In fact, relatively minor increases in the sales and various nuisance taxes were enacted during only two of the four biennials during which Rosellini served as governor, the last by the 1961 legislature.

Despite this modest raise in tax rates over the eight Rosellini years, a booming state economy brought in such increased revenues that the previous deficits were wiped out and when he left office in 1965, Rosellini presented his young successor with a record treasury surplus of $115.4 million.

The worst of the social and physical deficits which had accumulated during the Langlie years had also been corrected, and Daniel Jackson Evans took over a seemingly healthy commonwealth at the start of his first term.

The conservative Republican legislative leader quickly metamorphized into the liberal Republican governor. Just as Democrats of 20 years earlier had labeled Clarence Martin "the best Republican we ever elected," numerous members of Evans' party came to the conclusion that he was the best Democrat *they* had ever elected.

Having previously denounced Rosellini budgets as too high, Evans decided that the one the outgoing governor had presented to the

GOOD FOR ONE MORE LAST DROP ?

As this Seattle *Times* cartoon of 1973 indicates, we've come a long and expensive way since the state of Washington went into the liquor business to keep prices as low as possible.

1965 legislature was "unrealistically low." He revised it upward and so during the first Evans biennium, the sales, cigarette, public utility and business and occupation taxes were all increased, along with motor vehicle, drivers' license and corporate registration fees. The pattern has continued over the intervening years with the sales tax up from three percent to five percent (including a .50 percent share for local governments) and a proliferation of nuisance tax raises until liquor and tobacco taxes in Washington are the highest in the nation . . . so high that legislators frequently dispatch a well-paid staff member to Nevada to smuggle back carloads of illegal but moderately priced booze.

The scenario of executive-legislative relations has resembled a series of reruns. The governor proposes a "minimum" budget to meet the needs of the state and announces that tax increases will be essential to balance it. The legislators celebrate thrift by crying that the governor's appropriations package is "out-of-line" and that, furthermore, he has grossly underestimated the revenues to be expected during the coming biennium. The governor, who is nothing if not "firm," insists that added funds will be needed and that he will follow in the footsteps of the last Republican governor, Langlie, and veto the entire budget unless he gets his tax increases. The legislature, after much talk of "boiling out the fat" and "trimming to the bone," brings forth a budget bill within a few percentage points of the governor's and balanced by increased nuisance taxes.

The first Evans budget was up from Rosellini's $1,795,600,000 to $2,146,900,000. That was increased in 1967 to $2,830,500,000, in 1969 to $3,847,800,000, in 1971 to $4,370,700,-000 and in 1973 to just under five billion dollars, plus a requested 1974 mid-biennial supplemental appropriation of a quarter billion dollars. By 1975 this request had approached seven billion dollars.

At the 1967 session the governor insisted on the usual round of tax increases, although the state treasury had a surplus of over $100 million. He wanted to use half of that for one-time capital improvements, and predicted that the surplus would be down to $81 million at the close of the coming biennium. He later revised the figure upward to $93 million, but house Democratic leader O'Brien insisted it would be nearer $119 million. Evans threatened to veto the budget unless the legislature either cut it or raised taxes. Democratic lawmakers, having complained bitterly that "for the second straight session Evans has demanded an un-needed sales tax increase," provided enough votes to the Republicans to pass the increases and end the session in order to "save the taxpayers money."

It was at this time that Evans, the legislative opponent of an income tax, came forth with his first "tax reform package," which called for a single-rate income tax and the reduction of the sales tax for 4.5 to 3.5 percent. When it wasn't accepted he turned to Langlie's preoccupation with forcing local property taxes upward to the constitutional limits. In this he was far more successful than his predeccessor had been.

In 1969 he presented the legislature with a budget which was about a billion dollars higher than the last one. *"This,"* he explained, *"is an austere budget. It is also a balanced budget. It is meant to be both so that this legislature and ultimately the people of the state can determine what is to be done about the fiscal crisis that is stalking this state."*

The legislature, he felt, should pass his "tax reform" package based on a flat 3.5 percent income tax rate for both individuals and corporations. What the people should do was approve it at the 1970 election. The legislature duly came forth with HJR-42 incorporating the governor's recommendations. And just in case, funds were appropriated, at Evans' request, to permit a property tax "reevaluation and equalization" program to be enforced by his tax commission. He warned voters that if they turned down HJR-42 their property taxes would probably go up.

The citizens overwhelmingly turned down "tax reform" in 1970 and the governor was right; their property taxes did go up . . . in some cases like 1,000 percent.

By 1972 the governor had come to the conclusion that a graduated net income tax might, after all, be more acceptable. The legislature labored mightily over a new proposal, HJR-82, which was strongly slanted toward the "trickle-down" theory of taxation advocated by the Seattle Chamber of Commerce. Business should be accorded a lighter tax burden than individuals so that it can afford to develop more jobs and provide the abundant life to more individuals. The measure became bogged down in a sea of conflicting opinions and failed to pass. The 1970 and 1971 sessions duly increased various nusiance taxes and, somewhat frightened by the piercing cries of wounded property tax-payers, embarked upon various "tax relief" measures, largely at the expense of school districts and local government.

In the meantime, Evans had won a second term in 1968. John O'Connell, who enjoyed almost as pure an image as the governor, bested Martin Durkan, who had achieved a major position of power in the state senate, in the Democratic primaries. Shortly before the general election the Seattle *Times,* by a remarkable coincidence, discovered that the state's attorney general enjoyed a "line of credit" at Las Vegas gambling casinos and front-paged a reproduction of a $10,000 check issued by him to one of them.

That left only one Straight Arrow on the ballot and Evans was back for another four years.

As a matter of fact, although Evans is a man of remarkable personal integrity, his years in office have not been unblemished. Things ccurred from time to time that, had they surfaced during the Rosellini administration, would have resulted in thunderous denunciations from the news media of the state.

During 1969 and 1970, for example, it was revealed that the state government was embarked on a major campaign of providing free college educations to favored employees at public expense. The department of public assistance, headed by a former second echelon Boeing executive, Sidney Smith, had 51 of them in colleges and universities receiving all or part of their salaries and free tuition. This reached public attention when an assistant director of Smith's department was sentenced in Thurston county district court to a suspended jail sentence on a charge of pointing and aiming a firearm at a person . . . the result of an altercation with his wife and another woman on the parking lot of a suburban restaurant and bar much frequented by upper level executives of the department. Shortly thereafter the erring bureaucrat disappeared from the capital city.

It was not until some months later, early in 1970, that the details of his sudden departure were revealed. Since the previous September he had been enrolled in the University of Washington law school at full salary of $18,000 a year plus all academic expenses. Also enrolled as a full-time student was a young woman case worker from Tacoma. The two were married while attending school at public expense. Public and legislative indignation forced the newlyweds to quit school, but the story had a happy ending after all. The bridegroom was given a new job in the state personnel department at a higher salary and the kindly Smith, who had made it all possible, soon became the highest paid laborer in the public vineyards of Olympia . . . higher paid than the governor.

This was followed by the indictment by a Seattle grand jury of the governor's entire state liquor board on charges of grand larceny. There were hints that the board members had removed more than just the customary free samples supplied by distillery representatives from the huge state liquor warehouse in Seattle. Evans conceded that some of the 44,000 or so bottles of free booze had found their way to the mansion.

While all this was going on, one of the board members was busted for drunken driving.

Such a situation would surely have resulted in demands for impeachment had it developed a few years earlier when a non-eagle scout was occupying the executive offices, but the press treated it all with remarkable equanimity, even when Evans reappointed board member Leroy Hittle, the former Associated Press capitol correspondent while he was still under indictment. For good measure, the governor announced with typical firmness that he would probably have reappointed him even if he had been convicted.

The liquor board indictments were subsequently quashed, largely on the technical argument that state officials can be tried only in Thurston county. Efforts to block the public release of the grand jury findings have been led, with apparent success, and it appears at

NO PAPER SHORTAGE HERE: A corner of legislative bill room showing a few of the thousands of printed bills introduced in a present-day session. Fortunately, only a fraction of them pass.

this writing that the question of guilt or innocence may never be revealed.

But without doubt the most unfortunate occurrence of the Evans era was the creation of a bureaucratic monstrosity called the department of social and health services.

Like Langlie, Evans is an advocate of combining state agencies into super-departments under gubernatorial control. The first of these, the department of ecology, was duly created, immediately increasing the pollution control budget by 2,135 percent.

In 1970 the governor unveiled his dream agency, the department of social and health services, combining the former departments of institutions, public assistance, health, vocational rehabilitation and veterans' affairs. A "blue ribbon" committee appointed by Evans during his first term had reported that the department of institutions was then already too big and cumbersome and should be divided in two. The governor dissolved that one and appointed another, which obediently echoed his own opinions.

The legislators, who certainly should have been sufficiently aware of Parkinson's Law to know better, were assured that the new super-agency would reduce costs to the taxpayer while "improving service to clients"; furthermore, it was essential to restructure the state's human resources programs in the image of that federal giant, the department of health, education and welfare, in order to grab off all the federal grants which might be available.

The total costs of all the so-called human resources programs during the Rosellini administration had never reached $250 million, although the greatest reforms in the state's history occurred during those years. In the last biennium before the new super-agency was created, costs had reached $585.6 million. In the 1969-1971 biennium, with the reorganization not completed, the cost went to $895.6 million. In 1971 to 1973, with Sidney Smith and a proliferating host of new and highly paid bureaucrats getting their feet firmly off the ground, the price tag had skyrocketed to $1,134,700,000!

The results have been catastrophic in the area of state institutions. The common sense penal reforms of Dr. Heyns have given way to ultra-liberal permissiveness. The prisons which Lawrence Delmore reclaimed from the con bosses have been returned to them. The penitentiary hospital became a narcotics center, staffed and patronized by addicts. The $14 million Washington Corrections Center, well on its way to becoming a model for the nation, has become an arena for racial strife and most of the highly successful forestry camps have been abandoned.

Idiocy reached tragic proportions in ill-planned programs to provide vacations outside prison walls. A sociopathic inmate out on "furlough" was stopped for a routine traffic violation by a state trooper. He gunned the officer down and fled, leaving a widow and two small children. A notorious escape artist with a 30-year federal sentence awaiting him was sent off with a kitchen assistant of three months seniority on a "take a lifer to dinner" jaunt outside the walls. The guest departed the feast, murdered a Tacoma pawnbroker, shot the man's wife, and the state was sued for $850,-000. A five-year-old Clark county girl was kidnapped by a furloughed inmate with a long record of sex crimes against children. A work releasee who had gotten into trouble as a member of a motorcycle gang was assigned to a repair shop patronized by motorcycle gangs and was killed in a subsequent "rumble" between motorcycle gangs.

And these are just a few of the more glaring examples.

In his first campaign against Rosellini, Evans had expressed dismay that anyone would even think of running for a third term. He considered the idea contrary to every tenet of healthy, democratic government.

In 1972, after a statewide junket to "sound out the public" on their attitude toward a revised "tax reform" package, he came to the conclusion that the state needed his services for another four years. The need was such that his previous feelings of revulsion toward third-term governors were now "inoperative."

It appeared that Senator Durkan, his groundwork solidly laid, was a shoo-in for the Democratic nomination this time . . . and that he would have a ready-made campaign issue; one that Evans himself had played for all it was worth a few years earlier. The only opposition seemed to be the young child psychiatrist and freshman representative, Dr. Jim McDermott, who possessed considerable charm but little political experience, organized backing or money.

Then, late in the game, Albert D. Rosellini returned to the fray. He was still good and mad at Dan Evans, and increasing public outrage at skyrocketing property taxes indicated that the time was ripe to gain revenge . . . and a third term as governor.

In a well financed if belated primary campaign, the old political pro, now 63 years of age, linked Evans and Durkan . . . as chairman of the all-powerful senate ways and means committee . . . as the "Evans-Durkan administration" of big spenders and big taxers.

It appeared that he had struck a responsive chord in the electorate. In the 1972 primary election Rosellini delivered a stunning upset to the seemingly unbeatable Durkan. Even with three attractive Democratic candidates in the field, he massively outpolled Evans, who was opposed only by veteran legislator Perry Woodall. Although virtually unknown outside political circles, the conservative Wapato lawyer took approximately one out of every three Republican primary votes. After the primary he evoked cries of outrage and threats of excommunication from the party faithful when he threw his support to Rosellini.

Campaigning on a pledge to cut governmental costs, abolish the department of social and health services and reduce taxes, it appeared that Rosellini was now the one who couldn't be beaten.

Then history began to repeat itself.

Although he had been convinced that it would be mortally dangerous to get on television with the wily Evans, he found himself entrapped. The governor tippytoed into what was supposed to be a Rosellini-only televised appearance at a Seattle community college. When the primly smiling governor suddenly bobbed up beside him, Rosellini let his temper get the better of him. Goaded by a planted claque of hostile hecklers, he scornfully referred to his opponent several times as "Danny boy."

Even people who didn't like Evans very well felt the contemptuous reference to the state's chief executive was in poor taste.

The polls which had shown Evans an almost certain loser began to move upward in his favor.

Then history repeated itself again. Both the *Times* and *Post-Intelligencer* came out with last-minute pre-election lead stories. Just what they were based upon remains unclear, except that they involved vague charges that Rosellini, in his capacity as a private attorney, had contacted a Honolulu policeman regarding a club license for a relative of a former client who was under indictment on gambling charges.

At about the same time bumper stickers began appearing with the message, *"Do We Need A Godfather?"*

And Daniel J. Evans became the first Washington governor to achieve a third consecutive term in office.

It was revealed that the chief assistant attorney general, one Keith Dysart, had arranged to have a private investigator look into Rosellini's affairs and that he had been involved for a long time in trying to find somebody in the news media willing to print or air his vague charges regarding telephone calls to Honolulu. It was subsequently revealed that a paid informer had been placed in the Rosellini campaign headquarters and that his private telephone had apparently either been tapped, or confidential records extracted from the telephone company. Dysart, who had been campaigning for Evans and spying on Rosellini on state time, was suspended by his boss, Gorton, who expressed utter amazement regarding the whole matter. He later resigned. More recently he was rewarded with a well-paid staff job with the parent agency of the National Governors' Conference.

Evans was chairman of the conference.

Although there would appear to be at least some slight similarity between what went on in

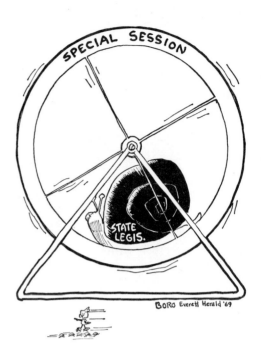

BORO Everett Herald '69

Slow pace of legislative activity has been a target of political cartoonists for seventy years. The Everett *Herald* was poking fun at the 1969 session.

the Washington state election of 1972 and what went on in the area of the Watergate complex in Washington, D.C., it has resulted in no comparable furor. The 1973 legislature appointed an investigating commission with limited budget and one-man staff to look into the affair.

At this writing they are still looking.

Through it all, Governor Evans, like Governor Langlie, has maintained his pure and saintly image . . . or did until the 1973 legislature, in the last hectic hours of the session, quietly raised his salary from $32,500 to $47,300 . . . and their own from $3,600 to $10,560.

The result was a tidal wave of voter outrage such as has never crashed upon the politicians of the state in the 86 years of its history.

A Snohomish county citizen named Bruce Helm proposed a referendum to roll the pay raises back to the 5.5 percent approved under federal pay board anti-inflation standards. After some delay, the courts announced that you can't abolish a pay raise with a referendum. (The judges all got fat pay raises, too.)

Undismayed, Helm drew up an initiative, which required a lot more signatures . . . some 120,000 of them. The secretary of state, who was also in for a massive pay raise, was doubtful of its legality. Attorney General Gorton, who was cut in for a $15,000 a year increment, had pedaled off into the sunrise on a bicycle headed for Boston, and was apparently lost somewhere in middle America.

By the time he was found and had given his consideration to Helm's initiative, less than three weeks remained before the filing deadline. No initiative had ever come close to gaining the needed signatures in that length of time and those who had received such generous infusions of taxpayers' money from the legislature breathed sighs of relief.

Then the tidal wave hit. Bruce Helm came to Olympia with his initiative petitions . . . which contained some *700,000 signatures* . . . many times the number needed and representing about one of every three active voters in the state.

It was logically impossible, but it had been done.

When Governor Evans, returning from an out-of-state trip to confer with President Nixon, was queried by reporters and television newsmen regarding his reaction to Helm's victory (and, incidentally, the loss of $13,000 of the salary increase he had been counting on to lift him from the financial level of a common laborer), he reacted with a verbal hip-shot . . . and wounded himself grievously.

"It appears," he sniffed, *"that elective officials' salaries are to be set at the whim of a furniture salesman from south Snohomish county."*

Public reaction caused Rosellini's "Danny boy" *faux pas* to fade into insignificance. It made all the furniture salesmen in the state mad. It made all the residents of south Snohomish county mad, it made the 700,000 taxpayers who had flocked to sign Helm's initiative mad. It probably made a large number of people who would have signed the petition if they had been given the chance mad too.

One man's whimsy – Another man's woe

"Nobody important, Dan. Just another one of those furniture salesmen from South Snohomish County."

The *Washington Teamster* poked fun at Governor Evans' unfortunate off-the-cuff remarks about Bruce Helm and his initiative to roll back salaries of state elective officials.

There are those who believe that if the chronology of events had been such that Evans' furniture salesman *faux pas* had been uttered a year earlier, Al Rosellini would currently be occupying the big leather chair in Olympia.

But that is in the realm of conjecture. We can only wonder what would happen if past events could be recalled . . . just as we can only wonder what comedies and dramas . . . and tragedies . . . are yet to be played out by new casts of rogues, buffoons and statesmen waiting in the wings of the future to tread the boards of that fascinating stage, the state capital.

505

Olympia the beautiful

Latest scandal to rock legislative halls is alleged pay-offs for passage of bill favorable to garbage collection interests, as dramatized in this *Washington Teamster* cartoon.

Lt. Gov. John A. Cherberg

A. Ludlow Kramer

Slade Gorton

Karl V. Herrmann

Bert Cole

Robert S. O'Brien

Robert V. Graham

INDEX

HOUSE OF REPRESENTATIVES STATE OF WASHINGTON 1911

Newell, Gordon R
        Rogues, buffoons & statesmen [by] Gordon
Newell. 1st ed.   Seattle, Hangman Press [1975]
        506p. illus. 27cm.

        Includes bibliographical references and index.

1.Olympia, Wash.-History. 2.Washington (State)-Politics
and government. I.Title.